SUPPLY CHAIN MANAGEMENT

Processes, Partnerships, Performance

SUPPLY CHAIN MANAGEMENT

Processes, Partnerships, Performance

Third Edition

Douglas M. Lambert, Editor
Fisher College of Business
The Ohio State University

Supply Chain Management Institute
Sarasota, Florida
www.scm-institute.org

For information:

Supply Chain Management Institute
2425 Fruitville Road
Sarasota, FL 34237
Phone: (941) 957-1510
Fax: (941) 957-0900
www.scm-institute.org

For Order Information:
sales@scm-institute.org

For Training on the Supply Chain Management Framework:
info@scm-institute.org

Printed in the United States of America.

Lambert, Douglas M.
Supply Chain Management: Processes, Partnerships, Performance
Douglas M. Lambert
        p. cm.
Includes bibliographical references and index.
   ISBN: 978-0-9759949-3-1

Project Manager: Nancy Bevier
Designer: Cynthia Klusmeyer
Printer: The Hartley Press, Inc.
                      4250 St. Augustine Road
                      Jacksonville, FL 32207

To General Raymond E. Mason and his wife, Margaret

Contributing Authors

Douglas M. Lambert is the Raymond E. Mason Chair in Transportation and Logistics and Director of The Global Supply Chain Forum at The Ohio State University. Dr. Lambert has served as a faculty member for over 500 executive development programs in North and South America, Europe, Asia and Australia. He is the author or co-author of seven books and more than 100 articles. In 1986, Dr. Lambert received the CLM Distinguished Service Award for his contributions to logistics management. He holds an honors BA and MBA from the University of Western Ontario and a Ph.D. from The Ohio State University.

Sebastián J. García-Dastugue is Assistant Professor at Universidad de San Andrés in Buenos Aires, Argentina. He is a member of the research team of the The Global Supply Chain Forum at The Ohio State University. His research deals with cross-functional integration and business-to-business relationships. He has more than 10 years of experience in industry. Dr. Garcia-Dastugue received his Ph.D. from The Ohio State University, his MBA from IAE - Universidad Austral, and his BA in MIS from Universidad CAECE.

Keely L. Croxton is an Associate Professor in the Department of Marketing and Logistics at The Ohio State University. Her research has been published in major academic journals. She has experience implementing supply chain management processes with several companies and has taught in executive development programs focused on the implementation of supply chain management. Her prior work experience is in the automotive, paper and packaging, and third-party logistics industries. Dr. Croxton holds a B.S. from Northwestern University and a Ph.D. from MIT.

A. Michael Knemeyer is an Assistant Professor in the Department of Marketing and Logistics at The Ohio State University. His research focuses on developing and implementing collaborative relationships in the supply chain. His work has been published in major academic journals and has been cited in leading practitioner journals. He received a BSBA in Business Logistics and Marketing from John Carroll University and a Ph.D. in Business Logistics from the University of Maryland.

Dale S. Rogers is Professor of Supply Chain Management and Director of the Center for Logistics Management at the University of Nevada, Reno. He is also, the chairman of the Reverse Logistics Executive Council, a professional organization devoted to the improvement of reverse logistics practices; and the E-Business Supply Chain Council, an organization that provides continued understanding of Internet technologies. He received his Ph.D. from Michigan State University.

Thomas J. Goldsby is an Associate Professor, Gatton College of Business and Economics at the University of Kentucky. Prior to entering academia, he worked for the Valvoline Company, the Transportation Research Board of the National Academy of Sciences in Washington, D.C. and at the University of Kentucky Transportation Research Center. His research interests focus on customer service and supply chain integration. He received his Ph.D. in Marketing and Logistics from Michigan State University. Dr. Goldsby holds a BS in Business Administration from the University of Evansville and MBA from the University of Kentucky.

John T. Gardner is a Professor of Marketing and Logistics at SUNY College of Brockport. He received his BS in Environmental Health and his MBA from East Carolina University, a MBA and a Ph. D. in Marketing from The Ohio State University. Professor Gardner was the recipient of the CLM Dissertation Award in 1990 for a dissertation which included both a set of structured case studies and a quantitative analysis of survey data.

Terrance L. Pohlen is an Associate Professor, University of North Texas. He has over 20 years of logistics experience in the United States Air Force. His research interests include supply chain metrics and the effect of more accurate cost information on supply chain structure. He received a BS in Marketing from Moorhead State University, a MS in Logistics from the Air Force Institute of Technology and an MA and Ph.D. from The Ohio State University.

Rudolf Leuschner is a Doctoral student in the Department of Marketing and Logistics at the Fisher College of Business, The Ohio State Universtiy. His research deals with managing work structure in the supply chain. He received a BS in International Business and a MBA from the University of Nevada, Reno.

Preface

In the fall of 2004, undergraduate students in the first class of a supply chain management course at The Ohio State University were asked what they thought a "supply chain" was. After considerable discussion, the class agreed that a supply chain was a network of companies. Next, they were asked to forget about a network of companies and identify the functions required to manage one company. Without much delay, the students agreed that all functions needed to be involved including: marketing, finance, production, purchasing, logistics, and research and development. Then, they were asked what functions must be involved in managing a supply chain and they quickly reached the conclusion that managing a network of companies requires, at a minimum, involvement of all of the functions that are necessary to manage one company. These bright young people knew that it was not possible to manage a supply chain, a network of companies, with only three functions: purchasing, operations, and logistics. This is the same conclusion that was reached by the executives and researchers involved with The Global Supply Chain Forum a decade earlier.

In 1992, with the encouragement of Gary Ridenhower of 3M, I decided to take the steps to develop a research center that we had been talking about for a number of years. On April 23 and 24, 1992, executives from six companies accepted my invitation to meet and begin a research center which, in 1996 when I moved to The Ohio State University, became The Global Supply Chain Forum. The mission of the Forum is to provide the opportunity for leading practitioners and academics to pursue the critical issues related to achieving excellence in supply chain management. Membership in the Forum consists of representatives of firms recognized as industry leaders. Balance is maintained both as to the nature of the firms and the specific expertise of their representatives. The membership is targeted at fifteen firms. It is expected that members actively participate in Forum activities.

The first research project funded by the Forum was on partnerships. The objective was to determine how to develop and maintain close business relationships with other members of the supply chain. In a progress report, the research team presented a description of characteristics of successful partnerships and the main reasons for failure. The members regarded the progress as positive, but they wanted an assessment tool to set the right expectations of both potential partners. In 1996, the Partnership Model was published followed by a Facilitator's Guide.

In 1994, while the development of the Partnership Model was being finalized, the supply chain management research project began. With the Partnership Model, managers had a tool to determine when a partnership was appropriate and what form the relationship should take. Now, they focused their interest on the development of a framework to assist them in coordinating activities across corporate functions and with other key members of the supply chain.

At its genesis, the Forum members viewed supply chain management within the context of the total business rather than as an initiative within a single function such as logistics or manufacturing. The goal of implementing supply chain management has been to develop competitiveness and to achieve a market advantage through the implementation of cross-functional processes. These processes are the mechanism through which internal and external activities are coordinated.

During the Forum meetings in 1994, the members presented the state of development of supply chain management in their companies and our definition of supply chain management and the corresponding framework were developed. The group's thinking on the processes that must be implemented to manage the supply chain was strongly influenced by the work that was being done at 3M.

In 1995, it was decided that an executive seminar as well as teaching material needed to be developed and the first seminar was offered at the Marriott Sawgrass Resort in February of 1996. The seminar was structured based on our supply chain management framework which included seven of the eight processes. The eighth process, returns management, was added prior to the second seminar held in April, 1997. With the encouragement of the Forum members, a definition and a framework for supply chain management were published in 1997, based on the contents of the seminars and Forum research to date. In 2000, an MBA course on supply chain management based on the Forum framework was offered for the first time at The Ohio State University. In 2004, the first edition of this book was published which represented a significant milestone in our research. The first Chinese edition was published by Peking University Press in 2007. The book is being used in degree programs at universities around the world as well as in executive development programs.

Since its beginning, the supply chain management framework presented in this book has represented the combined knowledge and experience of the executives who are members of the Forum and the research team. The current state of development of the framework is the result of thousands of hours of reading and writing, uncountable hours of discussions involving executives and researchers during the Forum meetings, and numerous site visits to identify and document best management practices. The supply chain management framework represents more than 15 years of joint effort between industry and academia.

Douglas M. Lambert

Acknowledgements

A number of people have contributed to this work. First and foremost, the members of The Global Supply Chain Forum who guided us in the supply chain management research and helped us develop the material in this book. The friendship and guidance provided by the executives who represent the Forum member organizations are a major part of my personal and professional life. Two representatives from the following organizations have attended the Forum meetings: 3M, Cargill, The Coca-Cola Company, Colgate-Palmolive Company, Defense Logistics Agency, Hallmark, Hewlett-Packard Company, International Paper, Limited Brands, Masterfoods USA, Moen Incorporated, Shell Global Solutions International B.V., TaylorMade-adidas Golf Company, and Wendy's International.

Colleagues who played a significant role in the development of the supply chain management framework are Keely L. Croxton, Sebastián J. García-Dastugue, A. Michael Knemeyer, Dale S. Rogers, John T. Gardner, and Thomas J. Goldsby. Terrance L. Pohlen and Yemisi Bolumole also contributed to this research. Martha C. Cooper and Janus Pagh are acknowledged for their help in writing the two initial pieces summarizing the early stages of the research. Yubei Hu, a graduate of the MBA and Master of Accounting programs at the Fisher College of Business, supported us in our work with the Forum part-time while she was a student and for eight months in 2004 when she worked as my office manager, before accepting a position in Supply Chain Services and Operations at 3M. It is also important to recognize the support of my administrative assistant, Shirley Gaddis.

Provost Joseph A. Alutto, formerly Dean of the Fisher College of Business, deserves recognition for his support of our vision for supply chain management. Professor Stephen Mangum, Interim Dean, and Professor Robert Burnkrant, Chair of the Department of Marketing and Logistics, have provided encouragement and support. It is also important to recognize our outstanding colleagues in the Fisher College of Business.

Special thanks are given to General Raymond E. Mason and his wife, Margaret, who are generous supporters of the Fisher College of Business and great examples of what makes being a Buckeye something special.

Finally, I would like to thank my wife, Lynne, for her love and friendship.

Douglas M. Lambert

Contents

3. The Supplier Relationship Management Process

4. The Customer Service Management Process

8. The Product Development and Commercialization Process

9. The Returns Management Process

10. Conducting Assessments of the Supply Chain Management Processes

11. Mapping for Supply Chain Management

12. Lean Thinking and Supply Chain Management

13. Implementing and Sustaining the Supply Chain Management Processes

14. Developing and Implementing Partnerships in the Supply Chain

15. Supply Chain Management Performance Measurement

16. Supply Chain Management: The Next Steps

Appendix A:

Appendix B:

CHAPTER

1

Supply Chain Management

Douglas M. Lambert

Overview

There is a great deal of confusion regarding what supply chain management involves.[1] In fact, many people using the name supply chain management treat it as a synonym for logistics or as logistics that includes customers and suppliers.[2] Others view supply chain management as the new name for purchasing or operations,[3] or the combination of purchasing, operations and logistics.[4] However, successful supply chain management requires cross-functional integration within the firm and across the network of firms that comprise the supply chain. The challenge is to determine how to successfully accomplish this integration.

...successful supply chain management requires cross-functional integration within the firm and across the network of firms that comprise the supply chain.

In this chapter, supply chain management is defined and the uniqueness of our framework is explained. Descriptions of the transactional and the relationship management views of business process management are provided. The supply chain management processes are described as well as the importance of standard business processes. Then, there is an explanation of how the supply chain management processes can be used to achieve cross-functional and cross-firm integration. There is a description of how customer relationship management and supplier relationship management form the critical supply chain management linkages and how their impact on the financial performance of the organization can be measured. Also, the partnership model is introduced as means of building high-performance relationships in the supply chain.

---

[1] This chapter is based on: Douglas M. Lambert, Martha C. Cooper and Janus D. Pagh, "Supply Chain Management: Implementation Issues and Research Opportunities," *The International Journal of Logistics Management*, Vol. 9, No. 2 (1998), pp. 1-19; Keely L. Croxton, Sebastián J. García-Dastugue, Douglas M. Lambert, and Dale S. Rogers, "The Supply Chain Management Processes," *The International Journal of Logistics Management*, Vol. 12, No. 2 (2001), pp. 13-36; and, Douglas M. Lambert, Margaret A. Emmelhainz and John T. Gardner, "Developing and Implementing Supply Chain Partnersips," *The International Journal of Logistics Management*, Vol. 7, No. 2 (1996), pp. 1-17.

[2] Simchi-Levy, David, Philip Kaminski, and Edith Simchi-Levy, *Designing and Managing the Supply Chain: Concepts, Strategies, and Case Studies*, Boston, MA: Irwin/McGraw Hill, 2000.

[3] Monczka, Robert M., Robert J. Trent and Robert B. Handfield, *Purchasing and Supply Chain Management*, Cincinnati, OH: South-Western College Publishing, 1998.

[4] Wisner, Joel D., G. Keong Leong and Keah-Choon Tan, *Supply Chain Management: A Balanced Approach*, Mason, OH: Thomson South-Western, 2004.

Introduction

One of the most significant paradigm shifts of modern business management is that individual businesses no longer compete as solely autonomous entities, but rather within supply chains. In this emerging competitive environment, the ultimate success of the business will depend on management's ability to integrate the company's intricate network of business relationships.[5]

Increasingly the management of relationships across the supply chain is being referred to as supply chain management (SCM). Strictly speaking, the supply chain is not a chain of businesses, but a network of businesses and relationships. SCM offers the opportunity to capture the synergy of intra- and inter-company integration and management. In that sense, SCM deals with business process excellence and represents a new way of managing the business and relationships with other members of the supply chain.

Thus far, there has been relatively little guidance from academia, which has in general been following rather than leading business practice.[6] There is a need for building theory and developing normative tools and methods for successful SCM practice. The Global Supply Chain Forum, a group of non-competing firms and a team of academic researchers, has been meeting regularly since 1992 with the objective to improve the theory and practice of SCM. The definition of SCM developed and used by the members of The Global Supply Chain Forum follows:[7]

> Supply chain management is the integration of key business processes from end-user through original suppliers that provides products, services, and information that add value for customers and other stakeholders.

This view of SCM is illustrated in Figure 1-1, which depicts a simplified supply chain network structure, the information and product flows, and the SCM processes that integrate functions within the company as well as other firms across the supply chain. Thus, standard supply chain management processes are necessary to manage the links across intra- and inter-company boundaries.

This chapter is organized as follows. First there is a description of what SCM is not. This is followed by a section describing supply chain management and a brief overview of business process management. Next, the supply chain management processes are described. Then, the need for standard business processes is introduced. Next, the need for cross-functional and cross-firm involvement in the supply chain management processes is described. This is followed by a section that illustrates how customer relationship management and supplier relationship management form the critical supply chain management linkages. Then, you will be shown how to measure the financial impact of customer relationship management and supplier relationship management. Building high-performance relationships in

...the ultimate success of the business will depend on management's ability to integrate the company's intricate network of business relationships.

---

[5] Drucker, Peter F., "Management's New Paradigms," *Forbes Magazine*, October 5, 1998, pp. 152-177; and, Martin G. Christopher, "Relationships and Alliances: Embracing the Era of Network Competition," in *Strategic Supply Chain Management*, ed. John Gattorna, Hampshire, England: Gower Press, 1998, pp. 272-284.

[6] Lambert, Douglas M., Martha C. Cooper, and Janus D. Pagh, "Supply Chain Management: Implementation Issues and Research Opportunities," *The International Journal of Logistics Management*, Vol. 9, No. 2 (1998), pp. 1-19.

[7] The Global Supply Chain Forum, Fisher College of Business, The Ohio State University. See: fisher.osu.edu/scm.

Figure 1-1
Supply Chain Management:
Integrating and Managing Business Processes Across the Supply Chain

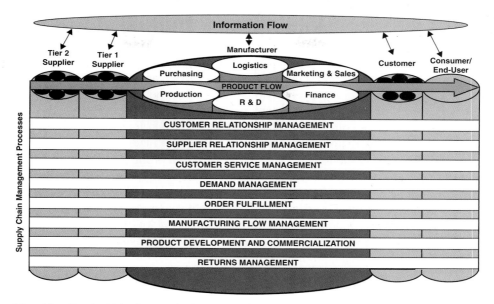

Source: Adapted from Douglas M. Lambert, Martha C. Cooper, and Janus D. Pagh, "Supply Chain Management: Implementation Issues and Research Opportunities," *The International Journal of Logistics Management,* Vol. 9, No. 2 (1998), p. 2.

the supply chain and a summary of the supply chain management framework are the last two topics covered. Finally, conclusions are presented.

What SCM Is Not

The term SCM was originally introduced by consultants in the early 1980's[8] and subsequently has become widely used.[9] Since the late 1980's, academics have attempted to give structure to SCM.[10] Bechtel and Jayaram[11] provided an extensive retrospective review of the literature and research on SCM. They identified generic schools of thought, and the major contributions and fundamental assumptions of SCM that must be challenged in the future.

Until recently most practitioners,[12] consultants[13] and academics[14] viewed SCM

---

[8] Oliver, R. Keith and Michael D. Webber, "Supply-Chain Management: Logistics Catches Up with Strategy," *Outlook,* (1982), cit. Martin G. Christopher, *Logistics, The Strategic Issue,* London: Chapman and Hall, 1992.

[9] La Londe, Bernard J., "Supply Chain Evolution by the Numbers," *Supply Chain Management Review,* Vol. 2, No. 1 (1998), pp. 7-8.

[10] For example, Graham C. Stevens, "Integration of the Supply Chain," *International Journal of Physical Distribution and Logistics Management,* Vol. 19, No. 8 (1989), pp. 3-8; and, Denis R. Towill, Mohamed M. Naim, and J. Wikner, "Industrial Dynamics Simulation Models in the Design of Supply Chains," *International Journal of Physical Distribution and Logistics Management,* Vol. 22, No. 5 (1992), pp. 3-13.

[11] Bechtel, Christian and Jayanth Jayaram, "Supply Chain Management: A Strategic Perspective," *The International Journal of Logistics Management,* Vol. 8, No. 1 (1997), pp. 15-34.

as not appreciably different from the contemporary understanding of logistics management, as defined by the Council of Logistics Management (CLM) in 1986.[15] That is, SCM was viewed as logistics that was integrated with customers and suppliers. Logistics as defined by the CLM always represented a supply chain orientation, "from point-of-origin to point-of-consumption." Then, why the confusion? It is probably due to the fact that logistics is a function within companies and is also a bigger concept that deals with the management of material and information flows across the supply chain. This is similar to the confusion over marketing as a concept and marketing as a functional area. Thus, the quote from the CEO who said, "Marketing is too important to be left to the marketing department." Everybody in the company should have a customer focus. The marketing concept does not apply just to the marketing department. Everyone in the organization should focus on serving the customer's needs at a profit.

Everyone in the organization should focus on serving the customer's needs at a profit.

The understanding of SCM has been re-conceptualized from integrating logistics across the supply chain to integrating and managing key business processes across the supply chain. Based on this emerging distinction between SCM and logistics, in 2003, CLM announced a modified definition of logistics. The modified definition explicitly declares CLM's position that logistics management is only a part of SCM. The revised definition follows:

> Logistics is that part of supply chain management that plans, implements, and controls the efficient, effective forward and reverse flow and storage of goods, services, and related information between the point-of-origin and the point-of-consumption in order to meet customers' requirements.[16]

SCM is not just confused with logistics. Those in the operations management area, such as APICS, are renaming what they do as supply chain management[17] as

---

[12] Davis, Tom, "Effective Supply Chain Management", *Sloan Management Review*, Vol. 34, No. 4, Summer (1993), pp. 35-46; Bruce C. Arntzen, Gerald G. Brown, Thomas P. Harrison and Linda L. Trafton, "Global Supply Chain Management Digital Equipment Corporation," *Interfaces*, Vol. 25, No. 1 (1995), pp. 69-93; and, Robert C. Camp and Dan N. Colbert, "The Xerox Quest for Supply Chain Excellence," *Supply Chain Management Review*, Spring (1997), pp. 82-91.

[13] Scharlacken, John W., "The Seven Pillars of Global Supply Chain Planning," *Supply Chain Management Review*, Vol. 2, No. 1 (1998), pp. 32-40; Gene Tyndall, Christopher Gopal, Wolfgang Partsch and John Kamauff, *Supercharging Supply Chains*, New York: John Wiley & Sons, Inc., 1998; and, William C. Copacino, *Supply Chain Management: The Basics and Beyond*, Boca Raton, FL: St. Lucie Press, 1997.

[14] Fisher, Marshall L., "What is the Right Supply Chain for Your Product?" *Harvard Business Review*, Vol. 75, No. 2, March-April (1997), pp. 105-116; Hau L. Lee and Corey Billington, "Managing Supply Chain Inventory: Pitfalls and Opportunities," *Sloan Management Review*, Vol. 33, No. 3, Spring (1992), pp. 65-73; Robert B. Handfield and Ernest L. Nichols, Jr., *Introduction to Supply Chain Management*, Upper Saddle River, New Jersey, Prentice Hall, 1999; and, Donald J. Bowersox and David J. Closs, *Logistical Management – The Integrated Supply Chain Process*, New York: McGraw-Hill Companies, 1996.

[15] CLM defined logistics management as: The process of planning, implementing, and controlling the efficient, cost-effective flow and storage of raw materials, in-process inventory, finished goods, and related information flow from point-of-origin to point-of-consumption for the purpose of conforming to customer requirements. *What's It All About?*, Oak Brook, IL: Council of Logistics Management, 1986.

[16] The definition is posted at the CSCMP's homepage: www.CSCMP.org.

[17] APICS, *Basics of Supply Chain Management*, CPIM Certification Review Course, Participant Guide, Version 2.1, Alexandira, VA: APICS, The Educational Society for Resource Management, 2001.

are those working in the procurement area.[18]   Some universities have created departments of supply chain management by combining purchasing, operations and logistics faculty, which is a perspective that has appeared in the literature.[19]

Just What is Supply Chain Management?

Figure 1-1 illustrates the supply chain network structure of a manufacturer with two tiers of customers and two tiers of suppliers, the information and product flows, and the supply chain management processes that must be implemented within organizations across the supply chain. All of the processes are cross-functional and cross-firm in nature. Every organization in the supply chain needs to be involved in the implementation of the same eight processes but corporate silos and functional silos within companies are barriers to this integration (see Figure 1-1). In most major corporations, functional managers are rewarded for behavior that is not customer friendly or shareholder friendly. This is because the metrics used focus on functional performance such as cost per case, asset utilization, and revenue goals, not on customer value or shareholder value. Successful management of the supply chain requires the involvement of all of the corporate business functions.[20] A network of companies cannot be managed with fewer functions than are necessary to manage one company.

Every organization in the supply chain needs to be involved in the implementation of the same eight processes but corporate silos and functional silos within companies are barriers to this integration.

In his keynote address to the International Association of Food Industry Suppliers in March 2005, Tom Blackstock, Vice President of Supply Chain Operations at Coca-Cola North America, confirmed the need to involve all business functions in supply chain management when he said: "Supply chain management is everybody's job".[21] In 2006, John Gattorna expressed a similar perspective on the breadth of management necessary for successful implementation of supply chain management:

"We have to embrace a far more liberal view of the supply chain."

> We have to embrace a far more liberal view of the supply chain. In effect, the supply chain is any combination of processes, functions, activities, relationships, and pathways along which products, services, information, and financial transactions move in and between enterprises. It also involves any and all movement of these from original producer to ultimate end-user or consumer, and everyone in the enterprise is involved in making this happen.[22]

In reality, a supply chain is much more complex than the row of silos depicted in Figure 1-1. For a company in the middle of the supply chain like a consumer goods manufacturer, the supply chain looks like an uprooted tree (see Figure 1-2) where the root system represents the supplier network and the branches of the tree

---

[18] Monczka, Robert M., Robert J. Trent and Robert B. Handfield, *Purchasing and Supply Chain Management*, Cincinnati, OH: South-Western College Publishing, 1998.

[19] Wisner, Joel D., G. Keong Leong and Keah-Choon Tan, *Supply Chain Management: Balanced Approach*, Mason, OH: Thomson South-Western, 2004.

[20] Blackstock, Thomas, Keynote Speech, International Association of Food Industry Suppliers, San Francisco, CA, March 11, 2005 and John Gattorna, Supply Chains Are the Business," *Supply Chain Management* Review, Vol. 10, No. 6 (2005), pp. 42-49.

[21] Blackstock, Thomas, Keynote Speech, International Association of Food Industry Suppliers, San Francisco, CA, March 11, 2005.

[22] Gattorna, John, "Supply Chains Are the Business", *Supply Chain Management Review*, Vol. 10, No. 6 (2006), pp. 42-49.

Figure 1-2

Figure 1-2
Supply Chain Network Structure

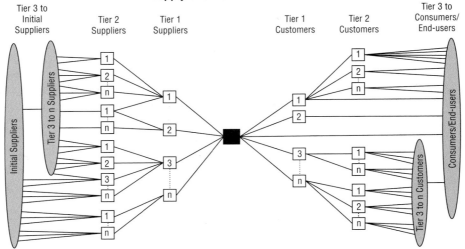

Source: Adapted from Douglas M. Lambert, Martha C. Cooper and Janus D. Pagh, "Supply Chain Management: Implementation Issues and Research Opportunities," *The International Journal of Logistics Management*, Vol. 9, No. 2 (1998), p. 3.

represent the customer network. The supply chain will look different depending on a firm's position in it. For example, in the case of a retailer, like Wal-Mart, the consumers would be next to the dark square (Wal-Mart) in the center of Figure 1-2 making them the only tier in the customer network. For an initial supplier, such as a shrimper, there would be no suppliers associated with the product flow.

Managing the entire supply chain is a very challenging task. Managing all suppliers back to the point-of-origin and all products/services out to the point-of-consumption might appear to be overwhelming. It is probably easier to understand why executives would want to manage their supply chains to the point-of-consumption because whoever has the relationship with the end-user has the power in the supply chain. Intel created a relationship with the end-user by having computer manufacturers place an "Intel inside" label on their computers. This affects the computer manufacturer's ability to switch microprocessor suppliers. However, opportunities exist to significantly improve profits by managing the supplier network as well. For example, Coca-Cola is one of the largest purchasers of PET resins in the world as a result of managing its suppliers of packaging materials beyond Tier 1. Because resin costs represent such a large portion of the package cost, Coca-Cola contracts for PET resins directly with the resin producer. This practice also results in improved availability and less price volatility.

At the end of the day, supply chain management is about relationship management. A supply chain is managed, link-by-link, relationship-by-relationship, and the organizations that manage these relationships best will win. The links in the chain are formed by the customer relationship management process of the seller organization and the supplier relationship management process of the buyer organization. The focus of the remainder of this chapter is on business process management, the eight supply chain management processes, how customer relationship management and supplier relationship management form

At the end of the day, supply chain management is about relationship management. A supply chain is managed, link-by-link, relationship-by-relationship, and the organizations that manage these relationships best will win.

the linkages for integrating companies in the supply chain, how the finanaical impact of each linkage is measured, and how a tool known as the partnership model, can be used to structure relationships with key customers and suppliers.

Business Process Management

Increasingly, managers want to implement business processes and integrate them with other key members of the supply chain.

Increasingly, managers want to implement business processes and integrate them with other key members of the supply chain.[23] A business process is a structured set of activities with specified business outcomes for customers.[24] Initially, business processes were viewed as a means to integrate corporate functions within the firm. Now, business processes are used to structure the activities between members of a supply chain. Hammer has pointed out that it is in the integration of business processes across firms in the supply chain where the real "gold" can be found.[25]

The concept of organizing the activities of a firm as business processes was introduced in the late 1980s[26] and became popular in the early 1990s, after the publication of books by Hammer and Champy,[27] and Davenport.[28]

The motivation for implementing business processes within and across members of the supply chain might be to make transactions efficient and effective, or to structure inter-firm relationships in the supply chain.

The motivation for implementing business processes within and across members of the supply chain might be to make transactions efficient and effective, or to structure inter-firm relationships in the supply chain. Both approaches are customer oriented. The first focuses on meeting the customer's expectations for each transaction, the other on achieving longer term mutual fulfillment of promises.

The transactional view of business process management is rooted in advances in information and communication technology which enabled time compression and availability of information throughout the organization.[29] The focus is not on automating the established business processes, but on redesigning businesses.[30] This transactional approach to redesigning business processes is based on Taylor's principles of scientific management which aim to increase organizational efficiency and effectiveness using engineering principles from manufacturing operations.[31] In this case, business process redesign is based on standardizing

[23] This section is based on material included in Douglas M. Lambert, Sebastián J. García-Dastugue and Keely L. Croxton, "An Evaluation of Process-Oriented Supply Chain Management Frameworks," *Journal of Business Logistics*, Vol. 26, No. 1 (2005), pp. 25-51.

[24] Davenport, Thomas H. and Michael C. Beers, "Managing information about processes," *Journal of Management Information Systems*, Vol. 12, No. 1 (1995), pp. 57-80.

[25] Hammer, Michael, "The Superefficient Company," *Harvard Business Review*, Vol. 79, No. 8 (2001), pp. 82-91.

[26] Hammer, Michael and Glenn E. Mangurian, "The Changing Value of Communications Technology," *Sloan Management Review*, Vol. 28, No. 2 (1987), pp. 65-71; and, Thomas H. Davenport, Michael Hammer and Tauno J. Metsisto, "How Executives Can Shape Their Company's Information Systems," *Harvard Business Review*, Vol. 67, No. 2 (1989), pp. 130-134.

[27] Hammer, Michael and James Champy, *Reengineering the Corporation: A Manifesto for Business Revolution*, 1st ed, New York, NY: Harper Business, 1993.

[28] Davenport, Thomas H., *Process Innovation: Reengineering Work through Information Technology*, Boston, MA: Harvard Business School Press, 1993.

[29] Hammer, Michael and Glenn E. Mangurian, "The Changing Value of Communications Technology," *Sloan Management Review*, Vol. 28, No. 2 (1987), pp. 65-71.

[30] Hammer, Michael, "Reengineering Work: Don't Automate, Obliterate," *Harvard Business Review*, Vol. 68, No. 4 (1990), pp. 104-112

[31] Taylor, Frederick W., *The Principles of Scientific Management*, New York, NY: Harper & Bros, 1911.

transactions and the transfer of information.[32] The goal is to improve outcomes for customers by making transactions more efficient and accurate.

The second view of business process management focuses on managing relationships in the supply chain and is based on an evolving view from the field of marketing. A significant amount of the marketing literature is concerned with market transactions (business transactions with customers) and the fulfillment of orders. Rooted in economic theory, researchers studied the efficiency of transactions with the customers, which raised awareness about the importance of customer retention.[33] Obtaining repeat business, that is to conduct multiple transactions with the same customer, is more cost efficient than obtaining a new customer.[34] This view of marketing, managing transactions with customers, is dominated by the "4Ps": product, price, promotion, and place.[35]

The early marketing channels researchers such as Alderson and Bucklin conceptualized why and how channels are created and structured.[36] From a supply chain standpoint, these researchers were on the right track in terms of: 1) identifying who should be a member of the marketing channel, 2) describing the need for channel coordination, and 3) drawing actual marketing channels. However, for the last 40 years most marketing channels researchers ignored two critical issues. First, they did not build on the early contributions by including suppliers to the manufacturer, and thus neglected the importance of a total supply chain perspective. Unlike the marketing channels literature, a major weakness of much of the SCM literature is that the authors appear to assume that everyone knows who is a member of the supply chain. There has been little effort to identify specific supply chain members, key processes that require integration or what management must do to successfully manage the supply chain. Second, channels researchers focused on marketing activities and flows across the marketing channel, and overlooked the need to integrate and manage cross-functionally within and across companies. In 1992, Webster[37] challenged marketers and marketing researchers to consider relationships with multiple firms. He also called for cross-functional consideration in strategy formulation.

During the 1990s, a paradigm shift occurred with the introduction of the concept of relationship marketing.[38] The goal of relationship marketing "…is to establish, maintain, and enhance… relationships with customers and other

> *The second view of business process management focuses on managing relationships in the supply chain and is based on an evolving view from the field of marketing.*

---

[32] Davenport, Thomas H. and James E. Short, "The New Industrial Engineering: Information Technology and Business Process Redesign," *Sloan Management Review*, Vol. 31, No. 4 (1990), pp. 11-27.

[33] Weld, Louis D. H., "Marketing Functions and Mercantile Organizations," *The American Economic Review*, Vol. 7, No. 2 (1917), pp. 306-318.

[34] Kotler, Philip, *Marketing Management: Analysis, Planning, Implementation and Control*, 7th ed, Englewood Cliffs, NJ: Prentice-Hall, 1991.

[35] McCarthy, E. Jerome, *Basic Marketing: A Managerial Approach*, Homewood, IL: R.D. Irwin, 1960.

[36] Alderson, Wroe, "Marketing Efficiency and the Principle of Postponement," *Cost and Profit Outlook*, Vol. 3, September (1950); Reavis Cox and Wroe Alderson (eds.) *Theory in Marketing*, Chicago, IL: Richard D. Irwin, Inc., 1950; and, Louis P. Bucklin, *A Theory of Distribution Channel Structure*, IBER Special publication, Berkeley, California, 1966.

[37] Webster, Frederick E. Jr., "The Changing Role of Marketing in the Corporation," *Journal of Marketing*, Vol. 56, No. 4 (1992), pp. 1-17; Atul Parvatiyar and Jagdish N. Sheth, Relationship Marketing: Theory, Methods, and Applications, Jagdish N. Sheth and Atul Parvatiyar (eds.), Atlanta: Emory University Center for Relationship Marketing, 1994.

[38] Grönroos, Christian, "Quo Vadis, Marketing? Toward a Relationship Marketing Paradigm," *Journal of Marketing Management*, Vol. 10, No. 5 (1994), pp. 347-360.

partners, at a profit, so that the objectives of the parties involved are met. This is achieved by mutual exchange and fulfillment of promises".[39] Thus, the focus of developing and maintaining relationships in the supply chain is beyond the fulfillment of one or a set of transactions. In the new environment, managers need to focus on helping customers achieve their objectives.

The field of relationship marketing is focused on the customer-side, looking downstream in the supply chain. However, the development and maintenance of relationships with key suppliers should be based on the same pillars, mutuality and fulfillment of promises, in order for suppliers to be profitable. Management needs the support of the firm's key suppliers to fulfill the promises made to customers and meet financial goals. In other words, corporate success is based on relationship management with both suppliers and customers. The management of inter-organizational relationships with members of the supply chain involves people, organizations, and processes.[40] In fact, the ability to manage inter-organizational relationships "… may define the core competence of some organizations as links between their vendors and customers in the value chain".[41]

In 1992, executives from a group of international companies and a team of academic researchers, began development of a relationship oriented and process-based SCM framework. In February 1996, the The Global Supply Chain Forum (GSCF) framework was presented in a three-day executive seminar co-sponsored by the Council of Logistics Management, and was later presented in the literature.[42] The eight GSCF processes are cross-functional and are meant to be implemented inter-organizationally across key members of the supply chain. The motivation for developing the framework was to provide structure to assist academics with their research on supply chain management and practitioners with implementation.

The Supply Chain Management Processes

Empirical research has led to the conclusion that "the structure of activities within and between companies is a critical cornerstone of creating unique and superior supply chain performance".[43] In our research, executives believed that competitiveness and profitability could increase if key internal activities and business processes are linked and managed across multiple companies. Thus, "corporate success requires a change from managing individual functions to

The management of inter-organizational relationships with members of the supply chain involves people, organizations, and processes.

"…corporate success requires a change from managing individual functions to integrating activities into supply chain management processes".

---

[39] Grönroos, Christian, *Service Management and Marketing, Managing the Moments of Truth in the Service Competition*, Lexington, MA: Free Press/Lexington Books, 1990.

[40] Webster, Frederick E. Jr., "The Changing Role of Marketing in the Corporation," *Journal of Marketing*, Vol. 56, No. 4 (1992), pp. 1-17.

[41] Webster, Frederick E. Jr., "The Changing Role of Marketing in the Corporation," *Journal of Marketing*, Vol. 56, No. 4 (1992), pp. 1-17.

[42] Cooper, Martha C., Douglas M. Lambert and Janus D. Pagh, "Supply Chain Management: More than a New Name for Logistics," *The International Journal of Logistics Management*, Vol. 8, No. 1 (1997), pp. 1-14; Douglas M. Lambert, Martha C. Cooper and Janus D. Pagh, "Supply Chain Management: Implementation Issues and Research Opportunities," *The International Journal of Logistics Management*, Vol. 9, No. 2 (1998), pp. 1-19; and, Keely L. Croxton, Sebastián J. García-Dastugue, Douglas M. Lambert and Dale S. Rogers, "The Supply Chain Management Processes," *The International Journal of Logistics Management*, Vol. 12, No. 2 (2001), pp. 13-36.

[43] Håkansson, Håkan and Ivan Snehota, *Developing Relationships in Business Networks*, London: Routledge, 1995.

integrating activities into supply chain management processes".[44] In many major corporations, such as Coca-Cola, management has reached the conclusion that optimizing the product flows cannot be accomplished without implementing a process approach to the business.[45] Several authors have suggested implementing business processes in the context of supply chain management, but there is not yet an "industry standard" on what these processes should be. The value of having standard business processes in place is that managers from organizations across the supply chain can use a common language and can link-up their firms' processes with other members of the supply chain, as appropriate. The supply chain management processes identified by The Global Supply Chain Forum and shown in Figure 1-1 are:

- Customer Relationship Management
- Supplier Relationship Management
- Customer Service Management
- Demand Management
- Order Fulfillment
- Manufacturing Flow Management
- Product Development and Commercialization
- Returns Management

Each supply chain management process has both strategic and operational sub-processes. The strategic sub-processes provide the structure for how the process will be implemented and the operational sub-processes provide the detailed steps for implementation. The strategic process is a necessary step in integrating the firm with other members of the supply chain, and it is at the operational level that the day-to-day activities take place. Each process is led by a management team that is comprised of managers from each business function, including: marketing, sales, finance, production, purchasing, logistics and, research and development. Teams are responsible for developing the procedures at the strategic level and for implementing them at the operational level. A brief description of each of the eight processes follows.

Customer Relationship Management

The customer relationship management process provides the structure for how the relationships with customers will be developed and maintained. Management identifies key customers and customer groups to be targeted as part of the firm's business mission. These decisions are made by the leadership team of the enterprise and the owner of the strategic process is the CEO. The goal is to segment customers based on their value over time and increase customer loyalty of target customers by providing customized products and services. Cross-functional customer teams tailor Product and Service Agreements (PSAs) to meet the needs of key accounts and for segments of other customers. The PSAs specify levels of performance. The teams work with key customers to improve processes and reduce demand variability and non-value-added activities. Performance

The customer relationship management process provides the structure for how the relationships with customers will be developed and maintained.

[44] Blackstock, Thomas, Keynote Speech, International Association of Food Industry Suppliers, San Francisco, CA, March 11, 2005.

[45] Blackstock, Thomas, Keynote Speech, International Association of Food Industry Suppliers, San Francisco, CA, March 11, 2005.

reports are designed to measure the profitability of individual customers as well as the firm's impact on the financial performance of the customer.[46]

Supplier Relationship Management

The supplier relationship management process provides the structure for how relationships with suppliers will be developed and maintained. As the name suggests, this is a mirror image of customer relationship management. Just as a company needs to develop relationships with its customers, it also needs to foster relationships with its suppliers. Close relationships are developed with a small subset of suppliers based on the value that they provide to the organization over time, and more traditional relationships are maintained with the others. Supplier teams negotiate PSAs with each key supplier that defines the terms of the relationship. For each segment of less critical suppliers, a standard PSA is provided and it is not negotiable. Supplier relationship management is about defining and managing these PSAs. Partnerships are developed with a small core group of suppliers. The desired outcome is a win-win relationship where both parties benefit.

Customer Service Management

Customer service management is the supply chain management process that deals with the administration of the PSAs developed by customer teams as part of the customer relationship management process. Customer service managers monitor the PSAs and proactively intervene on the customer's behalf if there is going to be a problem delivering on promises that have been made. The goal is to solve problems before they affect the customer. Customer service managers will interface with other process teams, such as supplier relationship management and manufacturing flow management to ensure that promises made in the PSA's are delivered as planned.

Demand Management

Demand management is the supply chain management process that balances the customers' requirements with the capabilities of the supply chain. With the right process in place, management can match supply with demand proactively and execute the plan with minimal disruptions. The process is not limited to forecasting. It includes synchronizing supply and demand, reducing variability and increasing flexibility. For example, it involves managing all of the organization's practices that increase demand variability, such as end-of-quarter loading and terms of sale which encourage volume buys. A good demand management process uses point-of-sale and key customer data to reduce uncertainty and provide efficient flows throughout the supply chain. Marketing requirements and production plans should be coordinated on an enterprise-wide basis. In advanced applications, customer demand and production rates are synchronized to manage inventories globally.

---

[46]Lambert, Douglas M. and Terrance L. Pohlen, "Supply Chain Metrics," *The International Journal of Logistics Management*, Vol. 12, No. 1, (2001), pp. 1-19.

Order Fulfillment

The order fulfillment process involves more than just filling orders. It includes all activities necessary to design a network and enable a firm to meet customer requests while minimizing the total delivered cost. At the strategic level, for example, it is necessary to determine which countries should be used to service the needs of various customers considering service requirements, tax rates and where profits should be earned as well as import and export regulations. While much of the actual work will be performed by the logistics function, it needs to be implemented cross-functionally and with the coordination of key suppliers and customers. The objective is to develop a seamless process from the various customer segments to the organization and then on to its suppliers.

Manufacturing Flow Management

Manufacturing flow management is the supply chain management process that includes all activities necessary to obtain, implement and manage manufacturing flexibility in the supply chain and to move products into, through and out of the plants. Manufacturing flexibility reflects the ability to make a wide variety of products in a timely manner at the lowest possible cost. To achieve the desired level of manufacturing flexibility, planning and execution must extend beyond the four walls of the manufacturer to other members of the supply chain.

Product Development and Commercialization

Product development and commercialization is the supply chain management process that provides the structure for developing and bringing to market products jointly with customers and suppliers. Effective implementation of the process not only enables management to coordinate the efficient flow of new products across the supply chain, but also assists other members of the supply chain with the ramp-up of manufacturing, logistics, marketing and other activities necessary to support the commercialization of the product. The product development and commercialization process team must coordinate with customer relationship management process teams to identify customer articulated and unarticulated needs; select materials and suppliers in conjunction with the supplier relationship management process teams; and, work with the manufacturing flow management process team to develop production technology to manufacture and implement the best product flow for the product/market combination.

Product development and commercialization is the supply chain management process that provides the structure for developing and bringing to market products jointly with customers and suppliers.

Returns Management

Returns management is the supply chain management process by which activities associated with returns, reverse logistics, gatekeeping, and avoidance are managed within the firm and across key members of the supply chain. The correct implementation of this process enables management not only to manage the reverse product flow efficiently, but to identify opportunities to reduce unwanted returns and to control reusable assets such as containers. While significant opportunities to reduce costs are possible through better management of reverse logistics, even greater potential to reduce costs and increase revenue are possible by eliminating those management practices and performance failures that cause returns.

The Requirement for Standard Business Processes

Thousands of activities are performed and coordinated within a company, and every company is by nature in some way involved in supply chain relationships with other companies.[47] When two companies build a relationship, some of their internal activities will be managed between the two companies.[48] Since both companies have linked some internal activities with other members of their supply chain, a link between two companies is thus a link in what might be conceived as a supply chain network. For example, the internal activities of a manufacturer can affect the internal activities of a distributor, which in turn have an effect on the internal activities of a retailer. Ultimately, the internal activities of the retailer are linked with and can affect the activities of the end-user.

Our research team has found that in some companies, executives emphasize a functional structure (see Figure 1-3, Tier 1 Supplier) and others a process structure (see Figure 1-3, Manufacturer, Tier 2 Supplier and both tiers of customers). Those companies with processes had different numbers of processes consisting of different activities and links between activities. Different names were used for similar processes, and similar names for different processes. This lack of inter-

Figure 1-3
Supply Chain Management: The Disconnects

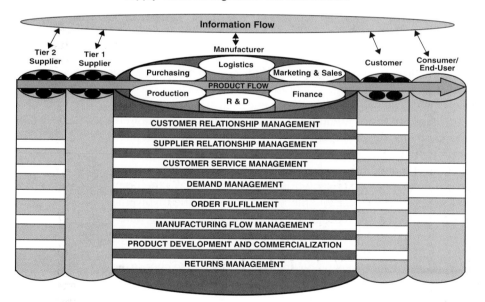

Source: Adapted from Douglas M. Lambert, Martha C. Cooper, and Janus D. Pagh, "Supply Chain Management: Implementation Issues and Research Opportunities," *The International Journal of Logistics Management,* Vol. 9, No. 2 (1998), p. 10.

[47] Bowersox, Donald J., "Integrated Supply Chain Management; A Strategic Perspective," *Annual Conference Proceedings*, Chicago, Illinois: Council of Logistics Management (1997), pp. 181-189; George E. Stigler, "The Division of Labor Is Limited by the Extent of the Market," *Journal of Political Economy*, Vol. 59, No. 3 (1951), pp. 185-193; and, R. H. Coase, "The Nature of the Firm," *Economica*, Vol. 4 (1937), pp. 386-405.

[48] Håkansson, Håkan and Ivan Snehota, *Developing Relationships in Business Networks*, London: Routledge, 1995.

company consistency is a cause of significant friction and inefficiencies in supply chains. It is important that managers in different firms speak the same language (use the same terminology). There is generally an understanding of what corporate functions like marketing, manufacturing and finance represent. If management in each firm identifies its own set of processes, how can these processes be linked across firms?

In some of the GSCF companies, business processes extended to suppliers and were managed to some extent between the two firms involved. This may imply that when a leadership role is taken, firms in the supply chain will use the same business processes. When this is possible, each member of the band is playing the same tune.

The number of business processes that should be integrated and managed between companies will likely vary. However, in each specific case, it is important that executives thoroughly analyze and discuss which key business processes to integrate and manage.

Achieving Cross-Functional and Cross-Firm Involvement Using the Supply Chain Management Processes

If the proper coordination mechanisms are not in place across the various functions, the process will be neither effective nor efficient. By taking a process focus, all functions that touch the product or are involved in the service delivery must work together. Figure 1-4 shows examples of how managers from each function within the organization provide input to the eight supply chain management processes. For example, in the customer relationship management process, marketing provides the knowledge of customers and marketing programs as well as the budget for marketing expenditures, sales provides the account management expertise, research and development provides the technological capabilities to develop product solutions that meet customer requirements, logistics provides knowledge of logistics and customer service capabilities, production provides the manufacturing capabilities, purchasing provides knowledge of supplier capabilities, and finance provides customer profitability reports. Customers and suppliers are shown in Figure 1-4 to make the point that each of these processes, to be properly implemented, requires the involvement of all business functions as well as customers and suppliers. When third-party logistics providers are used, representatives from these firms should serve on the process teams to provide their logistics expertise.

In order to achieve cross-firm integration, management needs to choose the type of relationship that is appropriate for each link in the supply chain.[49] Not all links throughout the supply chain should be closely coordinated and integrated. The most appropriate relationship is the one that best fits the specific set of circumstances.[50]

If management in each firm identifies its own set of processes, how can these processes be linked across firms?

If the proper coordination mechanisms are not in place across the various functions, the process will be neither effective nor efficient.

---

[49] Lambert, Douglas M. and A. Michael Knemeyer, "We're in This Together," *Harvard Business Review*, Vol. 82, No. 12 (2004), pp. 96-108 and Lambert, Douglas M., Margaret A. Emmelhainz, and John T. Gardner, "Developing and Implementing Supply Chain Partnerships," *The International Journal of Logistics Management*, Vol. 7, No. 2 (1996), pp.1-17.

[50] Cooper, Martha C. and John T. Gardner, "Good Business Relationships: More Than Just Partnerships or Strategic Alliances," *International Journal of Physical Distribution and Logistics Management*, Vol. 23, No. 6 (1993), pp. 14-20.

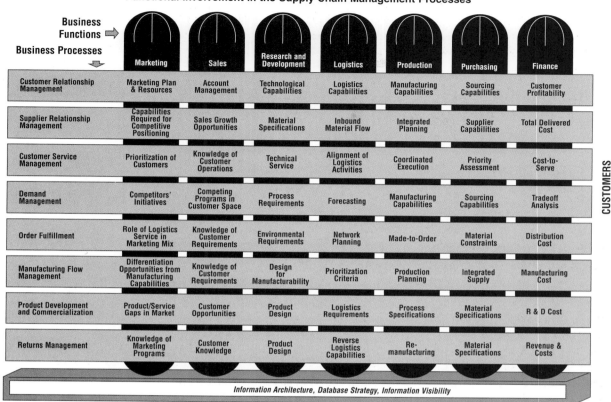

Figure 1-4
Functional Involvement in the Supply Chain Management Processes

Business Processes	Marketing	Sales	Research and Development	Logistics	Production	Purchasing	Finance
Customer Relationship Management	Marketing Plan & Resources	Account Management	Technological Capabilities	Logistics Capabilities	Manufacturing Capabilities	Sourcing Capabilities	Customer Profitability
Supplier Relationship Management	Capabilities Required for Competitive Positioning	Sales Growth Opportunities	Material Specifications	Inbound Material Flow	Integrated Planning	Supplier Capabilities	Total Delivered Cost
Customer Service Management	Prioritization of Customers	Knowledge of Customer Operations	Technical Service	Alignment of Logistics Activities	Coordinated Execution	Priority Assessment	Cost-to-Serve
Demand Management	Competitors' Initiatives	Competing Programs in Customer Space	Process Requirements	Forecasting	Manufacturing Capabilities	Sourcing Capabilities	Tradeoff Analysis
Order Fulfillment	Role of Logistics Service in Marketing Mix	Knowledge of Customer Requirements	Environmental Requirements	Network Planning	Made-to-Order	Material Constraints	Distribution Cost
Manufacturing Flow Management	Differentiation Opportunities from Manufacturing Capabilities	Knowledge of Customer Requirements	Design for Manufacturability	Prioritization Criteria	Production Planning	Integrated Supply	Manufacturing Cost
Product Development and Commercialization	Product/Service Gaps in Market	Customer Opportunities	Product Design	Logistics Requirements	Process Specifications	Material Specifications	R & D Cost
Returns Management	Knowledge of Marketing Programs	Customer Knowledge	Product Design	Reverse Logistics Capabilities	Re-manufacturing	Material Specifications	Revenue & Costs

SUPPLIERS · Business Functions ⇒ · CUSTOMERS

Information Architecture, Database Strategy, Information Visibility

Note: Process sponsorship and ownership must be established to drive the attainment of the supply chain vision and eliminate the functional silo mentality.

Source: Adapted from Keely L. Croxton, Sebastian J. García-Dastuque and Douglas M. Lambert, "The Supply Chain Management Processes," *The International Journal of Logistics Management*, Vol. 12, No. 2 (2001), p.31.

Determining which members of the supply chain deserve management attention is based on their importance to the firm's success. In some companies, management works closely with second-tier members of the supply chain in order to achieve specific supply chain objectives, such as product availability, improved quality, improved product introductions, or reduced overall supply chain costs. For example, a tomato ketchup manufacturer in New Zealand conducts research on tomatoes in order to develop plants that provide larger tomatoes with fewer seeds. Their contracted growers are provided with young plants in order to ensure the quality of the output. Since the growers tend to be small, the manufacturer negotiates contracts with suppliers of equipment and agricultural chemicals such as fertilizer and pesticides. The farmers are encouraged to purchase materials and machinery using the manufacturer's contract rates. This results in higher quality tomatoes and lower prices without sacrificing the margins and financial strength of the growers.

Customer relationship management and supplier relationship management form the critical linkages throughout the supply chain.

The Critical Supply Chain Management Linkages

Customer relationship management and supplier relationship management form the critical linkages throughout the supply chain (see Figure 1-5). For each

Figure 1-5
Customer Relationship Management (CRM) and Supplier Relationship Management (SRM):
The Critical Supply Chain Management Linkages

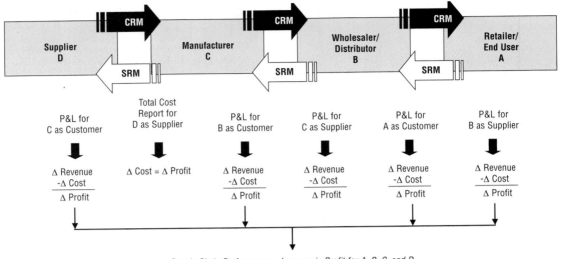

Supply Chain Performance = Increase in Profit for A, B, C, and D

Source: Adapted from Douglas M. Lambert and Terrance L. Pohlen, "Supply Chain Metrics," *The International Journal of Logistics Management,* Vol. 12, No. 1 (2001), p. 14.

supplier in the supply chain, the ultimate measure of success for the customer relationship management process is the positive change in profitability of an individual customer or segment of customers over time. For each customer, the most comprehensive measure of success for the supplier relationship management process is the impact that a supplier or supplier segment has on the firm's profitability. The goal is to increase the profitability of each organization by developing the relationship. The biggest potential roadblock is failure to reach agreement on how to split the gains that are made through joint improvement efforts. The overall performance of the supply chain is determined by the combined improvement in profitability of all of its members from one year to the next.

Typically, large sums of money are spent by corporations to attract new customers; yet these same companies are often complacent when it comes to nurturing existing customers to build and strengthen relationships with them.[51] However, for most companies existing customers represent the best opportunities for profitable growth. There are direct and strong relationships between profit growth; customer loyalty; customer satisfaction; and, the value of goods delivered to customers.[52] In a business-to-business environment, the customer relationship management process is the supply chain management process that provides the structure for how relationships with customers are developed and maintained. The decision regarding who is a key customer requires evaluation of the profitability and

The decision regarding who is a key customer requires evaluation of the profitability and potential profitability of individual customers.

[51] Berry, Leonard L. and A. Parasuraman, "Marketing to Existing Customers" in *Marketing Services: Competing Through Quality,* New York, NY: The Free Press, 1991, p.132.

[52] Heskett, James L., W. Earl Sasser, Fr. and Leonard A. Schlesinger, *The Service Profit Chain,* New York, NY: The Free Press, 1997, p.11.

potential profitability of individual customers. Then, cross-functional customer teams tailor PSAs to meet the needs of key accounts and segments of other customers.[53] PSAs come in many forms, both formal and informal, and may be referred to by different names. However, for best results they should be formalized as written documents. Teams work with key accounts to improve processes, and reduce demand variability and non-value-added activities.

Supplier relationship management is the mirror image of customer relationship management. All suppliers are not the same. Some suppliers contribute disproportionately to the firm's success and with these organizations, it is important to have cross-functional teams interacting. There will be teams established for each key supplier and for each segment of non-key suppliers. The teams are comprised of managers from several functions, including marketing, finance, research and development, production, purchasing and logistics. At the strategic level, the team is responsible for developing the strategic process, and seeing that it is implemented. Supplier teams have the day-to-day responsibility for managing the process at the operational level.

Some suppliers contribute disproportionately to the firm's success and with these organizations, it is important to have cross-functional teams interacting.

Since, there will be a customer team and a supplier team for each key customer and supplier, and for each segment of non-key customers/suppliers, it is important that teams calling on competitors do not have overlapping members. It will be very hard for team members to not be influenced by what has been discussed as part of developing a PSA for a competitor of the firm with which they are working. Given the current spotlight on business ethics, it is important to reach agreement on what data to share and there is a fine line between using process knowledge gained versus using competitive marketing knowledge gained from a customer or supplier. Firm employees outside of the team might execute parts of the process, but the team still maintains managerial control.

Customer relationship management and supplier relationship management are the key processes for linking firms across the supply chain and each of the other six processes is coordinated through this linkage. For example, if the customer relationship management and supplier relationship management teams decide that there is an opportunity to improve performance by focusing on the demand management process, the demand management process teams from the two companies are involved. When the process is improved, product availability is improved. If this is important, revenue for the customer increases. In addition, inventories are reduced, thereby reducing the inventory carrying cost charged to the customer's profitability report. There also may be fewer last minute production changes and less expediting of inbound materials which will impact the costs assigned to each customer. It is important that metrics are in place for the demand management process teams so that members can be compensated for the improvements derived. However, if profitability reports by customer are properly developed, they will capture improvements made in all of the processes. So having accurate profitability reports is key.

---

[53] Seybold, Patrica B., "Get Inside the Lives of Your Customers", *Harvard Business Review*, Vol. 78, No. 5 (2001), pp. 81-89.

Measuring the Financial Impact of Customer Relationship Management and Supplier Relationship Management

The development of customer profitability reports enables the customer relationship management process teams to track performance over time. These reports should reflect all of the cost and revenue implications of the relationship. Variable manufacturing costs are deducted from net sales to calculate a manufacturing contribution. Next, variable marketing and logistics costs, such as sales commissions, transportation, warehouse handling, special packaging, order processing and a charge for accounts receivable, are deducted to calculate a contribution margin. Assignable non-variable costs, such as salaries, customer related advertising expenditures, slotting allowances and inventory carrying costs, are subtracted to obtain a segment controllable margin. The net margin is obtained after deducting a charge for dedicated assets. Because these statements contain opportunity costs for investments in receivables and inventory and a charge for dedicated assets, they are much closer to cash flow statements than traditional profit and loss statements. They contain revenues minus the costs (avoidable costs) that disappear if the revenue disappears.

Sysco, a $23.4 billion food distributor, implemented profitability reports by customer in 1999. These reports enabled management to make strategic decisions about the allocation of resources to accounts, such as which customers receive preferred delivery times, which customers receive value-added services free and which ones must pay for them. The result was increased profit growth as illustrated in Figure 1-6. The five-year cumulative annual growth rate for the period 1999 to 2003 was 11.3% for sales and 19.1% for net earnings. As shown in Figure 1-6, the

The development of customer profitability reports enables the customer relationship management process teams to track performance over time.

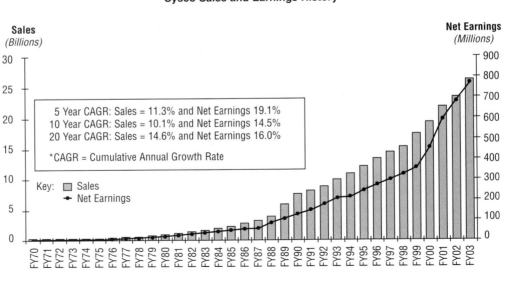

Figure 1-6
Sysco Sales and Earnings History

5 Year CAGR: Sales = 11.3% and Net Earnings 19.1%
10 Year CAGR: Sales = 10.1% and Net Earnings 14.5%
20 Year CAGR: Sales = 14.6% and Net Earnings 16.0%

*CAGR = Cumulative Annual Growth Rate

Key: Sales
Net Earnings

Source: Neil Theiss, Senior Director, Supply Chain Management, Sysco Corporation.

rate of growth in net earnings improved sharply after the profitability reports were implemented.

In the case of retailers and wholesalers, profitability reports also can be developed for each supplier. However, for manufacturers who purchase materials, total cost reports are used to evaluate suppliers. In addition to measuring current performance, these profitability reports and total cost reports can be used to track performance of customers and suppliers over time and to generate pro-forma statements that can be used to evaluate potential process improvement projects. Decision analysis can be performed to consider "what if" scenarios such as best, worst and most likely cases.

Figure 1-7 shows how the customer relationship management process can affect the firm's financial performance as measured by economic value added (EVA®).[54] It illustrates how customer relationship management can impact sales, cost of goods sold, total expenses, inventory investment, other current assets, and the investment in fixed assets. For example, customer relationship management can lead to higher sales volume as a result of strengthening relationships with profitable customers, selling higher margin products, increasing the firm's share of the customer's expenditures for the products/services sold, and/or improving the mix, that is, aligning services and the costs to serve. The same approach can be

Figure 1-7
How Customer Relationship Management Affects Economic Value Added (EVA®)

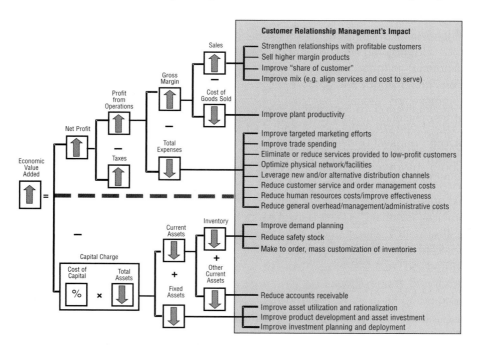

Source: Adapted from Douglas M. Lambert and Terrance L. Pohlen, "Supply Chain Metrics," *The International Journal of Logistics Management*, Vol. 12, No. 1 (2001), p. 10.

[54] Stewart, III, G. Bennett, *The Quest for Value*, New York: Harper Collins Publishers, Inc., 1999.

used for each of the eight SCM processes to measure its impact on EVA®.

Management should implement processes that increase the profitability of the total supply chain not just the profitability of a single firm. Implementing supply chain management should benefit the whole supply chain while members share equitably in the risks and the rewards. If the management team of a firm makes a decision that positively affects that firm's EVA® at the expense of the EVA® of customers or suppliers, every effort should be made to share the benefits in a manner that improves the financial performance of each firm involved and thus give each one an incentive to improve overall supply chain performance.

Implementing supply chain management should benefit the whole supply chain while members share equitably in the risks and the rewards.

Building High-Performance Relationships in the Supply Chain

Successful implementation of The Global Supply Chain Forum Supply Chain Management Framework is dependent on developing close relationships with key customers and suppliers. In other words, supply chain management is relationship management. For this reason, there is a need for a tool that can be used to structure the key relationships that are identified when implementing customer relationship management and supplier relationship management. This tool is the partnership model and the GSCF definition of partnership follows.

> A partnership is a *tailored* business relationship based on mutual trust, openness, shared risk and shared rewards that results in business performance greater than would be achieved by the two firms working together in the absence of partnership.[55]

Partnerships can take multiple forms and the degree of partnership achieved can reflect tight integration across the firm boundaries, or only limited integration across the boundaries. Since partnership implementation requires significant managerial time commitments and often other resource commitments, the goal is to fit the type of partnership to the business situation and the organizational environment. The types of partnership are Type I, Type II and Type III. These are called "types," not "levels" because there should be no implication that higher levels are better than lower levels. The goal should be to have the correct amount of partnering in the relationship. Figure 1-8 illustrates the range of possible relationships.

Figure 1-8
Types of Relationships

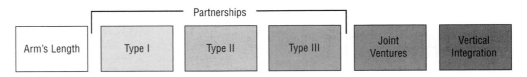

Source: Douglas M. Lambert, Margaret A. Emmelhainz and John T. Gardner, "Developing and Implementing Supply Chain Partnerships," *The International Journal of Logistics Management*, Vol. 7, No. 2 (1996), p. 2.

---

[55] Lambert, Douglas M., and A. Michael Knemeyer, "We're In This Together," *Harvard Business Review*, Vol. 82, No. 12 (2004), pp. 114-122 and Douglas M. Lambert, *Supply Chain Management; Processes, Partnerships, Performance*, Sarasota, Florida: Supply Chain Management Institute, 2006, p. 169.

The Partnership Model

The model separates the drivers of partnership, the facilitators of partnership, the components of partnership and the outcomes of partnership into four major areas for attention (see Figure 1-9). Drivers are the compelling reasons to partner, and must be examined first when approaching a potential partner. Facilitators are characteristics of the two firms that will help or hinder the partnership development process. Components are the managerially controllable elements that should be implemented at a particular level depending on the type of partnership. Outcomes measure the extent to which each firm achieves its drivers. The partnership model provides a structure for assessing the drivers and facilitators, and component descriptions for the prescribed type of partnership.

Drivers. Why add managerial complexity and commit resources to a supply chain relationship if a good, long-term contract that is well specified will do? To the degree that business as usual will not get the supply chain efficiencies needed, partnership may be necessary. By looking for compelling reasons to partner, the drivers of partnership, management in the two firms may find that they both have an interest in tailoring the relationship. The model separates the drivers into four categories: asset/cost efficiencies, customer service improvements, marketing advantage, and profit stability and growth. All businesses are concerned with these four issues, and the four can capture the goals of managers for their relationships.

Facilitators. The nature of the two firms involved in partnership implementation will determine how easy or hard it will be to tailor the relationship. If the two firms mesh easily, the managerial effort and resources devoted to putting the correct relationship in place will be lower for the same results. The elements that make partnership implementation easy or hard are called facilitators. They represent the environment of the partnership; those aspects of the two firms that will help or hinder partnership

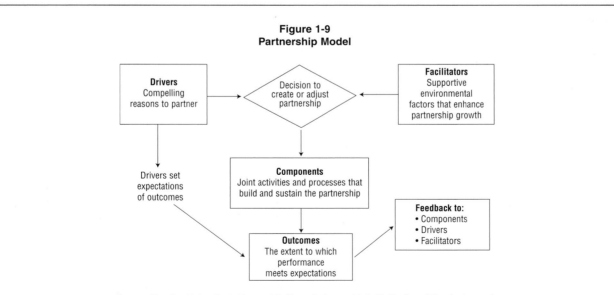

Figure 1-9
Partnership Model

Source: Douglas M. Lambert, Margaret A. Emmelhainz and John T. Gardner, "Developing and Implementing Supply Partnerships," *The International Journal of Logistics Management*, Vol. 7, No. 2 (1996), p. 4.

activities. There are four major categories of facilitators: corporate compatibility, management philosophy and techniques, mutuality and symmetry.

Components. While drivers and facilitators determine the potential for partnership, the components are the building blocks of partnership. They are universal across firms and across business environments and unlike drivers and facilitators, are under the direct control of the managers involved. In other words, they are the activities that managers in the two firms actually perform to implement the partnership. There are eight components of partnership: planning, joint operating controls, communications, risk/reward sharing, trust and commitment, contract style, scope and investment. The components are implemented differently for Type I, Type II and Type III partnerships. Action items are identified for the drivers and components so that both partners' expectations are met.

Outcomes. A partnership, if appropriately established and effectively managed, should improve performance for both parties. Profit enhancement, process improvements, and increased competitive advantage are all likely outcomes of effective partnerships. Specific outcomes will vary depending upon the drivers which initially motivated the development of the partnership. It should be noted, however, that a partnership is not required to achieve satisfactory outcomes from a relationship. Typically, organizations will have multiple arm's length relationships which meet the needs of and provide benefits to both parties.

A partnership, if appropriately established and effectively managed, should improve performance for both parties.

The Partnership Building Session

Using the partnership model to tailor a relationship requires a one and one-half day session. The correct team from each firm must be identified and committed to a meeting time. These teams should include top managers, middle managers, operations personnel and staff personnel. A broad mix, both in terms of management level and functional expertise, is required in order to ensure that all perspectives are considered.

The success of the partnership building process depends on the openness and creativity brought to the session. The process is not about whether to have a business relationship; it is about the style of the relationship. The partnership building session is only a first step in a challenging but rewarding long-term effort to tailor your business relationship for enhanced results.

Summary of the Supply Chain Management Framework

Figure 1-10 illustrates the inter-related nature of SCM and the need to proceed through several steps to design and successfully manage a supply chain. The SCM framework consists of three closely inter-related elements: the supply chain network structure, the supply chain management processes, and the supply chain management components. The supply chain network structure is comprised of the member firms and the links between these firms. Business processes are the activities that produce a specific output of value to the customer. The supply chain management components are the managerial methods by which the business processes are integrated and managed across the supply chain. These topics will be covered in detail in the chapters of this book that follow.

Figure 1-10
Supply Chain Management: Elements and Key Decisions

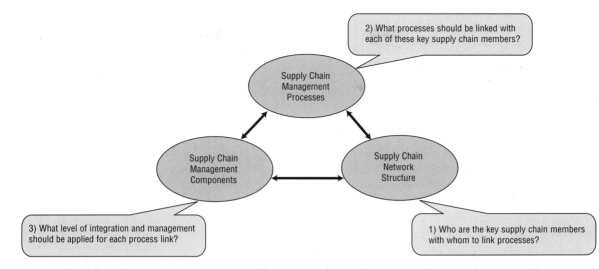

Source: Adapted from Douglas M. Lambert, Martha C. Cooper and Janus Pagh, "Supply Chain Management: Implementation Issues and Research Opportunities," *The International Journal of Logistics Management*, Vol. 9, No. 2 (1998), p. 4.

Conclusions

Executives are becoming aware of the emerging paradigm that the successful integration and management of key supply chain management processes across members of the supply chain will determine the ultimate success of the single enterprise.

Executives are becoming aware of the emerging paradigm of inter-network competition, and that the successful integration and management of the supply chain management processes across members of the supply chain will determine the ultimate success of the single enterprise. Organizations exist in supply chains whether the relationships are managed or not. Managing the supply chain cannot be left to chance.

Research with member firms of The Global Supply Chain Forum indicates that successful SCM requires integrating business processes with key members of the supply chain. Considerable waste of valuable resources results when supply chains are not integrated, appropriately streamlined and managed. The structure of activities/processes within and between companies is vital for creating superior competitiveness and profitability. A prerequisite for successful SCM is to coordinate activities within the firm by implementing the eight supply chain management processes using cross-functional teams. The partnership model is a tool that can be used to structure these cross-functional relationships with key customers and suppliers.

Failure to implement cross-functional business processes will result in missed opportunities that with the level of competitiveness faced by most firms can no longer be tolerated. For example, a manufacturer of consumer durable goods implemented a rapid delivery system that provided retailers with deliveries in 24 or 48 hours anywhere in the United States. The rapid delivery system was designed to enable the retailers to improve service to retail consumers while holding less inventory and thus improving per unit profitability. Six years later, the company had not seen the anticipated reductions in retailers' inventories and reduced the service promise to 48 or 72 hours depending on the retailer's location. The rapid delivery system never achieved its full potential because the sales and marketing organizations still provided customers with incentives to buy in large volumes.[56] This example should make it clear that failure to manage all the touches will diminish the impact of initiatives within the supply chain. Implementing the eight supply chain management processes will increase the likelihood of success because all functions as well as key customers and suppliers will be involved in the planning and implementation of the initiative. The penalty for not gaining the full involvement of all functions and aligning the metrics is dealing with the actions of those who maliciously or inadvertently undermine the initiatives.

The implementation of SCM involves identifying: the supply chain members, with whom it is critical to link; the processes that need to be linked with each of these key members; and, the type/level of integration that applies to each process link. The objective of SCM is to create the most value not simply for the company but the whole supply chain network including the end-customer. Consequently, supply chain process integration and reengineering initiatives should be aimed at boosting total process efficiency and effectiveness across members of the supply chain.

At a meeting of The Global Supply Chain Forum, a series of break-out sessions were devoted to the topic "the supply chain of the future". At the end of the day, the conclusion of the group was that when an organization's management had successfully implemented all eight of the SCM processes, they would have achieved the supply chain of the future and would be able to respond to whatever challenges the business might face. Where is your company in terms of successful implementation of cross-functional business processes? In order to create the most value for the company's shareholders and the whole supply chain including end users/consumers, management must take action to integrate the supply chain. The time for action is now.

The remaining 15 chapters of this book are organized as follows. Chapters 2 through 9 contain detailed descriptions of the eight supply chain management processes: customer relationship management, supplier relationship management, customer service management, demand management, order fulfillment, manufacturing flow management, product development and commercialization, and returns management. Chapter 10 deals with how to conduct assessments of the supply chain management processes using the assessment tools at the end of the book. Chapter 11 deals with mapping for supply chain management. In Chapter 12, the authors describe lean thinking and supply chain management. Chapter 13 contains material on implementing and sustaining the supply chain management processes and in Chapter 14 a systematic process for developing, implementing and continuously improving relationships with key members of the supply chain is presented. Chapter 15 deals with supply chain management performance measurement. Finally, Chapter 16, Supply Chain Management: The Next Steps, provides a comparison of The Global Supply Chain Forum and Supply Chain Council supply chain management frameworks as well as guidelines for implementing the GSCF framework.

The implementation of SCM involves identifying: the supply chain members, with whom it is critical to link; the processes that need to be linked with each of these key members; and, the type/level of integration that applies to each process link.

---

[56] Lambert, Douglas M. and Renan Burduroglu, "Measuring and Selling the Value of Logistics", *The International Journal of Logistics Management*, Vol. 11, No. 1 (2000), pp. 1-17.

CHAPTER

2

The Customer Relationship Management Process

Douglas M. Lambert

Overview

The customer relationship management process provides the structure for how relationships with customers will be developed and maintained. The goal is to segment customers based on their value over time and increase customer loyalty by providing customized products and services. In this chapter, the importance of customer relationship management as a supply chain management process is explained and detailed descriptions of the strategic and operational sub-processes that comprise customer relationship management are given. The interfaces that are necessary with the other seven supply chain management processes are identified and guidelines for successful implementation are provided.

Introduction

In a business-to-business environment, customer relationship management is the supply chain management process that provides the structure for how relationships with customers are developed and maintained.

Typically, large sums of money are spent to attract new customers; yet management is often complacent when it comes to nurturing existing customers to build and strengthen relationships with them.[1] However, for most companies, existing customers represent the best opportunities for profitable growth. There are direct and strong relationships between profit growth; customer loyalty; customer satisfaction; and, the value of goods delivered to customers.[2] "Relationship marketing concerns attracting, developing, and retaining customer relationships".[3] In a business-to-business environment, customer relationship management is the supply chain management process that provides the structure for how relationships with customers are developed and maintained. Management identifies key customers and customer groups to be targeted as part of the firm's business mission. The decision regarding who represents key customers requires evaluation of the profitability and potential profitability of individual customers. Often it is assumed that the marketing function is responsible for creating, maintaining and strengthening relationships with business-to-business customers because it does

---

[1] Berry, Leonard L. and A. Parasuraman, "Marketing to Existing Customers" in *Marketing Services: Competing Through Quality*, New York, NY: The Free Press, 1991, p.132.

[2] Heskett, James L., W. Earl Sasser, Fr. and Leonard A. Schlesinger, *The Service Profit Chain*, New York, NY: The Free Press, 1997, p.11.

[3] Berry, Leonard L. and A. Parasuraman, "Marketing to Existing Customers" in *Marketing Services: Competing Through Quality,* New York, NY: The Free Press, 1991, p.133.

this with consumers. However, for two large organizations to be able to coordinate their complex operations, all corporate functions must be involved and actively participate in the relationship in order to align corporate resources with the profit potential of each relationship. The customer teams tailor product and service agreements (PSAs) to meet the needs of key accounts and segments of other customers.[4] PSAs come in many forms, both formal and informal, and may be referred to by different names from company to company. However, for best results they should be formalized as written documents. Teams work with key accounts to improve processes, and eliminate demand variability and non-value-added activities. Performance reports are designed to measure the profitability of individual customers as well as the firm's financial impact on those customers.

The customer teams tailor product and service agreements (PSAs) to meet the needs of key accounts and segments of other customers.

Customer relationship management has become a critical business process as a result of: competitive pressures; the need to achieve cost efficiency in order to be a low-cost, high-quality supplier; a recognition of the fact that customers are not equal in terms of their profitability; and, knowledge that customer retention can significantly affect profitability. Customer relationship management is one of the eight supply chain management processes (see Figure 2-1) and it must interface with each of the other seven. In this chapter, a description of the strategic and operational processes that comprise customer relationship management is provided along with the sub-processes and the activities that comprise each sub-

Figure 2-1
Supply Chain Management:
Integrating and Managing Business Processes Across the Supply Chain

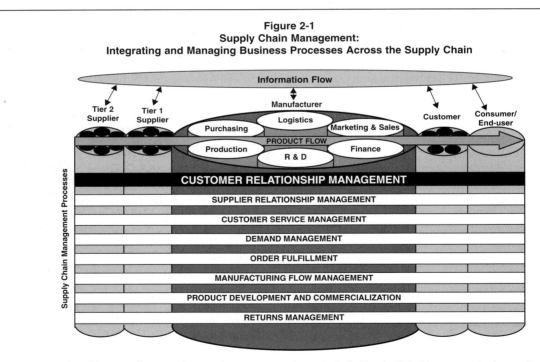

Source: Adapted from Douglas M. Lambert, Martha C. Cooper, and Janus D. Pagh, "Supply Chain Management: Implementation Issues and Research Opportunities," *The International Journal of Logistics Management,* Vol. 9, No. 2 (1998), p. 2.

---

[4] Seybold, Patrica B., "Get Inside the Lives of Your Customers", *Harvard Business Review,* Vol. 78, No. 5 (2001), pp. 81-89.

process. Also, there are descriptions of the interfaces with functions, the other supply chain management processes and other firms. Finally, conclusions are presented.

Customer Relationship Management as a Supply Chain Management Process

Customer relationship management and supplier relationship management provide the critical linkages throughout the supply chain.

Customer relationship management and supplier relationship management provide the critical linkages throughout the supply chain (see Figure 2-2). For each supplier in the supply chain, the ultimate measure of success for the customer relationship management process is the change in profitability of an individual customer or segment of customers. For each customer, the most comprehensive measure of success for the supplier relationship management process is the impact that a supplier or supplier segment has on the firm's profitability. The goal is to increase the joint profitability by developing the relationship. The biggest potential roadblock is failure to reach agreement on how to split the gains that are made through joint process improvement efforts. The overall performance of the supply chain is determined by the combined improvement in profitability of all of its members from one year to the next.

While there are a great number of software products that are being marketed as customer relationship management, these technology tools should not be confused with the relationship-focused supply chain management process. Customer relationship management software has the potential to enable management to gather customer data quickly, identify the most valuable customers over time, and provide the customized products and services that should increase

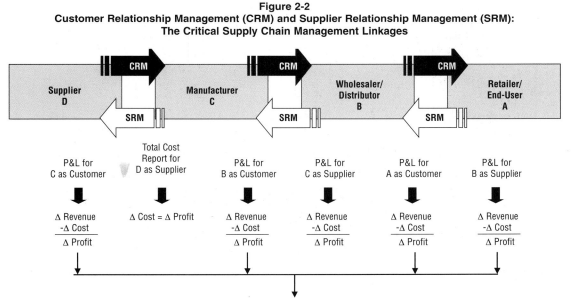

Figure 2-2
Customer Relationship Management (CRM) and Supplier Relationship Management (SRM):
The Critical Supply Chain Management Linkages

Supply Chain Performance = Increase in Profit for A, B, C, and D

Source: Adapted from Douglas M. Lambert and Terrance L. Pohlen, "Supply Chain Metrics," *The International Journal of Logistics Management,* Vol. 12, No. 1 (2001), p. 14.

customer loyalty.[5] When it works, the costs to serve customers can be reduced making it easier to acquire more, similar customers. However, according to Gartner Group, 55% of all customer relationship management (software solutions) projects do not produce results.[6] In a Bain Survey of 451 senior executives, 25% reported that these software tools had failed to deliver profitable growth and in many cases had damaged long-standing customer relationships. One firm spent over $30 million only to scrap the entire project.[7] There are four major reasons for the failure of customer relationship management software projects: (1) implementing software solutions before creating a customer strategy; (2) rolling out software before changing the organization; (3) assuming that more technology is better; and, (4) trying to build relationships with the wrong customers.[8] To be successful, management must place its primary focus on the customer relationship management process and the people and the procedures that make the technology effective. Relying on the technology by itself will most often lead to failure.[9]

Unfortunately, there are a wide range of views as to what constitutes customer relationship management. At one extreme, it is about the implementation of a specific technology solution and at the other, it is a holistic approach to selectively managing relationships to create shareholder value.[10] It is the former perspective that results in so many failures. In order to develop mutually beneficial business relationships, customer relationship management should be positioned in a broad strategic context and be consistently implemented throughout the organization.[11] According to Payne and Frow, customer relationship management must be viewed as strategic, cross-functional and process-based in order to avoid the potential problems associated with a narrow technology oriented definition.[12] However, the functions that they included appear to be limited to executives working in sales, marketing and information technology. There was no indication that managers from finance, research and development, production/operations, purchasing, logistics or other functions had been included or even considered. It is imperative that all corporate functions are involved in complex, high-value business relationships. As identified in *The Service-Dominant Logic of Marketing*, knowledge is the fundamental source of competitive advantage, the customer is a

...customer relationship management must be viewed as strategic, cross-functional and process-based in order to avoid the potential problems associated with a narrow technology oriented definition.

---

[5] Rigby, Darrell K., Frederick F. Reichheld and Phil Scheffer, "Avoid the Four Perils of CRM,", *Harvard Business Review*, Vol. 80, No. 2 (2002), pp. 101-109.

[6] Rigby, Darrell K., Frederick F. Reichheld and Phil Scheffer, "Avoid the Four Perils of CRM,", *Harvard Business Review*, Vol. 80, No. 2 (2002), pp. 101-109.

[7] Rigby, Darrell K., Frederick F. Reichheld and Phil Scheffer, "Avoid the Four Perils of CRM,", *Harvard Business Review*, Vol. 80, No. 2 (2002), pp.101-109.

[8] Rigby, Darrell K., Frederick F. Reichheld and Phil Scheffer, "Avoid the Four Perils of CRM,", *Harvard Business Review*, Vol. 80, No. 2 (2002), pp. 101-109.

[9] Turchan, Mark P. and Paula Mateus, "The Value of Relationships," *Journal of Business Strategy*, Vol 22, No. 6 (2001), pp. 29-32.

[10] Payne, Adrian and Pennie Frow, "A Strategic Framework for Customer Relationship Management," *Journal of Marketing*, Vol. 69, No. 4 (2005), pp. 167-176.

[11] Swift, Ronald S., *Accelerating Customer Relationships - Using CRM and Relationship Technologies*, Upper Saddle River, New Jersey: Prentice Hall, 2000; and Atul Parvatiyar and Jagdish N. Sheth, "Customer Relationship Management: Emerging Practice, Process and Discipline," *Journal of Economic and Social Research*, Vol. 3, No. 2 (2001), pp. 1-34.

[12] Payne, Adrian and Pennie Frow, "A Strategic Framework for Customer Relationship Management," *Journal of Marketing*, Vol. 69, No. 4 (2005), pp. 167-176.

co-producer, and a service-centered view is customer oriented and relational.[13] In order to generate knowledge of the customer that will lead to the co-production of value, all business functions should be involved in the relationship. The more business functions that are involved in key customer relationships, the more useful the knowledge that will be generated.

The customer relationship management process has both strategic and operational elements. For this reason, the process has been divided into two parts, the strategic process in which management establishes and strategically manages the process, and the operational process in which implementation takes place (see Figure 2-3). Implementation of the strategic process within the firm is a necessary step in integrating the firm with other members of the supply chain, and it is at the operational level that the day-to-day activities take place. The strategic process is led by a management team that is comprised of executives from several functions: marketing, sales, finance, production, purchasing, logistics and, research and development. The team is responsible for making decisions about how relationships with customers will be developed and maintained. At the operational level, there will be a customer team for each key account and for each segment of other customers. It is important that teams calling on competitors do not have

Figure 2-3
Customer Relationship Management

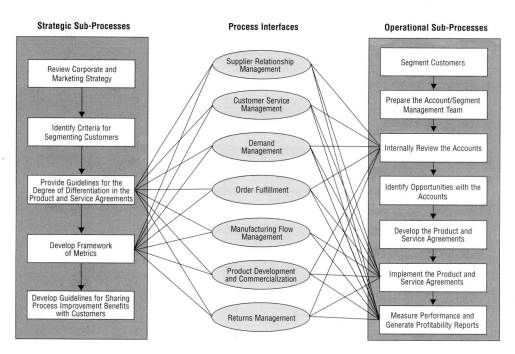

Source: Adapted from Keely L. Croxton, Sebastián J. García-Dastugue, Douglas M. Lambert and Dale S. Rogers, "The Supply Chain Management Processes," *The International Journal of Logistics Management,* Vol. 12, No. 2 (2001), p. 15.

[13] Lusch, Robert F. and Stephen L. Vargo, *The Service-Dominant Logic of Marketing,* Armonk, New York: M.E. Sharpe, Inc., 2006.

overlapping members since it will be very hard for these individuals to not be influenced by what has been discussed as part of developing a PSA for a competitor of the customer. Business ethics dictate that it is important to reach agreement on what data to share and there is a fine line between using process knowledge gained versus using competitive marketing knowledge gained from a customer. The account teams will have day-to-day responsibility for managing the process at the operational level. Firm employees outside of the team might execute parts of the process, but the team still maintains managerial control.

The Strategic Customer Relationship Management Process

At the strategic level, the customer relationship management process provides the structure for how relationships with customers will be developed and managed. An objective is to align functional expertise from the supplier and the customer to support implementation of the other seven supply chain management processes. This alignment is necessary in order to identify and achieve improvment opportunities. The strategic customer relationship management process is comprised of five sub-processes (see Figure 2-4).

Review Corporate and Marketing Strategies

The customer relationship management process team reviews the corporate strategy and the marketing strategy in order to identify markets and target segments

The customer relationship management process team reviews the corporate strategy and the marketing strategy in order to identify markets and target segments that are critical to the organization's success now and in the future.

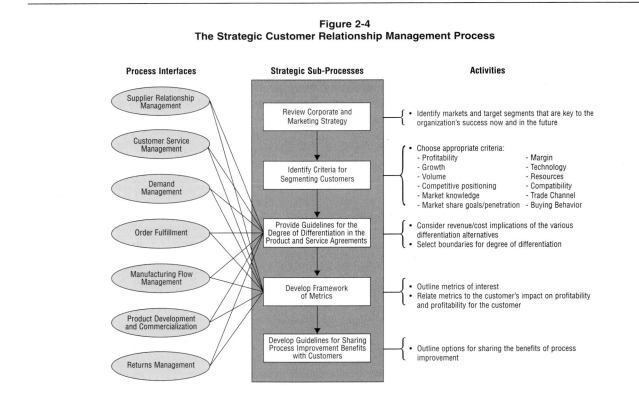

Figure 2-4
The Strategic Customer Relationship Management Process

that are critical to the organization's success now and in the future. Strategies are directional statements that provide guidance in terms of: (1) the markets to serve and customer segments to target; (2) the positioning theme that differentiates the business from its competitors; (3) the channels used to reach the market; and, (4) the appropriate scale and scope of activities to be performed.[14]

Identify Criteria for Segmenting Customers

In the second sub-process, the team identifies the criteria that will be used to segment customers within the markets and target segments identified in the first sub-process. For example, grocery retail may be viewed as an important segment, but all grocery retailers will not be of equal importance to the organization's success. This second level of segmentation provides guidelines for determining which customers qualify for tailored PSAs and which customers will be grouped into segments and offered a standard PSA that is developed to provide value to the segment. Customer segments must have clear differences in their PSAs or they are not distinct segments. Potential segmentation criteria include: profitability, growth potential, volume, competitive positioning issues, access to market knowledge, market share goals, margin levels, level of technology, resources and capabilities, compatibility of strategies, channel of distribution and buying behavior (what drives their buying decision). As part of this sub-process, the team develops the firm's strategy for dealing with segments of customers who do not qualify for individually tailored PSAs.

Provide Guidelines for the Degree of Differentiation in the Product and Service Agreements

The goal is to offer PSAs that enhance the profitability of the firm and its customers.

In the third sub-process, the team develops guidelines for the degree of differentiation in the PSA. This involves developing the differentiation alternatives and considering the revenue and cost implications of each. The output is the degree of customization that can be offered to customers based on the potential of the customer(s). The goal is to offer PSAs that enhance the profitability of the firm and its customers. For some customers, PSAs will be enhanced and in other cases the offerings included in the PSAs will be trimmed. It is a matter of matching the company's resources to the customers' short-term and long-term value to the firm. Profitability reports by customer are a key input when making these decisions. In order to find and understand the opportunities to customize the PSAs, in this sub-process the team will interface with all of the other processes.

At 3M, PSAs contain: the contacts including name, title, telephone, e-mail for both 3M and the customer representatives; details related to transportation including deliveries, order minimums, driver instructions, will calls and appointments; bills of lading (combine or do not combine purchase orders); pallets to be used; purchase order confirmations; order status including names of contact individuals, Internet order status website with user name and password; details related to pricing inquires; availability of market development funds; marketing promotional allowances; acceptability of backorders and how they will be handled; and contract items. For key customers, the PSAs are customized and for segments of other customers standard values are provided for each parameter.

---

[14] Day, George, S., *Market Driven Strategy: Processes for Creating Value,* New York, NY: The Free Press, 1990, p. 6.

Develop Framework of Metrics

Developing the framework of metrics involves outlining the metrics of interest and relating them to the customer's impact on the firm's profitability as well as the firm's impact on the customer's profitability. The customer relationship management process team has the responsibility for assuring that the metrics used to measure the performance of the other processes are not in conflict. Management needs to insure that all internal and external measures are driving consistent and appropriate behavior.[15]

Figure 2-5 shows how the customer relationship management process can affect the firm's financial performance as measured by economic value added (EVA). It illustrates how customer relationship management can impact sales, cost of goods sold, total expenses, inventory investment, other current assets, and the investment in fixed assets. For example, customer relationship management can lead to higher sales volume as a result of strengthening relationships with profitable customers, selling higher margin products, increasing the firm's share of the customer's expenditures for the products/services sold, and/or improving the mix, that is, aligning services and the costs to serve.

Developing the framework of metrics involves outlining the metrics of interest and relating them to the customer's impact on the firm's profitability as well as the firm's impact on the customer's profitability.

Figure 2-5
How Customer Relationship Management Affects Economic Value Added (EVA®)

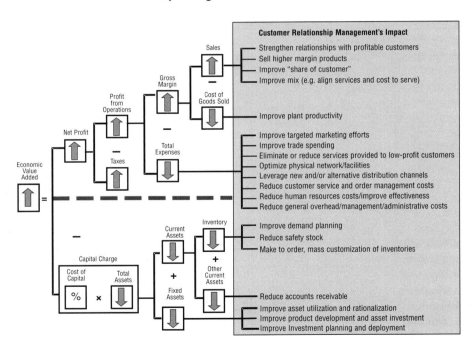

Source: Adapted from Douglas M. Lambert and Terrance L. Pohlen, "Supply Chain Metrics," *The International Journal of Logistics Management,* Vol. 12, No. 1 (2001), p. 10.

[15] Lambert, Douglas M., Martha C. Cooper, and Janus D. Pagh, "Supply Chain Management: Implementation Issues and Research Opportunities," *The International Journal of Logistics Management,* Vol. 9, No. 2 (1998), pp. 1-19.

Cost of goods sold can be reduced as a result of the better planning that comes from collaboration with customers. Cost savings occur due to fewer last-minute production changes and, less expediting of inbound materials and shipments to customers. For wholesalers, significant cost savings can occur as a result of fewer order changes.

Customer relationship management leads to better targeting of marketing expenditures. A number of expenses can be reduced as a result of better tailoring of the firm's marketing and logistics programs to customer needs while giving full consideration to the profitability of each customer. Trade spending also can be improved. Services to low profit customers can be eliminated or reduced and reallocated to more profitable customers to drive revenue growth. Better knowledge of customer requirements and the reduction of services to low-profit customers can lead to a reconfiguration of the physical network of facilities resulting in cost savings. Less profitable customers may be served using wholesalers/distributors which may represent a new channel of distribution. Reductions are also possible in the costs of customer service and order management, human resources, and general overhead and administrative. In addition to reducing expenditures, there is the opportunity through customer relationship management to better allocate resources to customers which can be measured in terms of increased revenue.

Properly implemented, customer relationship management can reduce current assets such as inventories and accounts receivable as well as fixed assets. Inventories can be reduced as a result of improved demand planning, lower safety stocks, and/or the shift to a make-to-order manufacturing environment. Accounts receivable can be reduced as a result of fewer disputed invoices that typically are caused by incomplete orders, missed deliveries, incorrect pricing, and/or products shipped in error. Finally, successful customer relationship management can lead to lower fixed assets as a result of improved utilization/rationalization of plant and warehousing facilities, and improved investment planning and deployment.

Once the team has an understanding of how customer relationship management affects the firm's financial performance as measured by EVA, metrics must be developed for each of the individual activities performed and these metrics must be tied back to the firm's financial performance. However, management should focus on those activities that increase the profitability of the total supply chain not just the profitability of a single firm. Management's goal when implementing supply chain management should be to encourage actions that benefit the whole supply chain while at the same time equitably sharing in the risks and the rewards. If the management team of a firm makes a decision that positively affects that firm's EVA at the expense of the EVA of customers or suppliers, every effort should be made to share the benefits in a manner that improves the financial performance of each firm involved so all involved parties have an incentive to improve overall supply chain performance.

The development of customer profitability reports enables the process team to track performance over time. If calculated as shown in Table 2-1, these reports reflect all of the cost and revenue implications of the relationship. Variable manufacturing costs are deducted from net sales to calculate a manufacturing contribution. Next, variable marketing and logistics costs, such as sales commissions, transportation, warehouse handling, special packaging, order processing and a charge for accounts receivable, are deducted to calculate a

Better knowledge of customer requirements and the reduction of services to low-profit customers can lead to a reconfiguration of the physical network of facilities resulting in cost savings.

Management's goal when implementing supply chain management should be to encourage actions that benefit the whole supply chain while at the same time equitably sharing in the risks and the rewards.

Table 2-1
Customer Profitability Analysis:
A Contribution Approach with Charge for Assets Employed

	Customer A	Customer B	Customer C	Customer D
Net Sales				
Cost of Goods Sold (Variable Manufacturing Cost)	———	———	———	———
Manufacturing Contribution				
Variable Marketing and Logistics Costs:				
Sales Commissions				
Transportation				
Warehousing (Handling in and out)				
Special Packaging				
Order Processing				
Charge for Investment in Accounts Receivable	———	———	———	———
Contribution Margin				
Assignable Nonvariable Costs:				
Salaries				
Segment Related Advertising				
Slotting Allowances				
Inventory Carrying Costs				
Controllable Margin				
Charge for Dedicated Assets Used				
Net Margin	══	══	══	══

contribution margin. Assignable nonvariable costs, such as salaries, customer related advertising expenditures, slotting allowances and inventory carrying costs, are subtracted to obtain a segment controllable margin. The net margin is obtained after deducting a charge for dedicated assets. These statements contain opportunity costs for investment in receivables and inventory and a charge for dedicated assets. Consequently, they are much closer to cash flow statements than a traditional profit and loss statement. They contain revenues minus the costs (avoidable costs) that disappear if the revenue disappears. For more information on profitability reports by customer see the Appendix to this chapter.

At Sysco, a $23.4 billion food distributor, profitability reports by customer were implemented in 1999. These reports enabled management to make strategic decisions about the allocation of resources to accounts including which customers receive the preferred delivery times and which customers must pay for value added services if they want to receive them. The results are illustrated in Figure 2-6. The five year cumulative annual growth rate for the period 1999 to 2003 was 11.3% for sales and 19.1% for net earnings. As shown in Figure 2-6, net earnings growth improved sharply after the profitability reports were implemented.

In addition to measuring current performance, these reports can be used to track the profitability of customers over time and to generate pro-forma statements that estimate the impact of potential process improvement projects. Decision analysis can be performed to consider what-if scenarios such as best case, worst case and most likely customers.

...these reports can be used to track the profitability of customers over time and to generate pro-forma statements that estimate the impact of potential process improvement projects.

Develop Guidelines for Sharing Process Improvement Benefits with Customers

In the final sub-process, the team develops the guidelines for sharing process improvement benefits with customers. The goal is to make process improvements win-win solutions for both the firm and the customer. If all of the parties involved

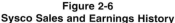

Figure 2-6
Sysco Sales and Earnings History

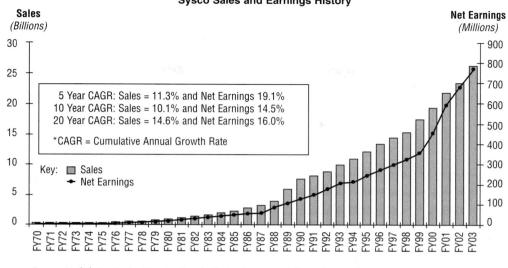

5 Year CAGR: Sales = 11.3% and Net Earnings 19.1%
10 Year CAGR: Sales = 10.1% and Net Earnings 14.5%
20 Year CAGR: Sales = 14.6% and Net Earnings 16.0%

*CAGR = Cumulative Annual Growth Rate

Key: ☐ Sales
      ● Net Earnings

Source: Neil Theiss, Senior Director, Supply Chain Management, Sysco Corporation

The customer relationship management team must quantify the benefits of process improvements in financial terms.

do not gain from process improvement efforts, it will be difficult to obtain their full and sustained commitment. The customer relationship management team must quantify the benefits of process improvements in financial terms.

For example, in a project that involved Cargill and a key customer, representatives from the two firms needed to address the following issue as they worked to develop a method for sharing the benefits:

- An agreement in principle on a fair allocation of benefits. For example, should it be 50% and 50% or 60% and 40%?
- Timeframe for benefit sharing. Should it be the life of the agreement, five years, or re-assessed annually?
- Decision on what benefits/costs to include.
- A fair approach to handling capital expenditure costs.
- Accurate baseline to use as a starting point for measuring savings.
- Common process to measure value captured and the cost to get.
- Benefit review and approval procedures.
- Mechanics to accrue for and transfer value (where, how, how often, etc.).
- Methodology review.

It was decided that a 50/50 split was in keeping with the overall spirit of the partnership, would motivate both parties to maximize the opportunities, and would acknowledge that neither party could achieve the savings without the other party. Both companies' process improvement teams agreed that benefits should be derived from supply chain initiatives, be explicitly recognized in supply chain project outcomes (e.g. reduced freight, reduced inventory carrying costs, reduced administrative transaction costs, etc.), and be in excess of a predetermined "baseline" for each area. The costs to be considered should be directly related to recommended supply chain initiatives (capital costs, transaction costs, system related costs, etc.), represent only incremental, full time staff adds, and be documented costs, greater than an agreed upon minimum dollar amount.

In the view of Cargill's management, it was important to identify the range of expectations that each team brought to the project. It was also necessary to agree on specific shared, realistic objectives with regard to process efficiency, growth/profit stability, costs savings, improved customer service, organizational alignment, clear metrics, and any other areas that were viewed as important by the parties.

The key learnings for the management team were summarized as follows:

- Determine gain sharing at the outset so it does not undermine the joint objectives. Collaborative projects pursue opportunities that cannot be achieved independently, so the value will only be captured if jointly implemented.
- Working between business units is challenging - adding an external trading partner is even harder – trust, culture, process and system differences have an impact.
- Skeptics abound – success requires focused leadership and management support.
- Partnerships work – they take longer and are harder, but they work. Once trust is established, there are many opportunities to learn from each other.
- All involved enhance their knowledge and capabilities, which will be applied outside of the partnership, which should be acknowledged and encouraged.
- Enhanced collaboration and cooperation between customers and Cargill has led to unique results.
- Next step is to consider opportunities to jointly approach the retailer or the next trading partner in the supply chain.

Determine gain sharing at the outset so it does not undermine the joint objectives.

In summary, the objective of customer relationship management at the strategic level is to identify markets and target segments, provide criteria for segmenting customers, provide customer teams with guidelines for customizing the product and service offering, develop a framework for metrics, and provide guidelines for the sharing of process improvement benefits with the customers.

The Operational Customer Relationship Management Process

At the operational level, the customer relationship management process deals with writing and implementing the PSAs. It is comprised of seven sub-processes: segment customers, prepare the account/segment management team, internally review the accounts, identify opportunities with the accounts, develop the product and service agreement, implement the product and service agreement, and measure performance and generate profitability reports (see Figure 2-7).

Segment Customers

All customers do not contribute equally to the firm's success and the goal is to identify those customers who desire and deserve special treatment so that the firm's offerings can be tailored to meet their needs while achieving the firm's profit goals for the customer. In the first sub-process, customers are segmented based on the criteria that were established in the strategic process. A key measure is the current profitability of each customer measured as shown in Table 2-1 combined

All customers do not contribute equally to the firm's success and the goal is to identify those customers who desire and deserve special treatment so that the firm's offerings can be tailored to meet their needs while achieving the firm's profit goals for the customer.

Figure 2-7
The Operational Customer Relationship Management Process

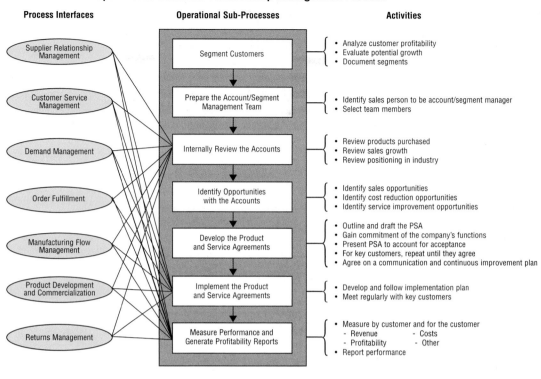

with growth potential. Other criteria for segmenting customers might include: competitive positioning, market knowledge, market share goals/penetration, margin, technological capabilities, resources, compatibility, and class of trade.

Table 2-2 shows how one major corporation has segmented customers based on profitability. The most profitable customers were classified as Platinum followed by Gold, Silver, Bronze and Lead (unprofitable). Platinum customers only represented 8.4% of the accounts but they produced 65% of the pretax earnings. At the other extreme, unprofitable customers represented 34.3% of the accounts and actually reduced overall pretax earnings by 6%. Management must determine which of the unprofitable customers have the potential to become profitable and which ones will likely remain unprofitable. This information is used to prioritize customers for the customer relationship management process. Table 2-3 shows how the profitability and thus segments can change from year to year. Not only did some Platinum customers turn to Gold, Silver, Bronze and Lead in 2003, but unprofitable customers became profitable with some even becoming Platinum. The goal is to understand what is driving the numbers and reassign resources on that basis.

Management must determine which of the unprofitable customers have the potential to become profitable and which ones will likely remain unprofitable.

Prepare the Account/Segment Management Teams

In this sub-process, the account or segment management teams are formed,

Table 2-2
Customer Segmentation Based on Pretax Profit Contribution

Segment	Percentage of Accounts	Percentage of Pretax Earnings
Platinum	8.4%	65%
Gold	17.1%	25%
Silver	18.2%	11%
Bronze	22.0%	5%
Lead (Unprofitable)	34.3%	-6%
Total	100%	100%

Table 2-3
Customer Segmentation for 2002 and 2003

	2002 Segmentation Percentage of Customers Mix	2003 Segmentation					
		Platinum	Gold	Silver	Bronze	Lead (Unprofitable)	Total
Platinum	7.71%	5.89%	1.35%	0.21%	0.09%	0.15%	7.71%
Gold	16.49%	1.74%	10.44%	2.82%	0.79%	0.70%	16.49%
Silver	17.90%	0.26%	3.61%	8.79%	3.47%	1.77%	17.90%
Bronze	22.05%	0.15%	0.93%	4.37%	11.59%	5.02%	22.05%
Lead (Unprofitable)	35.85%	0.32%	0.80%	2.04%	6.06%	26.04%	35.85%
Total	100%	8.36%	17.13%	18.23%	21.99%	34.29%	100%

including the salesperson who will be the account or segment manager. The teams are cross-functional with representation from each of the functional areas including marketing, research and development, manufacturing, logistics, information systems, finance and purchasing. Some team members may be more important to a specific customer relationship. For example, if the business drivers for both firms are to collaborate on the development of new products, personnel from research and development will play a key role on the teams. In the case of key accounts, each team is dedicated to a specific account and meets regularly with the customer's team. In most instances, the team members, with the exception of the account representatives, will have full-time positions in one of the functions. For very large customers, such as Wal-Mart, suppliers such as Colgate-Palmolive have dedicated team members who work full-time on the customer team and are located near the customer's corporate headquarters. In the case of customer segments, a team develops and manages a standard PSA for a group of customers.

In the case of key accounts, each team is dedicated to a specific account and meets regularly with the customer's team.

Internally Review the Accounts

Each account team reviews their account or segment of accounts to determine the products purchased, sales growth and their position in the industry. The value that the firm brings to the customer is based on the customer relationship management team's ability to understand and meet the customer's priorities. The customers' top priorities are so important that they will pay a premium for them or, when they are not being provided, they will switch some or all of their business to another supplier.[16] The link between understanding customers' priorities and the firm's profitability is established by the following sequence of activities:

- Understand priorities (the objective of the next sub-process).
- Design products and services that address these priorities.
- Sell the value proposition to the customers and within the firm.
- Measure the impact on the profitability of customers and customer segments.

Identify Opportunities with the Accounts

With a business-to-business customer, there are many individuals throughout the customer's organization who must be identified in order to gain knowledge about the customer's needs, behavior, decision-making process, price sensitivities and preferences.

In order to understand the customer, the team must ask the right people the right questions. With a business-to-business customer, there are many individuals throughout the customer's organization who must be identified in order to gain knowledge about the customer's needs, behavior, decision-making process, price sensitivities and preferences.[17] A major part of this effort is to identify customer priorities that are being ignored and find a way to profitably respond to them. Once the team has an understanding of the customer(s), they work with each account or segment of accounts to develop improvement opportunities in sales, costs and service. These opportunities might arise from any part of the business, so the account teams need to interface with each of the other supply chain management process teams.

In a supply chain management context, it is also important to understand what brings value to customers beyond Tier 1. For example, "a component supplier must understand the economic motivations of the manufacturer who buys the components, the distributor who takes the manufacturer's products to sell, and the end-use consumer".[18]

Develop the Product and Service Agreements

In the fifth sub-process, each team develops the PSA for their account or segment of accounts. The PSA is an agreement that matches the requirements of the customer with the capabilities of the firm and the firm's profit goals for the customer. Each team first outlines and drafts the PSA, and then gains commitment from the internal functions. For key accounts, they present the PSA for acceptance, and work with the customer until agreement has been reached. It is important that the PSA for key accounts include a communication and continuous improvement plan. For other accounts, the PSA is presented to the customer by a salesperson. This sub-process aligns the business goals of the customer and the firm so that the expectations of each side are realistic and understood by both organizations.

Implement the Product and Service Agreements

In the sixth sub-process, the team implements the PSA, which includes holding regular planning sessions with key customers. The customer relationship management teams provide input to each of the other supply chain management processes that are affected by the customizations that have been made in the PSAs. Customer relationship management teams must work with the other process teams to make sure

[16] Slywotzky, Adrian J. and David J. Morrison, *The Profit Zone,* New York, NY: Times Books, 1997.

[17] Slywotzky, Adrian J. and David J. Morrison, *The Profit Zone,* New York, NY: Times Books, 1997.

[18] Slywotzky, Adrian J. and David J. Morrison, *The Profit Zone,* New York, NY: Times Books, 1997.

that the PSA is being implemented as planned, and schedule regular meetings with customers to review progress and performance. Implementation of the PSA might require an investment in new information systems, the re-engineering of a transactional activity, or a new employee such as a dedicated person for planning.

Measure Performance and Generate Profitability Reports

In the last operational sub-process, the team captures and reports the process performance measures and makes certain that they are not in conflict with metrics from each of the other processes. Customer profitability reports are also generated. These profitability reports provide information for measuring and selling the value of the relationship to each customer and internally to upper management. Value should be measured in terms of costs, impact on sales, and associated investment, or the efforts incurred will go unrewarded.[19]

The other process teams communicate customer-related performance to the customer relationship management teams who tie these metrics back to the profitability of the firm as well as to the profitability of the customer. For example, Heinz in the United Kingdom has the capability of generating reports that show the profitability of customers such as Tesco and Sainsbury to Heinz. Also, reports are provided to key customers that show how much Heinz has contributed to their profit. The ability to generate profitability reports of this type is a powerful tool that enables fact-base negotiation between the process teams of each firm.

Conclusions

Customer relationship management provides the structure for how relationships with customers are developed and maintained, including the establishment of PSAs between the firm and its customers. It is a key supply chain management process which along with the supplier relationship management process form the critical linkages that connect firms in the supply chain. Supply chain management is about relationship management and thus an organization's success depends to a large extent on the individual relationships that are developed with customers and suppliers. A top-to-top relationship is necessary to achieve buy-in and the resources to support the relationship but there must be multiple one-to-one relationships "where the rubber meets the road." Successful customer relationship management requires trust, open books, senior executives who walk the talk, key connections and quick wins.

The ultimate measure of success for each relationship is the impact that it is having on the financial performance of the firms involved. Consequently, it is necessary for each firm to have the capability to measure the performance of both customer relationship management and supplier relationship management in terms of their impact on incremental revenues and costs as well as incremental investment. The supply chain is managed relationship-by-relationship, link-by-link. With the proper information regarding the costs and benefits associated with process improvement and a willingness to share the gains, over time the supply chain should migrate to the most efficient and effective structure.

The ultimate measure of success for each relationship is the impact that it is having on the financial performance of the firms involved.

---

[19] Lambert, Douglas M. and Renan Burduroglu, "Measuring and Selling the Value of Logistics," *The International Journal of Logistics Management,* Vol. 11, No. 1 (2000), pp. 1-17.

APPENDIX:

CUSTOMER AND PRODUCT PROFITABILITY REPORTS

The best overall measure of performance for the customer relationship management process is the profitability of individual customers and customer segments overtime...

Knowledge of the profitability of customers and products is a requirement for informed management of a business. The best overall measure of performance for the customer relationship management process is the profitability of individual customers and customer segments overtime and these profitability reports should be generated using revenues and avoidable costs. When developing customer profitability reports the first question that must be answered deals with whether the cost is dependent on unit volume (see Figure 2A-1). If the answer is yes, then it is appropriate to charge it to the applicable customer or customer segment. If the answer is no, then it is necessary to determine if the cost is dedicated to a specific customer segment. If Procter and Gamble was developing a profitability report on Wal-Mart, this is where the costs of the Wal-Mart customer team would be deducted: salaries, benefit costs, travel budgets, etc. The goal is to deduct from revenue all costs that would disappear if the revenue disappeared. If the answers

Figure 2A-1
Assigning Costs to Customers and Customer Segments

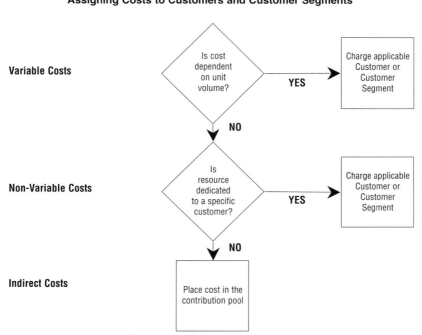

to both questions in Figure 2A-1 are no, the cost is placed in the contribution pool. While no customer must cover any specific amount of these costs, all customers must generate a net segment margin that covers these costs in total and provides the desired earnings per share. The size of the net segment margin will determine the relative contribution of each customer (customer group) from the standpoint of financial performance. This information, combined with estimates of future growth for each segment, enables management to develop strategies that will maximize profitability. The overriding rule is to include in segment reports, only those costs that will disappear if the sales disappear.

Many people will argue that the contribution approach should not be used because all costs need to covered in order to earn a profit. However, since any method of allocation is arbitrary by definition, these costs should not be allocated to individual customers or products. To argue that these costs will not be managed if they are not allocated to individual customers is naive. It is an issue of aggregation. For example, customer profitability analysis begins with lines on an order. For each line, costs that are specific to the SKU should be deducted (variable manufacturing costs, sales commission if they vary by SKU, etc.) from the sales for the SKU. All of the lines of the order should be summed and the order specific costs should be deducted (order picking costs and shipping costs for example). At this point, it is possible to determine if the order is profitable.

The next step is to total the sales and costs of all orders for a specific customer or customer segment and deduct the customer specific costs such as the dedicated account team, co-operative advertising and the cost of carrying inventory to support the customer. The next level of aggregation is customers in a class of trade (grocery retail) or geographic area. At this point, all of the joint costs that support the class of trade or geographic area are deducted. Finally, all classes of trade or all geographic areas are combined and at this level since all revenues are accounted for in the sales of the total company, all remaining corporate costs and joint costs are deducted. Therefore, all of the costs are considered at the total company level and the reason why the leadership team is compensated so generously in most companies is that they are responsible for managing these costs.

Now, we will consider the example of a division of a multi-division corporation with sales of $42.5 million, where traditional accounting data showed a net profit of $2.5 million before taxes. While management believed that this profit was not adequate, traditional accounting gave few clues regarding how profitability might be improved. In the absence of fact, the managers from various business functions within the division would have conflicting ideas about how profitability could be improved. The marketing manager would like to increase the advertising budget to increase sales. The representative from finance might argue that the company is spending twice as much as it should on advertising. The sales and marketing representatives would like more products but managers from manufacturing and logistics argue there are too many SKU's and that it is impossible to achieve the necessary efficiencies in operations. Sales people want lower prices and the manager from finance argues that prices are too low, that a five percent increase in prices would improve profitability by $ 2 million. Everyone has a suggestion for improving profitability that is based on his/her experience and based on that experience each is sure that he/she is right. Without good information, it is difficult if not impossible to determine the course of action that will have the best results. However, a contribution approach to profitability analysis by customer type can be used to specifically identify where performance is inadequate (see Table 2A-1).

In this example, drugstore sales were the largest of the four customer types and represented 45% of net sales, but the segment controllable margin-to-sales ratio was the lowest at 15.7%; it was less than one-half of that of the second most profitable segment, discount stores at 31.7%, and only 37% as large as the most profitable segment, department stores at 42.1%. However, at $3.1 million the segment controllable margin was substantial. It is doubtful that discontinuing sales to drugstores would be a wise decision. An analysis of product profitability by customer segment showed that product mix was not the source of the problem. But, all drugstore customers were not the same. The drugstore customers were comprised of national drug chains, regional drug chains and independent pharmacies. Further segmentation of the drugstores into these three groups revealed that national drugstore chains had a segment controllable margin-to-sales ratio of 34.9%, which was almost as large as that of the grocery chains (36.9%) and better than discount stores (31.7%), that regional drugstore chains (30.9%) were almost as profitable as discount stores (31.7%), and that small independent pharmacies were losing $85,000 per year (see Table 2A-2).

Sales to the independent pharmacies were resulting in a loss of $85,000 per

Table 2A-1
Profitability by Type of Account: A Contribution Approach

	Total Company	Department Stores	Grocery Chains	Drug Stores	Discount Stores
			Type of Account		
Sales	$ 42,500	$ 6,250	$ 10,500	$ 19,750	$ 6,000
Less discounts, returns and allowances	2,500	250	500	1,750	—
Net Sales	40,000	6,000	10,000	18,000	6,000
Cost of goods sold (variable manufacturing costs)	20,000	2,500	4,800	9,200	3,500
Manufacturing Contribution	20,000	3,500	5,200	8,800	2,500
Variable selling and distribution costs:					
Sales commissions	800	120	200	360	120
Transportation costs	2,500	310	225	1,795	170
Warehouse handling	600	150	—	450	—
Oder-processing costs	400	60	35	280	25
Charge for investment in accounts receivable	700	20	50	615	15
Contribution margin	15,000	2,840	4,690	5,300	2,170
Assignable nonvariable costs (costs incurred specifically for the segment during the period):					
Sales promotion and slotting allowances	1,250	60	620	400	170
Advertising	500	—	—	500	—
Bad debts	300	—	—	300	—
Display racks	200	—	—	200	—
Inventory carrying costs	1,250	150	200	800	100
Segment controllable margin	$ 11,500	$ 2,530	$ 3,870	$ 3,100	$ 1,900
Segment controllable margin-to-sales ratio	27.1%	42.1%	36.9%	15.7%	31.7%

Note: This approach can be modified to include a charge for the assets employed by each of the segments, as well as a deduction for the change in market value of these assets. The result would be referred to as the net segment margin (residual income).

Source: Douglas M. Lambert and Jay U. Sterling, "Educators Are Contributing to Major Deficiencies in Marketing Profitability Reports," *Journal of Marketing Education* Vol. 12, No 3 (1990), pp. 44-45.

Table 2A-2
Profitability by Type of Drug Store Account: A Contribution Approach

		Type of Account		
	Drug Store Channel	National Drug Chains	Regional Drug Chains	Independent Pharmacies
Sales	$ 19,750	$ 4,250	$ 5,500	$ 10,000
Less discounts, returns and allowances	1,750	250	500	1,000
Net Sales	18,000	4,000	5,000	9,000
Cost of goods sold (variable manufacturing costs)	9,200	2,100	2,600	4,500
Manufacturing Contribution	8,800	1,900	2,400	4,500
Variable selling and distribution costs:				
Sales commissions	360	80	100	180
Transportation costs	1,795	120	200	1,475
Warehouse handling	450	—	100	350
Oder-processing costs	280	25	55	200
Charge for investment in accounts receivable	615	20	35	560
Contribution margin	5,300	1,655	1,910	1,735
Assignable novariable costs (costs incurred specifically for the segment during the period):				
Sales promotion and slotting allowances	400	90	110	200
Advertising	500	—	—	500
Bad debts	300	—	—	300
Display racks	200	—	—	200
Inventory carrying costs	800	80	100	620
Segment controllable margin	$ 3,100	$ 1,485	$ 1,700	$ (85)
Segment controllable margin-to-sales ratio	15.7%	34.9%	30.9%	—

Note: This approach can be modified to include a charge for the assets employed by each of the segments, as well as a deduction for the change in market value of these assets. The result would be referred to as the net segment margin (residual income).

Source: Douglas M. Lambert and Jay U. Sterling, "Educators Are Contributing to Major Deficiencies in Marketing Profitability Reports," *Journal of Marketing Education* Vol. 12, No 3 (1990), pp. 43-44.

year as a result of: the costs associated with overnight package service, third-party warehousing costs, inventory carrying costs, the costs associated with small orders, the slow payment of customer bills and high bad debts. This information enabled management to estimate the impact on corporate profitability if the independent pharmacies were served by drug wholesalers or if other cost cutting efforts such as inside sales and scheduled deliveries might give the best results. The alternative that would lead to the greatest improvement in long-term profitability should be selected. In this case, the relationships with independent pharmacies were outsourced by shifting the business to wholesalers.

Rather than using contribution reports, the accounting systems in most firms allocate fixed costs to individual segments which provides incorrect information because costs "common" to multiple segments are allocated based on arbitrary measures of activity.[20] Consequently, vital information about the controllability and behavior of costs is lost. For example, if a segment of customers or products is found to be unprofitable and is discontinued, the joint-fixed costs will be reallocated to the remaining segments.

---

[20] Douglas M. Lambert and Jay U. Sterling, "What Types of Profitability Reports Do Marketing Managers Receive?" *Industrial Marketing Management,* Vol. 16, No.4 (1987), pp. 295-303.

	Total Company	Type of Account			
		Department Stores	Grocery Chains	Drug Stores	Discount Stores
Net Sales	$ 40,000	$ 6,000	$ 10,000	$ 18,000	$ 6,000
Cost of goods sold (variable manufacturing costs)	25,000	3,750	6,250	11,250	3,750
Manufacturing Margin	15,000	2,250	3,750	6,750	2,250
Less Expenses					
Sales commissions	800	120	200	360	120
Transportation costs ($/case)	2,500	375	625	1,125	375
Warehouse handling ($/cu. ft)	600	90	150	270	90
Order-processing costs ($/order)	400	30	50	300	20
Sales promotions (% of sales)	1,250	187	312	563	188
Advertising (% of sales)	500	75	125	225	75
Bad Debts (% of sales)	300	45	75	135	45
General Overhead and Administrative Expense (% of sales)	6,150	922	1,538	2,768	922
Net Profit (before taxes)	$ 2,500	$ 406	$ 675	$ 1,004	$ 415
Segment controllable margin	6.3%	6.8%	6.8%	5.6%	6.9%

Source: Douglas M. Lambert and Jay U. Sterling, "Educators Are Contributing to Major Deficiencies in Marketing Profitability Reports," *Journal of Marketing Education*, Vol. 12, No 3 (1990), pp. 49.

Table 2A-3 shows how the customer profitability analysis in Table 2A-2 would change if it were calculated using typical methods of cost allocation. Drugstores would show a profit of over $1 million significantly larger than the other customer groups. At 5.6%, the profit-to-sales ratio for drugstore customers would compare favorably with the other customer groups (82% of the profit-to-sales ratio for grocery chains), whereas the segment controllable margin-to-sales ratio of the drugstores at 15.7% was less than half (43%) of that earned by the grocery stores (see Table 2A-1). The two methods of accounting would result in much greater differences in the profitability of products because manufacturing, marketing, and logistics costs typically vary more across products than customers. If the drugstore customers in Table 2A-3 were analyzed by type of drugstore, the profit-to-sales ratios for the three groups of customers would be approximately equal because average costs were being used.

A similar approach can be used to measure the profitability of products. Once product contribution reports are implemented, managers can begin to accurately assess strategic options such as which products to drop or whether prices can be raised on inelastic products or reduced on high-volume products. More attention can be directed to those products that are most profitable. The 80-20 rule can be used to identify candidates for elimination. Managers in companies that have implemented segment profitability reports have been able to identify products and customers that were either unprofitable or did not meet corporate financial objectives. Ironically many of these products/customers were previously thought to be profitable, due either to their sales volumes or to manufacturing margins. It is difficult to compete even when firms have good financial information. It is almost impossible to compete with bad information.

Figure 2A-2 shows how management can combine customer profitability and product profitability to identify candidates for elimination from the product line (the challenge quadrant). Every effort should be made not to incur service failures

It is difficult to compete even when firms have good financial information. It is almost impossible to compete with bad information.

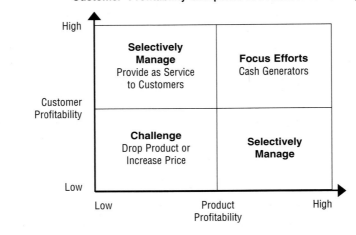

Figure 2A-2
Customer Profitability Compared to Product Profitability

on quality problems on those products that are highly profitable and are being purchased by the most profitable customers.

Table 2A-4 contains an example that shows in many cases only a few key costs can be used to identify underperforming products at the SKU level. Product Group A was comprised of 340 SKUs with total inventory of $6,309,800. The annual unit sales were 148,527 and inventory turns equaled 4x. It was decided to consider every SKU with less than 2x to be a slow-moving item and these SKUs totaled 135 of the 340 in the product line. Average inventory turns on these products was 0.6x and the inventory of these products was 28.9% of total inventory ($1,823,900). The total product contribution generated from the 340 SKUs was $19,947,200 but the contribution from the 135 slow-moving items was only $149,500 or 0.7% of the total. The next step was to determine which customers were purchasing these products and an analysis similar to that in Figure 2A-2 was performed in order to indentify SKUs for elimination from the product line.

In summary, cost allocations can distort profitability reports for customers and products. "Seriously distorted product costs can lead managers to choose a losing competitive strategy by de-emphasizing and overpricing products that are highly profitable and by expanding commitments to complex, unprofitable lines. The company persists in the losing strategy because executives have no alternative sources of information to signal when product costs are distorted."[21]

...cost allocations can distort profitability reports for customers and products.

Limitations of Profitability Reports

Research has shown that the segment profitability reports used by managers have serious shortcomings since most reports are based on average cost allocations rather than on the direct assignment of costs at the time a transaction occurs.[22] Period costs (e.g., fixed plant overhead and general/administrative costs) are

---

[21] Kaplan, Robert S., "One Cost System Isn't Enough," *Harvard Business Review*, Vol. 66, No. 1 (1988), pp. 61-66.

[22] Douglas M. Lambert and Jay U. Sterling, "What Types of Profitability Reports Do Marketing Managers Receive?" *Industrial Marketing Management*, Vol. 16, No. 4 (1987), pp. 295-303.

Product Group A	No. of Items (1)	Annual Volume (2)	Invent. Turns (3)	Average $ Inventory (4)	Sales Price (5)	Manufact. Contrib. (6)	Contrib. Margin (7)	Annual Contrib. (8)	% Contrib. Margin to Price (9)	% Slow Mover Contrib. to Total (10)	% Slow Mover Volume to Total (11)	% Slow Mover Inventory to Total (12)
Total Product Line	340	148,527	4	$6,309,800	$459.95	$181.90	$134.30	$19,947,200	29.2%			
Slow Movers (<2 times)	135	7,422	0.6	$1,823,900	$406.98	$153.63	$ 20.14	$ 149,500	4.9%	0.7%	5.0%	28.9%

Many of the problems encountered by manufacturing companies are the result of using a "full cost" approach whereby indirect costs (such as overhead and general administrative expenses) are allocated to each customer or product.

allocated to customers and products using arbitrary bases such as direct labor hours, sales revenue, or cost of sales. Opportunity costs related to investments in inventories and accounts receivable are not included. Finally, key marketing and logistics costs frequently are ignored.

Many of the problems encountered by manufacturing companies are the result of using a "full cost" approach whereby indirect costs (such as overhead and general administrative expenses) are allocated to each customer or product. As a result, many managers use control mechanisms that focus on the wrong targets: direct manufacturing labor or sales volume. Reward systems based on these control mechanisms drive behavior toward either simplistic goals that represent only a small fraction of total cost (labor) or single-minded sales efforts (volume). These systems cause managers to ignore more effective ways to compete, such as product quality, on-time delivery, short lead times, rapid product innovations, flexible manufacturing, and efficient deployment of scarce capital.

Many managers do not know the true cost of their company's products or services, how to most effectively reduce expenses, or how to direct resources to the most profitable customers because of the following factors:[23]

- Accounting systems are designed to report the aggregate effects of a firm's operations to stockholders, creditors, and governmental agencies and for these uses, costs can be aggregated in a few large categories.
- Accounting costs are computed to provide a historical record of the company's operations and costs common to multiple segments are allocated, using subjective and arbitrary bases.
- Accounting systems typically record marketing and logistics costs in aggregated accounts and seldom are costs attached to individual products or customers at the time the transactions are recorded. When the detail is captured, it is frequently lost because only aggregated data are carried forward to subsequent accounting periods. Once data are aggregated, the only way to disaggregate them is by allocation methods that distort the profitability.
- Profitability reports do not show a segment's contribution to overall

---

[23] Thomas S. Dudick, "Why SG&A Doesn't Always Work," *Harvard Business Review*, Vol. 65, No. 1 (1987), pp. 30-35; Robert S. Kaplan, "How Cost Accounting Distorts Product Costs," *Management Accounting*, April 1988, pp. 20-27; John J. Wheatley, "The Allocation Controversy in Marketing Cost Analysis," *University of Washington Business Review*, Vol. 30, No. 4, (1971), pp. 61-70; Ford S. Worthy, "Accounting Bores You? Wake Up," *Fortune*, October 12, 1987, pp. 43-50; and Douglas M. Lambert and Jay U. Sterling, "What Types of Profitability Reports Do Marketing Managers Receive?" *Industrial Marketing Management*, Vol. 16, No. 4 (1987), pp. 295-303.

corporate profitability, but rather include fixed costs, joint product/service costs, and corporate overhead cost allocations. Often top management encourages this approach because of the fear that sales force knowledge of variable costs will lead to lower selling prices. However, prices should be determined by the marketplace and not based on costs.

- In many standard cost systems, fixed costs are treated as variable costs, which masks the true behavior of the fixed costs.

The Importance of Accurate Cost Data

Accurate cost data are required for development of product and customer profitability reports so that scarce corporate resources can be directed to the products and customers that will provide the greatest return on those resources. The accounting system must be capable of providing information to answer questions such as the following:

- How do marketing, research and development, operations and logistics costs affect contribution by product, by territory, by customer, and by salesperson?
- How should resources be used to support customers and customer segments?
- What are the costs associated with providing additional levels of customer service?
- What is the optimal amount of inventory?
- What mix of transport modes/carriers should be used?
- How many field warehouses should be used and where should they be located?
- How many production setups are required?
- Which plants will be used to produce each product?
- What are the optimum manufacturing plant capacities based on alternative product mixes and volumes?
- What product packaging alternatives should be used?
- To what extent should information systems be automated?
- What distribution channels should be used?
- What products should be dropped from the product line?

To answer such questions, management must know what costs and revenue will change as a result of the decision that is being made. That is, the determination of a product's (customer's) contribution should be based on how corporate revenues, expenses, and profitability would change if the product (customer) were dropped. Any costs or revenue that are unaffected by this decision are irrelevant. For example, relevant costs might include sales commissions, promotional allowances, and transportation costs associated with a product's sales. Irrelevant costs are the overhead associated with the corporate head office and security guards at the plant. Implementation of this approach to decision making is severely hampered by the unavailability of accounting data, or the inability to use the right data when they are available. The best and most sophisticated models are only as good as the accuracy of the numbers used.

Segment profitability reports become more useful as a management tool when they are developed on pro-forma basis and actual results are compared to the budget as shown in Table A2-5. Table 2A-5 shows a level of aggregation that would be of interest to the firm's president. This report allows that president to see that a

Segment profitability reports become more useful as a management tool when they are developed on pro-forma basis and actual results are compared to the budget...

Table 2A-5
Segmental Analysis Using a Contribution Approach ($000)

	Budget	Explanation of Variation from Budget			Actual Results
		Variance Due to Ineffectiveness	Standard Allowed for Output Level Achieved	Variance Due to Inefficiency	
Net Sales	$45,000	$5,000	$40,000	—	$40,000
Cost of goods sold (variable manufacturing cost)	20,250	2,250	18,000	—	18,000
Manufacturing contribution	24,750	$2,750	$22,000	—	$22,000
Variable marketing and logistics costs (costs that vary directly with sales to the segment)*	11,250	1,250	10,000	$700	10,700
Segment contribution margin	$13,500	$1,500	$12,000	$700	$11,300
Assignable nonvariable costs (costs incurred specifically for the segment during the period)**	3,000	—	3,000	—	3,000
Segment controllable margin	$10,500	$1,500	$9,000	$700	$8,300

Assumption: Actual sales revenue decreased, a result of lower volume. The average price paid per unit sold remained same.(If the average price per unit changes then an additional variance—the marketing variance— can be computed.) Difference in income of $2,200 ($10,500-8,300) between budgeted and actual results can be explained by the following variances:
a. Ineffectiveness—inability to reach target sales objective $1,500
b. Inefficiency at operating level achieved of $40,000...... $700

$2,200

* These costs might include: sales commissions, transportation costs, warehouse handling costs, order processing costs, and a charge for accounts receivable.

** These costs might include: salaries, segment-related advertising, bad debts, and inventory carrying costs. The fixed costs associated with corporate-owned and operated facilities would be included if, and only if, the warehouse was solely for this segment of the business.

---

glance why targeted net income has not been reached. There is a $1.5 million difference due to ineffectiveness, which is a measure of the net income the company has forgone because of its inability to meet its budgeted level of sales. There is also an inefficiency factor of $0.7 million. The difference between $9 million and the actual outcome of $8.3 million is a $0.7 million variation due to inefficiency within the marketing and logistics functions. This analysis can be performed for segments such as products, customers, geographic areas, or divisions.

The key to successful implementation of a flexible budget lies in the analysis of cost behavior patterns. It is necessary to determine the fixed and variable components of costs. For example, regression analysis can be used to determine a variable rate per unit of activity and a total fixed cost component. Once this is accomplished, the flexible budget for control becomes a reality. One caution is that cost estimates that are based on past cost behavior patterns will contain inefficiencies. The predicted measure of cost may not be a measure of what the activity should cost but an estimate of what it will cost, based on the results of previous periods.

While substantial savings can be generated when management is able to compare actual costs to a set of predetermined standards or budgets, there are even greater opportunities for profit improvement in the area of decision making.

Information System Requirements for Measuring Profitability by Customer and Product

While substantial savings can be generated when management is able to compare actual costs to a set of predetermined standards or budgets, there are even greater opportunities for profit improvement in the area of decision making. If manageers are to make informed decisions, they must have accurate data. The addition or deletion of territories, salespeople, products, or customers requires a knowledge of how well existing segments are performing, and how revenues and costs will change with the alternatives under consideration. Management needs a database that is capable of providing on a routine basis information on individual segments such as customers, salespeople, products, territories, or channels of distribution. The system must be able to store data by fixed and variable components so that the incremental revenues and costs associated with alternative strategies can be identified.

Several types of transactions occur in a business, and each transaction results in the creation of source documents such as customer orders, shipment bill of lading, sales invoices to customers, and invoices from suppliers/vendors. In addition, a variety of internal transactions and activities are documented (e.g., "trip reports" for private fleet activities and salespeople "call reports"). Other costs may be identified from standard cost systems, engineering time studies, or statistical estimating (e.g. multiple regression techniques). In any case, source documents must be computerized. Data inputs must be coded with details such as function, customer, territory, product, revenue expense, channel of distribution, transportation mode, carrier, revenue, and expense. The system must be capable of filing large amounts of data and providing rapid aggregation and retrieval of various modules of information for decision making or external reporting. Combined with standard costs, the database makes it possible to generate both functional cost reports and segment contribution reports. The system works by charging functions with actual costs and the costs are compared to predetermined standards. Individual segments such as customers or products are credited with segment revenues and charged the standard cost, plus controllable variances. Figure 2A-3 shows the source documents that are used, the management reports, and the profitability reports that can be generated from a database.

The database should be capable of collecting the revenues and costs for every transaction and aggregating them by functional activity (e.g., selling, advertising/promotion, transportation, warehousing, and order processing). This technique is commonly referred to as responsibility accounting and is used primarily to develop annual budgets and monthly variance reports by major categories and subcategories of corporate activities, such as manufacturing, research development, marketing/sales, and logistics. Cost data must be recorded at the time of the transaction with enough detail to identify fixed-variable and direct-indirect components. The data must be sufficiently defined to permit the formulation of meaningful modules (see Figure 2A-4). Knowledgeable decision-making in the areas of strategic and operational planning require a sophisticated management information system.

The contribution approach has been described in the literature for more than 40 years, but surveys of corporate practices and a review of marketing management texts indicate that there are relatively few integrated operating systems that report segment profits on a timely and accurate basis.[24] Why does this condition exist? Many managers mistakenly feel that the same accounting practices (i.e., the allocation of all costs) used to value inventories and report results to the

> **The system must be able to store data by fixed and variable components so that the incremental revenues and costs associated with alternative strategies can be identified.**

---

[24] Douglas M. Lambert and Jay U. Sterling, "Educators are Contributing to Major Deficiencies in Marketing Profitability Reports," *Journal of Marketing Education*, Vol. 12, No. 3 (1990), pp. 42-52.

Figure 2A-3
Source Documents, Management Reports, and Profitability Reports

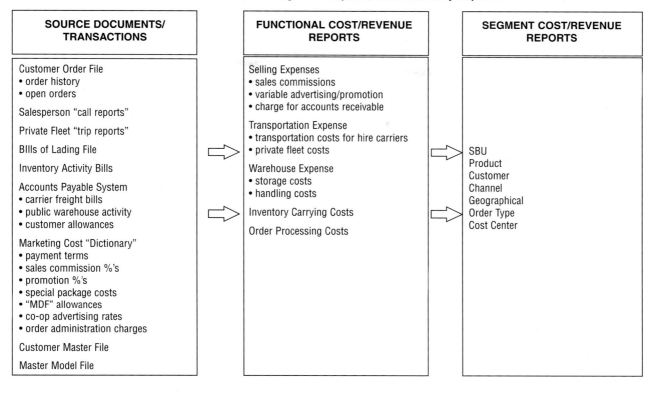

SOURCE DOCUMENTS/ TRANSACTIONS	FUNCTIONAL COST/REVENUE REPORTS	SEGMENT COST/REVENUE REPORTS
Customer Order File • order history • open orders Salesperson "call reports" Private Fleet "trip reports" Bills of Lading File Inventory Activity Bills Accounts Payable System • carrier freight bills • public warehouse activity • customer allowances Marketing Cost "Dictionary" • payment terms • sales commission %'s • promotion %'s • special package costs • "MDF" allowances • co-op advertising rates • order administration charges Customer Master File Master Model File	Selling Expenses • sales commissions • variable advertising/promotion • charge for accounts receivable Transportation Expense • transportation costs for hire carriers • private fleet costs Warehouse Expense • storage costs • handling costs Inventory Carrying Costs Order Processing Costs	SBU Product Customer Channel Geographical Order Type Cost Center

---

Figure 2A-4
Information Required to Develop Segment Profitability Reports

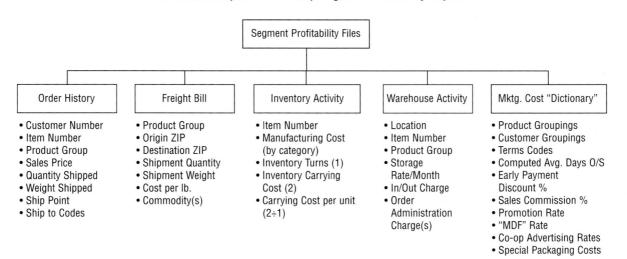

Segment Profitability Files

Order History	Freight Bill	Inventory Activity	Warehouse Activity	Mktg. Cost "Dictionary"
• Customer Number • Item Number • Product Group • Sales Price • Quantity Shipped • Weight Shipped • Ship Point • Ship to Codes	• Product Group • Origin ZIP • Destination ZIP • Shipment Quantity • Shipment Weight • Cost per lb. • Commodity(s)	• Item Number • Manufacturing Cost (by category) • Inventory Turns (1) • Inventory Carrying Cost (2) • Carrying Cost per unit (2÷1)	• Location • Item Number • Product Group • Storage Rate/Month • In/Out Charge • Order Administration Charge(s)	• Product Groupings • Customer Groupings • Terms Codes • Computed Avg. Days O/S • Early Payment Discount % • Sales Commission % • Promotion Rate • "MDF" Rate • Co-op Advertising Rates • Special Packaging Costs

Internal Revenue Service or Securities and Exchange Commission should be used to generate reports for managing the business. Also, managers may feel that using only variable and direct fixed costs might encourage sub-optimal pricing by salespeople. Top management and accountants may feel more comfortable if they can tie the cumulative results of the various segments to total company profit-and-loss data. Managers often fail to recognize the behavioral differences of fixed and variable costs, as well as the distinction between direct and indirect expenses. As a result, they fail to understand the usefulness and purpose of contribution reports. Finally, data processing personnel often discourage the development of such reports by citing the difficulties in creating the databases and operating systems required to assign direct costs to specific product and market segments. With the information technology that is available, these reasons are no longer valid.

Summary

Marketing, operations and logistics costs can have a significant impact on the profitability of a firm's customers and products. Yet in many firms, managers do not have accurate data for measuring customer and product profitability, managing day-to-day operations and making capital budgeting decisions. Successful management of the business depends on having full knowledge of the costs and revenue associated with customers and products.

Managers responsible for customer profitability need to understand the financial implications of their decisions. Executives must be able to talk the language of accountants, understand the benefits of contribution analysis, recognize the difference between good and bad accounting data, and have the capability of accessing relevant data on an ongoing basis. The support and active participation by top management, including the chief executive, is necessary since resistance to change is one of the major barriers facing organizations. According to Michael Dell: "Until you look inside and understand what's going on by business, by customer, by geography, you don't know anything".[25]

One company that has developed customized profitability reports by customer is 3M. Managers are able to see how manufacturing, distribution and marketing costs affect customer profitability and which products contribute the most. According to 3M's Karen Madsen, the key enablers are: data availability, data accuracy and state-of-the-art system capabilities. An extensive data warehouse combined with activity-based costing allows 3M to track the costs associated with serving customers and selling individual products.[26] In this appendix, we saw how costs and revenues assigned by class of trade, can be used to identify a business segment that is unprofitable and how contribution reports can point the direction for improvement. We also saw how erroneous decisions result when traditional full cost reports are used. Finally, we examined the use of flexible budgets to control performance and described the information systems necessary for the development of profitability reports by customer and product.

Successful management of the business depends on having full knowledge of the costs and revenues associated with customers and products.

---

[25] Magretta, Joan, "The Power of Virtual Integration: An Interview with Dell Computer's Michael Dell," *Harvard Business Review*, Vol. 76, No. 2 (1998), p. 77.

[26] Karen K. Madsen, "Integrated Supply Chain Metrics: An Industry Perspective," Measuring Logistics Performance Seminar, The Ohio State University /University of North Florida, May 19-21, 1999.

The Supplier Relationship Management Process

Douglas M. Lambert

Overview

The supplier relationship management process provides the structure for how relationships with suppliers are developed and maintained. Close relationships are developed with a small set of key suppliers based on the value that they provide to the organization over time, and more traditional relationships are maintained with the others. In this chapter, detailed descriptions of the strategic and operational sub-processes that comprise supplier relationship management are given. The interfaces that are necessary with the other seven supply chain management processes are identified and guidelines for successful implementation of the process are provided.

Introduction

The cost of materials as a percentage of sales has been estimated at approximately 53 percent for all types of manufacturing in the United States. These costs range from a low of 27 percent for tobacco products to a high of 83 percent for petroleum and coal products but most industries are in the 45 – 60 percent range.[1] For wholesalers and retailers, the cost of goods sold is higher than the materials costs of manufacturers. These numbers indicate the magnitude of the benefits that are possible through better management of the supplier network.

Supplier relationship management is the supply chain management process that provides the structure for how relationships with suppliers are developed and maintained.

Supplier relationship management is the supply chain management process that provides the structure for how relationships with suppliers are developed and maintained. As the name suggests, it is similar to customer relationship management. Just as close relationships need to be developed with key customers, management should forge close cross-functional relationships with a small number of key suppliers, and maintain more traditional buyer and salesperson relationships with the others.[2] Management identifies those suppliers and supplier groups to be targeted as part of the firm's business mission. Supplier relationship management teams work with key suppliers to tailor product and service agreements (PSA) to meet the organization's needs, as well as those of the selected suppliers. Standard PSAs are crafted for segments of other suppliers. Supplier relationship

---

[1] Stock, James R. and Douglas M. Lambert, *Strategic Logistics Management*, 4th Ed., New York, NY: McGraw Hill/Irwin, 2001.

[2] Dyer, Jeffery H., Dong Sung Cho and Wujin Wu, "Strategic Supplier Segmentation: The Next 'Best Practice' in Supply Chain Management," *California Management Review,* Vol. 40, No. 2 (1998), pp. 57-77.

management is about developing and managing the PSAs. Teams work with key suppliers to improve processes, and eliminate demand variability and non-value-added activities. The goal is to develop PSAs that address the major business drivers of both the organization and the supplier. Performance reports are designed to measure the profit impact of individual suppliers as well as the firm's impact on the profitability of suppliers.

Supplier relationship management represents an opportunity to build on the success of strategic sourcing and traditional procurement initiatives. It involves developing partnership relationships with key suppliers to reduce costs, innovate with new products and create value for both parties based on a mutual commitment to long-term collaboration and shared success. For complex relationships such as Coca-Cola and Cargill, it is necessary to coordinate multiple divisions spread across multiple geographic areas. Coca-Cola and Cargill both have revenue in excess of $80 billion per year, one represents the largest beverage and bottling system and the other the largest ingredient and nutritional company. Cross-functional teams from each of the companies meet on a regular basis to identify projects that will create joint value in areas such as new markets, new products, productivity and sustainability. The relationship involves the CEOs of both companies.

Supplier relationship management has become a critical business process as a result of: competitive pressures; the need to achieve cost efficiency in order to be cost competitive; and, the need to develop closer relationships with key suppliers who can provide the expertise necessary to develop innovative new products and successfully bring them to market. Supplier relationship management is one of the eight processes (see Figure 3-1) and it must interface with each of the other seven. In this chapter, a description of the strategic and operational processes that

Supplier relationship management represents an opportunity to build on the success of strategic sourcing and traditional procurement initiatives. It involves developing partnership relationships with key suppliers to reduce costs, innovate with new products and create value for both parties based on a mutual commitment to long-term collaboration and shared success.

Figure 3-1
Supply Chain Management:
Integrating and Managing Business Processes Across the Supply Chain

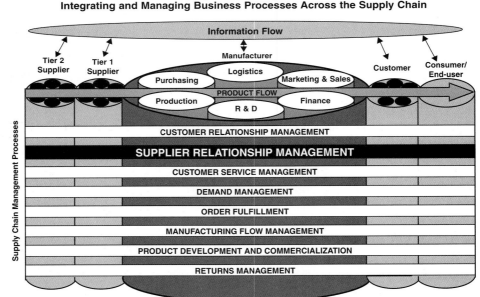

Source: Adapted from Douglas M. Lambert, Martha C. Cooper, and Janus D. Pagh, "Supply Chain Management: Implementation Issues and Research Opportunities," *The International Journal of Logistics Management,* Vol. 9, No. 2 (1998), p. 2.

comprise supplier relationship management is provided along with the sub-processes and their activities. Also, the interfaces with the other supply chain management processes are identified. Finally, conclusions are presented.

Supplier Relationship Management as a Supply Chain Management Process

Supplier relationship management and customer relationship management provide the critical linkages throughout the supply chain.

Supplier relationship management and customer relationship management provide the critical linkages throughout the supply chain (see Figure 2-2 on page 27). For each supplier, the ultimate measure of success for the customer relationship management process is the change in profitability of the customer. For each customer, the measure of success for the supplier relationship management process is the impact that the supplier has on the firm's profitability. The supplier relationship management process has both strategic and operational elements. Therefore, we have divided the process into two parts, the strategic process in which the firm establishes and strategically manages the process, and the operational process which is the actualization of the process once it has been established (see Figure 3-2). Implementation of the strategic process within the firm is a necessary step in integrating the firm with suppliers, and it is at the operational level that the day-to-day activities take place. The strategic process is led by a management team which is responsible for developing the structure that will guide the operational teams. At the operational level, there will

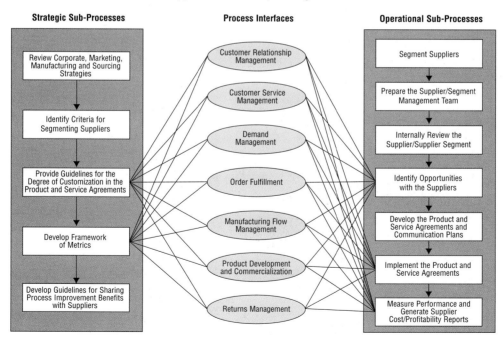

Figure 3-2
Supplier Relationship Management

Source: Adapted from Keely L. Croxton, Sebastián J. García-Dastugue, Douglas M. Lambert and Dale S. Rogers, "The Supply Chain Management Processes," *The International Journal of Logistics Management,* Vol. 12, No. 2 (2001), p. 15.

be a team established for each key supplier and for each segment of other suppliers. The teams are comprised of managers from several functions, including marketing, finance, production, purchasing and logistics, and they have the day-to-day responsibility for managing the process. Firm employees outside of the teams might execute parts of the process, but the teams still maintain managerial control.

The Strategic Supplier Relationship Management Process

At the strategic level, the supplier relationship management process provides the structure for how relationships with suppliers will be developed and managed. It is comprised of five sub-processes (see Figure 3-3).

Review Corporate, Marketing, Manufacturing and Sourcing Strategies

The supplier relationship management process team reviews the corporate strategy, and the marketing, manufacturing and sourcing strategies, in order to identify supplier segments that are critical to the organization's success now and in the future. The supplier network is a key part of profitable business development since it will impact: the quality of products, product availability, the time to market for new products, and access to critical technology. By reviewing these strategies, management identifies the supplier types with whom the firm needs to develop long-term relationships. For example, at Colgate-Palmolive Company stretch financial goals led management in the oral care business to the conclusion that closer, partnership type, relationships were necessary with key suppliers. Management believed that these relationships would result in product innovations that would enable the business to achieve the financial goals.

The supplier relationship management process team reviews the corporate strategy, and the marketing, manufacturing and sourcing strategies, in order to identify supplier segments that are critical to the organization's success now and in the future.

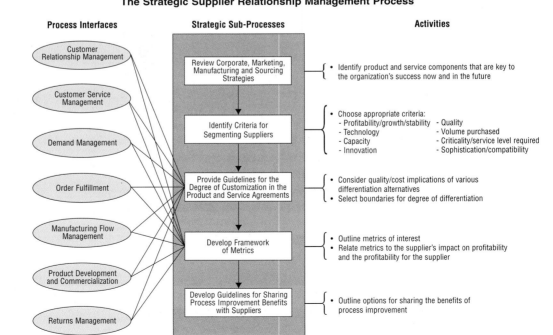

Figure 3-3
The Strategic Supplier Relationship Management Process

Identify Criteria for Segmenting Suppliers

In the second sub-process, the team identifies the criteria that can be used to segment suppliers. The results of the segmentation are used to determine with which suppliers the firm should develop tailored PSAs and which suppliers should be grouped and offered a standard PSA that meets the firm's goals as well as generates a reasonable profit for the suppliers. Potential criteria include: profitability; growth and stability; the criticality of the service level necessary; the sophistication and compatibility of the supplier's process implementation; the supplier's technology capability and compatibility; the volume purchased from the supplier; the capacity available from the supplier; the culture of innovation at the supplier; and, the supplier's anticipated quality levels.[3] The team determines which criteria to use and how suppliers will be evaluated on each criterion. A segmentation scheme is developed that will be used at the operational level to identify key suppliers and segments of other suppliers.

A segmentation scheme is developed that will be used at the operational level to identify key suppliers and segments of other suppliers.

At Wendy's International, a matrix is used to compare suppliers on the basis of the complexity of the commodity for Wendy's and the volume of the spend (see Figure 3-4). Items that are low in complexity and low in terms of the expenditure are *non-critical* items such as straws. *Leverage* items are those for which Wendy's spend is high but the items are not complex or strategic to the business. The goal for these items is to improve service by such things as reducing lead times. For non-critical and leverage items, it is not necessary to have cross-functional teams interacting with the supplier. Salespeople from companies providing these commodities call

Figure 3-4
Comparing Suppliers on Complexity and Volume

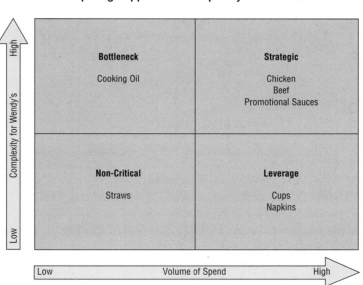

Source: Judy Hollis, Vice President, Wendy's International

---

[3] Burt, David, N., Donald W. Dobler and Stephen L. Starling, *World Class Supply Management,* New York, NY: McGraw-Hill/Irwin, 2003.

on buyers as they traditionally have done and buyers select suppliers based on price and service. *Bottleneck* items are those for which Wendy's spend is low but they are very complex such as cooking oil. Finally, *strategic* items are those that are both high in complexity and high in the amount spent per year. These items for Wendy's include chicken, beef and promotional sauces. Generally, Wendy's management tries to move items from the bottleneck quadrant to the non-critical or to the leverage quadrant. Management's goal was to move cooking oil from the bottleneck segment to the leverage segment, but it was actually moved to the strategic segment as a result of product innovation with Cargill, a key supplier. Suppliers of strategic items are candidates for partnership relationships (see Chapter 14). Cross-functional teams from the supplier and Wendy's work on initiatives that will increase revenues and reduce costs thereby improving the financial performance of both firms.

Masterfoods USA uses a matrix that is similar to Wendy's, but substitutes "supply risk" for "complexity" and "contribution potential" for "volume of spend." The fewer the number of suppliers, the more Masterfoods moves up on the low to high scale for supply risk. The mid point on the low to high "contribution potential" scale is $500,000. The savings potential must exceed $500,000 for the supplier to be in either of the segments on the right side of the matrix (Strategic and Leverage quadrants).

The Coca-Cola Company is implementing the supplier relationship management process and Figure 3-5 shows the supplier segmentation matrix

Bottleneck items are those for which Wendy's spend is low but they are very complex such as cooking oil.

Figure 3-5
Supplier Segmentation Matrix for The Coca-Cola Company

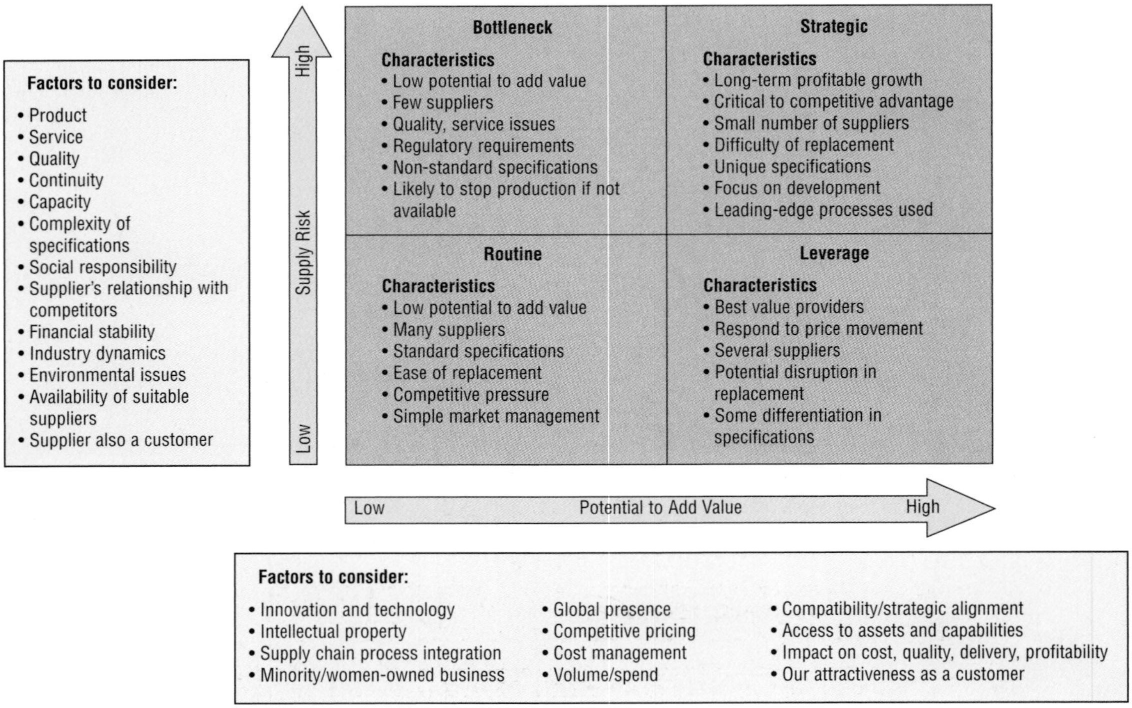

Factors to consider:

- Product
- Service
- Quality
- Continuity
- Capacity
- Complexity of specifications
- Social responsibility
- Supplier's relationship with competitors
- Financial stability
- Industry dynamics
- Environmental issues
- Availability of suitable suppliers
- Supplier also a customer

Supply Risk — High / Low

Bottleneck

Characteristics
- Low potential to add value
- Few suppliers
- Quality, service issues
- Regulatory requirements
- Non-standard specifications
- Likely to stop production if not available

Strategic

Characteristics
- Long-term profitable growth
- Critical to competitive advantage
- Small number of suppliers
- Difficulty of replacement
- Unique specifications
- Focus on development
- Leading-edge processes used

Routine

Characteristics
- Low potential to add value
- Many suppliers
- Standard specifications
- Ease of replacement
- Competitive pressure
- Simple market management

Leverage

Characteristics
- Best value providers
- Respond to price movement
- Several suppliers
- Potential disruption in replacement
- Some differentiation in specifications

Potential to Add Value — Low / High

Factors to consider:

- Innovation and technology
- Intellectual property
- Supply chain process integration
- Minority/women-owned business
- Global presence
- Competitive pricing
- Cost management
- Volume/spend
- Compatibility/strategic alignment
- Access to assets and capabilities
- Impact on cost, quality, delivery, profitability
- Our attractiveness as a customer

Source: Courtesy of The Coca-Cola Company

developed at the strategic level to guide in the segmentation of suppliers. At Coca-Cola the strategic SRM team decided that supply risk and potential to add value would be used as the segmentation criteria. Under supply risk there are 13 factors to consider and under potential to add value there are 12 factors. It is possible to rate suppliers on each of the factors and then based on the relative importance of each factor, develop two scores for each supplier that are used to position the supplier on the matrix. The team also specified the characteristics of firms for each of the four quadrants of the matrix (see Figure 3-5). In addition, business objectives were defined for each segment as well as the expected result from achieving these objectives (see Figure 3-6). For example, the business objectives for the strategic segment are:

- manage risk and vulnerability
- maximize supply performance
- develop preferential relationships
- have close supplier management.

The result is profitable long-term growth for both parties. The team also identified relationship implication guidelines for each of the four segments that specify the level of engagement, the amount of resources necessary, the depth of involvement and how the relationship should be measured (see Figure 3-7).

In order to provide Coca-Cola employees with details on the progress that is being made implementing supplier relationship management and the results that are being achieved, the Global SRM Program Manager at The Coca-Cola Company produces a SRM newsletter on a quarterly basis. Topics covered in the newsletter include the SRM framework, updates on activities and results, SRM tools, and how success is measured. Partnership sessions are held with key suppliers identified in the segmentation. The partnership model that is being used at Coca-Cola is described in detail in Chapter 14.

Figure 3-6
Business Objectives by Segment

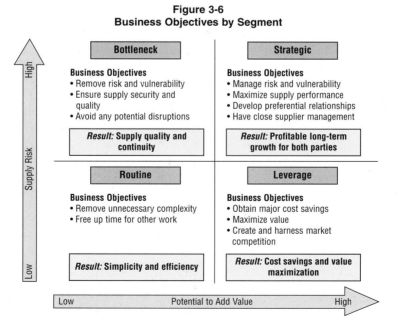

Source: Courtesy of The Coca-Cola Company

Figure 3-7
Relationship Implication Guidelines by Segment

	Bottleneck		Strategic
Resources	• Director or senior level leadership • Non-dedicated relationship manager • Semi-annual business review meetings • Dedicated quality or technical resources	Resources	• VP up to Executive level leadership • Dedicated relationship manager • Quarterly reviews; top-to-top meetings • On-site or dedicated supplier resources
Strategic Planning	• Semi-annual business planning • Share forecasts and demand plans	Strategic Planning	• Extensive business planning • Direct linkage to S&OP process
Customer/ Market	• Effort to change specifications or develop substitutes to reduce supply risk	Customer/ Market	• Involvement in new product development • Knowledge of our business strategy
Measurement/ Knowledge	• Standard supplier metrics (one-way) • Some strategic information sharing	Measurement/ Knowledge	• Customized supplier metrics (two-way) • Use **Partnership Model** to align strategies
	Tactical		**Leverage**
Resources	• Tactical management resources	Resources	• Director level leadership • Non-dedicated relationship manager • Use cross-functional commodity councils • Annual business review meetings
Strategic Planning	• Transactional focus to planning	Strategic Planning	• Annual business planning • Standard volume forecasts
Customer/ Market	• May or may not be opportunities for product or service development	Customer/ Market	• May or may not be opportunities for product development
Measurement/ Knowledge	• Transactional supplier metrics • Commercial information sharing	Measurement/ Knowledge	• Standard supplier metrics (one-way) • Some strategic information sharing

(Vertical axis: Supply Risk, Low to High. Horizontal axis: Potential to Add Value, Low to High.)

Note: These implications show the level of engagement, amount of resources, and depth of involvement focused on managing the performance of suppliers in each quadrant.

Source: Courtesy of The Coca-Cola Company

Provide Guidelines for the Degree of Differentiation in the Product and Service Agreements

In the third sub-process, the team develops guidelines for the degree of differentiation in the PSA. This involves developing the differentiation alternatives and considering the revenue and cost implications of each. To do this, the team considers the quality and cost implications of various differentiation alternatives, and selects the boundaries for the degree of customization. The team must interface with each of the other processes in order to understand the degree of differentiation that is desirable as well as be ready to design supporting systems to aid in implementation. For example, the demand management process team may want to share with key suppliers demand information from Collaborative Planning, Forecasting and Replenishment (CPFR) implementations with customers. Investments in technology may be necessary for this to be successful.[4] At Masterfoods USA, the PSA represents a letter of intent that covers five key areas: cost, innovation, supply chain, quality, and environment. Supplier teams must set specific guidelines for suppliers within these areas.

…the team develops guidelines for the degree of differentiation in the PSA. This involves developing the differentiation alternatives and considering the revenue and cost implications of each.

---

[4] Skjoett-Larsen, Tage, Christian Thernoe and Claus Andresen, "Supply Chain Collaboration: Theoretical Perspectives and Empirical Evidence", *International Journal of Physical Distribution & Logistics Management*, Vol. 33, No. 6 (2003), pp. 531 – 549; and, Gene Fliedner, "CPFR: An Emerging Supply Chain Tool", *Industrial Management and Data Systems*, Vol. 103, No. 1 (2003), pp.14-21.

Develop Framework of Metrics

Developing the framework of metrics involves outlining the metrics of interest and relating them to the supplier's impact on the firm's profitability as well as the firm's impact on the supplier's profitability. The supplier relationship management process team has the responsibility for assuring that the metrics used to measure supplier performance do not conflict with the metrics used in the other processes. Management needs to insure that all internal and external measures are driving consistent and appropriate behavior.[5]

Figure 3-8 shows how the supplier relationship management process can affect the firm's financial performance as measured by economic value added (EVA). It illustrates how supplier relationship management can impact sales, cost of goods sold, total expenses, inventory investment, other current assets, and the investment in fixed assets. For example, supplier relationship management can lead to higher sales volume by improving the quality of materials and the service obtained from suppliers. Higher quality products will enable the firm to charge higher prices and/or increase unit sales. Improved service from suppliers might enable the firm to provide better service to its customers and thus lead to increased sales.

Cost of goods sold can be reduced as a result of better planning and fewer last minute production changes, less expediting of materials as well as lower costs for direct materials. In Wendy's case, these savings occur in suppliers' operations and they share the savings with Wendy's through price reductions.

> *The supplier relationship management process team has the responsibility for assuring that the metrics used to measure supplier performance do not conflict with the metrics used in the other processes.*

Figure 3-8
How Supplier Relationship Affects Economic Value Added (EVA®)

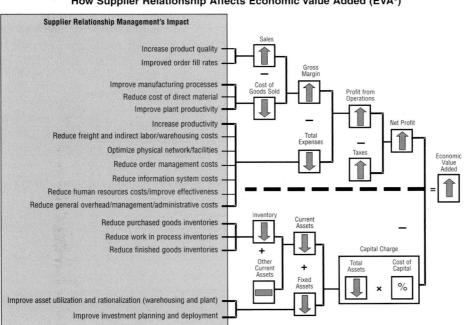

Source: Adapted from Douglas M. Lambert and Terrance L. Pohlen, "Supply Chain Metrics," *The International Journal of Logistics Management,* Vol. 12, No. 1 (2001), p. 11.

[5] Lambert, Douglas M. and Terrance L. Pohlen, "Supply Chain Metrics", *The International Journal of Logistics Management,* Vol. 12, No. 1 (2001), pp.1-19.

A number of expenses can be reduced as a result of: increased productivity; lower freight and receiving costs; realignment of network facilities; lower order management costs; lower information system costs; improved management of human resources; and, lower general overhead and administrative costs.

Supplier relationship management can lead to lower inventories of purchased materials, in-process inventories and finished goods inventories. Improvement in suppliers' order fulfillment and on-time delivery performance will result in lower safety stock needs for all three types of inventory. Finally, better supplier relationship management can lead to lower fixed assets as a result of improved asset utilization and rationalization (warehousing and plant facilities), and improved investment planning and deployment.

When the team has developed an understanding of how supplier relationship management can impact the firm's financial performance as measured by EVA, metrics must be developed for each of the individual activities that must be performed and these metrics must be tied to financial performance. Management should implement initiatives that increase the profitability of the total supply chain not just the profitability of a single firm. Management should encourage actions that benefit the whole supply chain while at the same time equitably sharing in the risks and rewards. If the management of a firm makes a decision that positively affects that firm's EVA at the expense of the EVA of a supplier or a customer, every effort should be made to share the benefits in a manner that improves the financial performance of each firm involved and so that managers in each firm have an incentive to improve supply chain performance.

At the wholesale and retail level, the development of supplier profitability reports enables the process team to track performance over time. If calculated as shown in Table 3-1, these reports reflect all of the cost and revenue implications of

When the team has developed an understanding of how supplier relationship management can impact the firm's financial performance as measured by EVA, metrics must be developed for each of the individual activities that must be performed and these metrics must be tied to financial performance.

Table 3-1
Supplier Profitability Analysis:
A Contribution Approach With Charge for Assets Employed

	Supplier A	Supplier B	Supplier C	Supplier D
Sales				
Cost of Goods Sold				
Gross Margin				
Plus: Discounts and Allowances				
Market Development Funds				
Slotting Allowances				
Co-operative Advertising Allowances				
Net Margin				
Variable Marketing and Logistics Costs:				
Transportation				
Receiving				
Order Processing				
Order Costs (will depend on situation)				
Controllable Margin				
Assignable Nonvariable Costs				
Salaries				
Advertising				
Inventory Carrying Costs Less:				
Charge for Accounts Payable				
Other Costs (will depend on situation)				
Segment Controllable Margin				

the relationship. Cost of good sold is deducted from net sales to calculate a gross margin. Then, revenue adjustments such as discounts and allowances, market development funds, slotting allowances and co-operative advertising allowances must be added to achieve a net margin. Next, variable marketing and logistics costs are deducted to calculate a contribution margin. Assignable non-variable costs, such as salaries, advertising, and inventory carrying costs less a charge for accounts payable, are subtracted to obtain a segment controllable margin. These statements contain opportunity costs for investment in inventory. Consequently, they are much closer to cash flow statements than a traditional profit and loss statement. They contain revenues minus the costs (avoidable costs) that disappear if the revenue disappears (see the Appendix to Chapter 2).

Supplier profitability reports can be constructed by wholesalers and retailers but it is not possible for manufacturers to develop these reports for the suppliers of undifferentiated components and materials.

Supplier profitability reports can be constructed by wholesalers and retailers but it is not possible for manufacturers to develop these reports for the suppliers of undifferentiated components and materials. In this case, total cost reports are used along with calculations of the total delivered cost per unit purchased. Total cost reports should include the purchase price plus transportation costs, inventory carrying costs, financial impact of terms of sale, ordering costs, receiving costs, quality costs and administrative costs. At the end of the day, it is the change in profits or costs (in the case of total cost reports) that management should focus on because it is the change in profits or costs that measures the impact of the relationship on earnings per share.

Develop Guidelines for Sharing Process Improvement Benefits with Suppliers

The goal is to make process improvements win-win solutions for both the firm and the supplier.

In the final sub-process, the team develops the guidelines for sharing process improvement benefits with suppliers. The goal is to make process improvements win-win solutions for both the firm and the supplier. If both parties do not gain from the relationship, it will be difficult to gain the supplier's full commitment to the firm's goals. The supplier relationship management team must find ways to quantify the benefits for process improvements in financial terms. At Masterfoods USA, suppliers are given a 100% of the benefits derived from cost savings projects until they recover the entire investment that has been made and make an agreed upon level of profit. After that point has been reached, 100% of the benefits go to Masterfoods USA. The goal is to encourage suppliers to keep improving and to avoid becoming complacent.

At Wendy's International, the following description of cost savings initiatives and gain sharing is attached to the terms and conditions of every PSA:

> Supplier shall in good faith endeavor, throughout the term of this Agreement, to continually reduce the cost of the services and products it provides hereunder and be responsible to present to Wendy's potential cost savings initiatives on a semi-annual basis. Cost savings may occur in specification changes (as agreed upon by both parties), changes in manufacturing capabilities or other potential cost efficiency areas to be agreed upon by the parties. Wendy's and Supplier agree to review, not less than semi-annually, Supplier's satisfaction of Wendy's reasonable cost and efficiency standards and to reasonably and in good faith improve the cost and efficiency of the Approved Products if and to the extent reasonable in light of the then applicable requirements as set forth by Wendy's, acting reasonably. Supplier shall use its commercially reasonable and good faith

efforts to satisfy any such heightened or more stringent standards that the parties agree to pursuant to such semi-annual reviews.

Gain sharing arrangement for multi-year Agreements:
- Supplier will deliver 2% minimum annual cost savings on controllable portion of costs.
- 1st year – cost savings generated in year 1 as a result of supplier idea or joint development will be retained by the supplier.
- 2nd year – cost savings generated in year 2 as a result of supplier idea or joint development will be shared between Wendy's and the supplier at a ratio of 50% : 50%.
- 3rd year – cost savings generated in year 3 as a result of supplier idea or joint development will be passed along to Wendy's.
- Any cost savings generated by an idea proposed exclusively by Wendy's that does not require capital investment by supplier will be immediately passed along to Wendy's.[6]

In summary, the objective of supplier relationship management at the strategic level is to identify key product and service components, provide criteria for segmenting suppliers, provide supplier teams with guidelines for customizing the product and service offering, develop a framework of metrics, and provide guidelines for the sharing of process improvement benefits with the suppliers.

The Operational Supplier Relationship Management Process

At the operational level, the supplier relationship management process deals with developing and implementing the PSAs. It is comprised of seven sub-processes: differentiate suppliers; prepare the supplier/segment management team; internally review the supplier/supplier segment; identify opportunities with the suppliers; develop the product/service agreements and communication plans; implement the product/service agreements; and, measure performance and generate supplier cost/profitability reports (see Figure 3-9).

At the operational level, the supplier relationship management process deals with developing and implementing the PSAs.

Segment Suppliers

In the first sub-process, suppliers are segmented based on the criteria that were established in the strategic process. At Wendy's International, management performs an industry analysis including consideration of strengths, weaknesses, opportunities and threats that helps differentiate among suppliers. For example, no single supplier can fill all of Wendy's needs for chicken. One supplier is a low cost supplier who gets 60 percent of Wendy's volume and guides Wendy's in its dealing with all chicken suppliers in terms of where there are opportunities for cost reduction. Another supplier, who has 30 percent of the volume, is a leader in research and development and generates new products for Wendy's. But, this supplier cannot meet all of Wendy's needs, and must share these innovations with Wendy's other suppliers. Since this supplier conducted the research, it will receive 40 percent of the first year volume of the new products. The final 10 percent of the volume goes to a minority supplier to satisfy Wendy's corporate goal to encourage diversity. The output of this sub-process is the identification of which suppliers are key to the firm and which suppliers are grouped into segments.

---

[6] Wendy's International, "Additional Terms and Conditions".

Figure 3-9
The Operational Supplier Relationship Management Process

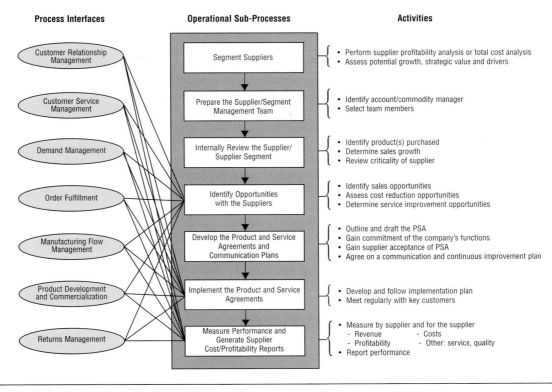

Process Interfaces	Operational Sub-Processes	Activities
Customer Relationship Management	Segment Suppliers	• Perform supplier profitability analysis or total cost analysis • Assess potential growth, strategic value and drivers
Customer Service Management	Prepare the Supplier/Segment Management Team	• Identify account/commodity manager • Select team members
Demand Management	Internally Review the Supplier/Supplier Segment	• Identify product(s) purchased • Determine sales growth • Review criticality of supplier
Order Fulfillment	Identify Opportunities with the Suppliers	• Identify sales opportunities • Assess cost reduction opportunities • Determine service improvement opportunities
Manufacturing Flow Management	Develop the Product and Service Agreements and Communication Plans	• Outline and draft the PSA • Gain commitment of the company's functions • Gain supplier acceptance of PSA • Agree on a communication and continuous improvement plan
Product Development and Commercialization	Implement the Product and Service Agreements	• Develop and follow implementation plan • Meet regularly with key customers

Returns Management	Measure Performance and Generate Supplier Cost/Profitability Reports	• Measure by supplier and for the supplier
		  - Revenue - Costs
		  - Profitability - Other: service, quality
		• Report performance

Prepare the Supplier/Segment Management Teams

In this sub-process, the account or segment management teams are formed, including the buyer who will be the supplier or supplier segment relationship manager. The teams are cross-functional with representation from each of the functional areas. In the case of key suppliers, each team is dedicated to a specific supplier and meets regularly with a team from the supplier organization. In the case of supplier segments, a team manages a group of suppliers and develops and manages the standard PSA for the segment. Each supplier/segment team is comprised of a team manager and a cross-functional group of members. At Wendy's International, the criteria that are used to identify the key suppliers are used to identify critical team members. For an example, Marzetti's is a supplier of promotional sauces which Wendy's management views as strategic. The development of new sauces is a critical component of this relationship which means that research and development personnel must be part of the Wendy's supplier relationship management team and the Marzetti's customer relationship management team.

In the case of key suppliers, each team is dedicated to a specific supplier and meets regularly with a team from the supplier organization.

Internally Review the Supplier/Supplier Segment

Each supplier/segment team reviews their supplier or segment of suppliers to determine the role that the supplier or segment of suppliers plays in the supply chain. A supplier team works with each supplier or segment of suppliers to identify improvement opportunities. The team examines each of the other supply chain management processes, both at the firm and at the supplier or supplier segment to identify opportunities for improvement.

Identify Opportunities with the Suppliers

Once the teams have an understanding of the supplier(s), they work with each supplier or segment of suppliers to develop improvement opportunities. These opportunities might arise from any of the supply chain management processes, so the supplier teams need to interface with each of the other process teams. Wendy's uses the partnership model, described in Chapter 14, to structure relationships with key suppliers. The partnership sessions enable both Wendy's and the supplier to gain knowledge about the business drivers for the other firm. This leads to goal setting that becomes an ongoing part of the quarterly business reviews between the firms. The Wendy's buyers prepare a scorecard for each of their suppliers in which the drivers are included. Coca-Cola, Colgate-Palmolive Company, Defense Logistics Agency and Masterfoods USA are also using the partnership model with key suppliers. In fact, Masterfoods USA has used it with a Tier 1 supplier and also with the Tier 2 supplier who provides the key ingredient to the Tier 1 supplier.

Develop the Product and Service Agreements and Communication Plans

In the fifth sub-process, each team develops the PSA for their supplier or segment of suppliers. For key suppliers, the team negotiates a mutually beneficial PSA, and then gains commitment from the supplier's internal functions. They work with the suppliers until agreement has been reached. It is important that the PSA for key suppliers include a communication and continuous improvement plan. For segments of non-key suppliers, a standard PSA is developed for each segment. These represent the minimum requirements to be a supplier and they are not negotiable. At Wendy's, supplier relationship management teams prepare a negotiation plan for meetings with key suppliers to develop the PSAs. What does Wendy's want to have versus what does it need to have? It is important to prioritize initiatives and negotiate the best solution if all of them are not possible. Items that Wendy's includes in the PSA include the cost savings initiatives described earlier as well as goals for spending with minority-owned businesses. Suppliers will make a good faith effort to competitively purchase goods and/or services directly related to the goods covered in this Agreement from Historically Underutilized Businesses (HUB's), also commonly referred to as minority-owned business. Supplier shall report all HUB sending on a quarterly basis to Wendy's.[7]

Additional items that may be included in Wendy's PSAs with suppliers are the following:

- **Open-book Costing.** Supplier shall provide a monthly detailed breakdown of all applicable actual costs as they relate to pricing and costs affecting Wendy's business and the Approved Products.
- **Key Business Review.** Supplier and Wendy's shall meet regularly for the purpose of conducting business reviews to review the plans and expectations as outlined in the Agreement.
- **Diversity Clause.** Supplier agrees to seek out first and second-tier diversity suppliers where applicable to the Wendy's business.

For key suppliers, the team negotiates a mutually beneficial PSA, and then gains commitment from the supplier's internal functions.

---

[7] Wendy's International, Exhibit B, "Additional Terms and Conditions".

- **Written Contingency Plans.** Supplier shall provide, in writing, detailed and executable contingency plans applicable for Supplier to insure continuity of supply.
- **Weekly Volume and Pricing Reports.** Supplier shall provide to Wendy's in writing at such time periods and in a form as reasonably required by Wendy's, volume and applicable prices sold to Wendy's Approved Distributors and restaurants.[8]

At Masterfoods USA the PSAs include an eight step vendor assurance program (shown in Table 3-2) that is described in company documents as follows:

Vendor Assurance requires that we seek and develop relationships with those suppliers who have the ability, currently or potentially, to meet Masterfoods USA standards and specifications consistently. This confidence building process is a joint activity between Masterfoods and the Supplier, and is grounded on the Mutuality Principle. As our partners, vendors need a thorough knowledge of the specific way in which we will use their product. Open communications will help them to understand our reasons to increasing conformance. Masterfoods' goal is a vendor certification of quality achievement which requires a minimum auditing by ourselves and which assures that materials will perform reliably over time.[9]

Table 3-2
Vendor Assurance: The Eight Steps

Step 1	**Specifications.** The concept of Vendor Assurance is explained to the vendor and the mutual commitment to Vendor Assurance established. The specifications of the goods or service to be purchased are explained and their content discussed.
Step 2	**Process Description.** Good manufacturing practices and environmental responsibility are demonstrated by the vendor. A detailed description of the vendor's normal process is provided in confidence and forms the basis of the Vendor File.
Step 3	**Risk Assessment.** Jointly, hazards are identified, risks are quantified, and Critical Control Points associated with the vendor's process are located.
Step 4	**Quality Management.** Existing quality systems to minimize risks are assessed and documented. Where necessary, additional methods to monitor and control key areas are implemented. A commitment and positive attitude to quality improvement are demonstrated by the vendor.
Step 5	**Conformance.** The vendor provides data that demonstrates his process is capable of consistently meeting his customers' requirements.
Step 6	**Review.** The periods' activities are reviewed, confirming that the customers' requirements are met, assuring incoming materials can be accepted based on vendor data, and identifying areas for improvement.
Step 7	**Mutual Development.** Exchanged visits between Mars, Incorporated and the vendor by relevant personnel from all parts of both companies occur, as appropriate, to better understand one another's processes, needs, limitations, specifications and quality performance.
Step 8	**Continue Commitment to Quality.** Enduring business relationships are established which motivate vendors to continuously improve quality, costs, and responsiveness to our mutual benefits. This will be assured by regular audits as part of normal communications between partners.

Source: Masterfoods USA

[8] Wendy's International, "Additional Terms and Conditions".

[9] Masterfoods USA.

Implement the Product and Service Agreements

In the sixth sub-process, the team implements the PSA, which includes holding regular planning sessions with key suppliers. The supplier relationship management teams provide input to each of the other supply chain management process teams that are affected by the customizations that have been made in the PSAs. Supplier relationship management teams must work with other process teams to assure that the PSAs are being implemented as determined, and meet with suppliers on a regular basis to monitor progress and performance. At Wendy's, the PSAs with key suppliers are reviewed at the quarterly business meetings to ensure that implementation is taking place as planned. Depending on the supplier involved, as many as 50 people can participate in these quarterly business reviews.

The supplier relationship management teams provide input to each of the other supply chain management process teams that are affected by the customizations that have been made in the PSAs.

Measure Performance and Generate Supplier Cost/Profitability Reports

In the last operational sub-process, the team captures and reports the process performance measures. Metrics from each of the other processes also are captured in order to generate the supplier cost/profitability reports. These reports provide information for measuring and selling the value of the relationship to each supplier and internally to upper management. The value provided should be measured in terms of costs, impact on sales, and associated investment, otherwise the process improvements will go unrecognized and unrewarded.[10]

The other process teams communicate supplier-related performance to the supplier teams who tie these metrics back to the profitability of the firm and the profitability of its suppliers. Wendy's regularly schedules comprehensive performance reviews with key suppliers at quarterly business meetings. Less critical suppliers might have biannual review meetings but all suppliers meet with Wendy's personnel at least once per year to review performance.

Conclusions

Supplier relationship management provides the structure for how relationships with suppliers are developed and maintained, including the establishment of PSAs between the firm and its suppliers. It is a key supply chain management process which along with the customer relationship management process forms the critical linkages that connect firms in the supply chain. Supply chain management is about relationship management and the supply chain is managed link-by-link, relationship-by-relationship. The ultimate measure of success for each relationship is the impact that it is having on the financial performance of the firms involved. Consequently, it is necessary for each firm to have the capability of measuring the performance of the supplier relationship management and customer relationship management teams in terms of their impact on incremental revenues and costs. With this knowledge, it will be possible to develop programs that improve supply chain performance and to negotiate sharing of benefits and costs so that all of the involved players have the incentive to participate.

The ultimate measure of success for each relationship is the impact that it is having on the financial performance of the firms involved.

---

[10] Lambert, Douglas M. and Terrance L. Pohlen, "Supply Chain Metrics", *The International Journal of Logistics Management*, Vol. 12, No. 1 (2001), pp.1-19.

The Customer Service Management Process

A. Michael Knemeyer, Douglas M. Lambert and Sebastián J. García-Dastugue

Overview

The customer service management process is responsible for administering the product and service agreements (PSAs) developed by customer teams as part of the customer relationship management process.[1] The key differentiating factor between the traditional customer service activity and the customer service management process is that the process is primarily proactive. The process involves the development of triggers and signals to identify situations that may become problems before they affect the customer so that the promises made in the PSA can be achieved without interruption. Standardized response procedures are developed to respond to recurring events and coordination mechanisms are put in place to deal with irregular events. Information systems are developed to provide visibility to the triggers and signals that identify events requiring a response. In this chapter, we describe the customer service management process in detail to show how it can be implemented and managed. To do this, we identify the activities of each strategic and operational sub-process; evaluate the interfaces with the business functions and the other seven supply chain management processes; and describe examples of successful implementation.

Introduction

In a competitive business environment, management needs to implement the customer service management process in order to proactively respond to situations before they negatively impact the customer.

In a competitive business environment, management needs to implement the customer service management process in order to proactively respond to situations before they negatively impact the customer. It is this proactive perspective that makes the customer service management process different from the customer service activity in logistics. The customer service group in logistics is where customers might call in to place orders; to inquire about an order that has not arrived as scheduled; to complain about damaged products, invoice errors, products shipped in error; and/or to change an order. It might be argued that the greater the number of calls to the customer service group, the more service failures customers are experiencing and thus a more appropriate name might be customer non-service group.

---

[1] This chapter is adapted from Yemisi A. Bolumole, A. Michael Knemeyer and Douglas M. Lambert, "The Customer Service Management Process," *The International Journal of Logistics Management,* Vol. 14, No. 2 (2003), pp. 15-31.

In contrast, the role of customer service managers within the customer service management process is to monitor the PSAs for customers, and intervene on their behalf to solve problems before they are affected. For example, a customer has planned a large promotion. When do the advertising materials need to be received by the customer? Are they being produced on schedule? When do products need to be shipped in order to arrive on-time? A trigger in the information system notifies the customer service manager that the order should have been scheduled for production, but it has not been scheduled. Investigation by the customer service manager reveals that the customer's order has not been scheduled for production because a key component has not arrived from the supplier. The customer service manager contacts the supplier relationship management team assigned to that supplier to find a solution as well as the manufacturing flow management process team to reschedule production and perhaps the order fulfillment process team to expedite delivery, if necessary. The goal is to deliver the promotional materials and products when promised so that the customer has no need to place a call. If, even with all this effort, the on-time delivery will not take place, the customer is given advance notice and an action plan is developed.

The motivation for management to proactively manage customer service comes from the need to avoid the costs of service failures and ultimately grow sales from demanding customers who are involved in their own complex businesses. In the words of a former Director of Customer Service at 3M, "The fact that 3M is a multi-national, multi-division, and multi-product company is not our customers' problem".[2] The goal of the customer service management process is to develop the necessary infrastructure and coordination mechanisms for implementing the PSAs, to proactively address potential service issues and to provide a key point of contact to the customer.[3]

"The fact that 3M is a multi-national, multi-division, and multi-product company is not our customers' problem".

In this chapter, we describe the sub-processes and activities of the customer service management process. Customer service management is one of the eight supply chain management processes and it requires interfaces with the other seven processes shown in Figure 4-1. Customer service management is described with particular emphasis on the distinction between customer service management as a supply chain management process and customer service from a logistics perspective. We also delineate the distinction between the customer service management process and the customer relationship management process, and describe the interface between the two processes. Next, we detail the strategic and operational sub-processes that comprise customer service management, and describe their activities, and the interfaces with business functions, the other supply chain management processes and other firms. Then, we provide examples of the operational customer service management process at Gillette Argentina and at Shell International Petroleum Company Limited. Finally, we present the conclusions.

---

[2] Fabozzi, Dennis S., "Customer Service Management," Supply Chain Management Seminar, Marriott Sawgrass, February 14, 1996.

[3] Croxton, Keely L., Sebastián J. García-Dastugue, Douglas M. Lambert, and Dale S. Rogers, "The Supply Chain Management Processes," *The International Journal of Logistics Management*, Vol. 12, No. 2 (2001), pp. 13-36.

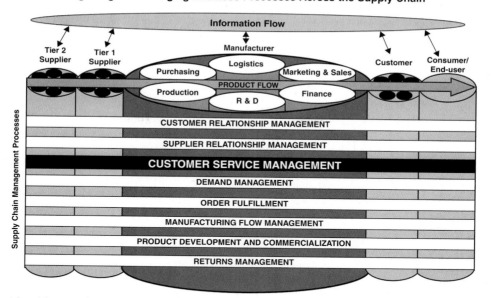

Figure 4-1
Supply Chain Management:
Integrating and Managing Business Processes Across the Supply Chain

Source: Adapted from Douglas M. Lambert, Martha C. Cooper, and Janus D. Pagh, "Supply Chain Management: Implementation Issues and Research Opportunities," *The International Journal of Logistics Management,* Vol. 9, No. 2 (1998), p. 2.

Customer Service Management as a Supply Chain Management Process

The customer service management process has both strategic and operational elements, as shown in Figure 4-2. In the strategic process, a management team establishes the structure for managing the process, and in the operational process it is implemented. Strategic sub-processes typically involve a longer time horizon, are closely linked to the corporate strategy and establish the framework for process implementation. Operational sub-processes focus on the implementation of the customer service management process on a day-to-day basis. Figure 4-2 also shows the interfaces between each sub-process and the other supply chain management processes. These interfaces might take the form of a transfer of data or might involve sharing information with other process teams to facilitate joint problem solving.

The customer service management process should not be confused with logistics customer service . . .

The customer service management process should not be confused with logistics customer service, which represents a measure of the logistics system's performance in creating time and place utility. In other words, how well the logistics function performs in terms of satisfying existing customers and attracting new ones.[4] From this perspective, customer service provides the key interface between the marketing and logistics functions. The customer service management process includes the proactive management and administration of PSAs, and provides a single point of contact and a source of information for the customer.

---

[4] Lambert, Douglas M., James J. Stock and Lisa M. Ellram, *Fundamentals of Logistics Management,* Burr Ridge, IL.: Irwin/McGraw-Hill, 1998.

Figure 4-2
Customer Service Management

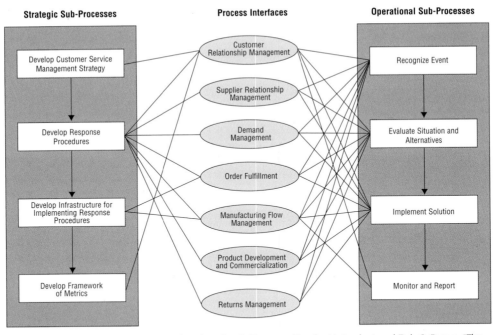

Source: Adapted from Keely L. Croxton, Sebastián J. García-Dastugue, Douglas M. Lambert, and Dale S. Rogers, "The Supply Chain Management Processes," *The International Journal of Logistics Management*, Vol. 12, No. 2 (2001), p. 17.

PSAs are documents that match specific customer or customer segment needs with a firm's products and services. They represent a firm's commitment to a customer based on a realistic understanding of customer requirements and the firm's own capabilities and profit goals. The customer relationship management process teams establish PSAs of varying complexity based on the customer segmentation developed in that process. The PSAs contain detailed information such as: the number and extent of products within the firm's portfolio; shipping locations; frequency of orders; contractual limitations; purchasing and delivery specifications; price/service guarantees; joint product development opportunities; preferred terms; and, advertising. The inclusion of some or all of these components in the PSA means that the agreement can range from a low level of customization, which would be typical for most segments of customers, to a high level of customization for a few key accounts (see Figure 4-3). As the level of customization increases, the PSAs include additional value-added services.

Management must prioritize the firm's investment strategies so these align with the diverse set of customer needs. Achieving this is a holistic, enterprise-wide responsibility, not just the job of sales and customer service. It involves understanding changing customer needs, focusing resources on the highest priority customers or customer segments, and reengineering transactional activities to develop products and services which are aligned with customer requirements.

In order to identify opportunities to more efficiently and effectively administer PSAs, it is necessary to work with the sales, marketing and manufacturing functions as well as customers and suppliers. Increasingly technology is being leveraged to

PSAs are documents that match specific customer or customer segment needs with a firm's products and services.

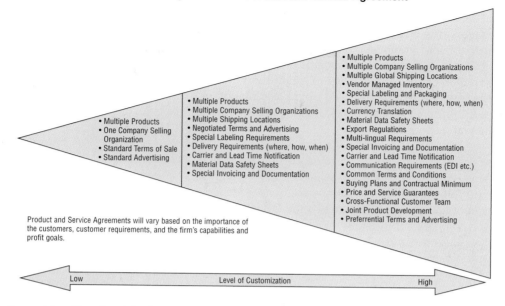

Figure 4-3
Potential Components of a Product and Service Agreement

- Multiple Products
- One Company Selling Organization
- Standard Terms of Sale
- Standard Advertising

- Multiple Products
- Multiple Company Selling Organizations
- Multiple Shipping Locations
- Negotiated Terms and Advertising
- Special Labeling Requirements
- Delivery Requirements (where, how, when)
- Carrier and Lead Time Notification
- Material Data Safety Sheets
- Special Invoicing and Documentation

- Multiple Products
- Multiple Company Selling Organizations
- Multiple Global Shipping Locations
- Vendor Managed Inventory
- Special Labeling and Packaging
- Delivery Requirements (where, how, when)
- Currency Translation
- Material Data Safety Sheets
- Export Regulations
- Multi-lingual Requirements
- Special Invoicing and Documentation
- Carrier and Lead Time Notification
- Communication Requirements (EDI etc.)
- Common Terms and Conditions
- Buying Plans and Contractual Minimum
- Price and Service Guarantees
- Cross-Functional Customer Team
- Joint Product Development
- Preferrential Terms and Advertising

Product and Service Agreements will vary based on the importance of the customers, customer requirements, and the firm's capabilities and profit goals.

Low ← Level of Customization → High

Source: Adapted from Dennis S. Fabozzi, "Customer Service Management," Supply Chain Management Seminar, Marriott Sawgrass, February 14, 1996.

provide on-line/real-time product, pricing and order status information in support of customer orders and inquiries. For example, Moen Inc. introduced CustomerNet, an interactive website designed to provide customers and customer service managers with visibility to customer orders and shipping status. This customer service management tool continues to evolve as Moen Inc. customizes the website functionality for specific customers and customer segments. Process teams need to understand and consider the implications of their solutions to meet customer requirements on the other members of the supply chain.

While the customer relationship management process teams develop the PSAs, customer service management teams service and support the PSAs.

While the customer relationship management process teams develop the PSAs, customer service management teams service and support the PSAs. TaylorMade-adidas Golf Company Inc. demonstrates this distinction through their use of a customer relationship management process team to establish the PSA that delineates a basic set of parameters for managing the relationship with each golf equipment retailer. This agreement involves a mutual understanding of each other's goals and requirements for the relationship. Then, customer service management process teams service and support these agreements. Based on the customers' PSA, the process teams serve as the internal advocate for the retailer by developing account-focused process improvements and value-added services.

The strategic customer service management process team is comprised of managers from all corporate functions including marketing, finance, production, purchasing and logistics. This team might also include members from key customers, key suppliers or third-party logistics providers. This team is not full-time, that is, members come together from different functions and firms to carry out process activities which cut across traditional functional responsibilities and expertise. The strategic process team is responsible for defining the customer service strategy and designing the infrastructure and framework to be used for its implementation, as well as for developing the response procedures and overseeing their implementation. The operational process can be managed by a team for large critical customers or by assigning an individual customer service manager the day-to-day responsibility for the process. The teams or customer service managers are responsible for implementing the activities as established by the strategic process team. Other employees might be involved in implementation of the process, but the customer service management process teams or customer service managers maintain managerial responsibility.

Customer service managers are dedicated full-time to a particular customer or segment of customers. They are necessary because, with the exception of very large customer accounts such as Wal-Mart for which suppliers might have a dedicated team, the only person other than the salesperson who is dedicated full-time to a particular customer or segment of customers is the customer service manager. The salesperson is the company's in-the-field representative who should be focused on growing customer business and finding solutions to customer problems that are unrelated to the company in its supplier role, not solving problems that the firm has created for the customer such as late deliveries. The customer service manager is the internal advocate for the customer or segment of customers. The success of an organization's customer service management process is only as effective as its knowledge of its customers and of its own internal capabilities. The PSAs articulate commitments based on customer requirements and expectations as well as the firm's capabilities and profit goals for the customer or customer segment.

The customer service manager is the internal advocate for the customer or segment of customers.

The role of the customer service manager within the customer service management process is different from that of a traditional customer service representative, an order entry clerk who might also provide information on order status and resolve invoicing problems. Customer service managers interface and work with other supply chain management process teams to provide effective solutions in order to avoid customer inquiries and complaints. Customer service managers with this expanded role must be compensated appropriately. At 3M, compensation for the customer service employees corresponds to the pay scale for field sales representatives. Top level customer service managers are compensated at a level equivalent to top level sales representatives which differentiates the position from traditional day-to-day order-taking responsibilities. This practice of matching extends across the pay scale connecting various levels of sales representatives with customer service representatives as they progress towards the managerial level.

The Strategic Customer Service Management Process

Strategic customer service management includes four sub-processes that deal with the necessary procedures and infrastructure for implementing PSAs. At this level, the process team is responsible for planning how each of the potential promises made to customers in the PSAs will be monitored and how exceptions will be managed. Figure 4-4 shows the strategic customer service management sub-processes, the activities that comprise each one, and the interfaces with the other seven supply chain management processes. The strategic process team is responsible for providing the structure that enables an effective proactive customer service management process.

...the process team is responsible for planning how each of the potential promises made to customers in the PSAs will be monitored and how exceptions will be managed.

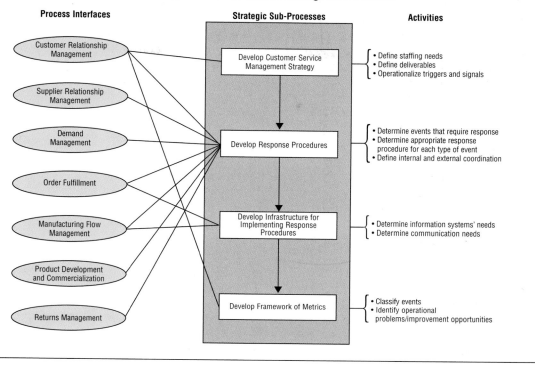

Figure 4-4
The Strategic Customer Service Management Process

Develop Customer Service Management Strategy

The strategic customer service management process is focused on developing an overall customer service strategy that enables the organization to meet the commitments made in the PSAs. A company's target markets will influence the development of the customer service management strategy. For example, TaylorMade-adidas Golf Company Inc. targets 0-10 handicap golfers, who typically have deeper technical questions about the company's products. To address the needs of this target market, the company provides in-depth technical information about its products on its corporate website. The website provides answers for typical inquires from this group of consumers and is a valuable resource for the company's retailers. Customer service managers understand the time-definite delivery requirements of golfers who are playing in tournaments. Therefore, customized golf orders for tournaments are constantly monitored to ensure that they are not delivered late.

In this sub-process, the team identifies the deliverables of the customer service management process, operationalizes the triggers and signals for initiating action, and defines the staffing needs. In order to become proactive, triggers and signals must identify tasks that were not performed as planned. In such cases, customer service managers must be notified as soon as possible in order to implement corrective measures before the event affects the customer. The deliverables of the process are standardized responses to standardized events that occur while administering the PSA. The output is a list of relevant events with corresponding

In order to become proactive, triggers and signals must identify tasks that were not performed as planned.

triggers, signals and deliverables. When implementing the first strategic sub-process, the customer service management team interfaces with the customer relationship management team. Because PSAs vary based on the importance of customers, customer requirements, and the firm's capabilities and profit goals, management should develop a tiered customer service strategy.

Next, the process team defines a customer service management structure that identifies the staffing, administrative, and technological resources needed and available, matching resource availability with the importance of individual customers and customer segments. The process team interfaces with the customer relationship management process teams to identify appropriate ways to deliver on the promises made in the PSAs.

Shell has developed a Customer Relationship Implementation Solution Pack (CRISP) as a way to provide consistency throughout its global operations. CRISP provides the framework for establishing accreditation levels, customer service staffing needs, infrastructure and deliverables. CRISP helps to catalog customer complaints and ensuing responses, thus building a database of response procedures which helps provide consistency in the responses and actions across all call centers. In addition, this information can be used by customer service managers as they look for ways to avoid future service problems.

Develop Response Procedures

In the second sub-process, the team determines the types of events that require responses and develops response procedures for each of these events. This includes developing the internal and external coordination required to respond, and distinguishing between customer and internal responses. The sub-process requires organizations to have adequate customer segmentation to allocate resources efficiently. Based on the PSA signed with each customer, there are situations that need to be monitored regularly. Events are triggered when these situations are under certain conditions. If the predetermined conditions are met, an event is triggered. The best case scenario is to trigger the event with enough time to resolve the situation so that the customer is not affected. This is part of managing the relationship with the customer proactively. Customer service managers need to monitor conditions based on the promises made in the PSA to each customer or customer segment. For each determined event, appropriate response procedures are established for the organization. For example, Gillette Argentina systematically monitors the product flow from Gillette to retailers and in each of the retailer's stores to avoid affecting sales to end-customers, and has developed response procedures for each of these potential events in order to ensure delivering on the promises made in the PSA. Figure 4-5 shows an example of the response procedures. The big arrow on the map represents the event that is triggered when there is an unexplainable reduction in sales. Each square represents an activity; squares with s-shaped bottoms represent reports; diamonds are decision points; and, rounded rectangles represent deliverables.

The flowchart in Figure 4-5 shows the standardized procedure if a store experiences a decline in sales. Every week, customer service managers download data from the retailer's private exchange including point-of-sale data, inventory levels and orders. The first activity is to compare weekly sales with sales of the last four weeks. At this point, an event is triggered if sales have declined unexplainably. In response, it is necessary to determine if the retailer's information system shows that

The best case scenario is to trigger the event with enough time to resolve the situation so that the customer is not affected.

Figure 4-5
Standardized Response Procedure for a Sales Decline

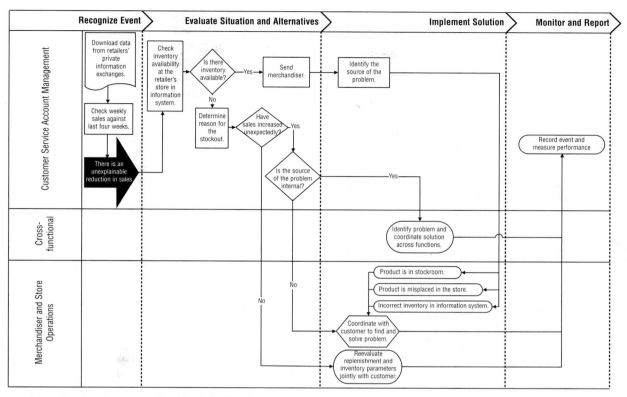

Source: Based on discussions with Pablo Bottinelli, Gillette Argentina

there is inventory available at that store. If there is no inventory at the store, then either sales have been higher than expected or Gillette had a stockout and could not replenish the customer adequately. If the information system shows that there is inventory available, then direct inspection is required to determine whether the information system is reporting incorrectly that there is inventory available, or that the product is misplaced in the store (customers cannot find it, thus, sales declined), or the product has not been replenished from the stockroom to the shelf. In any case, the appropriate corrective action is coordinated with the customer. This example shows how inter-organizational information sharing enabled the organizations to provide better service to the end-customer.

Moen Inc. also develops detailed response procedures at a strategic level. For example, if a supplier's manufacturing operation goes down for an extended period of time, the customer service manager contacts the customers whose orders are affected and communicates the problem, expected consequences to the customers in the most factual way possible, and provides them with a solution. Typical response procedures are scripted and integrated into customer service manager training activities. Moen's customer service management process team determines the events that require a response by assessing the severity of the issue to

Typical response procedures are scripted and integrated into customer service manager training activities.

customers. When determining an appropriate response procedure, Moen has found internal and external communication to be critical. When necessary, management assembles a response team that coordinates the message to the customer, with the goal of maintaining the integrity of the product as well as the company's reputation. The response team may include representatives from marketing, logistics, business planning, sales and other affected functional areas.

Develop Infrastructure for Implementing Response Procedures

Once the customer service management process team decides on appropriate response procedures to the relevant events, the team identifies the infrastructure for implementing them. The sources of the information needed to handle each event and appropriate communication protocols for internal and external coordination must be identified. The customer service management process team must determine the information technology and communication needs for managing the PSAs. These information systems must be capable of identifying problems associated with delivering on the promises made in the PSAs. If there are technical constraints, the components of the PSA that are affected have to be re-evaluated and eventually modified to make them feasible.

Once the customer service management process team decides on appropriate response procedures to the relevant events, the team identifies the infrastructure for implementing them.

Customer service tracking software can be used to identify when there is non-compliance, provide documentation of this occurrence as well as establish the immediate action required. Responsibility for this action is then assigned to individual customer service managers and tracked until an effective solution is provided. For example, FAW-Volkswagen Automotive Company Ltd. - a large-scale, joint-venture car manufacturing collaboration between First Automobile Works of China and German automakers Volkswagen and Audi - has utilized SAP to integrate all customer service functions on a single platform, from the contact center through sales, service, and marketing. The system allows customer service managers to get the latest product information and address customer issues at any time, anywhere. Moen Inc. also uses SAP to formalize a "work list" that enables recurring process information to reach all internal and external parties who need to act on the information. They utilize a process specialist who can assist in laying out the appropriate administrative and technological infrastructure for implementing response procedures, mapping the process, and defining the appropriate work steps to respond to events.

Develop Framework of Metrics

Finally, the team develops the framework of metrics to be used to measure and monitor the performance of the process, and sets goals for performance improvement. A uniform approach should be used throughout the firm to develop these metrics.[5] The customer service management process metrics should provide managers with the information necessary to identify problems and improvement opportunities in the administration of the PSA. These measurements are used for managing the process and for improving its efficiency. The team interfaces with the customer relationship management team to assure that the metrics developed are consistent with the firm's objectives.

---

[5] Lambert, Douglas M. and Terrance L. Pohlen, "Supply Chain Metrics," *The International Journal of Logistics Management,* Vol. 12, No. 1 (2001), pp. 1-19.

Metrics selected should reflect the customer's perspective and expectations. These metrics should measure the impact of customer service management on the organization's efficiency, its return on assets and ultimately, on its financial performance as measured by Economic Value Added (EVA).[6] Figure 4-6 illustrates how customer service management can impact sales, cost of goods sold, total expenses, inventory investment, other current assets and fixed assets. Implementing the customer service management process can result in higher sales by strengthening relationships with key customers thereby reducing turnover in these key accounts. The information that is obtained about customers can be used to identify opportunities to sell higher margin products or increase the overall "share of customer" through superior service delivery. Similarly, improved customer service management may increase overall sales by avoiding lost sales associated with inadequate performance. Close monitoring of the PSAs should result in fewer last minute production changes, thereby reducing cost of goods sold. Several expenses can be reduced through the improved planning and communication including: reducing returns, order processing and transaction costs; minimizing or eliminating claims; improved management of warranty, replacement, and repair programs; and, reducing the number of expedited shipments.

Close monitoring of the PSAs should result in fewer last minute production changes, thereby reducing cost of goods sold.

Figure 4-6
How Customer Service Management Affects Economic Value Added (EVA®)

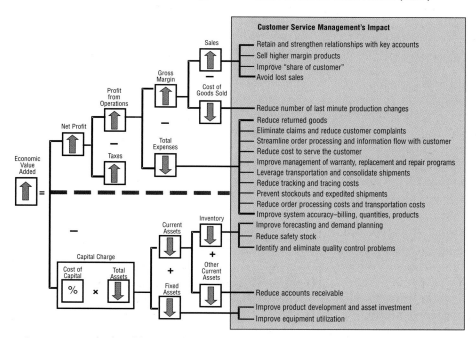

Source: Framework adapted from Douglas M. Lambert and Terrance L. Pohlen, "Supply Chain Metrics," *The International Journal of Logistics Management,* Vol. 12, No. 1 (2001), p. 10.

[6] Stewart, G. Bennet III, *The Quest for Value: A Guide for Senior Managers*, 2nd Edition, New York, NY: Harper Collins, 1999; and, Joel M. Stern, "One Way to Build Value in Your Firm, a la Executive Compensation," *Financial Executive*, Vol. 3, No. 6 (1990), pp. 51-54.

Implementation of this process can lead to better forecasting and demand planning which will result in lower levels of safety stock. These benefits arise from an increased level of confidence that customers will have in the promises made in the PSA. Customers who are confident in the firm's ability to deliver on its commitments will be less likely to over order to protect against stockouts. Also, the data collected will enable an improved ability to identify and eliminate quality control problems. Accounts receivables can be improved since fewer invoices will be disputed as a result of incomplete orders and missed delivery dates. Finally, increased customer involvement facilitated by the process can lead to improved product development efforts, better asset investment planning and better equipment utilization. Although other activities and processes in the supply chain affect these holistic metrics, the team responsible for customer service management needs to estimate how this process affects the firm's financial performance. The determination of potential financial implications will help to justify future investments in the process and to determine rewards for superior performance.

Once the team has an understanding of the impact that customer service management can have on financial performance as measured by EVA, metrics need to be developed for the activities performed and these metrics must be tied back to financial measures. These metrics enable management to measure the value created for the firm. Typical process measures include the number of events detected early and solved before the customer was affected, the number and type of customer inquires received, number and associated costs of not fulfilling promises made to customers in PSAs, accessibility of customer service representatives, and the ability to effectively respond to customer inquiries.

It is important that firms implement processes that positively affect the profitability of the supply chain as a whole, not just that of an individual firm. There are advantages to using aligned metrics throughout the supply chain as these enable each organization to encourage the right behaviors from the other members. A primary goal of supply chain management should be to encourage behavior that benefits the entire supply chain while sharing the risks and rewards among its members. If management of one firm makes a decision that positively affects their firm's EVA but negatively affects the EVA of a key supplier or customer, the two firms should work out an agreement where the benefits are shared so that both firms' management teams have the incentive to implement the improvements.

The Operational Customer Service Management Process

At the operational level, customer service management process teams are responsible for the execution of the process as it was designed by the strategic process team. Figure 4-7 shows the four operational sub-processes, the activities within each of these, and the interfaces of each sub-process with the other supply chain management processes.

Recognize Event

Timely recognition of events by the customer service management process team is critical for successfully implementing the PSAs. In order to recognize events, it is necessary to systematically monitor operational activity. Examples of customer service events include missed production runs, stockouts, component

...the team responsible for customer service management needs to estimate how this process affects the firm's financial performance.

Timely recognition of events by the customer service management process team is critical for successfully implementing the PSAs.

Figure 4-7
The Operational Customer Service Management Process

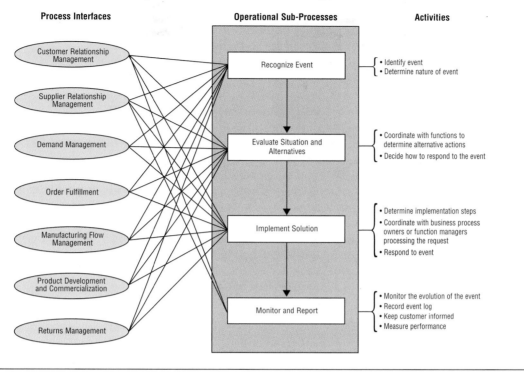

quality issues, technical questions, order amendment requests, materials not received from suppliers in time, and products not scheduled for production in time. The team needs to have a thorough understanding of the firm's operations, and try to foresee the effects of a given event on the customer and on the internal operations of the firm. As an example, Moen Inc. treats large or significant orders with unique requirements in packaging, quantity or shipping execution over and above the normal stock replenishment orders as an event. When such an order enters the system, a cross-functional team is alerted. The team works with sales and marketing, and communicates internally the customer requirements. Internal communication is critical for identifying potential obstacles to fulfilling the customers' unique requirements.

Evaluate Situation and Alternatives

Once the event is recognized, the customer service management process team evaluates alternatives for managing the event with the least disruption to the customer and internal operations. If there is a standardized response procedure for the event no evaluation is required. For non-standard events a set of alternative actions must be considered working jointly with the specialists in each of the functions that are affected by the event as well as those who can contribute to implementing the solution. This requires interfacing with other processes that might be affected by the alternative responses. At Moen Inc., customer service managers gather information to effectively evaluate potential alternatives for

SUPPLY CHAIN MANAGEMENT   81

handling the event. Another key consideration when evaluating the situation and alternatives is to fully understand both the customer's operational limitations as well as Moen's. For example, a Moen customer service manager alerted a customer of the potential negative consequences of a decision to scale back some existing orders which would have caused a significant shipping delay because of the customer's requirement to ship in full truckloads. A shipping delay might have adversely affected the level of stock availability at the store level.

Implement Solution

The implementation of the selected solution is coordination intensive, since other business process owners or functional managers often need to participate in the implementation. Possible solutions include expediting materials from a supplier, buying materials on the spot market, scheduling an unplanned manufacturing run, scheduling a manufacturing run of a smaller batch size than the minimum quantity, or expediting an order to the customer. At TaylorMade-adidas Golf Company Inc., a response might be to refer the consumer back to a member of the company's retailer network. While the customer service manager might have the ability to respond to the event, the nature of the golf industry supply chain dictates the need to refer the customer back to the retailer. The fear of disintermediation within the retailer network requires that managers recognize the implications of their solutions on other members of the supply chain.

The implementation of the selected solution is coordination intensive, since other business process owners or functional managers often need to participate in the implementation.

Monitor and Report

The customer service management process includes monitoring and reporting performance. This includes identifying possible process improvements to avoid future events or improve the responses to them. The sub-process involves recording the event in a database that can be used to identify recurring events. Also, monitoring the evolution of the event in order to know to what extent the response has been implemented. Part of the sub-process is informing the customer about how the open issues are being resolved. Performance of the process is measured and conveyed to the customer relationship management and supplier relationship management process teams. The most effective feedback occurs in a continuous stream, providing guidance and direction for process improvements.

A periodic review can be performed using specific metrics defined in the strategic process. Every identified opportunity for process improvement should be considered. TaylorMade-adidas Golf Company Inc. improved its monitoring and reporting capabilities through the implementation of an i2 system. The system provides real-time customer service information that more closely monitors the evolution of events and increases management's ability to access timely customer service information.

Examples of the Operational Customer Service Management Process

In this section, we present two examples of implementation of the customer service management process. The first example, based on Gillette Argentina, shows the importance of systematically monitoring the flow of products and transactions in order to detect situations that are likely to affect the customer unless corrective

Gillette's example shows how events can be triggered internally and how solutions can be implemented to avoid affecting the customer.

actions are taken. Gillette's example shows how events can be triggered internally and how solutions can be implemented to avoid affecting the customer. The second example, based on Shell, highlights that for customer-initiated events, standard response procedures are required to provide consistent responses efficiently.

Standardized Response Procedures at Gillette Argentina

At Gillette Argentina, customer service managers monitor the flow of product and orders to proactively manage the promises made in the PSAs to customers.

At Gillette Argentina, customer service managers monitor the flow of product and orders to proactively manage the promises made in the PSAs to customers. The implementation of Collaborative Planning, Forecasting and Replenishment (CPFR) between Gillette Argentina and customers enabled management to proactively manage product flow to CPFR customers. Figure 4-8 shows how the four sub-processes of the operational customer service management process were implemented to deliver on the commitment made in terms of product availability to customers with whom CPFR was implemented. The big arrows represent the event that is triggered. Each square represents an activity, squares with s-shaped lines represent reports, diamonds are decision points; and rounded rectangles represent deliverables to customers.

Recognize Event. Every week, an analyst who is part of the customer service management team monitors internal inventory reports to determine if there are products that are likely to stockout in the near future. This event is critical in order to deliver on the promises made to the customer in the PSA. If the analyst determines that there could be a stockout in the next four weeks, a response is triggered to avoid or minimize the impact to the customer.

Figure 4-8
Procedure for Monitoring Product Availability in Order to Deliver on Commitments Made in PSAs

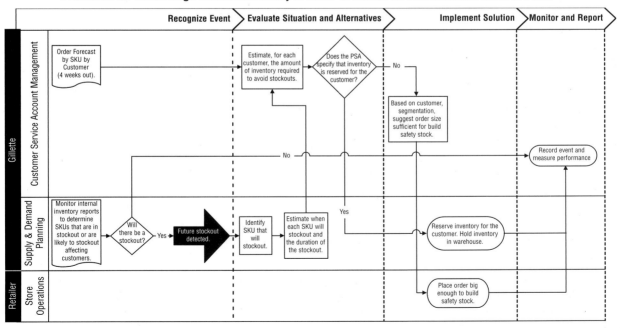

Source: Based on discussions with Pablo Bottinelli, Gillette Argentina.

Evaluate Situation and Alternatives. The customer service management team evaluates the implications of the event and the alternative course of actions that can be taken to avoid or minimize the impact on the customer. Gillette's inventory reports are combined with the customer's order forecast. The order forecast shows the details for orders that the customer is expected to place during the next four weeks. The analyst estimates the timing and the duration of the stockout to determine how much product is needed to avoid the stockout to the customer. The solution to implement depends on the terms in the PSA with the customer.

Implement Solution. Customer service managers can reserve inventory for a key customer in Gillette's warehouse. In order to offer the service of reserving inventory for the customer, the information system must be able to isolate the inventory so that it cannot be sold to another customer.

If the PSA does not specify that Gillette will reserve inventory for the customer, then the customer is notified to increase safety stocks to cover the shortage. The customers that have implemented CPFR have empowered Gillette to determine the appropriate order sizes and to increase inventory to avoid stockouts. For the customers who have not implemented CPFR, customer service managers communicate that a stockout is possible in the next four weeks so that the customer can deal with this situation.

Monitor and Report. When an event is triggered, systematic monitoring is performed because customer service managers know that this situation requires management's attention. The recorded information becomes very useful for determining patterns of the events. For example, are the potential stockouts related to the same SKUs? Are they associated with the same customer? Are stockouts likely to occur at the same time of the month or year? Event tracking is also useful for reporting performance internally and to the customer.

Standardized Response Procedures at Shell

Standard response procedures are also necessary for events initiated by the customer. Figure 4-9 shows the service process map to manage a customer order amendment at Shell. The customer request to amend an order triggers an event which requires coordination across functions. The arrows on the map represent the customer event; each rectangle details the set of response procedures for the particular event; circles establish a required intermediate step; diamonds are decision points; and rounded rectangles represent deliverables.

Recognize Event. At Shell, recognizing customer service events includes receiving calls and requests from customers who wish to make changes to their order. The sub-process used for delivering this service applies to all products. Customer service managers verify the customer's identity to ensure they have the authority to carry out the inquiry and determine ship to location information. Capturing the order amendments involves establishing and categorizing the details of changes required by the customer.

Evaluate Situation and Alternatives. Shell utilizes a customer service impact scale to classify the potential severity of events. High impact events are assigned an 'S' (stoppage) where the service promised is not delivered and the effect upon, and potential damage to, the customer relationship is severe. Events with mid-level severity are assigned a 'D' (disruptions) where the service promised is disrupted or significantly hampered. The impact on the customer relationship is less severe, but nonetheless potentially damaging to the relationship. Events with the least severe

Shell utilizes a customer service impact scale to classify the potential severity of events.

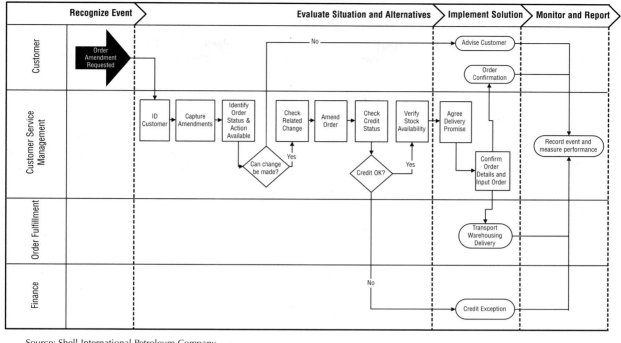

Source: Shell International Petroleum Company

impact where the service promised does or could result in a minor inconvenience to the customer are assigned an 'A' (annoyance). Using this customer service impact scale, amending customer orders is awarded an 'S', to demonstrate the potential severity of this situation on the customer relationship, indicating that not fulfilling the service promise would have a severe impact on the customer relationship. The next level of evaluation is to determine whether the sub-process changes (in terms of actions, people, IT, product, etc.) depending on the customer classification. In this example, it varies by product and is differentiated according to the service level agreements defined in the PSAs. Decisions on the most appropriate service response, available media, and standard/specific application types to be used remain the responsibility of the operating unit involved.

Implement Solution. At Shell, there is an interface with the team that is charged with standardizing data that are used and transferred across the organization, as defined in CRISP. Within the standardized response procedure (see Figure 4-9) other internal functional interfaces and external interfaces, necessary for resolving customer inquiries, are also identified. The customer service management process team interfaces with the manufacturing flow management and order fulfillment process teams in order to provide adequate visibility to support the firm's customer service efforts.

Following the procedure shown in Figure 4-9, customer service managers implement a resolution of the customer request. Major steps taken include identifying where the order is in the delivery process; understanding and advising the customer of any associated changes; amending the order with new details, and

The customer service management process team interfaces with the manufacturing flow management and order fulfillment process teams in order to provide adequate visibility to support the firm's customer service efforts.

ascertaining stock and transportation availability. This sub-process requires a knowledge of any issues that could affect the firm's ability to meet the requirements of the amended order. When implementing an order amendment process, customer service managers refer to the PSAs to insure that the solution conforms to the promises that have been made. These rules must be applied to each situation and monitored for compliance.

Monitor and Report. Cost measures are used to determine and compare the cost to serve individual customer segments. Key performance indicators used within Shell UK to measure performance and monitor the evolution of the customer order amendment sub-process include:

- Total number of amendments by customer.
- Speed of acknowledgment.
- Percentage of calls with live resolution.
- Percentage of calls receiving a date and time commitment.
- Total number of rework activities.
- Number of amended orders as a percentage of total orders.

Conclusions

The customer service management process is responsible for administering the product and service agreements (PSAs) developed by customer teams as part of the customer relationship management process. The process involves strategic and operational sub-processes focused on the development of triggers and signals to identify situations that may become problems before they are noticed by the customer. Addressing potential service events proactively is critical so that the promises made to customers in the PSAs can be achieved. Standardized response procedures are developed to respond to recurring events and mechanisms are put in place to deal with irregular events. Information systems and coordination mechanisms among the corporate functions are developed to assist in implementation of the process.

A well thought-out implementation and seamless execution of the customer service management process can have substantial impact on the firm's EVA through, for example, increased revenue, lower expenses, reduced inventory levels, improved asset utilization and improved product availability. Customer service managers monitor PSAs to minimize service failures. Implementation of the process increases operational flexibility and facilitates the development of an effective system and infrastructure so that management can proactively respond to events before they impact the customer. The customer service management process enables management to find ways to improve both the internal and external coordination that needs to take place in order to deliver on the promises made to customers.

The customer service management process enables management to find ways to improve both the internal and external coordination that needs to take place in order to deliver on the promises made to customers.

The Demand Management Process

Keely L. Croxton, Douglas M. Lambert, Sebastián J. García-Dastugue
and Dale S. Rogers

Overview

Demand management is the supply chain management process that balances the customers' requirements with the capabilities of the supply chain.[1] With the right process in place, management can match supply with demand proactively and execute the plan with minimal disruptions. The process is not limited to forecasting. It includes synchronizing supply and demand, increasing flexibility, and reducing variability. In this chapter, we describe the demand management process in detail to show how it can be implemented within a company and managed across firms in the supply chain. We examine the activities of each sub-process; evaluate the interfaces with corporate functions, processes and firms; and provide examples of successful implementation.

Introduction

The demand management process is concerned with balancing the customers' requirements with the capabilities of the supply chain. This includes forecasting demand and synchronizing it with production, procurement, and distribution capabilities. A good demand management process can enable a company to be more proactive to anticipated demand, and more reactive to unanticipated demand. An important component of demand management is finding ways to reduce demand variability and improve operational flexibility. Reducing demand variability aids in consistent planning and reduces costs. Increasing flexibility helps the firm respond quickly to internal and external events. Most customer-driven variability is unavoidable, but one of the goals of demand management is to eliminate management practices that increase variability, and to introduce policies that foster smooth demand patterns. Another key part of demand management is developing and executing contingency plans when there are interruptions to the operational plans. The goal of demand management is to

A good demand management process can enable a company to be more proactive to anticipated demand, and more reactive to unanticipated demand.

---

[1] This chapter is based on Keely L. Croxton, Douglas M. Lambert, Sebastián J. García-Dastugue and Dale S. Rogers "The Demand Management Process," *The International Journal of Logistics Management*, Vol. 13, No. 2 (2002), pp. 51-66.

meet customer demand in the most effective and efficient way.

The demand management process can have a significant impact on the profitability of a firm, its customers and suppliers. Improving the process can have far-reaching implications. Having the right product on the shelves will increase sales and customer loyalty.[2] Improved forecasting can reduce raw materials and finished goods inventories. Smoother operational execution will reduce logistics costs and improve asset utilization. These improvements will be realized not only within the firm, but will extend to other members of the supply chain.

Demand management is one of the eight processes and it requires interfaces with the other seven (see Figure 5-1). We describe the strategic and operational processes that comprise demand management, including the sub-processes and their activities. In addition, we identify the interfaces with the corporate functions, the other supply chain management processes and other firms. Finally, we present conclusions.

Demand Management as a Supply Chain Management Process

The demand management process has both strategic and operational elements, as shown in Figure 5-2. In the strategic process, the team establishes the structure for managing the process. The operational process is the actualization of demand management. Implementation of the strategic process is a necessary first

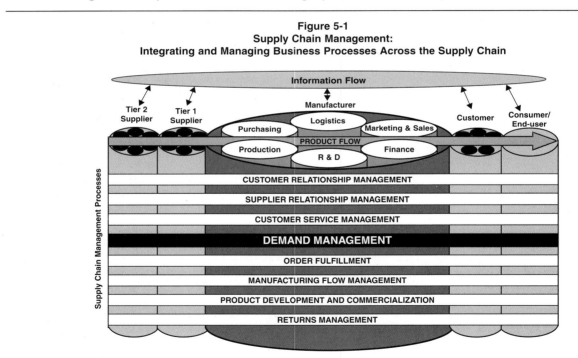

Figure 5-1
Supply Chain Management:
Integrating and Managing Business Processes Across the Supply Chain

Source: Adapted from Douglas M. Lambert, Martha C. Cooper, and Janus D. Pagh, "Supply Chain Management: Implementation Issues and Research Opportunities," *The International Journal of Logistics Management*, Vol. 9, No. 2 (1998), p. 2.

---

[2] Zinn, Walter and Peter C. Liu, "Customer Response to Retail Stockouts" *Journal of Business Logistics,* Vol. 22, No. 1 (2001), pp. 50-53; Mike Duff, "Loyalty Wanes when Stock is Low," *DSN Retailing Today,* Vol. 40, Issue 20 (2001), pp. 37-38.

Figure 5-2
Demand Management

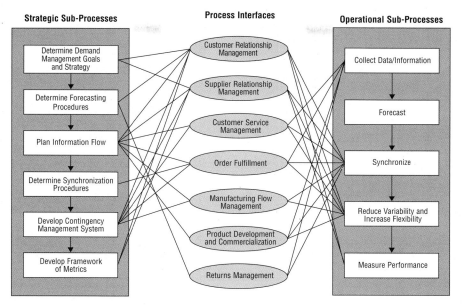

Strategic Sub-Processes   **Process Interfaces**   **Operational Sub-Processes**

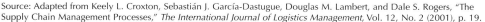

Source: Adapted from Keely L. Croxton, Sebastián J. García-Dastugue, Douglas M. Lambert, and Dale S. Rogers, "The Supply Chain Management Processes," *The International Journal of Logistics Management*, Vol. 12, No. 2 (2001), p. 19.

step in integrating the firm with other members of the supply chain, and it is at the operational level that the day-to-day activities are executed. Figure 5-2 also shows the interfaces between each sub-process and the other seven processes. These interfaces might take the form of a transfer of data that other processes require, or might involve sharing information or ideas with another process team.

A process team comprised of managers from several functions including marketing, finance, production, purchasing and logistics, leads both the strategic and operational processes. The team might also include members from outside the firm. For example, the team might include customers as well as representatives from a key supplier or a third-party provider. The team is responsible for developing the procedures at the strategic level and seeing that they are implemented. This team also has day-to-day responsibility for managing the process at the operational level. Firm employees outside of the team might execute parts of the process, but the team maintains managerial responsibility.

The Strategic Demand Management Process

Demand management is about forecasting and synchronizing. The strategic process is comprised of six sub-processes that are aimed at designing an efficient operational system for matching supply and demand. Figure 5-3 shows the sub-processes, the activities that comprise each one, and the interfaces with the other seven supply chain management processes.

There is an abundance of technology on the market to help managers with components of the demand management process. The team needs to determine how the firm will use technology within the demand management process, and

Figure 5-3
The Strategic Demand Management Process

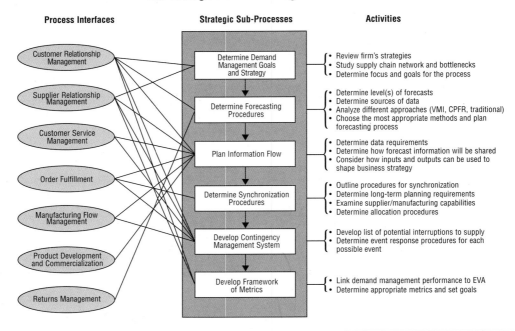

how information systems will need to be integrated with other members of the supply chain to facilitate the process. It is important that the technology solution is consistent with the expected benefits. Some firms will require more investment in information technology than others.[3] It is critical that managers concentrate on the people and the procedures that make the technology effective and not rely simply on the technology.

Determine Demand Management Goals and Strategy

The demand management process is focused on predicting customer demand and determining how that demand can be synchronized with the capabilities of the supply chain. The process team must have a broad understanding of the firm's strategy, the customers and their needs, the manufacturing capabilities, and the supply chain network. In order to accomplish this, information is required from individuals in functions as well as the customer relationship management and supplier relationship management processes.

With this understanding, the process team can have a high-level discussion about the goals and the focus of the process, which may vary across different firms and industries. For instance, business in the telecommunications industry has become so unpredictable that Lucent Technologies, a global network provider, has decided to place priority on increasing flexibility in response to the demand, and put less focus on trying to accurately forecast it. In industries, where demand is

It is critical that managers concentrate on the people and the procedures that make the technology effective and not rely simply on the technology.

[3] Smith, Todd, Jay Mabe and Jeff Beech, "Components of Demand Planning: Putting Together the Details for Success" *Strategic Supply Chain Alignment*, John Gattorna, Editor; Aldershot, England: Gower Publishing Limited, 1998, pp. 123-137.

more stable, reducing forecast error might be more cost effective than increasing flexibility. The discussion that the process team has in this sub-process will set the tone for how demand management is structured.

Determine Forecasting Procedures

In the second sub-process, the process team develops a critical piece of demand management; that is, forecasting. The team needs to select the appropriate forecasting approaches. This includes determining the levels and time frames of the forecasts needed throughout the firm, identifying the sources of data, and then defining forecasting procedures for each forecast required.

Different parts of the firm might need different levels of the forecast.[4] For instance, manufacturing planning might require an SKU-level forecast. Transportation planning, on the other hand, might need a forecast aggregated at the product-family level but disaggregated by region. Marien[5] suggested five levels of forecasting, all based on the time frame of the forecast. However, the decision should not be based solely on the time frame required. Other factors play a role, such as the units being forecasted and the use of the forecasts. Ross Products, a division of Abbott Laboratories and a market leader in pediatric and adult nutritionals, found that the forecasting needs of the entire firm could be met with three forecasts, one for operations, one for marketing and one for finance.[6]

A firm might also use different forecasting procedures for new products or limited-time promotional offers than they do for their standard products. For instance, the management team at a global beverage company recognized the difficulty in developing long-term forecasts for new products. Consequently, when introducing a new product, the forecasting team now works with key suppliers and the sales organization to develop a pipeline-fill forecast; that is, a gross sales figure for the duration of the supply chain lead-time. Based on cross-functional input and risk assessment, they determine an initial production quantity. This quantity is produced before the introduction of the product so that the beverage company can meet demand through the initial stage of the introduction. Once management observes the level of demand in the first few weeks, they can begin to generate a reasonably accurate forecast for the future.

It is important that these strategic decisions regarding the number of forecasts used are made collectively by a team of managers and that the resulting forecasts are coordinated. Although there might be several forecasts used in the firm, they should be consistent and represent one truth. If managers of each function develop their own forecasts independently, the firm will lose control over the forecasting process.

If managers of each function develop their own forecasts independently, the firm will lose control over the forecasting process.

Next, the team determines the sources of the data required to generate each forecast. These might include historical data, sales projections, promotion plans, corporate objectives, market share data, trade inventory, and market research. In order to determine how to use these data, the team should understand the value of

---

[4] Helms, Marilyn M., Lawrence P. Ettkin and Sharon Chapman, "Supply Chain Forecasting - Collaborative Forecasting Supports Supply Chain Management," *Business Process Management Journal*, Vol. 6, No. 5 (2000), p. 392.

[5] Marien, Edward J., "Demand Planning and Sales Forecasting: A Supply Chain Essential," *Supply Chain Management Review,* Vol. 2, No 4, (1999), pp. 76-86.

[6] Robeano, Steven, "Demand Forecasting: Reality vs. Theory," unpublished speech at the National Management Science Roundtable, Nashville, 1991.

the information from each source; for instance, determining how good each source is at predicting demand.

Most forecast methods use past demand information as an input to predict future sales. However, many managers overlook the fact that past sales might not equal past demand. For example, if a firm faced a stockout, then perhaps not all the demand was met in that time period. Relying on sales data in the forecast underestimates the true demand and might result in a low forecast, increasing the probability of another stockout in the next time period. Therefore, when considering how data will be used for forecasting, the team should examine ways to estimate past unmet demand and include this information in the calculation of the statistical forecast. One way to estimate this is to multiply the average daily sales of the product by the number of days there was a stockout.

It is at this point that the team might also consider Collaborative Planning, Forecasting and Replenishment (CPFR) or Vendor Managed Inventory (VMI).[7] If these systems are being implemented, the customer is a direct source of data. If this is the case, the team needs to interface with the customer relationship management process team to determine what systems will be used to efficiently transfer data between the firms.

Once the team has an understanding of what type of forecast is needed, and what data are available, they can select a forecasting method and define a process to follow for each required forecast. There are many methods from which to choose, from quantitative, such as time series methods, to more people-driven, such as focus groups and the Delphi approach.[8] The appropriate method will depend on the environment in which the forecasting is taking place. In fact, different methods might be used for different products. In one company, management segments products according to demand uncertainty and demand volume in order to make decisions about the appropriate forecasting approaches. Each product is plotted using a two-by-two matrix as shown in Figure 5-4. The quadrant of the matrix in which a product is categorized will determine the appropriate forecasting approach. Quantitative methods based on historical data are used for products with low demand uncertainty. Products with high uncertainty and high volume require more human input, perhaps from the sales force or the customers themselves. If a product has low volume and high uncertainty, make-to-order production is used, which avoids the need for an SKU-level forecast and allows management to concentrate on an aggregated forecast for raw-materials or components.

Products with high uncertainty and high volume require more human input, perhaps from the sales force or the customers themselves.

After the appropriate forecasting approach is determined, the team selects the specific forecasting method. When making this decision, it is important for the team to understand the nature of the demand. For instance, if the demand is seasonal, they will want to select a method that incorporates seasonality. Should the team decide to use a quantitative approach like time series or regression, they might consider using forecasting software. There are numerous stand-alone

---

[7] Sherman, Richard J., "Collaborative Planning, Forecasting & Replenishment (CPFR): Realizing the Promise of Efficient Consumer Response through Collaborative Technology," *Journal of Marketing Theory & Practice*, Vol. 6, No. 4 (1998), pp. 6-9; and, Matt Waller, Eric M. Johnson and Tom Davis, "Vendor-Managed Inventory in the Retail Supply Chain," *Journal of Business Logistics*, Vol. 20, No. 1 (1999), pp. 183-203.

[8] Makridakis, Spyros, Steven C. Wheelwright and Rob J. Hyndman, *Forecasting: Methods and Applications*, New York: John Wiley & Sons, Inc., 1998.

Figure 5-4
Segmenting Products to Determine Appropriate Forecasting Approaches

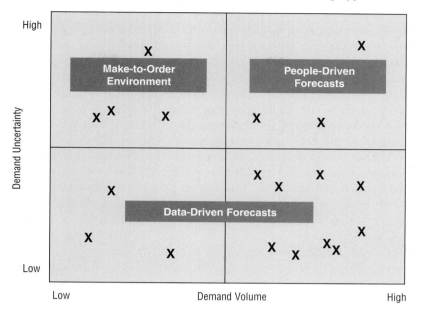

software packages on the market that can handle the forecasting component of demand management and do not require significant financial investments.[9] It is important that the capabilities of the software package align with the forecasting needs of the firm. Considerations when selecting a software package include the span of statistical methods that the system uses, the ability to adjust the forecast, the ability to use the software in a collaborative mode (either internally or externally), and the sophistication of the output reports that are offered.[10]

The team also needs to determine how often the forecasting procedures will be reevaluated. For instance, if the nature of the demand changes or the forecast errors begin to worsen, the team will need to convene and make necessary changes to the procedures being used.

Plan Information Flow

Once the team decides on the method of forecasting and the sources of data, they plan the information flow; that is, how the input data will be transferred, and what output needs to be communicated to whom.

Once the team decides on the method of forecasting and the sources of data, they plan the information flow; that is, how the input data will be transferred, and what output needs to be communicated to whom. Input to the forecasting process will likely come from several functions, the customer relationship management process, and in a CPFR environment, the customers themselves. The forecasts are communicated internally to the other process teams that are affected by them.

---

[9] Yurkiewicz, Jack, "Forecasting: Helping to Fine-tune Your Choices," *OR/MS Today*, Vol. 33, No. 4 (2006), pp. 40-49; and Chaman L. Jain, "Benchmarking Forecasting Software & Systems," *Journal of Business Forecasting*, Vol. 25, Issue 4 (2006/2007), pp. 28-30.

[10] Safavi, Alex, "Choosing the Right Forecasting Software and System," *Journal of Business Forecasting Methods & Systems*, Vol. 19, Issue 3 (2000), pp. 6-10.

In addition, the firm needs to determine what data will be shared with other members of the supply chain. For instance, in a CPFR environment, SKU-level forecasts are jointly developed with next-tier customers. Management might decide to share these forecasts in an aggregated form with suppliers, perhaps including key second tier suppliers. For example, Wendy's International, a quick service restaurant chain, shares its forecasts with both their lettuce processors and their lettuce growers.

The team also needs to consider if information systems need to be developed or enhanced in order to efficiently transfer appropriate information. Within a single firm, Enterprise Resource Planning (ERP) systems can provide consistent data that can be used throughout the company. In many cases, however, the demand management process needs information to flow between firms in the supply chain. For instance, information systems can be put into place to provide inventory visibility in the supply chain or manage the information flow of a VMI or CPFR implementation. Considerable effort is often required to integrate systems between firms. In some cases, web-based applications, which do not require integration of information systems between supply chain members, provide an effective means for sharing information with suppliers and customers. Companies like Moen Inc., the world's largest manufacturer of plumbing products, have developed applications to share forecasts, production schedules and inventory levels with their supplier base through the Internet. A web-enabled application can be a first point of contact for status reports.

As an extension to the information flow, the team should consider ways in which both the inputs and outputs of demand management can be used to define the future business strategy. Langabeer[11] differentiates the tactical use of demand information from its strategic uses. He argues that the same information that is used in the demand management process can be used to shape the marketing strategy and the direction the firm takes. For instance, analyzing demand and forecast data allows management to plan the life cycle of products, including the determination of when to introduce new products and phase out existing ones. Data on where the bottlenecks in the supply chain are can be used in conjunction with product profitability reports to guide management on its investment strategies. The process team should look for ways to share insight that is gained as part of executing the demand management process with other key decision makers in the firm.

> *As an extension to the information flow, the team should consider ways in which both the inputs and outputs of demand management can be used to define the future business strategy.*

The activities and learnings of the demand management process can also influence the supply chain strategy. Supply chain strategy should be determined, at least in part, by the supply and demand uncertainty that exists in the firm's supply chain.[12] As shown in Figure 5-5, managers need to align their firm's supply chain strategy with the uncertainties inherent in the system. Since firms often have products with different levels of uncertainty, managers should follow different supply chain strategies for different products. As the demand management team gains an understanding of system uncertainties and works to reduce them, the information they glean can be used to guide and perhaps evolve the supply chain strategies so that they maintain proper alignment.

---

[11] Langabeer, Jim R. II, "Aligning Demand Management with Business Strategy," *Supply Chain Management Review,* Vol. 4, No. 2 (2000), pp. 66-72.

[12] Lee, Hau L., "Aligning Supply Chain Strategies with Product Uncertainties," *California Management Review,* Vol. 44, No. 3 (2002), pp. 105-119.

Figure 5-5
Aligning Supply Chain Strategies with Uncertainty

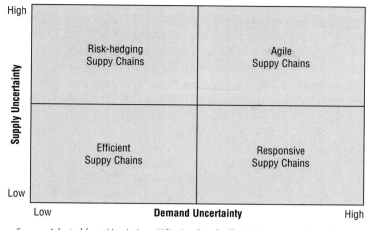

Source: Adapted from Hau L. Lee, "Aligning Supply Chain Strategies with Product Uncertainties," *California Management Review*, Vol. 44, No. 3 (2002), pp. 105-119. Copyright © 2002, by The Regents of the University of California. Reprinted by permission of The Regents.

Determine Synchronization Procedures

Next, the team determines the synchronization procedures required to match the demand forecast to the supply chain's manufacturing, supply and logistics capabilities. Frequently, this is referred to as sales and operations planning (S&OP). As shown in Figure 5-6, the synchronization requires coordination with marketing, manufacturing and sourcing, logistics and finance. When executed at the operational level, this synchronization sub-process includes examining the forecasted customer demand and determining the requirements back through the

Figure 5-6
Synchronization

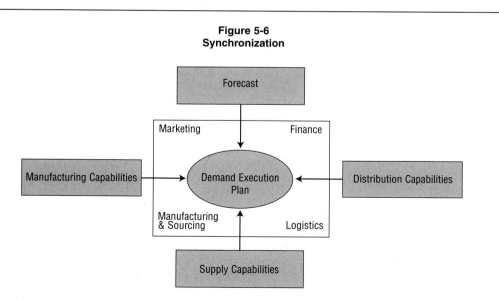

supply chain. It requires not only understanding the level of demand, but also the velocity at which product is required at each touch point in the supply chain. The output of this synchronization will be a single execution plan that will balance the needs and costs of manufacturing, logistics, sales, and the suppliers to meet anticipated demand. This execution plan will provide the basis for the detailed manufacturing and sourcing plan that is developed within the manufacturing flow management process through manufacturing requirement planning (MRP), and the detailed distribution plan that is developed within order fulfillment through distribution requirement planning (DRP).

At the strategic level, the team is responsible for developing the synchronization procedures that will be used at the operational level, including who will be included and the structure for how they will meet. Some firms have a two-stage procedure whereby a cross-functional team of managers will meet, for instance monthly, to develop an initial demand execution plan. If there are any unresolved issues from this meeting, they will be directed to a meeting of upper-level managers who resolve them and sign-off on a final demand execution plan.

Once a firm has effective internal synchronization procedures, management should consider integrating key suppliers and customers directly into it. For instance, a beverage company includes internal suppliers in their monthly S&OP meeting. These suppliers are under the company's corporate umbrella, but they are different strategic business units and they have their own income statements and balance sheets.

Part of determining the synchronization procedures is defining policies about stockpiling and allocating; that is, where to stock inventory when supply is greater than demand, and how to reposition inventory when demand is greater than supply. These guidelines will be rather generic. Within the order fulfillment process, the customer-specific rules will be developed. It is critical that the team is cross-functional because these decisions could impact the customers, the financial statements, and the planning processes. For instance, if demand is lower than anticipated, a manufacturing manager acting alone might choose to use the extra capacity to make whichever product is easiest to manufacture. A logistics manager might choose to move inventory where it is the cheapest to move or store. But of course the decision should be made to maximize future profit, not minimize the costs of a single function. Therefore, all key functions should be represented in the decision-making.

The team needs to gain a complete understanding of the capacity and flexibility available at key points along the supply chain. They also need to determine the long-term planning requirements, particularly in the case of demand with high seasonality or long-term changes, such as sustained growth. In the case of limited capacity and a product with seasonal demand, it might be necessary to ramp-up production several months prior to the high demand periods. At this point in the process, the team might also recognize future capacity issues and make recommendations to proactively address them before they cause problems.

The team needs to gain a complete understanding of the capacity and flexibility available at key points along the supply chain.

It is important to realize that different product-lines might require different synchronization procedures. This is part of aligning supply chain strategy with product characteristics. For instance, for a product with high demand uncertainty, and therefore expected high forcast errors, managers should not rely too heavily on the forecast, and instead designs supply chain flexibility into the system. To Moen Inc., this has meant developing different procedures for core, custom and new products. For new products, the focus is on attaining the most flexibility possible, as the demand of new products is the most uncertain. For Moen's core product-lines, management is interested in driving the costs out since products are mature and competitive price pressure is high. For custom products that are low-volume, the goal is asset optimization, which suggests an assemble-to-order system. When Moen used the same procedures for all products, they had problems because the goals of all three classifications could not be attained with one set of procedures. This is why they moved to a differentiated system where the methods vary over the three classifications. In fact, even the organizational structure is differentiated; that is, different people are responsible for planning in each area.

Systems such as those provided by i2, Manugistics, and SAP[13] can be implemented to facilitate synchronization and help develop the demand execution plan. These systems are designed to examine the real-time constraints on the sources of supply and match them with the forecasted demand. Combining the functionality of information flow and synchronization, some of these systems can offer inventory deployment tools that provide real-time decision support for managing inventory in the supply chain. Although these systems are useful, they should be used in conjunction with human decision-making in a team setting. There are too many factors involved in the synchronization procedures to leave it entirely to an automated system.

Develop Contingency Management System

Another important component of the strategic demand management process is developing contingency plans to respond to significant internal or external events that disrupt the balance of supply and demand.

Another important component of the strategic demand management process is developing contingency plans to respond to significant internal or external events that disrupt the balance of supply and demand.[14] For example, how should the firm react if a manufacturing facility is unexpectedly shut down, or a port strike interrupts the flow of raw materials? Determining reaction procedures prior to the possible events will allow management to respond quickly in the case that one of these events occurs. In addition, the process team should consider what will be done if there is an interruption to any portion of data flow through the supply chain due to system errors.

The goal in this sub-process is to have documented plans ready in case of any likely disruption. Developing these plans with a cross-functional team and assuring everyone has access to the plans should lead to smoother operations and less silo-oriented fire-fighting when a disruption does occur. Learning from the hurricanes of 2005, managers at a global beverage company spent more time fine-tuning their contingency plans. Now as soon as there is a serious threat of a hurricane, they have specific directions about how to change production plans and reposition inventory.

This contingency management system should be developed in accordance with the expectations of the customers outlined in the customer relationship management process, and with input from the order fulfillment, manufacturing flow management and supplier relationship management processes. Once developed, the contingency plans need to be communicated to the affected process teams.

---

[13] See: www.i2.com; www.manugistics.com; www.sap.com.

[14] Dobie, Kathryn, L. Milton Glisson and James Grant, "Terrorism and the Global Supply Chain: Where Are Your Weak Links?" *Journal of Transportation Management,* Vol. 12, No. 1 (2000), pp. 57-66.

Develop Framework of Metrics

Finally, the team develops the framework of metrics to be used to measure and monitor the performance of the process, and sets the goals for performance improvement. A uniform approach should be used throughout the firm to develop these metrics.[15] The team should start by understanding how demand management can influence key performance metrics that directly affect the firm's financial performance, as measured by economic value added (EVA).[16] Figure 5-7 provides a framework for examining these relationships. It shows how demand management can impact sales, cost of goods sold, total expenses, inventory investment, other current assets, and fixed assets. For example, better demand management can result in higher sales by increasing customer loyalty and repeat business due to better forecasting and the associated customer service improvements. Also, improved product availability can lead to higher levels of retail sales and/or lower inventory carrying costs which can lead to a larger portion of the customer's purchases in this category. Product freshness results in better assortment and consumer appeal. A reduction in returns and markdowns can lead to the company becoming a more preferred supplier.

The team should start by understanding how demand management can influence key performance metrics that directly affect the firm's financial performance, as measured by economic value added (EVA).

Figure 5-7
How Demand Management Affects Economic Value Added (EVA®)

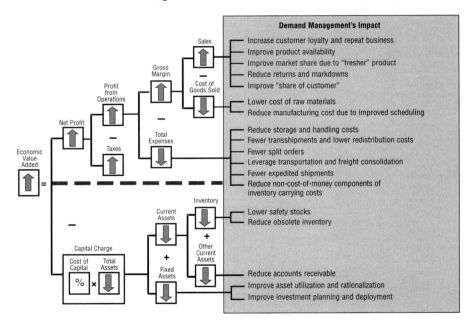

Source: Adapted from Douglas M. Lambert and Terrance L. Pohlen, "Supply Chain Metrics," *The International Journal of Logistics Management*, Vol. 12, No. 1 (2001), p. 10.

---

[15] Lambert, Douglas M. and Terrance L. Pohlen, "Supply Chain Metrics," *The International Journal of Logistics Management*, Vol. 12, No. 1 (2001), pp. 1-19.

[16] Stewart, G. Bennett III, *The Quest for Value: A Guide for Senior Managers*, 2nd Edition, New York, NY: Harper Collins, 1999; and, Joel M. Stern, "One Way to Build Value in Your Firm, a la Executive Compensation," *Financial Executive*, November-December 1990, pp. 51-54.

Cost of goods sold can be reduced as a result of lower cost of raw materials due to fewer expedited shipments and fewer last minute production changes by the supplier. Manufacturing costs can decrease as a result of improved scheduling.

A number of expenses can be reduced through better planning and scheduling that comes from less demand variability, including: storage and handling, transportation, order processing and the non-cost of money components of inventory carrying cost.

Better demand management can lead to lower safety stocks and less obsolete inventory which delivers higher inventory turns and lower inventory investment. Accounts receivable can be improved since fewer invoices will be disputed as a result of incomplete orders and missed delivery dates. Finally, better demand management can lead to lower fixed assets as a result of improved asset utilization and facility rationalization, and better investment planning and deployment.

Although these holistic metrics are affected by other activities and processes in the supply chain, the team responsible for demand management needs to estimate how this process impacts the firm's financial performance. Doing so will help to justify future investments in the process and to determine rewards for good performance.

Once the team has an understanding of the impact that demand management can have on financial performance as measured by EVA, metrics need to be developed for the activities performed and these metrics must be tied back to financial measures. Typical process measures for demand management include forecast error and capacity utilization. If steps are taken to actively reduce variability or increase flexibility, it is appropriate to include metrics that monitor the results of these activities, as well as to measure how improvements in these non-financial measures affect financial performance. The role of the customers in reducing demand variability and the role of suppliers in increasing flexibility need to be measured and their contributions rewarded. The team needs to confirm these measures with the customer relationship management team to assure consistency across the firm.

Management should implement processes that positively affect the profitability of the supply chain as a whole, not just that of their firm. It is the goal of supply chain management to drive behavior that benefits the entire supply chain while sharing risks and rewards among its members. If management of one firm in the supply chain makes a decision that positively affects their firm's EVA but negatively affects the EVA of a key supplier or customer, the two firms should work out an agreement where the benefits are shared so that the bottom lines of both firms improve.

If steps are taken to actively reduce variability or increase flexibility, it is appropriate to include metrics that monitor the results of these activities, as well as to measure how improvements in these non-financial measures affect financial performance.

The Operational Demand Management Process

At the operational level, the process team must execute the forecasting and synchronization as it was designed at the strategic level. In addition, they will identify ways to reduce demand variability and increased flexibility. Figure 5-8 shows the five operational sub-processes, the activities within each of these, and the interfaces between processes.

Collect Data/Information

At the strategic level, the data requirements for developing the forecast were determined, and the information systems were put in place to facilitate this data collection. In order to collect the relevant data that were specified in the strategic

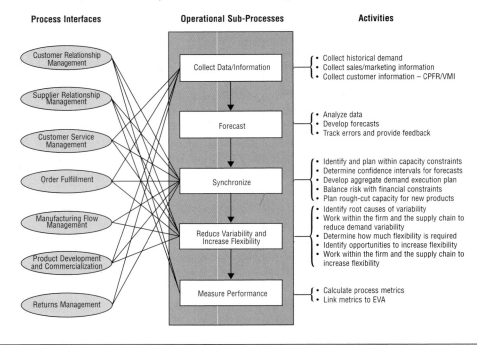

Figure 5-8
The Operational Demand Management Process

process, the team must interface with the marketing function as well as the order fulfillment, customer service management, product development and commercialization, and returns management processes. When designing the forecasting system at the strategic level, important input comes from the customer relationship management team, but at the operational level, it is the order fulfillment and customer service management processes that provide the most relevant information on anticipated demand. The product development and commercialization process team provides information regarding the rollout of new products. Data from the returns management process are used for generating the forecast because it provides input to understanding the actual demand. If a forecaster only uses sales figures as a measure of past demand, and does not consider what was returned, the forecast will be based on inflated numbers.

Data from the returns management process are used for generating the forecast because it provides input to understanding the actual demand.

Forecast

With all the required data in hand, the team develops the forecasts. It is important that they track and analyze the forecast error and incorporate this feedback to fine-tune the forecasting methods. This is an important component of the learning process associated with good forecasting. For example, at a global beverage company, managers examine forecast errors and perform a root-cause analysis when errors are unusually large. This analysis involves tracing the source of the unexpected demand (or shortage of demand) to see if it is a particular customer, brand, region, or product. Once the source is known, it is necessary to determine what the cause was and how long the change in demand will last. This provides a starting point for improving future forecasts.

Synchronize

The forecast provides one input for matching demand with supply. The synchronization sub-process follows the procedures determined at the strategic level. This is where the team turns the forecast into a demand execution plan (see Figure 5-6); that is, a plan for how the firm will meet the demand. In addition to the forecast, the team must consider capacities throughout the supply chain, financial limitations, and current inventory positioning (including saleable product that is being repositioned as a result of returns).

Understanding the capacity limitations requires the team to look both upstream and downstream. Ideally, the team should know both the capacity and the current inventory levels for key members of the supply chain. Comparing this information to the forecast will tell the team what constraints are in the system. Once the constraints are identified, the team can work with the other process teams to determine how to resolve the bottlenecks, or to allocate the available resources and prioritize demand.

Once the constraints are identified, the team can work with the other process teams to determine how to resolve the bottlenecks, or to allocate the available resources and prioritize demand.

Although most forecasting methods are focused on determining the point forecast, calculating confidence intervals can provide management with valuable information on which to base their decisions.[17] Using past forecast error values, the team can calculate confidence intervals for the forecasts. For instance, a manufacturing firm might forecast the demand to be 100 units and the 95% confidence interval to be 80 to 120 units. This means they are 95% sure the actual demand will fall in this range. In addition to the point forecast, this range could be shared with suppliers to provide information that they can use for planning, or even to negotiate available capacity. Management can also use this information to determine how much demand they want to meet. To offer high customer service, they should produce 120, but if the cost of inventory or risk of obsolescence is high, they might choose to produce only 80. In order to make this determination, the team needs to understand the firm's cost structure and strategic objectives.

In addition to supply and manufacturing constraints, the forecast might introduce a financial constraint. In turning the forecast into a demand plan, the team might need to practice risk management. This is the practice of balancing risk with financial rewards. When it is not financially feasible to meet all the demand, management must decide how to most effectively allocate resources. The contingency management plans developed at the strategic level might also need to be considered if an internal or external event causes a disruption to supply or large forecast errors.

The team also develops a rough-cut capacity plan for any new products soon to be launched. At Moen, Inc., management not only determines existing capacities, but talks to key suppliers to understand how quickly they could respond if demand exceeds the forecast for a new product.

The output of the synchronization sub-process is a demand execution plan that includes aggregate production plans and inventory-positioning plans, which need to be communicated internally and to key members of the supply chain. Developing and communicating these plans requires interfaces with the customer relationship management, customer service management, order fulfillment,

---

[17] Makridakis, Spyros, Steven C. Wheelwright and Rob J. Hyndman, *Forecasting: Methods and Applications*, New York: John Wiley & Sons, Inc., 1998.

manufacturing flow management, supplier relationship management, and product development and commercialization processes.

A cross-functional management team at a global beverage company improved their synchronization procedures by getting better and more consistent involvement from the sales managers. One benefit has been more thoughtful planning of sales promotions to account for any potential supply constraints. As a result, they have provided higher product availability at lower cost during promotions.

Reduce Variability and Increase Flexibility

Many people see variability as the enemy of planning. It is easy to plan for the average, but it is the deviations from the norm that cause problems. Managers spend substantial time and money dealing with the consequences of demand and supply variability. There are two things managers can do to minimize the negative impact of variability. One is to reduce the variability itself, and the other is to increase the flexibility to react to it. A key component of demand management is an ongoing effort aimed at doing both these things. Increasing flexibility helps the firm respond quickly to internal and external events and reducing demand and supply variability aids in consistent planning and reduces costs.

Management should first try to reduce variability and then manage the unavoidable variability by building-in flexibility.[18] Flexibility usually comes with a price tag so it should not be used as a Band-Aid to fix problems that can otherwise be avoided. There are many sources of variability in the supply chain. One of the most problematic is demand variability. Many managers see demand as an uncontrollable input. Bolton states that demand management "actively seeks to ensure that the customer demand 'profile' that is the input into the demand-planning process is as smooth as possible".[19] This is the difference between demand planning and demand management. Within the demand management process, the team should look for sources of variability and implement solutions to reduce it.

Table 5-1 provides examples of sources of demand variability and potential solutions.[20] For example, the team might work with the customer relationship management team and help customers better plan promotions, or implement scheduled ordering policies.[21] The team might also find that internal practices are driving demand variability, such as end-of-quarter loads. If the demand for new products is highly variable, they could work with the product development teams to implement controlled roll-outs where the products are introduced first in test markets where demand patterns can be evaluated. In some scenarios, it could be the competition that is driving demand variability. For instance, demand could be affected

There are two things managers can do to minimize the negative impact of variability. One is to reduce the variability itself, and the other is to increase the flexibility to react to it.

---

[18] Slack, N.D.C., *The Manufacturing Advantage*, London: Mercury, 1991.

[19] Bolton, Jamie, "Effective Demand Management: Are You Limiting the Performance of Your Own Supply Chain?" *Strategic Supply Chain Alignment*, John Gattorna, Editor; Aldershot, England: Gower Publishing Limited, 1998, p. 139.

[20] Bolton, Jamie, "Effective Demand Management: Are You Limiting the Performance of Your Own Supply Chain?" *Strategic Supply Chain Alignment*, John Gattorna, Editor; Aldershot, England: Gower Publishing Limited, 1998, p. 139.

[21] Cachon, Gerard, "Managing Supply Chain Demand Variability with Scheduled Ordering Policies," *Management Science*, Vol. 45, No. 6, pp. 843-856.

Table 5-1
Sources of Variability and Possible Solutions

Causes of Lumpy Demand	Possible Supply Chain Solutions
Consumer promotions	Plan promotions collaboratively with customers.
Sales metrics	Design consistent metrics that avoid actions such as end-of-quarter loads.
Credit terms	Revise credit terms with customer input to ensure that the terms of sale are not negatively affecting purchase patterns.
Pricing/Incentives	Work with sales/marketing to only offer incentives that truly increase long-term sales.
Minimum order quantities	Assure that all costs are included when calculating the appropriate minimum order size.
Long distribution channels	Incorporate demand volatility into network design decisions.

by a competitor engaged in end-of-quarter loading or offering a promotion. In these cases, the variability is unavoidable, but can often be planned for when developing the forecast. Likewise, the team should also look for ways to reduce supply variability and work with the supplier relationship management team and the purchasing function to implement changes. It is easier to manage supply chains that fall towards the bottom and left portions of Figure 5-5, so the demand management process team should look for ways to reduce uncertainties in both dimensions.[22] Then they should assure that the company's executives adjust the supply chain strategies accordingly. "The supply chain which best succeeds in reducing uncertainty and variability is likely to be the most successful in improving its competitive position."[23]

Gaining flexibility allows a company to better manage the system variability that cannot be eliminated – both anticipated and unanticipated variability. When a beverage company introduced one of its new products, demand was more than double the amount forecasted. Because management had developed a flexible system, they were able to manage through this without affecting customer service. Increasing flexibility can influence the reliability, quality, cost and speed of the process and its products.[24] The team should first determine how much flexibility is needed. Because building flexibility into a system is often expensive, it is important that the level of flexibility developed is consistent with the needs of the supply chain. To make this determination, the process team needs to fully understand customers' needs, demand patterns, and the capabilities of the entire supply chain.

Because building flexibility into a system is often expensive, it is important that the level of flexibility developed is consistent with the needs of the supply chain.

Once the team understands how much flexibility is needed, they should look for ways to attain it. This involves working with the other process teams within the firm, as well as with suppliers and customers to determine where there are opportunities to add flexibility into the supply chain. For example, the team might work with the manufacturing flow management team to find ways to introduce postponement into

---

[22] Lee, Hau L., "Aligning Supply Chain Strategies with Product Uncertainties," *California Management Review*, Vol. 44, No. 3 (2002), pp. 105-119.

[23] Towill, Denis R. and Peter McCullen, "The Impact of Agile Manufacturing on Supply Chain Dynamics," *The International Journal of Logistics Management*, Vol. 10, No. 1 (1999), p. 86.

[24] Correa, Henrique Luiz, *Linking Flexibility, Uncertainty and Variability in Manufacturing Systems*, Aldershot, England: Avebury Publishing, 1994.

the manufacturing process, implement agile manufacturing practices, or find ways to multi-source.[25] They might work with the customer relationship management team to stratify customers so that the firm can be most responsive to a small set of key customers, or work with the product development teams to standardize materials. The team might work with the order fulfillment team to make changes to the network, such as reducing lead-times or increasing capacity at buffers. Solutions might also exist from within the demand management process, such as implementing VMI.

In order to find ways to increase flexibility and reduce variability, the process team works with the sales, marketing and manufacturing functions, customers and suppliers. To increase flexibility, they identify bottlenecks and pinch points, and develop cost-effective solutions. To reduce variability, the team highlights root causes and develops solutions that are consistent with the business strategy. Identifying these opportunities involves process interfaces with manufacturing flow management, supplier relationship management, customer relationship management and customer service management, as well as the corporate functions. In all cases, the team needs to consider the implications of the solutions on the other members of the supply chain.

Measure Performance

Finally, the process team is responsible for measuring the performance of the process with the metrics developed at the strategic level. These metrics are used internally to improve the process and are provided to the customer relationship management team and supplier relationship management team who will convey the firm's performance to the key members of the supply chain and generate the customer profitability and supplier profitability or cost reports.[26]

Conclusions

Demand management is an important component of successful supply chain management. A well thought-out implementation and seamless execution of the process can have substantial benefits to the firm's EVA through, for example, reduced inventory levels, improved asset utilization and improved product availability. It is not enough to forecast well and have a good operations planning system. Demand management should include finding ways to reduce demand variability and increase operational flexibility, and implementing a good contingency management system so that the firm can quickly react to unplanned issues.

Although it is possible to implement many portions of the demand management process without going outside the four walls of the firm, the real opportunities come when management reaches out to the other members of the supply chain and integrates this process with the processes of suppliers and customers. It is through these integration efforts that the benefits of supply chain management will be achieved.

Although it is possible to implement many portions of the demand management process without going outside the four walls of the firm, the real opportunities come when management reaches out to the other members of the supply chain and integrates this process with the processes of suppliers and customers.

---

[25] van Hoek, Remko I., "The Rediscovery of Postponment: A Literature Review and Directions for Research," *Journal of Operations Management*, Vol. 19, No. 2 (2001), pp. 161-184; and, Y. Y. Yusef and A. Gunasekaran, "Agile Manufacturing: A Taxonomy of Strategic and Technological Imperatives," *International Journal of Production Research*, Vol. 40, No. 6 (2002), pp. 1357-1385.

[26] Lambert, Douglas M. and Terrance L. Pohlen, "Supply Chain Metrics," *The International Journal of Logistics Management*, Vol. 12, No. 1 (2001), pp. 1-19.

CHAPTER

6

The Order Fulfillment Process

Keely L. Croxton

Overview

Order fulfillment is a key process in managing the supply chain.[1] It is the customers' orders that put the supply chain in motion, and filling them efficiently and effectively is the first step in providing customer service. However, the order fulfillment process involves more than just filling orders. It is about designing a network and a process that permits a firm to meet customer requests while minimizing the total delivered cost. In this chapter, the order fulfillment process is described in detail to show how it can be implemented cross-functionally within a company, and managed across firms in the supply chain. The activities of each sub-process are examined; the interfaces with corporate functions, processes and firms are evaluated; and, examples of successful implementations are provided.

Introduction

Order fulfillment involves generating, filling, delivering and servicing customer orders. In some cases, it is only through this process that the customer interacts with the firm, and therefore, the order fulfillment process can determine the customer's experience.[2] To accomplish these tasks, management must design a network and a fulfillment process that permits a firm to meet customer requests while minimizing the total delivered cost. This requires integration of logistics, marketing, finance, purchasing, research and development, and production within the firm, and coordination with key suppliers and customers. At the operational level, the order fulfillment process focuses on transactions, while at the strategic level, management can focus on making critical improvements to the process that influence the financial performance of the firm, its customers and its suppliers. For instance, order fulfillment directly affects product availability which influences total sales volume. An optimized network minimizes total delivered costs, including sourcing costs. A streamlined process reduces the order-to-cash cycle which frees up capital, and reduces the delivery lead-time which allows for reduced inventory levels. Thus, order fulfillment can affect the financial performance of the focal-firm, as well as other members of the supply chain.

> *At the operational level, the order fulfillment process focuses on transactions, while at the strategic level, management can focus on making critical improvements to the process that influence the financial performance of the firm, its customers and its suppliers.*

---

[1] This chapter is based on Keely L. Croxton, "The Order Fulfillment Process," *The International Journal of Logistics Management*, Vol. 14, No. 1 (2002), pp. 19-32.

[2] Shapiro, Benson P., V. Kasturi Rangan, and John J. Sviokla, "Staple Yourself to an Order," *Harvard Business Review*, Vol. 40, No. 4 (1992), pp.113-122.

In this chapter, the framework for implementing the order fulfillment process is developed. The process is described as it would be implemented at a firm in the middle of the supply chain, for instance a manufacturer or distributor. For a retailer, the process is similar in some respects, but it would need to be adapted before being implemented. Order fulfillment is one of the eight supply chain management processes and it requires interfaces with the other seven (see Figure 6-1). The strategic and operational processes that comprise order fulfillment are described, including the sub-processes and their activities. In addition, the interfaces with the corporate functions, the other supply chain management processes and other firms are identified. Finally, conclusions are presented.

Order Fulfillment as a Supply Chain Management Process

The order fulfillment process has both strategic and operational elements, as shown in Figure 6-2. Therefore, the process has been divided into two parts, the strategic process in which management establishes the structure for managing the process, and the operational process that is the execution of the process once it has been established. Implementation of the strategic process within the firm is a necessary first step in integrating the firm with other members of the supply chain, and it is at the operational level that the day-to-day activities take place. Figure 6-2 also shows the interfaces between each sub-process and the other seven supply chain processes. These interfaces might take the form of a transfer of some data that the other process requires, or might involve sharing information or ideas with another process team.

Figure 6-1
Supply Chain Management:
Integrating and Managing Business Processes Across the Supply Chain

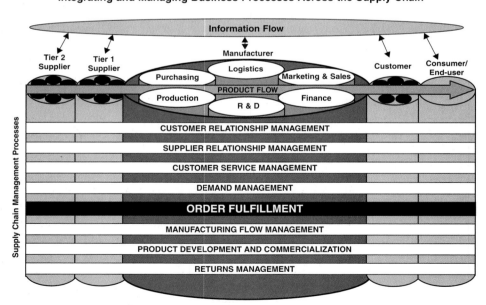

Source: Adapted from Douglas M. Lambert, Martha C. Cooper, and Janus D. Pagh, "Supply Chain Management: Implementation Issues and Research Opportunities," *The International Journal of Logistics Management,* Vol. 9, No. 2 (1998), p. 2.

Figure 6-2
Order Fulfillment

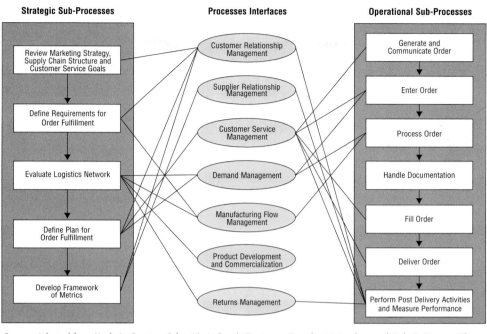

| Strategic Sub-Processes | Processes Interfaces | Operational Sub-Processes |

Source: Adapted from Keely L. Croxton, Sebastián J. García-Dastugue, Douglas M. Lambert and Dale S. Rogers, "The Supply Chain Management Processes," *The International Journal of Logistics Management,* Vol. 12, No. 2 (2001), p. 21.

A cross-functional process team comprised of managers from several functions, including logistics, marketing, finance, purchasing and production, leads both the strategic and operational processes. The team might also include members from outside the firm. For example, the team might include representatives from a key customer or a third-party provider. The team is responsible for developing the procedures at the strategic level and seeing that they are implemented. This team also has day-to-day responsibility for managing the process at the operational level. Firm employees outside of the team might execute parts of the process, but the team still maintains managerial responsibility.

Firm employees outside of the team might execute parts of the process, but the team still maintains managerial responsibility.

The Strategic Order Fulfillment Process

At the strategic level, the process team designs the operational order fulfillment process. This includes designing the network, establishing policies and procedures, and determining the role of technology in the process. This requires interfacing and communicating with multiple functional areas within the firm, and can be enhanced by working with suppliers and customers to develop a network and a process that meets the customers' requirements in a cost effective manner. Although many managers consider order fulfillment to fall within the role of the logistics function, it is the integration with other functions in the firm and other firms in the supply chain that becomes key in defining order fulfillment as a supply

Figure 6-3
The Strategic Order Fulfillment Process

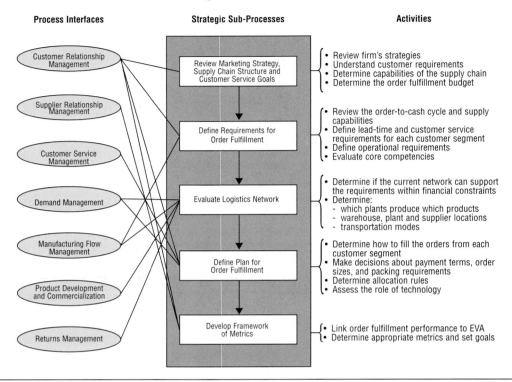

chain process. Figure 6-3 shows the sub-processes, activities and interfaces for the strategic order fulfillment process.

Review Marketing Strategy, Supply Chain Structure and Customer Service Goals

In this first sub-process the process team reviews the marketing strategy, supply chain structure, and customer service goals. By examining the marketing strategy and customer service goals, they are seeking to understand the requirements of the customer and the role that customer service plays in the overall strategy of the firm. To fully understand the customers, the team should interface with the customer relationship management team to understand what is most important to the customer. Often this information is identified through a customer service audit.[3] Together, the two teams will determine which services are necessary to achieve and maintain corporate/supply chain goals.

The order fulfillment process needs to be designed around the customer, but within the limits of the firm's business and marketing strategy. The team also needs to understand the firm's order fulfillment budget. That is, determining how much is acceptable to spend on fulfilling the order. A firm might be able to most quickly

The order fulfillment process needs to be designed around the customer, but within the limits of the firm's business and marketing strategy.

---

[3] Stock, James R. and Douglas M. Lambert, *Strategic Logistics Management*, New York, NY: McGraw-Hill, 2001, pp. 110-126.

deliver a product to the customer with an express air shipment, but the costs associated with that policy erodes profits and could be unacceptable. Likewise, financial issues might dictate a minimum order size or something about the selling terms. Throughout the design of the fulfillment process, the team needs to trade-off the costs of the solution with the benefits to the customer and the impact on the financial performance of the firm, and its customers and suppliers.

Throughout the design of the fulfillment process, the team needs to trade-off the costs of the solution with the benefits to the customer and the impact on the financial performance of the firm, and its customers and suppliers.

The supply chain structure is another important input into the design of the order fulfillment process. Both the sourcing and the distribution sub-networks that are in place impose limits on the cost and the lead-time of the fulfillment process. The team needs to examine the current network to understand its limitations and how cost is added as product moves through the supply chain.

The sub-process sets the foundation for the rest of the strategic process. Teams that fail to execute this step will struggle with the rest of the process because they will not understand the goals nor the constraints on the system. It is imperative that the team understands the role that order fulfillment plays in attaining the corporate goals.

Define Requirements for Order Fulfillment

Once the customer requirements and the limits imposed by the network structure are understood, the team can focus on defining the requirements for the order fulfillment process. This includes reviewing the order-to-cash cycle, understanding the supply capabilities, and defining the lead-time and customer service requirements. The customer relationship management and manufacturing flow processes provide input to accomplish this. In addition, the team needs to understand the operational requirements of the order fulfillment environment, including such details as how many orders need to be filled per day and how many dock-doors will be needed. There might also be legal requirements that need to be adhered to, for instance, handling requirements for hazardous materials, or customs requirements for international shipments. The process team should get a full understanding of all the requirements and make sure that the process is designed to adhere to them.

Customer differences might require management to develop an array of order fulfillment procedures. For instance, the customer relationship management team might have identified key customers that need a shorter lead-time than others. In this case, the team would develop multiple sets of requirements and assure that the fulfillment process can meet all the variations. International Paper, the world's largest paper and forest products company, categorizes its customers into four segments, according to their sales and profitability. Within each segment, customer service profiles are defined. While these activities are part of the customer relationship management process, the order fulfillment team has to plan for those parts of the profile that pertain to order fulfillment such as order cut-off times and delivery times.

In addition, the team needs to evaluate the core competencies within order fulfillment and determine which aspects of the process are potentially service differentiating. For instance, Wendy's International, a quick service restaurant chain, has focused on its order delivery to drive-through customers, offering the fastest delivery among fast-food restaurants for five straight years.[4] If a firm offers

---

[4] Gereffi, Paul, *"What the Numbers Tell Us,"* QSR, October 2002.

guaranteed service levels, the order fulfillment team needs to consider how the process can be structured to accommodate these expectations. The team should determine what value-added services will be provided, to whom those services will be offered, who will pay for them, and their impact on the profitability of the firm and the supply chain. At Shell, a global energy company, the salesperson is responsible for the cost the firm incurs for the services offered to customers. Each salesperson then decides whether to pass these costs along to the customer.

After completing this sub-process, the team should understand what the order fulfillment process will need to accomplish at the operational level. They should be able to articulate the specific order fulfillment goals for each customer segment and know the degree to which the process can be customized for specific customers or customer segments.

Evaluate Logistics Network

After the first two sub-processes, the team knows the capabilities of the supply chain and the requirements of the customers. If the capabilities cannot support the requirements, the next step is to evaluate the supply chain network to determine if the network could be redesigned to resolve the gaps.

The design and operation of the network has a significant influence on the cost and performance of the system. One study showed that network modeling projects identify cost reductions of an average of 11.6% of controllable logistics costs,[5] but the structure of the network affects more than logistics costs. It can affect customer service levels, lead times and component costs. Network design tools can be used to determine which plants will produce which products, where warehouses, plants, and suppliers should be located, and which transportation modes should be used. In addition, customers need to be efficiently assigned to networks of supply. These decisions affect the capabilities, the cost, and the timeframe of the order fulfillment process. In some cases, these decisions can have significant impact on other members of the supply chain. For example, DowBrands, which at the time was the consumer products affiliate of Dow Chemical Company, found that they could reduce transit-time variability by designing the distribution system so that less-than-truckload shipments avoided break-bulk terminals.[6] This variability reduction allowed customers to hold less inventory. In a supply chain management environment, they could work with key customers to see if the increase in distribution cost would be offset by the reduction in inventory cost in the supply chain.

Historically, managers have focused their network design efforts on the internal portion of their supply chain;[7] that is, where the facilities they manage should be located. Increasingly, managers are broadening the scope of their network design projects to include a greater portion of the supply chain, such as

Network design tools can be used to determine which plants will produce which products, where warehouses, plants, and suppliers should be located, and which transportation modes should be used.

---

[5] Jimenez, Sue, Tim Brown and Joe Jordan, "Network modeling tools: Enhancing supply chain decision making," *Strategic Supply Chain Alignment,* John Gattorna, Editor; Gower, 1998.

[6] Robinson, E. Powell, Li-Lian Gao and Stanley D. Muggenborg, "Designing an Integrated Distribution System at DowBrands, Inc." *Interfaces,* Vol. 23, No. 3 (1993), pp. 107-117.

[7] Pooley, John, "Integrated Production and Distribution Facility Planning at Ault Foods," *Interfaces,* Vol. 24, No. 4 (1994), pp. 113-121; Camm, Jeffrey D., et. al, "Blending OR/MS, Judgment, and GIS: Restructuring P&G's Supply Chain," *Interfaces,* Vol. 27, No. 1 (1997), pp. 128-142.

first and second tier suppliers and customers.[8]

These network models require data from every functional area within the firm. Obtaining accurate data often involves gathering data from upstream and downstream members of the supply chain. Particularly important input to this sub-process comes from the demand management, manufacturing flow, product development and commercialization, and returns management processes. Likewise, the resulting network has implications throughout the firm and the supply chain. The order fulfillment team is responsible for assuring that the new network is communicated and implemented appropriately.

While developing a formal network design model is time-consuming and requires expertise, many managers have found that once the model is developed, they can use it to monitor their network and identify potential issues early. This allows them to proactively modify their network structure before problems arise. Models can also be used to study the impact of high-level business decisions on the firm's ability to continue to meet order fulfillment needs.

Define Plan for Order Fulfillment

The next strategic sub-process defines the plan for order fulfillment, determining how orders from various customers or segments of customers will be taken and filled. This is largely where the operational order fulfillment process is defined. The team also determines which portions of the process will be outsourced to a third party.

The team needs to make decisions about payment terms, allowable order sizes, and picking and packing operations. Increasingly, customers are requesting customized packing; for instance, the size of the pallet, or the way the pallets are configured. The team needs to consider these customer requirements.

The team also needs to consider the impact of their decisions on demand variability.[9] The effectiveness of the order fulfillment process can be strained by demand that is highly variable. During this sub-process, the team should work with the demand management process team, as they are responsible for finding ways to reduce demand variability.[10] For instance, payment terms might lead customers to place orders at certain times of the month, creating lumpy demand. Large order sizes could have similar effects. Smoothing out demand will make it easier to manage the operational order fulfillment process efficiently.

An important consideration in designing the order fulfillment system is to determine what will be done when an order cannot be filled. The order fulfillment team needs to develop rules about how demand is allocated, or possibly when an order should not be accepted at all. At Colgate-Palmolive, a consumer packaged goods company, the team develops "Risk and Opportunity Grids" that provide operational guidelines about what to do in the case that demand cannot be met.

An important consideration in designing the order fulfillment system is to determine what will be done when an order cannot be filled. The order fulfillment team needs to develop rules about how demand is allocated, or possibly when an order should not be accepted at all.

[8] Arntzen, Bruce C., Gerald G. Brown, Terry P. Harrison and Linda L. Trafton, "Global Supply Chain Management at Digital Equipment Corporation," *Interfaces,* Vol. 27, No. 1 (1997), pp. 69-93.

[9] Bolton, Jamie, "Effective demand management: Are you limiting the performance of your own supply chain?" *Strategic Supply Chain Alignment,* John Gattorna, Editor; Gower, 1998.

[10] Croxton, Keely L., Douglas M. Lambert, Sebastián J. García-Dastugue, and Dale S. Rogers, "The Demand Management Process," *The International Journal of Logistics Management,* Vol. 13, No. 2 (2002), pp. 51-66.

For instance, which customers should receive priority, when to short a customer's order, etc? International Paper has rules in place that will only allow safety stock to be used to fill orders from its key customers. In another example, the management at Dell, a global computer manufacturer, takes a revenue management approach to order fulfillment.[11] They implemented a "sell what you have policy" where order-takers are encouraged to sell configurations that are readily available. They are given the flexibility to adjust the price on these available configurations to encourage customers to buy products that would be "easy" on the supply chain rather than ones that would incur extra costs and erode profitability.[12] For Dell, this has been an appropriate way to balance supply and demand through its order fulfillment process.

Before deciding to implement any allocation system, management needs to understand the customer service and customer satisfaction implications. The team should work with the customer relationship management team in developing these policies. Once the team determines the procedures, it is important to communicate them to the customer service management team, who addresses the concerns of the customers when these events occur. There is also a close interface with the demand management process at this point because these allocation rules need to be aligned with the contingency management system developed in the strategic demand management process.[13]

An important component of designing an order fulfillment process is determining the flow of order information; in other words, how the order information will be captured and fed to the demand management process. For instance, manufacturing is outsourced at Lucent Technologies, a global communications network provider, so orders are sent directly to suppliers. At Moen Inc., a manufacturer of plumbing products, customers can place orders directly into Moen's SAP system, bypassing the traditional, and very manual, order entry process. At Taylor Made-adidas Golf Company, a manufacturer of golf equipment, sales people carry handheld computer units which allow them to enter orders from the customer site and download them into the Taylor Made-adidas order management system. In some supply chains, point-of-sale data are communicated between firms to allow suppliers to place orders with distributors. Each of these examples requires a unique information flow that needs to be developed by the order fulfillment process team. Because this usually involves data transfer between firms, which is increasingly accomplished with technology, the team should consider the role of technology in order fulfillment and how it should be used to aid each step of the process and integrated with other members of the supply chain. Although decisions regarding technology need to be made at the strategic level, the technological options and issues will be explored later in this chapter, in the section on the operational order fulfillment process, since the technology supports the operational activities.

An important component of designing an order fulfillment process is determining the flow of order information; in other words, how the order information will be captured and fed to the demand management process.

---

[11] Harris, Frederick H. deB. and Jonathan P. Pinder, "A revenue management approach to demand management and order booking in assemble-to-order manufacturing," *Journal of Operations Management,* Vol. 13 (1995), pp. 299-309.

[12] Byrnes, Jonathan, "The Bottom Line: Who's Managing Profitability?" *HBS Working Knowledge,* September 2, 2002.

[13] Croxton, Keely L., Douglas M. Lambert, Sebastián J. García-Dastugue, and Dale S. Rogers, "The Demand Management Process," *The International Journal of Logistics Management,* Vol. 13, No. 2 (2002), pp. 51-66.

Develop Framework of Metrics

As with all the supply chain management processes, metrics should be tied back to the firm's economic value added (EVA).

In the final sub-process a framework of metrics must be developed to measure and monitor the performance of the process. As with all the supply chain management processes, metrics should be tied back to the firm's economic value added (EVA).[14] Figure 6-4 shows how improvements in the order fulfillment process can affect the firm's EVA by influencing sales, cost of goods sold, total expenses, inventory investment, other current assets and fixed assets. A streamlined order fulfillment process can reduce expenses such as handling, freight and overhead. However, the execution of the order fulfillment process has less obvious implications. For example, improved product availability increases sales and market share. Efficient supply chain design can reduce component costs which can reduce the cost of goods sold, and reduce inventory levels throughout the supply chain. If the order-to-cash cycle is reduced, payments are made more quickly, which reduces the current assets on the books. The process team needs to understand these implications and understand how the process affects financial performance.

Once the team has an understanding of the impact that order fulfillment can have on the financial performance of the firm, metrics need to be developed for the activities performed. Typical process measures include order-to-cash cycle time, order fill rate, and order completeness. Many companies measure perfect orders,

Figure 6-4
How Order Fulfillment Affects Economic Value Added (EVA®)

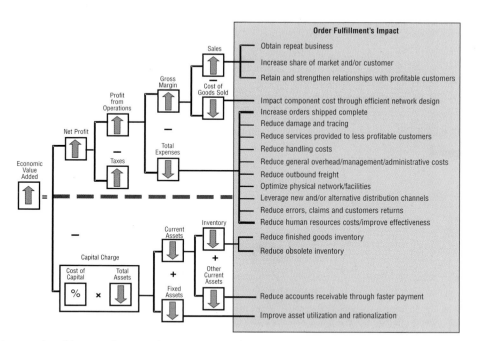

Source: Adapted from Douglas M. Lambert and Terrance L. Pohlen, "Supply Chain Metrics," *The International Journal of Logistics Management,* Vol. 12, No. 1 (2001), p.13.

---

[14] Lambert, Douglas M. and Terrance L. Pohlen, "Supply Chain Metrics," *The International Journal of Logistics Management,* Vol. 12, No. 1 (2001), pp. 1-19.

which usually incorporate the accuracy, the condition upon arrival, and the punctuality of orders. Some companies, like Hewlett-Packard, a global provider of technology products and services, track the number of order-touches to measure the efficiency of the order fulfillment process.

The team should work with the customer relationship management process team to make sure that they are not only aligning the order fulfillment metrics with the other metrics used throughout the firm, but that they are measuring what the customers deem important. It is important to assure that the firms in the supply chain implement processes that positively affect the EVA of the supply chain, not just an individual firm within it. It is the goal of supply chain management to drive behavior that benefits the entire supply chain while sharing the risks and rewards incurred. The team should share the framework of metrics with the customer relationship management and supplier relationship management processes and set goals for process improvement.

Developing the metrics is the last sub-process at the strategic level, but this does not mean that the work is done. The team should review the execution of the order fulfillment process periodically to assure that it is as effective and efficient as possible. Shapiro et. al. recommend that management "staple themselves to an order" to look for horizontal and vertical gaps in the process.[15] The team should map the order flow and then follow several orders through the system. The average and variability in the time it takes to execute each step should be measured. This will help the team understand where orders might get stuck or where the process needs more standardization. This careful examination of the process once it is being executed at the operational level might lead the team back to the strategic sub-processes to re-design the network, the plan for order fulfillment, or the metrics.

It is important to assure that the firms in the supply chain implement processes that positively affect the EVA of the supply chain, not just an individual firm within it.

The Operational Order Fulfillment Process

Figure 6-5 shows the seven sub-processes and activities that comprise the operational order fulfillment process. At the operational level, order fulfillment is very transactional. It is focused on managing the customer order cycle and the specific activities are executed primarily within the logistics function. In fact, a customer order is said to serve "as the communications message that sets the logistics process in motion".[16] However, managers need to focus attention on managing the interfaces with the other supply chain management processes and with other functional areas within the firm, and finding opportunities to integrate with other members of the supply chain.

Because order fulfillment begins with the customer's order, it is natural to integrate with key customers to streamline the order-to-cash cycle and make it as cost-effective for the supply chain as possible. The growth of technology in the supply chain environment has had significant impact on the order fulfillment process. Much of what used to be very manual steps has been automated by the advent and adoption of technology such as electronic data interchange (EDI), the

Because order fulfillment begins with the customer's order, it is natural to integrate with key customers to streamline the order-to-cash cycle and make it as cost-effective for the supply chain as possible.

---

[15] Shapiro, Benson P., V. Kasturi Rangan, and John J. Sviokla, "Staple Yourself to an Order," *Harvard Business Review,* Vol. 40, No. 4 (1992), pp.113-122.

[16] Stock, James R. and Douglas M. Lambert, *Strategic Logistics Management,* New York NY: McGraw-Hill, 2001, p. 146.

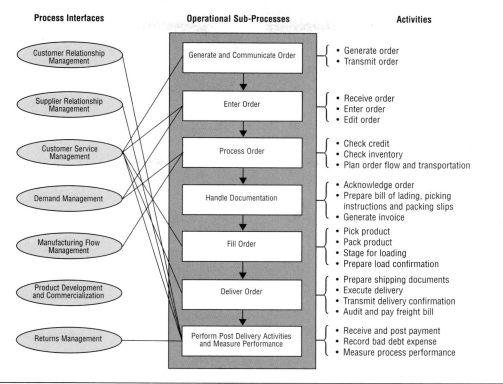

Figure 6-5
The Operational Order Fulfillment Process

Process Interfaces	Operational Sub-Processes	Activities
Customer Relationship Management	Generate and Communicate Order	• Generate order • Transmit order
Supplier Relationship Management	Enter Order	• Receive order • Enter order • Edit order
Customer Service Management	Process Order	• Check credit • Check inventory • Plan order flow and transportation
Demand Management	Handle Documentation	• Acknowledge order • Prepare bill of lading, picking instructions and packing slips • Generate invoice
Manufacturing Flow Management	Fill Order	• Pick product • Pack product • Stage for loading • Prepare load confirmation
Product Development and Commercialization	Deliver Order	• Prepare shipping documents • Execute delivery • Transmit delivery confirmation • Audit and pay freight bill
Returns Management	Perform Post Delivery Activities and Measure Performance	• Receive and post payment • Record bad debt expense • Measure process performance

Internet, available-to-promise (ATP) and capable-to-promise (CTP) systems, and enterprise resource planning (ERP) and advanced planning and scheduling (APS) systems. These technologies, along with others such as transportation management systems (TMS) and inventory visibility tools, can provide managers information that can be used throughout the supply chain to streamline the order fulfillment process.

The implementation of these technologies has had two significant effects on the order fulfillment process. One is the streamlining of the operational process which has taken days out of the order-to-cash cycle. Ingram Macrotron Distribution, a subsidiary of Ingram Micro, implemented an electronic ordering system that reduced order processing costs by 60%, reduced order processing time by 30%, and decreased the average order fulfillment time by 60%.[17] In addition to the faster order fulfillment, it reduced the ordering costs of its customers by 12%, thereby providing benefit to other members of the supply chain.

The other effect that technology has had is on improving the ability for companies in the supply chain to integrate more effectively. Within order fulfillment, this integration usually takes place between the focal-firm and its customers. For instance, with the use of integrated technologies, the first two sub-processes can often

---

[17] "Ingram Macrotron Increases Electronic Sales and Decreases Order Processing Costs Using Microsoft Solution," 2002. See: www.microsoft.com/resources/casestudies/

be handled in one step. At Colgate-Palmolive, approximately 90% of orders are accepted through either EDI or the Internet and dropped directly into the SAP system for processing, where the order-flow and transportation planning is automatically executed. This not only reduces steps in the process, but reduces order entry errors which can be costly and time consuming to correct. Giving track-and-trace capabilities to customers is another way to integrate them into the process and reduce the workload on the customer service team. Streamlining the process improves customer service, allows inventory reductions, and improves cash flow. Implementing these technologies can be win-win for multiple members in the supply chain.

However, technology comes with a price, often not only for the focal firm but for other members of the supply chain. For instance, in the case of Colgate-Palmolive, the customers' technology needs to be integrated with Colgate-Palmolive's to streamline the transfer of data. It is paramount that management understands the financial impact of implementing these systems. Many companies faced failure after rushing into the e-commerce business because management believed that the internet would revolutionize order fulfillment. In determining which technologies to adopt, the order fulfillment team needs to weigh the costs against the value added by each technology. The technology should be judged by its ability to streamline the process and integrate the supply chain.

In determining which technologies to adopt, the order fulfillment team needs to weigh the costs against the value added by each technology. The technology should be judged by its ability to streamline the process and integrate the supply chain.

Generate and Communicate Order

As we trace an order through the operational order fulfillment process, the first step is to generate and communicate the order. Orders generally come through customer service, the sales organization, or directly from the customer. In some cases this is automated, for instance in an EDI or VMI environment, or other systems in which orders are automatically placed when the inventory level reaches a pre-set level. For other companies, the sales process is very labor intensive. Firms often lose valuable time in this sub-process and can reduce its duration by days using technology and automated information sharing.

The key functional interfaces for this sub-process are between the logistics, marketing and sales areas. At Herman Miller, a leading manufacturer of office furniture, management redesigned the sales process so that customers can lay-out a design for an office space on a salesperson's laptop. The customer can see how everything will fit and how colors will look together, and view it from any angle. Once the customer has the design as they want it, the software creates an order list and provides a final price. The order can be easily downloaded over the Internet into the order system. This software application was designed primarily as a sales and marketing tool, but it also streamlined the order generation and order entry processes and reduced errors. Errors were reduced from more than 20% to near zero, and customers received order confirmation with shipping and installation dates within two hours of placing the order, as opposed to the old process where this would take over a week.[18] The integration of the sales process into the order fulfillment process yielded Herman Miller substantial benefits to their operational performance.

---

[18] Sucher, Sandra J. and Stacy E. McManus, "Herman Miller (A): Innovation by Design," Harvard Business School Case Study, 2002; and, David Rocks, "Reinventing Herman Miller," Business Week Online, April 3, 2000.

Enter Order

Once received, the order needs to be entered and edited, if necessary. Errors in receiving and entering an order can be very costly. The process team should measure and track error levels and look for root causes of the errors. Often, orders that are received do not contain all the required information. This might be due to an issue with the sales process or with the customers. For instance, it might be that orders are incomplete because the sales people are providing customers with incomplete quotes.[19] If this is the case, the process team should work with the sales force to improve order quotes and give customers complete information for their orders.

The team might work directly with customers to help streamline the process to reduce errors, perhaps by integrating technologies. Some companies have found that while giving customers the capability to enter orders directly into their system has streamlined the process, it has also increased the number of errors, perhaps because the customers are not as well trained as the firm's internal people. The process team should carefully monitor this and perhaps employ more checks and balances in the system.

Data regarding the orders are transmitted to the customer service management and demand management processes. The customer service management process needs to have data on order status to help customers. The demand management process uses the order entry information as input for generating future forecasts. Both process teams benefit if the information is received in a timely and error-free fashion.

Process Order

The first step to processing the order is to check the customer's credit. The credit check requires an interface with finance and is another common source of delay in the process. If orders are getting to this stage and not passing the credit check, the process team should work with the sales force to make sure they have information on which customers have credit problems. Also, a system should be put in place so that customers can easily determine how much credit they have available.[20] In some cases, systems can be designed so that this credit check occurs before orders are placed. For instance, if customers are placing orders over the internet, the system could prevent them from ordering if their credit situation is not good. New customers could establish credit on-line before being allowed to place orders.

For orders that are not filled directly from inventory, the DRP process will determine where the order will be manufactured or assembled and how it will be shipped to the customer by the due date.

Once the credit issue is resolved, inventory levels are checked and the order flow is planned. It is determined how the order will be routed through the supply chain which is commonly referred to as the distribution requirements planning (DRP) process. If the order will be filled from inventory, the inventory location is determined, inventory levels are updated, and the distribution plan is executed. If the order is composed of several products from different locations, the shipments will have to be coordinated.[21] For orders that are not filled directly from inventory, the DRP process will determine where the order will be manufactured or assembled and how it will be shipped to the customer by the due date. This

---

[19] Waller, Matthew A., Dennis Woolsey and Robert Seaker, "Reengineering Order Fulfillment," *The International Journal of Logistics Management,* Vol. 6, No. 2 (1995), pp. 1-10.

[20] Waller, Matthew A., Dennis Woolsey and Robert Seaker, "Reengineering Order Fulfillment," *The International Journal of Logistics Management,* Vol. 6, No. 2 (1995), pp. 1-10.

[21] Croxton, Keely L., Bernard Gendron and Thomas L. Magnanti, "Models and Methods for Merge-in-Transit Operations," *Transportation Science,* Vol. 37, No. 1 (2003), pp. 1-22.

information is an important input for the demand management and manufacturing flow processes.

Handle Documentation

Once the order has been processed and planned, the documentation related to that order is prepared, including order acknowledgement, bill of lading, picking instructions, packing slips and the invoice. If the order will be shipped internationally, the customs and duty forms will be prepared. Note that in some warehouse management systems (WMS), the documentation is prepared after the order is filled, reversing the order of this sub-process and the following one.

Many firms are providing customers with order visibility and tracking capabilities. In this case, part of the documentation is electronic in nature and needs to be updated throughout the remainder of the order fulfillment process.

Fill Order

The next stage of the order fulfillment process is filling the order. Usually, order filling occurs on the plant floor or in a warehouse and involves picking, packing, staging, and load configuration. It is important for the personnel who fill the orders to know if there are customer-specific specifications, such as particular packing requirements or pallet configurations. This information should be part of the picking instructions that were generated in the previous sub-process. Once the order is filled and confirmed, the order status is communicated to the customer service management team so that they can provide information to the customer if requested.

Key issues in this sub-process are the accuracy and timeliness with which these activities are performed. The adoption of warehouse technologies, particularly bar code and wireless radio frequency technology, has improved the accuracy of filling orders. Warehouse layout and material handling can have significant impact on timeliness. Changes to the physical layout, racking system, or item locations can make the process more efficient.[22] Therefore, the process team should continuously examine the potential impact of new technologies and layout changes.

The adoption of warehouse technologies, particularly bar code and wireless radio frequency technology, has improved the accuracy of filling orders.

Deliver Order

The final step in the order-to-delivery process is to arrange delivery of the order. In this sub-process, shipping documents are prepared, the transportation plan is executed, delivery is confirmed, and the freight bill is audited and paid. In order to help the customer plan, advance shipping notices (ASN) should be sent.

Delays and errors in these steps can be costly, because there is little chance to make-up for the mistakes without impacting the customer. For most firms, it is also the point in the order fulfillment process where control of the order is relinquished, as it is usually handed over to a transportation company. Effective

---

[22] Ackerman, Kenneth, "Designing Tomorrow's Warehouse: A Little Ahead of the Times," *Journal of Business Logistics*, Vol. 20, No. 1 (1999), pp. 1-4; Che-Hung Lin and Iuan-Yuan Lu, "The Procedure of Determining the Order Picking Strategies in Distribution Center," *International Journal of Production Economics*, Vol. 60/61, Issue 3 (1999), pp. 301-307; and, Simon J. Dennis, "Order Picking: An Overlooked Option?" *Logistics Focus*, Vol. 7, No. 3 (1999), pp. 3-8.

relationships with transportation companies can play an important role in executing the delivery sub-process.

As part of the information flow, track-and-trace documentation is made available to the customer service management team who will use this information when a customer inquires about an order. Alternatively, it might be sent directly to customers so that they can track their orders themselves.

Perform Post-Delivery Activities and Measure Performance

In the final steps of the order fulfillment process, payment is received and posted, discrepancies are addressed, and bad debt expense is recorded. The process of receiving and posting payment can often be labor intensive. If, for example, a customer sends in payment of an invoice but subtracts out deductions without explanation, the customer service management team needs to call the customer and follow-up on what the issues are and how they can be resolved. This becomes time-consuming for both parties. If firms can work with customers to minimize these types of issues, the total cost of delivery will be reduced.

An ongoing part of the order fulfillment process is to measure the process and communicate the results throughout the firm and to key members of the supply chain.

An ongoing part of the order fulfillment process is to measure the process and communicate the results throughout the firm and to key members of the supply chain. Because the order fulfillment process has such direct impact on the customer, it is important to track the timeliness of the process. Two important metrics of the order fulfillment process are the order-to-cash cycle time and the customer cycle time. The order-to-cash cycle time measures the elapsed time from the receipt of the customer's order to the time that the proper payment is posted, while the customer cycle time is a measure of the elapsed time from the order being placed to the receipt of the order into the customer's inventory. It is important to examine not only the average duration of these cycles, but also the variability. The variability of the customer cycle time is particularly important to the customer, as they need to hold more safety stock when there is high variability. For the customer, reduction in the variability has more financial impact than a reduction in the average cycle time[23]. Measuring both the average and the variation in the time required to complete each operational sub-process will allow the team to see where they should focus their attention.

Conclusions

The order fulfillment process is often viewed as transactional and part of the logistics function within a firm. However, it is important that managers recognize its strategic components, its cross-functional needs, and its role within the management of the supply chain.

At the strategic level, the order fulfillment process involves understanding the internal and external requirements and assuring that the system has adequate capabilities. This includes understanding the business strategy and the customer service requirements, and designing a supply chain network to meet customers' needs efficiently. Another important component of the process is to have a

---

[23] Stock, James R. and Douglas M. Lambert, *Strategic Logistics Management*, New York NY: McGraw-Hill, 2001; Tomkins, James A., et. al., Facilities Planning, New York, NY: John Wiley and Sons, Inc., 1996.

responsive system in place for when demand exceeds supply and some orders cannot be filled. Assuring that this system still manages to meet at least the minimum needs of customers is critical to achieving good customer service even in the face of adversity. The other very important strategic piece comes in designing the metrics. There are numerous examples of bad metrics driving misguided behavior. The process team needs to examine the effects of order fulfillment on the financial performance of the firm and assure that the metrics used are consistent with improving the financial performance of the entire supply chain.

While the order fulfillment process is often viewed as a logistics activity, the process cannot be designed without input from other functional areas including marketing, finance, purchasing, and production, as well as support groups like information technology. Therefore, it is important that the process team be cross-functional. To achieve strong performance, the requirements of all functional areas must be met.

Although it is possible to implement many portions of the order fulfillment process without going outside the four walls of the firm, the real opportunities come when a firm reaches out to other members of the supply chain. Integrating key customers and suppliers can help streamline and improve the order fulfillment process. Whether it is through idea sharing or information sharing, the role of the other supply chain members takes the order fulfillment activities from a single-firm process to a supply chain management process.

While the order fulfillment process is often viewed as a logistics activity, the process cannot be designed without input from other functional areas including marketing, finance, purchasing, and production, as well as support groups like information technology.

CHAPTER

7

The Manufacturing Flow Management Process

Thomas J. Goldsby and Sebastián J. García-Dastugue

Overview

Manufacturing flow management is the supply chain management process that includes all activities necessary to obtain, implement, and manage manufacturing flexibility in the supply chain and to move products through the plants.[1] Manufacturing flexibility reflects the ability to make a variety of products in a timely manner at the lowest possible cost and respond to changes in demand. To achieve the desired level of manufacturing flexibility, planning and execution must extend beyond the four walls of the factory. In this chapter, we describe the manufacturing flow management process in detail to show how it can be implemented within a company and managed across firms in the supply chain. We examine the activities of each sub-process; evaluate the interfaces with corporate functions, processes, and firms; and provide examples of successful implementation.

Introduction

Firms that perform the manufacturing activities in a supply chain face several challenges, one of which is to produce products in varieties and quantities that are in synch with the marketplace. Connecting production management to actual demand represents a sizable opportunity for most organizations. For example, the potential savings from Efficient Consumer Response, an effort to connect production management with the market in the grocery industry, have been estimated at $30 billion.[2] Disconnects are often cited in the U.S. automotive industry with inventories on dealer lots averaging two months' supply and sometimes exceeding four months' supply.[3]

> *Connecting production management to actual demand represents a sizable opportunity for most organizations.*

---

[1] This chapter is based on Thomas J. Goldsby and Sebastián J. García-Dastugue, "The Manufacturing Flow Management Process," *The International Journal of Logistics Management,* Vol. 14, No. 2 (2003), pp. 33-52.

[2] Kurt Salmon Associates, Inc., *Efficient Consumer Response: Enhancing Consumer Value in the Grocery Industry,* Washington, D.C.: Food Marketing Institute, 1993.

[3] Silke Carty, Sharon, "Chrysler Wrestles with High Levels of Inventory," *USA Today,* (November 3, 2006), pp. 1B-2B.

The costs and expertise required to match market dynamics can be prohibitive, leading some manufacturers to rely on outsourced production activities. Contract manufacturing in the electronics industry grew from $60 billion in 1998[4] to $190 billion in 2006, with the figure expected to double by 2013.[5] In pharmaceutical chemicals and agrochemicals, contract manufacturing represents approximately half of the manufacturing capacity.[6]

In large part, outsourced manufacturing is growing as a result of the need for manufacturing flexibility.[7] Manufacturing flexibility enables greater responsiveness to changes in customers' product preferences and quantities demanded.[8] Determining the right degree of flexibility is important to virtually any company involved in the supply, production, distribution or sales of goods, and is at the center of the manufacturing flow management process. While manufacturing activities might be outsourced to suppliers, the commitment to quality and the managerial responsibility has to be retained at the firm. This is underscored by massive recalls initiated by U.S. companies resulting from offshore supply and manufacturing in 2007.

Determining the right degree of flexibility is important to virtually any company involved in the supply, production, distribution or sales of goods, and is at the center of the manufacturing flow management process.

The manufacturing flow management process team coordinates all activities necessary to obtain, implement, and manage manufacturing flexibility in the supply chain and to move products through the plants. The process involves much more than production. For example, the efficiency of the product flow through the plants depends on the reliability of the inbound logistics activity as well as the suppliers' ability to deliver orders on time and complete. Therefore, the logistics and procurement functions should work closely with production. Similarly, the degree of manufacturing flexibility partly depends on the flexibility of all suppliers. There are several ways to provide flexibility, including reserving available capacity, and standardizing components while maintaining inventory of subcomponents. Suppliers need to be involved because they will be affected by these tactics. In sum, several factors both internal and external to the firm affect the firm's ability to achieve the desired degree of manufacturing flexibility.

In this chapter, a framework for implementing an efficient and effective manufacturing flow management process is presented. Because manufacturing flow management is one of the eight supply chain management processes, it requires interfaces with the other seven (see Figure 7-1). We describe the strategic and operational processes that comprise manufacturing flow management, including the sub-processes and their activities. In addition, we identify the interfaces with the corporate functions, the other supply chain management processes, and other firms. Finally, conclusions are presented.

---

[4] Meeks, Paul, "Heard From the Buy Side," *Red Herring*, (September 1999), p. 4.

[5] Deffree, Suzanne, "Outsourcing Drives EMS, ODM Growth," *Electronic News*, Vol. 52, No. 31 (2007), p. 7.

[6] Van Arnum, Patricia, "Bulls or Bears? Outlook in Contract Manufacturing," *Chemical Market Reporter*, (February 14, 2000), pp. 3-6.

[7] Panchuk, Patricia, "The Future of Manufacturing: An Exclusive Interview with Peter Drucker," *Industry Week*, (September 21, 1998), pp. 36-42.

[8] Christopher, Martin and Denis R. Towill, "Developing Marketing Specific Supply Chain Strategies," *The International Journal of Logistics Management*, Vol. 13, No. 1 (2002), pp. 1-14.

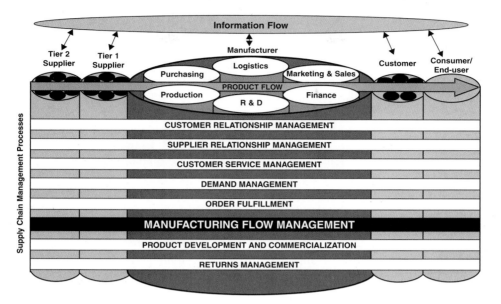

Figure 7-1
Supply Chain Management:
Integrating and Managing Business Processes Across the Supply Chain

Source: Adapted from Douglas M. Lambert, Martha C. Cooper, and Janus D. Pagh, "Supply Chain Management: Implementation Issues and Research Opportunities," *The International Journal of Logistics Management,* Vol. 9, No. 2 (1998), p. 2.

Manufacturing Flow Management as a Supply Chain Management Process

The manufacturing flow management process deals with establishing the manufacturing flexibility needed to serve the target markets and making the products.

The manufacturing flow management process deals with establishing the manufacturing flexibility needed to serve the target markets and making the products such that quality and cost objectives are accomplished. Manufacturing flexibility is defined as "the ability to respond to environmental changes with less time and cost".[9] The concept and significance of flexibility, broadly defined and as it applies to manufacturing operations, receive treatment in a subsequent section of the chapter. Flexibility is important to most operations and particularly so when the manufacturer faces demand variation across a wide assortment of products. Less stable demand environments place a premium on flexible accommodation. The challenge is determining the right degree of flexibility to build into the manufacturing system given that increased flexibility typically is accompanied by higher costs or increased investment.

Manufacturing flow management, like the other supply chain management processes, relies on external connectivity to accomplish its objectives. While it initially might appear relevant only to the finished goods manufacturer (or assembler), the process is significantly influenced by the up- and downstream members of the supply chain. Downstream members influence the process through the demand for product assortments that meet expectations in terms of

[9] Upton, D.M., "The Management of Manufacturing Flexibility," *California Management Review,* Vol. 96, No. 2 (1994), pp. 72-89.

specific attributes, quality, cost, and availability as well as through changes to plans. Upstream members affect the manufacturer's ability to fulfill the customers' expectations. It might be argued that the potential of the manufacturing capabilities of the firm is limited by the capabilities of upstream suppliers. It is important to view the manufacturing flow management process as one that extends beyond the four walls of the final assembler.

It is important to view the manufacturing flow management process as one that extends beyond the four walls of the final assembler.

The process presented here is not industry- or context-specific but rather provides guidance to companies that influence, or are influenced by, the process. For example, a grocery retailer that offers private label products should consider implementing the manufacturing flow management process with its manufacturers. In this sense, a retailer may not perform manufacturing itself but rely on the manufacturing capabilities of suppliers to ensure its success. This example illustrates that the manufacturing flow management process is not the domain of manufacturers alone.

The manufacturing flow management process has both strategic and operational elements (see Figure 7-2). The strategic portion of manufacturing flow management provides the structure for managing the process within the firm and across key supply chain members. The operational portion of the process represents the day-to-day execution of manufacturing flow management. Developing the strategic process is necessary to integrate the firm with other members of the supply chain. It is at the operational level that the day-to-day activities are executed.

Figure 7-2
Manufacturing Flow Management

Strategic Sub-Processes	Process Interfaces	Operational Sub-Processes
Review Manufacturing, Sourcing, Marketing, and Logistics Strategies	Customer Relationship Management	Determine Routing and Velocity through Manufacturing
Determine Degree of Manufacturing Flexibility Required	Supplier Relationship Management	Plan Manufacturing and Material Flow
Determine Push/Pull Boundaries	Customer Service Management	Execute Capacity and Demand
Identify Manufacturing Constraints and Determine Capabilities	Demand Management	Measure Performance
Develop Framework of Metrics	Order Fulfillment	
	Product Development and Commercialization	
	Returns Management	

Source: Adapted from Keely L. Croxton, Sebastián J. García-Dastugue, Douglas M. Lambert, and Dale S. Rogers, "The Supply Chain Management Processes," *The International Journal of Logistics Management*, Vol. 12, No. 2 (2001), p. 22.

Much of the richness associated with the framework is found in the interfaces among processes for it is here that the processes extend to other functions within the firm and other key members of the supply chain.

Much of the richness associated with the framework is found in the interfaces among processes for it is here that the processes extend to other functions within the firm and other key members of the supply chain. These interfaces might take the form of data transfer, or the sharing of information and ideas with other process teams during regular planned or ad hoc meetings.

A process team comprised of managers from several corporate functions, including production, purchasing, logistics, marketing, and finance, leads both the strategic and operational processes. The team also might have representation from outside the firm, including key customers, suppliers, and/or third-party service providers. The process team is responsible for developing the procedures at the strategic level and seeing that they are implemented at the operational level. Involvement on the operational level is typically limited to addressing exceptions or problems in execution. While employees outside of the process team might execute parts of the process, the team maintains managerial control.

The Strategic Manufacturing Flow Management Process

The strategic portion of manufacturing flow management consists of five sub-processes that collectively represent the decision-making infrastructure for the process. This infrastructure embodies the development of the manufacturing plan, the means of execution, limits to execution, and the appropriate measures of performance. We address each of the five sub-processes in order as depicted in Figure 7-3. This figure includes the activities within each of the sub-processes as

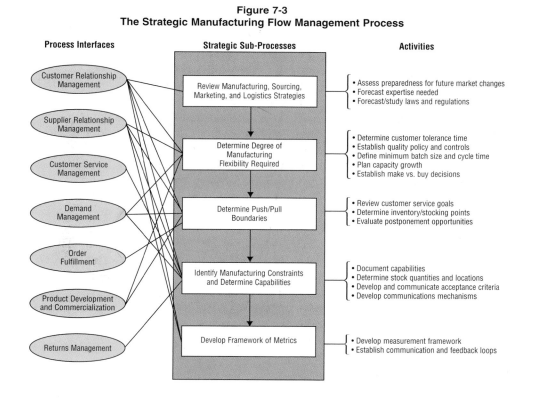

Figure 7-3
The Strategic Manufacturing Flow Management Process

well as the interfaces between manufacturing flow management and the other supply chain management processes.

Review Manufacturing, Sourcing, Marketing, and Logistics Strategies

In this sub-process, the manufacturing flow management process team reviews the functional strategies that have an effect on manufacturing flexibility and on the flow of products through the plants. The functional strategies that are reviewed include the manufacturing, sourcing, marketing, and logistics. This review dictates the priorities of the production function and the roles of its suppliers and supporting service providers.[10] In this sub-process, the strategy starts to be translated into required capabilities and deliverables. If these deliverables are below the customers' expectations, the firm will lose some business opportunities. On the other hand, if these deliverables exceed what the customers actually expect, the firm might be consuming resources for which the customer will fail to offer commensurate reward.

Relating the strategy to the capabilities marks a shift in mentality from "We sell what we make," to, "We make what we sell." This important distinction leads to an assortment of products that satisfy the needs of distinct market segments. The production capabilities of the firm play an important role in the determination of a firm's competitive basis, whether that basis is cost, quality, service, or time.[11] When competitive advantage is to be gained by adopting a unique manufacturing strategy or by employing a common strategy more effectively, it is even more critical that the manufacturing strategy and corporate strategy are aligned. The key is to ensure that the strategy results in value to customers and, ultimately, shareholders.

The production capabilities of the firm play an important role in the determination of a firm's competitive basis, whether that basis is cost, quality, service, or time.

Strategy determination may be driven, in part, by the manufacturing philosophy of the firm. Two manufacturing philosophies that have gained much interest in recent years are lean manufacturing and agility. These two philosophies, while distinct, share a common objective: to satisfy customer demand at the least total cost. It is in the means by which this objective is accomplished that the two philosophies differ. Leanness embodies the relentless elimination of "muda" (the Japanese term for "waste") and is modeled primarily after the Toyota Production System developed by Taiichi Ohno. Ohno identified seven critical wastes to eliminate; these include overproduction, waiting, unnecessary transportation, overprocessing, inventory, unnecessary movement, and defective parts.[12] Meanwhile, agility is oriented toward mass customization or quick, responsive accommodation of varied demand in terms of volume, variety, and mix through flexible operations.[13] Dell Computer is a commonly cited example of agile manufacturing. The company employs a rapid configuration system for its custom-built computer products in support of its consumer-direct marketing strategy.

Lean principles tend to be favored when products are standard (i.e., offer low variety) and demand is somewhat stable over long product life cycles. This allows

---

[10] Demeter, Krisztina, "Manufacturing Strategy and Competitiveness," *International Journal of Production Economics,* Vol. 81-82 (2003), pp. 205-213.

[11] Naylor, J. Ben, Mohamed M. Naim, and Danny Berry, "Leagility: Integrating the Lean and Agile Manufacturing Paradigms in the Total Supply Chain," *International Journal of Production Economics,* Vol. 62 (1999), pp. 107-118.

[12] Womack, James P. and Daniel T. Jones, *Lean Thinking,* New York, NY: Simon & Schuster, 1996.

extensive planning and a focus on efficient, defect-free production.[14]   An agile approach is preferred when there is a large amount of product variety, demand is highly unpredictable, and product life cycles are short.

Situations arise where a combination of the two philosophies is appropriate. This hybrid is referred to as "leagile". Appropriate situations for "leagile" manufacturing might include products as they proceed through their life cycle (i.e., agile in infancy, lean in growth and maturity, and agile in decline), diverse products made of standard components or sub-assemblies (i.e., lean production of components with agile assembly of finished goods), or across product lines (i.e., fast-moving products produced in a lean manner and slow-moving products are produced using agility). Therefore, it is not wise to identify oneself as a "lean" or "agile" manufacturer given that either philosophy (or a combination of the philosophies) might be embraced as the situation evolves.[15]   It is important that the manufacturing strategy fits the corporate strategy and the strategies of key supply chain members given the prevalence.

Looking beyond paradigms of lean and agile manufacturing are five generic manufacturing strategies.   These five strategies from least to most flexible are described briefly below:

- Ship to Stock (STS). Products are standardized and pre-positioned in the market; customers' expectations of immediate availability support the maintenance of speculative safety stock at all points of distribution.
- Make to Stock (MTS). Products are standardized but not necessarily allocated to specific locations; demand is anticipated to be stable or readily forecasted at an aggregate level.
- Assemble to Order (ATO). Products can be customized within a range of possibilities, usually based upon a standard platform; final form of the product is postponed until demand is known.
- Make to Order (MTO). Raw materials and components are common but can be configured into a wide variety of products.
- Buy to Order (BTO). Products can be unique right down to the raw material level; product variety is virtually limitless, though lead time is long as materials are procured, processed into finished goods, and delivered.[16]

> ...it is not wise to identify oneself as a "lean" or "agile" manufacturer given that either philosophy (or a combination of the philosophies) might be embraced as the situation evolves.

[13] Naylor, J. Ben, Mohamed M. Naim, and Danny Berry, "Leagility: Integrating the Lean and Agile Manufacturing Paradigms in the Total Supply Chain," *International Journal of Production Economics,* Vol. 62 (1999), pp. 107-118; and, Martin Christopher and Denis R. Towill, "Developing Market Specific Supply Chain Strategies," *The International Journal of Logistics Management,* Vol. 13, No. 1 (2002), pp. 1-14.

[14] Mason-Jones, Rachel, Ben Naylor, Denis R. Towill, "Engineering the Leagile Supply Chain," *International Journal of Agile Management Systems,* Vol. 2, No. 1 (2000), pp. 54-61.

[15] To read more about lean, agile and leagile philosophies, see J. Ben Naylor, Mohamed M. Naim, and Danny Berry, "Leagility: Integrating the Lean and Agile Manufacturing Paradigms in the Total Supply Chain," *International Journal of Production Economics,* Vol. 62 (1999), pp. 107-118; Rachel Mason-Jones, Ben Naylor, Denis R. Towill, "Engineering the Leagile Supply Chain," *International Journal of Agile Management Systems,* Vol. 2, No. 1 (2000), pp. 54-61; and, Martin Christopher and Denis R. Towill, "Developing Market Specific Supply Chain Strategies," *The International Journal of Logistics Management,* Vol. 13, No. 1 (2002), pp. 1-14.

[16] These five strategies are identified and described in J. Ben Naylor, Mohamed M. Naim, and Danny Berry, "Leagility: Integrating the Lean and Agile Manufacturing Paradigms in the Total Supply Chain," *International Journal of Production Economics,* Vol. 62 (1999), pp. 107-118.

Figure 7-4 illustrates the relationship among these five generic strategies. Selection of the best strategy depends largely upon the perceived levels of demand variability across the assortment of products offered by the manufacturer and the ability to forecast long-, medium-, and near-term demand accurately. If demand is certain and stable, there is very little need to employ flexibility to delay activities in order to learn from the behavior of the demand and, consequently, make more accurate decisions. Rather, the manufacturer can buy materials in large batches and enjoy long production runs, recognizing that inventories will be depleted at a known rate. However, given the shrinking product life cycles experienced by many products, greater flexibility is necessary to accommodate uncertainty in demand. Determining the appropriate degree of manufacturing flexibility will be described further in the next sub-process.

...given the shrinking product life cycles experienced by many products, greater flexibility is necessary to accommodate uncertainty in demand.

In addition to monitoring current market conditions is the need to develop preparedness for foreseeable changes that might affect the market. These changes might include the advent of radically new products that make current offerings obsolete, or the development of new materials or technologies that revolutionize a manufacturing process. One such example is found in the common usage of carrageenan, a seaweed extract used by toothpaste manufacturers to thicken and stabilize the toothpaste formula. It is believed that a substitute for carrageenan is being developed. The substitute will cost half of what carrageenan costs per unit of finished product. Carrageenan suppliers face the challenge of reacting to the impending threat in order to retain their customers. Should the threat become

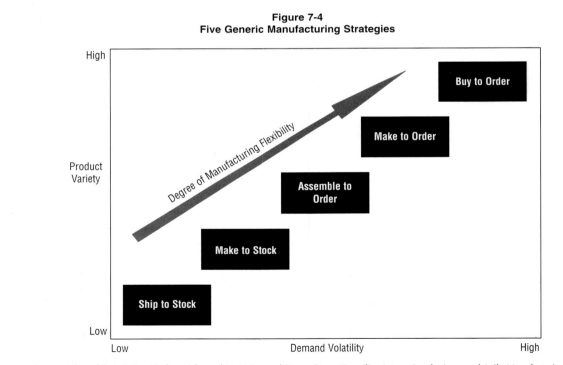

Figure 7-4
Five Generic Manufacturing Strategies

Source: Adapted from J. Ben Naylor, Mohamed M. Naim, and Danny Berry, "Leagility: Integrating the Lean and Agile Manufacturing Paradigms in the Total Supply Chain," *The International Journal of Production Economics*, Vol. 62, (1999), pp. 107-118.

imminent, the suppliers will have to invest heavily in either a new process or product to retain the relationships with their customers.

Thus, the team needs to predict the technological changes expected for the medium- and long-term future. Changes in technology might be accompanied with new expertise needed. These changes, depending on their impact, might not only be regarded as a strategic manufacturing decision, but also as a shift in business strategy. Forces that affect the manufacturing strategy might stem from competitive forces, but also from environmental policies and other regulations. For instance, government support for the advancement of hydrogen fuel cell technology can invigorate an industry. However, regulations can extinguish an industry just as easily - as has been seen with asbestos-based products, lead-based paints, and R-12 refrigerant, among others.

In reviewing the corporate and functional strategies, the manufacturing flow management team works in close collaboration with the customer relationship management team to ensure that production capabilities match market demands.

In reviewing the corporate and functional strategies, the manufacturing flow management team works in close collaboration with the customer relationship management team to ensure that production capabilities match market demands. In fact, it is the responsibility of the customer relationship manager team to communicate market conditions and opportunities that establish the competitive priorities for the marketing, purchasing, and logistics functions as well as manufacturing.

Determine Degree of Manufacturing Flexibility Required

The second strategic sub-process builds upon the first by determining the degree of manufacturing flexibility required to accommodate demand. Manufacturing flexibility ensures the company's ability to manage resources and uncertainty to meet various customer requests. Flexibility can have different meanings in different contexts. Table 7-1 summarizes types of flexibility and provides the definition for each. The most frequently cited views of flexibility are those that refer to the production function, such as mix, volume, and expansion flexibility. However, the supply chain management processes are both cross-functional and cross-firm. Within this cross-functional context, other organizational aspects need to be considered and will influence the firm's degree of flexibility such as the customer differentiation strategy. Therefore, we have included in Table 7-1 a broader view of flexibility that transcends the production function.

There are several factors that drive the need for manufacturing flexibility. Demand characteristics factor in the determination of manufacturing flexibility. Demand volume, variation, and predictability of the variation are at the top of the list of considerations. Also important to consider is the customer's tolerance for waiting and reaction to an out-of-stock situation by either switching to a substitute product, back-ordering, delaying the purchase, or getting the item from an alternative supplier/store.[17] Characteristics associated with the product itself include the variety (i.e., the level of standardization or differentiation), stage and expected duration of the product life cycle, complexity of the product, and profit margin of the product. Finally, the lead times that can be achieved in different levels of the supply chain will influence the degree of manufacturing flexibility that will be

---

[17] Zinn, Walter, and Peter C. Liu, "Consumer Response to Retail Stockouts," *Journal of Business Logistics,* Vol. 22, No. 1 (2001), pp.49-72.

Table 7-1
Types of Flexibility

Type of Flexibility	Definition
Organizational Flexibility	
Manufacturing or Operations	The ability of the organization to manage production resources and uncertainty to meet various customer requirements
Market	The ability to mass-customize and build close relationships with customers, including designing new products and modifying existing ones
Supply	The ability to reconfigure the supply chain (geographically) as sources of supply and customers change
Information Systems	The ability to align information systems with changing customer demands
Production Flexibility	
Mix	The ability to change over to a different product quickly and economically without changes in capacity
Volume	The ability to operate at various batch sizes and/or at different production volumes economically and effectively
Expansion	Modular building and expanding capacity
Material Handling	The ability to effectively transport different work pieces between various processing centers over multiple paths
Process (routing)	The ability to process a given set of part types using multiple routes effectively
Machine	The ability of a machine to perform different operations economically and efficiently
Work-center (labor)	The ability of the workforce to perform a broad range of tasks economically and effectively

Source: adapted from Duclos, Leslie K., Robert J. Vokurka and Rhonda R. Lummus, "A Conceptual Model of Supply Chain Flexibility," *Industrial Management & Data Systems*, Vol. 103, No. 6 (2003), pp. 446-456; and Zhang, Qingyu, Mark A. Vonderembse and Jeen-Su Lim, "Manufacturing Flexibility: Defining and Analyzing Relationships among Competence, Capability, and Customer Satisfaction," *Journal of Operations Management*, Vol. 21, No. 2 (2003), pp. 173-191.

required to satisfy demand. For example, a flexible manufacturing system might be required to offset long inbound lead times or long outbound delivery times.

Quality policies and required degrees of control add to the lead times. Some controls such as inspection upon receiving a shipment might be removed by assigning control to the source, or removing inspections altogether by developing quality protocols jointly with suppliers, certifying their processes. In some cases, quality controls are mandated such as tests required by the Food and Drug Administration. For example, baby-food products require an incubation period before they are released to the market. This incubation-time requirement limits some aspects of flexibility by forcing the manufacturer to maintain higher inventories than would be necessary in the absence of such a mandate.

Generally, more flexibility is preferred. However, there is a cost associated with developing manufacturing flexibility. The targeted type and degree of flexibility should fit the overall business strategy.[18] Management may pursue the implementation of higher degrees of flexibility and/or specific types of flexibility for key customers.

[18] Gaimon, Cheryl and Vinod Singhal, "Flexibility and the Choice of Manufacturing Facilities under Short Product Life Cycles," *European Journal of Operational Research,* Vol. 60, No. 2 (1992), pp. 211.

The ability of the demand management process to recognize demand volatility and to manage it effectively, might reduce the need for manufacturing flexibility.

Additionally, managers must be confident that the firm will be rewarded by its customers for providing heightened degrees of manufacturing flexibility. The ability of the demand management process to recognize demand volatility and to manage it effectively, might reduce the need for manufacturing flexibility.

Once the desired degree of manufacturing flexibility has been determined, attention turns to how best to achieve it. Batch sizes and cycle times, which can vary by product, customer, market, or life-cycle phase, must be defined. The customer relationship management team provides critical input toward these determinations. Avery Dennison's Graphics division has established distinct approaches to accommodate fast-moving and slow-moving products. Fast-moving products are produced in large batches in a lean manner - knowing that demand will exist for them. Slower-moving products are produced on an as-needed or MTO basis. Prior to implementing this mixed-mode strategy, Avery struggled to achieve next-day service (from order receipt to shipping). Today, the business achieves same-day service across the product line at a very high level. This improved accommodation of demand has helped a market contender become the market leader.[19]

The TaylorMade-Adidas Golf Company employs mixed-mode approach to create a made-to-order, custom golf club deliverable in 24 hours. While make-to-stock clubs still represent the primary share of the company's business, demonstrating that custom clubs can be produced quickly and at a reasonable cost has reinforced the company's reputation as a best-in-class manufacturer.[20] Further reinforcement was found in 2002 when the United States Golf Association (USGA) revised its standards for clubs' coefficient of restitution (or "springiness"). The USGA extended the acceptable limit only to revert to its original level less than three months later, thereby making the company's top-selling product a non-compliant club in USGA-sanctioned events. By integrating research and development (R&D) and manufacturing, and involving key suppliers in the initiative, management at TaylorMade was able to market a redesigned, compliant club within twelve days of the USGA's reversed decision.[21]

Beyond consideration of the manufacturer's current capabilities, there must be consideration of the manufacturing strategy's complete time horizon to determine whether current capacity is sufficient to support sales objectives. Incorporating information developed by the customer relationship management team and the marketing function regarding market growth, penetration of new markets, and sustained growth, the manufacturing flow management team should assess the ability to respond to anticipated growth and determine future capacity needs.

A final, critical consideration in this sub-process is whether the manufacturer can and should perform the value-added processing in-house. As indicated in the introduction to this chapter, companies often will hire an external, contract manufacturer to fulfill specific manufacturing needs or to supplement supply during rapid growth or seasonal demand. In other instances, however, the company may choose to outsource its traditional manufacturing responsibilities entirely. Many firms

---

[19] Roche, Terry, Manufacturing and Supply Chain Consultant, Avery Dennison, personal interview, conducted at Montgomery, Ohio on May 21, 2003.

[20] Bowman, Robert J., "TaylorMade Drives Supply-Chain Efficiency with 24-Hour Club," *Global Logistics & Supply Chain Strategies* (October 2002), pp. 38-43.

[21] Bowman, Robert J., "TaylorMade Drives Supply-Chain Efficiency with 24-Hour Club," *Global Logistics & Supply Chain Strategies* (October 2002), pp. 38-43.

focus on building brands rather than physical products, outsourcing the full scope of manufacturing responsibilities to one or more contract manufacturers who can provide desired products at a lower cost. Companies such as The Limited, Nike, Lucent Technologies, Sara Lee, Ericsson, and Alcatel rely extensively on outsourced manufacturing to focus on new product development, marketing, and distribution.[22]

Determining when and what to outsource is a challenge. Masterfoods USA outsources production when the company either lacks a production capability or simply prefers not to own the technology. Masterfoods also employs contract manufacturers for temporary capacity during peak sales seasons. The 3M Company employs a similar logic but refuses to outsource manufacturing activities for which it has a competitive advantage. Given the importance of this decision, input should be received from purchasing, logistics, finance, and senior executives in the company.

Even when management chooses to "buy" rather than "make" key components or finished goods, it is important that the strategic planning responsibilities remain in the firm.[23] When outsourcing production, significant responsibilities shift from manufacturing flow management to the supplier relationship management process. Manufacturing expertise must remain in the company to ensure that the supplier operates in a manner consistent with the company's competitive priorities and within legal and social boundaries. The manufacturing flow management process team remains an important voice, protecting the company's interests when outside sources provide critical manufacturing services.

The process team will interact frequently with the supplier relationship management process team even when no manufacturing activities are outsourced. The manufacturing flexibility of a firm will be influenced by the flexibility of key suppliers. Therefore, the supplier relationship management process team will provide assessment of suppliers' flexibility. They will also use this interaction with the manufacturing flow management process team to identify opportunities for improvement among the suppliers.

Determine Push/Pull Boundaries

The degree of manufacturing flexibility of each member of the supply chain influences the placement of push/pull boundaries. Push/pull boundaries refer to the positioning of a decoupling point in the supply chain — up to which supply is pushed forward as make-to-stock but beyond which demand drives make-to-order execution.[24] The key to determining a push/pull boundary is recognizing the stage of value-added processing in which differentiation from a standard configuration

> *Even when management chooses to "buy" rather than "make" key components or finished goods, it is important that the strategic planning responsibilities remain in the firm.*

---

[22] Lynch, Grahame, "Telecom's New Role Model: Nike," *America's Network*, Vol. 105, No. 14 (2001), p. 58; Serant, Claire, "Selectron Opts to Lease Lucent Plant in Three-Year, $2B Ousourcing Deal," EBN, No. 1273 (2001), p.10; Susan Reda, "Customer Service, Brand Management Seen as Key spects of On-Line Fulfillment," *Stores Magazine*, Vol. 82, No. 10 (2000), pp. 40-43; and, Gretchen Morgenson, "Been There, Tried That," *Forbes*, Vol. 106, No. 9 (1997), pp.60-61.

[23] Singhal, Jaya and Kalyan Singhal, "Supply Chains and Compatibility among Components in Product Design," *Journal of Operations Management*, Vol. 20 (2002), pp. 289-302.

[24] Frequently, the push/pull boundaries are presented as determining the location of "*the*" decoupling point. This view of a single decoupling point is a conceptual simplification that, in practice, will be found only when the focus is internal to a firm or to a limited section of the product flow. When multiple members of a supply chain are involved, it is likely that more than one decoupling point is needed; see: Graves, Stephen C. and Sean P. Willems, "Optimizing Strategic Safety Stock Placement in Supply Chains," *Manufacturing and Service Operations Management*, Vol. 2, No. 1 (2000), pp. 68-83.

takes place. In a buy-to-order arrangement, manufacturing flexibility is at a premium and the primary decoupling point is upstream from the manufacturer given that raw materials are unique to the individual finished good. At the other extreme, ship-to-stock strategies generate a standardized product, allowing the decoupling point inventories to reside in the manufacturer's distribution channel.[25]

In ship-to-stock and make-to-stock arrangements, the customer can usually enjoy immediate satisfaction of an in-stock product (even though the product may not exactly match the customer's specific needs). If longer lead times can be negotiated with customers through the product and service agreement (PSA) developed by the customer relationship management team, greater opportunities for postponement become possible. Postponement reduces speculation and risks associated with finished goods inventories.[26] Should short or immediate lead times be set forth in the PSA, the manufacturer will have little choice but to pursue a speculative arrangement, position goods in the marketplace in advance of demand, and hope that the goods sufficiently meet customers' expectations in terms of appearance, performance, and quantity.

Supply chains that lack the ability to respond quickly to changes in customer demand incur the costs of oversupply and the opportunity costs of undersupply common with the bullwhip effect.

Supply chains that lack the ability to respond quickly to changes in customer demand incur the costs of oversupply and the opportunity costs of undersupply common with the bullwhip effect.[27] The primary responsibility for ensuring that the manufacturer responds to customer demand rests with the customer relationship management team in collaboration with the demand management process team. The product development and commercialization process is also involved to the extent that different product designs can be developed to accommodate manufacturing better and perhaps make postponement opportunities viable. Meanwhile, the supplier relationship management team is responsible for ensuring that suppliers understand their roles in the manufacturing flow management process.

Once the primary decoupling point is determined, the order fulfillment process must act in support of the push-pull decision to ensure that customers' expectations are fulfilled appropriately. In fact, the postponement of manufacturing activities might shift processing responsibilities typically performed by production to the logistics function of the business. Responsibilities would be limited ordinarily to light processing, such as packaging, labeling, and assembling display units. For instance, Hewlett-Packard (HP) has long performed the bundling of power supplies and users' manuals with print-imaging equipment in the distribution operation to support international sales. This effort is critical given that users in different nations will have different needs. Delaying the bundling of these items until demand is recognized by region prevents HP from speculating the nations from which demand originates. General Mills employs a similar strategy by bundling promotional items such as children's coloring books with breakfast cereals at the company's distribution centers throughout the U.S. By performing

---

[25] For more information regarding decoupling point determination, see J. Ben Naylor, Mohamed M. Naim, and Danny Berry, "Leagility: Integrating the Lean and Agile Manufacturing Paradigms in the Total Supply Chain," *International Journal of Production Economics*, Vol. 62 (1999), pp. 107-118.

[26] Cooper, Martha C. and Janus D. Pagh, "Supply Chain Postponement and Speculation Strategies: How to Choose the Right Strategy," *Journal of Business Logistics*, Vol.19, No. 2 (1998), pp. 13-33.

[27] Lee, Hau L., V. Padmanabhan and Seungjin Whang, "The Bullwhip Effect in Supply Chains," *Sloan Management Review*, Vol. 38, No. 3 (1997), pp. 93-102.

these activities closer (in terms of time and proximity) to the retail customer, General Mills experiences less uncertainty in short-term demand and reduces its risks of inventory obsolescence.[28]

Identify Manufacturing Constraints and Determine Capabilities

After the push-pull boundaries are determined, the strategic process team addresses the roles and responsibilities of the supply chain members to identify manufacturing constraints and requirements for desired performance. Recognizing bottlenecks in the manufacturing process is critical in achieving this objective. Among the more common constraints are labor and equipment resources. Ensuring that existing resources meet current and future demand ranks among the greatest difficulties for manufacturers.

Products that experience significant demand seasonality are particularly susceptible to periods of substantial under- and over-capacity. Manufacturers often hire temporary workers to offset the problem of insufficient labor on a short-term basis. With regard to equipment and facility resources, manufacturers will outsource excess production, build in advance, or use overtime capacity to ensure ready inventory availability when demand peaks. The ability to forecast these changes in demand patterns accurately is essential to providing adequate supply at the lowest possible cost. Therefore, the demand management process team not only must be aware of potential bottlenecks or problems in the flow of products through the plants but also must communicate demand forecasts well in advance, with continuous updates that provide greater accuracy in the near-term.

The manufacturing flow management process team identifies the manufacturing constraints and capabilities, and translates them into deliverables to the customers. The identification of the manufacturing constraints will lead to the development of the inventory policy for each facility in the supply chain network. The inventory policy will include how much inventory is to be held in the form of raw materials, subcomponents, work-in-process, and finished goods, and how often inventory will be replenished. Also, the inventory policy will determine the appropriate actions in the event of a stockout, which will be coordinated with demand management and, eventually, incorporated with contingency plans. Contingency plan development is imperative in minimizing disruption when problem situations cannot be anticipated or avoided.[29]

The identification of the manufacturing constraints will lead to the development of the inventory policy for each facility in the supply chain network.

Manufacturing technology sometimes poses constraints to manufacturing capabilities, such as the minimum manufacturing lead times. Other limits to the lead times that a firm can promise to its customers might be set, for example, by the planning process. Consequently, these constraints need to be identified

---

[28] For more information regarding postponement strategies, see Zinn, Walter, and Donald J. Bowersox, "Planning Physical Distribution with the Principle of Postponement," *Journal of Business Logistics,* Vol. 9, No. 2 (1988), pp. 117-136; Van Hoek, Remko I., Harry R. Commandeur, and Bart Vos, "Reconfiguring Logistics Systems through Postponement Strategies," *Journal of Business Logistics,* Vol. 19, No. 1 (1998), pp. 33-54; and, Cooper, Martha C. and Janus D. Pagh, "Supply Chain Postponement and Speculation Strategies: How to Choose the Right Strategy," *Journal of Business Logistics,* Vol.19, No. 2 (1998), pp. 13-33.

[29] Croxton, Keely L., Douglas M. Lambert, Dale S. Rogers and Sebastián J. García-Dastugue, "The Demand Management Process," *The International Journal of Logistics Management,* Vol. 13, No. 2 (2002), pp. 51-66.

explicity and translated into possible deliverables for customers. These deliverables should be incorporated in the development of the customer service strategy and the PSAs. Furthermore, since management should identify key customers and group other customers in segments, different manufacturing capabilities might be offered to the different key customers and segments. For example, a supplier to a US-based quick-service restaurant chain will accept rush orders from this customer; even if it means delaying production of another customer's order. Obviously, this service policy cannot be adopted for all customers. In addition, the costs associated with delaying other customers' orders must be determined. Management must assess the costs of offering prioritized customer service. The manufacturing flow management and customer relationship management teams need to discuss the possible features that can be included in PSAs. The capabilities are communicated to the demand managment, order fulfillment, and returns management process teams. Further, the customer service management team receives the order acceptance guidelines. The team uses these guidelines every time a customer has a request. The order acceptance guidelines help to identify which requests can be fulfilled without any further evaluation. Some requests might require additional management time to evaluate their economic and technical viability though the majority can be done based solely on the order acceptance guidelines.

Manufacturing flow management is enhanced as upstream supply chain members understand their roles and engage in coordinated flow to support the manufacturer's value-added processing.

Manufacturing flow management is enhanced as upstream supply chain members understand their roles and engage in coordinated flow to support the manufacturer's value-added processing. The process team is responsible for developing communication mechanisms that make coordination possible across companies. In addition, the team develops criteria for acceptable quality throughout the manufacturing processes. The supplier relationship management process facilitates this interaction with key suppliers. The supplier relationship management team is charged not only with coordinating responsibilities with suppliers, but also jointly developing and implementing process improvement initiatives. Opportunities for process improvement often can be more easily identified by upstream supply chain members than by the manufacturer. For example, Cargill, Inc., works closely with its food processing customers to develop better products and better processes for improved product flow.

The manufacturing flow management process team will also participate in the development of the disposition requirements and returns management strategy. The disposition guidelines are developed in the returns management process.[30] However, the manufacturing flow management team will possess know-how regarding the methods for disassembling and disposing of the manufactured products. Disposition options include sending the product to landfill but the more preferable option is recapturing value. Therefore, the manufacturing flow management team participates in the feasibility analysis of the disposition options, including the determination of materials that can be reused or recycled, as well as the development of refurbishing and remanufacturing capacity.

---

[30] Rogers, Dale S. , Douglas M. Lambert, Keely L. Croxton and Sebastián J. García-Dastugue, "The Returns Management Process," *The International Journal of Logistics Management,* Vol. 13, No. 2 (2002), pp. 1-18.

Develop Framework of Metrics

In the final strategic sub-process, the process team develops the framework of metrics to be used to measure and improve the performance of the process. A uniform approach should be used throughout the firm to develop these metrics.[31] The team should start by understanding how the manufacturing flow management process can directly affect the firm's financial performance, as measured by economic value added (EVA).[32] The true test of the process' effectiveness is found in the value it creates. Figure 7-5 provides a framework that shows how manufacturing flow management can impact sales, cost of goods sold, total expenses, inventory investment, other current assets, and fixed assets.

Though the financial implications of production operations typically focus on cost reduction, the manufacturing flow management process should be credited with revenue enhancement associated with successful execution as well. For example, better manufacturing flow management can result in higher sales and healthier margins through consistent availability of products that meet customers' specific needs. Manufacturing flexibility that accommodates changes in product attributes and volume allows the company to meet demand better than rivals and to do so with lower inventory investment. Together, these factors strengthen customer loyalty and support repeat business. Loyal customers are also more likely to direct a greater proportion of their business to the proven manufacturer, improving the company's "share of customer." The value provided to the customer through manufacturing flexibility should be measured and sold both to upper management and to the customer. This value should be traded-off with the cost of obtaining, developing, and managing flexibility.

Though the financial implications of production operations typically focus on cost reduction, the manufacturing flow management process should be credited with revenue enhancement associated with successful execution as well.

Cost of goods sold can be reduced as a result of reduced labor and material expenses. Improving manufacturing processes increases plant productivity. Reducing waste and rework, and increasing labor utilization are other potential sources of savings. Non-manufacturing expenses also can be reduced through improved manufacturing flow management. A responsive manufacturing process leads to better order fill rates and orders shipped complete. Not only will order fill increase but it will be achieved faster and with fewer expedited shipments. A process focused on quality in execution will reduce damage and handling expense and perhaps investment in packaging. In addition, a well designed and implemented manufacturing flow management process can reduce human resource costs and improve the effectiveness of employees.

Better manufacturing flow management increases inventory turns and reduces component, work in process, and finished goods inventories. Manufacturing flexibility accommodates demand with less inventory obsolescence. More responsive supply and improved order fill leads to fewer disputes with customers, and reductions in accounts receivable. Finally, better manufacturing flow management improves asset utilization, as well as better investment planning and deployment. It is only through

---

[31] Lambert, Douglas M. and Terrance L. Pohlen, "Supply Chain Metrics," *The International Journal of Logistics Management*, Vol. 12, No. 1 (2001), pp. 1-19; and Croxton, Keely L., Douglas M. Lambert, Dale S. Rogers and Sebastián J. García-Dastugue, "The Demand Management Process," *The International Journal of Logistics Management*, Vol. 13, No. 2 (2002), pp. 51-66.

[32] Bennett, Stewart G., III, *The Quest for Value: A Guide for Managers,* 2nd Edition, New York: Harper Collins, 1999; and Joel M. Stern, "One Way to Build Value in Your Firm, a la Executive Compensation," *Financial Executive*, November-December 1990, pp. 51-54.

Figure 7-5
How Manufacturing Flow Management Affects Economic Value Added (EVA®)

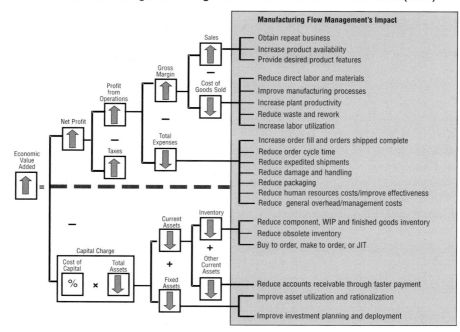

Source: Adapted from Douglas M. Lambert and Terrance L. Pohlen, "Supply Chain Metrics," *The International Journal of Logistics Management*, Vol. 12, No. 1 (2001), p. 10.

Upon recognizing the impact of manufacturing flow management on the firm's financial performance, as measured by EVA, the team must develop operational metrics that guide behavior in production operations and yield desired performance.

demonstrating the manufacturing flow management process' contribution to the greater success of the firm and supply chain that further investments in the process will be justified and rewards for good performance will be determined.

Upon recognizing the impact of manufacturing flow management on the firm's financial performance, as measured by EVA, the team must develop operational metrics that guide behavior in production operations and yield desired performance. The metrics assess efficiency and effectiveness in terms of important performance criteria such as product quality, productivity, cycle time, inventory levels, cost, and safety. The importance of these measures should correlate closely with the prioritization of competitive bases, as determined by the manufacturing strategy and must be tied back to financial measures. The manufacturing flow management team coordinates the metrics with the aid of the customer relationship management team to ensure appropriateness and importance to customers. To the extent possible, the manufacturer should gather both formal and informal input from customers (next-tier customers and end users should they not be the same). Metrics for upstream performance might also be devised for the supplier relationship management team to assess the contribution of suppliers to process performance. In the same way metrics are coordinated with customer relationship management so that the customers reward the firm, metrics are also communicated to supplier relationship management to reward suppliers' efforts to firm success. The manufacturing flow management process will generate input to guide the supplier relationship management team in seeking process improvements from the supply base.

Finally, the framework for metrics should provide the basis for aligning the efforts of the corporate functions. Traditionally, interfaces between functions are difficult because functional metrics are not tied to financial metrics or focused on the customer. This type of conflict may be resolved through better communication, teamwork, better understanding of the other one's responsibilities, and clarification of goals.[33] The appropriate framework for metrics should facilitate internal integration; it should enable viewing the firm's activities holistically across the corporate functions.

The Operational Manufacturing Flow Management Process

The operational portion of manufacturing flow management is the realization of the process developed at the strategic level. Despite the apparent similarities between the operational sub-processes and the planning and scheduling activities of the production function internal to most manufacturers, key differences exist. These differences include the guidance provided by the infrastructure developed at the strategic level and the interfaces that link the operational sub-processes in a structured way to the other seven supply chain management processes. There are four sub-processes that represent the operational flow. Each is depicted in Figure 7-6.

Determine Routing and Velocity through Manufacturing

The first operational sub-process establishes the execution of the plan set forth in the strategic portion of the process. Determining the routing and velocity of materials and goods through manufacturing is the first step. The demand management process provides critical input to this sub-process, primarily though sharing the demand execution plan. This plan is based on historical demand, marketing and sales strategies, and general market intelligence and is developed at the product family or group level.

Upon reviewing the aggregate production plan, production management assesses the volume capacity across the manufacturing network and allocates volume to each plant. To the extent that production is outsourced to contract manufacturers, the supplier relationship management team will be instrumental in communicating with these external service providers. Each plant then develops its own master production schedule (MPS) that dictates which products to produce, when, and in what quantities. The MPS reflects the manufacturing priorities set forth at the strategic level, recognizing the products and customers that are most important to the manufacturer's profitability by granting them higher priorities. In addition, it reflects the manufacturing strategy among the range of possibilities (buy to order, make to order, assemble to order, make to stock, and ship to stock). Factors such as capacity limitations, manufacturing constraints, production setup time and costs, and inventory carrying costs are considered when developing the MPS.[34] There is communication with the supplier relationship management team to ensure

To the extent that production is outsourced to contract manufacturers, the supplier relationship management team will be instrumental in communicating with these external service providers.

---

[33] Shaw, Vivienne , Christopher T. Shaw and Margit Enke, "Conflict Between Engineers and Marketers: the Experience of German Engineers," *Industrial Marketing Management,* Vol. 32, No. 6 (2003), pp. 489-499.

[34] Krajewski, Lee J. and Larry P. Ritzman, *Operations Management: Strategy and Analysis*, 7th Edition, Upper Saddle River, NJ: Prentice Hall, 2004.

Figure 7-6
The Operational Manufacturing Flow Management Process

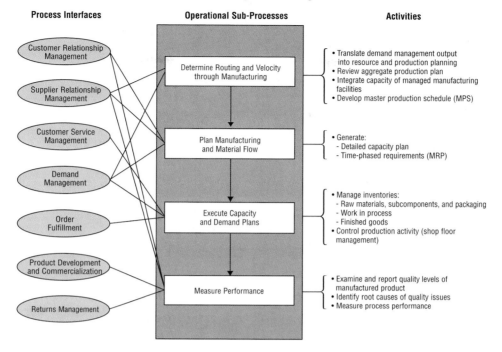

that the supply base is committed to the accommodation of the manufacturing priorities.

As manufacturing firms gain greater flexibility in their operations, less reliance will be placed on advanced planning.

As manufacturing firms gain greater flexibility in their operations, less reliance will be placed on advanced planning. Rather, agility will be emphasized where rapid accommodation of varied customer demands proves both efficient and valued in the marketplace. While flexibility is regarded among the most promising opportunities in manufacturing, most operations remain driven by sales forecasts that subsequently determine routing and velocity.

Plan Manufacturing and Material Flow

Once the MPS is determined, focus shifts to the detailed planning of capacity and inbound materials necessary to "feed" the production schedule. The material requirements plan (MRP) identifies the quantities and timing of all subassemblies, components, and raw materials needed to support production of the end-items.[35] The MRP, therefore, serves as the prime operational interface between manufacturing flow management and supplier relationship management. Along with the MPS, product-specific bills of materials and on-hand inventories drive the MRP explosion that yields the desired quantities of input materials required at any given time to support product flow. The MRP includes not only material inputs for the product but also packaging material.

---

[35] Krajewski, Lee J. and Larry P. Ritzman, *Operations Management: Strategy and Analysis*, 7th Edition, Upper Saddle River, NJ: Prentice Hall, 2004.

Next, production management develops the capacity resource plan, which represents a time-phased plan of the capacity needed from each resource. Should a capacity or materials shortage be identified, the team will interact, on the one hand, with the demand management team to find possible solutions to the bottleneck from the demand side. On the other hand, the process team will interact with the supplier relationship management process team to work with materials suppliers or with contract manufacturers, if manufacturing activities are outsourced.

The supplier relationship management team not only prepares suppliers for future material needs but keeps manufacturing informed of any potential hazards or disruptions that might be encountered upstream in the supply chain. Similarly, supplier relationship management will coordinate changes to the MRP in response to changes of demand, rush orders, or capacity-related issues. Management should be aware of other types of contingencies that are not related to daily operational activities. For instance, many North American manufacturers were affected by the West Coast port closures of October 2002, essentially cutting off supply from Asia for a period of several weeks. During such times, customer relationship management may be involved to the extent that problems arise in fulfilling demand. Should capacity prove insufficient to meet the needs of all customers, the demand management team will designate the order of manufacturing priorities.

Execute Capacity and Demand Plans

Execution follows the completed planning process. This sub-process involves frequent interface with the demand management and order fulfillment process teams to maintain efficient flow of materials, work-in-process, and finished goods. Daily verification ensures that schedule attainment is achieved - providing adjustments as necessary. In addition, the supply of packaging materials must be sufficient to ensure that shortages do not disrupt the flow of inbound materials and outbound goods. This is particularly challenging for manufacturers using returnable packaging in a closed-loop system.

Synchronizing available capacity and demand represents the on-going effort to provide sufficient, timely supply with minimal inventories, asset and labor productivity consistent with established standards, and high quality. Timely execution relies on well developed plans and an ability to adapt to variation in the process. Quality programs such as Six Sigma and its associated blackbelt training are popular means to reduce process variance. To the extent that processing time can be lessened and the variance minimized, the manufacturer can better meet customers' changing needs with less disruption and lower costs.[36]

Timely execution relies on well developed plans and an ability to adapt to variation in the process.

Beyond demand management and order fulfillment, the synchronization of capacity and demand calls for interaction with customer service management. This primarily will take the form of executing the order acceptance guidelines established in the strategic sub-process associated with manufacturing capabilities. Customer service failures will be minimal in number and severity if promises made to customers are within the capability of the firm, as established in the order acceptance guidelines. Problems only worsen when unreasonable promises are

---

[36] George, Michael L., *Lean Six Sigma: Combining Six Sigma Quality with Lean Production Speed*, New York: McGraw-Hill, 2002.

extended or when problem resolution requires time and resources already dedicated to existing orders. The extension of "reasonable" orders can be facilitated through order promising, a common feature of manufacturing resource planning (MRP II) systems. MRP II is an expansion of closed-loop MRP to include information to all corporate functions, and order promising is a way to tie customers' orders to product availability.[37] Order acceptance guidelines, developed at the strategic level of manufacturing flow management, should extend beyond product availability and include other order parameters such as required lead time, order size, or changes to existing orders. These guidelines might change based on situational factors. For example, if working below capacity it is likely that the firm may behave more flexibly than if working at full capacity.

Measure Performance

The final operational sub-process involves process assessment and identification of improvement opportunities. The manufacturing flow management process, like all of the other supply chain management processes, spans beyond the four walls of the company. Therefore, the manufacturing flow management team not only must measure performance within the firm's manufacturing plants but also must relate this performance to the broader supply chain.

The manufacturing flow management team regularly tracks performance measures and conveys these metrics to the customer relationship management and supplier relationship management teams.

The manufacturing flow management team regularly tracks performance measures and conveys these metrics to the customer relationship management and supplier relationship management teams. Recognition of improvement opportunities may only be possible through external measurement of performance. With regard to customer satisfaction, for instance, internal measures alone will not capture the disparity between what a customer expects and what is actually delivered. This information can only be obtained by communicating with the customer. The customer relationship management team is well positioned to gather this information on behalf of manufacturing flow management and order fulfillment. The same might be true of problems on the inbound side of the manufacturing operation. For this reason, regular conversation with suppliers through the supplier relationship management team ensures that inbound materials flow with minimal disruption. The customer relationship management and supplier relationship management teams can then use these metrics to generate cost and profitability reports. These reports are valuable when negotiating services with key material and service providers, and when determining rewards for customers and suppliers who have positively influenced the performance of the manufacturing flow management process.[38]

The manufacturing flow management process team must interact with other process teams. For instance, product design flaws or inconsistencies between product design and manufacturing would require the imput of the product development and commercialization process team. In addition, the returns management process can provide important indications of design or manufacturing problems based upon the unfortunate situation of customers recognizing flaws before they can be reconciled internally. Once a root cause is

---

[37] Markland, Robert E., Shawnee K. Vickery and Robert A. Davis, *Operations Management: Concepts in Manufacturing and Services*, 2nd ed., Cincinnati, Ohio: South-Western College, 1998.

[38] Lambert, Douglas M. and Terrance L. Pohlen, "Supply Chain Metrics," *The International Journal of Logistics Management*, Vol. 12, No. 1 (2001), pp. 1-19.

determined, the process teams resolve the problem and informs those within and outside the company that are affected.

Conclusions

The manufacturing flow management process deals with establishing and implementing the capabilities for the management of the conversion of materials and components into finished goods demanded by the market. The areas of operations management, operations research, and industrial engineering are well versed in recognizing new, better ways to perform the conversion activities within the four walls of the manufacturer. Supply chain management, on the other hand, seeks ways to improve performance by leveraging the capabilities of not only the production function within the firm but the diverse capabilities of supply chain members. While manufacturing flow management represents only one of the eight supply chain management processes, it is a critical driver of success for all supply chain members.

Successful implementation requires the involvement of customers and suppliers in the manufacturing flow management process. This involvement is coordinated through the customer relationship management and supplier relationship management teams, respectively. In fact, customer relationship management interfaces with all five of the strategic sub-processes and two of the four operational sub-processes. Supplier relationship management is involved in four of five strategic sub-processes and three of four operational sub-processes. It is not only through internal efforts of the manufacturer but through the efforts of material and service providers that the desired degree of manufacturing flexibility is achieved.

Capturing demand information and better managing demand is critical to the manufacturing flow management process. The close relationship between manufacturing flow management and demand management is characterized by the many interfaces between these two processes. The ability of the demand management process to anticipate demand with precision alleviates the need of the manufacturing system to be flexible. However, the trend in most industries is one of frequent and often dramatic change, driving the need for greater flexibility.

When value can be demonstrated, management wants to know how quickly the benefits can be achieved.

Economic value added analysis was introduced as a way to help sell the value of manufacturing flow management as a supply chain management process. The financial benefits must be clear within the firm and with other members of the supply chain to gain buy-in and long-term commitment. When value can be demonstrated, management wants to know how quickly the benefits can be achieved.

CHAPTER

8

The Product Development and Commercialization Process

Dale S. Rogers, Douglas M. Lambert and A. Michael Knemeyer

Overview

Product development and commercialization is the supply chain management process that provides structure for developing and bringing to market new products jointly with customers and suppliers.[1] Effective implementation of the process not only enables management to coordinate the efficient flow of new products across the supply chain, but also assists supply chain members with the ramp-up of manufacturing, logistics, marketing and other related activities to support the commercialization of the product. In this chapter, the product development and commercialization process is described in detail to show how it can be implemented. To do this, the process is described in terms of its strategic and operational sub-processes and associated activities, and the interfaces with business functions, other supply chain management processes and other firms. Examples of successful implementation are provided.

Developing products rapidly and moving them into the marketplace efficiently is important for long-term corporate success.

Introduction

The product development and commercialization process requires effective planning and execution throughout the supply chain, and if managed correctly can provide a sustainable competitive advantage. Developing products rapidly and moving them into the marketplace efficiently is important for long-term corporate success.[2] In many markets, 40 percent or more of revenues come from products introduced in the prior year.[3]

While the creation of successful products is a multidisciplinary process,[4]

---

[1] This chapter is based on Dale S. Rogers, Douglas M. Lambert and A. Michael Knemeyer, "The Product Development and Commercialization Process," *The International Journal of Logistics Management*, Vol. 15, No. 1 (2004), pp. 43-56.

[2] Cooper, Robert G., Scott J. Edgett, and Elko J. Kleinschmidt, *Portfolio Management for New Products*, Reading, MA: Perseus Books, 1998.

[3] Handfield, Robert B. and Ernest L. Nichols, Jr., *Supply Chain Redesign*, Upper Saddle River, NJ: Financial Times Prentice Hall, 2002.

[4] Olson, Eric M., Orville C. Walker, Jr., Robert W. Ruekert, and Joseph M. Bonner, "Patterns of Cooperation During New Product Development Among Marketing, Operations and R&D: Implications for Project Performance," *The Journal of Product Innovation Management*, Vol. 18, No. 4 (2001), pp. 258-271.

product development and commercialization from a supply chain management perspective integrates both customers[5] and suppliers[6] into the process in order to reduce time to market. The ability to reduce time to market is key to innovation success and profitability[7] as well as the most critical objective of the process.[8] As product life cycles shorten, the right products must be developed and successfully launched in ever-shorter time frames in order to remain competitive[9] and achieve differentiation in the marketplace.

Product development and commercialization is one of the eight supply chain management processes (see Figure 8-1) and it must interface with the other seven. It requires the integration of customers and suppliers and the alignment of their activities. Successful implementation of the process requires metrics that measure the financial impact on the firm and on other members of the supply chain. In this chapter, we review the different types of product development and relevant definitions. Then, we describe the strategic and operational sub-processes that comprise the product development and commercialization process. Finally, we present conclusions.

Types of Product Development Projects

Product development projects can be classified as one of the following four types:[10]

- **New product platforms:** This type of project involves a major development effort to create a family of products based on a new, common platform. The product family addresses familiar markets and product categories. Moen Incorporated's project involving the Revolution Massaging Showerhead is an example. This product offers several features not available with any of their other products.
- **Derivatives of existing product platforms:** These projects extend an existing product platform to better address familiar markets with one or more new products. Sony Corporation, by using common components in successive generations of the Sony Walkman, achieved higher quality throughout the platform life.[11]
- **Incremental improvements to existing products:** These projects involve

> *...product development and commercialization from a supply chain management perspective integrates both customers and suppliers into the process in order to reduce time to market.*

---

[5] Karkkainen, Hannu and Petteri Piippo, "Ten Tools for Customer-driven Product Development in Industrial Companies," *International Journal of Production Economics*, Vol. 69, No. 2 (2001), pp. 161-176.

[6] Schilling, Melissa A. and Charles W. L. Hill, "Managing the New Product Development Process: Strategic Imperatives," *Academy of Management Executive*, Vol. 12, No. 3 (1998), pp. 67-82.

[7] Dröge, Cornelia, Jayanth Jayaram and Shawnee K Vickery, "The Ability to Minimize the Timing of New Product Development and Introduction: An Examination of Antecedent Factors in the North American Automobile Supplier Industry," *The Journal of Product Innovation Management*, Vol. 17, No. 1 (2000), pp. 24-37.

[8] Schilling, Melissa A. and Charles W. L. Hill, "Managing the New Product Development Process: Strategic Imperatives," *Academy of Management Executive*, Vol. 12, No. 3 (1998), pp. 67-82.

[9] Zacharia, Zach G., "Research and Development in Supply Chain Management," in *Supply Chain Management*, ed. John T. Mentzer., Thousand Oaks, CA: Sage Publications, Inc., 2001.

[10] Ulrich, Karl T. and Steven D. Eppinger, *Product Design and Development- 3rd Edition*, New York, NY: McGraw-Hill/Irwin, 2004.

[11] Sanderson, S. and M. Uzumeri, "A Framework Model and Product Family Competition," *Research Policy*, (1995), pp. 24.

Figure 8-1
Supply Chain Management:
Integrating and Managing Business Processes Across the Supply Chain

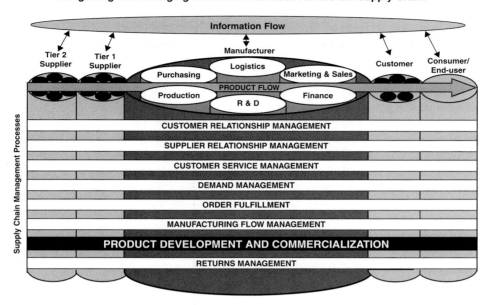

Source: Adapted from Douglas M. Lambert, Martha C. Cooper, and Janus D. Pagh, "Supply Chain Management: Implementation Issues and Research Opportunities," *The International Journal of Logistics Management,* Vol. 9, No. 2 (1998), p. 2.

adding or modifying some features of existing products in order to keep them current and competitive. As an example, TaylorMade-adidas Golf introduced, in its Rossa putters, two new versions of its popular mallet-style Monza putter: the Monza Long and Monza Mid. While the new products maintain the features of the original Monza putter, the heads of the new putters were engineered to work best with a long and mid-length shaft respectively.

- **Fundamentally new products:** These projects involve radically different product or production technologies and might help to address new and unfamiliar markets. In late 2001, Apple Computer rolled out the iPod, a small digital music player weighing just 6.5 ounces and capable of holding about 1,000 songs[12] which was different from other Apple products.

Product development and commercialization might include the integration of services. The combination of a physical product with services makes the product more valuable. Services such as maintenance or training might be integrated into the product development process. For example, Lucent Technologies includes specific review criteria relating to the development of customer documentation and training plans in the process. Supply chain considerations might drive innovative customer-focused solutions which differentiate the product from competitors' offerings, particularly in saturated markets.

Product development and commercialization may include the integration of services. The combination of a physical product with services makes the product more valuable.

[12] Walker, Rob, "The Guts of a New Machine," *The New York Times Magazine,* (November 30, 2003), pp. 78.

Product Development and Commercialization as a Supply Chain Management Process

Each of the eight supply chain processes defined by The Global Supply Chain Forum contains strategic and operational elements. The strategic portion of the product development and commercialization process establishes a structure for developing a product and moving it to the market, providing a template for implementation within the firm. The operational portion is the realization of the process that has been established at the strategic level. Figure 8-2 shows the sequence of sub-processes that comprise the strategic and operational product development and commercialization processes. The lines connecting the sub-processes to the other seven supply chain management processes in the center of the diagram depict the interfaces between each sub-process and the other processes.

Both the strategic and operational processes are led by cross-functional teams. The teams are comprised of managers representing product engineering, research and development, marketing, finance, production, purchasing and logistics. Usually, the teams will include members from outside the firm such as representatives from key customers and/or suppliers. For example, Visteon, a supplier of automotive components, is a key player on the product development and commercialization team of the Ford Motor Company. Similarly, a user advocate is part of the product development and commercialization team at Lucent

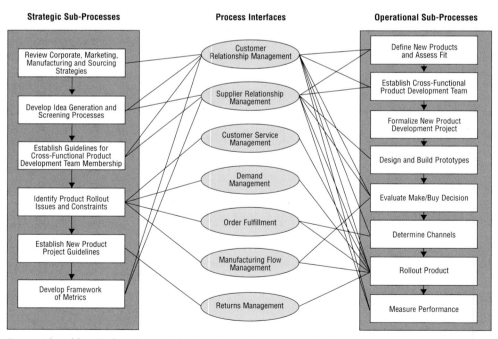

Figure 8-2
Product Development and Commercialization

Source: Adapted from Keely L. Croxton, Sebastián J. García-Dastugue, Douglas M. Lambert, and Dale S. Rogers, "Supply Chain Management: Implementation Issues and Research Opportunities," *The International Journal of Logistics Management*, Vol. 12, No. 2 (2001), p. 27.

Technologies. The user advocate helps identify the customer value proposition for the product during the early stages of development and assists with the formulation of appropriate documentation and training as the product reaches commercialization.

At the strategic level, a process team is responsible for developing the framework for product development and commercialization within the firm. Multiple operational teams have day-to-day responsibility for managing the process for specific development projects. While these various teams have project responsibility, the strategic team maintains control of the overall process.

The Strategic Product Development and Commercialization Process

The objective of the strategic portion of the product development and commercialization process is to construct a formalized structure through which management executes the operational process. That is, the strategic process provides the blueprint for the implementation and is composed of six sub-processes, as shown in Figure 8-3.

Review Corporate, Marketing, Manufacturing and Sourcing Strategies

The first sub-process in the strategic portion of the product development and commercialization process is to review the corporate, marketing, manufacturing and sourcing strategies to determine how they will impact products to be developed and sold. For example, the marketing strategy contains the key customer segment needs assessment.

Corporate and marketing strategies should influence idea generation for products.

Corporate and marketing strategies should influence idea generation for products. These strategies guide budget priorities that are examined to determine specific product development and commercialization objectives. General business strategies are honed into explicit plans that define how the firm's strategy translates into product development and commercialization requirements. The time frames of these strategies are aligned with expected product development cycle times. This gives the product development and commercialization team detailed objectives that are aligned with overall firm strategies and budgets, and include time to market objectives. Research has shown that managers in successful firms clearly communicate the organization's overall strategic direction, and then implement the product development and commercialization process in a manner consistent with their business strategies.[13] For example, a review of a firm's marketing strategy should allow the product development and commercialization team to more effectively identify projects that address customer needs. While the marketing strategy identifies customers, the product development and commercialization process implements the activities to meet the needs of those customers.[14]

The review of corporate, marketing, manufacturing and sourcing strategies is particularly relevant as management establishes the objectives for the product development and commercialization process and examines how resources and competencies support achievement of these objectives. For example, the product

---

[13] Schilling, Melissa A. and Charles W. L. Hill, "Managing the New Product Development Process: Strategic Imperatives," *Academy of Management Executive*, Vol. 12, No. 3 (1998), pp. 67-82.

[14] O'Dwyer, Marie and Tom O'Toole, "Marketing-R&D Interface Contexts in New Product Development," *Irish Marketing Review*, Vol. 11, No. 1 (1998), pp. 59-68.

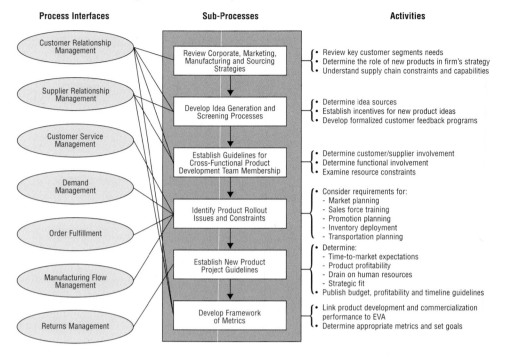

Figure 8-3
The Strategic Product Development and Commercialization Process

Process Interfaces	Sub-Processes	Activities
Customer Relationship Management	Review Corporate, Marketing, Manufacturing and Sourcing Strategies	• Review key customer segments needs • Determine the role of new products in firm's strategy • Understand supply chain constraints and capabilities
Supplier Relationship Management	Develop Idea Generation and Screening Processes	• Determine idea sources • Establish incentives for new product ideas • Develop formalized customer feedback programs
Customer Service Management	Establish Guidelines for Cross-Functional Product Development Team Membership	• Determine customer/supplier involvement • Determine functional involvement • Examine resource constraints
Demand Management	Identify Product Rollout Issues and Constraints	• Consider requirements for: - Market planning - Sales force training - Promotion planning - Inventory deployment - Transportation planning
Order Fulfillment	Establish New Product Project Guidelines	• Determine: - Time-to-market expectations - Product profitability - Drain on human resources - Strategic fit • Publish budget, profitability and timeline guidelines
Manufacturing Flow Management	Develop Framework of Metrics	• Link product development and commercialization performance to EVA • Determine appropriate metrics and set goals
Returns Management		

development and commercialization team at Moen Incorporated is driven by a corporate edict that SKU growth will be proportional to sales growth. Therefore, as the team reviews the organization's three-year product strategy to identify and prioritize new product opportunities, they rank the revenue potential and operational complexity of the opportunities. The revenue potential is provided by the marketing function and is based on market intelligence. Market intelligence is largely driven by gap analyses of the current product portfolio which management uses to identify style and/or price point gaps within the current product mix. The operational complexity rankings are developed through consultations among the sourcing, manufacturing, logistics and engineering functions. These complexity rankings reflect the ability of the organization to source, make and deliver the desired product. The product design can simplify or complicate the execution of the other supply chain management processes. A proliferation of products and product variations might cause complications with little or no payoff.

In addition to reviewing the overall product strategy, the product development and commercialization team reviews the sourcing, manufacturing and marketing strategies in order to assess the fit of the product development objectives with current capabilities. Then, the team provides feedback of future product development requirements to the sourcing, manufacturing and marketing functional areas so that the acquisition of needed capabilities can be integrated into their future strategies.

The product design can simplify or complicate the execution of the other supply chain management processes.

Develop Idea Generation and Screening Procedures

The idea generation and screening procedures are developed next. The outputs of the first sub-process are objectives that will drive the idea generation and screening procedures. This can include determining sources for ideas, considering incentives for developing products for: the focal firm, suppliers, and customers. In addition, this sub-process will begin to develop formalized customer feedback programs. At this point in the product development and commercialization process, there needs to be an interface with the customer relationship management process to determine how new products will impact key customers and whether those products will be accepted.

Ideas for new products may come from several sources, including:[15]
- Marketing and sales personnel.
- Research and technology development teams.
- Product development and commercialization teams.
- Manufacturing and operations organizations.
- Customers and potential customers.
- Suppliers and third parties.
- Competitors and potential competitors.

The product development and commercialization process team should explicitly develop a methodology for generating these opportunities. As an example, 3M has implemented the lead user methodology to generate new ideas. Lead users are defined as users of a given product that expect attractive innovation related benefits and whose needs for a given innovation are typically earlier than the majority of the target market.[16] The lead user method as conducted at 3M involves identifying and learning from lead users both within the target market and in advanced analog markets that have similar needs in a more extreme form.[17] Lead users provide information on both needs and ideas for solutions.

Establish Guidelines for Cross-Functional Product Development Team Membership

It is critical to have the right people from the internal functions along with key customers and suppliers involved in the product development and commercialization process.

Next, the process team establishes guidelines for the membership of the cross-functional product development team. It is critical to have the right people from the internal functions along with key customers and suppliers involved in the product development and commercialization process. The involvement of the process teams from customer relationship management and supplier relationship management is central to managing the relationships across the supply chain. Business rules related to the product development and commercialization process should be included in the product and service agreements (PSAs).

While the strategic product development and commercialization process team is a standing team, the operational level teams are formed on a project by project basis.[18] There are two types of operational product development teams.

---

[15] Ulrich, Karl T. and Steven D. Eppinger, *Product Design and Development*, 3rd Edition, New York, NY: McGraw-Hill/Irwin, 2004.

[16] von Hippel, Eric, *The Sources of Innovation*, New York, NY: Oxford University Press, 1988.

[17] Lilien, Gary L., Pamela D. Morrison, Kathleen Searls, Mary Sonnack, and Eric von Hippel, "Performance Assessment of the Lead User Idea-Generation Process for New Product Development," *Management Science*, Vol. 48, No. 8 (2002), pp. 1042-1059.

Operating and innovating teams[19] are identified based on the underlying objectives of their project. The operating teams are concerned with evolutionary development of current product and service offerings. Operating teams span boundaries, but tend to be more internally focused. Innovating teams, which pursue new business opportunities that are distinct from existing offerings, span organizations and have a wider perspective. Innovating teams interact with consumers, retailers, wholesalers and suppliers. Guidelines established by the strategic level team should take these differences into consideration in terms of establishing the guidelines for team membership.

The strategic product development and commercialization process team works to determine the extent of involvement from key customers and suppliers. Partnerships might be formed with customers and suppliers to complement internal knowledge as well as to learn about new markets and technologies, and reduce overall risk.[20] Relative strengths, weaknesses and roles of personnel within the internal functions are assessed to determine their involvement. Resource constraints are examined to determine which resources can be utilized on specific new product projects.

As part of the product development and commercialization process at Lucent Technologies, specific involvement guidelines by functional area are established for each stage of the process. Functional representatives on the team are identified as either deliverable owner, input provider, or consultant. Functional representatives might include corporate, legal/contract management, development, sales, marketing, services, finance, product management, logistics, intellectual property and standards, quality management as well as an advocate for the user.

Identify Product Rollout Issues and Constraints

The fourth sub-process is the identification of product rollout issues and constraints. Pinch points that will hamper the product development and commercialization process are determined. This sub-process includes considerations of market and promotion planning, sales force training, inventory deployment planning, transportation planning and capacity planning. Each of the internal business functions needs to be involved to avoid poor product rollouts. In addition, the team should get input from the order fulfillment process to assess how new products will impact this process.

It is critical to identify potential commercialization problems and think about solutions to these problems. As part of this sub-process, the team works with the supplier relationship management and manufacturing flow management teams to determine if there are constraints related to components for the new product. In the case of completely outsourced manufacturing, the manufacturing flow management team still helps to identify problems with scheduling or production. A linkage to

It is critical to identify potential commercialization problems and think about solutions to these problems.

---

[18] Pitta, Dennis A., Frank Franzak and Lea P. Katanis, "Redefining New Product Development Teams: Learning to Actualize Consumer Contributions," *Journal of Product & Brand Management*, Vol. 5, No. 6 (1996), pp. 48-60.

[19] Barczak, Gloria and David Wilemon, "Leadership Differences in New Product Development Teams," *Journal of Product Innovation Management*, Vol. 6, No. 4 (1989), pp. 259-267.

[20] McDermott, Richard, "How to Build Communities of Practice in Team Organizations: Learning Across Teams," *Knowledge Management Review*, Vol. 2, No. 2 (1999), pp. 32-37.

order fulfillment assists in the consideration of rollout issues. Typical decisions to be made at this point are initial inventory levels and the positioning of the inventory.

Unisys has standardized product rollout procedures because of the complexity and high cost of their products and the difficulties and expenses associated with sourcing, manufacturing and distribution. Utilizing project management tools that allow all of the key issues to be considered is important when the price of a computer can be greater than $1,000,000. Anticipating pinch points and developing a solution in advance can determine a product's success.

Anticipating pinch points and developing a solution in advance can determine a product's success.

As part of their product development and commercialization process, Lucent Technologies produces a detailed financial assessment, product description and execution plan for a successful rollout. This enables management to examine rollout issues and constraints when making the business decision to commit significant resources to the project.

Establish New Product Project Guidelines

Next, new product project guidelines are established. In this sub-process, expectations for time to market are developed. Product profitability scenarios are developed and the implications for human resources resulting from new product projects are determined. The guidelines for evaluating the strategic fit of new products are established. Ritchey Bicycle Components, a high-end bicycle parts company, provides an example of establishing new product project guidelines. Before a new product is approved, the team must submit a detailed plan that includes budgets and project guidelines to the Chief Operating Officer. If it does not appear that the project will be a strategic fit and successful in the marketplace, the proposed project will not move forward without changes. Finally, budget, profitability, and timeline guidelines are published.

At Unisys after the customer need is identified, the product management process (PMP) begins, encompassing the feasibility, design, development, qualification, support and termination stages of the identified product. To ensure that supply chain requirements are defined and included, Unisys generates detailed documents and provides them to engineering to be embedded in the marketing statement of requirements, the starting point of the PMP process.

Develop Framework of Metrics

The final sub-process is to develop the framework of metrics. Typical process metrics might include time to market, time to profitability and initial sales. As with the other processes, the metrics that are chosen need to be coordinated with the customer relationship management and the supplier relationship management process teams to assure that they do not conflict with other metrics or the firm's overall objectives.

As part of this sub-process, the team develops procedures for analyzing the total cost of product development and commercialization and the impact of new products on current ones. Product development and commercialization can be a key driver of profitability. At Colgate-Palmolive, the development of innovative products with key suppliers has been identified as a strategy for achieving their stretch financial goals.

Figure 8-4 depicts the relationship between product development and commercialization and the firm's financial performance as measured by EVA. EVA

Figure 8-4
How Product Development and Commercialization Affects Economic Value Added (EVA®)

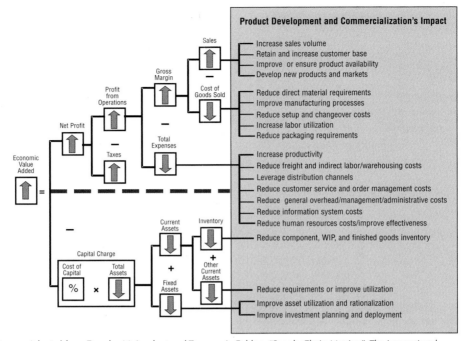

Source: Adapted from Douglas M. Lambert and Terrance L. Pohlen, "Supply Chain Metrics," *The International Journal of Logistics Management,* Vol. 12, No. 1 (2001), p. 10.

considers revenues, costs and profit, as well as the cost of assets required to generate the profits. For example, better management of the product development and commercialization process can lead to sales increases as a result of rolling out successful new products, improving product availability, retaining existing customers, and attracting new customers. Cost of goods sold can be reduced by lowering material requirements, reducing production setup and changeover costs, increasing labor utilization, and reducing packaging requirements.

Expenses can be reduced by increasing productivity, optimizing the physical network of facilities, and leveraging new and/or alternative distribution channels. Management can leverage product development and commercialization to help reduce the costs of freight and warehouse labor, customer service, order management, information, human resources, overhead and/or administrative costs. In many companies, managers not only focus the product development and commercialization activities on developing products to take to market, but find ways to more effectively and efficiently perform supporting processes.

Better management of product development and commercialization can result in reductions in component, work-in-process and finished goods inventories. Other current assets can be reduced as a result of better new product planning and introduction. Finally, better management of new product development and commercialization can lead to lower fixed assets as a result of improved asset utilization and rationalization, and better investment planning and deployment.

The product development and commercialization process can have a significant impact on the profitability of customers.

The product development and commercialization process can have a significant impact on the profitability of customers. For this reason, every attempt should be made to identify and report the revenue, cost, and asset implications of this process on the profitability of key customers and segments of customers. The cost of customer specific assets can be reflected in customer profitability reports by incorporating a charge for assets employed.

The Operational Product Development and Commercialization Process

The operational portion of the product development and commercialization process is the implementation of the structure developed at the strategic level. It is a template for the synchronization of product development and commercialization activities and consists of eight sub-processes as shown in Figure 8-5.

Define New Products and Assess Fit

The objective of this sub-process is to define new products and assess their fit. New product ideas are generated and screened. A market assessment is completed, key customers and suppliers are consulted, and the fit with existing channels, manufacturing, and logistics is determined. This sub-process involves interfaces with customer relationship management and supplier relationship management processes, as well as with the business functions in the firm.

As an example, Moen Incorporated utilizes various forms of customer input in the product development and commercialization process. Moen has used retailer input as a means for identifying new product opportunities. Retail buyers along with their Moen sales representative have identified new product opportunities while reviewing current products within the store aisle. The retail buyer requested a product that was similar to a previously successful product but had certain stylistic adjustments that reflected changes in consumer preferences. The Moen sales representative and the retail buyer contacted a product development and commercialization process team to determine the potential feasibility of the request.

Establish Cross-Functional Product Development Team

Using the guidelines developed at the strategic level, the cross-functional product development and commercialization teams are established. Internal and external parties such as suppliers or customers whose input is necessary for the success of the new product need to be included on the team as early as possible. These teams will be responsible for formalizing the new product development project.

One of the barriers to including suppliers and customers on the product development and commercialization team is the geographical separation of the potential members. Virtual teaming has been proposed as a model and practice that can overcome this geographical barrier.[21] This approach utilizes technology to form collaborative relationships, unconstrained by geography that can quickly

---

[21] Bal, Jay, Richard Wilding, and John Gundry, "Virtual Teaming in the Agile Supply Chain," *The International Journal of Logistics Management*, Vol. 10, No. 2 (1999), pp. 71-82.

Figure 8-5
The Operational Product Development and Commercialization Process

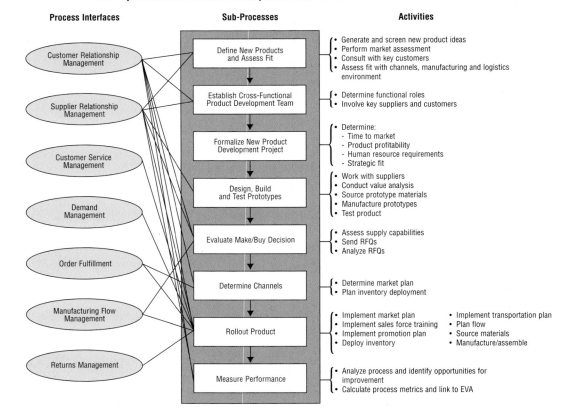

apply knowledge and expertise that affect the product development and commercialization process.

Differences in corporate culture represent another barrier that affects the involvement of suppliers and customers on the team. A culture must exist in each of the organizations involved on the team that facilitates and encourages joint problem solving and decision making across organizational boundaries. The internal functions of the individual organizations must be willing to pursue collaborative relationships. This requires a culture permeating each organization that encourages and values collaboration.[22]

At Unisys, the product development and commercialization team has the involvement of marketing, engineering, sales, operations, logistics, procurement, field service, and external suppliers. The establishment of cross-functional, boundary spanning teams at Unisys is driven by the dedication to the principles of supply chain management and concurrent engineering. When they adhere to these principles, design time and cost is reduced while maintaining product quality and reliability.

Differences in corporate culture represent another barrier that affects the involvement of suppliers and customers on the team.

---

[22] McIvor, R. and P. Humphreys, "Early Supplier Involvement in the Design Process: Lessons from the Electronics Industry," Omega: *The International Journal of Management Science*, Vol. 32, No. 3 (2004), pp. 179-199.

Formalize New Product Development Project

Using the guidelines established at the strategic level, the cross-functional product development teams examine the strategic fit of the new product within the organization's current product portfolio.

Using the guidelines established at the strategic level, the cross-functional product development teams examine the strategic fit of the new product within the organization's current product portfolio. The team works with key suppliers to formalize time to market expectations, product profitability goals, and budget requirements. Any potential implications for human resources are identified and addressed.

The formation of budget and resource needs within this sub-process are particularly relevant given that 75 percent of new product development programs fail commercially,[23] while 55 percent of managers report that product development efforts in their companies failed to meet its sales and profit objectives.[24] The reasons for failure include lack of market information, a failure to listen to the voice of the customer, poor up-front pre-development homework, unstable product definition, poor quality of execution of key product development tasks, and poorly structured, ineffectual project teams.[25] A closer examination of these reasons combined with recent benchmarking studies suggests that many problems are interlinked, and traceable to resource deficiencies.[26] Devoting adequate resources to the project is important for increasing the likelihood of success.

Design, Build and Test Prototypes

The team manages the process of designing, building and testing prototypes of the product ideas. For example, auto companies develop concept cars to test new product ideas. In this phase, teams work with suppliers and perform a value analysis to determine what portions of the product design and rollout process truly add value. Then, they source prototype materials and manufacture product samples. The final step of this sub-process is to test the product.

Ford Motor Company invested in a prototype optimization model with its related expert systems to budget, plan and manage prototype test fleets, and to maintain testing integrity. The model reduced annual prototype costs by more than $250 million.[27] This has shortened the planning process, established global

---

[23] Griffin, A. and Albert L. Page, "PDMA Success Measurement Project: Recommended Measures for Product Development Success and Failure," *Journal of Innovation Management*, Vol. 13, No. 6 (1996), pp. 478-496.

[24] Cooper, Robert G., Scott J. Edgett, and Elko J. Kleinschmidt, "Best Practices for Managing R&D Portfolios," *Research Technology Management*, Vol. 41, No. 4 (1998), pp. 20-33.

[25] See drivers of new product development success in: Mitzi M. Montoya-Weiss, and Roger Calantone, "Determinants of New Product Performance: A Review and Meta Analysis," *Journal of Product Innovation Management*, Vol. 11, No. 5 (1994), pp. 397-417; Sanjay Mishra, Dongwook Kim, and Dae Hoon H. Lee, "Factors Affecting New Product Success: Cross Country Comparisons," *Journal of Product Innovation Management*, Vol. 13, No. 6 (1996), pp. 530-550; and, Robert G. Cooper, "New Products: What Separates the Winners from the Losers," in *PDMA Handbook for New Product Development*, ed. Milton D. Rosenau Jr., New York, NY: John Wiley & Sons, 1996.

[26] Cooper, Robert G. and Scott J. Edgett, "Overcoming the Crunch in Resources for New Product Development," *Research Technology Management*, Vol. 46, No. 3 (2003), pp. 48-58.

[27] Chelst, Kenneth, John Sidelko, Alex Przebienda, Jeffrey Lockledge, and Dimitrios Mihailidis, "Rightsizing and Management of Prototype Vehicle Testing at Ford Motor Company," *Interfaces*, Vol. 31, No. 1 (2001), pp. 91-108.

procedures for prototype development, and created a common structure for communication between budgeting and engineering.[28]

At Harley-Davidson, suppliers that only provide prototypes have been eliminated. Harley-Davidson works exclusively with ultimate production suppliers for the supply of prototypes. While these suppliers will either build prototypes or contract them out to an outside organization, they nonetheless are directly involved in this stage of the process. Management believes that product development success has been improved by having direct design input and oversight from suppliers at the prototype stage.[29]

Evalute Make/Buy Decision

Once the prototypes have been evaluated, the team needs to determine whether the product should be manufactured in-house, or purchased from suppliers. Part of the make/buy decision is to determine how much of the new product should be made in-house and how much by different members of the supply base. In many firms, management has a short-term perspective for make/buy decisions that erodes long-term profitability. These decisions might have strategic implications for the firm and should be formulated from a strategic perspective with senior management involvement.[30]

The decision to outsource or keep the product sourcing and manufacturing within the firm is a critical one. There might be strategic reasons for keeping the product in-house. The need to control costs or to retain product knowledge within the firm might lead management to keep the product in-house. This decision involves interfacing with other supply chain management processes including customer relationship management, manufacturing flow management and supplier relationship management. Once it is determined what will be sourced, supply capabilities are assessed and requests for quotations are sent, received and analyzed.

The need to control costs or to retain product knowledge within the firm might lead management to keep the product in-house.

Determine Channels

In the sixth sub-process, the marketing and distribution channels for the new product are determined. The customer relationship management and order fulfillment process teams provide input at this stage. Then, the market plan for the product is developed, and initial inventory planning is performed.

The team needs to consider the channel choice decision carefully. In some cases, the channel decision is the primary factor in determining a product's success. Strengths and weaknesses of various channels need to be analyzed. Consumer packaged goods companies are often faced with the choice of moving product through mass-merchandise channels where price is low and vendor compliance demands are high, or through lower volume channels where price is

---

[28] Chelst, Kenneth, John Sidelko, Alex Przebienda, Jeffrey Lockledge, and Dimitrios Mihailidis, "Rightsizing and Management of Prototype Vehicle Testing at Ford Motor Company," *Interfaces*, Vol. 31, No. 1 (2001), pp. 91-108.

[29] Fitzgerald, Kevin R., "Purchasing at Harley Links Supply with Design," *Purchasing*, Vol. 122, No. 2 (1997), pp. 56-58.

[30] Humphreys, P. and R. McIvor, and G. Huang, "An Expert System for Evaluating the Make or Buy Decision," *Computers and Industrial Engineering*, Vol. 42, No. 2-4 (2002), pp. 567-585.

protected and logistics requirements are lower. The products might have cost or physical requirements that necessitate specific channel characteristics. It may be useful for the team to work with the customer relationship management team to determine how current and potential customers will react to the new products that will flow through existing or new channels.

At Moen Incorporated, the channel implications of the product development and commercialization process is a critical consideration. Depending on the channel used to rollout the new product, the inventory loading curves will vary. The retail channel requires that minimum inventory levels of the new product are available in their stores at launch. The wholesale channel is characterized by a much slower ramp-up period, but demonstrates a higher level of demand volatility. Moen's retail channel is becoming more demanding with regard to new products. In order to maintain shelf space, Moen must consistently provide retailers with a flow of new product offerings that are specific to their organizations. The wholesale channel is also looking for new products that are specific to individual firms.

Rollout Product

Many products are unsuccessful because of poor product rollout. Materials need to be sourced, inbound materials positioned, and products manufactured and/or assembled. The market plan is implemented, the sales force is trained on the new product offering, and the promotion plan is executed. Inventory is deployed using methodologies developed through the transportation plan. It is important that all of the other processes are involved in planning and executing the product rollout.

In the early 1990s, Coca-Cola developed Fruitopia and Powerade which were juice-based, non-carbonated products. The group responsible for the rollout did not adequately consider the manufacturing and sales requirements for pasteurized beverages. With the majority of their other products, the bottlers would buy concentrate, use a cold-fill process, and distribute the product to stores and restaurants. For juice-based products that required pasteurization, new equipment was needed that the bottling network was not ready to purchase themselves. So, the burden of producing bottled finished product was shifted back to a group that was unfamiliar with rolling out products that did not move in tank trucks. Because they did not anticipate the complexity involved, it took longer to establish Fruitopia and Powerade as strong brands. After rethinking the rollout, they were able to successfully relaunch the brands.

A successful rollout can enhance the impact that a new product has in the marketplace. Having the right amount of product available at the right time in the right place are key elements of product success. No matter how much potential a new product has, if it is not moved to market efficiently and effectively, it is likely that the product development process will not be successful.

Measure Performance

In the final sub-process, performance is measured using the metrics developed at the strategic level, and communicated to the appropriate individuals both within the organization and across the supply chain. Communications with other members of the supply chain are coordinated through the customer relationship management and supplier relationship management processes.

Tracking new product performance is important at Moen Incorporated which has established three distinct product groups: core products, custom products and new products. Moen requires a 95% fill rate for three consecutive months in order to move new products into the core product category.

Conclusions

Product development and commercialization is one of the eight supply chain management processes that transcend the boundaries of the firm. Effectively implementing product development and commercialization can reduce a firm's costs, increase revenues and positively impact Economic Value Added (EVA). The need for managers to implement product development and commercialization across the supply chain is increasingly necessary for business success and value creation. By tapping into the knowledge and skills of other supply chain members, a firm can expand its information resources and gain access to ideas for product development or increased development efficiency.

By tapping into the knowledge and skills of other supply chain members, a firm can expand its information resources and gain access to ideas for product development or increased development efficiency.

The Returns Management Process

*Dale S. Rogers, Douglas M. Lambert, Keely L. Croxton
and Sebastián J. García-Dastugue*

Overview

Returns management is the supply chain management process by which activities associated with returns, reverse logistics, gatekeeping, and avoidance are managed within the firm and across key members of the supply chain.

Returns management is the supply chain management process by which activities associated with returns, reverse logistics, gatekeeping, and avoidance are managed within the firm and across key members of the supply chain.[1] The correct implementation of this process enables management not only to manage the reverse product flow efficiently, but to identify opportunities to reduce unwanted returns and to control reusable assets such as containers. In this chapter, we describe how the returns management process is implemented. The process is described in terms of its sub-processes and activities, and the interfaces with corporate functions, other supply chain management processes and other firms. Examples of successful implementation are provided.

Introduction

The management of returns is important for many firms. In the United States, retail customer returns for general merchandise are estimated to be approximately six percent of revenue.[2] At this rate, returns for the top 30 U.S. non-grocery retailers for 2006 were approximately $67 billion. Return rates can be even higher for specialty retailers. For example, one catalog apparel retailer has experienced return rates of up to 40 percent. Logistics costs associated with managing returns have been estimated at four percent of a firm's total logistics costs.[3] For 2006, this would represent about $52 billion to the U.S. economy. The magnitude of these numbers demonstrates the need for management attention to the returns process.

---

[1] This chapter is based on Dale S. Rogers, Douglas M. Lambert, Keely L. Croxton and Sebastián J. García-Dastugue, "The Returns Management Process," *The International Journal of Logistics Management*, Vol. 13, No. 2 (2002), pp. 1-18.

[2] Rogers, Dale S. and Ron S. Tibben-Lembke, *Going Backwards: Reverse Logistics Trends and Practices*, Pittsburgh, PA: Reverse Logistics Executive Council, 1999.

[3] Rogers, Dale S., Ronald S. Tibben-Lembke, Kasia Banasiak, Karl Brokmann, and Timothy Johnson, "Reverse Logistics Challenges," *Proceedings of the 2001 Council of Logistics Management Annual Conference*, Oak Brook, IL: Council of Logistics Management, 2001, p. 1.

Returns management is a critical supply chain management process that requires planning and effective execution across the firms in the supply chain. Effective implementation of returns management enables executives to identify productivity improvement opportunities. Returns management is a boundary spanning process that requires interaction between members of the supply chain. It encompasses activities such as avoidance and gatekeeping, which are central elements to effective management of the return flow. As part of implementing the process, management needs to measure the financial impact of returns on the firm and on other members of the supply chain.

Returns management is a critical supply chain management process that requires planning and effective execution across the firms in the supply chain.

The chapter is organized as follows. We review the different types of returns and relevant definitions. We then describe the strategic and operational processes that comprise returns management, and present the sub-processes and their activities. Returns management is one of the eight processes and it requires interfaces with the other seven (see Figure 9-1). Therefore, we identify the interfaces with the corporate functions, the other supply chain management processes and other firms. Finally, we present the conclusions.

Types of Returns

There are many types of returns that need to be managed within this process, each of which poses unique challenges. Based on input from The Global Supply Chain Forum, we group returns into five categories: consumer returns, marketing returns, asset returns, product recalls and environmental returns.

Figure 9-1
Supply Chain Management:
Integrating and Managing Business Processes Across the Supply Chain

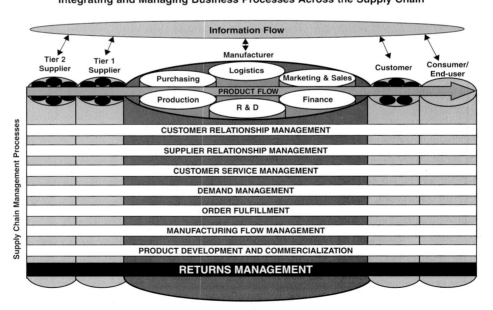

Source: Adapted from Douglas M. Lambert, Martha C. Cooper, and Janus D. Pagh, "Supply Chain Management: Implementation Issues and Research Opportunities," *The International Journal of Logistics Management,* Vol. 9, No. 2 (1998), p. 2.

Consumer Returns

Consumer returns due to buyers' remorse or product defects are generally the largest category of returns. Many companies have liberal returns policies that make it easy for consumers to return products. This is based on the belief that consumers will continue to purchase from a retailer with liberal returns policies which increase the retailer's revenues. For the Christmas 2002 season, Circuit City, a large U.S. retailer of consumer electronics, made returns easier for the customer by not requiring receipts for credit card purchases, since they keep information of past purchases linked to each customer's credit card number. Some companies such as L.L. Bean, a large U.S. based catalog retailer, even have lifetime warranties that allow consumers to return a product after years of ownership.

Marketing Returns

Marketing returns consist of product returned from a position forward in the supply chain. These returns are often due to slow sales, quality issues, or the need to reposition inventory. Other examples of marketing returns include: close-out returns, which are first quality products that the retailer or distributor has decided to no longer carry; buy-outs or "lifts", where one manufacturer purchases a retailer's supply of a competitor's product to get access to shelf space; job-outs, where seasonal merchandise is returned after the season's end; and, surplus and overruns. In many cases, marketing returns can represent a significant percentage of sales.

In addition to returns driven by market issues, some marketing returns are driven by management practices.

In addition to returns driven by market issues, some marketing returns are driven by management practices. For example, end-of-quarter loads to the channel in order to achieve short-term financial results can produce high return rates. Management should identify the costs associated with these returns to evaluate the benefits from artificially loading the channel. Inappropriate incentive systems drive undesired behavior such as loading the channel unnecessarily by misaligning the firm's objectives and those of the sales force. For example, when sales force bonuses are linked to revenues and returns are not taken into account, the objective of some salespeople is to ship products out to the channel. This practice often results in high return rates.

Asset Returns

Asset returns consist of the recapture and repositioning of an asset. These returns are typically characterized as items that management wants to see returned. Categories that fall within asset returns are repositioning of an asset such as oil drilling equipment, and reusable containers. For example, the Ford Customer Service Division of the Ford Motor Company uses a closed-loop reusable collapsible rack system to deliver automobile parts to their dealerships. A truck driver delivers the order in a wheeled cage that collapses to facilitate shipping the cage back to the Ford Customer Service Division distribution center. The driver makes the delivery of the parts and picks up the collapsed cages from the previous order. This racking system has reduced the overall delivery cost and is also environmentally friendly.

Reusable totes are another example of a desirable return that has become a standard in many industries. At Baker and Taylor, a book, music, and video wholesaler, reusable plastic totes are used to move product between Baker and

Taylor and some of its customers such as Amazon. These totes are stackable, protect the product better than corrugated cardboard and are less expensive on a per movement basis. The use of reusable pallets, racks or totes should be coordinated with customer relationship management and/or supplier relationship management process teams.

Product Recalls

Product recalls are a form of return that are usually initiated because of a safety or quality issue. Recalls can be voluntary or mandated by a government agency. They require more up-front planning than most other return types, and this planning is central to managing them effectively.[4] Information technology and effective communications play a central roll in the management of product recalls. For industries that are susceptible to recalls, like the automotive or food industries, part of designing an effective returns management process is developing procedures for informing customers of a recall and efficiently handling the return.

Environmental Returns

Environmental returns include the disposal of hazardous materials or abiding by environmental regulations. Environmental returns are different from other types of returns because they might include regulatory compliance that limits the set of options. Additionally, there are often stringent documentation and audit requirements. For example, the Environmental Protection Agency in the United States has banned computer monitors that use cathode ray tubes from landfills since 1992 because of the lead content in the components.[5] Due to this regulation, the firms responsible for the cathode ray tubes need to have a process in place to dispose of the unusable computer monitors.

In the European Union (EU), producer responsibility regulations have been adopted. For example, the EU Packaging Waste Directive established the concept of the "polluter pays" by sharing the responsibility for waste packaging recovery across the whole supply chain. This legislation has helped to dramatically reduce packaging waste. In 2001, German firms recovered 80 percent of packaging and Dutch firms recovered 65 percent.[6]

Summary

When designing a returns management process, managers need to consider each type of return and develop procedures that are appropriate for each one. The type of return might have a different impact within the firm and on other firms in the supply chain. For instance, a return that affects a consumer could have a long lasting effect on the market's perception of the firm; thus, management might take marketing considerations into account to find the best procedure to handle the event. In contrast, for a return in which there is no direct effect on the consumer, the key

When designing a returns management process, managers need to consider each type of return and develop procedures that are appropriate for each one.

---

[4] Smith, N. Craig, Robert J. Thomas and John A. Quelch, "A Strategic Approach to Managing Product Recalls," *Harvard Business Review*, Vol. 74, No. 5 (1997), pp. 102-112.

[5] Raymond Communications, *Transportation Packaging and the Environment*, College Park, MD: Raymond Communications, 1997.

[6] Fernie, John, and Cathy Hart, "UK Packaging Waste Legislation Implications for Food Retailers," *British Food Journal*, Vol. 103, No. 3 (2001), pp. 187-199.

considerations might be limited to finding the most cost effective return flow option. Similarly, returns due to product failure might require interfaces with the supplier relationship management and/or product development and commercialization process teams, while returns due to consumer remorse might not.

Defining Returns Management

Terms such as reverse logistics, closed-loop supply chain management, and returns have been used to describe some of the activities in returns management. However, these terms do not adequately describe the returns management process.

Terms such as reverse logistics, closed-loop supply chain management, and returns have been used to describe some of the activities in returns management. However, these terms do not adequately describe the returns management process. For example, reverse logistics has been defined to be:

> The process of planning, implementing, and controlling the efficient, cost effective flow of raw materials, in-process inventory, finished goods and related information from the point of consumption to the point of origin for the purpose of recapturing value or proper disposal.[7]

Reverse logistics is the process of moving goods from their typical final destination for the purpose of capturing value, or proper disposal. Remanufacturing and refurbishing activities also may be included in the definition of reverse logistics, as well as processing returned merchandise due to damage, seasonal inventory, salvage, recalls, and repositioning of inventory. It also includes recycling programs, hazardous material programs, obsolete equipment disposition, and asset recovery. While reverse logistics is a useful term, it does not include all activities involved in managing the return flow of materials and information through the supply chain. Reverse logistics is limited to the movement of goods or materials "backward" through the supply chain. Returns management is much broader in scope.

Another phrase that has been coined to attempt to describe these activities is closed-loop supply chain management, which has been defined as:

> Supply chains that are designed to consider the acquisition and return flows of products, reuse activities, and the distribution of the recovered products.[8]

This definition is helpful because it recognizes that both forward and backward flows need to be managed in the supply chain. However, it does not help in understanding the activities that make up the management of the return flows.

Another term often used to describe the backward flow of goods is returns. The Supply Chain Council expanded their definition of the SCOR model to include returns in 2000. The Council has defined returns to be:

> Processes associated with returning or receiving returned products for any reason. These processes extend into post-delivery customer support.[9]

This definition appears to focus on the physical movement of goods backwards in the supply chain and does not include critical activities such as gatekeeping and avoidance. Also, the SCOR returns process does not include activities required for the financial management of returns nor does it link returns

---

[7] Rogers, Dale S. and Ron S. Tibben-Lembke, *Going Backwards: Reverse Logistics Trends and Practices,* Pittsburgh, PA: Reverse Logistics Executive Council, 1999, p. 2.

[8] Guide, Jr., Daniel., "The Development of Closed-Loop Supply Chains," Presentation to CIMSO Supply Chain Forum, Insead, November 20, 2001.

[9] Supply-Chain Operations Reference-model: SCOR Overview Version 8.0, Pittsburgh PA: Supply-Chain Council, 2006, p. 7.

to the financial performance of the firm.

The term used throughout this article to describe the process is returns management which we define as follows:

> Returns management is that part of supply chain management that includes returns, reverse logistics, gatekeeping, and avoidance.

This definition includes activities that are critical to supply chain management such as avoidance and gatekeeping. Avoidance involves finding ways to minimize the number of return requests. It can include ensuring that the quality of product and user friendliness for the consumer is at the highest attainable level before the product is sold and shipped, or changing promotional programs that load the trade when there is no realistic chance that the product shipped to the customer will be sold.

Gatekeeping means making decisions to limit the number of items that are allowed into the reverse flow. Successful gatekeeping allows management to control and reduce returns without damaging customer service. Gatekeeping eliminates the cost associated with returning products that should not be returned or the cost of products returned to the inappropriate destination. The point of entry into the reverse flow is the best point to eliminate unnecessary cost and management of materials by screening unwarranted returned merchandise.

Returns Management as a Supply Chain Management Process

Each of the eight supply chain management processes defined by The Global Supply Chain Forum contains strategic and operational elements.[10] The strategic portion of returns management establishes a structure for implementation of the process within the firm and across key members of the supply chain. The operational portion is the realization of the process that has been established at the strategic level. Figure 9-2 shows the sequence of sub-processes that comprise strategic and operational returns management. The lines connecting the sub-processes to the other seven supply chain management processes in the center of the diagram depict the interfaces between each sub-process and these processes.

Both the strategic and operational processes are led by a management team that is comprised of managers from several functions including marketing, finance, production, purchasing and logistics. In some cases, the team may include members from outside the firm such as customers, suppliers or representatives from third-party service companies. For example, Genco, a third-party provider, is a key player on the returns management team of Sears, a U.S. retailer. When management of Sears considers a change in their returns process, Genco is usually part of the team that analyzes the data and develops options.

The process team is responsible for developing the procedures at the strategic level and seeing that they are implemented. This team also has day-to-day responsibility for managing the process at the operational level. While firm employees outside of the team might execute parts of the process, the team maintains managerial control.

> **Returns management is that part of supply chain management that includes returns, reverse logistics, gatekeeping, and avoidance.**

---

[10] Croxton, Keely L., Sebastián García-Dastugue, Douglas M. Lambert and Dale S. Rogers, "The Supply Chain Management Processes," *The International Journal of Logistics Management,* Vol. 12, No. 2 (2001), pp. 13-36.

Figure 9-2
Returns Management

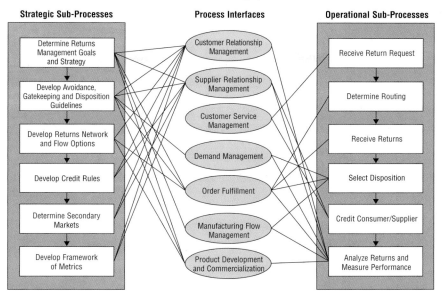

Strategic Sub-Processes	Process Interfaces	Operational Sub-Processes
Determine Returns Management Goals and Strategy	Customer Relationship Management	Receive Return Request
Develop Avoidance, Gatekeeping and Disposition Guidelines	Supplier Relationship Management	Determine Routing
Develop Returns Network and Flow Options	Customer Service Management	Receive Returns
Develop Credit Rules	Demand Management	Select Disposition
Determine Secondary Markets	Order Fulfillment	Credit Consumer/Supplier
Develop Framework of Metrics	Manufacturing Flow Management	Analyze Returns and Measure Performance
	Product Development and Commercialization	

Source: Adapted from Keely L. Croxton, Sebastián García-Dastugue, Douglas M. Lambert, and Dale S. Rogers, "The Supply Chain Management Processes," *The International Journal of Logistics Management*, Vol. 12, No. 2 (2001), p. 19.

The Strategic Returns Management Process

The objective of the strategic portion of the returns management process is to construct a formalized structure through which the operational process is executed. It provides the blueprint for the implementation of returns management. The strategic process is composed of six sub-processes, as shown in Figure 9-3.

Determine Returns Management Goals and Strategy

A firm's returns management capabilities can be used strategically to enhance the overall performance of the company.

A firm's returns management capabilities can be used strategically to enhance the overall performance of the company. For example, returns policies can be used to improve customer loyalty, improve profits, and enhance the brand or firm's public image.

Returns policies can be used to improve customer loyalty by reducing risk to the customer. A buyer for a retailer will be more likely to purchase a new product if he/she knows that it can be returned if the product does not sell. For example, an electronics distributor facing a period of volatile memory chip prices used their returns policy to help resellers better control inventories. By allowing resellers to return anything within a reasonable timeframe, customers' risk is reduced.[11] Consumers are also more likely to buy a product that can be returned if they experience buyer's remorse.[12] Allowing returns is critical to the catalog apparel

---

[11] Rogers, Dale S. and Ron S. Tibben-Lembke, *Going Backwards: Reverse Logistics Trends and Practices,* Pittsburgh, PA: Reverse Logistics Executive Council, 1999.

[12] Banker, Steve, "e-Business and Reverse Logistics," ebizQ, ITQuadrant, Inc. December 24, 2001 (b2b.ebizq.net).

Figure 9-3
The Strategic Returns Management Process

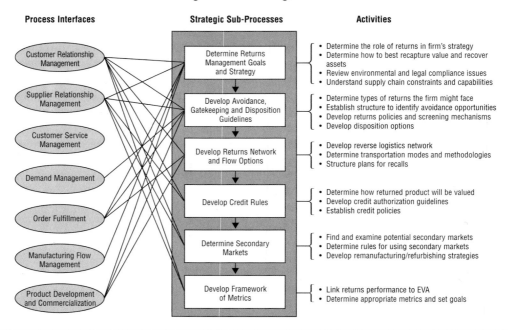

Process Interfaces	Strategic Sub-Processes	Activities
Customer Relationship Management	Determine Returns Management Goals and Strategy	• Determine the role of returns in firm's strategy • Determine how to best recapture value and recover assets • Review environmental and legal compliance issues • Understand supply chain constraints and capabilities
Supplier Relationship Management	Develop Avoidance, Gatekeeping and Disposition Guidelines	• Determine types of returns the firm might face • Establish structure to identify avoidance opportunities • Develop returns policies and screening mechanisms • Develop disposition options
Customer Service Management	Develop Returns Network and Flow Options	• Develop reverse logistics network • Determine transportation modes and methodologies • Structure plans for recalls
Demand Management	Develop Credit Rules	• Determine how returned product will be valued • Develop credit authorization guidelines • Establish credit policies
Order Fulfillment	Determine Secondary Markets	• Find and examine potential secondary markets • Determine rules for using secondary markets • Develop remanufacturing/refurbishing strategies
Manufacturing Flow Management	Develop Framework of Metrics	• Link returns performance to EVA • Determine appropriate metrics and set goals
Product Development and Commercialization		

business because most consumers need the assurance that they can return something if it does not fit or otherwise meet their expectations.

Management can also use returns policies to improve loyalty from small wholesalers or retailers by helping them control their inventories. Often these customers will buy large quantities of one product on a deal offered by a salesperson, but then are unable to purchase other products later from the same company because their inventory levels are too high or their credit lines are full. It may be in the best interest of the supplier to allow customers to return product that is not selling to help reduce these inventory and credit-line constraints.

In addition, return policies can be used to directly improve profits. For example, manufacturers can use returns management capabilities to protect marketing channels. They may pull product off the shelf and bring it back for refurbishment or disposal in order to make certain that the product is not sold through channels that might damage the value of the brand. For some high-end brands, it is critical for the long-term value of the brand to protect the channel and not allow leakage into inappropriate channels. For example, when Federated Department Stores rebranded some of its Florida stores as Burdines, Mitchell & Ness, a high-end manufacturer of authentic throwback sports jerseys, pulled its products from the Burdines' stores to protect its brand image. Mitchell & Ness management used the company's returns management abilities to reposition the inventory in the appropriate chanels.

In addition, return policies can be used to directly improve profits.

Recapturing value and recovering assets is another strategic use of returns that can reduce costs and improve profits. Innovative ways of reusing materials, or refurbishing and reselling products, whether through primary or secondary channels, can be an important source of revenue. In interviews, we found that firms with asset recovery programs achieve significant bottom-line profits as a result.

Another way a firm can improve profits is using returns capabilities to adjust which products are being offered to the consumer. The most important asset a retail store has is its retail space. To maximize profit per square foot of selling space, management needs the flexibility to take slow-moving items off the shelf and replace them with fast-movers. Traditionally, retailers compensated for mistakes with markdowns. Increasingly, the returns management capabilities of the supply chain are being used to keep the products fresh and other outlets are being used for the slow-moving products.[13]

Management can also use returns to enhance the firm's public image or exhibit good citizenship by doing what they believe is the right thing. For example, some companies engage in voluntary recycling programs with their products. Nike, Inc. established the Reuse-A-Shoe program where old athletic shoes are collected and sorted, and those that are in good condition are donated to charity. The remaining shoes are shipped to Nike's shredding facility. The recycled material is used to make running tracks, athletic courts and playground surfaces.[14]

In order to design a returns management system, the process team needs to first consider the role that returns play in their firm's overall customer service strategy and the ways returns management might contribute to improved profits.

In order to design a returns management system, the process team needs to first consider the role that returns play in their firm's overall customer service strategy and the ways returns management might contribute to improved profits. This should be done in conjunction with the customer relationship management process team who will best understand the needs and expectations of the customers.

Another key consideration in determining the goals of the returns management process is to understand the environmental and legal compliance issues that impact the firm and the supply chain. In many firms, environmental and legal issues are the impetus to start improving returns management. Laws that apply to used product and product planned for disposal need to be understood by team members. For example, in one U.S. state, Minnesota, it has been ruled that automotive shocks and struts cannot be placed in landfills.[15] Various computer components are banned from landfills, including circuit boards with high lead content and computer monitors with cathode ray tubes. Each member of the supply chain needs to understand and minimize the environmental impact of returned materials. This step could also include developing guidelines for measuring the environmental impact of particular modes of transport, obtaining ISO 14000 certification, reducing usage of hazardous materials and decreasing unnecessary packaging. In many cases, there will be an interface with the product development and commercialization process because the product and packaging will have to be designed with these environmental issues in mind.

Compliance with legal requirements is a minimum baseline. Firms that appear to be environmentally careless risk offending a large portion of the

---

[13] Rogers, Dale S. and Ron S. Tibben-Lembke, *Going Backwards: Reverse Logistics Trends and Practices,* Pittsburgh, PA: Reverse Logistics Executive Council, 1999.

[14] Goldfield, Robert, "Nike tests curbside recycling of shoes," *The Business Journal Portland,* June 1, 2001.

[15] Rogers, Dale S. and Ron S. Tibben-Lembke, *Going Backwards: Reverse Logistics Trends and Practices,* Pittsbugh, PA: Reverse Logistics Executive Council, 1999.

consumer base. For example, firms that wish to sell to the European market need to be aware of the Green Dot initiative. The Green Dot is the logo for the Duales System Deutschland which is a joint effort by 400 firms in Germany to try to meet the German government's quotas for recycling packaging. When the Green Dot trademark was implemented in Germany, it set a new standard for extended producer responsibility. For example, to obtain the right to place the Green Dot symbol on their product packaging, German beverage brand owners must ensure that at least 72 percent of their bottles are refillable and that deposits are charged on all non-refillable containers. A package stamped with a Green Dot indicates the brand owner is paying its fair share of waste recovery.[16]

In industries that could be subject to product recalls, the team also needs to review the legal issues that arise in the event of a recall. Product recalls can either be mandated by a government agency, or they can be initiated by one of the members of the supply chain. Either way, there are legal and ethical issues that need to be addressed. For example, in the infant care industry, product recalls occur frequently. Firms that operate in this industry need to identify and remove affected product from the supply chain quickly when a product recall issue develops.

Part of developing the returns management strategy is understanding the constraints and capabilities of the firm and the supply chain. This requires interfaces with the order fulfillment and manufacturing flow management processes. Order fulfillment assists the returns management process team in understanding the boundaries around the physical flow and the information technology capabilities and constraints of the logistics system. Manufacturing flow management provides costs and capacity available for remanufacturing and refurbishing in order to identify the best options to recapture value and recover assets.

There is also an interface with the supplier relationship management process. Firms such as large retailers determine their returns management strategy in conjunction with their buying group. The PSAs that are developed with suppliers include policies regarding returns.

Develop Return Avoidance, Gatekeeping and Disposition Guidelines

The second step in the strategic returns management process is to develop return avoidance, gatekeeping and disposition guidelines. This step includes determining the types of returns the firm might face, and developing policies and screening mechanisms to handle those anticipated returns. The team in conjuction with suppliers and customers will develop disposition options for returned items and establish the structure to identify avoidance opportunities.

The use of effective avoidance, gatekeeping and disposition procedures minimizes the cost of moving returned items back through the supply chain. Avoidance aims at reducing the number of return requests. The goal of gatekeeping is to identify as early as possible what products should be accepted as a return. The disposition procedures will enable quick routing of a return to the most appropriate destination.   Interfaces with order fulfillment, demand management, supplier relationship management, and product development and commercialization facilitate the construction of these guidelines. Order fulfillment assists the returns

The use of effective avoidance, gatekeeping and disposition procedures minimizes the cost of moving returned items back through the supply chain.

---

[16] Menzies, David, "Reduce, Reuse, Reject," *Canadian Business*, Vol. 73, No. 24 (2000), pp. 135-136.

management process with developing disposition guidelines that reflect the capabilities of the distribution system. Demand management provides long-term forecasts which can be used to structure the disposition guidelines. Supplier relationship management coordinates with suppliers to determine appropriate avoidance and gatekeeping procedures. The link between this sub-process and product development and commercialization facilitates communication about product quality which is critical to return avoidance.

Return avoidance means developing and selling the product in a manner such that return requests are minimized. This is a critical part of returns management and differentiates this process from reverse logistics and the traditional view of returns.

Return Avoidance. Return avoidance means developing and selling the product in a manner such that return requests are minimized. This is a critical part of returns management and differentiates this process from reverse logistics and the traditional view of returns.

Avoidance can be accomplished in a number of ways. For example, it can be derived from improved quality by having fewer items that are defective, or by giving better instructions to the consumer regarding how to properly operate the product. In some consumer electronics categories, over half of the products returned are classified as "no-fault found." In many of these cases, the product was returned because the consumer did not know how to operate it properly. In the computer industry, return avoidance has been improved through "ease-of-use" initiatives,[17] such as a setup poster included inside a computer's shipping box. Because consumers are often intimidated by the complexity of the computer and the accompanying setup manuals, or refuse to read the setup manuals, PC manufacturers include an easy to understand poster that includes pictures and minimal text to improve the consumer's experience and reduce the number of unnecessary support calls and returns. For the TIVO tapeless video recorder and player, many consumers were unaware of the product complexity, that it required a phone line and there was a recurring monthly charge. This misunderstanding by the consumer resulted in many first quality, fully functional TIVO machines being returned to the store. The high return rate could have been reduced if retail sales personnel had been better trained to explain to the consumer how the product functioned.

Black and Decker integrates the returns process with product development to learn from the returns how to develop better products, increase ease-of-use, and minimize future returns. Most Black and Decker returns from around the U.S. flow back to the National Disposition Center in Nashville, Tennessee. The National Disposition Center includes a laboratory for product engineers so that they can evaluate the defective products and work to develop solutions to improve quality or ease-of-use. This has decreased the time it takes to make engineering changes, and reduced the amount of defective product sold.

Consistency of product can be critical in return avoidance. For the catalog business at Victoria's Secret, a lingerie retailer, many returns are a result of sizing issues. If their suppliers do not consistently size the product, consumers might order the wrong size. Victoria's Secret incurs the cost of shipping the item back to the distribution center and putting it back into stock. In order to reduce the number of returns, management works with suppliers to apply sizing guidelines across all

---

[17] Brown, Bruce, "PC Ease of Use: Getting Better ~or Worse?" *Extreme Tech*, July 10, 2001 Ziff Davis Media Inc. (www.extremetech.com).

products in a uniform manner. This reduces the costs associated with returns and improves customer satisfaction. In situations where suppliers have a direct effect on the amount of returns, the returns management team must coordinate with the supplier relationship management team so that suppliers know their role in avoidance.

Internal procedures and metrics can lead to returns. For example, if sales people engage in end-of-quarter loads, some customer firms will accept the product and return unsold product later, despite the fact that both seller and buyer anticipated that some of the product would be returned. In some cases, internal procedures that drive returns reach the end-customer. For instance, catalog retailers frequently offer free shipping if customers spend more than a set minimum. Some customers will spend more than the required amount only to get the free shipping, with intentions to return some of the items. At the strategic level, the process team develops procedures that will be used to identify avoidance opportunities. At the operational level, the team will look for sources of these unnecessary returns and try to change the internal policies to limit them.

Gatekeeping. Gatekeeping is the screening of both the return request and the returned merchandise.[18] When the return request is initiated, it might be possible to divert it to technical support to assist the customer on the appropriate use of the product to avoid the need for the return. If a product is returned, gatekeeping is the screening of the product to determine if it is a valid return. The gatekeeping guidelines include the description of returns that are allowed. Gatekeeping assures that only product that should be returned to a specific point in the returns network is allowed to enter the return flow. Preventing unwarranted returned merchandise from entering the channel improves the disposition of the warranted goods. By gatekeeping at the point of entry into the reverse flow, unnecessary costs can be eliminated. However, there might be more than one gatekeeping point in the supply chain.

Gatekeeping is the screening of both the return request and the returned merchandise.

Failure in gatekeeping can create significant friction between supplier and customer firms, not to mention lost revenue and higher costs. Store-level clerks and front-line personnel are often unwilling or unable to gatekeep returns. Once a sales associate makes a decision about a return, it is usually not overturned. Unwarranted return problems are exacerbated because items that should not be in the return flow continue to pick up additional costs as they travel back through the supply chain. Thus, the sales associates have the power and the responsibility to avoid unnecessary cost. Management has to make sure that sales associates are aware of this and have the necessary information and empowerment to make the right decisions.

Nintendo, the electronic game manufacturer, has developed a particularly innovative gatekeeping system. They encourage retailers to register the game machine at the point of sale. If the game machine is returned to the store, Nintendo and the retailer can determine if the product is covered by warranty, and if it is being returned inside the allotted time. A window was added to the package that allows the product's serial number to be scanned at the point-of-sale. This information updates a database that a retailer can access when the customer brings

---

[18] Rogers, Dale S. and Ron S. Tibben-Lembke, *Going Backwards: Reverse Logistics Trends and Practices,* Pittsburgh, PA: Reverse Logistics Executive Council, 1999.

back a Nintendo machine.[19] This gatekeeping system has become so successful for Nintendo that a spin-off firm, SiRas, has been established to sell the Nintendo gatekeeping solution commercially.

The implementation of effective gatekeeping usually involves integrating some activities with other members of the supply chain. Thus, the involvement of the customer relationship management and supplier relationship management process teams is central to managing the relationships across the supply chain. Considerations related to returns are likely to be an item to be included in the product and service agreements (PSAs).

Disposition refers to the decision about what to do with returned product, which might include resale through secondary markets, recycle, remanufacture or transfer to a landfill.

Disposition. Disposition refers to the decision about what to do with returned product, which might include resale through secondary markets, recycle, remanufacture or transfer to a landfill. The disposition guidelines define the returned items ultimate destiny. A firm forward in the supply chain should make disposition decisions quickly, particularly with products that have date codes or lose value over time. Rules need to be developed for disposition options in conjunction with other members of the supply chain, as well as with input from other processes, such as customer relationship management, product development and commercialization, and supplier relationship management. For example, returning an item to the vendor needs to be accomplished in accordance with the PSA with the supplier that was developed through the supplier relationship management process.

Develop Returns Network and Flow Options

Next, the returns network and flow options are determined. The team develops the reverse logistics network and evaluates if it is appropriate to outsource any of the returns management activities to third-party logistics providers. Transportation modes and methodologies are determined during this sub-process. For example, managers might decide that utilizing backhauls is the most efficient way of transporting returns. For some firms, a network of central return centers might be established to handle returned product separately from products moving forward toward the consumer. Rogers and Tibben-Lembke found that for many firms, distribution centers do not effectively handle both forward and reverse flows.[20]

The customer relationship management team helps assure that the returns management process meets customers' expectations.

This step in the process is completed with input from the customer relationship management, order fulfillment, and product development and commercialization process teams. The customer relationship management team helps assure that the returns management process meets customers' expectations. Input from the order fulfillment process team is important because both forward and reverse flows might use the same resources or systems. If management wants to analyze the returned product and provide feedback into the development of new products, then the product development and commercialization process team should be involved in designing the returns network.

When developing the returns network, the team must consider the different

---

[19] Rogers, Dale S. and Ron S. Tibben-Lembke, *Going Backwards: Reverse Logistics Trends and Practices,* Pittsburgh, PA: Reverse Logistics Executive Council, 1999.

[20] Rogers, Dale S. and Ron S. Tibben-Lembke, *Going Backwards: Reverse Logistics Trends and Practices,* Pittsburgh, PA: Reverse Logistics Executive Council, 1999.

types of returns and develop procedures that meet the needs of each one. For instance, product recalls usually require an efficient communication system with consumers, and a well thought-out process for how material will be returned and handled. Having the ability to respond to the unexpected can be critical. In 1982, cyanide was put into unopened bottles of Tylenol, poisoning several people in the Chicago area. McNeil Laboratories' response was to immediately recall approximately 31 million bottles of the pain reliever, with a retail value of more than $100 million. The company quickly took the product off the shelf, analyzed all of it for further tampering, and offered consumers incentives such as free replacement of capsules with caplets and coupons for future purchases. The recall was executed with a returns management system that immediately cleansed the channel of any possibly tainted product. Because they acted quickly and competently, long-term sales were not affected negatively and the perception of the brand was strengthened.[21]

Develop Credit Rules

The next sub-process in strategic returns management is to develop credit rules. In this sub-process, general guidelines are established with input from suppliers and customers that will determine how returned merchandise will be valued. Credit authorization guidelines will be developed and credit policies established. Since this involves customers and suppliers, the customer relationship management and the supplier relationship management process teams should be involved in determining the rules that will be included in the PSAs. Determining the value of used items that are returned and unused items that have not sold well also takes place in this sub-process.

Determine Secondary Markets

Once it has been determined where in the supply chain the returned product will be shipped, the process team can examine potential secondary markets. The team will determine which secondary markets are most appropriate. These secondary markets can include Internet-based auctions, or retailers that specialize in returned goods or "seconds." Often, manufacturers that utilize outlet malls as a secondary market will require that the store selling their second products not be located near a retailer for their first quality or new product.

Firms that choose to obtain additional value from items that have been returned must consider sales cannibalization of first quality items and the impact of secondary markets on brand image. For many years the large American automobile companies did not sell remanufactured or refurbished aftermarket parts because they did not want to damage sales of new parts. When they chose not to sell remanufactured parts, an entire industry of salvage dealers and remanufacturers grew to fill the need for less expensive auto parts. The large automobile companies recognized that selling refurbished parts could be as profitable as the new parts business and have now entered this business. If cannibalization is an issue, the team should interface with the customer relationship management and supplier relationship management processes to develop programs that benefit all concerned parties.

Firms that choose to obtain additional value from items that have been returned must consider sales cannibalization of first quality items and the impact of secondary markets on brand image.

---

[21] Roberts, Sally, "Tragedy Spurred Innovation," *Business Insurance*, Vol. 36, No. 42 (2002), pp. 1, 54.

Develop Framework of Metrics

The team should develop procedures for analyzing return rates and tracing the returns back to the root causes.

The last sub-process of strategic returns management is developing the framework of metrics. Metrics that might be used include return rates and financial impact of returns. The team should develop procedures for analyzing return rates and tracing the returns back to the root causes. Measures such as amount of product to be reclaimed and resold as is, or percentage of material recycled are examples of such metrics. For example, at Victoria's Secret Catalog, managers track the cost of returns, what items customers are returning and why, the return percentage, and the percentage of the garments that may be resold. This analysis of returns, in an industry that traditionally has high returns costs, has resulted in a more effective system. For catalog retailers, returns can be a key driver of profitability.

Key metrics should be developed in conjunction with the customer relationship management and supplier relationship management processes, and be included in the PSAs. These agreements might include policies and procedures for handling returns from the customers. Returns management can impact critical firm metrics such as economic value added (EVA). Figure 9-4 depicts the relationship between returns management and EVA. EVA considers not only revenues, costs and profit, but also the cost of assets required to earn stated profits.[22]

For example, better returns management can increase sales through removing

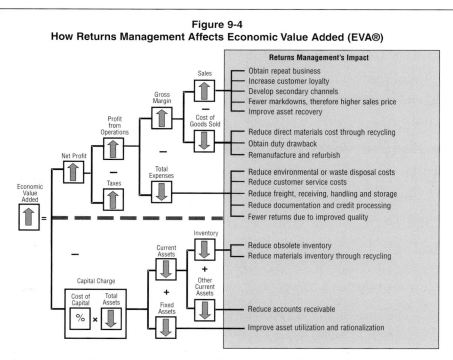

Figure 9-4
How Returns Management Affects Economic Value Added (EVA®)

Source: Framework adapted from Douglas M. Lambert and Terrance L. Pohlen, "Supply Chain Metrics," *The International Journal of Logistics Management*, Vol. 12, No. 1 (2001), p. 10.

---

[22] Bennett, Stewart G., III, *The Quest for Value: A Guide for Managers*, 2nd Edition, New York, NY: Harper Collins, 1999.

risk from the customer and transferring it back to the firm. This will increase customer loyalty and the probability of obtaining repeat business. Also, sales are increased by the sale of returned products through secondary channels. Returns management improves product freshness by moving slow selling items off of the sales floor and keeping the channel clear. Through avoidance efforts, policies that load the trade will be questioned which also leads to lower markdowns, as well as reduced demand variability which is an objective of the demand management process. Cost of goods sold can be reduced through recycling. The use of remanufactured and refurbished product also reduces the cost of materials. A firm might be entitled to duty drawback for imported products that are returned which reduces the cost of goods sold.

Expenses can be reduced through better management of packaging or products with less negative environmental impact and lower waste disposal costs. Using better returns management can reduce customer service costs, freight and handling costs, documentation and credit processing, and the costs of returns related to poor quality.

Better management of returns can lead to reduction of obsolete inventory both within the firm and throughout the supply chain. Sometimes recycled materials can be used in place of new raw materials so that the value of raw materials inventories can be reduced. Accounts receivable can be improved through better credit management. Better returns management can result in lower fixed assets for investments such as buildings and equipment, particularly if the volume of returns is significantly reduced or third-party providers are used.

The returns management process can have a significant impact on the profitability of customers. For this reason, every attempt should be made to identify and report the revenue, cost, and asset implications of returns management on the profitability of key customers and segments of customers. Changes in assets can be reflected in customer profitability reports by incorporating a charge for assets employed.

The returns management process can have a significant impact on the profitability of customers.

The Operational Returns Management Process

The operational portion of returns management is the realization of the process developed at the strategic level. For returns management, the operational portion is a template for managing returns transactions. It consists of six sub-processes, as shown in Figure 9-5.

Receive Return Request

The process is initiated when a return request is received from the customer who could either be a consumer or another firm downstream in the supply chain. Returns might result from consumers bringing an item back to the store, or they might be marketing returns from retailers or distributors due to slow sales, clearing credit lines, or stock rotation. In some cases, the return requests will come through the customer service management process. For firms with catalog business such as Victoria's Secret, the consumer can submit a return request through the Internet, over the phone, or simply return the item through the mail.

At Hewlett-Packard, when a customer needs to replace a used printer toner cartridge, the returns management process begins when a customer calls a local

Figure 9-5
The Operational Returns Management Process

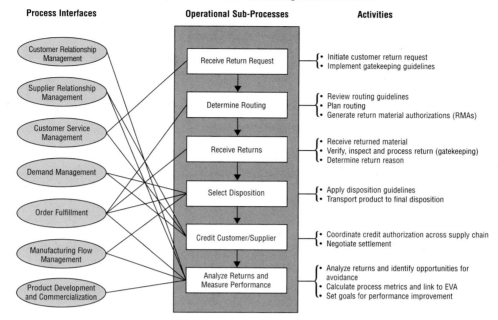

Process Interfaces	Operational Sub-Processes	Activities

Receive Return Request
- Initiate customer return request
- Implement gatekeeping guidelines

Determine Routing
- Review routing guidelines
- Plan routing
- Generate return material authorizations (RMAs)

Receive Returns
- Receive returned material
- Verify, inspect and process return (gatekeeping)
- Determine return reason

Select Disposition
- Apply disposition guidelines
- Transport product to final disposition

Credit Customer/Supplier
- Coordinate credit authorization across supply chain
- Negotiate settlement

Analyze Returns and Measure Performance
- Analyze returns and identify opportunities for avoidance
- Calculate process metrics and link to EVA
- Set goals for performance improvement

Process Interfaces: Customer Relationship Management, Supplier Relationship Management, Customer Service Management, Demand Management, Order Fulfillment, Manufacturing Flow Management, Product Development and Commercialization

phone number for collection of their boxed, empty toner cartridges. In some cases, a third-party firm handles the customer's calls and picks up the used cartridges from the customer's site. Hewlett-Packard has a 16 percent worldwide return rate on used toner cartridges and 31 percent in the United States. Since 1991, over 47 million toner cartridges have been recycled.

The first gatekeeping should occur when the return requests are received in order to identify items that should not be returned. When a customer calls seeking authorization for a return, the employees can work with the customer to determine if an option other than return may be acceptable. For example, a direct computer retailer may require the customer to speak with a technical support person to assist in determining whether the computer is defective before granting authorization for the return. Most retail stores do not perform this technical support gatekeeping function. For the manufacturer, it is much more difficult to implement gatekeeping when the consumer can bring an item back to the retail store without having to talk to a technical support person that can analyze the problem.

Determine Routing

Once a return request is received, routing is determined based on the guidelines and policies established in the strategic portion of the process.

Once a return request is received, routing is determined based on the guidelines and policies established in the strategic portion of the process. The routing activity is primarily a planning function. During this stage of the process, return material authorizations (RMA) derived from the return requests are generated and advanced ship notices are sent signaling to the receiving location that the returns are on their way. The order fulfillment process may assist in determining the routing.

In many cases, a third party performs this service. Genco, a third-party provider that specializes in reverse logistics and returns management, runs centralized return centers for several customer firms. As part of their end-to-end returns management service offerings, they can manage both the inbound and outbound transportation of the reverse flow. For a few of their large customers, Genco coordinates with carriers to pick up returned merchandise at the retail stores in consolidated milk-run shipments, and then deliver the consolidated loads to the return center at a lower cost than if the store shipped back returned products independently.

Receive Returns

If the return item is sent to a warehouse or central return center, products need to be verified, inspected, and processed. It might be that the order fulfillment process assists in managing the return flow. Generally this is a manual process that should be completed as quickly as possible to improve cash flow. Although gatekeeping is performed at the point of entry to the reverse flow, a thorough evaluation of returned goods must be performed at the warehouse or central return center.

When a product is returned, a reason code should be assigned to it. Typical reason codes developed by the Reverse Logistics Executive Council fall into the categories of repair/service codes, order processing errors, damaged/ defective product, and contractual issues.[23] Returns should be tracked by reason codes to develop more meaningful performance metrics that can provide valuable information both within the firm and to suppliers and customers. In some cases, it is not cost effective to track return reasons in great detail because it is costly to examine and track every return. However, failure to examine products carefully and establish reasons for returns may lead to even higher costs.

Returns should be tracked by reason codes to develop more meaningful performance metrics that can provide valuable information both within the firm and to suppliers and customers.

Select Disposition

The next sub-process in the operational returns management process is to examine each return and select the appropriate disposition. Rules developed in the strategic returns management process and contained in a database that is available to workers processing returns are used to determine the final disposition. The dispositioning of the product can include refurbish, remanufacture, recycle, resell as is, resell through a secondary market, or send the product to a landfill. The order fulfillment and manufacturing flow management processes can assist returns management in determining how and where the disposition is executed. In addition, information about where recoverable product is in the system needs to be communicated with the demand management process.

Short disposition cycle times are a critical element of good returns management, so the speed of disposition should be measured. For electronic items such as computers, product value decreases quickly with time, so it is imperative that the product move quickly into the returns channel. Equally important is that the disposition guidelines are clear and the employees are well-trained to assure that the correct disposition is made.

---

[23] Brothers, Jacob and Dale S. Rogers, Presentation to the Reverse Logistics Executive Council, Chicago, 1997.

It is often less expensive to refurbish returned product than it is to manufacture items from new materials. With the growth of the Internet, secondary markets for refurbished products, such as Internet-enabled auctions, have developed. Companies such as Hewlett-Packard utilize the Internet to sell remanufactured and refurbished product to derive revenues from returned items. The largest secondary market, ebay, now accounts for approximately 25 percent of the dollars spent in e-commerce in the United States and over 55 percent of the e-commerce expenditures in Germany.[24]

Credit Customer/Supplier

Once the returns have been processed, credit needs to be given to the appropriate customer, consumer or supplier. This process can be difficult and requires negotiation between members of the supply chain. Clear rules in the PSAs, will make it easier to determine the appropriate credit. Credit authorization guidelines that were developed in the strategic returns sub-processes are implemented. If the return is complex and has not been negotiated in the PSA, this portion of the process can involve the customer relationship management and supplier relationship management processes, several functions within the firm, and other firms in the supply chain.

Financial issues related to credit to customers and suppliers can impact the efficiency of the returns management process. Much like the push to increase sales near the end of the quarter, some retailers try to shift the ownership of their returned goods and slow moving inventory back to suppliers before closing their books.

Some downstream supply chain members use chargebacks to get credited by the supplier more quickly. Chargebacks are deductions, discounts or short payments from a supplier's invoice. A retailer may deduct from a supplier's current invoice the amount of the item that they have returned or are planning to return.

Much like the push to increase sales near the end of the quarter, some retailers try to shift the ownership of their returned goods and slow moving inventory back to suppliers before closing their books.

Analyze Returns and Measure Performance

The final step in the operational process is to analyze the returns and measure performance. An important component of this step is to use the data on returns to identify opportunities for avoidance in order to make improvements to the product and the other processes. This analysis might result in feedback to order fulfillment, demand management, manufacturing flow management, product development and commercialization, or supplier relationship management. It should also be used in the ongoing strategic returns process to help develop avoidance guidelines.

The rates of defective products can be given to the supplier relationship management process team so that quality can be improved, and/or to the product development and commercialization process team so that product designers can quickly identify problems with their designs. Other key measures are return rates and disposition cycle time. Costs related to returned product and the recovery of value derived from resale or recycling are also critical metrics.

Every effort should be made to document the impact of the returns management process on the financial performance of the firm as measured by EVA

---

[24] Todd Lutwak, Presentation of the Reverse Logistics Executive Council, December 11, 2003.

(see Figure 9-4). While measuring the sales implications will be more difficult than measuring cost and asset implications, potential sales increases should not be ignored since they might have the greatest impact on profitability. Cost reductions and asset reductions are usually much easier to measure and for this reason they are often the only areas where financial performance is measured.

The final activity of the sub-process is to set goals for performance improvement. Following a thorough analysis of firm performance, objectives for improvement are established and communicated within the firm and to relevant portions of the supply chain. These communications with other members of the supply chain are coordinated through the customer relationship management and supplier relationship management processes.

While measuring the sales implications will be more difficult than measuring cost and asset implications, potential sales increases should not be ignored since they might have the greatest impact on profitability.

Conclusions

Returns management as a supply chain management process includes several features that can make an individual firm more effective and efficient. However, the process will provide the most benefits when implemented across members of the supply chain. The returns management process can reduce costs, increase revenues and increase customer satisfaction.

Returns management includes the implementation of avoidance, gatekeeping, disposition guidelines, and the measurement of the financial aspects of returns. Avoidance of unnecessary returns through improved policies and better understanding of the sources and reasons behind returns can reduce the number of return requests which will reduce costs and increase customer satisfaction. Gatekeeping can reduce the cost of doing business by identifying as early as possible the products that should not be returned. Developing disposition guidelines and implementing them across the supply chain will reduce costs by increasing the speed in the reverse flow and assisting in the selection of the destination of the returned product. Linking the performance of the process with the firm's financial measures will help in the appropriate identification of the benefits from returns management which can be used internally to reward managers and, in the supply chain, to reward customers and suppliers.

Measuring the benefits from returns management may be used to justify investments for future improvements to the process. Returns management can be used strategically to increase switching costs and reduce risk to the customer. Overall, the returns management process can increase customer satisfaction by avoiding returns, and in the case of unavoidable or desirable returns, by handling returns quickly and effectively.

Overall, the returns management process can increase customer satisfaction by avoiding returns, and in the case of unavoidable or desirable returns, by handling returns quickly and effectively.

10 Conducting Assessments of the Supply Chain Management Processes

Sebastián J. García-Dastugue and Douglas M. Lambert

Overview

The eight supply chain management processes provide a comprehensive framework to guide cross-functional teams in their efforts to achieve the integration necessary for managing relationships with customers and suppliers. However, the successful implementation of any of the supply chain management processes requires that management from all corporate functions understand their role in the process. The challenge is finding a way to bring all the necessary parties together and start the dialogue. In this chapter, we describe a methodology designed to assist management in the implementation of the supply chain management processes using the assessment tools contained in Appendix A through Appendix H. The assessment of a process will enable management to benchmark the practices of the firm with those prescribed in the process and prioritize the identified improvement opportunities.

Introduction

Where should we start in terms of implementing the cross-functional supply chain management processes? How can I evaluate my organization's level of maturity in terms of the eight supply chain management processes? These are questions that executives frequently struggle with answering. In order to help answer these questions, an assessment tool was developed for each of the eight processes. Completion of an assessment enables management to identify opportunities to improve performance on specific activities within a process and to set the appropriate priorities.

Completion of an assessment enables management to identify opportunities to improve performance on specific activities within a process and to set the appropriate priorities.

The discussion that takes place during the assessment enables management to understand how their decisions and actions affect others in the organization. Since work is done inside corporate functions, managers interact primarily with others in the same function. Thus, mental models, assumptions and opinions about what is important for the organization as well as how other functional areas perform or should perform their activities are developed based on managers' experiences in a function. Even specific terminology is used inside each function that makes communication between or among functions challenging. This results in a certain degree of detachment between corporate functions that can result in a feeling of "handing off" activities instead of viewing activities as a continuous flow. The consequence is that the flows of product and information are broken. The assessment of a supply chain management process provides a non-threatening environment to build the cohesion across the organization that is necessary for achieving corporate success.

In this chapter, a methodology for conducting cross-functional assessments is provided to assist management in the implementation of the supply chain management processes. These tools enable a cross-functional team to evaluate the degree of implementation of a process. The assessment also serves as a benchmark so that management can track progress in implementation. In addition, the assessment makes it possible for managers to prioritize opportunities for improvement. The assessment tools are provided in Appendix A through Appendix H.

The assessment also serves as a benchmark so that management can track progress in implementation.

Conducting an Assessment

Management can assess from one to eight processes depending on priorities, resources and internal support. Because each assessment requires broad cross-functional involvement, it is best to begin by focusing on one or a small subset of the processes. The assessment of a process includes having all of the participants complete the assessment tool individually and then holding a face-to-face meeting to generate consensus among the respondents. When completing the assessment, participants provide their individual perspectives of how the organization is performing each activity of the process, how important that activity is to the organization's success now and in the future, and an explanation for their evaluation of the activity. Individual assessments are dicusssed in a consensus building meeting, during which the participants are asked to discuss the dispersion of the scores. The full power of the assessment is achieved only when it is conducted with adequate cross-functional representation. Developing a common view among managers of the state of management practices and how important these practices are to the organization as a whole establishes a baseline from which opportunities for improvement can be identified and progress can be measured.

The assessment of a supply chain management process provides an opportunity for managers from multiple functions to discuss opportunities and problems without assigning blame. Frequently, the consensus building session is the first time a cross-functional group with such broad representation has met for something other than dealing with an emergency situation or problem. Dealing with problems often includes assigning responsibilities and in these situations management may behave defensively, undermining the objective identification of improvement opportunities.

The assessment of a supply chain management process provides an opportunity for managers from multiple functions to discuss opportunities and problems without assigning blame.

Frequently, what people identify as problems are actually symptoms because the source of the problem is beyond their line of sight. Conducting the assessment provides managers with the opportunity to broaden their view by listening to others' opinions about each activity of the process and sharing their own. This exchange of ideas in a constructive environment results in the development of a common perspective in terms of areas of opportunity and leads to potential courses of action. The structure provided by each supply chain management process guides the cross-functional team in the identification and prioritization of the improvement opportunities. For example, if forecasting is identified as an area that needs to improve, the structure of the demand management process leads the team to evaluate the data collection activities first; because the forecast only will be as good as the data that are used to develop it. Then, the team will evaluate the remaining activities in the demand management process.

Performing an assessment involves the following 10 steps:

- Gain commitment for an assessment.
- Select the process to assess.
- Choose the participants for the assessment.
- Schedule the assessment.
- Acquaint participants with the framework and the supply chain management process that will be assessed.
- Complete the assessment tool individually.
- Summarize responses to use for discussion in the consensus-building meeting.
- Hold the consensus building meeting.
- Prepare a summary of scores, importance, justifications and potential action items.
- Develop a plan for action.

Gain Commitment for an Assessment

The main reason to conduct a cross-functional assessment of a process is to capture the perspectives of managers from all key corporate functions when determining a baseline of current performance and identifying opportunities for improvement. Thus, support from top-management and the vice-presidents of the functions are important for success. Lack of adequate support can result in low participation in the assessment which will jeopardize the initiative. If adequate cross-functional representation is not achieved, the assessment will lose effectiveness because the consensus will not represent the perspectives of all parties that need to be involved for successful implementation of the process. Also, those who participated in the assessment may leave the meeting feeling that the objectives for the meeting were not accomplished, because key people were not involved. This may discourage their participation in future cross-functional initiatives.

If adequate cross-functional representation is not achieved, the assessment will lose effectiveness because the consensus will not represent the perspectives of all parties that need to be involved for successful implementation of the process.

Select the Process to Assess

Management must decide which process or processes to select for the assessment. There might be a recognized problem and the solution requires a cross-functional initiative. For example, if it has been recognized that there is a need to improve customer service, the first process to assess could be customer service management. A customer service survey that indicates customers are unsatisfied with consistency of deliveries or with the organization's proactiveness might become the burning platform to assess the customer service management process and/or the order fulfillment process. If forecasting is recognized as a problem area, then demand management may be the place to start.

In some situations, organizational politics will dictate where to start. For example, the customer relationship management process might be viewed as the domain of marketing or sales; similarly, the supplier relationship management process might be viewed as the domain of the procurement function. If the individual driving the assessment is not from one of these areas, it may be difficult to gain support. If a logistics executive is the one who has suggested that an assessment should be done, order fulfillment could be a good place to start. Manufacturing flow management might be a good place to start, if an executive from operations is the champion. Regardless of the process chosen, including all functions is necessary for a successful assessment and will allow managers to see that all functional areas are required for the appropriate implementation of the eight business processes. A successful assessment should increase support for the cross-functional assessment of other processes.

A successful assessment should increase support for the cross-functional assessment of other processes.

Choose the Participants for the Assessment

Each process has cross-functional activities and completing an assessment requires that the team members have a complete picture of the organization's management practices. The challenge is that an organization is made up of individuals and they may not act in concert and may not communicate as needed within the organization or with other members of the supply chain.

The assessment participants should include representatives from all functions including marketing, sales, logistics, production, finance, purchasing, IT, and research and development. They should represent enough levels of the organization to adequately assess the process. Normally, this would require senior level excecutives as well as people that execute the daily activities. In our experience, when assessment teams did not have adequate cross-functional representation, the sessions were less effective. A number of times, during the consensus building meeting, it was clear that someone who was not present should have been part of the assessment. Since conducting an assessment requires considerable time from participants, it is necessary to determine if all of the appropriate individuals have been invited to participate. We have not found a case were someone invited to participate in an assessment did not benefit from their involvement or did not contribute to the discussion.

In order to guide the discussion that will take place during the consensus building meeting, the facilitator needs to gather data about the participants including names, e-mail addresses, organizational positions and their primary responsibilities in the organization. Table 10-1 shows an example of the data collected about participants for an assessment. The facilitator of the consensus building session needs this information to determine whether the necessary cross-functional involvement is being achieved.

Schedule the Assessment

An assessment needs to be planned at least a month in advance of the consensus building meeting. The appropriate length of time depends on the agendas of the executives that need to be part of the assessment. Most frequently, planning starts 60 days before the consensus building meeting. The activities that are involved in conducting the assessment usually occur during a period of 10 to 14 days. Figure 10-1 shows a sample timeline of the activities that are required to conduct an assessment.

Figure 10-1 shows that the description of the process is planned for a Tuesday

Table 10-1
Background of the Assessment Participants

		Assessment of the Demand Management Process at Global Corporate Auckland, New Zealand - August 7, 2007		
Last Name	**First Name**	**e-Mail Address**	**Position**	**Main Responsibilities**
Doe	Joe	Joe.Doe@GlobalCorporate.com	Director of Operations	Responsible for all manufacturing operations
Cantropus	Peter	Peter.Cantropus@GlobalCorporate.com	Consultant/Staff	SC Consulting business units globally
Johnson	Jay	Jay.Johnson@GlobalCorporate.com	Director of Sales	Sales Planning to retail customers
Ramirez	Juan	Juan.Ramirez@GlobalCorporate.com	Demand and Supply Planning	Demand, Supply, Infrastructure Planning
Fitzgerald	Catherine	Catherine.Fitzgerald@GlobalCorporate.com	Director of Marketing	Brand Management and product introduction
Bolton	Isaac	Isaac.Bolton@GlobalCorporate.com	Director of Customer Service	Runs all inside service
Kara-Rima	John	John.Kara-Rima@GlobalCorporate.com	IT Support Analyst	Support for Corporate ERP demand and supply
Hoyer	Michael	Michael.Hoyer@GlobalCorporate.com	Supply Planning Manager	Supply Planning
Berdiner	Mark	Mark.Berdiner@GlobalCorporate.com	Sales Director	Manager Sales Force
Carter	Patricia	Patricia.Carter@GlobalCorporate.com	Demand Manager	Demand Planning and promotions planning
Quito	Esteban	Esteban.Quito@GlobalCorporate.com	Financial Analyst	Cash flow analysis
Reid	Yolanda	Yolanda.Reid@GlobalCorporate.com	Logistics Services Manager	Runs third party services
Thomson	Paul	Paul.Thomson@GlobalCorporate.com	Supply Chain Planner	Planning and Scheduling the Plant #1
Stevenson	Louis	Louis.Stevenson@GlobalCorporate.com	Sales Support Representative	Inside support for outside sales reps + customers
Robertson	Martin	Martin.Robertson@GlobalCorporate.com	Business Analysis Manager	Brand Analysis
Reid	Pete	Pete.Reid@GlobalCorporate.com	Key Account Manager	Calls on top customer accounts

Figure 10-1
Sample Schedule for Conducting an Assessment

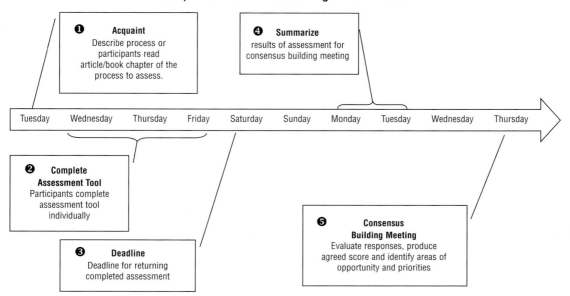

❶ **Acquaint**
Describe process or participants read article/book chapter of the process to assess.

❹ **Summarize**
results of assessment for consensus building meeting

Tuesday Wednesday Thursday Friday Saturday Sunday Monday Tuesday Wednesday Thursday

❷ **Complete Assessment Tool**
Participants complete assessment tool individually

❸ **Deadline**
Deadline for returning completed assessment

❺ **Consensus Building Meeting**
Evaluate responses, produce agreed score and identify areas of opportunity and priorities

(❶ in Figure 10-1). Participants are given 3 days, between Wednesday and Friday, to complete the assessment tool (❷ in Figure 10-1). This might seem like a short time; however, our experience shows that if individuals cannot find 45 minutes to complete the assessment in a period of three days, the probability is high that they will not find the time. Exceptions include when individuals are away from the office during those three days.

It is necessary to establish a deadline for completing the assessment (❸ in Figure 10-1) to maximize the number of responses. Figure 10-1 shows that Monday and Tuesday are assigned to prepare for the consensus building meeting (❹ in Figure 10-1). Wednesday can be a day for traveling if participants are coming from multiple locations. The consensus building meeting is held on Thursday (❺ in Figure 10-1). It is possible to compress this timeline as well as to extend it if necessary. It is our experience that this length of time works well.

Acquaint Participants with the Framework and the Supply Chain Management Process that Will Be Assessed

Those participating in the assessment need to be well acquainted with the supply chain management framework and the process being assessed. Team members need to understand that the framework is based on the management of long-term relationships with key customers and suppliers, on the importance of customizing products and services for each key customer or segment of customers, and the need to involve all functions adequately. Participants need to feel comfortable with these concepts in order to complete the assessment. The participants also need to understand the concepts embedded in the process being assessed. For example, the demand management process includes synchronization, reducing variability and increasing flexibility. If these concepts are not well understood, respondents may view the importance of these activities lower than they should be scored. Also, because the same terminology often is used to refer to different concepts, terms can be easily confused. For example, when conducting an assessment of the customer service management process, some respondents may base their response on the activities performed in the call center. If this happens, the power of the proactiveness that is embedded in the customer service management process would not be appreciated. In fact, they would not be evaluating the supply chain management process, but rather the performance of the customer service activity.

Those participating in the assessment need to be well acquainted with the supply chain management framework and the process being assessed.

Each team member should read Chapter 1 of this book to understand the overall framework, and then the chapter describing the process that is being assessed. Alternatively, an expert may describe the concepts to the participants. If this is done internally, a facilitator should be identified and given the resources to become an expert on the process and be able to explain it to the respondents.

Complete the Assessment Tool Individually

The assessment tool needs to be completed individually without the influence of co-workers. This will assure that the individuals' views concerning the organization's management practices related to the process are captured. Figure 10-2 shows, as an example, one of the operational customer relationship management sub-processes, Sub-process 0-1 - Segment Customers.

The assessment tool needs to be completed individually without the influence of co-workers.

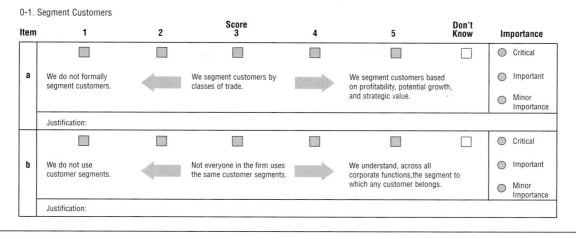

Figure 10-2
Example of the Customer Relationship Management Assessment Tool

For each of the items in the assessment tool, as shown in Figure 10-2, respondents must choose a score from **1** to **5** for the description that best represents the organization's management practices. Note that only the scores **1**, **3**, and **5** are anchored in a short description. If the respondent believes that the item is implemented between two descriptions (**1-3** or **3-5**), then the value between those descriptions should be chosen (**2** or **4**). Using Figure 10-2 as an example, if the respondent believes that the organization is between a **3** (We segment customers by classes of trade) and **5** (We segment customers based on profitability, potential growth and strategic value), then the appropriate response is a **4**.

There might be items in the assessment tool that cannot be answered by a particular individual. This may occur because the respondent is not familiar with the organization's approach to a particular item. Each item in the assessment tool includes a box with the option **Don't Know**. Respondents should choose this option if appropriate, rather than leaving the item blank. The fact that someone does not know about a particular issue is useful information. If that person must know more about the activity, providing them with the necessary information offers the opportunity for a quick fix.

Because the assessment tool was designed to be used in any organization, it is possible that an individual activity may not be important to a specific organization at a point in time. For this reason, we ask participants to rate the importance of each item on a three-point scale: minor importance, important, critical. Rating depends on the individual's perception of the importance of the item to the organization's success now and in the future.

It is important that respondents take the time to include a short justification for the score and the importance they give to each item.

It is important that respondents take the time to include a short justification for the score and the importance they give to each item. This justification will be necessary during the consensus-building session in order to explain their scores to the other participants. Completing the assessment tool individually takes between 45 minutes and one hour. It is recommended that respondents complete the assessment without interruption because the structure of the process requires a sequence of thought that if interrupted might result in the respondent forgetting the reasoning behind previous responses.

Summarize Responses to Use for Discussion in the Consensus-building Meeting

After all responses are collected, the facilitator needs to process them for the consensus building meeting. At a minimum, the facilitator needs to calculate basic descriptive statistics of the scores and the importance values for each assessment item (average, mode, range, and histogram/frequency). The facilitator should have the list of justifications in case there is a need to foster discussion. If the group of respondents is sufficiently large and there are multiple respondents from each functional area, the facilitator may calculate an average score and importance by function. These data may identify differences by function which can be used to encourage discussion.

Table 10-2 shows the basic data that are needed for facilitating the consensus building meeting. The table shows data for the order fulfillment process. For each item, the average, maximum and minimum are calculated. Also, it is helpful to have the count of each score (histogram) including how many people responded that they did not know how to score the item as well as how many left the item

Table 10-2
Summary of Responses for the Consensus Building Meeting

Process	Sub Process	Item	Description	Score Average	Max	Min	Count 1	Count 2	Count 3	Count 4	Count 5	"Don't Know"	Count Blank	Importance Average	Max	Min	Count 1	Count 2	Count 3	Count Blank	Responses
OF	S1	a	Marketing strategy	3.6	5	2	0	1	4	4	2	0		2.4	3	2	0	7	4		11
OF	S1	b	Customer service strategy	3.5	5	2	0	2	3	5	1	0		2.3	3	2	0	5	3		11
OF	S1	c	Customer service goals	3.8	5	2	0	1	2	5	2	1		2.4	3	2	0	7	4		11
OF	S1	d	Core competencies within order fulfillment	3.4	5	1	1	0	6	2	2	0		2.7	3	2	0	3	8		11
OF	S1	e	Budget for order fulfillment	4.2	5	1	1	0	0	3	5	2		2.3	3	1	1	6	4		11
OF	S2	a	Customers' order fulfillment requirements	2.9	5	1	2	2	3	3	1	0		2.9	3	2	0	1	10		11
OF	S3	a	Network analysis	3.7	5	2	0	3	1	2	4	1		2.6	3	2	0	4	7		11
OF	S4	a	P...	3.7	5	2	0	1	4	3	3	0		2.2	3	2	0	8	2		11
OF	07	a	Process efficiency	4.3	5	3															10
OF	07	b	Process time and variability	4.0	5	3	0	0	2	6	2	0		2.3	3	1	1	5	4		10
OF	07	c	Complaints due to process variability	3.1	5	2	0	2	3	1	1	3		2.2	3	2	0	8	2		10
OF	07	d	Order status	4.2	5	3	0	0	1	5	3	1		2.4	3	2	0	6	4		10
OF	07	e	Competitive advantage	3.5	58	2	0	2	1	4	1	2		2.6	3	2	0	4	6		10
OF	07	f	Communication of performance	3.7	5	3	0	0	4	4	1	1		2.1	3	1	2	5	3		10
OF	07	g	Reward customers and suppliers	1.8	4	1	5	2	1	1	0	1		2.1	3	2	0	9	1		10

blank. The same calculations for importance are shown in Table 10-2. The last column on the right shows how many people completed the assessment.

Hold the Consensus Building Meeting

The main objective of the consensus building meeting is to have the team agree on a score for each item in the assessment tool.

The main objective of the consensus building meeting is to have the team agree on a score for each item in the assessment tool. Usually, it is helpful to have a projector showing the item of the assessment tool; that is, the text used for anchors on the values **1**, **3** and **5**, so that participants can read them during the discussion. The facilitator shows the assessment tool one item at a time on the screen, reads the descriptions that serve as anchors, reports the distribution of scores including the number of people that responded for each value, and queries the group to offer opinions to help the team reach a consensus score.

A consensus building meeting requires four hours. There are situations in which calling executives in for a four-hour-long meeting results in lower attendance. However, experience indicates that this type of meeting rarely takes less than four hours. It is strongly recommended that the organizer of the assessment explains the purpose of the meeting, the value of the time dedicated, and that participation is critical for the assessment to achieve its full potential. In our experience, participants agree that the time dedicated to the consensus building meeting was time well spent given the learning that takes place through the sharing of perspectives and the opportunities for improvement that are identified.

...the richness of the consensus building meeting is derived from the discussion among the participants to produce the consensus scores rather than from the scores themselves.

The facilitator of the consensus building meeting needs to manage the pace of the meeting and make sure that all individuals participate. The purpose of the consensus building meeting is to generate a consensus score for each item and its importance. However, the richness of the consensus building meeting is derived from the discussion among the participants to produce the consensus scores rather than from the scores themselves. During the meeting, the facilitator needs to record the consensus score and importance, the group's justification, and comments that indicate areas of opportunity and potential action items.

Consensus building meetings start by discussing the strategic process item by item; the operational process follows. The strategic portion of the supply chain management process defines the structure for implementation and the operational portion is where the day-to-day activities take place. Because of the importance of putting the correct structure in place, the majority of the time of a consensus building meeting is dedicated to the strategic portion of the process. Frequently, three hours of the four-hour consensus building meeting are dedicated to the assessment of the strategic sub-processes.

It is possible to characterize the dynamics in the consensus building meetings in three stages: 1) beginning, 2) core discussion, and 3) final hour. The discussion in a consensus building meeting tends to begin slowly, particularly if it is the first assessment in which the participants have been involved. During the beginning stage, many participants observe each other, evaluate each other's participation and reactions, and eventually contribute a comment. A slow beginning is more likely if managers from multiple levels are in the room. In order to shorten this initial stage of the meeting, the highest level person in attendance or the facilitator may comment at the beginning that openness and candor are key to a successful consensus building meeting.

The second stage of the consensus building meeting is when the core discussion takes place. By this time, everyone in the meeting is participating actively. It is important that the facilitator provides the opportunity for all participants to give their comments, examples and anecdotes. During this stage, most of the main improvement opportunities and potential courses of action result from the discussion. It is possible that participants will try to find the solution to the issue being discussed during the consensus building session. In order to keep the session on the schedule, once the group has agreed on the direction or potential course of action, the facilitator should move the group on to the next item in the assessment.

The final hour of the consensus building meeting, which is devoted to the operational process has two characteristics that are worth mentioning. First, the participants reach consensus quickly compared to the time required to reach consensus during the discussion of the strategic portion of the process. During this stage, participants look at each other and refer to previous discussions; which leads to agreement on the score and importance more quickly. Second, the meeting time is running out. For this reason, some people may believe that the meeting is being rushed. To deal with this issue, the facilitator should explain early in the meeting and at the start of the discussion on the operational process that the strategic sub-processes requires more time and that the meeting is likely to go faster when generating consensus on the operational items.

It is important that the facilitator provides the opportunity for all participants to give their comments, examples and anecdotes.

Prepare a Summary of Scores, Importance, Justifications and Potential Action Items

The scores, importance ratings and justifications must be summarized for the report on the assessment. The management team responsible for implementing the process will use the results to prioritize opportunities and develop action items. The summary report should provide a general description of the context of the assessment including the list of participants, the consensus scores and importance ratings, and the justification for the group's view. It is worthwhile to include the list of justifications and scores of the individual respondents without identifying who said what. This information provides a sense of the breadth of perspectives and internal practices, which could become indicators of actions required. The facilitator may suggest potential action items as well as recommendations regarding the improvement opportunities. An example of a summary report is provided in the Appendix at the end of this chapter.

Develop a Plan for Action

The output of the consensus building meeting is, for each item in the assessment tool: 1) an agreed score, 2) an agreed importance rating, and 3) a justification for why the group agreed on the score and the importance. It is advisable that the facilitator also records the discussion related to the potential courses of action for the improvement opportunities that were identified during the consensus building. In order to establish priorities for action, the items of the assessment can be mapped in a 3-by-5 matrix as shown in Figure 10-3.

Management should give the highest priority to those items whose agreed scores are 1 or 2 and for which the agreed importance is 3. Next in priority are the actionable items; those that have a score of 1 or 2 and importance of 2, or scores

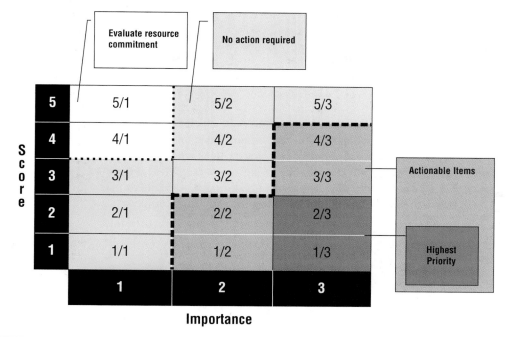

Figure 10-3
Establishing Priorities with the Results of an Assessment

of 3 or 4 and an importance of 3. Management does not need to include in the agenda for action the items with scores and importance that fall in the area identified as no action required in Figure 10-3. However, if an item falls in the upper-left corner of the matrix (score of 4 or 5 and importance of 1), management should evaluate whether these activities are a drain of resources. It appears that performance is beyond what it needs to be based on the fact that these activities are of minor importance to the success of the firm. However, we have not experienced an item in this region.

Having identified the items that require action, the executive driving the assessment should lead the development of action items required to implement the improvement opportunities identified.

Having identified the items that require action, the executive driving the assessment should lead the development of action items required to implement the improvement opportunities identified. If possible, action items should be articulated for all opportunities discussed during the consensus building session. While this may increase the length of the session, it is advisable that responsibilities be assigned as part of the consensus building session. Action items should include: 1) a description of the improvement opportunity, 2) the name of the person responsible for the improvement initiative, 3) the next step, and, 4) a deadline for accomplishing the next step. As an aid in the development of action items, the assessment team should refer to the sub-processes and activities that comprise the process.

The purpose of articulating action items as part of the consensus building meeting should not be to determine the solution to be implemented, but to get started on establishing a project that will result in the improvement. It is a good practice to define action items that can be achieved in a short period of time, within 3 months, and others that require a year or more to implement. In order to insure the implementation of action items, the sponsor of the project should consider establishing a regular schedule where every manager responsible for action items presents the progress made and describes future actions. This type of meeting will enable everyone to understand that progress is being made in the implementation of the supply chain management process and will bring in the perspectives of all corporate functions.

Conclusions

The supply chain management framework presented in this book is a comprehensive model designed to assist executives in the management of relationships with customers and suppliers, and to achieve the necessary integration across corporate functions. The supply chain management processes are designed to guide the cross-functional efforts. It is likely that some parts of the processes are implemented to some degree in any organization. The eight assessment tools, one for each of the cross-functional processes described in this chapter (see Appendixes A to H at the end of the book.), and the methodology to conduct an assessment were developed to assist management to: 1) benchmark management practices in the firm with those prescribed in the processes, 2) identify where to start with the implementation of a process, and, 3) assess improvements over time as the implementation unfolds.

The assessment tools are designed to be applicable in any business environment. Because the tools and the methodology to assess practices in the firm are standardized, management may conduct assessments across locations, divisions, or geographies to identify the best-in-class for each process and transfer improvements to the rest of the organization. Finally, this benchmarking experience can be used between non-competing firms with similar business challenges.

We observed multiple benefits that result from conducting an assessment of a cross-functional process. First, we found that an assessment of a process provides an environment where representatives from all corporate functions are encouraged to provide their perspective on the management practices of the firm as a whole, rather than just focusing on what is happening inside a single corporate function. The consensus building meeting provides a constructive environment for exchanging ideas because the cross-functional team is not trying to solve a problem or contingency. Second, we found situations where representatives from functional areas were invited for the first time to become involved in the evaluation of the activities of a process. In these situations, it was clear to everyone that the functional perspective provided by these representatives was necessary and valuable. Furthermore, executives wondered why these representatives were not involved in the past discussions. Third, the discussion developed during the consensus building meeting enables participants to view others' perspectives as well as explain their own, which results in a broader understanding of how their decisions and actions affect others in the organization. Finally, we found that the output of an assessment provides an objective basis for prioritizing action items across the organization and can be used to gain the support from upper-management that is necessary to realize the improvement opportunities.

...the output of an assessment provides an objective basis for prioritizing action items across the organization and can be used to gain the support from upper-management that is necessary to realize the improvement opportunities.

APPENDIX: Example Report of a Cross-Functional Assessment

The assessment of the demand management process at the ABC Company took place at Miami on March 6, 2007. The consensus building session had cross-functional participation and included John Stevenson, regional manager, and Carlos Gimenez, vice president of marketing, 16 people were invited to complete the assessment using a web-based tool and it was completed by 15 of them. All 15 participated in the consensus building meeting. The meeting was facilitated by Doug Lambert and Sebastián García-Dastugue.

The leadership team of the division has decided that supply chain management represents an opportunity to achieve the corporate goals to gain cost efficiencies and increase market share. John Stevenson believed that it was necessary to better coordinate activities with customers and suppliers and that the supply chain management processes represented the vehicle for achieving the desired coordination. The demand management process is a good place to start because integration across all of the business functions is required for implementation of the eight processes. Also, John and Carlos believed that managers from each function would be able to recognize the importance of their involvement in this process.

After facilitating the assessment of the demand management process, it is our perception that a number of sophisticated management systems are in place but there is a substantial opportunity to increase cross-functional integration. This opportunity is similar to those found in other major corporations where we have conducted the assessment of cross-functional business processes.

The demand management process has a significant impact on supply chain costs and on the firm's ability to respond to changes in the marketplace. Based on the assessment, the following opportunities were identified:

- As in many other companies, there are sophisticated information systems that produce metrics, but there is an opportunity to better utilize these metrics to manage the business.
- Sales and marketing executives are rewarded for revenue generated and not for the profitability of the business. Decisions would improve if profitability measures were used. At a minimum country managers need to be rewarded based on profitability of the business generated in their countries rather than on revenue.
- There is an opportunity to improve cross-functional integration and the following should be considered: 1) use cross-functional business processes to define the activities performed within a function and those that must be coordinated in cross-functional teams; 2) link operational metrics to profitability; and, 3) develop the capability to produce profitability reports (based on revenue minus avoidable costs plus a charge for asset utilization) for key customers and customer segments.

The power of the assessment of any of the supply chain management processes comes from the cross-functional participation and the discussion of divergent views. The assessment scores and importance are completed individually and, during the consensus building meeting, the group discusses each question in the assessment tool. After some discussion, a group score and an importance value are produced with justifications to support the scores. The scoring and comments that resulted from the assessment of the demand management process are attached to this report. If the group agrees that a score is low and the item is critical, that item is likely to represent an opportunity for improvement. A high score and low importance usually indicates that no action is required. A low score and low importance may mean that the item is not relevant for the organization and nothing needs to be done. In short, opportunities stem from low scores and high importance; and the items in this category become priorities for improvement. During the assessment of the demand management process, a number of specific improvement opportunities were identified and they are described in the following sections of this report.

The Strategic Demand Management Process

All participants in the assessment of the demand management process agreed that "we have a good understanding of our corporate strategy and how it affects our strategy for demand management". All participants viewed this as critical which is the starting point for a good demand management process. In addition, other items that are the cornerstones of an efficient demand management process were scored high. For example, the group agreed that there was a general understanding of the bottlenecks within the company. But, there is an opportunity to identify the bottlenecks associated with suppliers, subsidiaries, third-party logistics providers and key customers. Successful implementation of the demand management process requires that the managers involved have a common understanding of the challenges associated with implementing the process across key members of the supply chain.

The demand management process is designed at the strategic level and it is executed at the operational level. Both portions of the process require cross-functional involvement. The strategic demand management process team puts the structure in place and the members of this team should be top managers from all functional areas. Without the appropriate top-management support, the implementation of the demand management process may be unsuccessful.

S1: Determine Demand Management Goals and Strategy
Item c: Demand Management Goals and Priorities

The score for this item was a 2 and the importance was a 3. The consensus was that a more cross-functional view of the demand management process was necessary. At present, each function uses their own metrics which may lead to conflicts. For example, if the sales organization is measured by revenue, marketing by market share, logistics by fill-rates and operations by cost, the functional objectives will be in conflict. Due to the metrics, management in each function will find it difficult to be sympathetic to the others' perspective, or do what is best for the shareholder or the customer. If the goals and priorities for the demand management process are set by a cross-functional team, this will generate a common understanding of what the organization is capable of doing in terms of reacting to changes in demand or implementing quick replenishment methodologies such as Collaborative Planning, Forecasting and Replenishment (CPFR).

Possible actions include:
- Map functional objectives based on the reward system and assess potential sources of functional conflicts since they affect the demand management process. The goal is to link demand management metrics to the financial performance of the organization and to profitability reports. These reports should be developed for each country and for each key customer or segment of customers.
- Design a demand management scorecard to be shared periodically with internal

operations and downstream members of the supply chain in order to encourage individuals to consider how their decisions and actions affect the process.
- Assess the problems and the costs associated with amplification of demand.

S2: Determine Forecasting Procedures
Item a: Forecasts and Functional Areas

The score for this item was a 4 and the importance was a 3. Despite the high score, the discussion in the consensus building meeting and the justification indicate that there might be at least three forecasts in use: 1) marketing and operations; 2) sales; and 3) finance. This item may be closely related to S1-c, which indicates the existence of cross-functional conflicts due to functional metrics.

Possible actions include:
- Understand the needs of each functional area and/or geography regarding the forecast.
- Institutionalize performance metrics related to forecasting in order to track improvements over time and relate improvements to financial results (such as lower costs or higher revenue as a result of fewer lost sales).
- Track forecasting accuracy (or variability of forecasting errors) to determine the cost associated with variability or forecast errors.

S2: Determine Forecasting Procedures
Item d: Forecasting Methods

The score for this item was a 4 and the importance was a 3. The forecasting methods used include quantitative analysis. However, as described in the consensus building meeting, the forecast is produced in Excel. If the forecasting process is predominately manual, there is an opportunity to explore software packages that may combine the best of quantitative and judgmental forecasting techniques.

Possible actions include:
- Determine the cost associated with variability in forecast errors; evaluate information flow to identify local information in each country that can be used in the forecasting process.
- Identify potential improvements to forecasting that are possible by using a forecasting software package that can be integrated with the ERP and advanced planning systems.

S3: Plan Information Flow
Item b: Sharing Forecasts

The score for this item was a 4 and the importance was a 3. The high score reflects the fact that the forecast is being shared upstream in the supply chain. There is consensus that there is less sharing of the forecast downstream in the supply chain. Sharing information with downstream members of the supply chain might improve the coordination of product flow.

Possible actions include:
- Determine how the forecasts can be used downstream in the supply chain, who benefits from having the forecasts available, and what information they need.
- If quick replenishment systems such as CPFR or VMI (Vendor Managed Inventory) are implemented, the requirements for the forecast lessen. For example, if CPFR is implemented with key customers that account for 20% of demand, then this portion of the demand does not need to be forecasted since an order forecast will be produced for that customer.
- While management has done a good job at sharing plans with suppliers, there have been few efforts directed at integrating with subsidiaries and key customers.

- Customers and subsidiaries might have what is referred to as local information. This is information about business opportunities available in the local market that are unlikely to be identified by a centralized forecasting group. There might be an opportunity to identify local information that needs to be shared. For example, the forecast is based on past sales plus other variables at the macro level. Usually, lost sales are not considered for forecasting purposes. During the consensus building meeting, a participant shared the experience that one of the regions did not take orders unless there was inventory on hand to fill the order. Recording the number of orders not taken and the size of each order is vital information for improved planning in future periods. This could become an action item for immediate implementation.

S4: Determine Synchronization Procedures
Item a: Synchronization Procedures

The score for this item was a 2 and the importance was a 3. The development of synchronization procedures is a significant opportunity. The process by which demand and supply are matched appears to be fragmented.

Possible actions include:
- Design synchronization procedures (sometimes referred to as Sales and Operations Planning) to include demand and the capabilities of the supply chain. The result of the synchronization process is a demand execution plan which is based on the business opportunities and the capabilities of the firm. The demand execution plan is a commitment from all of the functions involved. Figure 10A-1 contains an illustration of the synchronization that must take place.
- Having appropriate synchronization procedures in place will reduce the number of exceptions and emergency situations such as rush orders, transshipments and stockouts. Generally, handling exceptions is time consuming for management.

S4: Determine Synchronization Procedures
Item c: Capacity and Flexibility Available

The score for this item was a 2 and the importance was a 3. During the consensus building meeting, participants expressed the belief that the flexibility of the supply chain was

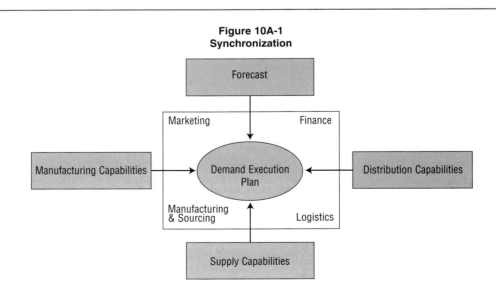

Figure 10A-1
Synchronization

approximately 20%. However, no one in the session felt confident about the actual degree of flexibility. The capacity of the supply chain needs to be assessed in order to determine to what extent the supply chain can respond to changes in demand or unforeseen situations.

Possible actions include:

- Assess available capacity and flexibility.
- Evaluate the organization's capability to respond to changes.

S5: Develop Contingency Management Systems
Item a: Event Management

The score for this item was a 1 and the importance was a 3. The group agreed that developing the capability to react to contingencies is an improvement opportunity. Participants of the consensus building meeting agreed that dealing with last minute changes and contingencies requires considerable management attention. To effectively manage changes, it is important, first, to have the capability to detect the contingency as early as possible and, second, to empower employees to determine the action plan. Dealing with contingencies requires determining all feasible alternatives, identifying the cost and revenue implications of each alternative, and implementing the chosen solutions.

Possible actions include:

- Define operational triggers that indicate the need for management's attention.

S6: Develop Framework of Metrics
Item a: Metrics

The score for this item was a 2 and the importance was a 3. It was agreed that data are available for developing metrics. The opportunity lies in identifying the best metrics to use. Functional conflicts can be minimized by developing appropriate performance metrics for each cross-functional process and tying these metrics back to financial performance as measured by Economic Value Added (EVA).

Metrics drive behavior, and appropriate metrics are needed to encourage functional managers to focus on customers and on the organization's financial results. At a minimum, country managers need to be judged on profitability because not all dollars of revenue are the same and country managers make decisions that contribute to the profitability of the organization.

Possible actions include:

- Evaluate the metrics that are available in the ERP system.
- Track forecast errors for each forecast and for all countries/regions/market segments to assess implications associated with variability of forecast errors.
- Ensure that metrics are shared and are used to drive behavior and decision making. Tracking performance over time is likely to change management behavior even if the reward system remains unchanged.

S6: Develop Framework of Metrics
Item c: Conflicting Functional Objectives

The score for this item was a 1 and the importance was a 3. Cross-functional initiatives need to include all functions involved (in the case of all processes at the strategic level and for demand management in particular, we believe that there needs to be representation from all functions). Failure to include all functions in the cross-functional demand management team may mean that individuals not involved will inadvertently or maliciously subvert the effort.

Possible actions include:

- Develop a map of potential conflicting functional objectives. Identify the objectives for each function and how they affect other functions. Then identify potential sources of conflict between the functions. This could be a series of 2-by-2 matrices, one for each function, to show each function's objective and the potential conflicts with other functions.

The Operational Demand Management Process

O2: Forecast
Item a: Variability of Forecast Errors

The score for this item was a 3 and the importance was a 3. The measures of variability of forecast errors and the costs associated with these errors may be used as a burning platform to improving the forecasting process.

Possible actions include:
- Determine variability of forecast errors at multiple levels of aggregation such as by product family, geography, dollars and time.
- Relate forecast accuracy to cost of added complexity.

O2: Forecast
Item b: Forecast Accuracy

The score for this item was a 3 and the importance was a 3. Determine the variability of forecast errors. The organization needs to build reactive capacity to respond to the variability of forecast errors.

Possible actions include:
- Automate the measurement of forecast accuracy.

O2: Forecast
Item c: Tracking Forecast Errors

The score for this item was a 3 and the importance was a 3. There was consensus that data to measure performance are available. The improvement opportunity is to understand how management can act based upon the performance of the forecasting process. There always will be forecast errors; the opportunity for the organization lies in understanding the underlying reasons why the forecast was not accurate.

Possible actions include:
- Evaluate potential organizational learning opportunities associated with conducting a root-cause analysis of the forecast.

O4: Reduce Variability and Increase Flexibility
Item d: Flexibility of Responses

The score for this item was a 2 and the importance was a 3. Building flexibility in the downstream portion of the supply chain will result in increased customer service levels (product availability).

Possible actions include:
- Evaluate the potential increase in flexibility that can be achieved by implementing advanced inventory management techniques such as quick response; CPFR and postponement and centralization of inventories.
- Link demand to supply to increase flexibility and reduce costs of the whole supply chain.

11 Mapping for Supply Chain Management

*Douglas M. Lambert, Sebastián J. García-Dastugue and
A. Michael Knemeyer*

Overview

As supply chain network structures become more complex and geographically dispersed, management can benefit from developing a relationship-based map of their company's supply chain. The visual representation and analysis of the complexities in a firm's direct and indirect supply chain relationships serves as a starting point for increasing the cross-functional and cross-firm communication that is necessary for implementation of the supply chain management processes. The mapping effort also enables management to identify internal and external improvement opportunities and establish the critical relationship linkages that must be closely managed. Once a relationship-based map is developed, a wide variety of activity-based mapping techniques can be used to identify and realize improvement opportunities across the network of companies that constitute the supply chain.

Introduction

*Firms exist within
supply chains
whether or not
executives decide to
look beyond the walls
of their own
organization and
actively manage the
network of
relationships with
customers and
suppliers.*

Firms exist within supply chains whether or not executives decide to look beyond the walls of their own organization and actively manage the network of relationships with customers and suppliers. Increasingly, firms are sourcing materials globally, outsourcing production to low-cost areas, and establishing marketing presence in countries where products must be adapted for the local preferences. Thus, a number of activities occur outside the direct visibility of management. In this complex environment, relationship-based supply chain maps help management determine how many resources and what types of resources should be dedicated to each business relationship.

In order to better understand a company's supply chain, management needs a relationship-based supply chain map. Creating this map requires data that might be scattered throughout the organization or are not currently available at the needed level of disaggregation. Relationship-based maps will require data about entities beyond Tier 1. While the need to examine relationships beyond Tier 1 increases the challenge of developing this type of map, the potential value of the mapping effort is significant. For example, supply bottlenecks that may exist beyond Tier 1 must be addressed to reduce risk exposure. A relationship-based map should result in a deeper understanding of the supply chain realities.

Mapping involves gathering, organizing and presenting data visually to facilitate analysis of a supply chain. There are several reasons why management may want to undertake a mapping effort including: 1) to determine how to better serve existing customers; 2) to improve competitive positioning; 3) to evaluate the potential for outsourcing; 4) to meet the requirements of a customer segment; 5) to improve up-stream performance; and 6) to improve down-stream inventory replenishment. Management can select from a variety of mapping techniques based on their understanding of the supply chain and the particular business challenges.

Mapping involves gathering, organizing and presenting data visually to facilitate analysis of a supply chain.

Several mapping techniques can be used to identify opportunities to improve a firm's supply chain. For the relationship-based view of supply chain management developed in this book, two general categories of maps are relevant: relationship-based maps and activity-based maps, which include time-based process maps, pipeline inventory maps, and extended value stream maps. The relationship-based map serves as a starting point for identifying the key members of the supply chain. Given the degree of complexity that exists within most supply chains, development of the relationship-based map provides the needed focus for management efforts to identify opportunities for using the activity-based mapping techniques. While there are several existing sources of information on activity-based maps,[1] to date very little has been written about relationship-based maps. Therefore, the focus of this chapter will be primarily on developing an understanding of relationship-based mapping.

In this chapter, we show how relationship-based mapping can be used to identify key members of the supply chain. Relationship-based maps are described and two examples are provided. This type of map represents a critical first step for managers who want to develop a deeper understanding of their supply chain. Next, three distinct types of activity-based maps are described that build upon the output of the relationship-based mapping effort. Finally, a description of how to conduct a mapping session and conclusions are provided.

Relationship-based Maps

Supply chain management is about managing business relationships with a diverse set of customers and suppliers from the point-of-origin to the point-of-consumption. Relationship-based maps are used to help allocate resources within this network of organizations. Thus, relationship-based maps are focused on the corporate entities and on the relationships between the two companies that form each link in the supply chain. These maps serve as a critical first step for managers wanting to better understand the functioning of their firm's supply chain.

Mapping the corporate entities in the supply chain will facilitate the identification of opportunities that otherwise might go undetected. Also, it is necessary to identify relationships beyond Tier 1 that need to be managed. Relationship-based mapping contributes to the evaluation of consolidation opportunities in the supplier base, as well as the identification of opportunities to streamline the marketing channel by reducing the customer base through

Mapping the corporate entities in the supply chain will facilitate the identification of opportunities that otherwise might go undetected.

---

[1] See for example, Handfield, Robert B. and Ernest L. Nichols, Jr., *Supply Chain Redesign*, Upper Saddle River, NJ: Financial Times Prentice Hall, 2002; and, Quarterman Lee and Brad Snyder, *Value Stream and Process Mapping: The Strategos Guide*, Bellingham, WA: Enna Inc., 2007.

restructuring of the distribution network. For example, smaller less profitable segments of customers might be more effectively served through distributors.

Understanding the complexity in a supply chain can be a challenge. For a manufacturer in the middle of a supply chain, the supply chain network looks more like an uprooted tree than a chain (see Figure 11-1). The manufacturer can be viewed as the trunk of the tree, the branches are the network of customers and the roots are the network of suppliers. In the uprooted tree, some branches and some roots are bigger than others. This is also true within a supply chain, where some customers and some suppliers are more critical to the success of the focal firm's business.

To make a firm's complex network more manageable, it seems appropriate to distinguish between primary and supporting members.

To make a firm's complex network more manageable, it seems appropriate to distinguish between primary and supporting members. The definitions of primary and supporting members are based on interviews and discussions with the members of The Global Supply Chain Forum, and by applying the definition of a business process.[2] Primary members of a supply chain are all those autonomous companies or strategic business units who carry out value-adding activities (operational and/or managerial) in the business processes designed to produce a specific output for a particular customer or market.

Supporting members are companies that provide resources, knowledge, utilities or assets for the primary members of the supply chain. For example, supporting companies include those that lease trucks to the manufacturer, banks

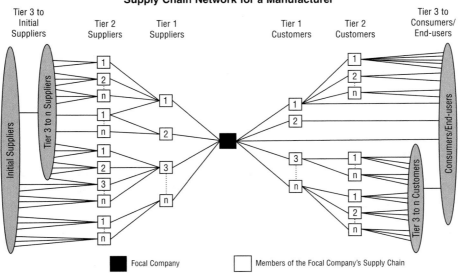

Figure 11-1
Supply Chain Network for a Manufacturer

Tier 3 to Initial Suppliers — Tier 2 Suppliers — Tier 1 Suppliers — Tier 1 Customers — Tier 2 Customers — Tier 3 to Consumers/End-users

Initial Suppliers — Tier 3 to n Suppliers — Consumers/End-users — Tier 3 to n Customers

■ Focal Company   ☐ Members of the Focal Company's Supply Chain

Source: Adapted from Douglas M. Lambert, Martha C. Cooper and Janus D. Pagh, "Supply Chain Management: Implementation Issues and Research Opportunities," *The International Journal of Logistics Management*, Vol. 9, No. 2 1998, p. 3.

[2] Davenport, Thomas H. and James E. Short, "The New Industrial Engineering: Information Technology and Business Process Redesign," *Sloan Management Review*, Vol. 31, No. 4 (1990), pp. 11-27.

that lend money to a retailer, the owner of the building that provides warehouse space, or companies that supply production equipment, print marketing brochures or provide temporary secretarial assistance. These supply chain members support the primary members.

The same company can perform both primary and supporting activities. Likewise, the same company can perform primary activities related to one process and supporting activities related to another process. Consider the case of an original equipment manufacturer (OEM) that buys some critical and complex production equipment from a supplier. When the OEM develops new products, managers work very closely with the equipment supplier to assure that they are using the supplier's equipment appropriately. Thus, the supplier is a member of the OEM's product development and commercialization process team. However, once the machinery is in place, the supplier is a supporting member for the manufacturing flow management process, since supplying the equipment does not in itself add value to the output of the process even though the equipment adds value.

The distinction between primary and supporting supply chain members is not obvious in all cases. Nevertheless, this distinction provides a reasonable managerial simplification and yet captures the essential aspects of who should be considered as key members of the supply chain. The definitions of primary and supporting members make it possible to define the point-of-origin and the point-of-consumption of the supply chain. The point-of-origin of the supply chain occurs where no previous primary suppliers exists. All suppliers to point-of-origin companies are supporting members. The point-of-consumption is where no further value is added, and the product and/or service is consumed.

Multiple Views of the Relationship-based Map

Since the map takes the perspective of the focal firm, it will look different depending on a company's position in the supply chain. The focal firm in Figure 11-1 could be a manufacturer such as Hewlett-Packard (HP), which has multiple tiers of suppliers. In the case of HP, the suppliers in Tier 1 include contract manufacturing firms; Tier 2 includes companies like Canon, who provides printer engines. Downstream in the supply chain, HP reaches end-customers through a distribution channel with multiple tiers (1 in Tier 1 Customers); sells to big-box retailers (2 in Tier 1 Customers) that sell to end-customers; and sells directly to end-customers through their web-site which is represented in Figure 11-1 with a straight line between the focal firm and Consumers/End-users.

The supply chain will look quite different from the perspective of one of HP's customers. Figure 11-2 depicts a supply chain network structure for a retailer (this could be the big-box retailer 2 in Figure 11-1). Note how the focal company is connected downstream solely to the end-customers and upstream with a network of suppliers; one of the boxes in Tier 1 – Suppliers is HP. On the other hand, Figure 11-3 illustrates the supply chain network structure for a supplier of original material, for example the company that extracts oil from the ground that will eventually become plastic resins for component parts. In the case of the oil company, the link between the focal company and the end-consumer will not exist because no consumer is likely to buy unprocessed crude oil. However, if the focal company was a shrimper or a farmer, it is possible that sales can be made directly to consumers.

Since the map takes the perspective of the focal firm, it will look different depending on a company's position in the supply chain.

Figure 11-2
Supply Chain Network Structure for a Retailer

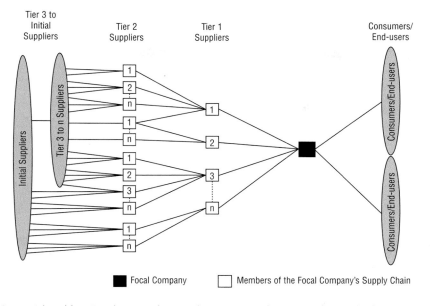

Source: Adapted from Douglas M. Lambert, Martha C. Cooper and Janus D. Pagh, "Supply Chain Management: Implementation Issues and Research Opportunities," *The International Journal of Logistics Management*, Vol. 9, No. 2 1998, p. 3.

Figure 11-3
Supply Chain Network Structure for a Supplier of Original Materials

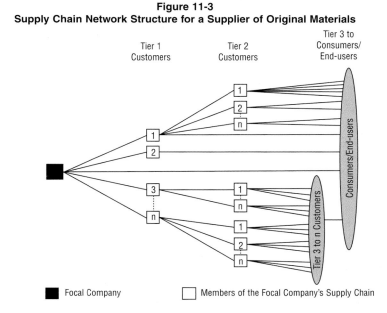

Source: Adapted from Douglas M. Lambert, Martha C. Cooper and Janus D. Pagh, "Supply Chain Management: Implementation Issues and Research Opportunities," *The International Journal of Logistics Management*, Vol. 9, No. 2 1998, p. 3.

The Structural Dimensions of the Network

The supply chain may be long, with numerous tiers, or short, with few tiers. As an example, the network structure for bulk cement is relatively short. Raw materials are taken from the ground, combined with other materials, moved a short distance, and used to construct buildings. The number of suppliers/customers represented within each tier also will vary (see Figure 11-2). The focal firm can have few companies at each tier or many suppliers and/or customers at each tier. Finally, the focal firm can be positioned at or near the initial source of supply (see Figure 11-3), be at or near to the ultimate customer (see Figure 11-2), or somewhere between these end points of the supply chain (see Figure 11-1).

Increasing or reducing the number of suppliers and/or customers affects the structure of the supply chain. As some companies move from multiple to single source suppliers, the supply chain may become narrower. Outsourcing logistics, manufacturing, marketing or product development activities is another example of decisions that change the supply chain structure. It may increase the length or width of the supply chain, and likewise influence the position of the focal company in the supply chain network because new tiers might be added to the supply chain.

Supply chains that burst to many Tier 1 customers/suppliers strain resources in terms of how many process links the focal company can integrate and closely manage beyond Tier 1. In general, our research team has found that in such cases only a few Tier 2 customers or suppliers are actively managed. Some of the companies studied have transferred servicing small customers to distributors, thus, adding a tier to the supply chain. This principle, known as functional spin-off,[3] is described in the marketing channels literature and can be applied to the focal company's network of suppliers.

Management of each company sees its firm as the focal company, and views membership and network structure differently. Because each firm is a member of the other's supply chain, it is important for management of each firm to understand their interrelated roles and perspectives. The integration and management of business processes across company boundaries will be successful only if it benefits each company.[4]

Complexity in a Supply Chain

The word "chain" suggests that supply chains are linear. In reality this is not the case. In practice, the network of relationships is more similar to those depicted in Figures 11-1, 11-2 and 11-3; in many cases supply chains are even more complex than these maps. Most companies are part of supply chains that overlap with those of competitors. Figure 11-4 represents the complexity found in a supply chain as a result of the focal firm being a seller to the same customers and a buyer from the same suppliers as its competitors (the other two boxes shown in the manufacturers' tier of the supply chain).

Some authors argue that the future of competition will not be company against company, but instead supply chains will compete directly against other

The integration and management of business processes across company boundaries will be successful only if it benefits each company.

---

[3] Stern, Louis W. and Adel El-Ansary, *Marketing Channels*, 5th Edition, Englewood Cliffs, NJ: Prentice Hall, 1995.

[4] Cooper, Martha C., Lisa M. Ellram, John T. Gardner and Albert M. Hanks, "Meshing Multiple Alliances," *Journal of Business Logistics*, Vol. 18, No. 1 (1997), pp. 67-89.

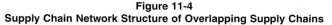

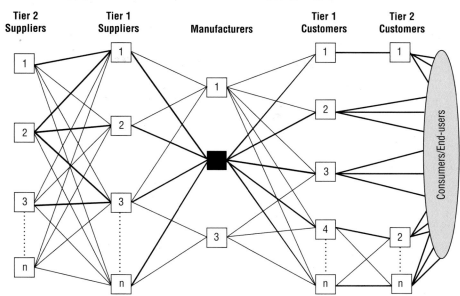

Source: Douglas M. Lambert and Terrance L. Pohlen, Supply Chain Metrics, *The International Journal of Logistics Management*, Vol. 12, No. 1 (2001), p. 9.

supply chains.[5] This is an over-simplification of the challenge in today's business environment. Supply chain versus supply chain can be the case only if management would not purchase from a supplier who sold to one of their competitors and would not sell to a competitor of an existing customer. Figure 11-4 illustrates the complexity in a real supply chain, where manufacturers of consumer packaged goods, such as Colgate-Palmolive, Procter & Gamble and Unilever, buy from the same suppliers (e.g. manufacturers of laminate for the toothpaste tubes) and sell to the same retailers (e.g. Carrefour and Wal-Mart). In this scenario, competition is based on how well the management of the focal firm and that of its competitors are able to leverage the relationships with customers and suppliers. In the long run, the most successful company will be the one whose management is able to tailor business relationships based on the expectations of the parties involved.

In the long run, the most successful company will be the one whose management is able to tailor business relationships based on the expectations of the parties involved.

Examples of Relationship-based Maps

In this section, we describe two cases of relationship-based mapping, one for a telecommunications company located in the USA and another for a supplier of beef products in Argentina. The cases provide insights on how to develop a relationship-based supply chain map and illustrate how strategic decisions can be made using the maps.

---

[5] Rice, James B. and Richard M. Hoppe, "Supply Chain vs. Supply Chain – The Hype and the Reality," *Supply Chain Management Review*, Vol. 79, No. 9-10 (2001), pp. 46-54; Hammer, Michael, "The Supperefficient Company," *Harvard Business Review*, Vol. 79, No. 9 (2001), pp. 82-91.

Supply Chain Relationship Mapping at Telecom Company. This example is based on a mapping session conducted at a telecommunications company headquartered in the United States. The focal firm, the wireless division, had two plants, one located in New Jersey and one located in Illinois, as well as a distribution center located in Illinois. The mapping session started with the identification of key Tier 1 suppliers that were determined to be critical to the firm based on a number of criteria such as volume purchased, availability of supply and potential risk. The goal when mapping the key Tier 1 suppliers was for management to determine the subset of suppliers that were the most important to the success of the firm. Figure 11-5 shows a disguised version of the supply chain map produced by executives from Telecom Company.

The mapping session started with the identification of key Tier 1 suppliers that were determined to be critical to the firm based on a number of criteria such as volume purchased, availability of supply and potential risk.

In this case, the mapping process required some investigation by the commodity managers, since not all Tier 2 suppliers were known. Commodity managers worked with the Tier 1 suppliers to identify Tier 2 suppliers of the most important materials and who offered the best opportunities for improvement. The development of the map revealed new information. For example, the map showed that Tier 1 suppliers, Supplier 1D and Supplier 1E, were buying components or materials from the same Tier 2 supplier, Supplier 2H. Despite the volume of each individual Tier 1 supplier being significant, the combined volume was larger. This discovery directed management to formalize a business relationship with Supplier 2H in order to leverage the volume of buy and gain efficiencies by sharing information and planning jointly. Also, if management decided to have two Tier 1 suppliers to diversify risk, the fact that both these suppliers buy from the same Tier 2 supplier reduces the effectiveness of this decision. A similar situation occurs with

Figure 11-5
Partial Supply Chain Map: Telecom Company

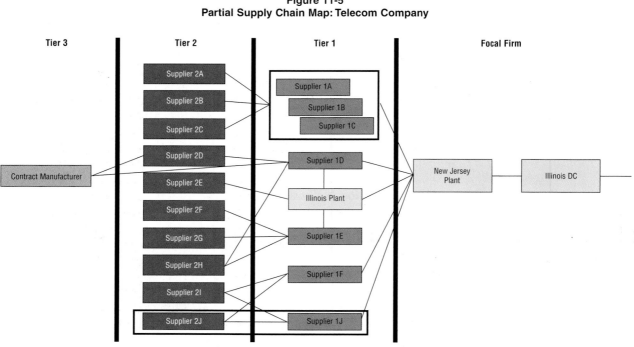

Supplier 2I and Supplier 2J, who both sold to Supplier 1F and Supplier 1J. Additionally, Supplier 1J and Supplier 2J are two divisions of the same company. In such a situation, management could evaluate the potential of managing a single business relationship with all divisions of the company.

The map shown in Figure 11-5 also illustrates that Supplier 1D and Supplier 1E ship materials to the plant owned by the focal company located in Illinois; then subassemblies were shipped to the plant in New Jersey; and finished products were shipped back to the Illinois distribution center located in the same city as the plant. Management could evaluate shifting production activities from Illinois to the New Jersey plant in order to reduce freight costs.

The next steps to further develop the supply chain map for Telecom Company would be to identify volumes in each link, the freight rates and prices of commodities or components to identify opportunities to leverage volume or increase service levels. These data would complete the relationship-based supply chain map, which could be used to develop a common understanding of the importance and the complexity found in each business relationship. This is required to achieve a coordinated effort among all corporate functions involved in the day-to-day activities supporting these relationships.

Diaz Herrera built a successful business based on integrating the beef supply chain in Argentina.

Supply Chain Relationship Mapping at Diaz Herrera. Diaz Herrera built a successful business based on integrating the beef supply chain in Argentina. Beef consumption in Argentina has a weekly spike in demand on the weekends. This spike in demand is attributable to a culture where people tend to connect entertaining and food. Grocery stores need to carry high quality beef products, have availability, and a wide assortment in order to generate traffic. The challenge is that the beef supply chain is fragmented and grocery chains struggle to fulfill end-customers' expectations.

Diaz Herrera built the business by managing relationships with both customers and suppliers. Figure 11-6 represents the supply chain for Diaz Herrera. Since the supply chain map always takes the perspective of the firm for which the map is being developed, the focal firm in this example is Diaz Herrera. Downstream in the supply chain, Diaz Herrera is vertically integrated, owning and renting slaughter houses. One of the Tier 1 customers included in the map is a food products distributor that provides the logistics service to distribute Diaz Herrera's meat products to other customers. By building a tailored business relationship, management at Diaz Herrera enabled the distributor to gain access to new customers (grocery retailers with whom Diaz Herrera already had business relationships) for the other services that the distributor offers. On the other hand, the distributor provided Diaz Herrera access to a network of medium size supermarkets that otherwise would have been difficult to serve. The other Tier 1 customer shown in the map represents a major portion of Diaz Herrera's slaughter services, but the same company is a supplier (cow/calf operation and grass-feeding) providing approximately 25% of Diaz Herrera's cattle purchase as well as holding a Hilton Quota. The Hilton Quota is the informal name of the tariff quota regulating beef exports destined for the European Union.[6]

The agricultural business in Argentina is dynamic for a number of reasons such as changing economic conditions, policies and trade quotas. In this environment, small and medium size farmers, in particular, may switch from

---

[6] For more information see http://en.wikipedia.org/wiki/Hilton_Quota.6

Figure 11-6
Supply Chain Map: Diaz Herrera

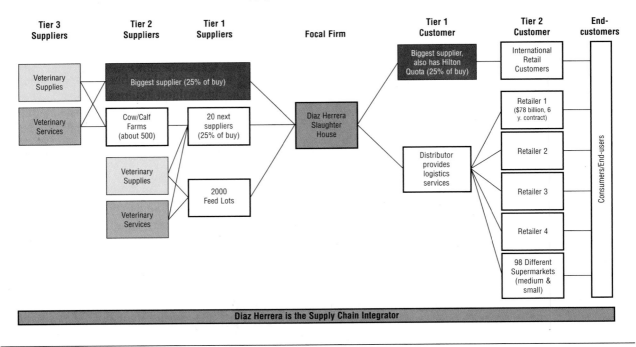

producing stock (cows) to growing crops, or vice versa, in a short period of time. Originally, Diaz Herrera was only in the beef business. But, at each of these swings in the business environment, the relationships that Diaz Herrera had built with both customers and suppliers were terminated because farmers would stop raising cattle. Livestock suppliers (cow/calf operations, veterinary suppliers and service providers) and customers (slaughter houses, distributors and retailers) suffered because farmers would unexpectedly switch from a cow/calf operation to a crop growing operation. In recent years, Diaz Herrera further developed his corporate strategy by broadening the scope of his business to both meat and crops. Now, Diaz Herrera capitalizes on the relationships with suppliers as a source of competitive advantage. When trade conditions are appropriate for exporting beef, Diaz Herrera leverages the buy on veterinary services and suppliers. When trade conditions favor crop exports, Diaz Herrera uses the same suppliers and supports them in the crop business.

Types of Business Process Links

Integrating and managing all business process links throughout the entire supply chain is likely not appropriate. Since the drivers for integration are situational and differ from process link to process link, the levels of integration should vary from link to link, and over time. Some links are more critical than others. As a consequence, the task of allocating scarce resources among the different business process links across the supply chain becomes crucial. The GSCF research indicates that four fundamentally different types of business process links

Since the drivers for integration are situational and differ from process link to process link, the levels of integration should vary from link to link, and over time.

can be identified between members of a supply chain: managed process links, monitored process links, not-managed process links, and non-member process links.

Managed Process Links. Managed process links are those that management of the focal company finds important to integrate and manage. In the supply chain shown in Figure 11-7, the managed process links are indicated by the thickest solid lines. The focal company will integrate and manage process links with Tier 1 customers and suppliers as well as with key firms beyond Tier 1.

Monitored Process Links. Monitored process links are not as critical to the focal company; however, it is important to the focal company that these process links are integrated and managed appropriately between the other member companies. Thus, the focal company, as frequently as necessary, simply monitors or audits how the process link is integrated and managed. The thick dashed lines in Figure 11-7 indicate the monitored process links.

Not-managed Process Links. Not-managed process links are links that the focal company is not actively managing, nor are they critical enough to use resources for monitoring. In other words, the focal company fully trusts the other members to manage the process links appropriately, or because of limited resources leaves it up to them. The thin solid lines in Figure 11-7 indicate the not-managed process links. For example, a manufacturer has a number of potential suppliers for cardboard shipping cartons. Usually the manufacturer will not choose to integrate and manage the links beyond the cardboard carton supplier all the way back to the

Figure 11-7
Types of Inter-Company Business Process Links

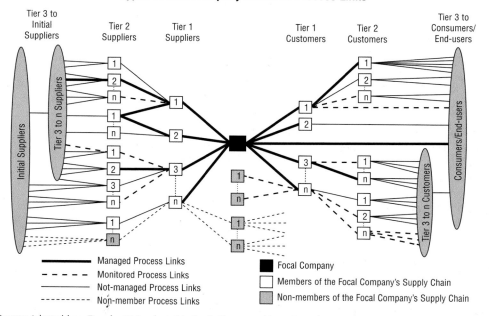

Source: Adapted from Douglas M. Lambert, Martha C. Cooper and Janus D. Pagh, "Supply Chain Management: Implementation Issues and Research Opportunities," *The International Journal of Logistics Management*, Vol. 9, No. 2 (1998), p. 7.

growing of the trees. The manufacturer wants certainty of supply, but it may not be necessary to integrate and manage the links beyond the cardboard carton supplier.

Non-member Process Links. Managers should be aware that their supply chains are influenced by decisions made in other connected supply chains. For example, a supplier to the focal company is a supplier to the chief competitor, which may have implications for the supplier's allocation of manpower to the focal company's product development and commercialization process, availability of products in times of shortage, and/or protection of confidentiality of information. Non-member process links are links between members of the focal company's supply chain and non-members of the supply chain. Non-member links are not considered as links of the focal company's supply chain structure, but they often affect the performance of the focal company and its supply chain. The thin dashed lines in Figure 11-7 illustrate examples of non-member process links.

Managers should be aware that their supply chains are influenced by decisions made in other connected supply chains.

Our research reveals variation in how closely companies integrate and manage links further away from the first tier. In some companies, management works through or around other members/links in order to achieve specific supply chain objectives, such as product availability, improved quality, or reduced overall supply chain costs. For example, a tomato ketchup manufacturer in New Zealand conducts research on tomatoes in order to develop plants that provide larger tomatoes with fewer seeds. Their contracted growers are provided with young plants in order to ensure the quality of the output. Since the growers tend to be small, the manufacturer negotiates contracts with suppliers of equipment and agricultural chemicals such as fertilizer and pesticides. The farmers are encouraged to purchase materials and machinery using the manufacturer's contract rates. This results in higher quality tomatoes and lower prices without sacrificing the margins and financial strength of the growers.

There are several examples of companies who, in times of shortage, discovered that it was important to manage suppliers beyond Tier 1 for critical items. One example involves a material used in the manufacturing of semiconductors. All six of the Tier 1 suppliers purchased from the same Tier 2 supplier. When shortages occurred, it became apparent that the critical relationship was with the Tier 2 supplier. It is important to identify the critical links in the supply chain and these may not be with the immediately adjacent firms.

The relationship-based map is used for making strategic decisions such as what are the critical companies with which a relationship needs to be developed and how much effort and resources need to be dedicated to each relationship. These decisions are likely to affect the structure of the supply chain both upstream (facing the network of suppliers) and downstream (facing the network of customers). Once management has decided with what other supply chain members they want to pursue managing business relationships, then there is an opportunity to look at the individual company's product flow structure to identify operational improvement opportunities.

Activity-based Maps

Opportunities in terms of product flow and costs may be identified through a more detailed understanding of the activities that represent the work that takes place within and between firms. An activity-based map identifies the specific steps and activities that make up the information, physical, or monetary flow of a process.[7] These maps can take a variety of forms and contain diverse sets of information.

From a systems point of view, an organization is a system that functions as a whole through the interaction of its parts. Process mapping is a managerial tool that uses systems thinking to determine how organizations perform the work. For every process, there is a functional sequence of events or actions. One action initiates another, which in turn initiates still another, until the process has completed its overall function by producing an output. Without understanding how the components of a process work together, it can be very difficult to predict what the consequences of an attempt to change the process might be. Everything in a process is connected to everything else. Thus, a change in one area of the process might produce unintended consequences in another area if the interrelationships are not well understood.

An activity-based map makes it easy for managers to understand the relationships among various processes, and among the steps within each process. A rigorously developed map should allow users to navigate throughout a process and its supporting processes. Through this increased visibility, managers should be able to make more informed decisions regarding any potential process changes.

Activity-based maps do not need to be limited only to activities within a facility. Supplier and customer activities can be represented as "supporting processes" to the facility's main processes. It is very important for managers of the facilities to understand how suppliers contribute to their overall processes. This knowledge should go well beyond having a life-cycle view of a product or service. If management truly understands the supplier's process, and the supplier's management understands the point where its contribution interacts with the focal company's process, then the two organizations will be better able to exchange information on best practices that can benefit them both.

Unfortunately, most organizations (and even some process improvement programs) treat suppliers as "outsiders." This view is not consistent with systems thinking. Most suppliers are happy to provide process information and discuss how best to use their products and services in their customers' processes. Suppliers realize that this promotes a much more favorable working relationship and can be the source of mutual gains.

The following sections will highlight some of the more popular activity-based mapping approaches: time-based process maps, pipeline inventory maps and extended value stream maps. As was the case with relationship-based maps, the visual definition of processes that are being performed in the supply chain can provide insights for maintaining control of the process and/or improving decision-making.

Without understanding how the components of a process work together, it can be very difficult to predict what the consequences of an attempt to change the process might be.

Time-based Process Mapping

Time-based process mapping (TBPM) is a tool for visually representing and analyzing the key interconnecting events and actions in relation to time.[8] Mangers can use this tool to compress the time required to perform these interacting processes. Time compression is the reduction of non-value added time throughout

---

[7] Bozarth, Cecil and Robert Handfield, *Introduction to Supply Chain Management*, Englewood Cliffs, NJ: Prentice Hall, 2005.

[8] Chapman, Paul, A. Harrison and V. Thayil, "Supply Chain Redesign at FinnForest Corp.," ECCH, Cranfield, UK. 2001.

a business in order to improve its competitiveness.[9] The primary goals of time compression are to increase productivity, improve quality, reduce cycle times and speed innovative products to market.[10] The achievement of these goals is dependent upon managing the entire supply chain and seeking to reduce pipeline length and/or to speed up flow through the pipeline.[11] As such, TBPM can be an effective tool for identifying activities in a process that add more cost than value.

In process mapping, time is a useful measure because it is a common unit of analysis and direct measure that, unlike cost, is not a lagging indicator. By using time as a process quality indicator, management is forced to a level of analysis on which they can focus their efforts. The key is for managers to systematically identify value- and non-value-adding time in the firm's processes. Value-adding time is time spent doing something that creates a benefit for which the customer is prepared to pay.[12] Whereas non-value-adding-time is time that is spent on activity whose elimination would lead to no reduction of benefit to the customer.[13] Figure 11-8 provides an example of a TBPM for a book printer.

As the TBPM is developed for a particular process, management must define

The primary goals of time compression are to increase productivity, improve quality, reduce cycle times and speed innovative products to market.

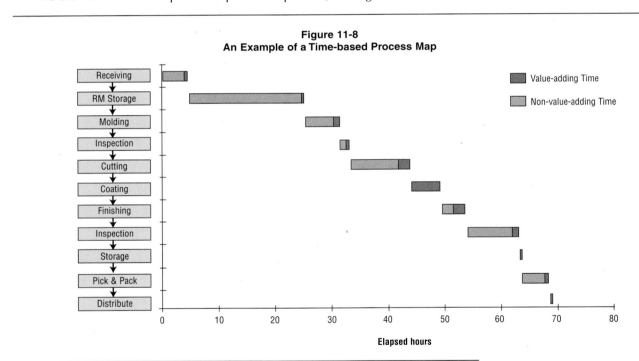

Figure 11-8
An Example of a Time-based Process Map

[9] Beesley, Adrian, "Time Compression in the Supply Chain," *Industrial Management and Data Systems*, Vol. 96, No. 2 (1996), pp. 12-17.

[10] Hui, Lou Tek, "Business Timeliness: The Intersection of Strategy and Operations Management," *International Journal of Productions & Operations Management*, Vol. 24, No. 6 (2004), pp. 605-624.

[11] Christopher, Martin, *Logistics and Supply Chain Management: Creating Value-Adding Networks*, 3rd Edition, London, UK: FT Press, 2005.

[12] Christopher, Martin, *Logistics and Supply Chain Management: Creating Value- Adding Networks*, 3rd Edition, London, UK: FT Press, 2005.

[13] Christopher, Martin, *Logistics and Supply Chain Management: Creating Value-Adding Networks*, 3rd Edition, London, UK: FT Press, 2005.

what a value-adding activity within the process is. An activity can be considered value adding if any of the following are true: 1) the customer cares about it; 2) it physically changes the item; and 3) it is done right the first time. While the definition of value-adding time may be context-dependent, managers must state clearly what is value adding, what is non-value adding and what is non-value adding but essential. This clarity is required in order to ensure those involved in the process will ultimately have confidence in the analysis of their activities. Inventory is associated with time and will depend on variability of lead-times. In the next section, we address pipeline inventory mapping.

Pipeline Inventory Process Mapping

A pipeline process map allows lead-times and inventory holdings for the supply chain to be shown together on the same page.

A pipeline process map allows lead-times and inventory holdings for the supply chain to be shown together on the same page. An example of this type of mapping is shown in Figure 11-9. The format of a pipeline process map is to show lead-time as a horizontal bar and inventory as a vertical bar. In both cases the length of the bar is proportional to the number of days of inventory it represents.

Using time to measure inventory and lead-time allows supply chain performance to be classified in the same units. There is an important relationship between lead-time and inventory. Specifically, supply chain lead-time increases the need for cycle stock and lead-time variability increases the requirements for safety stock. Therefore, reducing lead-time allows inventory levels to be reduced, thus reducing working capital, and improving responsiveness to changes in customer demand.[14] One of the problems with pipeline inventory mapping is that inventory builds in value as it moves closer to the point of consumption.

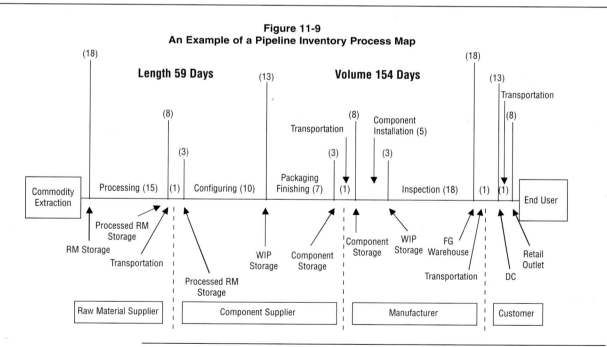

Figure 11-9
An Example of a Pipeline Inventory Process Map

[14] Chapman, Paul, A. Harrison and V. Thayil, "Supply Chain Redesign at FinnForest Corp.," ECCH, Cranfield, UK. 2001.

Consequently, a day of inventory is not equal to a day of inventory at a different location in the supply chain in terms of financial impact to the supply chain. This topic is covered in more detail in Chapter 15, Supply Chain Management Performance Measurement.

Extended Value Stream Maps[15]

Value stream maps are tools typically used within the four walls of manufacturing plants, for the identification and removal of waste that exists in the product flow.[16] But the value stream includes all actions necessary for bringing a product to market starting at the point where the product is designed and carrying through to production and ultimate delivery to the customer.[17] For this reason, there are opportunities to apply the use of value stream mapping to the entire supply chain. An extended value stream map (EVSM) exceeds the boundaries of the firm, usually extending to first-tier suppliers and customers.[18] While this scope will rarely represent the whole supply chain, the opportunities are often substantial within this scope. When scope must expand further up or downstream, the supply chain relationship-based map can help to identify which additional parties should be included.

Value stream maps are tools typically used within the four walls of manufacturing plants, for the identification and removal of waste that exists in the product flow.

The determination of the unit of analysis is critical to any mapping effort. For an EVSM, management should focus on a specific product or service. This focus is necessary because the map must reflect all variations, not only in the output and provisions but in inputs, time, and resources committed to the outputs. It is advisable to focus on a single product or service and typically one in which management feels significant improvement opportunities exist. Scope may expand or shift to other products or services over time. The key is to start simple and add breadth and scope based on the initial results.

Figure 11-10 shows a sample EVSM which will be described in greater detail in the next chapter. The company is a small manufacturer of surfboards and sells its products to consumers through a surf shop. Most of the surfboards are made-to-order. The map shows the activities of three key suppliers of raw materials. Each supplier fulfills weekly orders from the manufacturer's material requirements plan (MRP) and ships the order. Only two major steps of assembly are illustrated in the diagram. The first stage of assembly yields a generic blank, the foam core of the surfboard. The second stage provides for the customization and finishing of the board. Much greater detail could be provided regarding the manufacturing aspects of the product. For example, a manager might decide to map the process activity within individual work cells. However, the purpose of the EVSM is to examine the larger system of material and information flows among the key members of the supply chain. Where questions or opportunities dictate, closer examination follows.

Managers should use the relationship-based supply chain maps to identify the most significant suppliers and customers and where opportunities for improvement may reside. The EVSM helps management to identify the sources of waste in the

---

[15] This section is adapted from material contained in Chapter 12.

[16] Hines, Peter, Nich Rich, John Bicheno, David Brunt and et al, "Value Stream Management," *The International Journal of Logistics Management,* Vol. 9, No. 1 (1998), pp. 25-42.

[17] Rother, M. and Shook, J. "Learning to See, Value Stream Mapping to Add Value and Eliminate Muda," (1998), Brookline: The Lean Enterprise Institute.

[18] Dolcemascolo, Darren, "Bringing Lean to the Extended Supply Chain," *Supply Chain Management Review,* Vol. 10 No. 5, (2006), p. 61.

Figure 11-10
An Example of an Extended Value Stream Map

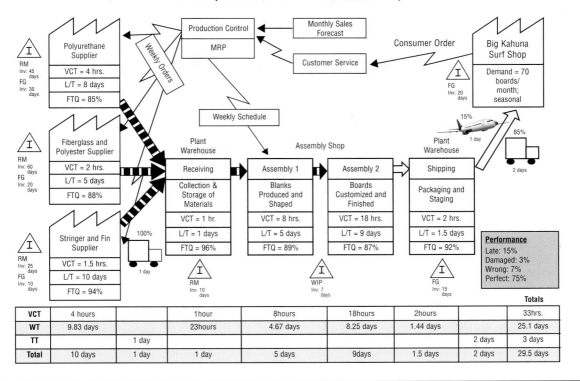

VCT	4 hours		1hour	8hours	18hours	2hours		33hrs.
WT	9.83 days		23hours	4.67 days	8.25 days	1.44 days		25.1 days
TT		1 day					2 days	3 days
Total	10 days	1 day	1 day	5 days	9days	1.5 days	2 days	29.5 days

value stream. In addition, by participating in the development of the current-state map, suppliers and customers could also benefit. Supplier and customer involvement could lead to the determination of how to improve quality while reducing wait time and non-value-added activity in yielding heightened customer satisfaction and healthier margins for the supply chain members. A future-state map captures the desired end state, where value is maximized, unnecessary steps are eliminated, and wastes are minimized.

Facilitating the Development of a Relationship-based Map

Typical mapping exercises can be structured around nine steps: 1) gain leadership support, 2) form the mapping team, 3) prepare for the mapping session, 4) identify key members of the supply chain, 5) determine critera for ranking suppliers and customers, 6) rank suppliers and customers, 7) identify opportunities, 8) establish implementation plan, and 9) reevaluate the map.

Step 1: Gain Leadership Support. It is critical that the mapping effort be supported at high levels within the organization and that a champion is identified early in the effort. It is necessary to communicate the power of visualizing the supply chain and of developing a consistent view of the relationships. The goals, perspective and scope of the effort should be clearly established.[19]

---

[19] Cooper, Martha C. and John T. Gardner, "Map Your Supply Chain", *CSCMP Explores...*, Vol. 2, Winter, (2005), pp. 1-16.

Step 2: Form the Mapping Team. Selecting the appropriate team members is a key to success. Management needs to identify the participants that will bring the knowledge that is necessary for developing the map. Participants may include executives from multiple functional areas. For example, R&D managers should know which suppliers are important in the development of new products. In addition, the potential involvement of suppliers and/or customers should be considered. In many cases, particularly on the supplier side, other supply chain members will provide visibility to relationships beyond Tier 1.

Step 3: Prepare for the Mapping Session. It is important to clearly delineate how the mapping session will be conducted. The session should be designed to facilitate the formation of the map of current relationships. Specific data that will be needed for the customer side of the supply chain include revenue, profitability, market segment, and cost-to-serve. For the supplier side, these data include volume of spend, products/materials purchased and cost.

Step 4: Identify Key Members of the Supply Chain. The objective of this step is to make an exhaustive list of customers and suppliers. In order to develop the relationship-based map, the best place to start is to identify the end-customers (segments or geographic regions) and build the map backward. Management needs to identify the target end-markets and move upstream identifying suppliers at each tier. If the mapping exercise starts with the supplier side of the supply chain, management should map Tier 1 suppliers and add key suppliers at each tier until the point-of-origin is reached.

Step 5: Determine Criteria for Ranking Suppliers and Customers. Generally, supply chains are very complex. For example, if a firm has 225 Tier 1 suppliers and each one of the 225 has on average 200 suppliers, there would be the potential for 45,000 Tier 2 suppliers. This complexity requires management to identify the customers and suppliers that are important enough to be part of the map. In order to make the mapping effort more manageable, criteria must be used to rank suppliers and customers to decide which ones should be placed on the map. Table 11-1 shows a list of potential criteria that might be use to rank suppliers. This list is meant only as an example, it is important for managers to identify the criteria that are most appropriate for their organization.

In order to make the mapping effort more manageable, criteria must be used to rank suppliers and customers to decide which ones should be placed on the map.

Step 6: Rank Suppliers and Customers. For each relationship identified in Step 4, use the criteria selected in Step 5, to evaluate each supply chain member. This is accomplished by recording the member's name and score on a spreadsheet. Table 11-2 contains a sample spreadsheet showing the data collected for Company A. As shown in Table 11-2, because not all criteria are going to be of equal importance, the team should identify the relative importance of each criterion on a scale of 1 to 3 were 3 indicates high importance. Then, for each supplier, there is a need to provide a rating on each criterion from 0 to 3, were 0 means that the criterion does not apply, 1 means low, 2 means medium, and 3 means high. The importance number multiplied by the rating provides a score for each criterion and summing the scores provides the total criticality score for each supply chain member.

Having calculated the criticality score for all the companies identified in Step 4, sort the relationships based on the criticality scores. Table 11-3 shows an example of the suppliers sorted by criticality; the table includes the company name, the criticality score, the map location (whether it is a customer or a supplier, and what tier is).

Table 11-1
Potential Criticality Criteria for Ranking Suppliers

- Volume of purchases
- Potential for partnership with supplier
- Potential to shut down production
- Potential to reduce total delivered cost
- Potential for joint development of new products
- Strategic importance of product/commodity
- Competitive threat - supplier becomes a competitor
- Long cycle time
- Potential for postponement/outsourcing
- Bottleneck (eliminate constraints, improve flow)
- Access to technology
- Product enhancements (quality, features, services)
- Large classes of members, each unimportant if taken alone, but collectively critical
- Special considerations unique to the industry

Table 11-2
Calculating Criticality Score for Company A

Criteria	Importance (1-3)	Rating (0-3)	Score
Potential partnership with supplier	2	2	4
Volume of purchases	3	3	9
Strategic importance of product/commodity	2	2	4
Potential to reduce total delivered cost	2	3	6
Potential to shutdown production	2	1	2
Potential for joint development of new products	3	2	6
Bottleneck (eliminate constraints, improve flow)	1	3	3
Total Criticality Score for Supply Chain Member			**34**

Table 11-3
Sorting Firms by Criticality Score

Firm Name	Criticality Score	Map Location (Supplier Tier e.g. C1, S2)
Company B	39	S1
Company C	36	S1
Company A	34	S1
Company Q	20	S2
Company D	27	S1
Company Y	25	S2

It may be necessary to schedule a number of meetings in order to obtain the data to complete the map. Management may find that there is a lack of visibility of relationships beyond Tier 1 and, thus, may need to obtain this information from key suppliers. Also, management may realize that in reality, the relationship with a key customer is being managed as multiple relationships. For example, in the mid 1990s, 3M found that the relationship with Target Corporation (a big retailer in the US) was managed like seven independent relationships; there was a corporate to corporate relationship and six divisions of 3M had relationships with six departments within Target. The output of this step is the "what is" map. The "what is" map represents the aggregated knowledge of all executives participating in the development of the map. This map becomes a powerful tool for identifying opportunities and risks.

Step 7: Identify Opportunities and Risks. Using the "what is" map, opportunities and risks are identified. Opportunities may include the need to formalize a relationship with customers and suppliers, develop a relationship with a Tier 2 company, or rationalize relationships. If there is a risk of supply, volatility in price or quality concerns, relationships may be managed beyond Tier 1. For example, The Coca-Cola Company is one of the largest purchasers of PET resins in the world. By combining their requirements across multiple suppliers, The Coca-Cola Company's worldwide volume exceeded that of any packaging supplier.

Step 8: Establish Implementation Plan. Based on the opportunities and risks identified, an action plan needs to be developed, responsibilities need to be assigned and timelines need to be established. Action items should include short-term and long-term projects. Short-term projects are the quick wins necessary to renew the support and show the value of the initiative. Long-term projects can include changes that will reshape the structure of the supply chain. Action items need to become agenda items at regularly scheduled meetings such as quarterly business reviews.

Step 9: Reevaluate Map. It is important to update and reanalyze the map. Once developed, the relationship-based map should become a dynamic document. The map should be revisited periodically to ensure that it is up-to-date and that it reflects any significant changes that have occurred in the supply chain (e.g., mergers, new suppliers, new customers, etc.).[20]

Conclusions

Many managers believe that supply chain maps, whether they are relationship-based or activity-based maps are not worth the effort to prepare. However, once management has these maps in hand, they often report that they cannot think of a better way to understand the nature of their supply chain—and the many interrelationships that exist within it. The maps are visual and provide managers with the basis for drilling down into particular processes in order to retrieve information that is critical to improve the functioning of the supply chain. As such, these types of maps can serve as a fundamental basis for a firm's entire supply chain improvement program.

The maps are visual and provide managers with the basis for drilling down into particular processes in order to retrieve information that is critical to improve the functioning of the supply chain.

[20] Cooper, Martha C. and John T. Gardner, "Map Your Supply Chain", *CSCMP Explores...*, Vol. 2, Winter, (2005), pp. 1-16.

12 Lean Thinking and Supply Chain Management

Thomas J. Goldsby and Sebastián J. García-Dastugue

Lean thinking in supply chain management is the use of lean principles to align activities across corporate functions within the firm and to manage business relationships with customers and suppliers.

Overview

Lean thinking provides principles and tools used to eliminate waste and to strive for perfection through continuous improvement. Though lean thinking was conceptualized to apply to all activities within the firm and across companies in the supply chain, usually lean is employed in operational settings within a single firm. Lean thinking in supply chain management is the use of lean principles to align activities across corporate functions within the firm and to manage business relationships with customers and suppliers. We show how lean principles and tools can be used in the context of the supply chain management framework. Also, we describe forms of waste that result from the lack of alignment in the supply chain – wastes that need to be eliminated in order to create greatest value for the end-customer.

Introduction

The term "lean" first appeared in The Machine that Changed the World[1] in reference to Toyota and its much heralded Toyota Production System (TPS). The book detailed the considerable differences observed between Toyota and its automotive rivals in an industry-wide study, where Toyota managed to achieve higher quality and greater output with less material, less space, and less equipment in less time– and was, hence, "leaner" than the competition. The study also documented the company's discipline and relentless pursuit of perfection through continuous improvement, or kaizen. Out of the original research conducted by Womack and Jones and others, a movement was born.

Since the mid-1990s, lean manufacturing has gained much attention in trade publications, industry reports, and case studies, where companies cite the benefits achieved through lean implementations. While reported benefits vary, a sample shows that lean principles successfully deployed in manufacturing can result in a 90% reduction in lead time, doubling of productivity, 75% reduction in inventory,

---

[1] Womack, James P., Daniel T. Jones, and Daniel Roos, *The Machine that Changed the World: The Story of Lean Production*, New York: Harper Perennial, 1991.

near-zero defects, reduced accidents, and improved morale.[2] In light of these benefits, it is easy to see why the lean movement has gained such a wide following. According to an annual survey conducted by *Industry Week* magazine, nearly 70% of U.S. manufacturers reported using lean principles as their primary method for improvement in 2007.[3] In a separate study, almost 90% of surveyed manufacturers indicated that they were pursuing Lean.[4]

In this chapter, we explore how lean thinking can be applied beyond the manufacturing function of a single company to the supply chain. We describe how to use lean thinking for the elimination of wastes that result from the lack of coordination among corporate functions within a firm and between firms. We start the chapter with the fundamental aspects of lean thinking. Second, we describe why lean thinking needs to be applied to operations of firms across the supply chain to create greater value for customers. This section includes a description of extended value stream mapping which is used to identify improvement opportunities across multiple firms. Third, we explain how lean thinking and supply chain management concepts and tools can be combined. Fourth, we describe forms of waste that can be identified when lean thinking is used in the context of managing business relationships. Finally, we present conclusions.

Fundamentals of Lean Management

The main premise of lean management is the elimination of muda, a Japanese expression for any activity that consumes resources without creating value in the eyes of the customer. Toyota engineer Taiichi Ohno identified seven forms of muda, or waste, in the development of the Toyota Production System. These wastes include: overproduction, waiting, unnecessary transportation, overprocessing, inventory, unnecessary movement and defective products[5]

In addition to muda, lean management is focussed on the elimination of mura and muri. Mura refers to unevenness in an operation, which causes operations to hurry at times and wait at others. Muri is the term that applies to the overburdening of equipment or the operator beyond management rules given the risks of equipment breakage or personal injury. The concepts of muda, mura, and muri are closely interrelated.[6] When asked to summarize the Toyota system for continuous improvement some years after creating TPS, Taiichi Ohno said, "All we are doing is looking at the time line from the moment the customer gives us an order to the point when we collect the cash. And we are reducing that time line by removing the non-value-added wastes."[7]

The main premise of lean management is the elimination of muda, a Japanese expression for any activity that consumes resources without creating value in the eyes of the customer.

---

[2] Liker, Jeffrey, The Toyota Way: 14 *Management Principles from the World's Greatest Manufacturer,* New York: McGraw-Hill, 2004.

[3] Blanchard, David, "Census of U.S. Manufacturers – Lean, Green, and Low Cost," *Industry Week,* (October 1, 2006); available at http://www.industryweek.com/ReadArticle.aspx?ArticleID=15009.

[4] Aberdeen Group, *The Lean Benchmark Report: Closing the Reality Gap,* 2006.

[5] Taiichi Ohno was the first to report these wastes, or forms of muda, in *Toyota Production System: Beyond Large-Scale Production,* New York: Productivity Press, 1988.

[6] Lean Enterprise Institute, *Lean Lexicon: A Graphical Glossary for Lean Thinkers,* 3rd Edition, Cambridge, MA: Lean Enterprise Institute, 2006.

[7] Ohno, Taiichi, *Toyota Production System: Beyond Large-Scale Production,* New York: Productivity Press, 1988, p. ix.

TPS includes an array of principles, and associated tools and practices. Though a comprehensive review of these principles and tools is beyond the scope of this chapter, some of the more prevalent aspects of lean manufacturing are presented in Table 12-1. It is through the disciplined adherence to these principles that Toyota has risen steadily to become the world's most admired manufacturing company and one of the most successful and profitable companies.[8]

Table 12-1
Lean Principles and Tools

Principle	Tools and Practices
Waste Reduction	Value Stream Mapping, Problem Solving, Genchi Genbutsu (go to where work is done), Five-Why's
Just-in-Time	Pull System, Quick Changeover, One-Piece and Continuous Flow, Kanban, Heijunka (Leveled Production), Takt Time Planning
Jidoka ("Make problems visible")	Visual Tools, 5S, Poka Yoke (error proofing), Andon (highlight and study the problem)
Single-Market Quality	Stable and Standardized Processes
Continuous Improvement	Kaizen (eye for wastes and improvement from everybody everyday), Discipline (to fight complacency and pursue perfection)
Respect for People	Safety, Teamwork, Training and Learning, Shared Rewards

Lean practices tend to focus on operational activities, and manufacturing activities in particular.

Lean practices tend to focus on operational activities, and manufacturing activities in particular. In a follow-up to The Machine that Changed the World, Womack and Jones[9] extended the principles of lean manufacturing and introduced the concept of "lean thinking". Lean thinking embodies an integrated approach to supply chain operations, dictating that the company: 1) specify value from the customer's perspective, 2) identify the value stream, 3) make value flow, 4) let customers pull their supply, and 5) strive toward perfection. The value stream refers to all of the actions required to bring a product from concept to launch and from order to delivery.[10] By assuming a "value stream" approach, lean thinking requires that the customer[11] not only play an integral role but drive the actions of all upstream supply chain members. This requires that management not only be aware of but actively manage the operational interfaces with key suppliers and customers in order to meet the needs of the end-customer. This integrated approach to materials management across the supply chain is what we refer to as lean supply chain operations, where the flows of materials and information are coordinated across primary members of the supply chain. Coordinated flow of materials helps to

---

[8] Liker, Jeffrey, *The Toyota Way: 14 Management Principles from the World's Greatest Manufacturer*, New York: McGraw-Hill, 2004.

[9] Womack, James P. and Daniel T. Jones, *Lean Thinking*, New York: Simon & Schuster, 1996.

[10] Lean Enterprise Institute, *Lean Lexicon: A Graphical Glossary for Lean Thinkers*, 3rd Edition, Cambridge, MA: Lean Enterprise Institute, 2006.

[11] When Womack and Jones (1996) refer to "the customer," we are to infer that they are speaking of the end customer and not the next-tier customer when a company sells through multiple tiers to reach the end-user market. In the case of Toyota, the next-tier customer are the dealers.

reduce the wastes identified by Ohno across involved companies.

Lean thinking must go beyond the factory if it is to achieve its objective of waste elimination across the supply chain; that is, both upstream with the suppliers' operations and downstream with customers. Failing to adopt a holistic view of the supply chain might result in the transfer of wastes to other members of the supply chain, thereby not eliminating waste but simply shifting it to others. For example, if management in the manufacturing company focuses internally to become leaner and pushes inventory away to customers and suppliers, the supply chain could be worse-off than if the manufacturing company holds the necessary amount of inventory to make the supply chain as a whole more efficient, particularly if the inventory costs are higher for other parties in the supply chain.[12] The manufacturing company might be leaner, but the costs and burdens associated with the supplier's waste ultimately will be passed along to the customer. The implementation of lean thinking requires extending its application across the operations of the key members of the supply chain.

Failing to adopt a holistic view of the supply chain might result in the transfer of wastes to other members of the supply chain, thereby not eliminating waste but simply shifting it to others.

Applying Lean Principles to Supply Chain Operations

Initiating lean in supply chain operations starts the same way that lean would be implemented within the company or even at the facility level – by instilling a culture of lean thinking. Management must establish the fundamental principles and tools of lean throughout the company in order that everyone be engaged every day in finding and eliminating waste. This culture should spread from the focal company to its key suppliers and customers, where wastes are identified and addressed collectively.

The benefits of lean grow with the involvement of multiple parties in the supply chain. The greatest value will be created where the discussions about improvement opportunities are open, honest, and encouraged. Toyota presents an excellent case for lean engagement with its suppliers. Toyota expects suppliers to support the just-in-time manufacturing at its plants and to identify opportunities for jointly improving operations. These opportunities are not limited to physical flow management and cost containment but include improved part engineering in what Toyota refers to as its Value Innovation Strategy.[13] This level of engagement, setting the right expectations and rewards, assures the company that suppliers bring forward innovation. For this reason, Toyota is regarded by automotive suppliers as the best original equipment manufacturer (OEM) to serve as well as the most demanding.[14]

Another example is provided by the 3M Company. Management at 3M extended lean to the relationship with xpedx, a major customer in the industrial consumable distribution business. The two companies collaborated on a project to reduce 3M's distribution costs and xpedx's inventory costs while improving the delivery service to xpedx customers. A joint solution was reached to handle fast-moving "A" items differently from slower-moving "B" and "C" items with 3M

---

[12] García-Dastugue, Sebastián J. and Douglas M. Lambert, Interorganizational Time-Based Postponement in the Supply Chain, *Journal of Business Logistics*, Vol. 28, No. 1 (2007), pp. 57-82.

[13] Anonymous, "The World's Most Innovative Companies," *Business Week* (April 24, 2006); available at: www.businessweek.com/magazine/content/06_17/b3981401.htm.

[14] Jackson, Bill and Michael Pfitzmann, "Win-Win Sourcing," *Strategy + Business*, Summer 2007; available at: http://www.strategy-business.com/press/article/07207?gko=04618.

assuming responsibility for inventory management and shipping of the slowest moving items directly to customers of xpedx. 3M's deployment of the company's expertise not only improved the order fulfillment process, establishing a template for future improvement efforts, but strengthened the relationship with a key customer.

A relationship-based supply chain map can help management to determine which suppliers and customers represent the best opportunities to eliminate waste, reduce cost, and create greater value (see Chapter 11). Candidates for lean collaboration may include the company's most valued customers where lean provisions can help to solidify good relationships. Customers providing below-average returns for the company also may represent good candidates. With respect to the engagement of upstream parties and service providers, the company's most critical suppliers are the most likely place to start to enhance mutual value and incite innovation in products and processes. Although all members of a company's supply chain should be considered eligible for inclusion in the lean effort and should be encouraged to pursue continuous improvement, the focus should be on those suppliers and customers that offer the greatest potential for improvement. Over time, as experience and maturity are gained and the benefits become more apparent, supply chain members outside the selected core will seek their own involvement.

Candidates for lean collaboration may include the company's most valued customers where lean provisions can help to solidify good relationships.

Extended Value Stream Mapping

Once good prospects for lean collaboration are identified using a relationship-based map, the parties should come together to map the value stream. The value stream includes all actions currently necessary for bringing a product to market from design to production and ultimate delivery to the customer.[15] A typical value stream map (VSM) focuses on the production activities, working backwards from the plant's shipping dock to the plant's receipt of materials. An extended value stream map (EVSM) has a scope that is beyond the boundaries of the firm, usually extending to first-tier suppliers and first-tier customers.[16] Substantial opportunities for improved operations and interface can be found within this broader scope. The EVSM could include selected customers or suppliers beyond the first tier that are critical to the success of the focal firm. Rarely, the whole of the supply chain, from the extraction of raw materials to end-user consumption, will be in a single EVSM because complexity increases as more members of the supply chain are included in the map.

An extended value stream map (EVSM) has a scope that is beyond the boundaries of the firm...

Critical to any mapping effort is the determination of the unit of analysis or scope. For an EVSM, the parties should choose a specific product or service to serve as the unit of analysis. The problem with not focusing on a specific product is that the map must address all variations, not only in the output but in inputs, time, and resources committed to the outputs. Therefore, it is advisable to focus on a single output and particularly one in which all parties feel significant improvement opportunities exist. Scope may expand or shift to other outputs over time. The key is to start simple, and add to the scope as experience is gained and value is perceived.

---

[15] Rother, Mike and John Shook, *Learning to See: Value-Stream Mapping to Create Value and Eliminate Muda*, Cambridge, MA: Lean Enterprise Institute, 2007.

[16] Dolcemascolo, Darren, *Improving the Extended Value Stream: Lean for the Entire Supply Chain*, New York: Productivity Press, 2006.

Figure 12-1 shows a sample EVSM that features a small manufacturer of handcrafted surfboards. The manufacturer sells products to consumers through a surf shop distribution channel, where most boards are customized. Upstream of the manufacturer the map includes the operations of three key suppliers of raw materials. Each supplier fulfills weekly orders from the manufacturer's material requirements plan (MRP) and ships by truck, taking one day for each shipment. Only two major steps of assembly are illustrated in the diagram. The first stage of assembly yields a generic blank, the foam core of the surfboard. The second stage provides for the customization and finishing of the board. More detail could be provided regarding the molding, shaping, laminating, and finishing of the product, and this is the level of detail that would be found in a conventional value stream map focused on the operations within the assembly facility. Also, it is possible to map the process activity within individual work cells when more detail is needed. The purpose of the EVSM is to examine the larger system of material and information flows among the key members of the manufacturer's supply chain. Where opportunities are identified, closer examination provided by value stream maps would follow.

The extended value stream map for the surfboard manufacturer yields many significant insights. For example, of the 29.5 pipeline days (days from first-tier supply to surf shop delivery) only 33 hours represent value creation time (VCT). Only 4.7% of the time that the material/product is in the system is value added,

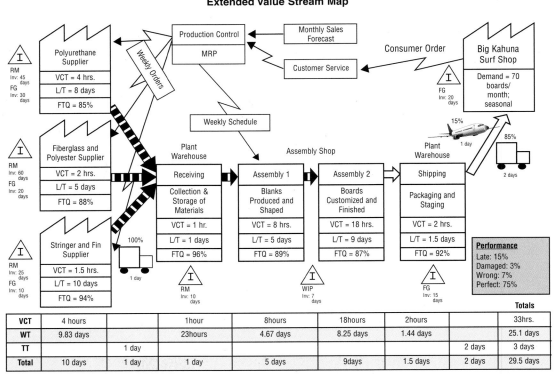

Figure 12-1
Extended Value Stream Map

VCT	4 hours		1hour	8hours	18hours	2hours		33hrs.
WT	9.83 days		23hours	4.67 days	8.25 days	1.44 days		25.1 days
TT		1 day					2 days	3 days
Total	10 days	1 day	1 day	5 days	9days	1.5 days	2 days	29.5 days

with the remaining 95.3% comprised of wait time (WT), non-value-added processing, and transit time (TT). This low level of throughput efficiency points to substantial improvement potential.

Also, the delivery performance experienced by the surf shop is poor. Lead times are quite long (usually 12.5 days when an appropriate semi-finished board is available and delivery is provided by truck), and yet 15% of shipments are late, 3% are damaged, and 7% are wrong or inaccurate, resulting in 75% perfect delivery. This level of delivery performance may not sound so bad, but compare it to the percentage of time in which all activities are performed according to specifications as measured by first-time quality (FTQ). The FTQ is listed for each stage in the value stream in Figure 12-1. When these are multiplied together (85% x 88% x 94% x 96% x 89% x 87% x 92%), we find that first-time quality is achieved only 48.1% of the time, with suppliers combining for first-time quality 70.3% of the time and the manufacturer providing first-time quality at a 68.4% level. How is it then that 48.1% FTQ results in 75% perfect delivery for the surf shop? The answer lies in the inventories held throughout the value stream. The map indicates that the suppliers, manufacturer, and the surf shop combine for 242 days of supply, with inventories in various states of completion. The 75% perfect delivery figure is disappointing in light of the substantial inventories maintained to back up the service commitment.

While further insight can be drawn from the extended value stream map, the example shows that opportunities for improvement are many and significant. Some opportunities rest with the manufacturer in isolation, while others might be found with the interactions between the manufacturer and its suppliers and customers. The EVSM helps management from all firms involved to identify the sources of waste in the value stream and serves as the starting point for broad-based lean implementation. After participating in the development of the current-state map, suppliers and customers should join the manufacturer in determining how to improve quality while reducing wait time and non-value-added activity in order to provide increased customer service and healthier margins for the supply chain members. A future-state map captures the desired end state, where value is increased, unnecessary steps are eliminated, and wastes are reduced and not transferred to others. It has been suggested that the desired future-state condition should be attainable within 12 months.[17]

> *The EVSM helps management from all firms involved to identify the sources of waste in the value stream and serves as the starting point for broad-based lean implementation.*

Coca-Cola conducted an EVSM session with a key supplier and customers in the non-carbonated beverage business. The exercise enabled management to identify improvement opportunities to serve Coca-Cola customers better and to be a better customer to the supplier. The EVSM is a powerful tool to engage involved parties, permitting them to see waste, collectively understand the opportunity for improvement, and act as a group. This premise of seeing, knowing, and acting as a group is a fundamental aspect of lean supply chain operations.[18]

To the extent that the benefits of the joint continuous improvement effort are shared, the spirit of cooperation will be reinforced. As described in more detail in the descriptions of customer relationship management and the supplier relationship management (Chapter 2 and 3, respectively), these two processes form

---

[17] Dolcemascolo, Darren, *Improving the Extended Value Stream: Lean for the Entire Supply Chain,* New York: Productivity Press, 2006.

[18] Dennis, Pascal, *Lean Production Simplified,* 2nd Edition, New York: Productivity Press, 2007.

the links in the supply chain. Initiatives that show favorable results for all parties help to sustain not only the relationship but the pursuit of innovation and continuous improvement. The challenge lies in determining how to share benefits with customers and suppliers with fair returns for all parties. Guidelines to share risk and rewards are necessary to obtain the full commitment of all parties. Relationships built on trust and commitment will have the foundation to focus on the long-term benefit of all involved and avoid opportunistic behavior. The guidelines for benefit sharing should be agreed upon before the opportunities are identified and be included in the product and service agreement.

Lean Thinking and Supply Chain Management

Lean principles should be applied beyond the realm of the manufacturing function and across companies in the supply chain to reduce the wastes commonly found in supply chain operations. To realize the full benefit of both lean thinking and supply chain management, the scope of lean implementations must exceed a single function and should be positioned as part of the management of relationships with customers and suppliers. Lean thinking in supply chain management embodies the management's efforts to adopt lean principles to align activities across corporate functions within the firm and to manage business relationships with customers and suppliers, where muda, mura and muri are eliminated from the supply chain as a whole. It involves continuous improvement through the elimination of wastes to increase the company's financial performance and that of customers and suppliers.

To realize the full benefit of both lean thinking and supply chain management, the scope of lean implementations must exceed a single function and should be positioned as part of the management of relationships with customers and suppliers.

While lean supply chain operations focus on the efficient flow of materials, goods and information across supply chain members, the application of lean to supply chain management goes beyond the physical flows of inventory to include the totality of the business relationship between firms. Table 12-2 illustrates the distinctions between lean applied solely to the manufacturing function and lean applied to the larger scope of supply chain management. Most pervasive in these differences is the recognition that to be "truly lean," management must focus on

---

Table 12-2
Lean Manufacturing vs. Lean Thinking and Supply Chain Management

Lean Manufacturing	Lean Thinking and SCM
• Focus: Operational efficiency within a plant	• Focus: Profitability; Efficiency and effectiveness across companies
• One business function involved	• All business functions involved
• Scope of activities: Receiving to shipping of a single facility represents the value stream	• Scope of activities: Raw material extraction to end user consumption i extended value stream
• Ohno's seven wastes in the operations of a single plant	• Ohno's seven wastes as well as others across the supply chain
• Customer demand is a given or there is arbitrary allocation	• Customer demand can be managed (Sales/Marketing involvement)
• Burdens and rewards are contained to production function	• Burdens and rewards are shared across funcations and into supply chain
• Cost reduction, asset efficiency, and inventory reduction are value drivers	• Revenue growth, cost reduction, asset efficiency, and working capital reduction as value drivers

efficiency and cost reductions, as well as profitability. For most implementations of lean manufacturing demand is taken as a given. As a result, the manufacturer may be very efficient (i.e., very "lean"), yet efficient in producing the wrong products when sales and marketing are not involved. Lean thinking and supply chain management is focused on cost reduction, asset efficiency, and inventory reduction as value drivers, as well as revenue growth and working capital reductions in inventory and non-inventory investments (e.g., accounts receivables).

The blending of lean thinking and supply chain management is natural in light of their complementary beliefs.

The blending of lean thinking and supply chain management is natural in light of their complementary beliefs. Some of the important commonalities between the two approaches include:

- Long-term perspective;
- Focus on the customer and creating value;
- Systems or holistic view, where emphasis is placed on performance of the whole and not the parts;
- Coordinated action and teamwork across work areas through process orientation;
- Standardized work and best-practice replication;
- Structured business relationships that are appropriate for short- and long-term needs; and,
- Reward systems that are fair and commensurate with burdens of work and risk.

This list of common characteristics indicates how much lean lends to supply chain management and vice versa. A closer look at lean thinking, its principles, and tools shows how the elements of lean relate to the supply chain management framework. Figure 12-2 illustrates how the lean principles relate to the management components of the framework. On one hand, the principles of waste reduction and respect for people overlap with the structural management components, namely control methods, knowledge management, and communication structure. The

Figure 12-2
Lean Principles and SCM Management Components

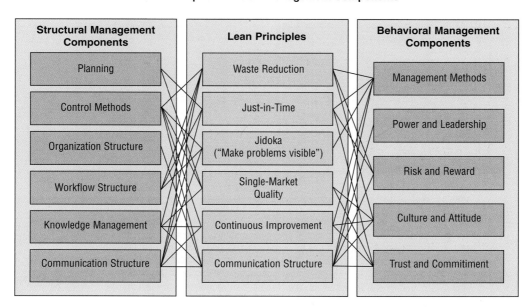

behavioral management components of management methods, culture and attitude, and trust and commitment contribute to lean's respect for people, focus on waste reduction, and continuous improvement.

The lean tools, some of which are referenced in Table 12-1, can be used for the implementation of the supply chain management processes. Figure 12-3 takes a sample of the lean tools and shows where they may be employed in the eight supply chain management processes. Value stream mapping may be employed across all eight processes, depending on the map's scope. Likewise, Five-Why's (the practice of asking "why?" five times to identify the root cause of defects), stable and standard processes, kaizen (continuous improvement), and shared rewards can find application in all eight processes. The application of kanban systems to signal replenishment needs in pull-based environments is a viable means of managing the physical flows found in order fulfillment, manufacturing flow management and returns management when returnable containers are involved. Kanban can be used in demand management, customer relationship management, and supplier relationship management. Finally, the concept of 5S (referring to five Japanese expressions that begin with an "s" sound) which provides for a safe, orderly, and efficient work environment could apply anywhere that work is done, though it is most often found in the operational environments of order fulfillment, manufacturing flow management, and returns management.

A Broader View of Waste

When one views lean principles in the wider scope of supply chain management, a set of wastes can be identified beyond the seven identified by

When one views lean principles in the wider scope of supply chain management, a set of wastes can be identified beyond the seven identified by Toyota's Taiichi Ohno.

Figure 12-3
Matching Lean Tools to SCM Processes

Process	Value Stream Mapping	Five Why's	Kanban	5S	Stable & Standard Process	Kaizen	Shared Rewards
CRM	+	+	+		+	+	+
SRM	+	+	+		+	+	+
CSM	+	+			+	+	+
DM	+	+	+		+	+	+
OF	+	+	+	+	+	+	+
MFM	+	+	+	+	+	+	+
PD&C	#	+			+	+	+
RM	+	+	#	+	+	+	+

"+" indicates common application
"#" indicates occasional application with broader application

Toyota's Taiichi Ohno. While Ohno's seven wastes remain relevant, other forms of waste exist beyond the purview of manufacturing management. Failing to eliminate these wastes will result in the forms of waste that Ohno identified. Using lean thinking only within the purview of manufacturing will not assist management in the identification of other wastes that will erode value to the customer. These wastes can be eliminated only through alignment of efforts across corporate functions with business objectives.

Management that adheres to lean thinking should strive to identify the sources of hidden costs and missed opportunities...

The challenge is that inefficiencies and missed opportunities that result from friction between corporate functions and friction with customers and suppliers generally take the form of hidden costs. We believe that the forms of waste suggested by Ohno represent the tip of an iceberg when compared to the larger collection of wastes found in organizations (see Figure 12-4). Management that adheres to lean thinking should strive to identify the sources of hidden costs and missed opportunities, which are represented by the portion of the iceberg that is below the surface in Figure 12-4. These below-the-surface wastes will usually become apparent only after they result in disappointing financial performance, disgruntled suppliers, or irate customers. The elimination of the following wastes will result in improving management practices so that all corporate functions become customer focused and financially driven:

- Cost allocations for decision making;
- Missed opportunities for value creation;
- Disconnects between promise making and promise keeping;
- Unclear expectations in business relationships;
- Late detection of action required;
- Misalignment of incentives; and,
- Excessive product proliferation.

Figure 12-4
Misalignment Results in Wastes Below the Surface

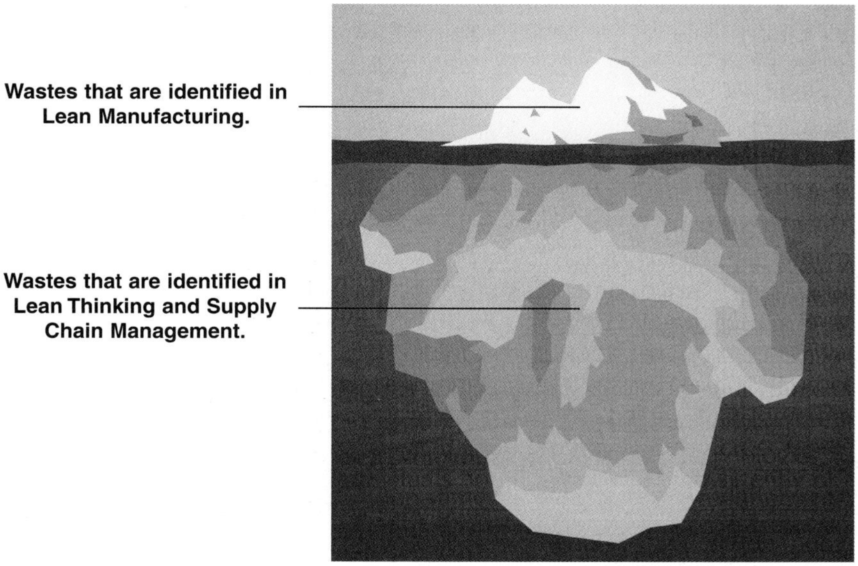

Wastes that are identified in Lean Manufacturing.

Wastes that are identified in Lean Thinking and Supply Chain Management.

Cost Allocations for Decision Making

Management often feels compelled to allocate all costs when making decisions regarding products, services, and customers. However, management should only consider avoidable out-of-pocket costs for such decisions. Out-of-pocket costs are those that go away if the unit of analysis is removed. The avoidable out-of-pocket costs are the variable costs and the direct fixed costs that can be attributed to a specific product, service, or customer. For instance, customer profitability reports should include the costs that are eliminated if the company stops selling to a particular customer. This includes all avoidable marketing costs, such as sales commissions, marketing discretionary costs (e.g., slotting allowances and marketing development funds), and the cost of dedicated resources (e.g., key account manager or a dedicated warehouse facility). Also, these reports should include costs that are direct to the flow of products, including transportation to the customer, and warehouse handling and order processing costs directly related to the products shipped to that customer. These reports should not include any portion of unassignable fixed costs like salaries of marketing, sales, and logistics executives; nor unassignable fixed costs of logistics and manufacturing operations, such as a fraction of warehouse or manufacturing plant costs (see Appendix to Chapter 2).

Management often feels compelled to allocate all costs when making decisions regarding products, services, and customers.

When evaluating profitability by product, only the costs that would be eliminated if that product (the specific stockkeeping unit [SKU]) is removed should be included in the analysis.[19] This includes the inventory investment of the item or any special advertisements for that item. If only one SKU is eliminated from a product line, and there is advertisement for the whole product line, the advertising budget will not be reduced if the SKU is eliminated.

The premise of not including all costs in decision making is not comfortable for many. A common argument is that "someone has to pay for the general and administrative costs." However, if the firm as a whole is the unit of analysis, all costs are direct to the entire firm; if the firm goes away then all costs are removed. So, cost data must be disaggregated at a level appropriate for the decision at hand; this is referred to as contribution analysis or segmental analysis.[20] Allocating costs that should have not been allocated produces lower-quality information for decision making, which, in turn, will result in poorer decision outcomes. The bigger the costs that are arbitrarily allocated, the more equal all customers/customer segments/products will appear in financial terms. Lean thinking applied to financial reports strives for the elimination of waste that reduces the quality of the information used for decision making.

Missed Opportunities for Value Creation

As competition intensifies, management may attempt to offer higher value propositions to customers. In ongoing business relationships, value provided to customers and the focus of the relationships often shifts away from the tangible product to services, the intangible aspects of the relationship. The services provided to customers, such as information sharing, product availability, customization of products or services, and advance notice of delays become central to vendor

---

[19] Lambert, Douglas M (1985), *The Product Abandonment Decision*, National Association of Accountants; Society of Management Accountants of Canada, Montvale, N.J.; Hamilton, Ont., Canada.

[20] Mossman, Frank H., Paul M. Fischer, W. J. E. Crissy, "New Approaches to Analyzing Marketing Profitability," *Journal of Marketing*, Vol. 38, No. 2 (1974), pp. 43-48.

selection and evaluation.[21] In this sense, every firm competes on services.[22] Consistent service delivery requires the adequate execution of activities based on knowledge and skills that reside in the corporate functions. Developing service components valued by the customer through understanding customer needs – and the resources consumed in providing the product/service bundle — requires the involvement of all the corporate functions.[23]

There are two main reasons that missed opportunities for value creation may result: 1) lack of adequate functional involvement, and 2) failure to sell the value of the services provided.

There are two main reasons that missed opportunities for value creation may result: 1) lack of adequate functional involvement, and 2) failure to sell the value of the services provided. When functional activities are focused internally on the fulfillment of functional objectives, management will lack the necessary customer interaction to be focused on the customer. In this case, the identification of opportunities for the development of services that would lead to value creation for both sides of the relationship will be undetected. When this is the case, customer segmentation and service differentiation may not be reaching all corporate functions. In other cases, where activities are tailored to the specific needs of a customer or group of customers, the value provided is not sold adequately. When management fails to sell the value, the firm does not get the appropriate reward for the value provided, resulting in margin erosion for the provider.

This waste is depicted by one consumer packaged goods (CPG) manufacturer when it failed to recognize that competitors had raised prices on capacity constrained items. As a result of failing to recognize this timely change in the market, the company lost margin potential on sold items and caused a run in demand that led to frequent out-of-stocks on its products. Though sales volume increased for a time, it was followed by a period of customer disappointment and miscues on demand, which result in demand amplification (also known as the "Forrester effect" or the "bullwhip effect").[24] Reacting to these miscues could result in the conventional wastes of overproduction and inventory buildup should the company raise prices to market levels (eroding demand) or prove slow in fulfilling customers' escalated demand at the reduced price (missing the market).

Disconnects between Promise Making and Promise Keeping

In many organizations, making promises to the customer is disconnected from the operation involved in fulfilling the promise. This represents a gap in the company's management of demand and supply. In such situations, the organization experiences stress handling exceptions, or promises are left unfulfilled. Frequently, this situation is related to: 1) poor information available to whoever makes the promise, or 2) poor understanding of how decisions and actions impact others in the organization. Both situations could be avoided by determining the information

---

[21] Lambert, Douglas M. and Thomas C. Harrington (1989), "Establishing Customer Service Strategies Within the Marketing Mix: More Empirical Evidence," *Journal of Business Logistics*, Vol. 10, No. 2, pp. 44-60.

[22] Webster, Frederick E., Jr. (1994), "Executing the New Marketing Concept", *Marketing Management*, Vol. 3, pp. 9–18.

[23] Vargo, Stephen L. and Robert F. Lusch, "Evolving to a New Dominant Logic for Marketing," *Journal of Marketing*, Vol. 68, No. 1 (2004), pp. 1-17.

[24] Forrester, Jay Wright (1961), *Industrial Dynamics*, Cambridge, Massachusets: M.I.T. Press and Lee, Hau L., V Padmanabhan and Seungjin Whang (1997), "Information Distortion in a Supply Chain: The Bullwhip Effect," *Management Science*, Vol. 43, No. 4, pp. 546-558.

that sales representatives need in order to make realistic commitments to customers. Over-promising will jeopardize the firm's ability to deliver on the promise, while under-promising might result in missing the opportunity of value creation. Both instances represent sources of waste.

For example, sales or customer service representatives responsible for taking orders might not have real-time data of product availability or capacity available to promise. An order might be accepted despite information somewhere in the organization indicating that accepting the order is unrealistic or unwise. In an attempt to close such a sale, promises could be made that would require additional effort, and cost, to be fulfilled. This is particularly common when sales representatives are rewarded for unit sales rather than profitable sales. Such functional metrics encourage making sales at any cost. Despite the apparent short-term gain, these situations often result in lower profits for the company.

This was the scenario at one consumer goods manufacturer that serves both consumer and institutional markets. Though the consumer market represents the vast majority of sales, the institutional sales division was eager to offer aggressive delivery terms for large, institutional purchases. This occurred despite the fact that these sales disrupted the planned provisions of the consumer channel and put this higher priority business at risk. This discrepancy in promise making and promise keeping will likely result in the muda of waiting, as customers wait to have their demand fulfilled. Mura (hurried operations) and muri (overburdening) may also occur. The greater risk, however, is not that waiting transpires in the supply chain, but that the waiting and frustration are experienced by the dominant customer segment for the manufacturer. Generally, this waste is not identified and addressed in conventional implementations of lean operations.

Unclear Expectations in Business Relationships

One of the main reasons business relationships end prematurely is because the expectations of one or both sides are not understood and, in turn, not satisfied.[25] Poorly articulated expectations are usually to blame. The challenge when setting expectations in close business relationships is that multiple functional areas and management levels must be involved. Otherwise, the relationship will be managed by a single salesperson from the supplier and a single purchasing agent from the customer. However, in close and complex business relationships, there are no two people that can grasp all aspects of the relationship.

As predicated by the partnership model (see Chapter 14), clear expectations establish the foundation for high performance relationships, with the product and service agreement (PSA) documenting those expectations. The formation and maintenance of critical business relationships require the involvement of multiple functions on both sides. In the absence of this dialogue, speculation and anxiety, give rise to wastes, reinforced by the frustration that erodes relations over time.

Management may find that the organization is prone to this form of waste both facing customers and suppliers. Unclear expectations likely will result in a few of the supply chain wastes already identified – such as missed opportunities for value creation or disconnects between promise making and promise keeping. It may also result in the waste of late detection of action required, described next.

Over-promising will jeopardize the firm's ability to deliver on the promise, while under-promising might result in missing the opportunity for value creation.

The challenge when setting expectations in close business relationships is that multiple functional areas and management levels must be involved.

---

[25] Lambert, Douglas M. and A. Michael Knemeyer, "We're In This Together," Harvard Business Review, Vol. 82, No. 12 (2004), pp. 114-122

Late Detection of Action Required

Emergency situations are inevitable in any business environment. Yet, the necessary inquiry commonly yields that someone somewhere in the organization is aware that something did not happen as planned, but does not initiate immediate corrective action when the problem could be minimized or mitigated altogether. Early detection of situations that require action provides actors with more time to respond to an exception or unplanned situation. The later a signal is identified and acted upon, the more difficult it will be to avoid or minimize the impact to the customer, and the higher the cost of the corrective action.

The later a signal is identified and acted upon, the more difficult it will be to avoid or minimize the impact to the customer, and the higher the cost of the corrective action.

Early detection and effective response to events, or outside-the-specification situations, reduce wastes in the form of costly action, customer disappointment, and even the recovery activity that must be enacted. To eliminate this waste, the lean concept of Jidoka (making problems visible) should be extended to customer interactions as well as the internal workflows of the organization. In many instances, bringing a problem to the attention of others who may be affected by the occurrence allows the problem to be managed before it affects the customer.

One consumer packaged goods manufacturer experienced a unique form of this waste by erroneously accumulating supplies of raw materials. The raw materials were stored at an off-site location where they were not visible to operations personnel. Through poor coordination, raw materials continued to be acquired at a high rate despite a slowdown in production. The raw materials with limited shelf lives went unused and resulted in an inventory write-off amounting to tens of millions of dollars. Lack of visibility and communication created considerable muda in the form of inventory as well as the unnecessary administrative activities of ordering and writing off the excess supplies.

Misalignment of Incentives

Misalignment of incentives can be found on two dimensions: 1) between firms in the supply chain, and 2) internally across corporate functions.

Misalignment of incentives can be found on two dimensions: 1) between firms in the supply chain, and 2) internally across corporate functions. Many of the misalignments of incentives between firms in the supply chain are related to a zero-sum proposition – what one side of the relationship gains is equal to what the other loses. As an example, consider price gaming, a primary source of demand amplification. In situations where sales representatives are rewarded solely by revenue generation (and not profitable revenue) with established monthly targets, sales tend to be concentrated on the last few days of the period. Indeed, buyers know that the sales representative is more "open" to negotiations as the end of the month approaches, and thereby delays the decision to buy as long as possible, even risking to run out of stock to adequately serve customers. Zero-sum games are characteristic of relationships that are oriented in the short-term and focused on price as the single negotiation criterion. This is likely to result in margin erosion to the supplier and the customer. Once this is recognized, top management can take action to encourage both the salesperson and the buyer to strive for win-win alternatives. The source of the waste is not in the way people behave, but the foundation of the relationship.

Similar gaming can occur between corporate functions inside a firm. Functional objectives will drive management's behavior at the expense of the performance of other functions. This type of situation usually sub-optimizes company and supply chain performance despite the powerful party's "favorable outcome." In organizations where incentives across functions are not aligned, managers do not consider the collateral damage and associated costs of their decisions and actions that result in wastes such as inventory costs or lost sales. This lack of shared accountability from misaligned incentives results in opportunistic behavior by the party in the most powerful position. Whether internal to the company or occurring across organizations in the supply chain, wastes, such as inventory, unnecessary or expedited transportation, and overproduction, can be attributed to these self-interested actions.

This waste was acknowledged in the description of the disconnect between promise making and promise keeping. As is typical with Ohno's forms of muda, interrelationships can be expected with wastes found in the larger supply chain perspective. For instance, Ohno's muda of overproduction will result in the muda of inventory and unnecessary transportation and movement (or handling). In our current analysis, a misalignment of incentives (say, between sales and operations) is likely to create disconnects between promise making and promise keeping.

One example of opportunistic behavior driven by misaligned incentives across members of the supply chain occurred at a consumer goods manufacturer that sold to "big box" retailers. One retail customer was renowned for incurring significant losses through product damage and pilferage at its stores. With these occurrences, the retailer took the liberty of discounting the value of the lost merchandise from the manufacturer's invoices, and hence was not inclined to reduce the frequency of loss and damage claims. As a corrective step, the manufacturer implemented vendor-managed inventory (VMI) where it shipped smaller quantities to the customer on a more frequent basis and assumed greater visibility and control for the inventory stocked at the stores. With VMI, the retail customer enjoyed improved service performance, as the manufacturer reduced its susceptibility to loss and damage claims.

In organizations where incentives across functions are not aligned, managers do not consider the collateral damage and associated costs of their decisions and actions that result in wastes such as inventory costs or lost sales.

Excessive Product Proliferation

Product proliferation[26] is a commonly cited source of complexity in the supply chain and a source of tension.[27] A tradeoff exists between developing new products to retain existing customers (or attract new customers) and carving the market into increasingly smaller, less profitable pieces. In making product-line decisions, management must trade off demand increases that result from offering a broader product line with the associated incremental costs.[28] Sometimes, line extensions are made in response to competitive pressure. Thus, product-line extension decisions need to be framed in the business context and made with the best possible information. One consumer packaged goods executive pointed out that for every product line extension, his operations must accommodate between 30 to 35 new SKUs — since the product must be provided in various formats and packages.

Product proliferation is a commonly cited source of complexity in the supply chain and a source of tension.

---

[26] Etymology of *proliferation*: back-formation from proliferation, from French prolifération, from proliférer to proliferate, from prolifère reproducing freely, from Latin proles + -fer –ferous (Merriam-Webster). Definition: to increase in number.

[27] Hayes, Robert H. and Steven G. Wheelwright (1979), "The Dynamics of Process-Product Life Cycles," *Harvard Business Review*, Vol. 57, No. 2, pp. 127-136.

[28] Bayus, Barry L. and William P. Putsis, Jr., "Product Proliferation: An Empirical Analysis of Product Line Determinants and Market Outcomes", *Marketing Science*, Vol. 18, No. 2. (1999), pp. 137-153.

Some companies have adopted strict rules for adding new items, such as requiring an existing item's removal for every new item introduced. In other companies, objectives have been established as a fraction of revenue that should be provided by products introduced in the last so many years. However, these rules prove difficult to enforce when good reasons are found to introduce new items as well as to keep products that are candidates for rationalization. Management from all functions needs to recognize that excessive product proliferation may increase substantially the strain on production and logistics resources, leading to higher costs and lower product availability. Additionally, excessive product proliferation can confuse end-customers.[29] Though new products are drivers of business growth, diminishing returns can be established when the costs and revenue implications associated with line extensions are estimated adequately. We believe that product decisions should be based on profitability. Measuring product profitability and customer profitability has the potential to provide invaluable insight. Identifying unprofitable products that are sold to unprofitable customers will provide a good starting point to eliminate waste. Product proliferation should be evaluated without any cost allocation as indicated with the first waste described previously (cost allocation for decision making). In addition, controls on excessive product proliferation provide a check on unconstrained complexity in managing the business.

Identifying unprofitable products that are sold to unprofitable customers will provide a good starting point to eliminate waste.

In sum, lean thinking applied in its conventional fashion within the operations area of a single firm will not address the root causes of the wastes described –wastes that result from poor coordination across functions or across supply chain members. For that reason, lean must be applied on the larger scope of supply chain management; it must apply to those activities that span the functions that support both supply and demand within and across companies in the supply chain. Blended with the supply chain management framework, lean thinking provides a means for preventing wastes as well as reducing manifest wastes. Together, lean thinking and supply chain management support the enhancement of value for all members of the supply chain and the challenge of continuous improvement for the benefit of the focal company and other supply chain members.

Conclusions

Lean thinking and supply chain management are two comprehensive methods for continuous performance improvement. Applied together, they can help to deliver the full benefits that each has to offer. Lean thinking offers a set of principles and tools that provide a lens through which to view the supply chain management framework. Extending the use of lean concepts and tools to other aspects of the business beyond a reduced set of corporate functions such as manufacturing and logistics, and administrative tasks has the potential to provide further benefits. In most organizations other forms of wastes can be found beyond those originally described by Taiichi Ohno. This is particularly true when the focus is on managing the entire business. The supply chain management framework provides the structure for managing business relationships and achieving the necessary cross-functional integration required to achieve customer satisfaction and long-term profitability.

---

[29] Narisetti, R., "P&G, Seeing Shoppers were being Confused, Overhauls Marketing," *The Wall Street Journal*, (January 15, 1997), pp. Al, A8.

In this chapter, we broadened the view of waste, or muda. Though the list of wastes formulated by Taiichi Ohno is still relevant, its most common application rests with observable wastes that manifest in the production function. There are other wastes that tend to be more latent and result from a lack of knowledge, from ineffective coordination of activities, or from misalignment across functions and companies. Supply chain management as presented in our framework is positioned to address – or better yet, prevent — these wastes. Therefore, lean thinking and supply chain management should be employed together.

Another way to express the connection between lean thinking and supply chain management is to recognize that lean helps to ensure that things are done right (i.e., most efficiently), and the supply chain management framework ensures that the right things get done (i.e., most effectively). Employed together, the focus is doing the right things right.[30] This simple mantra holds powerful implications for increasing the company's performance and that of all members of the supply chain.

Another way to express the connection between lean thinking and supply chain management is to recognize that lean helps to ensure that things are done right (i.e., most efficiently), and the supply chain management framework ensures that the right things get done (i.e., most effectively).

---

[30] Goldsby, Thomas and Robert Martichenko, *Lean Six Sigma Logistics: Strategic Development to Operational Success*, Boca Raton, FL: J. Ross, 2005.

13 Implementing and Sustaining the Supply Chain Management Processes

Douglas M. Lambert, Rudolf Leuschner, and Dale S. Rogers

Overview

There are eleven management components that must be considered in order to implement the eight supply chain management processes. The management components apply to all of the supply chain management processes. In this chapter, we describe each of the management components as well as how they can be used to coordinate implementation of the supply chain management processes and institutionalize the processes once they have been implemented.

Introduction

The management components provide guidance for implementation of each process and are divided into two groups: structural components and behavioral components.

Supply chain management is the integration of key business processes across the supply chain and the processes can be linked successfully only if the relationships with the other members of the supply chain are managed properly. To implement the processes, a number of management components are necessary.[1] The management components provide guidance for implementation of each process and are divided into two groups: structural components and behavioral components. The structural components include planning, control methods, knowledge management, workflow structure, organization structure, and communication structure. The behavioral components include management methods, power and leadership, risk and reward, culture and attitude, and trust and commitment. The behavioral components are often not as visible as the structural components, but they are essential for the successful implementation of the eight supply chain management processes. Quite often, when managers try to implement business processes, they only focus on the structural components. These efforts have a high failure rate because even though the right structure is put in place, the right behaviors are not encouraged. There is evidence from studies of business process reengineering that the behavioral components are critical success factors.[2]

---

[1] Cooper, Martha C., Douglas M. Lambert, and Janus D. Pagh, "Supply Chain Management: More Than a New Name for Logistics," *The International Journal of Logistics Management*, Vol. 8, No. 1 (1997), pp. 1-13.

[2] Teng, James T.C., Seung Ryul Jeong, and Varun Grover, "Profiling Successful Reengineering Projects," *Communications of the ACM*, Vol. 41, No. 6 (1998), pp. 96-102 and Paper, David and Ruey-Dang Chang, "The state of business process reengineering: a search for success factors," *Total Quality Management & Business Excellence*, Vol. 16, No. 1 (2005), pp. 121-133.

The management components are summarized in Figure 13-1. In this chapter, we describe each management component and its role in the implementation of the eight supply chain management processes. We begin with the structural and behavioral components. Then, we describe how a process can be implemented and institutionalized. The chapter ends with conclusions.

Structural Management Components

In this section, the structural management components are presented and their role in implementation of the supply chain management processes is explained. The structural management components are important because structure drives behavior. These components are generally the easiest to recognize in organizations and include planning, control methods, workflow structure, organization structure, knowledge management, and communication structure.

The structural management components are important because structure drives behavior.

Planning

Planning is the anticipation of likely occurrences in the supply chain and preparing potential responses to those events. Planning "begins with objectives; defines strategies, policies and detailed plans to achieve them; which establishes an organization to implement decisions; and includes a detailed review of performance and feedback to introduce a new planning cycle".[3] Planning is critical during all phases of the development of relationships with suppliers and customers.

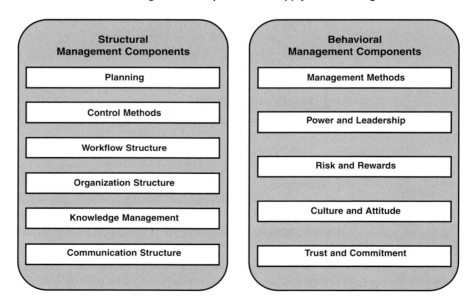

Figure 13-1
The Management Components of Supply Chain Management

Structural Management Components	Behavioral Management Components
Planning	Management Methods
Control Methods	Power and Leadership
Workflow Structure	Risk and Rewards
Organization Structure	Culture and Attitude
Knowledge Management	Trust and Commitment
Communication Structure	

Source: Adapted from Lambert, Douglas M., Martha C. Cooper and James D. Pagh, "Supply Chain Management: Implementation Issues and Research Opportunitites," *The International Journal of Logistics Management, Vol. 9, No. 2 (1998), p. 12.*

---

[3] Steiner, George A., *Top Management Planning*, New York: MacMillan, 1969, p. 7.

Planning is required to successfully implement each of the eight supply chain management processes.

Planning within an organization exists at many levels as well as in all functional areas.[4] Planning is required to successfully implement each of the eight supply chain management processes. It is important to have plans for different time frames and these time-phased plans are rolled up into the long-range plan. There are three levels of planning: strategic, tactical, and operational.[5] Strategic plans are of the highest level, stretch over multiple-year time frames, and typically focus on competition, resources, and stakeholders. Tactical plans are more specific and include important capital expenditures like new plant and equipment. Operational plans are more detailed and generally focus on a one-year range, creating efficiency, and have a financial orientation.

Steiner advocated the following five-step approach to long-range planning: plan to plan, specify objectives, develop strategies, develop detailed plans, and integrate plans.[6] The first step is planning to plan. It involves getting the right people together for planning, which in the case of supply chain management means identifying the members of the cross-functional process teams. The second step is to specify the objectives. This includes anticipating future requirements for the process and identifying performance gaps. For each of the supply chain management processes there is an assessment tool that can be used to identify performance gaps. How to conduct an assessment is described in Chapter 10. The third step is to develop strategies. The strategies developed by the process teams should address the major performance gaps that were discovered during the assessment. The fourth step is to develop detailed plans. This means translating the work of the strategic process team into an action plan for the operational process team(s). The last stage is to integrate the different levels of planning. The strategic process team provides direction to and receives feedback from the operational process team(s). The five planning steps and their implications for supply chain management are summarized in Table 13-1.

Table 13-1
The Five Steps for Planning in the Supply Chain Management Processes

Steps	Level	Supply Chain Management Implications
1 Plan to plan	Strategic	Process team involvement
2 Specify objectives	Strategic	Process assessment
3 Develop strategies	Strategic	Plan for the strategic sub-processes
4 Develop detailed plans	Operational	Plan for the operational sub-processes
5 Integrate plans	Strategic & Operational	Integration of strategic and operational plans

Source: Adapted from Steiner, George A., "Making Long Range Company Planning Pay Off," *California Management Review*, Vol. 4, No. 2 (1962), pp. 28-42

[4] Lambert, Douglas M., James R. Stock, and Lisa M. Ellram, *Fundamentals of Logistics Management*, Burr Ridge, IL: Irwin/McGraw-Hill, 1998, p. 549.

[5] Cooper, Martha C., Daniel E. Innis, and Peter R. Dickson, *Strategic Planning for Logistics*, Oak Brook, IL: Council of Logistics Management, 1992, p. 28.

[6] Steiner, George A., "Making Long Range Company Planning Pay Off," *California Management Review*, Vol. 4, No. 2, (1962), pp. 28-42.

Control Methods

Control is achieved by developing and implementing the best metrics. The problem is that often metrics are in conflict across functions within the firm and across companies in the supply chain. Because supply chains are comprised of many firms, it is difficult to develop metrics that maximize the performance of the entire supply chain. Most metrics that are referred to as supply chain metrics encourage local optimization and lead to sub-optimization of the overall supply chain.[7] For example, marketing managers want to increase the number of SKU's because they believe it will boost sales and they are rewarded for revenue increases. Finance managers want to improve EVA®, so they want to minimize investments in new assets such as manufacturing facilities. At the same time, manufacturing and logistics managers are expected to reduce the cost per unit. This situation creates conflict because achieving the performance goals on all three metrics is not possible. Usually, the most powerful individual wins which is generally not the best solution for the company or the supply chain.

In addition, managers strive to maximize the performance of their own firms, at the expense of the other firms in the supply chain. For example, a car manufacturer achieves high inventory turns by shipping finished cars to the dealers without consumer orders. This causes the dealers to have low inventory turns. Ford has 19 inventory turns and their dealers have approximately three to four turns.[8] Dealers have to absorb the higher inventory carrying cost and frequently product is discounted to reduce inventory. If the manufacturer was willing to hold regional inventories, dealer inventory turns could be increased. However, lower inventory turns would be experienced by the manufacturer which would increase its costs. But, these costs would be more than offset by the savings that the dealers experience. The cost of a car to the manufacturer is the cost of assembling it, while the dealer's cost is the manufacturer's selling price. Holding lower-cost inventory reduces the total inventory cost in the supply chain. Overall supply chain performance is improved if the manufacturer holds more inventory. However, for this to happen, management of the manufacturer needs to focus on total supply chain performance.

A framework for developing supply chain metrics is described in Chapter 15. This framework consists of seven steps that guide the implementation of relevant supply chain metrics.[9] Profit and loss statements that measure the impact of individual customer/supplier relationships provide the "best measure of supply chain management performance and can be used to align performance across processes and between firms".[10] When a buyer and seller negotiate, this metric allows them to understand the impact of changes on the profitability of both companies. Another advantage is that when managers in two firms collaborate on supply chain process improvements, the P&Ls for each side make the gains and losses clear so that burdens and benefits can be split equitably.

Control is achieved by developing and implementing the best metrics. The problem is that often metrics are in conflict across functions within the firm and across companies in the supply chain.

---

[7] Beamon, Benita, "Measuring Supply Chain Performance," *International Journal of Operations & Production Management*, Vol. 19, No. 3 (1999), pp: 275-292.

[8] Ford Motor Company, *2006 Annual Report*, 03/07/2007.

[9] Lambert, Douglas M. and Terrance Pohlen, "Supply Chain Metrics," *The International Journal of Logistics Management*, Vol. 12, No. 1 (2001), pp. 1-19.

[10] Lambert, Douglas M. and Terrance Pohlen, "Supply Chain Metrics," *The International Journal of Logistics Management*, Vol. 12, No. 1 (2001), p. 11.

Metrics must be aligned across firms in the supply chain and the processes of each firm must be aligned.[11] Without this alignment suboptimal behavior is rewarded. There are two sources of misalignment. One is that performance metrics may be measured differently across firms. What is called an on-time delivery by the supplier may not be viewed as an on-time delivery by the buyer. Another source of misalignment occurs when performance is measured similarly in each firm but managers take action that maximizes the performance of their own firm at the expense of the other. For example, managers at the auto manufacturer achieved inventory turns of 19, even though performance of the entire supply chain was diminished by this practice. Misaligned metrics can create conflicts in the supply chain. It is important for managers across the supply chain to compare the metrics that their firms use and ensure that they are aligned.

Workflow Structure

The goal of managing workflow structure is to streamline the supply chain so that total costs are minimized.

Workflow structure determines how and where the work within the supply chain is executed. The goal of managing workflow structure is to streamline the supply chain so that total costs are minimized. In order to do that, it is necessary to identify the specific locations in the supply chain where work should be completed. Management in each firm must understand how workflow in their organization has developed. Each firm develops a workflow structure because of unique circumstances in its environment and it is often unclear why work is completed in a certain way.[12] Before the workflow structure of the supply chain can be streamlined, senior managers in each firm must understand why their firm operates as it does and evaluate the efficiency of current operations.

A useful tool to understand the workflow structure of the supply chain is value stream mapping. The first step is to select an ingredient or component and map the supply chain. Next, the specific activities that are performed at each location are classified as either value-adding or non-value-adding. Value stream mapping provides a systematic approach to understanding what work is done at each stage in the supply chain so that non-value adding activities can be minimized. Value stream mapping is described in more detail in Chapter 11.

Managers must determine where in the supply chain the work should be located. For example, clothes sold in retail stores may need to be put on hangers and have a price ticket placed on them. The costs associated with this work may be lower at the plant or a distribution center than at the retail store, but the supplier's cost would increase. A mechanism must be in place to identify and adequately share the costs and benefits of a change in workflow. In another example, color is added to paint at the retail store so that it is not necessary for the retailer to hold large inventories of every possible paint color. In this example, moving a manufacturing activity, mixing the paint color, to the retail store lowers the total costs in the supply chain.[13]

---

[11] Novack, Robert A., "Quality and Control in Logistics: A Process Model," *International Journal of Physical Distribution and Materials Management*, Vol. 19, No. 11 (1989), p. 40.

[12] Rondeau, Patrick J., Mark A. Vonderembse, and T.S. Ragu-Nathan. "Expolring work system practices for time-based manufacturers: their impact on competitive capabilities," *Journal of Operations Management*, Vol. 18, No. 5 (2000), pp. 509-529.

[13] Lambert, Douglas M., James R. Stock, and Lisa M. Ellram, *Fundamentals of Logistics Management*, Burr Ridge, IL: Irwin/McGraw-Hill, 1998, p. 512.

Organization Structure

Implementation of the GSCF supply chain management processes does not mean that processes will replace functions such as marketing, sales, research and development, logistics, production, purchasing and finance. If a company manufactures products, it needs people who know how to operate factories. If money is spent on advertising, someone needs to evaluate the sales response to that advertising. And, someone needs to understand the tax code so that taxes are legally minimized. This expertise resides in the functions. Knocking down the functional silos is not the answer, rather they should be ventilated by implementing cross-functional teams. Functional managers bring their expertise to these teams and take a more holistic view of the company and the supply chain back to their functional role which makes the function less silo-like.

The planning and coordinating is done in the processes, while the execution is done in the functions. The amount of work that a function must complete is the same with or without the supply chain management process, but the processes ensure that the functions do the right work. For example, the logistics function still needs to ensure that all orders get to customers. In process implementation, the functional representatives must be able to devote adequate time and resources to the process teams. It is critical for process performance that employees understand that their work on the cross-functional teams is an important part of their job. Initially, everyone has to work harder for the process to succeed. This might create some discontent in the function, but at the same time it will motivate the teams to produce results quickly.

Cross-functional teams provide a firm with the ability to quickly respond to issues[14] and they are necessary for implementing the GSCF processes. The cross-functional teams may include key customer and supplier representatives. The work that should be performed by the cross-functional teams is described in each of the eight process chapters. The cross-functional teams play an important role in coordinating the work that is done in the functions so that it is focused on meeting customer needs and corporate goals. Figure 13-2 provides an example of how each function can contribute to the eight supply chain management processes.

In many organizations, customers are considered to be the domain of marketing and sales. However, all of the business functions should be involved in managing relationships with customers. For example, at the operational level of customer relationship management, managers from each function can make valuable contributions to the process. If a customer wants an exclusive flavor of the product, marketing and sales do not have the knowledge to understand how this request affects the company. Representatives from R&D, logistics, production, purchasing and finance need to be involved. The representative from R&D understands what is required to develop the new product. The representative from logistics understands how the increased volume affects warehousing and transportation cost. The representative from purchasing understands how to obtain the materials for the new product. The representative from finance understands

> *Knocking down the functional silos is not the answer, rather they should be ventilated by implementing cross-functional teams.*

> *In many organizations, customers are considered to be the domain of marketing and sales. However, all of the business functions should be involved in managing relationships with customers.*

---

[14] Dumaine, B., "The bureaucracy buster," *Fortune*, June 17, 1991, pp. 36-50, Mohrman S.A., "Integrating roles and structures in the lateral organization," in J.R. Galbraith and, E.E. Lawler III (Eds.), *Organizing for the Future*, San Francisco, CA: Jossey-Bass, 1993; and Parker, G.M., *Cross-functional teams: Working with allies, enemies, and other strangers*, San Francisco: Jossey-Bass, 1994.

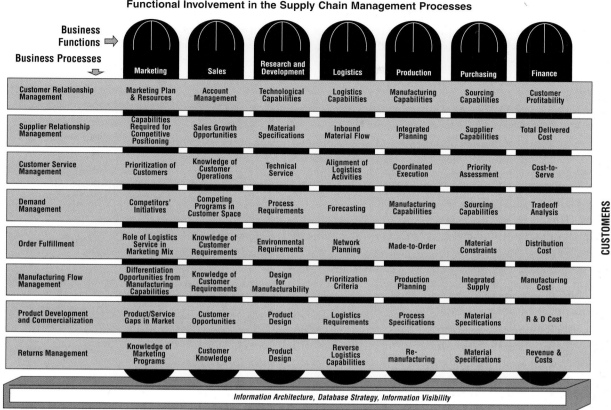

Figure 13-2
Functional Involvement in the Supply Chain Management Processes

Business Functions → Business Processes ↓	Marketing	Sales	Research and Development	Logistics	Production	Purchasing	Finance
Customer Relationship Management	Marketing Plan & Resources	Account Management	Technological Capabilities	Logistics Capabilities	Manufacturing Capabilities	Sourcing Capabilities	Customer Profitability
Supplier Relationship Management	Capabilities Required for Competitive Positioning	Sales Growth Opportunities	Material Specifications	Inbound Material Flow	Integrated Planning	Supplier Capabilities	Total Delivered Cost
Customer Service Management	Prioritization of Customers	Knowledge of Customer Operations	Technical Service	Alignment of Logistics Activities	Coordinated Execution	Priority Assessment	Cost-to-Serve
Demand Management	Competitors' Initiatives	Competing Programs in Customer Space	Process Requirements	Forecasting	Manufacturing Capabilities	Sourcing Capabilities	Tradeoff Analysis
Order Fulfillment	Role of Logistics Service in Marketing Mix	Knowledge of Customer Requirements	Environmental Requirements	Network Planning	Made-to-Order	Material Constraints	Distribution Cost
Manufacturing Flow Management	Differentiation Opportunities from Manufacturing Capabilities	Knowledge of Customer Requirements	Design for Manufacturability	Prioritization Criteria	Production Planning	Integrated Supply	Manufacturing Cost
Product Development and Commercialization	Product/Service Gaps in Market	Customer Opportunities	Product Design	Logistics Requirements	Process Specifications	Material Specifications	R & D Cost
Returns Management	Knowledge of Marketing Programs	Customer Knowledge	Product Design	Reverse Logistics Capabilities	Re-manufacturing	Material Specifications	Revenue & Costs

SUPPLIERS — *CUSTOMERS*

Information Architecture, Database Strategy, Information Visibility

Note: Process sponsorship and ownership must be established to drive the attainment of the supply chain vision and eliminate the functional silo mentality.

Source: Adapted from Keely L. Croxton, Sebastian J. García-Dastuque and Douglas M. Lambert, "The Supply Chain Management Processes," *The International Journal of Logistics Management*, Vol. 12, No. 2 (2001), p.31.

how the additional growth can be funded. Managers from all of the functions are necessary to estimate the potential impact on profit of a customer's request for an exclusive flavor of the product. While marketing and sales representatives may understand the price the customer will pay for the product, without input from all functions, it is unlikely that they will understand the profit implications of meeting the customer's request.

As previously noted, processes will not replace functions because the work is done in the functions. For example, in the strategic order fulfillment management process, the cross-functional team decides how to fill orders for each customer segment, including manufacturing locations, payment terms, order sizes and packing requirements. At the operational level, employees in the logistics function execute most of the work of the order fulfillment process; they pick, pack, stage, load, and make arrangements for the transportation of the product. Functional expertise is necessary.

Communication Structure

Communication structure describes the flow of information that is necessary to link two organizations and ensure that the right people talk to each other. Four basic questions that must be answered when determining the communication structure are:

- Who needs to communicate with whom?
- What should be communicated?
- How should communication take place?
- When is communication necessary?

A major challenge in supply chain management is developing and maintaining information and communication systems. This means more than implementing state of the art information technology. For example, Wendy's International schedules quarterly business reviews for strategic suppliers and requires vice president-level representation in these meetings. Agenda items for the quarterly business reviews include: strategic business plans, supplier evaluation, project status review, shared expectations, developing joint objectives, and next steps. Suppliers at the next level of importance to Wendy's are scheduled for semi-annual business reviews. All other suppliers have an annual business review. For the most critical suppliers, the CEOs from both companies might attend the meetings.[15]

A major challenge in supply chain management is developing and maintaining information and communication systems.

This example illustrates how communication can be structured between a customer and its suppliers. The question of who needs to talk to whom helps to make decisions such as requiring vice president level representation for strategic suppliers and only having a buyer meet with a sales person for a non-critical supplier. The question of what needs to be communicated leads to sharing growth plans with strategic suppliers and reviewing all the problems that came up since the last meeting with non-critical suppliers. Business results should be communicated face-to-face in a business review meeting. The question of when is communication necessary addresses what suppliers participate in quarterly business reviews and what suppliers participate in annual business reviews.

Knowledge Management

Knowledge management refers to the acquisition, storage, and distribution of information and expertise that is required for operating the company. It also involves managing access to that knowledge and expertise within the firm and across firms in the supply chain. When collaborating with customers and suppliers, management must decide how much knowledge will be shared. There is a fine line between giving away important competitive advantages and contributing to a partnership for the benefit of both firms.[16]

There is a fine line between giving away important competitive advantages and contributing to a partnership for the benefit of both firms.

Management maintains knowledge inside the firm by writing it into books, procedures, and manuals. At a very basic level, these documents make up the identity of a company. Maintaining consistent processes is a critical success factor. When the knowledge of the company becomes independent of the individual,

---

[15] Scherer, Tony, "Supplier Relationship Management at Wendy's," CLM Conference Presentation, Chicago, IL, 2003.

[16] Dyer, Jeffrey, and Kentaro Nobeoka, "Creating and Managing a High-Performance Knowledge-Sharing Network: The Toyota Case," *Strategic Management Journal*, Vol. 21, No. 3 (2000), pp. 345-367.

anyone can be taught to do a job if the person who developed the procedure is not available.[17] The longer that an individual works at a job, the more knowledge he/she acquires, but the organization loses that knowledge if the person leaves or changes assignments. In many cases, the loss of that knowledge represents a high cost to the firm. Also, new team members need to be brought up to the standards of the company and delays are costly. There is knowledge that supports each supply chain management process and that knowledge needs to be managed.

There are several tools available that aid in developing a knowledge management system, like expert systems,[18] intranet/extranet and corporate virtual libraries.[19] An expert system is created through the collective knowledge of several individuals in a firm who are experts in an area. It allows non-experts to make decisions similar to those of the experts. Intranets are used to distribute knowledge and information within an organization. If suppliers and customers have access, it becomes an extranet. An example of an extranet is Wal-Mart's retail link,[20] through which information is shared with suppliers.

Behavioral Management Components

The behavioral management components are less tangible than the structural management components and are more difficult to synchronize between firms in the supply chain.[21] These components include management methods, power and leadership, risk and reward, culture and attitude, and trust and commitment.

Management Methods

Managers must get things done through people. Peter Drucker described the role of managers as follows:

> The manager is the dynamic, life-giving element in every business. Without his leadership, the "resources of production" remain resources and never become production. In a competitive economy, the quality and performance of the managers determine the success of a business, indeed they determine its survival. For the quality and performance of its managers is the only effective advantage an enterprise in a competitive economy can have.[22]

Managers must encourage people to work effectively and efficiently. Most people are strongly influenced by their compensation and managers must understand the behavior they are promoting by the compensation plan. Salespeople who are compensated based on the amount of sales that they generate

Most people are strongly influenced by their compensation and managers must understand the behavior they are promoting by the compensation plan.

---

[17] Nonaka, Ikujiro, "The Knowledge-Creating Company," *Harvard Business Review*, Vol. 69, No. 6 (1991), pp. 96-104.

[18] Kumar, Sameer, and Ganesh Thondikulam, "Knowledge management in a collaborative business framework," *Information Knowledge Systems Management*, Vol. 5, No. 3 (2005-2006), pp. 171-187.

[19] Boyd, Stephanie, "What's Next for Corporate Virtual Libraries?" *Online*, Vol. 28, No. 6 (2004), pp. 14-24.

[20] Staff Writer, "Competitive Advantage Lies in Systems Efficiencies," *Chain Store Age*, Vol. 78, No. 8 (2002), pp. 74-76.

[21] Cooper, Martha C., Douglas M. Lambert, and Janus D. Pagh, "Supply Chain Management: More Than a New Name for Logistics," *The International Journal of Logistics Management*, Vol. 8, No. 1 (1997), pp. 1-13.

[22] Drucker, Peter F., *The Practice of Management*, New York, NY: Harper & Row, 1954, p. 3.

typically will try to maximize their own income by maximizing revenue, even if their firm's profitability suffers. The right supply chain metrics help employees to focus on behavior that benefits the firm and the entire supply chain.[23]

Another consideration is how to reward people for the work they do on cross-functional teams. It is very important to recognize that such work has to be tied to the compensation system. People working on process teams should not feel that they are performing some kind of extra-curricular activity, but that it is a regular part of their job that is important to the whole organization. Therefore, designing a compensation plan that rewards employees for their work on the supply chain management processes is a necessary part of the implementation cycle.

Power and Leadership

A manager at any level of the organization must be an effective leader. Supply chain management "connects" companies and requires individuals from those companies to work together. Individuals may differ with respect to their understanding of leadership due to their organization's philosophy and approach to leadership.

Early work on leadership by French and Raven, that is still considered relevant, identified the five sources of power that leaders have available in an organization: reward, coercion, legitimacy, reference, and expert. Reward power is based on the ability to provide positive consequences. Coercive power is based on the ability to punish. Legitimate power is based on the position in the organization. Referent power is based on association with powerful entities. Expert power is based on knowledge and ability. The first three bases of power are determined by the position that a manager holds and the last two are dependent on the person. Research has shown that leaders who base their influence on the two personal power bases supported by reward power are most effective. Least effective are leaders who rely on coercion and legitimate power.[24]

Typically, managers representing the various functions within a firm do not have the same amount of power. Functional managers must be aware of power imbalances and understand how to overcome them. For example, a vice president of operations and logistics may decide to implement the eight supply chain management processes and that the best place to start is with customer relationship management. But managers in the marketing function have a dominant position within the firm due to the strength of the brand and believe that customers are their domain. They may perceive that the manager from operations and logistics is invading their space and object. It might be easier to implement processes that seem to be in the domain of operations and logistics, like demand management, order fulfillment, or manufacturing flow management and involve marketing and sales representatives on the cross-functional teams. This way, managers from the marketing function may develop an understanding of the value of the supply chain management framework and they will be more likely to support implementing a process such as customer relationship management when it is their idea to do so.

Typically, managers representing the various functions within a firm do not have the same amount of power. Functional managers must be aware of power imbalances and understand how to overcome them.

---

[23] Pfeffer, Jeffrey, "Producing sustainable competitive advantage through the effective management of people," *Academy of Management Executive*, Vol. 19, No. 4 (2005), pp. 95-106.

[24] French, J.R.P., and B. Raven, "The bases of social power," In D. Cartwright (Ed.) *Studies in Social Power*, Ann Arbor: Institute for Social Research, University of Michigan, 1959, pp. 150-167.

It may be difficult to implement processes that are perceived to be "owned" by managers in a functional area that is different from that of the champion of the idea.

In addition to varying levels of power within the firm, there are different levels of power in the firms that comprise the supply chain. For example, if a customer represents most of a supplier's business and the supplier represents a small amount of the customer's purchases, the customer will have more power. Management can use its power in ways that only benefit the firm or in ways that benefit the entire supply chain. Also, when a firm's metrics reward managers for short-run success, it is difficult for them to make short-term sacrifices for long-term gains.[25]

Risk and Reward

Risks and rewards may not be equitably shared across the supply chain or within the company. Because of channel power, management may expect suppliers and customers to assume most of the risks, while taking most of the benefits. If the other firm cannot make a sufficient profit, the relationship will not last. Before entering into a relationship with another firm, an analysis of potential risks and rewards should be completed. In many companies there is not an adequate analysis of the potential risks and rewards associated with contractual relationships because management lacks the analytical ability to do so.[26]

In one supply chain, the focal firm may have a great deal of inventory risk, but have significant potential for profit generation. In another supply chain, the focal firm may shoulder little risk, but not have many opportunities for profit improvements. One of the firms in a supply chain may not have the ability to make much profit, but because of the strength of the channel captain is expected to bear a large amount of risk. For example, managers may ask a third-party logistics company to purchase trucks and warehouses to manage the distribution process. The hiring firm does not want to compensate the third party for the full risk they are taking by purchasing the asset. When the business changes and the warehouses or the number of trucks become unnecessary, the third party bears the cost of the assets and not the customer. A critical question is what should suppliers and customers risk? In supply chains where there is a very powerful channel leader, such as Wal-Mart or General Motors, there may be pressure on suppliers or customers to absorb more of the risk. To receive the long-term support of customers and suppliers, risks and rewards should be equitably distributed.

In supply chains where there is a very powerful channel leader, such as Wal*Mart or General Motors, there may be pressure on suppliers or customers to absorb more of the risk.

Culture and Attitude

Culture is the pattern of basic assumptions that an organization has invented, discovered, or developed, and that have worked well enough to be considered valid. Corporate culture is taught to new members of the firm as the correct way to perceive, think, and feel.[27] The values and norms held by top management determine the culture of the organization.

An organization's culture becomes firmly embedded and is difficult to change.

---

[25] Ganesan, Shankar, "Determinants of Long-Term Orientation in Buyer-Seller Relationships," *Journal of Marketing*, Vol. 58, No. 2 (1994), pp. 1-19.

[26] Huntsman, Jon M., *Winners Never Cheat: Everyday Values We Learned as Children (But May Have Forgotten)*, Upper Saddle River, NJ: Wharton School Publishing, 2005.

[27] Schein, Edgar H., *Organizational Culture and Leadership*, San Francisco, CA: Jossey-Bass, 1985.

Mergers between firms often face problems because of the incompatibility of corporate cultures. For example, in May 1998 Daimler-Benz AG acquired Chrysler Corporation for $36.4 billion. Management struggled for several years with challenges based on differences in the two organizations' cultures as well as the differences in the two national cultures. Changing an organization's culture requires changes in basic assumptions and values which is difficult to achieve. In the spring of 2007, Daimler-Benz sold the majority of Chrysler (80%) to a U.S. private equity firm for $7.4 billion. For Daimler-Benz the purchase of Chrysler was a bad investment. One of the main barriers to successful integration of the two companies was the difference in cultures.

When Toyota and Honda began assembling vehicles in the United States, they chose to bring their Japanese suppliers with them.[28] This strategy helped them quickly ramp up production. Management believed that it would be easier to bring suppliers that knew their culture, than to train American suppliers because Japanese corporate culture is very different from American corporate culture. Culture and attitude are very important factors in the relationship between suppliers and manufacturers.

Trust and Commitment

Trust is based on the belief that the individuals in each company will act in a way that is mutually beneficial. Commitment is the level of effort that management invests in a relationship. Commitment is usually a result of trust. For proper implementation of a partnership both trust and commitment are necessary.[29] Managers in the two firms must determine how to develop trust and commitment.

Research has shown five factors influence trust and commitment among companies in the supply chain.[30] First, managers in both organizations must experience satisfaction with the relationship. They have to believe that both sides win by building more closeness into the relationship. Second, companies that are more highly regarded in the marketplace will be trusted more by their customers and suppliers and are able to establish more effective relationships. Third, relationships with less conflict will show a higher degree of trust. Fourth, better communication leads to a higher level of trust. Fifth, the higher the level of trust between the managers of two firms, the greater the commitment to the relationship. The same factors are true for the relationships between employees and management. Tensions between unions and management have lead to confrontations and mistrust, which disrupted operations of the firms. Other research shows that as managers become more comfortable working together, trust and commitment increases and this is known as bilateral convergence.[31] The goal is to create a balanced relationship in which both sides are dependent on each other.

The goal is to create a balanced relationship in which both sides are dependent on each other.

[28]Banerji, Kunal, Rakesh B. Sambharya, "Vertical Keiretsu and International Market Entry: The Case of the Japanese Automobile Ancilliary Industry," *Journal of International Business Studies*, Vol. 27, No. 1 (1996), pp. 89-113.

[29] Lambert, Douglas M., and A. Michael Knemeyer, "We're in This Together," *Harvard Business Review*. Vol. 82, No. 12 (2004), pp. 114-122.

[30] Chu, Suh-Yueh, and Wen-Chang Fang, "Exploring the Relationships of Trust and Commitment in Supply Chain Management," *The Journal of American Academy of Business*, Vol. 9, No. 1 (2006), pp. 224-228.

[31] Kumar, Nirmalya, Lisa K. Scheer and Jan-Benedict E. M. Steenkamp, "The effects of perceived interdependence on dealer attitudes," *Journal of Marketing Research*, Vol. 32, No. 3 (1995), pp. 348-356.

Process Implementation and Maintenance

Once a process has been implemented, there is a need to maintain it over time.

The eleven management components are necessary to implement and sustain all of the supply chain management processes described in this book. Once a process has been implemented, there is a need to maintain it over time. Process implementation incudes finding the right people, incenting them for their work on the process teams, and providing the necessary resources. Process maintenance deals with implementing the right metrics and providing the structure to sustain the effort over time. A process is successfully implemented when an assessment using the assessment tool at the end of this book results in no opportunities for improvement on each activity that is rated as critical or important. Figure 13-3

Figure 13-3
Process Implementation and Maintenance

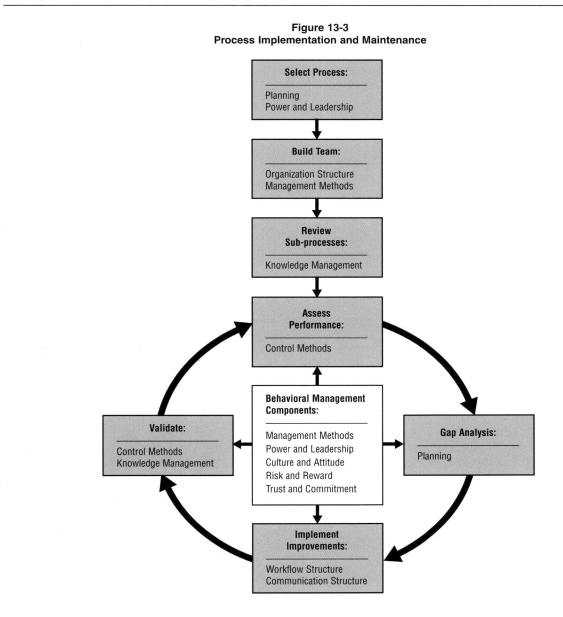

shows the necessary steps for implementing and maintaining a supply chain management process. The figure also shows which management components are relevant at each stage of process implementation and maintenance.

In order to successfully implement each of the eight supply chain management processes, there are seven steps that must be completed. The first step is to decide which process to implement. This requires planning and consideration of the power and leadership in the company. In addition, it is necessary to have the support of senior management and managers of each of the business functions. Then, it is necessary to build the process teams, which requires establishing cross-functional teams and implementing management methods that support this structure. The third step is to review the sub-processes described in the chapters. This is followed by an assessment of the performance of the current process and metrics must be developed for control purposes. The fifth step is to perform a gap analysis and plan for process improvements. Then, the identified improvement opportunities are addressed by changing the workflow structure and the communication structure. The final step is to validate the process. Control methods are used to measure the success of process improvements and experience is captured in the knowledge management system. All of the behavioral management components apply to the last four steps. In order to sustain the process, it is necessary to periodically repeat the cycle starting with a review of the sub-processes. Also, the organization's knowledge management system must capture learnings so that they are available for new team members. Next, each of the steps shown in Figure 13-3 is described.

In order to successfully implement each of the eight supply chain management processes, there are seven steps that must be completed.

Select Process

The first step is to pick the process to implement. The best place to start is with customer relationship management and supplier relationship management. They form the links in the supply chain and the segmentation of customers and suppliers that takes place in these processes is useful input to the other six processes. However, power and leadership should be considered before a decision on the order of process implementation is made. If the implementation of the first process is not successful, the chance for success of other process implementations is diminished. It is critical that managers in the company believe that the supply chain management processes add value and that the effort required for their implementation is worthwhile.

The senior executive sponsor of the SCM framework within each firm must understand who in the organization believes the framework should be implemented and who in the organization needs to be convinced. Some processes might be perceived as in the domain of a function. For example, customer relationship management deals with customers, and managers in the marketing and sales functions might believe that customers are their responsibility. Because supplier relationship management deals with suppliers, managers in the purchasing function may believe that they are responsible for this process. Other processes, such as order fulfillment and demand management might be viewed as within the domain of logistics. Regardless of which process is implemented first, managers from all functions must be involved and must understand that the process adds value in order to support its implementation.

It is critical that managers in the company believe that the supply chain management processes add value and that the effort required for their implementation is worthwhile.

Build Team

The leadership of the company must recognize the value of the process and communicate this value to the employees.

Once management decides which process to implement, the next step is to select the members of the strategic process team and the team leader. Implementation of any of the supply chain management processes should be supported by senior management. The leadership of the company must recognize the value of the process and communicate this value to the employees. Selecting the team is a very important decision since the success of the process implementation will be dependent on the team's performance. There are several points that should be considered when building a cross-functional team:[32]

- Limit the number of team members, so that each individual function has an appropriate level of importance.
- Ensure adequate levels of complementary skills by including at least one representative from each function.
- Identify how each function and the whole organization can benefit from implementation of the process.
- Set specific goals and a timeline.
- Have regular meetings to review progress.
- Create mutual accountability by rewarding team members based on process improvement.

The team leader may help select the team. The ideal team leader for each supply chain management process could come from any function. An exception is the customer relationship management process team which should be lead by the CEO of the company. The starting point in implementing the strategic customer relationship management process is to review the corporate and marketing strategies and determine what customers are key to the company's success now and in the future. In essence, the question that is being answered is "what business is the firm in"? Who should be making this decision, if it is not the CEO and the leadership team? For the other supply chain management processes, the team leader is not as clear. For example, it might seem to many that the manufacturing flow management process should be lead by the vice president of manufacturing, but the danger is that the process begins to look like the manufacturing function and the importance of the input from other functional managers is diminished. This will limit the effectiveness of the manufacturing flow management process implementation.

Each supply chain management process requires a different number of cross-functional teams. Table 13-2 provides a summary of the number of strategic and operational teams that are necessary for each of the processes. At the strategic level, each process generally requires one cross-functional team. However, depending on the firm's organization structure, more than one strategic team may be necessary. For example, 3M is made up of more than 35 business units that are organized into six businesses.[33] Because of the very different technologies and markets involved, 3M would need more than one strategic team to manage each process. This does not mean that each business unit needs a strategic team. If several business units sell to the same customers, then only one strategic team is

---

[32] Katzenbach, Jon R. and Douglas K. Smith, *The Wisdom of Teams: creating the high-performance organization*, New York, NY: McKinsey & Company, 2005, p. 62.

[33] 3M, "3M Facts," http://solutions.3m.com/wps/portal/3M/en_US/our/company/information/financial-facts/, accessed: 8/29/2007.

Table 13-2
Strategic and Operational Teams for Supply Chain Management Processes

Supply Chain Management Process	Strategic Level Teams	Operational Level Teams
Customer Relationship Management	One team comprised of the CEO and the functional VPs	One team for each key customer and for each segment of other customers
Supplier Relationship Management	One team	One team for each key supplier and for each segment of less critical suppliers
Customer Service Management	One team	Multiple teams
Demand Management	One team	Number of teams is determined by the complexity of the business in terms of products and customers
Order Fulfillment	One team	One team for each business unit
Manufacturing Flow Management	One team	One team for each distinct manufacturing technology
Product Development and Commercialization	One team	One team per project
Returns Management	One team	Number of teams is determined by the complexity of the business in terms of products and customers

necessary for these businesses. However, at the operational level multiple teams are necessary. For example, a relationship with an important customer is managed by a single team. The goal is to avoid unnecessary complexity.

The process owners can come from any function but they must be good managers who can build cross-functional support. The role of each member of the cross-functional team is to represent his/her function by providing functional expertise. If a decision that the team is about to make negatively affects a function, that representative must voice his/her concerns so that the team can make certain that the benefits exceed the costs. Similarly, managers who are on a cross-functional team must be able to explain to their functional colleagues why decisions made by the process team were good for the total organization.

The process owners can come from any function but they must be good managers who can build cross-functional support.

How the process teams are rewarded is a critical part of process implementation. There is an important balancing act between the individual's responsibilities in the function and his/her responsibilities in the cross-functional team. Team members should not be incented to abandon one for the other. The key to designing an effective reward system is to understand how the actions of the team affect the company's performance. The impact of the team's actions on economic value added (EVA®) should be measured as shown in each of the chapters that describe the processes.

Review Sub-processes

In each chapter where the supply chain management processes are described, a set of strategic and operational sub-processes and the associated activities are presented which provide direction for the cross-functional teams. Each team member should be familiar with the chapter in this book that describes the process targeted for implementation.

Each supply chain management process is divided into strategic and operational sub-processes. There are activities associated with each sub-process, which show the decisions that must be made for implementation. At the strategic level, the objective is to provide the structure to guide the operational teams. The operational teams plan the activities that functional employees execute. Everyone involved must be familiar with the activities in each of the stratagic and operational sub-processes.

After the first three steps have been completed, the implementation moves to a continuous cycle that is meant to institutionalize the process. The cycle is made up of four steps: assess performance, gap analysis, implement improvements, and validate. At the strategic level, the cycle might be repeated once a year. At the operational level, the process team might repeat the cycle every month or every quarter.

Assess Performance

The next step is to assess how well the process is being performed. In this stage, the control methods that were described earlier in this chapter are used. There are two types of performance assessments. The first uses the assessment tool that is provided in this book to perform a detailed assessment of the process. The second type of assessment reviews performance using the metrics that have been developed for the process. The assessment tool should be used at the beginning of process implementation in order to provide a benchmark against which progress in can be measured. It should be used again after the process is implemented in order to identify additional opportunities for improvement. Chapter 10 describes in detail how to conduct an assessment. Assessments should be conducted of the strategic and operational supply chain management processes every one or two

Managers must assess performance of the operational supply chain management processes at regular intervals using the appropriate metrics.

years using the assessment tool. Managers must assess performance of the operational supply chain management processes at regular intervals using the appropriate metrics. When repeating the cycle for process maintenance on a monthly or quarterly basis, it is not necessary to use the assessment tool. We identified several key metrics in the chapters describing each process but a summary of potential metrics follows:

- Customer Relationship Management: profitability by customer.
- Supplier Relationship Management: contribution of supplier to the company's profitability.
- Customer Service Management: the number of times the company was unable to identify a problem before it affected the customer and the number of times the company was able to identify a problem before it affected the customer.[34]

---

[34] Bolumole, Yemisi A., A. Michael Knemeyer, and Douglas M. Lambert, "The Customer Service Management Process," *The International Journal of Logistics Management*, Vol. 14, No. 2 (2003), pp. 15-31.

- Demand Management: planning accuracy, forecasting error and capacity utilization.[35]
- Order Fulfillment: distribution costs, order-to-cash cycle time, order fill rate, and order completeness.[36]
- Manufacturing Flow Management: WIP inventory levels, inventory velocity, manufacturing cost, product quality, productivity, cycle time, and safety.[37]
- Product Development and Commercialization: time to market, stockout percentage, total cost of product development and commercialization, and impact of new products on existing ones.[38]
- Returns Management: gatekeeping rate, asset recovery percentage, return rates, rate of product resold as is, percentage of materials recycled.[39]

These metrics are meant as guidelines that must be adapted to the requirements of the individual firm and supply chain. Each process must have its own set of metrics that best defines success. The metrics must be tracked over time to ensure the processes are adding value for the firm. For example, in customer relationship management the strategic team reviews overall profitability and the operational teams will review profitability of their customers or customer segments and compare it to projected profitability. As mentioned in the section on control methods, it is critical to find metrics that maximize the performance of the entire supply chain and that are aligned across firms.

Each process must have its own set of metrics that best defines success. The metrics must be tracked over time to ensure the processes are adding value for the firm.

Gap Analysis

In the gap analysis stage, the process teams evaluate the results of the assessment. Gap analysis is part of the planning that takes place when implementing and sustaining the supply chain management processes. The teams plan which process improvements will be implemented in the next stage. Depending on the type of performance assessment that was used, the results of the assessment tool or the metrics will be considered. After a supply chain management process assessment has been conducted, the areas that need improvement can be identified. The areas where the scores differ the most from the ideal score and are viewed as important or critical, represent the first gaps that the process teams will want to close. However, the team members should understand which areas can be influenced immediately and which ones cannot. There may be some areas where improvements can be made with relatively little effort. The process teams should identify the resources that are required to improve

[35] Croxton, Keely L., Douglas M. Lambert, Sebastián J. García-Dastugue, and Dale S. Rogers, "The Demand Management Process," *The International Journal of Logistics Management*, Vol. 13, No. 2 (2002), pp. 51-66.

[36] Croxton, Keely L., "The Order Fulfillment Process," *The International Journal of Logistics Management*, Vol. 14, No. 1 (2002), pp. 19-32.

[37] Goldsby, Thomas J., and Sebastián J. García-Dastugue, "The Manufacturing Flow Management Process," *The International Journal of Logistics Management*, Vol. 14, No. 2 (2003), pp. 33-52.

[38] Rogers, Dale S., Douglas M. Lambert, and A. Michael Knemeyer, "The Product Development and Commercialization Process," *The International Journal of Logistics Management*, Vol. 15, No. 1 (2004), pp. 43-56.

[39] Rogers, Dale S., Douglas M. Lambert, Keely L. Croxton, and Sebastián J. García-Dastugue, "The Returns Management Process," *The International Journal of Logistics Management*, Vol. 13, No. 2 (2002), pp. 1-18.

a score and what the improvements mean to the overall profitability of the firm. After all relevant performance gaps in the assessment have been identified, an action plan must be created. This five-step procedure may be used to develop an action plan:

- List all deviations from the ideal score.
- Rank by criticality.
- Rank by magnitude of deviation from target score.
- Rank by ease of implementation.
- Develop the action plan with timetable and responsibilities.

If the process team did not use the assessment tool and only reviewed metrics, then performance gaps must be determined using the metrics. The results must be compared to the goal. Then, depending on which goals are not met, areas for improvement can be identified. Since the gap analysis on the process metrics is done monthly or quarterly in the operational teams, the gaps are more operational than the gaps that are discovered using the assessment tool.

The strategic teams must decide if changes to the activities in the strategic sub-processes are necessary. As input for this decision, it is critical to talk to the operational teams and learn what problems they have encountered. For example, if in order fulfillment the logistics network was designed to deliver products with a 10-day lead-time, the operational teams could only offer a 10-day lead-time to a customer. However, if customers demand an eight-day lead-time because competitors offer eight days, the strategic team is responsible for making the decision to offer an eight day lead-time but it is not offered to customers until it can be provided profitably. In contrast, if a customer receives orders in 12 days and wants to shorten it to 10 days, this is a decision that is within the boundaries of the operational customer team. At this stage, process teams may decide if specific programs are to be implemented. For example, the demand management team may approach a customer or supplier to implement Collaborative Planning Forecasting and Replenishment (CPFR) or Vendor Managed Inventory (VMI). These programs will impact the way demand management is organized and changes will need to be made at the implement improvements stage.

Implement Improvements

At the implement improvements stage, the cross-functional teams convert the action plan that was established in the gap analysis into improvements for the process. In the initial process implementation, the sub-processes must be implemented at this stage. Also as part of the operational processes, the operational teams are built. Building the operational teams requires similar steps as building the strategic teams.

Once a supply chain management process is implemented, there is the need to continuously improve it.

Once a supply chain management process is implemented, there is the need to continuously improve it. The GSCF supply chain management framework is described in a way that makes it applicable to a wide range of businesses. The supply chain management processes may require some adaptation for each individual business. For example, a possible improvement could be the implementation of CPFR with a customer. However, this does not mean that every firm must implement CPFR. The question of how a process must look should be answered by the people who work on the process every day. After process improvements have been implemented, validation is the next stage in the cycle.

Validate

In the validate stage of the cycle, it is necessary to determine if the planned improvements have been successfully implemented. In order to decide whether a process has been implemented successfully, several measures of success are necessary. The specific measures are different from company to company and from process to process but generally a process is considered to be fully implemented when five scores are achieved on critical and important attributes during an assessment. Implementing a supply chain management process requires a significant investment in time and resources, and managers might be inclined to assume a process is implemented after the first four steps are completed.

An important aspect of a successful process improvement is whether the desired benefits have been achieved. For example, if VMI was implemented in order to reduce inventory levels in the supply chain, the process team must determine if inventory was actually reduced and by how much. This information must flow into the knowledge management system in order to be able to better quantify the success of similar programs in the future.

An important aspect of a successful process improvement is whether the desired benefits have been achieved.

At this stage, team membership should be evaluated. That is, the process teams must ask "do we have the right people"? It may happen that people move into new positions or leave the company. Then, new managers must fill that void on the cross-functional teams. Or when new managers join the firm, management might feel they should be involved in supply chain management and ask them to join a cross-functional team. Another possibility is that a customer becomes more important and a team is necessary to manage the relationship. The right people are critical for successful implementation of the supply chain management processes. After this step has been completed, a new cycle begins with assess performance.

Conclusions

The management components presented in this chapter are necessary to implement and maintain the supply chain management processes. The structural management components must be recognized and managed so that firms across the supply can work as an integrated whole. The behavioral management components are difficult to assess objectively but they often determine the success or failure of the supply chain management process implementation. It is critical for managers to analyze how the management components are manifested in their own company and in the other organizations that are part of their firm's supply chains.

The success of the firm's supply chain depends on the implementation and maintenance of the supply chain management processes. Well-designed processes will fail to be successful if the implementation and maintenance efforts are ineffective. Institutionalizing a supply chain management process requires rigor and discipline. Managers must be able to devote enough resources to the cross-functional process teams, but they still must accomplish their work in the functions. Institutionalizing the processes makes them sustainable.

Well-designed processes will fail to be successful if the implementation and maintenance efforts are ineffective. Institutionalizing a supply chain management process requires rigor and discipline.

CHAPTER

14 Developing and Implementing Partnerships in the Supply Chain

Douglas M. Lambert, A. Michael Knemeyer and John T. Gardner

Overview

An important aspect of implementing supply chain management is the formation of appropriate linkages between members of the supply chain.

An important aspect of implementing supply chain management is the formation of appropriate linkages between members of the supply chain.[1] While practitioners and academics have championed the value of partnerships for this purpose, the challenge is to find effective methods for developing the appropriate type of relationship. In this chapter, we describe a model that can be used to structure business relationships. Implementation issues are documented and direction is provided for managers interested in using this tool for tailoring key supply chain relationships.

Introduction

In an environment characterized by scarce resources, increased competition, higher customer expectations, and faster rates of change, executives are turning to partnerships to strengthen supply chain integration and provide sustainable competitive advantage. Partnering provides a way to leverage the unique skills and expertise of each partner and may increase switching costs. According to Rosabeth Moss Kanter, "…being a good partner has become a key corporate asset…In the global economy, a well-developed ability to create and sustain fruitful collaborations gives companies a significant competitive leg up".[2] But exactly what is a partnership, and when is one appropriate? At first glance, the answers to these questions might appear straight-forward, but they are not.

---

[1] This chapter is based on Douglas M. Lambert, Margaret A. Emmelhainz and John T. Gardner, "Developing and Implementing Supply Chain Partnerships," *The International Journal of Logistics Management,* Vol. 7, No. 2 (1996), pp. 1-17; Douglas M. Lambert, A. Michael Knemeyer and John T. Gardner, "Supply Chain Partnerships: Model Validation and Implementation," *Journal of Business Logistics,* Vol. 25, No. 2 (2004), pp. 21-42; and Douglas M. Lambert and A. Michael Knemeyer, "We're in This Together," *Harvard Business Review,* Vol. 82, No. 12 (2004), pp. 114-122.

[2] Kanter, Rosabeth M., "Collaborative Advantage: The Art of Alliances", *Harvard Business Review,* Vol. 72, No. 4 (1994), pp. 96-108.

There is considerable confusion over the definition of partnerships. As an example, one executive from a major manufacturer in the health care industry identified a relationship with a small-package express delivery company as a partnership. When analyzed in detail, it became apparent that the relationship was not a partnership; rather it was simply a long-term contract with volume guarantees. Managers from both firms believed that they were involved in a partnership because each firm was achieving the desired outcomes from the relationship. The transportation firm received a large revenue increase as the single-source provider of the service and the manufacturer achieved the service improvement and cost reductions that were promised. The initial reaction of an executive from the manufacturer was that she ought to work to turn the relationship into a partnership. This executive's reaction is understandable and fairly common. A basic premise is that partnerships are essential elements of business strategy and managers should strive to achieve such relationships with every customer and supplier. This is not only flawed thinking, it is dangerous thinking. The lesson here is that a partnership is not necessarily a requirement for achieving business success.

When analyzed in detail, it became apparent that the relationship was not a partnership; rather it was simply a long-term contract with volume guarantees. Managers from both firms believed that they were involved in a partnership because each firm was achieving the desired outcomes from the relationship.

Partnerships, while beneficial, are costly in terms of the time and effort required for successful implementation.[3] Consequently, a firm cannot and should not partner with every supplier, customer or third-party provider. It is important to ensure that scarce resources are dedicated only to those relationships which will truly benefit from a partnership. Yet, many organizations become involved in relationships that do not meet management expectations and/or which end in failure. How can managers determine, in advance, if a potential relationship is one which will result in competitive advantage, and is worthy of the time and resources needed to fully develop into a partnership? Further, all partnerships are not the same. How does management know what type of partnership would provide the best pay-off? These questions may be answered by utilizing the partnership model presented in this chapter.

The partnership model represents a systematic process for developing, implementing and continuously improving corporate relationships. Without a foundation of effective relationships, efforts to manage the flow of materials and information across the supply chain are likely to be unsuccessful.[4] Partnering between firms is one way to find and maintain competitive advantage for both firms.[5] The partnership model provides a structured and repeatable process to effectively and efficiently build and maintain tailored business relationships that might become an asset for executives looking for competitive advantage.

---

[3] Gardner, John T., Martha C. Cooper and Tom Noordewier, "Understanding Shipper-Carrier and Shipper-Warehouser Relationships: Partnerships Revisited," *Journal of Business Logistics*, Vol. 15, No. 2 (1994), pp. 121-143; and, F. Ian Stuart, "Supplier Partnerships: Influencing Factors and Strategic Benefits," *International Journal of Purchasing and Material Management*, Vol. 29, No. 4 (1993), pp. 22-28.

[4] "Supply Chain Challenges: Building Relationships – A Conversation with Scott Beth, David N. Burt, William Copacino, Chris Gopal, Hau L. Lee, Robert Porter Lynch and Sandra Morris," *Harvard Business Review*, Vol. 81, No. 7 (2003), pp. 64-74.

[5] Mentzer, John T., Soonhong Min and Zach G. Zacharia, "The Nature of Interfirm Partnering in Supply Chain Management," *Journal of Retailing*, Vol. 76, No. 4 (2000), pp. 549-568; and, Jakki Mohr and Robert E. Spekman, "Characteristics of Partnership Success: Partnership Attributes, Communication Behavior, and Conflict Resolution Techniques," *Strategic Management Journal*, Vol. 15, No. 2 (1994), pp. 135-152.

What is a Partnership?

Relationships between organizations can range from arm's length relationships (consisting of either one-time exchanges or multiple transactions) to vertical integration of the two organizations, as shown in Figure 14-1. Most relationships between organizations are at arm's length. Two organizations conduct business with each other, often over a long period of time and involving multiple exchanges. However, there is no sense of joint commitment or joint operations between management teams in the two organizations. In arm's length relationships, a seller typically offers standard products/services to a wide range of customers who receive standard terms and conditions. When the exchanges end, the relationship ends. While arm's length represents an appropriate option in many situations, there are times when a closer, more integrated relationship, referred to as a partnership, provides significant benefits to both firms.

While the word partnership has been interpreted by some to mean any business-to-business relationship, it is still the most descriptive term for closely integrated, mutually beneficial relationships that enhance supply chain performance. We believe that a partnership is most appropriately defined as follows:[6]

A partnership is a tailored business relationship based on mutual trust, openness, shared risk and shared rewards that results in business performance greater than would be achieved by the two firms working together in the absence of partnership.

A partnership is a *tailored* business relationship based on mutual trust, openness, shared risk and shared rewards that results in business performance greater than would be achieved by the two firms working together in the absence of partnership.

A key point of this definition is that the relationship is customized. It is not standard fare, that is, something that would be done for any customer of a particular size. Another key point is that incremental benefits must be gained from the tailoring effort. The tailoring process consumes managerial time and talent, thus it must yield measurable benefits.

A partnership is not the same as a joint venture which involves some degree of shared ownership across the two parties. Nor is it the same as vertical integration. Yet a well managed partnership can provide benefits similar to those found in joint ventures or vertical integration without the problems associated with ownership. For instance, a few years ago PepsiCo chose to acquire restaurants such as Taco Bell, Pizza Hut and KFC. One of the benefits of these acquisitions

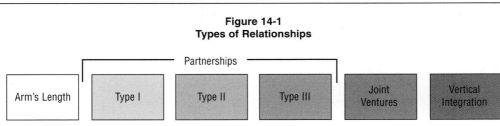

Figure 14-1
Types of Relationships

Source: Douglas M. Lambert, Margaret A. Emmelhainz and John T. Gardner, "Developing and Implementing Supply Partnerships," *The International Journal of Logistics Management*, Vol. 7, No. 2 (1996), p. 2.

---

[6] Lambert, Douglas M., Margaret A. Emmelhainz and John T. Gardner, "Developing and Implementing Supply Chain Partnerships," *The International Journal of Logistics Management*, Vol. 7, No. 2 (1996), pp. 1-17; and, Douglas M. Lambert, Margaret A. Emmelhainz and John T. Gardner (1999), "Building Successful Logistics Partnerships," *Journal of Business Logistics*, Vol. 20, No. 1 (1999), pp. 165-181.

was that PepsiCo could ensure that Coca-Cola would not be sold in these outlets. Coca-Cola achieved a similar result, without the cost of ownership, through its partnership with McDonald's. In the late 1990's, PepsiCo got out of the restaurant business saying that it detracted management attention from the core businesses: snacks and beverages.

Research shows that partnerships enable the firms involved to achieve cost savings and reduce duplication of efforts.[7] For suppliers, partnerships with industry leaders can enhance operations and prestige,[8] and provide stability in unstable markets.[9] For buyers, partnerships can improve profitability, reduce purchasing costs, and increase technical cooperation.[10]

While most partnerships share some common elements and characteristics, there is no one ideal or "benchmark" relationship which is appropriate in all situations. Because each relationship has its own set of motivating factors driving its development as well as its own unique operating environment, the duration, breadth, strength and closeness of the partnership will vary from case to case and over time. Three types of partnerships exist:

- **Type I** - The organizations involved recognize each other as partners and, on a limited basis, coordinate activities and planning. The partnership usually has a short-term focus and typically involves only one division or a limited number of functional areas within each organization.
- **Type II** - The organizations involved progress beyond coordination of activities to integration of activities. Although not expected to last "forever" the partnership has a long-term horizon. Multiple divisions and functions within the firm are involved in the partnership.
- **Type III** - The organizations share a significant level of operational integration. Each party views the other as an extension of their own firm. Typically no "end date" for the partnership exists.

Normally, a firm will have a wide range of relationships spanning the entire spectrum, the majority of which will not be partnerships at all but arm's length relationships. The largest percentage of partnerships will be Type I with only a limited number of Type III. Type III partnerships should be reserved for two or three percent of suppliers or customers who are critical to an organization's long-term success.

Normally, a firm will have a wide range of relationships spanning the entire spectrum, the majority of which will not be partnerships at all but arm's length relationships.

---

[7] Herbing, Paul A. and Bradley S. O'Hara, "The Future of Original Equipment Manufacturers: A Matter of Partnerships," *Journal of Business and Industrial Marketing,* Vol. 9, No. 3 (1994), pp. 38-43; Judith S. Whipple, Robert Frankel and David J. Frayer, "Logistical Alliance Formation Motives: Similarities and Differences with the Channel," *Journal of Marketing Theory and Practice,* Vol. 4, No. 2 (1996), pp. 26-36; and, Walter Zinn and A. Parasuraman, "Scope and Intensity of Logistics-Based Strategic Alliances: A Conceptual Classification and Managerial Implications," *Industrial Marketing Management,* Vol. 26, No. 2 (1997), pp. 137-147.

[8] Anderson, James C. and James A. Narus, "Partnering as a Focused Marketing Strategy," *California Management Review,* Vol. 33, No. 3 (1991), pp. 95-113; and, Robert E. Spekman, "Strategic Supplier Selection: Understanding Long-Term Buyer Relationships," *Business Horizons,* Vol. 31, No. 4 (1988), pp. 75-81.

[9] Fram, Eugene H. and Martin L. Presberg, "Customer Partnering: Suppliers' Attitudes and Market Realities," *Journal of Business and Industrial Marketing,* Vol. 8, No. 4 (1993), pp. 43-51.

[10] Ailawadi, Kusum L., Paul W. Farris and Mark E. Parry, "Market Share and ROI: Observing the Effect of Unobserved Variables," *International Journal of Research in Marketing,* Vol. 16, No. 1 (1999), pp. 17-33; and, Sang-Lin Han, David T. Wilson and Shirish P. Dant, "Buyer-Supplier Relationships Today," *Industrial Marketing Management,* Vol. 22, No. 4 (1993), pp. 331-338.

Development of the Model

The partnership model was initially developed using detailed case studies of relationships involving members of The Global Supply Chain Forum who identified 18 relationships which they believed reflected good partnerships that we could learn from (see Table 14-1). These case studies, along with a detailed literature review, and Forum members' input were used as the basis for the development of the partnership model. Over the past few years, the model has been used to structure more than 50 partnerships in a wide variety of contexts. Twenty of these relationships were used for a systematic validation of the model which provided support for the value of using the model as well as a number of specific guidelines on implementation issues.[11]

Of the 20 partnership meetings facilitated to validate the model, a major retailer provided an opportunity to use the model with nine product and service suppliers that involved a diverse set of relationships. Both critical component

---

Table 14-1
Relationship Cases Used to Develop the Model

Lucent Technologies (formerly known as AT&T Network Systems) and Panalpina for freight forwarding services of telecommunications equipment in the South American Market. Lucent Technologies manufactures and installs telecommunications systems, high-tech fibers, and switching technologies. The systems are shipped in the form of component parts with final assembly and installation in-country. As Lucent entered the Latin America market, it found customs documentation requirements to be particularly burdensome. For instance, the Brazilian government required that the documentation describe every separate part and item. For large systems this was equivalent to taking an automobile apart and shipping it by every nut, bolt, screw, fender, and bumper. Panalpina is a forwarder with offices in facilities in Central and South America and with a well established in-country infrastructure.

A small package express delivery company and a manufacturer for national distribution of healthcare products. This involved an offering of both air and ground transportation on the part of the carrier and a guaranteed volume on the part of the manufacturer.

McDonald's and Martin-Brower for the distribution of products and supplies to franchisees and company stores Martin-Brower is the largest of McDonald's six distributors, handling approximately 40% of McDonald's locations. Martin-Brower

distributes a complete range of products from food supplier to paper items.

McDonald's and OSI for the supply of hamburger patties to McDonald's restaurants. OSI is a manufacturer of beef patties, supplying approximately 25% of McDonald's volume. McDonald's is OSI's only customer.

McDonald's and Coca-Cola for the supply of beverages to McDonald's restaurants. McDonald's is Coke's largest customer and Coke is McDonald's largest supplier. Coca-Cola is the only cola beverage sold in any McDonald's store.

Xerox and Ryder for the delivery, installation, and removal of copiers. In this relationship, Ryder truck drivers deliver, set-up, test, and demonstrate copiers for Xerox. In addition, the drivers also perform initial customer training and remove old equipment.

Xerox and Ryder for inbound transportation services to Xerox's manufacturing locations. Xerox depends upon Ryder Dedicated Logistics to manage the Xerox in-bound network so that JIT requirements are met.

Whirlpool and ERX for the warehousing an distribution of Whirlpool appliances to dealers and customers within 24-48 hours of order placement. Quality Express is a program through which Whirlpool sought to improve its customer service levels by partnering with third party providers. ERX

is a joint venture between MARK VII, a transportation company, and Elston-Richards, a warehousing company, and operates six of eight Quality Exporess programs.

Whirlpool and IP Logistics for the warehousing and distribution of Whirlpool appliances to dealers and customers in one of eight Quality Express program. KP Logistics is a partnership between Kenco, a warehousing company, and Premier Transportation.

Whirpool and TRMTI (Leaseway) for the warehousing and distribution of appliances to dealers and customers from one of eight Quality Express locations. TRMTI is a division of Leaseway Transportation and had been providing delivery services to builders in Florida for Whirlpool prior to the initiation of Quality Express.

3M and Yellow Freight for less-than-truckload outbound transportation services. This was a relationship which extended from 1981 until 1993 and evolved from a one-year contract to a long-term based arrangement.

Target and 3M for a wide range of consumer products. This arrangement involves seven distinct relationships: one between the two corporations and six others between 3M divisions and Target departments.

Source: Douglas M. Lambert, Margaret A. Emmelhainz and John T. Gardner, "Developing and Implementing Supply Chain Partnerships," *The International Journal of Logistics Management*, Vol. 7, No. 2 (1996), p. 3.

---

[11] Lambert, Douglas M., A. Michael Knemeyer and John T. Gardner, "Supply Chain Partnerships: Model Validation and Implementation, *Journal of Business Logistics*, Vol. 25, No. 2 (2004), pp. 21-42.

suppliers and support product suppliers were included in the sample. Another nine partnership cases were completed with three companies in the consumer goods sector and their suppliers. These relationships included suppliers of raw materials and packaging materials as well as a vertically integrated internal relationship between two wholly owned subsidiaries of the same company who also conducted business with companies outside of the relationship. The final two cases involved a major company in the technology sector and two service suppliers.

The methodology used to develop and validate the model addresses a number of frequently cited criticisms of partnership research. For instance, Baba complained that most partnership research was based only on a limited number of interviews, often with just one executive, from only one party to the relationship.[12] Another concern is that much partnership research is based upon mail surveys. While mail surveys enable the gathering of large amounts of data from numerous sources, the extent and richness of the data collected are limited. Also, with a mail survey, there is no assurance that all participants are interpreting the questions in the same way or really understand what is meant by partnership.

The methodology used to develop and validate the model addresses a number of frequently cited criticisms of partnership research.

While case studies of partnerships do provide a fuller picture at the micro organizational level, such studies have not followed a unified research framework that would permit replication and generalization of findings. Partnership studies would benefit from research designs aimed at identification and explication of integrative processes that serve to bond partners and strengthen interorganizational relationships. Future research on partnerships must have the partnership dyad as the minimum unit of analysis. Investigations that capture only from one side of a given partnership (even if both partner types are represented in a sample) will fail to reflect accurately the dynamic forces that bond or break partnerships in the long run.[13]

The Partnership Model

The partnership model is comprised of four parts: the drivers of partnership, the facilitators of partnership, the components of partnership, and the outcomes of partnership.[14] Drivers are the compelling reasons to partner, and must be examined first when approaching a potential partner. Facilitators are the characteristics of the two firms that will help or hinder the partnership development process. It is the combination of facilitators and drivers that prescribes the appropriate type of partnership. Components are the managerially controllable elements that can be implemented at various levels depending on the type of partnership desired. How they are actually implemented will determine the type of partnership that exists. Outcomes are the extent to which each firm has achieved its expected drivers (see Figure 14-2). Partnerships in practice require a repeatable managerial process that will guide the analysis and implementation of appropriate levels of partnership

---

[12] Baba, Maretta L., "Two Sides to Every Story: An Ethnohistorical Approach to Organizational Partnerships", *City and Society*, Vol. 2, No. 2 (1988), pp. 71-104.

[13] Baba, Maretta L., "Two Sides to Every Story: An Ethnohistorical Approach to Organizational Partnerships", *City and Society*, Vol. 2, No. 2 (1988), p. 75.

[14] Lambert, Douglas M., Margaret A. Emmelhainz and John T. Gardner, "Building Successful Logistics Partnerships," *Journal of Business Logistics*, Vol. 20, No. 1 (1999), pp. 165-181.

Figure 14-2
Partnership Model

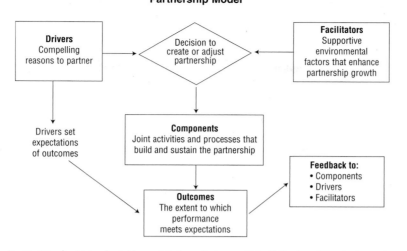

Source: Douglas M. Lambert, Margaret A. Emmelhainz, and John T. Gardner, "Developing and Implementing Supply Chain Partnerships," *The International Journal of Logistics Management*, Vol. 7, No. 2 (1996), p. 4.

components. The successes attributed to the use of the model indicate that it is a valuable tool for implementing partnerships in the supply chain. Managers consistently report that they would not have considered as many issues and would not have done so as holistically without the structure provided by the model. Some of the outcomes have surprised the users. A retailer used the model with a supplier who subsequently acquired a west coast manufacturing capability to provide full national coverage. The investment had been resisted before the partnership meeting. In another example, a consumer products manufacturer used the model in order to increase the flow of innovation opportunities from key suppliers. During one partnership meeting, a supplier committed to assigning a dedicated salesperson as well as dedicating an employee in their research and development area to this customer. This commitment was made because the partnership meeting identified the concerns of the customer's vice president of R&D regarding how the confidentiality of joint innovations between the companies would be handled.

Both qualitative and quantitative measures provided by managers support the value of using the model to tailor relationships within the supply chain.

Both qualitative and quantitative measures provided by managers support the value of using the model to tailor relationships. Management of a consumer products manufacturer identified that one of the outcomes of using the model was the implementation of a vendor managed supply system that produced $4.3 million in annual savings. Another case involving this manufacturer resulted in $2.8 million in annual savings by identifying an opportunity to work with the supplier to restructure its supply network. Managers of another company attributed the acceleration of a plant opening (a reduction of 2 months) to using the model.

The next section provides guidance on how to use the partnership model. First, a description of the preparation that must take place prior to using the model is outlined. Next, the partnership facilitation process is reviewed with a focus on providing suggestions on how to maximize its effectiveness as a managerial tool. Finally, a set of broader issues concerning the use of the model is detailed.

Preparation for Meeting

All parties involved, including meeting facilitators and participants, have activities that should be completed prior to the meeting. These activities include participant selection, meeting scheduling, meeting planning issues and groundwork issues.

The management team must determine which business relationship(s) are candidates. Management should consider the word-of-mouth issues associated with the decision to use the model with specific companies. In particular, what might be the reaction within a supplier or customer organization when it is discovered that a competitor has gone through the process and they have not? During several of our facilitations, managers from the company invited to participate in the meeting asked who else had gone through the process.

The meetings are greatly enhanced by the presence of individuals from multiple levels within the organizations who represent diverse functional expertise. The make-up of the group sends a message to those in the other firm about the importance of the relationship. It is important to involve the highest-level executives possible and still have the meeting. The more levels of management above the people in the room, the more likely a change in one of the more senior managers will negatively impact the commitments made in the meeting.

The meetings are greatly enhanced by the presence of individuals from multiple levels within the organizations who represent diverse functional expertise.

The need to have the involvement of multiple levels of employees with diverse functional expertise makes scheduling difficult. As was stated by one participant, "this is the first time all of these people have been together in the same room." The best way to handle this challenge is to have a high-level executive both state that the meeting is a priority and also attend the meeting. During our use of the model, the presidents of several of the firms attended the entire meeting.

Additional considerations when preparing for the meeting include:

- Publish a detailed agenda in order to establish expectations and maintain focus.
- Schedule sessions of one and a half days (back-to-back partnership meetings are not recommended).
- Schedule a dinner at the end of the first day to enable networking and clarification of the discussions that took place during the day.
- Review the model in advance (this is a must do for all participants).
- Make sure that meeting facilitators are conversant in the business situation.
- Provide a neutral location, spacious rooms, and proper supplies for recording and communicating the process.
- Provide participants with materials that include an agenda, a list of participants, and copies of forms used for the session.

While the preparation details appear to be intuitive, some meetings were hampered by a lack of attention to these issues.

The Partnership Meeting

The partnership meeting is a complex, multi-session process in which expectations are set, the environment is examined, and action plans are developed and assigned. Specific details related to the partnership meeting are described in the following sections. We describe the sessions as outlined in Table 14-2. The primary sessions include: 1) introduction and expectation setting session; 2)

Table 14-2
Partnership Facilitation – Key Points and Challenges

Process Stage	Key Points	Challenges
Preparation for Meeting	- review model prior to the meeting - invite appropriate participants to include multiple levels and functions	- scheduling difficulties
Introduction and Expectation Setting Session	- communicate that the business is not at risk - establish expectations of the process	- ensuring candid discussion
Drivers Session	- communicate the need to be selfish when establishing drivers - ensure confidentiality of session - be prepared to present ideas to the other party	- establishing solid driver metrics - explaining the customer service driver to the supplier - learning how to score the drivers
Facilitators Session	- establish environment for the joint session - learn how to jointly score the facilitators	- ensuring candid discussion - establishing the need to provide examples of past behavior
Targeting Session	- explain the need to use lowest driver score	- communicating to the parties that the goal is the appropriate level of partnership, not to have the highest level
Components Session	- connect to drivers and prescribed level of partnership - formulate action plans that address components and drivers	- connecting action items to drivers - prioritizing action items - incorporating driver metrics
Wrap-up Session	- establish appropriate follow-up schedule - establish appropriate assessment	- maintaining momentum - ensuring the allocation of managerial resources in order to execute action plans

Source: Douglas M. Lambert, A. Michael Knemeyer and John T. Gardner, "Supply Chain Partnerships: Model Validation and Implementation," *Journal of Business Logistics*, Vol. 25, No. 2 (2004), pp. 21-42.

drivers session; 3) facilitators session; 4) targeting session; 5) components session; and 6) the wrap-up session. We include a general overview of the session and where appropriate discuss assessment issues. Information on conducting each of the sessions is provided.

Introduction and Expectation Setting Session. The partnership meeting should begin with an introduction that reinforces the motivations for undertaking the process, a review of the model, and a discussion about expectations. For example, the vice president of one company detailed the corporate goals of increased innovation and profit margin growth as the underlying reason for using the model to build more structure into their relationships with key suppliers. In another firm, the vice president stated that the motivation for using the model was to achieve a structured and consistent approach to relationship management. It is critical for those in attendance to understand that the business is not at risk.

It is common for participants from one of the companies to want more partnership because they feel that somehow it relates to the security of the business. It is important for the meeting facilitator to establish from the very beginning of the session that the goal is to tailor the partnership to the most efficient and effective type. It should be made clear that the goal is NOT to have a Type III partnership but to determine the most appropriate type of partnership. The goal should be to obtain the desired business results for the least amount of effort. Incremental benefits must accrue to both firms, if management is going to invest incremental effort. This point should be reinforced throughout the meeting. The managerial time wasted on an unneeded Type III partnership would have large opportunity costs.

It should be made clear that the goal is NOT to have a Type III partnership but to determine the most appropriate type of partnership. The goal should be to obtain the desired business results for the least amount of effort.

Some additional issues concerning the role of the meeting facilitators are:

- Two individuals from outside the relationship are needed for the session that develops the drivers for each company.
- The individuals serve as the lead trainers and pace setters for the process.
- The individuals must be skilled in building consensus, probing for more information, assuring closure, and reinforcing agreements on action plans.

These recommendations were drawn from multiple cases. For instance, during a meeting at their customer's location, one supplier stated that the driver session felt like it was taking place back at their own headquarters. This comfort level would be difficult to achieve without unbiased meeting facilitators.

Drivers Session. Both parties must believe that they will receive significant benefits in one or more areas and that these benefits would not be possible without a partnership. The potential benefits which drive the desire to partner are categorized as: asset/cost efficiency, customer service, marketing advantage, and profit stability/growth. In addition, it is important to clarify how best to assess these drivers and how to conduct a drivers session.

Both parties must believe that they will receive significant benefits in one or more areas and that these benefits would not be possible without a partnership.

- **Asset/Cost Efficiency.** A potential for cost reduction provides a strong reason to partner. Closer integration of activities might lead to reductions in transportation costs, handling costs, packaging costs, information costs, or product costs and may increase managerial efficiencies. A partnership may enhance the development and use of specialized equipment and processes between the parties, without fear of technology transfer to a competitor.[15] McDonald's found that by establishing partnerships with regional distributors who serve as the single distributor for all products to all stores within a region, delivery and ordering costs were reduced.

- **Customer Service.** Integrating activities in the supply chain through partnerships can often lead to service improvement for customers in the form of reduced inventory, improved availability, and more timely and accurate information.[16] After discovering that they were significantly slower in deliveries to dealers and had more damage than competitors, Whirlpool developed a partnership with ERX, a logistics service provider. According to a Whirlpool executive, "Our original goal was to be 95% on-time, within the first year. By the fourth month we were at 99%".

---

[15] Williamson, Oliver E., *Markets and Hierarchies: Analysis and Antitrust Implications*, New York: The Free Press, 1975.

[16] Weitz, Barton and Sandy Jap, "Relationship Marketing and Distribution Channels", *Journal of the Academy of Marketing Science*, Vol. 23, No. 4 (1995), pp. 305-320.

- **Marketing Advantage.** A third reason for entering into a partnership is to gain a marketing advantage. A stronger integration between two organizations can: (1) enhance an organization's marketing mix; (2) ease entry into new markets; and, (3) provide better access to technology and innovation.[17] Through its partnership with Ryder for delivery and installation of copiers, Xerox was able to reduce its costs and thus become more price competitive. Target chose to partner with 3M in order to gain access to special packaging, and creative promotional and product strategies.
- **Profit Stability/Growth.** The potential for stabilizing profit is a strong driver for most partnerships. Strengthening of a relationship often leads to long-term volume commitments, reduced variability in sales, joint use of assets, and other improvements which reduce variability of profits.[18]

While the presence of strong drivers is necessary for successful partnerships, the drivers by themselves do not ensure success. The benefits derived from the drivers must be sustainable over the long term. If, for instance, the marketing advantage or cost efficiencies resulting from the relationship can be easily matched by a competitor, the probability of long-term partnership success is reduced.

Assessing Drivers. In evaluating a relationship, how does a manager know if there are enough drivers to pursue a partnership? First, drivers must exist for each party. It is unlikely that the drivers will be the same for both parties, but they need to be strong for both. For instance, in the Whirlpool/ERX partnership, improved service was a driver for Whirlpool, while stable, guaranteed volume was a driver for ERX. Second, the drivers must be strong enough to provide each party with a realistic expectation of significant benefits through a strengthening of the relationship.

...drivers must exist for each party. It is unlikely that the drivers will be the same for both parties, but they need to be strong for both.

Each party should independently assess the strength of their specific drivers by using the assessment guide shown in Table 14-3. The guide lists the four drivers and provides examples of each. These examples are not meant to be all inclusive, but rather should be used only as a starting point. Both parties to the potential relationship must develop and agree upon the specific descriptors of each driver that are appropriate for the relationship. Further, parameters for measuring each descriptor must be developed. For instance, under the driver Asset/Cost Efficiency, the parties must decide whether a product cost reduction target should be established. It is important that the descriptors of each driver be specified and agreed upon because the success of the partnership will be measured based upon whether the desired improvements are actually achieved.

The guide provides a rating scheme with a maximum score of 24. A very low score (below 8) indicates that the potential pay-off from a partnership is so low that it should not be pursued. Therefore, it is not necessary to proceed with the model and evaluate the facilitators. A score of 8 or above indicates that facilitators should be examined. A high score (16 or above) indicates a potential for significant benefits and suggests that a partnership should be pursued.

---

[17] Oliver, Christine, "Determinants of Inter-organizational Relationships: Integration and Future Directions", *Academy of Management Review*, Vol. 15, No. 2 (1990), pp. 241-265.

[18] Noordeweir, Thomas G., George John and John R. Nevin, "Performance Outcomes of Purchasing Arrangements in Industrial Buyer-Vendor Relationships", *Journal of Marketing*, Vol. 54, No. 4 (1990), pp. 80-93.

Table 14-3
Assessment of Drivers

Drivers are strategic factors which result in a competitive advantage and which help to determine the appropriate level of a business relationship. For each driver, circle the boxed number which reflects the probability of your organization **realistically** achieving a benefit **through forming a tighter relationship**.

	No Chance 0%	25%	50%	75%	Certain 100%
ASSET/COST EFFICIENCY	Probability				
1. What is the probability that this relationship will substantially reduce channel costs or improve asset utilization?	1	2	3	4	5

-product costs savings
-distribution costs savings, handling costs savings
-packing costs savings, information handling costs savings
-managerial efficiencies
-assets to the relationship

If you rated efficiencies in the shaded area and if the advantage is either a sustainable competitive advantage or it allows your firm to match benchmark standards in your industry, circle the I to the right. [1]

	No Chance 0%	25%	50%	75%	Certain 100%
CUSTOMER SERVICE	Probability				
2. What is the probability that this relationship will substantially improve the customer service level as measured by the customer?	1	2	3	4	5

-improved on-time delivery
-better tracking of movement
-paperless order processing
-accurate order deliveries
-improved cycle times
-improved fill rates
-customer survey results
-process improvements

If you rated customer service in the shaded area and if the advantage is either a sustainable competitive advantage or if it allows your firm to match benchmark standards in your industry, circle the I to the right. [1]

	No Chance 0%	25%	50%	75%	Certain 100%
MARKETING ADVANTAGE	Probability				
3. What is the probability that this relationship will lead to substantial marketing advantages?	1	2	3	4	5

-new market entry
-promotion joint advertising, sales promotion)
-price (reduced price advantage)
-product jointly developed product Innovation, branding opportunities)
-place (expanded geographic coverage, market saturation)
-access to technology
-innovation potential

It you rated marketing advantage in the shaded area and it the advantage is either a sustainable competitive advantage or if it allows your firm to match benchmark standards in your industry, circle the I to the right. [1]

	No Chance 0%	25%	50%	75%	Certain 100%
PROFIT STABILITY/GROWTH	Probability				
4. What is the probability that this relationship will result in profit growth or reduced variability in profit?	1	2	3	4	5

-growth
-cyclical leveling
-seasonal leveling
-market share stability
-sales volume
-assurance of supply

It you rated profit stability/growth in the shaded area and if the advantage is either a sustainable competitive advantage or if it allows your firm to match benchmark standards in your industry, circle the 1 to the right. [1]

Add all the boxed numbers which you have circled and place the total in the box to the right. This represents the strength of your motivation to partner. [ ]

Source: Douglas M. Lambert, Margaret A. Emmelhainz and John T. Gardner, "Developing and Implementing Supply Chain Partnerships," *The International Journal of Logistics Management,* Vol. 7, No. 2 (1996), p. 6.

*Representatives of
the two firms should
evaluate drivers
separately and the
evaluation must be
from a selfish
perspective.*

Conducting a Drivers Session. Representatives of the two firms should evaluate drivers separately and the evaluation must be from a selfish perspective. There are several other issues that must be addressed during the session. Since profits are a function of costs, service and marketing, there is a possibility for double counting. If a supplier hopes to market better as a result of increased partnership, they will also expect higher profit. A key for success is to warn the participants not to double count. They should use the first three drivers whenever they are appropriate. Only those potential drivers of profit that do not overlap with the others or do not focus on any one of the others should be included in profit stability and growth. If a customer service improvement by the seller yields lower inventories for the buyer, this is asset/cost efficiency for the buyer. If it yields better customer service to the buyer's customers, then it should be counted as a customer service improvement for the buyer. If a joint effort can level volumes, then it should be recorded in profit stability and growth.

Another difficulty with identifying and scoring drivers comes from the need to consider only the incremental gains possible through partnership. Thus, if a cost savings could be gained through hard bargaining or competitive bidding, it should not be scored high as a driver. If a savings due to deploying new technology could only be contemplated in the context of a close, long-term cooperative relationship, then it should be counted. Making this distinction is often difficult.

It can be challenging to get suppliers to think in terms of their own self-interest particularly if the buyer initiated the partnership meeting. Since they respond to the customer in a customer-oriented way in most discussions, taking a selfish perspective is sometimes difficult.

Evaluation of the customer service driver often poses a problem for sellers. They want to score as a driver, customer service improvements to the potential partner. While these are advantages to the potential partner, they are not compelling reasons for the seller to want a closer relationship. In order for the evaluation to be selfish on the part of the seller, only customer service improvements that can be offered to other customers as a result of more closeness in this relationship should be counted. If a firm, through partnership, can develop a customer service delivery approach that can later be rolled out for non-partner accounts, then the seller can score customer service as a compelling reason to partner.

When evaluating a driver each side should define specific bullets that apply to their business situation. It is important to put measurable goals on each specific bullet identified by the participants. An example for cost efficiency could be to reduce controllable costs in the component parts by five percent per year. A marketing advantage that would be harder to quantify in dollars would be to come up with at least five new product ideas over a two-year period, one of which would reach commercialization. After the group comes up with drivers specific to their situation, the meeting facilitator should challenge them to come up with measurable goals.

For each partnership driver, the managers of the buying firm and the managers of the selling firm must independently decide on a probability. For the first driver, the question is "What is the probability that this relationship will substantially reduce channel costs or improve asset utilization?" The scoring is on a five-point basis from 1 to 5 ranging from zero percent chance to 100 percent chance. Thus, the managers from each firm will determine four driver scores based on the probability of making substantial gains for their firm. There is no expectation that the drivers will be in the same categories for each firm, nor will the total scores be the same. Each side must assess their own self-interest independently and honestly, which is why the business cannot be at risk.

Drivers are assessed on "the probability that this relationship will substantially..." with the key word being substantially. If the driver bullets within one of the four drivers are collectively weak on substantiality, then a probability of getting a substantial advantage should be low before factoring uncertainty into the judgment. When one buyer organization assessed the potential for cost avoidance through partnership, they found a large number of potential savings. However, the total savings would only amount to a small part of one percent of the overall costs for the firm. Therefore, the rating had to be a low score even though managers thought achieving the savings was relatively certain.

It is important to have a blank driver form for the recording of driver elements specific to the relationship rather than use the generalized bullet points in the original model. The group should develop an exhaustive list of descriptors for each specific driver and then reduce it to a parsimonious list that can be summarized in a few bullet points. Each category should be evaluated and scored. Evaluating and weighting each bullet point, then coming up with a probability for each may add a false sense of accuracy, slow the process, and/or defy consensus. The participants should seek consensus for the final number for each of the four drivers. It is not reasonable to average the numbers, since one person's reason to choose a low or high probability may not have been considered by the others. Talking about differences and coming to consensus is useful and facilitates implementation later. Issues come out in the defense of specific ratings that otherwise would not emerge. There must be buy-in from the participants if the drivers are to be achieved.

Drivers for the supplier and the buyer will rarely match up in strength by category. It is important to emphasize this to the seller, as they often feel that their score on a particular driver should match their counterpart's score. In fact, often sellers have low customer service scores while buyers often have high customer service scores. It is not important that the scores match, just that both sides have compelling reasons to commit more resources to the relationship than is typical of an arm's-length relationship.

Once each side has scored their drivers, the next step is to come together and present these drivers. It is important to explain why the drivers were selected and how they were scored. This represents an expectations-setting session that is critical for partnership success. One of the reasons that partnerships fail is unrealistic expectations on the part of one or both of the parties.[19] What each bullet point means and the thinking behind the score needs to be understood by both sides of the relationship. If the representatives of the other firm indicate that they cannot or will not help achieve a particular driver, the driver should be reevaluated. If no one in the session objects to the other side's drivers, then management is obligated to help the other firm achieve its drivers.

There is a direct connection between drivers and outcomes. If the drivers are quantified during in the driver assessment, the evaluation of the partnership over

[19] Foster, Thomas A., "Lessons Learned," *Logistics*, No. 4 (1999), pp. 67-70.

There is no expectation that the drivers will be in the same categories for each firm, nor will the total scores be the same. Each side must assess their own self-interest independently and honestly, which is why the business cannot be at risk.

time is made much easier. An example for asset/cost efficiency is the goal of reducing product costs by 7% per year over the next three years. By knowing the exact expectation, there is more realistic buy-in and better tracking of progress when outcomes are measured.

Facilitators Session. Drivers provide the motivation to partner. But even with a strong desire for building a partnership, the probability of success is reduced if both corporate environments are not supportive of the relationship. A supportive environment which enhances integration of the two parties will improve the success of the partnership.

Facilitators are elements of a corporate environment which allow a partnership to grow and strengthen. They serve as a foundation for a good relationship. Facilitators either exist or they do not. And the degree to which they exist often determines whether a partnership succeeds or fails. Facilitators include: corporate compatibility, managerial philosophy and techniques, mutuality, and symmetry.

- **Corporate Compatibility.** For a relationship to succeed, partners must share values. The cultures and business objectives of the two firms must mesh. They do not have to be the same, but they cannot clash. For instance, the value placed on strategic planning and the approaches used for planning should be similar. The more similar the culture and objectives, the more comfortable the partners are likely to feel, and the higher the chance of partnership success.[20]
- **Managerial Philosophy and Techniques.** Another important facilitator is the compatibility of management philosophy and techniques. Such things as organizational structure, attitude toward employee empowerment, the relative importance of teamwork and the level of commitment to continuous improvement are examples of management philosophies.[21] The strong similarities in basic values as well as operating styles between McDonald's and Coca-Cola provides a strong foundation for a highly integrated Type III partnership.
- **Mutuality.** The ability of a management team to put themselves in their partner's shoes is critical in partnering. This ability is usually expressed as a willingness to develop joint goals, share sensitive information, and take a long-term perspective.[22] According to one manager, "…in a partnership you are taking on your partner's goals and aspirations… You have to be willing to give up your own identity. You loose your identity, but you grow with your partner." Another executive expressed mutuality this way. "A partnership has to benefit both parties. It cannot be a one way relationship because if you are going to weaken the other side, eventually you are going to weaken the whole operation."

[20] Deshpande, Rohit, and Fedrick E. Webster, "Organizational Culture and Marketing: Defining a Research Agenda", *Journal of Marketing*, Vol. 53, No. 1 (1989), pp. 3 -15.

[21] Mohr, Jakki and Robert Spekman, "Characteristic of Partnership Success: Partnership Attributes, Communication Behavior, and Conflict Resolution Techniques", *Strategic Management Journal*, Vol. 15, No. 2 (1994), pp. 135 – 152.

[22] Cooper, Martha C., and John T. Gardner, "Good Business Relationships: More than Just Partnerships or Strategic Alliances", *International Journal of Physical Distribution and Logistics Management*, Vol. 23, No. 6 (1993), pp. 14-36.

Drivers provide the motivation to partner. But even with a strong desire for building a partnership, the probability of success is reduced if both corporate environments are not supportive of the relationship.

"A partnership has to benefit both parties. It cannot be a one way relationship because if you are going to weaken the other side, eventually you are going to weaken the whole operation".

- **Symmetry.** The probability for success is increased when the partners are "demographically" similar. Symmetry in terms of the importance of each firm to the other's success, relative size, market share, financial strength, productivity, brand image, company reputation, and level of technological sophistication leads to stronger relationship. When firms are relatively symmetrical, there is no junior partner and none of the insecurity, defensiveness and fear which is often found in an unequal relationship.[23] In partnership between McDonald's and Coca-Cola, both have strong brand images and each is the number one firm in its industry. Further, McDonald's is Coca-Cola's largest customer and Coca-Cola is McDonald's largest supplier, adding more symmetry to the relationship.

Additional Facilitators. The four primary facilitators are universal in that they should exist in any relationship. Their presence strengthens the probability of success and their absence increases the chance of failure. In addition, situation-specific facilitators may be present. While the presence of these facilitators is likely to increase the probability of success, their absence does not mean failure. The additional facilitators include exclusivity, shared competitors, physical proximity, a prior history of working with the partner, and a shared high value end user.

- **Exclusivity.** When managers of both firms are willing to entertain the possibility of exclusivity, then the opportunities for and the likely advantages of the partnership are broadened. In the case of a branded product where exclusivity is not possible, exclusivity can be addressed by establishing a separate division that deals solely with the large partner, for example Coca-Cola's McDonald's USA division, or by providing unique packaging.
- **Shared Competitors.** In the relatively rare case when both parties face a common competitor, the partnership is likely to have a stronger foundation. When PepsiCo owned Taco Bell, Pizza Hut and KFC, it was the primary competitor for McDonald's and Coca-Cola.
- **Close Proximity.** If key players from both firms are located near each other, this can enhance the relationship. The relationship between Target and 3M reflects the influence of proximity. According to a 3M representative, "[the relationship] developed over time since both companies are based in the Twin cities."
- **Prior History.** Firms with a prior history of positive interaction will have an advantage when building partnerships. Having worked closely and successfully in the past strengthens the chance of successful future interactions.[24]
- **Shared End User.** When both partners are serving the same end user, and that end user is of high value, the partnership is likely to be strengthened. For example, both McDonald's and Coke place emphasis on the young consumer market and this strengthens their relationship.

---

[23] Langley, John C. and Mary C. Holcomb, "Creating Logistics Customer Value", *Journal of Business Logistics*, Vol. 13, No. 2 (1992), pp. 1-27.

[24] Graham, T. Scott, Patricia J. Daugherty and William N. Dudley, "The Long-term Strategic Impact of Purchasing Partnerships", *International Journal of Purchasing and Material Management*, Vol. 30, No. 4 (1994), pp. 13-18.

Facilitators apply to the combined environment of the two potential partners. Unlike drivers which are assessed by managers in each firm independently, facilitators should be assessed jointly.

Assessing Facilitators. Facilitators apply to the combined environment of the two potential partners. Unlike drivers which are assessed by managers in each firm independently, facilitators are assessed jointly. The discussion of corporate values, philosophies, and objectives often leads to an improved relationship even if no further steps toward building a partnership are taken. The strength of facilitators can be assessed using a 25 point rating guide shown in Table 14-4. The higher the facilitators, the better the chance of partnership success. A very low score (below 8) would suggest that even with strong drivers, a partnership is likely to fail.

Conducting a Facilitators Session. The facilitators should not be examined at the outset of a relationship. After a period of working together, the two firms will have a much easier time assessing each facilitator. In a new relationship, a logistics service provider and a large telecommunications manufacturer went through the process when the relationship was just beginning. The managers felt it was not possible to complete the facilitators because they lacked experience working together and decided to wait six months. The experience gained over these months sharpened the managers' views about how well the two firms would naturally mesh.

It is critical that the person leading the session emphasize the disfunctionality of painting an overly positive picture of the environment. The result will be to move the firms into more partnership than the situation demands and consume more managerial resources than necessary. The participants should be challenged to give examples of each claim to reduce the likelihood that they will overscore a facilitator. If both sides claim employee empowerment, then a concrete example of empowered decision-making is in order. In one case, both sides were indicating a strong quality focus, but one was a six sigma supporter and the other was focused on relationships not process. Both firms were very successful with their approach, but the differences could make joint work more difficult.

Bonus points are given for environmental factors that cannot be reasonably expected in every relationship but when they are present strengthen the relationship. Managers regularly want to claim close proximity based on something other than the two headquarters being in the same metropolitan area. A field office for one firm located close to the headquarters of the other or an on-site account manager is not close proximity as defined by the model. It is hard to have informal and social contacts between top management and others in both organizations if they are not closely co-located. When claims of prior experience with partnership are made, they should be based on the style of relationship described previously. It is important to gain consensus on the facilitator scores.

The appropriateness of any one type of partnership is a function of the combined strength of the drivers and facilitators.

Targeting Session. If both parties expect benefits from a partnership and if the corporate environments are supportive, a partnership is warranted. But, not all partnerships are the same. Three types of partnership exist, each with different degrees of integration. The appropriateness of any one type of partnership is a function of the combined strength of the drivers and facilitators. Strong drivers and strong facilitators suggest a Type III partnership while low drivers and low facilitators suggest an arm's length relationship, as shown in Figure 14-3.

While it might seem that managers should make all corporate relationships into Type III partnerships, this is not the case. In partnering, more is not always better. The objective should not be to have a Type III partnership, rather it should be to have the most appropriate type of partnership given the specific drivers and facilitators. In fact,

Table 14-4
Assessment of Facilitators

Facilitators are factors which provide a supportive environment for the growth and maintenance of a partnership. For each facilitator, indicate the probability of it being a factor in this relationship, by circling one of the boxed numbers.

	Probability				
CORPORATE COMPATIBILITY	**No Chance** 0%	25%	50%	75%	**Certain** 100%
1. *What is the probability that the two organizations will mesh smoothly in terms of.,*	1	2	3	4	5

   (a) CULTURE?
      -Both firms place a value on keeping commitments
      -Constancy of purpose
      -Employees viewed as long term assets
      -External stakeholders considered important

   (b) BUSINESS?
      -Strategic plans and objectives consistent
      -Commitment to partnership ideas
      -Willingness to change

	Probability				
MANAGEMENT PHILOSOPHY AND TECHNIQUES	**No Chance** 0%	25%	50%	75%	**Certain** 100%
2. *What is the probability that the management philosophy and techniques of the two companies will match smoothly?*	1	2	3	4	5

      -Organizational structure
      -Commitment to continuous improvement
      -Degree of top management support
      -Types of motivation used
      -Importance of teamwork
      -Attitudes toward "personnel churning"
      -Degree of employee empowerment

	Probability				
MUTUALITY	**No Chance** 0%	25%	50%	75%	**Certain** 100%
3. *What is the probability both parties have the skills and predisposition needed for mutual relationship building?*	1	2	3	4	5

   Management skilled at:
      -two-sided thinking and action
      -taking the perspective of the other company
      -expressing goals and sharing expectations
      -taking a longer term view
      -mutual respect

   Management willing to:
      -share financial information
      -integrate systems

	Probability				
SYMMETRY	**No Chance** 0%	25%	50%	75%	**Certain** 100%
4. *What is the probability that the parties are similar on the following important factors that will affect the success of the relationship:*	1	2	3	4	5

      -Relative size in terms of sales
      -Relative market share in their respective industries
      -Financial strength
      -Productivity
      -Brand imagetreputation
      -Technological sophistication

ADDITIONAL FACTORS (BONUS POINTS)

	Yes	No
5. *Do you have shared competitors which will tend to unite your efforts?*	1	0
6. *Are the key players in the two parties in close physical proximity to each other?*	1	0
7. *Is there a willingness to deal exclusively with your partner?*	1	0
8. *Do both parties have prior experience with successful partnerships?*	1	0
9. *Do both parties share a high value end user?*	1	0

Add all the boxed numbers which you have circled on this page aid place the total in the box to the right. This represents the strength/ability to sustain and grow the partnership.

Source: Douglas M. Lambert, Margaret A. Emmelhainz and John T. Gardner, "Developing and Implementing Supply Chain Partnerships," *The International Journal of Logistics Management*, Vol. 7, No. 2 (1996), p. 9.

Figure 14-3
Propensity to Partner Matrix

		DRIVER POINTS		
		8-11 Points	12-15 Points	16-24 Points
FACILITATOR POINTS	8-11 Points	Arm's Length	Type I	Type II
	12-15 Points	Type I	Type II	Type III
	16-25 Points	Type II	Type III	Type III

Source: Douglas M. Lambert, Margaret A. Emmelhainz and John T. Gardner, "Developing and Implementing Supply Chain Partnerships," *The International Journal of Logistics Management*, Vol. 7, No. 2 (1996), p. 10.

in situations with low drivers and/or facilitators, trying to achieve a Type III partnership is likely to be counterproductive. Having determined that a partnership is warranted, the next step is to actually put the partnership into place. This is done through the management components of partnership (see Figure 14-2).

Conducting a Targeting Session. The model uses a three-by-three matrix to prescribe partnership type and is subject to the difficulties present with any grid approach. The meeting facilitator needs to be sensitive to the fact that a single point change on either drivers or facilitators can move a relationship from a Type II partnership to a Type III or to a Type I. The prescriptions near the intersections of the matrix need to be evaluated with care. The goal is to tailor the relationship to fit the drivers and the environment not to match the grid.

Since the drivers are assessed independently, it is possible for the firms to have driver scores that fall into two different categories (low, medium, or high). When one firm has a driver score in a higher category than the other, the low driver score is used. Like any relationship, the party that wants it the least determines the outcome and it is important that both parties realize this. The relationship is only as strong as the weakest commitment. There is only one facilitator score since facilitators are evaluated jointly.

Another issue is how to handle a mismatch in driver scores. Initially, there was concern about the potential for disparity in driver scores. After experiencing two cases of large disparity in scores, it appears that this situation need not damage an otherwise good business relationship. It is important for the meeting facilitator to note the disparity as it emerges and encourage the representatives of the lower-scoring organization to emphasize how their drivers were scored. The reason for using the lowest driver score is because the firm with the least amount to gain will determine the level of focus on the relationship.

By the end of the targeting session, both parties should have a clearer understanding of the joint expectations of their relationship.

By the end of the targeting session, both parties should have a clearer understanding of the joint expectations of their relationship. This is critical for partnership success and if a partnership is not indicated. In the latter case, both parties benefit from understanding why an arm's length relationship is the best fit.

In summary, the assessment of the drivers and facilitators is used to determine the potential for a partnership. That is, should a partnership be implemented and if so what type of partnership is appropriate? However, it is the components and how they are implemented which determine the type of relationship that is actually in place.

Components Session. Components are the activities and processes that management establishes and controls throughout the life of the partnership. Every partnership has the same basic components, but the way in which the components are implemented and managed varies. Components include: planning, joint operating controls, communications, risk/reward sharing, trust and commitment, contract style, scope, and financial investment.[25]

- **Planning.** Joint planning, a key component of effective partnerships, can range from the sharing of existing plans to the joint development of strategic objectives. Effective joint planning adds both flexibility and strength to a relationship. In the McDonald's and Coca-Cola relationship, joint planning is done at multiple levels, on both a periodic and continual basis.[26]

- **Joint Operating Controls.** In a partnership, either party should be able to change the operations of the other for the good of the partnership. The ability to make changes can range from being encouraged to suggest changes to being empowered to operationalize a change without needing prior approval or notification from the partner. Within the Whirlpool Quality Express partnership, ERX could change the delivery schedule to a customer, without first obtaining approval, or even notifying Whirlpool.[27]

- **Communications.** Effective communication, on both a day-to-day and a non-routine basis, is a key component of successful partnerships. Integrated E-mail systems, regularly scheduled meetings and phone calls, and the willingness to share both good and bad news, as well as communication systems such EDI, all contribute to the success of a partnership. The more breadth and depth that exists in communication patterns, the stronger the partnership. Communication links should be across all levels of the organizations.[28]

- **Risk/Reward Sharing.** At the core of a partnership is the concept of "shared destiny". Mechanisms need to be in place to ensure that the benefits and rewards as well as the costs and risks are shared. A strong commitment to shared risk is evident when either party is willing to take a short-term "hit" in order to help out the partner and to strengthen the relationship. In one of our cases, a firm delayed a planned price increase because its partner was not meeting its financial goals due to competitive pressures. In another case, productivity gains above a stated level are shared 50/50.[29]

---

[25] Macneil, Ian R., *The New Social Contract, an Inquiry into Modern Contractual Relations*, New Heaven, CT: Yale University Press, 1980; and, Robert Dwyer, Paul H. Schurr and Sejo Oh, "Developing Buyer-Seller Relationships", *Journal of Marketing*, Vol. 51, No. 2 (1987), pp. 11-27.

[26] La Londe, Bernard J. and Martha C. Cooper, *Partnerships in Providing Customer Service: A Third Party Perspective*, Oak Brook, IL: Council of Logistics Management, 1989.

[27] Gardner, John T., Martha C. Cooper and Thomas G. Noodewier, "Understanding Shipper-Carrier and Shipper-Warehouser Relationships: Partnerships Revised", *Journal of Business Logistics*, Vol. 15, No. 2 (1994), pp. 121-143.

[28] Ellram, Lisa M., "A Managerial Guideline for the Development and Implementation of Purchasing Partnerships", *Journal of Purchasing and Materials Management*, Vol. 27, No. 3 (1991), pp. 2-8.

[29] Cooper, Martha C. and Lisa M. Ellram, "Characteristics of Supply Chian Management and the Implications for Purchasing and Logistics Strategy", *The International Journal of Logistics Management*, Vol. 4, No. 2 (1993), pp. 13-24.

- **Trust and Commitment.** No partnership can exist without trust and commitment. Loyalty to each other and a long-term focus are elements of trust and commitment. True partners do not need to worry about being replaced. While most executives involved in partnerships found it difficult to precisely define trust, they all intuitively knew when it existed.
- **Contract Style.** The type of contract which governs a partnership speaks volumes about the relationship. The strongest partnerships generally have the shortest and least specific agreements or no written agreement at all. A one to two-page document, outlining the basic philosophy and vision for the partnership, is all that is needed when the parties are truly integrated. The partnership contract for the Quality Express program was only about three pages long, and most managers operating under the contract had not seen it and were not aware that it existed. The "contract" between McDonald's and Coca-Cola was not in writing. It was an agreement based on trust and sealed with a handshake.[30]
- **Scope.** A partnership is made stronger by including more of the economic activities of each firm within the relationship. The number and complexity of the value-added steps covered and the amount of business involved are key elements of a partnership. In the partnership between Xerox and Ryder, Ryder performed light assembly and testing of equipment and Ryder truck drivers delivered the new machines, set them up, demonstrated them for customers, and removed the old equipment.[31]
- **Financial Investment.** A partnership can be strengthened by the sharing of financial resources. Shared assets, joint investment in technology, exchange of key personnel, and joint research and development reflect a high degree of financial interdependence which leads to a stronger partnership.[32]

Each of the eight components will be evident in every partnership. However, the amount of each component, ranging from low to high, and the way in which the component is managed will vary depending upon the type of the partnership. While every partnership will have some degree of joint planning, that planning can range from infrequent, ad-hoc sharing of individual plans (low) to systematic, multi-level, joint strategic planning (high). Table 14-5 shows the components can be implemented at different levels.

After determining appropriate type of partnership and the associated level of component implementation, the parties must agree on how each component is going to be put into place and managed.

Assessing the Components. After determining the appropriate type of partnership and the associated level of component implementation, the parties must agree on how each component is going to be put into place and managed. For instance, if it is determined that a Type III partnership is appropriate, this means that the majority, but not necessarily all, of the components should be implemented at a high level. Some decisions must be made on which of the components will be implemented at a high level, and which may be more appropriately implemented at a medium level, as well as a timetable for implementation and the resources needed.

---

[30] Gundlatch, Gregory T. and Patrick C. Murphy, "Ethical and Legal Foundations of Relational Marketing Exchanges", *Journal of Marketing*, Vol. 57, No. 4 (1993), pp. 36-46.

[31] Harrigan, Kathryn Rudie, "Matching Vertical Integration Strategies to Competitive Conditions", *Strategic Management Journal*, Vol. 7. No. 4 (1996), pp. 535-555.

[32] Heide, Jan B. and George John, "The Role of Dependence Balancing in Safeguarding Transaction-Specific Assets in Conventional Channels", *Journal of Marketing*, Vol. 52, No. 1 (1988), pp. 20-35.

Table 14-5
Partnership Component Levels

Partnership Component		Low	Medium	High
PLANNING	• Style	• On ad-hoc basis	• Regularly scheduled	• Systematic: Both scheduled and ad hoc
	• Level	• Focus on projects or tasks	• Focus is on process	• Focus is on relationship
	• Content	• Sharing of existing plans	• Performed jointly, eliminating conflicts in strategies	• Performed jointly and at multiple levels, including top management; objective is to mesh strategies; each party participates in other's business planning
JOINT OPERATING CONTROLS	• Measurement	• Performance measures are developed independently and results are shared	• Measures are jointly developed and shared; focused on individual firm's performance	• Measures are jointly developed and shared; focused on relationship and joint performance
	• Ability to make changes	• Parties may suggest changes to other's system	• Parties may make changes to other's system after getting approval	• Parties may make changes to other's system without getting approval
COMMUNICATIONS	NON-ROUTINE	• Very limited, usually just critical issues at the task or project level	• Conducted more regularly, done at multiple levels; generally open and honest	• Planned as part of the relationship; occurs at all levels; sharing of both praise and criticism; parties "speak the same language"
	DAY-TO-DAY			
	• Organization	• Conducted on ad-hoc basis, between individuals	• Limited number of scheduled communications; some routinization	• Systematized method of communication; may be manual or electronic; communication systems are linked
	• Balance	• Primarily one-way	• Two-way but unbalanced	• Balanced two-way communications flow
	• Electronic	• Use of individual system	• Joint modification of individual systems	• Joint development of customized electronic communications
RISK/REWARD SHARING	• Loss tolerance	• Very low tolerance for loss	• Some tolerance for short-term loss	• High tolerance for short-term loss
	• Gain commitment	• Limited willingness to help the other gain	• Willingness to help the other gain	• Desire to help other party gain
	• Commitment to fairness	• Fairness is evaluated by transaction	• Fairness is tracked year to year	• Fairness is measured over life of relationship
TRUST AND COMMITMENT	• Trust	• Trust is limited to belief that each partner will perform honestly and ethically	• Partner is given more trust than others, viewed as "most favored" supplier	• There is implicit, total trust; trust does not have to be earned
	• Commitment to each other's success	• Commitment of each party is to specific transaction or project; trust must be constantly "re-earned"	• Commitment is to a longer-term relationship	• Commitment is to partner's long-term success; commitment prevails across functions and levels in both organizations
CONTRACT STYLE	• Timeframe	• Covers a short time frame	• Covers a longer time frame	• Contracts are very general in nature and are evergreen, or alternatively the entire relationship is on a handshake basis
	• Coverage	• Contracts are specific in nature	• Contracts are more general in nature	• Contract does not specify duties or responsibilities; rather, it only outlines the basic philosophy guiding the relationship
SCOPE	• Share	• Activity of partnership represents a very small share of business for each partner	• Activity represents a modest share of business for at least one partner	• Activity covered by relationship represents significant business to both parties
	• Value-added	• Relationship covers only one or a few value-added steps (functions)	• Multiple functions, units are involved in the relationship	• Multiple functions and units are involved; partnership extends to all levels in both organizations
	• Critical activities	• Only activities which are relatively unimportant for partner's success	• Activities that are important for each partner's success are included	• Activities that are critical for each partner's success are included
INVESTMENT	• Financial	• There is low or no investment between the two parties	• May jointly own low value assets	• High value assets may be jointly owned
	• Technology	• No joint development of products/technology	• There is some joint design effort and there may be some joint R&D planning	• There is significant joint development; regular and significant joint R&D activity
	• People	• Limited personnel exchange	• Extensive exchange of personnel	• Participation on other party's board

Source: Douglas M. Lambert, Margaret A. Emmelhainz and John T. Gardner, "Developing and Implementing Supply Chain Partnerships," *The International Journal of Logistics Management*, Vol. 7, No. 2 (1996), p. 12.

At Texas Instruments, this model was used with a major supplier. After deciding that a Type II partnership was appropriate, the parties agreed on how communications were to take place, what type of joint planning was to be done, the operations which would be jointly managed and other aspects of the components. Each partner then determined what resources were necessary in terms of dollars, time and personnel; and commitments were obtained from top management for those resources. As a result, both parties understood and accepted the expectations and requirements of the partnership.

Conducting a Components Session. The component session is critical since it involves developing the action plan. The first three components, planning, joint operating controls, and communications, are the keys to a successful relationship. To help the process along each participant should have the table of partnership components available and record the current and desired level of implementation, action items, timelines and responsible parties.

The first step is to assess the current relationship component by component. In fact, the level of the analysis should be bullet by bullet within the components, as each component can be implemented at different levels. Thus, a relationship can entail joint planning on a regularly scheduled basis but focus on tasks. A typical review of the current state of the components found many of them with bullet points in different columns. The current implementation of the components reveals the amount of partnership that has been implemented in the relationship. This review provides initial guidance on the components that need more or less focus depending on the desired level of partnership.

The eight components should be reviewed again to determine the level of implementation based on the targeted partnership type. The participants determine action items such as forming a task force to set up communications links that support the attainment of the targeted partnership. In one relationship, management chose to form a steering committee charged with developing a vision for the relationship. This committee was responsible for ensuring that progress was made towards reaching the desired levels of implementation.

If specific actions are properly identified, then responsibility can be placed on individuals and due dates established.

If specific actions are properly identified, then responsibility can be placed on individuals and due dates established. It is not enough to say that metrics for a particular hard-to-measure driver should be jointly developed. The parties need to determine who should be involved, who leads, when the work will be completed, and to whom they will report. If this level of detail is achieved in the components session, the outcomes assessment will be easier and the probability of the relationship staying on track is higher. The action items from the components session need to become part of the ongoing operations planning process, such as a quarterly business review.

The final step in the components session is to review the drivers to ensure that each has been addressed. Drivers from each side should be available to all participants. If a driver for the seller (as is often the case) is to gain access to other business units within the parent company, then the trust and commitment components need to have specific action items. An example item would be to communicate the level of commitment and trust in the relationship within their respective company newsletters. This was an action item in one relationship which was added after a review of the drivers indicated that the marketing driver of the seller was not fully covered in the components.

For each partnership component, we recommend the following:

- **Planning.** Participants often have difficulty with the distinction between process and relationship as the focus of planning. An example of a process focus is the development of a method for making changes to the partner's delivery parameters. A relationship focus institutionalizes the partnership by putting the maintenance of the relationship within senior managers' job descriptions for each firm.
- **Joint Operating Controls.** Participants should be clear that this component refers to the operations at the interface between the firms. It is unlikely that management would allow a key value-adding step to be modified by a partner independently. It is important to give realistic examples. The distinction between suggesting changes and making changes after approval is subtle.
- **Communications.** The electronic component remains an important consideration, however it is becoming less of a question about whether electronic communication is used. The new differentiator is the types of electronic communication taking place between the organizations and the degree of tailoring of these tools to the specific relationship.
- **Risk and Reward Sharing.** When addressing this item the managers should be challenged to provide examples of what sharing will take place and how it will take place. Will there be a gain-sharing program developed? How would management in each firm react to some fairly realistic hypothetical scenarios regarding the sharing of the potential costs and benefits of jointly developed initiatives?
- **Trust and Commitment.** Trust is managerially built as a spiral of commitment, performance, and communications throughout the organizations. These three are repeated as the spiral raises the level of trust. Each of these three is under managerial control and should be considered.
- **Contract Style.** If no supplier or no customer operates on a contract, then the absence of a contract should not be interpreted as a Type III partnership. Conversely, if the legal department requires a detailed contract, but the parties do not use it to manage the relationship, then the existence of the contract is not the issue either. The key is how the contract is used to manage the business relationship.
- **Scope.** Including more value-added steps in the relationship typically makes the bonds tighter. The key issue to be considered is what would happen if this partner disappeared. How would the loss of the partner affect the business unit or the corporation?
- **Investment.** As mentioned above, financial commitment only makes sense if there is a need to make an investment in order to achieve relationship drivers.

Components need to be examined three times, each with a different goal: 1) to determine the current state; 2) to determine desired state; and, 3) to make sure nothing was omitted. The determination of the current state is best achieved through a group discussion of Table 14-5 as it relates to the relationship. Table 14-5 also provides a good overview of the amount of effort it will take to get to the desired state. After developing action plans, a quick review of the components is beneficial.

Components need to be examined three times, each with a different goal: 1) to determine the current state; 2) to determine desired state; and, 3) to make sure nothing was omitted.

Wrap-up Session. A key aspect of the wrap-up session is to reinforce to the participants that the outcomes of the process should result directly from the drivers, which is why it is so important to articulate with detail each organization's drivers. If both parties are achieving their drivers, the partnership will be viewed as a success. Therefore, during the components session it is important to review the drivers and establish action plans for achieving them. The most common approach is to establish a set of action items with assignment of responsibility and due dates. This is needed in order to maintain the momentum gained in the meeting.

In one meeting, managers failed to develop action plans. Their plan was to follow-up the partnership meeting with a videoconference focused on developing the action plan and assigning time frames and responsibilities for achieving the drivers. The follow-up videoconference failed to demonstrate the same level of focus and energy that existed during the partnership meeting. According to one of the managers, "we had to schedule an additional team building meeting in order to regain the momentum that was lost by waiting to establish an action plan."

A partnership, if appropriately established and effectively managed, should improve performance for both parties.

Assessing Outcomes. A partnership, if appropriately established and effectively managed, should improve performance for both parties. Profit enhancement, process improvements, and increased competitive advantage are likely outcomes of effective partnerships. Specific outcomes will vary depending upon the drivers which initially motivated the development of the partnership. It should be noted, however, that a partnership is not required to achieve satisfactory outcomes. Typically, organizations will have multiple arm's length relationships which meet the needs of and provide benefits to both parties. One of our case study relationships, between an express delivery company and a national manufacturer, was viewed by both parties at the beginning of the research as a partnership, since both parties were receiving their desired outcomes: a service improvement and cost reduction for the manufacturer and a revenue increase for the delivery company. At the completion of the research, it was clear to management in the manufacturing firm and the researchers that this relationship was not a partnership. The components of a partnership were not present. The desired benefits resulted from the fact that the parties were appropriately using an effective arm's length relationship.

Applications of the Model

The model was designed primarily as a tool to identify and develop partnerships with suppliers and customers. However, it can be used to assess an existing relationship, resolve conflicts in a relationship and to create a common vision of partnership within the organization.

Establishing a Partnership with a Supplier or Customer

When a major transportation company conducted a partnership session with a key customer, two very positive results emerged. First, the model clearly indicated to the parties the difference between a partnership and a long-term contract with volume and price guarantees (which is often mistakenly thought of as a partnership). According to one manager, "…the model identified eight or nine behaviors which we needed to change, as well as eight or nine behaviors we thought they could change."

Second, in a multi-division firm it is difficult to put a single-face forward. The model helped the transportation company coordinate the response of different business units to a partnership opportunity. In the words of a manager, "If we are looking at a corporate solution for the customer, one unit might have to do something that in the short run will be suboptimal, but in the long run will be positive for corporation as a whole as a result of positive gains made by other units. Or we may have to gamble and set rates and service commitments, which we know the competitor will match; and we will have to rely on the customer's integrity to deliver on their promise."

Assessing an Existing Relationship

The partnership model can be used to assess existing relationships. It works as an excellent check to ensure that a relationship is the appropriate type. By jointly working through the model, managers can determine if the relationship needs to be recalibrated.

The partnership model can be used to diagnose existing relationships.

For example, Goodyear and Yellow Freight had a strong relationship for a number of years, closely coordinated efforts and participated in numerous joint activities for distribution of tires. Although no problems existed in the relationship, managers at Goodyear decided to evaluate the relationship using the model. The assessment of the drivers and facilitators confirmed that a Type II partnership was appropriate. The components were reviewed and management from both firms believed that working through the model strengthened the partnership and helped management identify areas for improvement.

Resolving Conflicts in a Relationship

Texas Instruments used the model to improve its relationship with Photronics, a key supplier of photomask. Texas Instruments purchased 99 percent of its domestic market photomask requirements from Photronics, which represented about 36 percent of Phonotronics' sales. Photronics had five facilities in the U.S., including one in Texas dedicated to Texas Instruments.

Realizing the importance of the relationship, the two firms used the model to determine how the partnership might more effectively be managed. Considerable time was spent in joint meetings agreeing upon the meanings of each element of the drivers, facilitators, and components. Then each party independently assessed the drivers. This was done by 10 individuals from Photronics and 25 from Texas Instruments. After assessing drivers and facilitators, the teams agreed that the most appropriate type of relationship was a Type II. In a meeting attended by vice-presidents from Texas Instruments, the president, the chairman and vice-presidents from Photronics, and numerous operational personnel from both firms, agreement was reached on the specific implementation of the components. The teams prioritized the components and developed a detailed action plan outlining what each party would do to ensure successful implementation. Over a four month period, the teams held five to six hours of meetings per week, involving eight to 10 people from each firm. Management from both firms were more satisfied with the direction of the partnership. They shared and meshed five year plans and each made a commitment to the other. Even though their existing contract had expired, they chose to move forward without a contract.

Creating a Common Partnership Vision

The model provides a way to systematize the approach to partnering throughout an organization. Coca-Cola used the model with key suppliers such as Cargill as part of implementing the supplier relationship management process. The common language of drivers, facilitators, and components helps executives see the importance and potential of partnerships.

The model also serves as a screening tool when deciding where to allocate scarce resources. A firm can have a Type III partnership with only a limited number of partners. This limitation makes it critical that the correct relationship style is used in each business-to-business link. The model can be used to identity which relationships offer the best potential pay-back and should be given the most attention and resources.

Institutionalizing the Partnership Process

Relationships are critical to long-term competitive success, and the partnership model can help managers develop and implement a cohesive, focused relationship management strategy.

Relationships are critical to long-term competitive success, and the partnership model can help managers develop and implement a cohesive, focused relationship management strategy. Based on our experiences with many firms, institutionalizing the partnership approach so that it will survive the departure/transfer of a key executive requires a recognition of the importance of: a champion, preselling, education, organization, empowering employees and reporting.

As with any major organizational change, systematizing the approach to relationship management requires a champion or change agent who will promote the partnership concept throughout the organization. The success of Wendy's International with the partnership model was due, in large part, to the aggressive leadership of a change agent, Judy Hollis, the vice-president of supply chain management.

The model has been most successful in firms where a change agent sold top management on the concept of partnering and then introduced the details at an operational level. Short presentations, customized to each individual firm, and emphasizing the systematic approach to partnering were used as a "hook" to gain the interest of managers, customers and/or suppliers, as well as to gain a commitment to further education. When the effort was made to educate managers about the details of the model, its use was a success. It is imperative that all parties on both sides of the partnership have a common understanding of language and terms. Everyone should be using the same meaning for a Type III partnership, for instance.

A partnership can enhance an organization's ability to empower its own employees as well as those of its partner.

A partnership can enhance an organization's ability to empower its own employees as well as those of its partner. In the partnership between Whirlpool and ERX, ERX drivers were empowered to evaluate shipping damage and negotiate settlement, thus solving a potentially damaging customer service issue immediately. This eliminated the need for a damage adjuster and enhanced customer goodwill. Both parties felt comfortable with this arrangement due to the partnership components which were in place.

Similarly, Xerox empowered Ryder delivery personnel to unpack, set-up and test copiers, thus eliminating the need for multiple visits from Xerox personnel including technical representatives, sales people, and technicians who removed the old equipment. Xerox was placing its quality reputation on the line and in the hands of Ryder personnel. Trust, planning, operating controls, and risk sharing all had to be in place for this to work.

In order to keep the partnering process on track, there needs to be regular reporting and communication about the partnership and its progress both within each firm and across the organizations. This reporting can be done at joint team meetings, through internal newsletters, and/or in managerial reports. For example, at The Coca-Cola Company, Martha Buffington, the Global SRM Program Manager, prepares and distributes a supplier relationship management newsletter which keeps other employees aware of developments with key suppliers such as Cargill.

Conclusions

Partnerships are an important aspect of successful supply chain management. A well-designed facilitation process for establishing the appropriate level of partnership with other members of the supply chain has substantial benefits. These benefits are especially relevant when addressing an organization's critical supply chain linkages. In today's competitive environment with leaner organizations, it is necessary to form closer relationships with key suppliers, customers and third-party providers in order to maintain a leadership position and to grow. But the same forces that provide the benefits of partnering make it impossible to develop these relationships with everyone. Trying to develop a partnership where one is not warranted will waste valuable resources while providing minimal return. Not having a partnership when one is appropriate squanders an opportunity for competitive advantage.

The partnership model provides a systematic method for ensuring that partnerships are developed and managed in the most beneficial way for both firms. Users have found that the most helpful aspect of the model is not the specific scores obtained, but rather that the process leads to a disclosure of all important issues. However, the partnership model alone is not sufficient to guarantee effective relationship management. Business will continue "as usual" unless managers are provided with incentives and are rewarded for building and maintaining effective partnerships. Top management must not only embrace partnership ideals, they must recognize and reward cooperative behavior.

The partnership model provides a systematic method for ensuring that partnerships are developed and managed in the most beneficial way for both firms.

15 Supply Chain Management Performance Measurement

Douglas M. Lambert and Terrance L. Pohlen

Overview

Most discussions and articles about supply chain metrics are, in actuality, about internal logistics performance measures.[1] The lack of a widely accepted definition for supply chain management and the complexity associated with overlapping supply chains make the development of supply chain metrics difficult. Despite these problems, managers continue to pursue supply chain metrics as a means to increase their "line of sight" over areas they do not directly control, but have a direct impact on their company's performance. We provide a framework for developing supply chain metrics that translates performance into shareholder value. The framework focuses on managing the interfacing customer relationship management and supplier relationship management processes at each link in the supply chain. The translation of process improvements into supplier and customer profitability provides a method for developing metrics that enable management to identify opportunities for improved profitability and align objectives across firms in the supply chain.

Introduction

It is generally believed that a well-crafted system of supply chain metrics can increase the chances for success by aligning processes across multiple firms, targeting the most profitable market segments, and obtaining a competitive advantage through differentiated services and lower costs. The lack of proper metrics for a supply chain will result in failure to meet consumer/end-user expectations, suboptimization of departmental or company performance, missed opportunities to outperform the competition, and conflict within the supply chain. However, there is no evidence that meaningful performance measures that span the entire supply chain actually exist. Many factors contribute to this situation including: the lack of a supply chain orientation, the complexity of capturing metrics across multiple organizations, the unwillingness to share information among organizations, and the inability to capture performance by customer,

...there is no evidence that meaningful performance measures that span the entire supply chain actually exist.

---

[1] This chapter is adapted from Douglas M. Lambert and Terrance L. Pohlen, "Supply Chain Metrics," *The International Journal of Logistics Management*, Vol. 12, No. 1 (2001), pp. 1-19.

product or supply chain. A major contributor to the lack of meaningful supply chain management performance measures is the absence of an approach for developing and designing such measures.

In most companies, the metrics that management refers to as supply chain metrics are primarily internally focused logistics measures such as lead time, fill rate, or on-time performance. In many instances, these measures are financial (inventory turns and overall profitability), but they do not provide insight regarding how well key business processes have been performed or how effectively the supply chain has met customer needs. In a growing number of firms, management is beginning to measure performance outside the firm, but these efforts have been limited to evaluating the performance of Tier 1 suppliers, customers, or third-party providers. These metrics do not capture how the overall supply chain has performed and fail to identify where opportunities exist to increase competitiveness, customer value, and shareholder value for each firm in the supply chain.

In this chapter, we present a framework for developing metrics that measure the performance of the supply chain management processes, identify how each firm affects supply chain performance, and can be translated into shareholder value. First, we describe the problems with current metrics. Second, we explain the need for comprehensive supply chain metrics. Third, we describe the relationship between supply chain metrics and strategy. Fourth, we present a framework for developing supply chain metrics. Finally, we provide conclusions.

Problems with Existing Metrics

The performance measures used in most companies have several problems that prevent them from effectively measuring supply chain performance. Many measures identified as supply chain metrics are actually measures of internal logistics operations such as fill rate, lead time, on-time performance, damage and responsiveness[2] and are not the multi-firm measures that are necessary to measure the performance of the supply chain.[3] Similar measures were provided in seminar programs held at multiple locations in the United States and abroad, when we asked executives to identify examples of supply chain metrics. Typically, the executives identified inventory turns as one of the measures of supply chain performance, a view shared by several authors.[4] However, as a supply chain metric, inventory turns is not an effective measure and provides a useful example

Many measures identified as supply chain metrics are actually measures of internal logistics operations such as fill rate, lead time, on-time performance, damage and responsiveness[2] and are not the multi-firm measures that are necessary to measure the performance of the supply chain.

---

[2] Gilmour, Peter, "A Strategic Audit Framework to Improve Supply Chain Performance," *Journal of Business and Industrial Marketing,* Vol. 14, No. 5/6 (1999), pp. 355-363.

[3] Beamon, Benita M., "Measuring Supply Chain Performance," *International Journal of Operations and Production Management,* Vol. 19, No. 3 (1989), pp. 275-292; and, James S. Keebler, Karl B. Manrodt, David A. Durtsche, and D. Michael Ledyard, *Keeping Score,* Oak Brook, IL: Council of Logistics Management, 1999.

[4] Lapide, Larry, "What About Measuring Supply Chain Performance?" *Achieving Supply Chain Excellence Through Technology,* David L. Anderson editor, San Francisco, CA: Montgomery Research, 1999, pp. 287-297; *Energizing the Supply Chain: Trends and Issues in Supply Chain Management,* New York, NY: Deloitte Consulting, 1999, p. 15; *Supply Chain Operations Reference Model Overview of SCOR Version 3.1,* Pittsburgh, PA: Supply Chain Council, 2000, p. 9; "High Performance Value Chains: A Report of the 2000 Value Chain Survey," New York, NY: Cap Gemini Ernst & Young and *Industry Week,* 2000, p. 7; Debra Seaman Langdon, "Measure the Whole," *iSource Business,* March 2001, pp. 33-36; and, David L. Anderson, Franke E. Britt, and Donavon J. Favre, "The Seven Principles of Supply Chain Management," *Supply Chain Management Review,* Vol. 1, No. 1 (1997), pp. 31-41.

of why new metrics are needed for managing the supply chain.

An inventory turns measurement fails to capture key differences in product cost, form, and risk within the supply chain. Figure 15-1, which illustrates inventory positions and flows across four tiers of a supply chain, helps make this point. As inventory moves closer to the point of consumption, it increases in value. That is, the out-of-pocket cash investment in the inventory increases. The cash value of inventory increases from $5 at the suppliers, to $25 at the manufacturers, to $62 at the wholesalers, to $72 at the retailers.

...an inventory turn improvement by the retailer has a much greater effect on overall supply chain performance than a turn improvement by the supplier...

If the opportunity cost of money and the inventory turns are similar for each of the four tiers of the supply chain, inventory carrying costs are much higher at the retail level, and an inventory turn improvement by the retailer has a much greater effect on overall supply chain performance than a turn improvement by the supplier, or manufacturer, and a greater impact than a turn improvement by the wholesaler. Referring to Table 15-1, if the supplier, manufacturer, wholesaler and retailer are all achieving six turns and have a similar inventory carrying cost of 36 percent, an improvement to seven turns would be worth $0.04, $0.21, $0.53, and $0.62 per unit sold for each of the parties, respectively. This example illustrates that the common practice of pushing inventory forward in the supply chain might reduce overall supply chain performance. Current inventory turns at each level within the supply chain also must be considered. Figure 15-2 shows how the inventory carrying cost per unit changes with the number of inventory turns. While Figure 15-2 reflects the manufacturer data from Table 15-1, the shape of the curve is identical for the supplier, distributor/wholesaler and retailer. Now, let's reconsider how existing inventory turns at various tiers in the supply chain will

Figure 15-1
Inventory Flows Within the Supply Chain

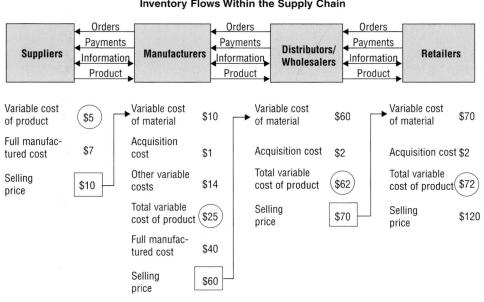

Source: Adapted from Douglas M. Lambert and Mark L. Bennion, "New Channel Strategies for the 1980s," in *Marketing Channels: Domestics and International Perspectives*, ed. Michael G. Harvey and Robert F. Lusch, Norman: Center for Economic Management Research, School of Business Administration, University of Oklahoma, 1982, p. 127.

Table 15-1
How Supply Chain Position Affects Inventory Carrying Cost

		Supplier	Manufacturer	Distributor/ Wholesaler	Retailer
Cash value of inventory:*		$5	$25	$62	$72
Inventory carrying cost %:		36%	36%	36%	36%
ICC/unit with:	1 turn	$1.80	$9.00	$22.32	$25.92
	2 turns	$0.90	$4.50	$11.16	$12.96
	3 turns	$0.60	$3.00	$7.44	$8.64
	4 turns	$0.45	$2.25	$5.58	$6.48
	5 turns	$0.36	$1.80	$4.46	$5.18
	6 turns	$0.30	$1.50	$3.72	$4.32
	7 turns	$0.26	$1.29	$3.19	$3.70
	8 turns	$0.23	$1.13	$2.79	$3.24
	9 turns	$0.20	$1.00	$2.48	$2.88
	10 turns	$0.18	$0.90	$2.23	$2.59
	11 turns	$0.16	$0.82	$2.03	$2.36
	12 turns	$0.15	$0.75	$1.86	$2.16

*Based on data provided in Figure 15-1

Figure 15-2
Annual Inventory Carrying Costs Compared to Inventory Turns

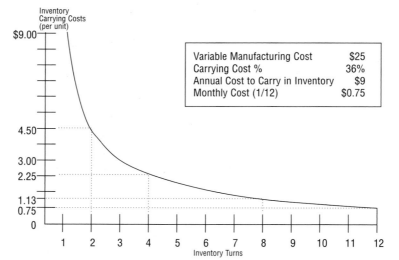

Variable Manufacturing Cost	$25
Carrying Cost %	36%
Annual Cost to Carry in Inventory	$9
Monthly Cost (1/12)	$0.75

Source: Adapted from Jay U. Sterling and Douglas M. Lambert as referenced in Douglas M. Lambert and James R. Stock, *Strategic Logistics Management*, Burr Ridge, IL: Irwin McGraw-Hill, 1993, p. 390.

affect the general rule that inventory, or inventory ownership, should be moved backward in the supply chain. If the manufacturer is only achieving five turns and wholesaler has eleven turns, a one turn improvement equates to $0.30 per unit sold for the manufacturer and $0.17 per unit sold for the wholesaler. In this case, the general rule is broken. The supply chain in total saves the most if the manufacturer achieves one more inventory turn. It is a matter of sharing the benefits so that members want what is best for the overall supply chain.

In addition, an inventory turn rate does not recognize the different forms or the risk of holding inventory. Raw materials held by the supplier might be used for multiple products or customers which makes it difficult to determine how downstream changes would affect the amount of inventory held by the supplier. The inventory turns metric does not consider risk. The further downstream the inventory, the greater the risk that it does not exactly meet consumers' requirements. Pushing the inventory backwards and postponing its final form permits the supply chain to avoid higher obsolescence costs and the cost of repositioning inventory when it has been deployed to the wrong location.

A single inventory turn metric for the supply chain cannot capture the differences that an improvement in turns will have at each level or for the total supply chain. Performance, as measured by total inventory carrying costs, would be a better measure since it considers both the cash value of the inventory at various positions in the supply chain as well as varying opportunity costs for inventory investments for various supply chain members.[5] Total inventory carrying cost is improved by pushing inventory backwards in the supply chain toward the point of origin. The further back, the lower the overall inventory carrying costs for the entire supply chain. In summary, inventory turns and other commonly used logistics measures are inadequate for evaluating and aligning performance across multiple companies in the supply chain.

...inventory turns and other commonly used logistics measures are inadequate for evaluating and aligning performance across multiple companies in the supply chain.

Another problem with metrics stems from the lack of a widely accepted definition of supply chain management. Many logistics practitioners, academics, and consultants view supply chain management as an extension of logistics outside the firm to include customers and suppliers.[6] However, the Council of Logistics Management (now the Council of Supply Chain Management Professionals) revised its definition of logistics in 2003 to reflect that logistics is only a part of supply chain management:

> Logistics is that part of Supply Chain Management that plans, implements and controls the efficient, effective forward and reverse flow and storage of goods, services, and related information between the point-of-origin and the point-of-consumption in order to meet customers' requirements.[7]

Supply chain management has a much broader scope and considers functions other than logistics:

> Supply chain management is the integration of key business processes from end user through original suppliers that provides products, services, and information that add value for customers and other stakeholders.[8]

---

[5] Stock, James R. and Douglas M. Lambert, *Strategic Logistics Management,* 4th Ed., Burr Ridge, IL: McGraw-Hill Irwin, 2001, pp. 187-221.

[6] Coyle, John J., Edward J. Bardi and Robert A. Novack, *Transportation,* 5th Ed., Cincinnati: South-Western College Publishing, 2000; William C. Copacino, *Supply Chain Management The Basics and Beyond,* Boca Raton, FL: St. Lucie Press, p. 7; Robert B. Handfield and Ernest L. Nichols, Jr., *Introduction to Supply Chain Management,* Upper Saddle, NJ: Prentice Hall Inc., 1999, p. 7; and, David Simchi-Levi, Philip Kaminsky, and Edith Simchi-Levi, *Designing and Managing the Supply Chain,* Boston, MA: Irwin McGraw-Hill, 2000, p. 1.

[7] Oak Brook, IL: Council of Logistics Management, 2003. See: www.cscmp.org

[8] Lambert, Douglas M. and Martha C. Cooper, "Issues in Supply Chain Management," *Industrial Marketing Management,* Vol. 29, No. 1 (2000), pp. 65-83.

Figure 15-1
Supply Chain Management:
Integrating and Managing Business Processes Across the Supply Chain

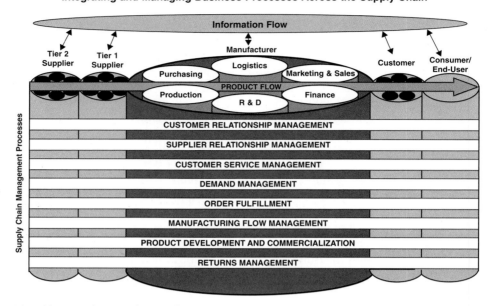

Source: Adapted from Douglas M. Lambert, Martha C. Cooper, and Janus D. Pagh, "Supply Chain Management: Implementation Issues and Research Opportunities," *The International Journal of Logistics Management,* Vol. 9, No. 2 (1998), p. 2.

Figure 15-3 shows the eight processes that must be implemented in the supply chain. The use of supply chain management as another name for logistics has led to observations that most companies have been using logistics metrics instead of measures that capture supply chain performance.[9]

Most of the literature has focused on analyzing and categorizing performance measurement systems.[10] More research is needed to develop supply chain metrics and to overcome the implementation barriers.[11] The supply chain must be viewed as one entity and any measurement system should span the entire supply chain.[12] Managers need to see the areas where supply chain performance can be improved, so they can focus their attention, and obtain higher levels of performance.[13]

[9] Lee, Hau L. and Corey Billington, "Managing Supply Chain Inventory: Pitfalls and Opportunities," *Sloan Management Review,* Vol. 33, No. 3 (1992), pp. 65-73; Larry Lapide, "What About Measuring Supply Chain Performance?" *Achieving Supply Chain Excellence Through Technology,* San Francisco, CA: Montgomery Research, 1999, pp. 287-297; Peter Gilmour, "A Strategic Audit Framework to Improve Supply Chain Performance," *Journal of Business and Industrial Marketing,* Vol. 14, No. 5/6 (1999), pp. 355-363; and, James S. Keebler, Karl B. Manrodt, David A. Durtsche and D. Michael Ledyard, *Keeping Score,* Oak Brook, IL: Council of Logistics Management, 1999.

[10] Beamon, Benita M., "Measuring Supply Chain Performance," *International Journal of Operations and Production Management,* Vol. 19, No. 3 (1989), pp. 275-292.

[11] Cooper, Martha C., Douglas M. Lambert and Janus D. Pagh, "Supply Chain Management: More Than a New Name for Logistics," *The International Journal of Logistics Management,* Vol. 8, No. 1 (1997), pp. 1-14.

[12] Holmberg, Stefan, "A Systems Perspective on Supply Chain Measurements," *International Journal of Physical Distribution and Logistics Management,* Vol. 30, No. 10 (2000), pp. 847-868.

[13] van Hoek, Remko I., "Measuring the Unmeasureable—Measuring and Improving Performance in the Supply Chain," *Supply Chain Management,* Vol. 3, No. 4 (1998), pp. 187-192.

Why Supply Chain Metrics?

Several factors are contributing to management's need for new types of measures for managing the supply chain...

Several factors are contributing to management's need for new types of measures for managing the supply chain including:

- The lack of measures that capture performance across the entire supply chain.
- The requirement to go beyond internal metrics and take a supply chain perspective.
- The need to determine the interrelationship between corporate performance and supply chain performance.
- The complexity of supply chain management.
- The requirement to align activities and share joint performance measurement information to implement strategy that achieves supply chain objectives.
- The desire to expand the "line of sight" within the supply chain.
- The requirement to allocate benefits and burdens resulting from functional shifts within the supply chain.
- The need to differentiate the supply chain to obtain a competitive advantage.
- The goal of encouraging cooperative behavior across corporate functions and across firms in the supply chain.

Measures spanning the entire supply chain do not exist,[14] and logistics or other functional measures do not adequately reflect the scope of supply chain management.[15] Managers can only determine whether they have met their corporate goals after the fact, by diagnosing poor financial results or when they lose a key customer.[16] The measures used have little to do with supply chain strategy and objectives and might actually conflict resulting in inefficiencies for the overall supply chain.[17] Metrics integrating performance across multiple companies are emerging,[18] but they are not comprehensive financial measures.

The adoption of a supply chain approach holds numerous consequences for the measurement and control of individual business activities[19] and the performance measures used. The shift from a functional to a process focus requires the development of new types of measures, financial as well as operational.[20] Supply chains, rather than the functional operations within a single company, become the new focus.[21] Supply chain members become accountable for the joint

---

[14] Mentzer, John T., editor, *Supply Chain Management,* edited by John T. Mentzer, Thousand Oaks, CA: Sage Publishing, 2001, p. 435.

[15] Caplice, Chris and Yossi Sheffi, "A Review and Evaluation of Logistics Performance Measurement Systems," *The International Journal of Logistics Management,* Vol. 6, No. 1 (1995), pp. 61-74.

[16] Lapide, Larry, "What About Measuring Supply Chain Performance?" *Achieving Supply Chain Excellence Through Technology,* David L. Anderson editor, San Francisco, CA: Montgomery Research, 1999, pp. 287-297.

[17] Lee, Hau L. and Corey Billington, "Managing Supply Chain Inventory: Pitfalls and Opportunities," *Sloan Management Review,* Vol. 33, No. 3 (1992), pp. 65-73.

[18] "Supply Chain Solutions: Linking the Chains," Kevin Francella and Katherine Doherty editors, Supplement to *Food Logistics,* March 1998.

[19] van Hoek, Remko I., "Measuring the Unmeasureable—Measuring and Improving Performance in the Supply Chain," *Supply Chain Management,* Vol. 3, No. 4 (1998), pp. 187-192.

[20] Kallio, Jukka, Timo Saarinen, Markku Tinnila and Ari P. J. Vepsalainen, "Measuring Delivery Process Performance," *The International Journal of Logistics Management,* Vol. 11, No. 1 (2000), pp. 75-87.

[21] Keebler, James S., Karl B. Manrodt, David A. Durtsche and D. Michael Ledyard, *Keeping Score,* Oak Brook, IL: Council of Logistics Management, 1999.

performance of these key business processes, and they require an integrated information system to enable multiple members of the supply chain to gain access to performance measures.[22] Management needs to understand the activities and costs of upstream and downstream supply chain members.[23]

In order for management to understand the interrelationship between corporate and supply chain performance, more holistic measures are required. These measures must integrate corporate financial and non-financial performance.[24] The translation of these measures into long-term shareholder value is critical for resolving conflicting objectives and supporting cost trade-offs across the supply chain especially in areas where cost or asset increases are required by some member(s). Existing measurement systems provide little assistance or insight regarding the question "What's in it for me?"[25] Future supply chain management innovations will come under increasing scrutiny to determine if and when they yield a positive impact on corporate performance.

Future supply chain management innovations will come under increasing scrutiny to determine if and when they yield a positive impact on corporate performance.

The complexity of the supply chain requires a different approach for designing metrics and measuring performance. In the case of a manufacturer, a supply chain can be represented as an uprooted tree, where the roots are the suppliers and the branches are the customers (see Figure 15-4). Managers require an understanding of what each branch or root adds to the value of the supply chain. The complexity of most supply chains makes it difficult to understand how activities at multiple tiers are related and influence each other. Performance measures must reflect this complexity and consider cross-company operations from original suppliers to the end customer.[26]

Relationship Between Supply Chain Metrics and Strategy

Implementing a supply chain strategy requires metrics that align performance with the objectives of other members of the supply chain.[27] Managers need to work collaboratively to generate the greatest mutual gains and savings.[28] Aligned metrics can assist in shifting managers' focus to attaining the operational goals of the enterprise-wide supply chain[29]. The alignment of metrics enables managers to identify and institutionalize the organizational, operational, and behavioral changes[30] needed

Implementing a supply chain strategy requires metrics that align performance with the objectives of other members of the supply chain.

[22] Lee, Hau L. "Creating Value Through Supply Chain Integration," *Supply Chain Management Review,* Vol. 4, No. 4 (2000), pp. 30-40.

[23] "Supply Chain Solutions: Linking the Chains," Kevin Francella and Katherine Doherty editors, Supplement to *Food Logistics,* March 1998.

[24] *Performance Measurement: Applying Value Chain Analysis to the Grocery Industry,* Joint Industry Project on Efficient Consumer Response, 1994.

[25] van Hoek, Remko I., "Measuring the Unmeasureable—Measuring and Improving Performance in the Supply Chain," *Supply Chain Management,* Vol. 3, No. 4 (1998), pp. 187-192.

[26] "Supply Chain Solutions: Linking the Chains," Kevin Francella and Katherine Doherty editors, Supplement to *Food Logistics,* March 1998.

[27] "Supply Chain Solutions: Linking the Chains," Kevin Francella and Katherine Doherty editors, Supplement to *Food Logistics,* March 1998.

[28] Keebler, James S., Karl B. Manrodt, David A. Durtsche and D. Michael Ledyard, *Keeping Score,* Oak Brook, IL: Council of Logistics Management, 1999.

[29] Walker, William T., "Use Global Performance Measures to Align the Enterprise Trading Partners," *Achieving Supply Chain Excellence Through Technology,* David L. Anderson, editor, San Francisco, CA: Montgomery Research, 1999.

[30] "Strategic Channel Management," *A Mercer Commentary,* Mercer Management Consulting, Undated.

Figure 15-4
Types of Inter-company Business Process Links

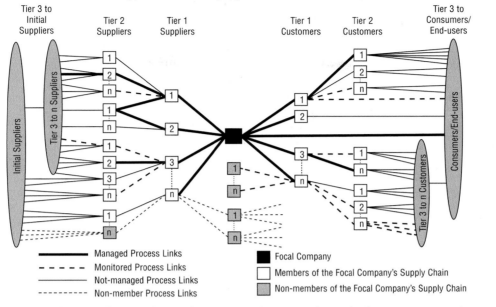

Source: Adapted from Douglas M. Lambert, Martha C. Cooper and Janus D. Pagh, "Supply Chain Management: Implementation Issues and Research Opportunities," *The International Journal of Logistics Management*, Vol. 9, No. 2 (1998), p. 7.

to manage relationships in the supply chain. Aligned metrics can direct management attention and effort to the areas requiring improvement leading to higher levels of performance for the supply chain.[31] By establishing metrics for the supply chain, managers will be more likely to reach overall corporate goals and business strategies.[32] Integrating business processes across the supply chain is difficult because of the many constituencies, each with their own metrics and individual objectives.[33] Their objectives might have little in common resulting in potential conflict and inefficiencies for the supply chain.[34] Conflicting objectives preclude managers from effectively managing trade-offs across functions[35] as well as across companies.

Managers need to extend their "line of sight" across the supply chain by measuring the performance of activities and companies they do not directly control.[36] Management of a single company rarely controls the supply chain from

[31] van Hoek, Remko I., "Measuring the Unmeasureable—Measuring and Improving Performance in the Supply Chain," *Supply Chain Management*, Vol. 3, No. 4 (1998), pp. 187-192.

[32] van Hoek, Remko I., "Measuring the Unmeasureable—Measuring and Improving Performance in the Supply Chain," *Supply Chain Management*, Vol. 3, No. 4 (1998), pp. 187-192.

[33] Sherman, Richard J., *Supply Chain Management for the Millennium*, Oak Brook, IL: Warehousing Education and Research Council, 1998.

[34] Lee, Hau L. and Corey Billington, "Managing Supply Chain Inventory: Pitfalls and Opportunities," *Sloan Management Review*, Vol. 33, No. 3 (1992), pp. 65-73.

[35] Lee, Hau L. and Corey Billington, "Managing Supply Chain Inventory: Pitfalls and Opportunities," *Sloan Management Review*, Vol. 33, No. 3 (1992), pp. 65-73.

[36] Lapide, Larry, "What About Measuring Supply Chain Performance?" *Achieving Supply Chain Excellence Through Technology*, David L. Anderson, editor, San Francisco, CA: Montgomery Research, 1999, pp. 287-297; and, Andrew K. Reese, "Metrics Mentality," *iSource Business*, June 2001, pp. 67-70.

point-of-origin to point-of-consumption and cannot see areas for improvement across the entire supply chain.[37] Increased visibility and shared metrics assist management with the integration, synchronization, and optimization of these inter-enterprise processes. The visibility makes the supply chain more transparent and can lead the way for performance improvements. Managers can determine how well the supply chain performed against the expectations of their customers[38] and use the information to determine where performance improvements need to occur. The identification of deficiencies outside of a company's span of control can lead to programs aimed at improving performance or taking some level of control of upstream or downstream supply chain activities. Managers rarely have face-to-face contact with the end users, and supply chain metrics enable all the linked members to better respond to changes in consumer demand.[39]

Functional shifts and cost trade-offs made across multiple firms require metrics capable of measuring the resulting benefits and burdens. Individual companies might have to sacrifice internal efficiencies or perform additional functions to reduce total supply chain costs.[40] Some firms will benefit from the realignment of activities while others will incur additional burdens or costs. Management needs the capability to measure where benefits or burdens have occurred and a mechanism for negotiating an equitable redistribution of the benefits and costs among firms.[41]

The commoditization of products and the number of competitive product offerings are forcing management to differentiate the firm's offerings through increased performance. Managers must examine the supply chain to determine additional revenue opportunities and where they can obtain the greatest leverage to differentiate the brand and/or to eliminate costs.[42] Integrated metrics allow management to assess the overall competitiveness of the supply chain and to determine which internal improvement efforts produce the greatest impact on overall competitiveness.[43]

Rewards and incentives are usually based on performance measurements that are focused internally rather than on the consumer or the supply chain.[44] The metrics used influence the behavior of individuals and determine supply chain

Integrated metrics allow management to assess the overall competitiveness of the supply chain and to determine which internal improvement efforts produce the greatest impact on overall competitiveness.

[37] van Hoek, Remko I., "Measuring the Unmeasureable—Measuring and Improving Performance in the Supply Chain," *Supply Chain Management,* Vol. 3, No. 4 (1998), pp. 187-192

[38] Reese, Andrew K., "Metrics Mentality," *iSource Business,* June 2001, pp. 67-70.

[39] Lummus, Rhonda R. and Robert J. Vokurka, "Managing the Demand Chain Through Managing the Information Flow: Capturing 'Moments of Information,'" *Production and Inventory Management Journal,* Vol. 40, No. 1 (1999), pp. 16-20.

[40] van Hoek, Remko I., "Measuring the Unmeasureable—Measuring and Improving Performance in the Supply Chain," *Supply Chain Management,* Vol. 3, No. 4 (1998), pp. 187-192.

[41] La Londe, Bernard J. and Terrance L. Pohlen, "Issues in Supply Chain Costing," *The International Journal of Logistics Management,* Vol. 7, No. 1 (1994), pp. 1-12.

[42] Keebler, James S., Karl B. Manrodt, David A. Durtsche and D. Michael Ledyard, *Keeping Score,* Oak Brook, IL: Council of Logistics Management, 1999.

[43] van Hoek, Remko I., "Measuring the Unmeasureable—Measuring and Improving Performance in the Supply Chain," *Supply Chain Management,* Vol. 3, No. 4 (1998), pp. 187-192.

[44] Neely, Andy, Mike Gregory and Ken Platts, "Performance Measurement System Design," *International Journal of Operations and Production Management,* Vol. 15, No. 4 (1995), pp. 80-116.

performance.[45] The behavior of managers in individual firms can be influenced by measurements such as increases in value or competitiveness, or through the use of rewards and sanctions.[46]

The focus on internal logistics metrics results in performance measures and activities not being aligned with supply chain strategy. The operational objectives of companies frequently conflict with one another leading to inefficiencies in the supply chain.[47] Many of the measurements used within firms are developed in isolation and incentives are linked to an individual's functional performance rather than strategy. The missing connection between strategy and measurements promotes an internal focus that becomes an obstacle to developing supply chain metrics[48] and contributes to many of the strategic level measures appearing unrelated or not actionable at lower levels in the corporate hierarchy.

Many of the measurements used within firms are developed in isolation and incentives are linked to an individual's functional performance rather than strategy.

Framework for Developing Supply Chain Management Metrics

Complexity makes the development of supply chain management metrics very difficult (see Figure 15-5). For example, consumer goods manufacturers such as Colgate-Palmolive, Procter & Gamble and Unilever sell to the same customers and in many cases purchase from the same suppliers. Competing supply chains appear more like interconnected or overlapping networks than a mutually exclusive "supply chain versus supply chain" form of competition. The overlap results in many instances of shared inventories, shared services, and shared assets between supply chains.[49] Managers cannot easily determine how business practices within specific companies drive total supply chain performance. As was pointed out earlier, you cannot simply add up inventory turns for participating firms and arrive at a total for the supply chain.

Despite the complexity and overlap existing in most supply chains, managers can develop metrics to align the performance of key business processes across multiple companies. We propose a framework that aligns performance at each link (supplier-customer pair) within the supply chain. The framework begins with the linkages at the focal company and moves outward a link at a time. The link-by-link approach provides a means for aligning performance from point-of-origin to point-of-consumption with the overall objective of maximizing shareholder value for the total supply chain as well as for each company. The framework consists of seven steps:

We propose a framework that aligns performance at each link (supplier-customer pair) within the supply chain.

[45] Lapide, Larry, "What About Measuring Supply Chain Performance?" *Achieving Supply Chain Excellence Through Technology,* David L. Anderson, editor, San Francisco, CA: Montgomery Research, 1999, pp. 287-297.

[46] Neely, Andy, Mike Gregory and Ken Platts, "Performance Measurement System Design," *International Journal of Operations and Production Management,* Vol. 15, No. 4 (1995), pp. 80-116.

[47] Holmberg, Stefan, "A Systems Perspective on Supply Chain Measurements," *International Journal of Physical Distribution and Logistics Management,* Vol. 30, No. 10 (2000), pp. 847-868.

[48] Mentzer, John T., editor, *Supply Chain Management,* Thousand Oaks, CA: Sage Publishing, 2001; Stefan Holmberg, "A Systems Perspective on Supply Chain Measurements," *International Journal of Physical Distribution and Logistics Management,* Vol. 30, No. 10 (2000), pp. 847-868; and, M. E. Kuwaiti and John M. Kay, "The Role of Performance Measurement in Business Process Reengineering," *International Journal of Operations, and Production Management,* Vol. 20. No. 12 (2000), pp. 1411-1426.

[49] Rice, James B. Jr. and Richard M. Hoppe, "Supply Chain vs. Supply Chain: The Hype & The Reality," *Supply Chain Management Review,* Vol. 5, No. 5 (2001), pp. 46-54.

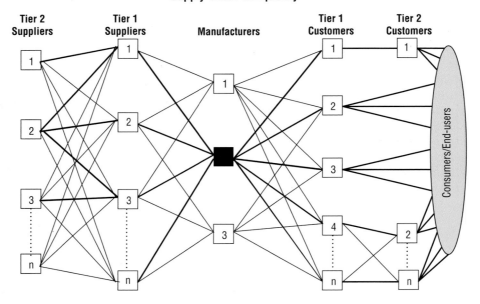

Figure 15-5
Supply Chain Complexity

- Map the supply chain from point-of-origin to point-of-consumption to identify where key linkages exist.
- Use the customer relationship management and supplier relationship management processes to analyze each link (customer-supplier pair) and determine where additional value can be created for the supply chain.
- Develop customer and supplier profit and loss (P&L) statements to assess the effect of the relationship on profitability and shareholder value of the two firms.
- Realign supply chain management processes and activities to achieve performance objectives.
- Establish non-financial performance measures that align individual behavior with supply chain management process objectives and financial goals.
- Compare shareholder value and market capitalization across firms with supply chain objectives and revise process and performance measures as necessary.
- Replicate steps at each link in the supply chain.

Map the Supply Chain

The framework begins with the mapping of the supply chain from point-of-origin to point-of-consumption. In the map, the various paths that materials, information and financial flows may take from source to the final consumer are identified (see Figure 15-4). Managers can use the map to identify the different companies and linkages comprising the supply chain. The key supply chain linkages are those that are most critical to success. The initial focus should be on

Customer relationship management (CRM) and supplier relationship management (SRM) are the two processes that capture the overall performance of a supplier-customer relationship and can be used to link up the entire supply chain.

managing those supplied/customer dyads with the greatest potential for increasing profitability and developing a sustainable competitive advantage. Customer relationship management (CRM) and supplier relationship management (SRM) are the two processes that capture the overall performance of a supplier-customer relationship and can be used to link up the entire supply chain.

Analyze Each Link

The supplier applies the CRM process to define how it will manage relationships with customers. Key customers are identified and the supplier's CRM teams work with these accounts to tailor product and service agreements that meet their requirements and specify the level of performance. The CRM process creates value by working with the customer to improve performance. For example, the CRM team may negotiate with the customer's team to implement supplier managed inventory (SMI). Successful SMI implementation might lead to increased revenues as the customer allocates a larger proportion of the business to that supplier. If the relationship reduces costs and can yield a price reduction for the consumer, revenues should increase as total sales for the supply chain increase. Revenues should increase as a result of better in-stock availability at the end of the supply chain. The cost of goods sold (COGS) should decrease through better scheduling of material requirements and more efficient utilization of plant capacity and labor. When SMI is implemented, the supplier experiences a one-time decrease in sales and the customer uses up existing inventory. The supplier's expenses will increase as the company assumes ownership of, and responsibility for, the customer's inventory; however, other expenses should decrease due to reduced order processing and forecasting costs. Inventory carrying costs should decrease as point-of-sale data are used to schedule shipments instead of forecasting requirements and maintaining safety stock. Better capacity utilization and collaborative planning and forecasting of requirements should reduce the need for customer specific assets. If these cost reductions in total do not more than offset the increased costs, then some other method of sharing benefits must occur. For example, the customer could write the supplier a check. The process improvements obtained through CRM can be translated into increased shareholder value through the use of an economic value-added (EVA) model as illustrated in Figure 15-6.

On the opposite side of the dyad, the customer uses the SRM process to manage supplier relationships. The customer selects and develops relationships with suppliers based on their criticality and contribution to profit goals. As with the CRM process, it is possible to identify how SRM affects EVA (see Figure 15-7). Referring to the previous example, the SRM process captures the value created through SMI implementation. The relationship might produce increased revenues through cost reductions, lower consumer prices, and improved quality obtained by working with a select group of suppliers. The COGS might be reduced through the leveraging of larger buys with a smaller number of suppliers. Expenses decrease as the supplier assumes responsibility for order placement and inventory management. Pushing the ownership of inventory backwards to the supplier reduces inventory carrying costs for the customer and for the total supply chain since the supplier owns the inventory at a lower cash value (see Figure 15-1). Together, the CRM and SRM processes capture the total value, adjusted for the cost

Figure 15-6
How Customer Relationship Management Affects Economic Value Added (EVA)

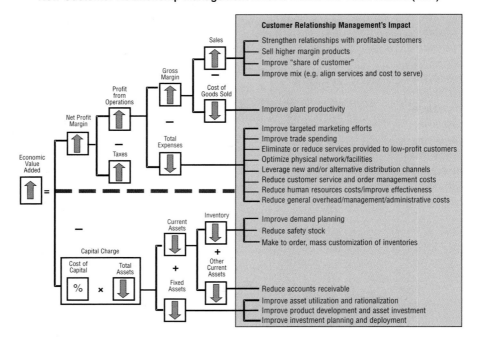

Figure 15-7
How Supplier Relationship Management Affects Economic Value Added (EVA)

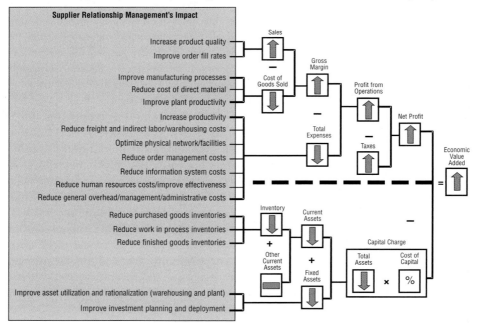

of money, created by the supplier-customer relationship. Exhibits similar to Figures 15-6 and 15-7 have been developed for the other six supply chain management processes and were included in prior chapters of this book.

Develop Profit and Loss Statements

The development of customer and supplier P&L statements provides a complete picture of how the relationship affects profitability for both firms (see Table 15-2). Initiatives undertaken by the two firms are reflected in these P&Ls, as are improvements in performance of the other six processes (see Figure 15-3). While performance metrics must be developed for all eight processes in order to motivate the desired behavior, the financial performance of all eight processes is captured in the customer P&Ls. When the customer P&Ls are aggregated for all customers and corporate joint costs deducted, the results represent overall firm performance.

When the customer P&Ls are aggregated for all customers and corporate joint costs deducted, the results represent overall firm performance.

Table 15-2 illustrates combined customer-supplier profitability analysis for a manufacturer selling to a wholesaler or retailer. In the case of the supplier (manufacturer), variable manufacturing costs are deducted from net sales to calculate a manufacturing contribution. Next, variable marketing and logistics costs are deducted to calculate a contribution margin. Assignable nonvariable costs, such as slotting allowances and inventory carrying costs, are subtracted to obtain a segment controllable margin. The net margin is obtained after deducting a charge for dedicated assets. In the case of the customer (wholesaler or retailer), product costs are deducted from sales to obtain a gross margin to which discounts and allowances are added to obtain the net margin. The remaining steps are similar to those taken by the supplier to obtain the net segment margin. These statements contain opportunity costs for investments in receivables and inventory

Table 15-2
Combined Customer-Supplier Profitability Analysis:
A Contribution Approach with Charge for Assets Employed

Supplier	Customer A	Customer	Supplier A
Net Sales		Sales	
Cost of Goods Sold (Variable Mfg. Cost)		Cost of Goods Sold	
Manufacturing Contribution		Gross Margin	
		Plus: Discounts and Allowances	
Variable Marketing & Logistics Costs:		Market Development Funds	
Sales Commissions		Slotting Allowances	
Transportation		Co-Op Advertising	
Warehousing (Handling in and out)		Net Margin	
Special Packaging		Variable Marketing & Logistics Costs:	
Order Processing		Transportation	
Charge for Investment in Accts. Rec.		Receiving	
Contribution Margin		Order Processing	
		Contribution Margin	
Assignable Nonvariable Costs:		Assignable Nonvariable Costs:	
Salaries		Salaries	
Segment Related Advertising		Advertising	
Slotting Allowances		Inventory Carrying Costs Less:	
Inventory Carrying Costs		Charge for Accounts Payable	
Segment Controllable Margin		Segment Controllable Margin	
Charge for Dedicated Assets Used		Charge for Dedicated Assets Used	
Net Segment Margin		Net Segment Margin	

and a charge for dedicated assets. Consequently, they are much closer to cash flow statements than a traditional P&L. They contain revenues minus the costs (avoidable costs) that disappear if the revenue disappears. If the supplier is selling an undifferentiated commodity to a customer that is another manufacturer, then the customer's report on the supplier is a total cost analysis unless revenue can be attributed to a source of supply (e.g., better quality or fewer returns). The customer compares the total cost for the current period to similar periods in the past or to comparable suppliers to determine the change in performance.

Realign Supply Chain Management Processes

The P&Ls provide the best measure of supply chain management performance and can be used to align performance across processes and firms. In our SMI example, implementation may cause the supplier to incur additional costs in some areas while obtaining cost reductions in others. The supplier's P&L reflects the resulting total cost as well as changes in assets (because of charges for assets employed), revenue, and profitability. Similarly, the customer's P&L reflects any changes due to SMI implementation. A combined profitability analysis captures the total effort and enables management to better understand how aligning their actions with supply chain objectives drives profitability in their firms. They can use this information as a basis for negotiating how to equitably split any benefits or burdens resulting from supply chain process improvements. In order to evaluate proposed programs, proforma P&Ls can be developed.

The P&Ls provide the best measure of supply chain management performance and can be used to align performance across processes and firms.

If the profitability reports are developed correctly, they will capture the impact of improved performance in all of the eight supply chain management processes (see Figure 15-8). The figure shows that the manufacturer (M) is generating profitabily reports for each customer and report C_1 represents retailer (R). While each process, such as order fulfillment, will have its individual metrics the overall performance is captured in the customer profit and loss statement. Figure 15-9 illustrates how management in the two organizations might identify process improvement opportunities by reviewing the activities performed in each process.

Functional measures, such as inventory turns, cannot capture the full extent of the cost trade-offs that must be considered and can be easily "gamed." Inventory carrying cost is a better measure, but it does not capture the costs incurred to achieve the reduction in inventory. Increases in production setup costs, transportation costs, ordering costs and lost sales costs might more than offset any gains made in inventory carrying costs. Typically, inventory reductions have a greater impact on total supply chain performance if they occur at the retail level. Generally speaking, making to order, pushing inventory backwards or pushing inventory ownership backwards in the supply chain improves overall performance. A combined customer-supplier profitability analysis will capture how the repositioning of inventory improves total supply chain performance, whereas inventory turns does not reflect any of the cost trade-offs within a firm or in the supplier-customer link.

Align Non-Financial Measures with P&Ls

P&Ls and EVA measures alone are not sufficient to effect improvements in supply chain performance or to align behavior. Supply chain and corporate metrics

Figure 15-8
Customer and Supplier Profitability Reports Should Capture the
Impact of Improved Performance in Each Process

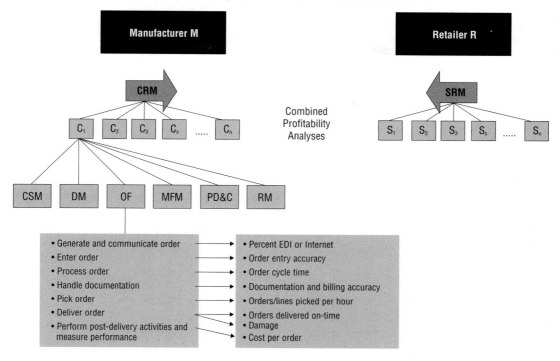

Figure 15-9
Identifying Process Improvement Opportunities

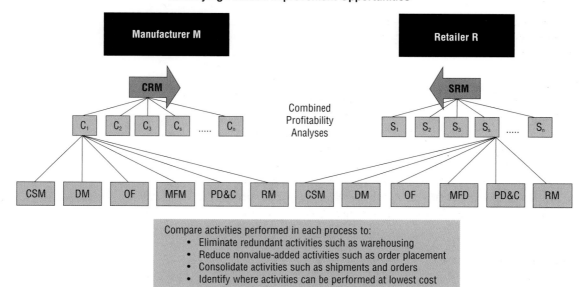

must be cascaded down to develop performance measures at the lowest level in the organization. For example, managers begin with the objectives identified in Figure 15-10 for developing performance measures for the order fulfillment process (see Order Fulfillment's Impact in Figure 15-10). These represent high level drivers of financial performance. It is necessary to develop more specific measures of performance (see Order Fulfillment's Performance Metrics in Figure 15-10).

A warehouseman or order fulfillment specialist supporting this process may not be able to relate how more efficient order picking and picking accuracy impact profitability or shareholder value, but they can focus on reducing order pick time and errors. Reducing order pick time while increasing productivity reduces the cost per order. Reducing order pick errors results in faster payment of customer invoices and reduces the cost of returned goods. By outperforming the competition, a faster order cycle time might lead to increased sales. Individual performance measures must be tied to the specific objectives required to improve profitability and shareholder value at each link in the supply chain. The relationship between improved non-financial performance and shareholder value can be accomplished by converting activities into costs through such means as activity-based costing, identifying any revenue or asset implications, and inserting this information into an EVA or profit analyses.

A combined customer-supplier profitability analysis will capture how the repositioning of inventory improves total supply chain performance, whereas inventory turns does not reflect any of the cost trade-offs within a firm or in the supplier-customer link.

Compare Across Firms and Replicate

The final steps in the framework compare the resulting shareholder value and market capitalization across firms (see Figure 15-11) and replicate these steps at every link in the supply chain. Overall performance might be measured by the

Figure 15-10
How Order Fulfillment Affects Economic Value Added (EVA®)

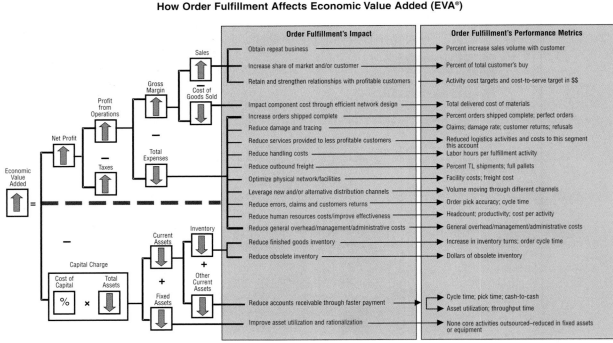

increase in profit or market capitalization for each firm in the supply chain. The wholesaler/distributor's P&L for C as a supplier and the manufacturer's cost saving for D as a supplier are not included in the market capitalization metric to avoid double counting as an increase in profit or expense reduction from a supplier is captured in the customer P&Ls. In the case of the retailer/end user, it would be unusual to have customer P&Ls so overall profitability is determined by summing supplier P&Ls and deducting corporate joint costs. While management's goal is to increase shareholder value, economic conditions or other events can lead to depressed price-earnings (P/E) multiples in the short run. In these situations, it may be better to simply sum the changes in net profits. In Figure 15-11, all firms show an increase in profits because management uses the financial data to negotiate an equitable sharing of the costs and benefits.

By analyzing the processes at each link and understanding the value the link creates, managers can align the supply chain management processes in order to provide the best value for consumers/end users and the highest profitability and shareholder value for each company.

Managers should assess whether the process changes and metrics employed have produced the targeted levels of profitability and shareholder value. They may need to refine the processes or make additional trade-offs to achieve the targets. In many instances, managers may find second or third tier customers and suppliers provide additional opportunities to reduce cost, increase quality, and accelerate product development. Some intermediaries that do not add value might be eliminated from the supply chain or others added if it can increase the profitability of certain segments; for example, a distributor may be used to service a large number of small accounts or to achieve distribution in a remote geographic region.

The customer-supplier profitability analysis should be applied at each link in the supply chain. By analyzing the processes at each link and understanding the value the link creates, managers can align the supply chain management processes in order

Figure 15-11
Profit and Market Capitalization Increases Measured Across Four Tiers of the Supply Chain

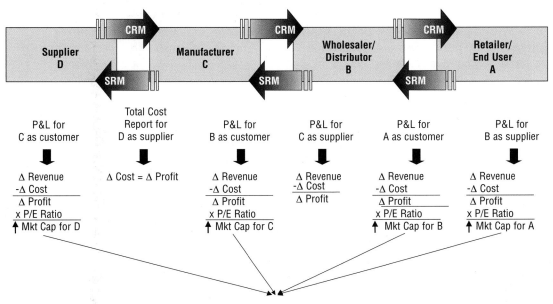

Supply Chain Performance = Increase in Market Cap for A, B, C, and D

to provide the best value for consumers/end-users and the highest profitability and shareholder value for each company. This framework increases management's understanding of how their firm contributes to the overall competitiveness and value created by the supply chain and provides the opportunity for a dynamic realignment of the supply chain. Management maximizes performance at each linkage and over time the processes become more efficient and effective and the supply chain naturally migrates to the point that maximizes profitability for each party and the whole. The process is on-going and requires continual adjustment. Managers can take proactive action within their firm as well as negotiate with other firms to further increase overall supply chain performance. Management must understand how value is created by each process at each link in the supply chain, take collaborative action to increase value, and replicate these steps across the entire supply chain. Ultimately, it is the value provided to retail customers or industrial end-users (product and service quality relative to price) that determines the competitiveness of the supply chain and the profitability of its members.

Conclusions

Most of the performance measures called supply chain metrics are logistics measures that have an internal focus and do not capture how the firm drives value or profitability in the supply chain. These measures may actually prove to be dysfunctional by attempting to optimize the firm's performance at the expense of the other firms in the supply chain, an approach that eventually decreases the value of the entire supply chain. The use of customer and supplier contribution reports avoids this situation. The customer-supplier P&Ls capture cost trade-offs as well as revenue implications, and any action taken by one firm is reflected in both firms' P&Ls. The combined P&Ls provide the necessary foundation for improving performance in the supply chain. Although one firm may incur additional costs, the combined analysis reflects whether the costs associated with a process improvement increased profitability through a larger share of the customer's business or increased supply chain competitiveness. By maximizing profitability at each link, supply chain performance migrates toward management's objectives and maximizes performance for the whole.

By maximizing profitability at each link, supply chain performance migrates toward management's objectives and maximizes performance for the whole.

16 Supply Chain Management: The Next Steps

Douglas M. Lambert, Sebastián J. García-Dastugue,
A. Michael Knemeyer and Keely L. Croxton

Overview

The preceding chapters have detailed The Global Supply Chain Forum (GSCF) process-based framework of supply chain management, described the partnership model which can be used to tailor key relationships, and presented a method for developing a performance measurement system to identify opportunities to improve profitability and to align objectives across firms in the supply chain. In this chapter, we provide additional insights on how to implement supply chain management. An alternative process-based supply chain management framework (Supply-Chain Operations Reference - SCOR) is compared and contrasted with the GSCF framework. Our goal is to provide management with an understanding of the strengths and weaknesses of both frameworks in order to determine which can bring the most value to their organization. Also, managerial guidelines for implementing the GSCF framework are detailed. These include an assessment tool for each of the eight processes to assist with the implementation of the GSCF framework and a model for facilitating the required organizational transformation.

Introduction

...managers who desire to implement a relationship-oriented supply chain management framework need to focus on implementing cross-functional business processes.

Given that a supply chain is the network of companies, or independent business units, from original supplier to end-users, management of this network is a broad and challenging task. As detailed in the previous chapters of this book, managers who desire to implement a relationship-oriented supply chain management framework need to focus on implementing cross-functional business processes. The GSCF processes provide the structure to manage the relationships with key members of the supply chain.

The focus of this chapter is to highlight considerations for managers who want to implement the supply chain management processes. The GSCF framework is compared to another supply chain management framework, SCOR, which also prescribes the implementation of business processes. While many authors have recognized the importance of implementing processes, these two frameworks represent the only alternatives available with sufficient detail to assist management in implementation. While both frameworks are process-based, they represent different approaches to supply chain management. Comparing them provides useful insight to management interested in implementation of one or both of the frameworks. The chapter contains guidelines for managers who adopt the GSCF framework. The guidelines deal with assessment and change management activities that support management's implementation efforts.

The chapter is organized as follows. First, the GSCF and SCOR frameworks are described. Second, the frameworks are compared and the strengths and weaknesses are identified. Third, guidelines for implementing the GSCF framework are suggested. Finally, conclusions are presented.

Process-Based Frameworks for Supply Chain Management

While there has been much discussion about the need to implement cross-functional business processes in the supply chain, there are only two frameworks that identify what processes are involved and provide enough detail for implementation. The SCOR and GSCF frameworks prescribe the implementation of business processes, but the goals of each are different. We briefly describe each framework and provide an evaluation of the strengths and weaknesses of each.

The SCOR and GSCF frameworks prescribe the implementation of business processes, but the goals of each are different.

The GSCF Framework

The GSCF defines supply chain management as *"the integration of key business processes from end user through original suppliers that provides products, services, and information that add value for customers and other stakeholders."* Implementation is carried out through three elements: the supply chain network structure, the business processes, and the management components. The following eight supply chain management processes are included in the GSCF framework.

- Customer Relationship Management - provides the structure for how relationships with customers are developed and maintained.
- Supplier Relationship Management - provides the structure for how relationships with suppliers are developed and maintained.
- Customer Service Management - provides the key point of contact for administering product and service agreements.
- Demand Management - provides the structure for balancing the customers' requirements with supply chain capabilities, including reducing demand variability and increasing supply chain flexibility.
- Order Fulfillment - includes all activities necessary to define customer requirements, design the logistics network, and fill customer orders.
- Manufacturing Flow Management - includes all activities necessary to obtain, implement and manage manufacturing flexibility and move products through the plants in the supply chain.
- Product Development and Commercialization - provides the structure for developing and bringing to market new products jointly with customers and suppliers.
- Returns Management - includes all activities related to returns, reverse logistics, gatekeeping, and avoidance.

Customer relationship management and supplier relationship management form the critical links of the supply chain and the other six processes are coordinated through them.

The GSCF framework is shown in Figure 16-1. Customer relationship management and supplier relationship management form the critical links of the supply chain and the other six processes are coordinated through them. Each of the eight processes is cross-functional and cross-firm, and can be broken down into a sequence of strategic sub-processes, and a sequence of operational sub-processes. Each sub-process is described by a set of activities. Cross-functional teams are used to define the structure for managing the process at the strategic level and to implement it at the operational level.

The Supply-Chain Operations Reference (SCOR) Framework

A second process-based framework, SCOR, was developed in 1996 by the Supply-Chain Council (SCC), a nonprofit organization founded by Pittiglio, Rabin, Todd & McGrath (PRTM), a consulting company, and AMR Research.[1] Initially, SCOR included four business processes: plan, source, make, and deliver, which are to be implemented within the firm and eventually connected across firms in the supply chain. Return, the fifth process, was added in 2001.[2] The SCOR framework has three components: business process reengineering, benchmarking and best practices analysis. SCOR prescribes the use of business process reengineering techniques to capture the current state of a process and then determine the "to-be" state.

Figure 16-1
Supply Chain Management:
Integrating and Managing Business Processes Across the Supply Chain

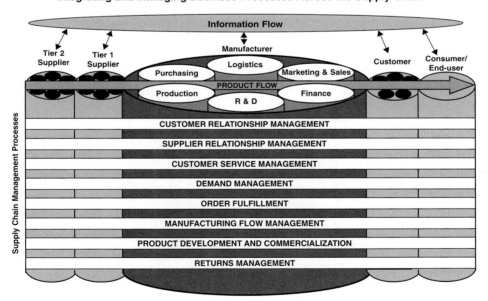

Source: Adapted from Douglas M. Lambert, Martha C. Cooper, and Janus D. Pagh, "Supply Chain Management: Implementation Issues and Research Opportunities," *The International Journal of Logistics Management,* Vol. 9, No. 2 (1998), p. 2.

---

[1] Supply-Chain Council, "Supply-Chain Operations Reference-model. Overview of SCOR Version 1.0," 1996.

[2] Supply-Chain Council, "Supply-Chain Operations Reference-model. Overview of SCOR Version 5.0," 2001.

Benchmarking is used to determine target values for operational performance metrics. Best practice analysis identifies management practices and software solutions used successfully by similar companies that are considered top performers.[3]

SCOR is organized around five processes (see Figure 16-2), which are:

- Plan - balances aggregate demand and supply to develop a course of action which best meets sourcing, production, and delivery requirements.
- Source - includes activities related to procuring goods and services to meet planned and actual demand.
- Make - includes activities related to transforming products into a finished state to meet planned or actual demand.
- Deliver - provides finished goods and services to meet planned or actual demand, typically including order management, transportation management, and distribution management.
- Return - deals with returning or receiving returned products for any reason and extends into post-delivery customer support.

Each of these processes is implemented in four levels of detail. Level One defines the number of supply chains as well as what metrics will be used. Level Two defines the planning and execution processes in material flow. Level Three defines the inputs, outputs and flow of each transactional element. At Level Four, the implementation details of the processes are defined.

Strengths and Weaknesses of the Two Frameworks

Each framework has its strengths and weaknesses which must be recognized for managers to understand the value that each can bring to their organizations, and the potential issues that must be addressed in implementing each.[4]

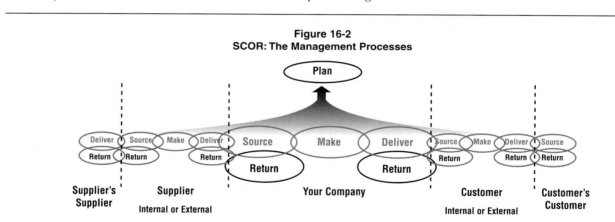

Figure 16-2
SCOR: The Management Processes

Source: Supply-Chain Operations Reference Model, Overview of SCOR Version 8.0, © Copyright 2006, Supply-Chain Council.

---

[3] The presentation of the SCOR framework is based on Supply-Chain Council, "Supply-Chain Operations Reference-model. Overview of SCOR Version 8.0," 2006; and, Peter Bolstorff and Robert Rosenbaum, *Supply Chain Excellence: a Handbook for Dramatic Improvement Using the SCOR Model*, New York: AMACOM, 2003.

[4] This section is based on material included in Douglas M. Lambert, Sebastián J. García-Dastugue and Keely L. Croxton, "An Evaluation of Process-Oriented Supply Chain Management Frameworks," *Journal of Business Logistics*, Vol. 26, No. 1 (2005), pp. 25-51.

Focus

The focus of the two frameworks can be summarized as follows: SCOR focuses on transactional efficiency, while GSCF focuses on relationship management.

The focus of the two frameworks can be summarized as follows: SCOR focuses on transactional efficiency, while GSCF focuses on relationship management. While managers need to aim for transactional efficiency, cost minimization across the supply chain cannot be achieved without managing key relationships. Failure to recognize the value of a relationship orientation will limit supply chain efficiency.

Several of the companies that have helped to develop the GSCF framework are also using SCOR.[5] Some managers find that SCOR is a useful tool for identifying areas of improvement to achieve quick pay-back opportunities that satisfy top-management's desire for cost reductions and asset efficiency. Identifying quick-hits is possible because the SCOR framework involves functions that are more easily integrated, and because the focus is on cost reduction and improved asset utilization. In many companies, opportunities still exist for transactional process improvements that might be found during the implementation of SCOR.

The GSCF framework is more strategic and focuses on increasing long-term shareholder value through cross-functional relationships with key members of the supply chain. The business settings that will tend to favor the implementation of the GSCF framework are those in which the capability to identify, build and maintain business relationships is considered to be a competitive advantage. In many businesses, management has begun to recognize the importance of intangibles in the marketing of products and that to succeed, interactivity, connectivity and ongoing relationships are needed.[6]

An executive summarized his experience working with both frameworks as follows:

> The difference between the SCOR and GSCF approaches lies in the fact that SCOR addresses symptoms through tactics. The GSCF framework provides a strategic approach to address supply chain management processes incorporating the knowledge, expertise and objectives of all functions (Ernie Elliot, Rear Admiral Retired, Supply Corps, USN; VP Supply Chain, xpedx, an International Paper Company).

Strategic Alignment

Each of the GSCF processes is aligned with the corporate strategy and the appropriate functional strategies either directly or indirectly through the customer relationship and supplier relationship management processes. For example, the manufacturing flow management process starts by reviewing the corporate, manufacturing, sourcing, marketing and logistics strategies. This link between the processes, and the corporate and functional strategies is needed in order to assure alignment and make functional activities responsive to the market.[7]

SCOR processes are developed based on the operations strategy.[8] While the

---

[5] The lists of members for both groups are available through the web. The list of members for GSCF: http://fisher.osu.edu/scm/members/index.html and for SCC: http://www.supply-chain.org/html/mlist_nolink.asp

[6] Vargo, Stephen L. and Robert F. Lusch, "Evolving to a New Dominant Logic for Marketing," *Journal of Marketing*, Vol. 68, No. 1 (2004), pp. 1-17.

[7] Day, George S., *Market Driven Strategy*, New York: Free Press, 1999.

[8] Bolstorff, Peter and Robert Rosenbaum, *Supply Chain Excellence: a Handbook for Dramatic Improvement Using the SCOR Model,* New York: AMACOM, 2003.

operations strategy should be developed based on the corporate strategy and be aligned with the other functional strategies,[9] SCOR does not explicitly consider this connection. A disconnect between functional and corporate strategies might jeopardize the organization-wide alignment of resources. Management pursuing the implementation of SCOR and interested in having the model provide the broadest impact should focus on positioning SCOR within the overall corporate strategy. This will help to align resources and goals, and prioritize implementation initiatives that result from the use of the framework.

Breadth of Activities

The GSCF framework is broad in its scope, including activities such as product development, demand generation, relationship management and returns avoidance. Some respond to the model with comments like, "It includes everything." This breadth is intentional. Since the focus of the framework is to provide a structure to maintain stable relationships in the supply chain, the framework provides direction on all the activities that need to be managed in order to identify, develop and maintain key relationships with both customers and suppliers.[10] This breadth is why participation of all the functional areas is so critical in the GSCF framework. The activities included in the eight processes will touch all aspects of managing the business.

In contrast, the scope of the SCOR framework is limited. As stated in the SCOR literature, "SCOR does not attempt to describe every business process or activity, including: sales and marketing (demand generation), research and technology development, product development, and some elements of post-delivery customer support."[11] The activities that are included are those related to the forward and backward movement of the products, and the planning required to efficiently manage these flows.

In some respects, the breadth of the GSCF framework might be both its biggest strength and its biggest weakness. It is a strength because it increases the opportunity for supply chain management to provide value. For instance, if managers implement the returns process as it is suggested in SCOR, they are focused on reverse logistics and might miss avoidance opportunities, such as improving the product or the processes so that there are fewer returns. The GSCF framework includes avoidance as a key part of implementing the returns process, so the potential for providing bottom-line value through the process is increased. As another example, the demand management process of the GSCF framework has a broader scope than the plan process of SCOR. The plan process views demand as an input while in demand management the team works to actively manage demand finding ways to reduce variability.

However, the breadth of the GSCF framework provides some implementation challenges. For some people, the concept of supply chain management has grown

"SCOR does not attempt to describe every business process or activity, including: sales and marketing (demand generation), research and technology development, product development, and some elements of post-delivery customer support."

---

[9] Berry, William L., Terry J. Hill and Jay E. Klompmaker, "Customer-driven manufacturing," *International Journal of Operations & Production Management*, Vol. 15, No. 3 (1995), pp. 4-15.

[10] Lambert, Douglas M., Martha C. Cooper and Janus D. Pagh, "Supply Chain Management: Implementation Issues and Research Opportunities," *The International Journal of Logistics Management*, Vol. 9, No. 2 (1998), pp. 1-19.

[11] Supply-Chain Council, "Supply-Chain Operations Reference-model. Overview of SCOR Version 8.0," 2006.

out of the logistics, production or purchasing function, and it is difficult to shift to this very broad view. The breadth also makes it challenging to start small because all functions are involved and interfaces exist among the eight supply chain management processes. To achieve the full benefits, management should commit to implementing all eight processes. However, if this is not possible, implementing one process at a time can result in enhanced performance. It might also be difficult to manage the interfaces between firms in the supply chain while there is substantial change going on within the focal firm. While the full value of these processes cannot be achieved without including customers and suppliers in the implementation, it is possible to improve the performance of the firm by implementing some of the activities and internal interfaces before implementing the full framework.

Cross-Functional Involvement

SCOR and GSCF are similar in that they both advocate cross-functional involvement and recognize that business processes will not replace corporate functions. However, the number of corporate functions included in each framework is different and the type of cross-functional involvement differs as well.

Because the GSCF framework touches all aspects of the business, it is critical that each process team includes representation from all incumbent functions including, but not limited to, marketing, production, finance, purchasing and logistics.

Because the GSCF framework touches all aspects of the business, it is critical that each process team includes representation from all incumbent functions including, but not limited to, marketing, production, finance, purchasing and logistics. The team members provide their functional expertise and assure that the decisions are the right ones for the whole firm. Figure 16-3 shows examples of how each functional area provides input to each business process. Working in cross-functional teams can be difficult to accomplish.[12] With long histories of a "functional silo" orientation, it is often difficult for management to put together cooperative cross-functional teams that can bring together the necessary functional expertise to successfully develop and implement innovative solutions for the supply chain. Top management has to commit to the vision and reward team activities in order to successfully achieve the cross-functional involvement necessary for the GSCF framework.

In the case of SCOR, the cross-functional involvement is pursued primarily within three functions: logistics, production and purchasing. Figure 16-4 shows what input each function provides into the SCOR processes.[13] Focusing on just three functions might make SCOR easier to implement since in many firms the activities of these three functions are more likely to be somewhat integrated within the corporate structure. The tradeoff is that management is attempting to manage the supply chain without critical input from marketing, finance and research and development. This limited functional involvement can yield sub-par performance and can even result in failed initiatives.

For example, a manufacturer of consumer durable goods implemented a rapid delivery system that provided retailers with deliveries in 24 to 48 hours anywhere in

---

[12] Webber, Sheila S., "Leadership and Trust Facilitating Cross-functional Team Success," *Journal of Management Development*, Vol. 21, No. 3 (2002), pp. 201-214.

[13] Evaluation based on Supply-Chain Council, "Supply-Chain Operations Reference-model. Overview of SCOR Version 8.0," 2006; and, Peter Bolstorff and Robert Rosenbaum, *Supply Chain Excellence: a Handbook for Dramatic Improvement Using the SCOR Model*, New York: AMACOM, 2003.

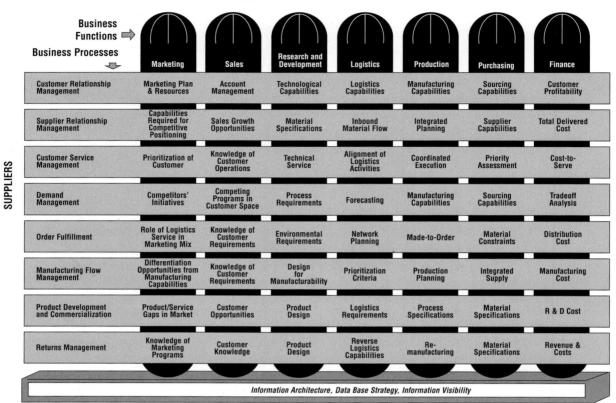

Figure 16-3
Functional Involvement in the GSCF Processes

Business Functions → / Business Processes ↓	Marketing	Sales	Research and Development	Logistics	Production	Purchasing	Finance
Customer Relationship Management	Marketing Plan & Resources	Account Management	Technological Capabilities	Logistics Capabilities	Manufacturing Capabilities	Sourcing Capabilities	Customer Profitability
Supplier Relationship Management	Capabilities Required for Competitive Positioning	Sales Growth Opportunities	Material Specifications	Inbound Material Flow	Integrated Planning	Supplier Capabilities	Total Delivered Cost
Customer Service Management	Prioritization of Customer	Knowledge of Customer Operations	Technical Service	Alignment of Logistics Activities	Coordinated Execution	Priority Assessment	Cost-to-Serve
Demand Management	Competitors' Initiatives	Competing Programs in Customer Space	Process Requirements	Forecasting	Manufacturing Capabilities	Sourcing Capabilities	Tradeoff Analysis
Order Fulfillment	Role of Logistics Service in Marketing Mix	Knowledge of Customer Requirements	Environmental Requirements	Network Planning	Made-to-Order	Material Constraints	Distribution Cost
Manufacturing Flow Management	Differentiation Opportunities from Manufacturing Capabilities	Knowledge of Customer Requirements	Design for Manufacturability	Prioritization Criteria	Production Planning	Integrated Supply	Manufacturing Cost
Product Development and Commercialization	Product/Service Gaps in Market	Customer Opportunities	Product Design	Logistics Requirements	Process Specifications	Material Specifications	R & D Cost
Returns Management	Knowledge of Marketing Programs	Customer Knowledge	Product Design	Reverse Logistics Capabilities	Re-manufacturing	Material Specifications	Revenue & Costs

SUPPLIERS — CUSTOMERS

Information Architecture, Data Base Strategy, Information Visibility

Note: Process sponsorship and ownership must be established to drive the attainment of the supply chain vision and eliminate the functional barriers that artificially separate the process flows.

Source: Adapted from Douglas M. Lambert, Larry C. Guinipero and Gary J. Ridenhower, "Supply Chain Management: A Key to Achieving Business Excellence in the 21st Century," unpublished manuscript.

the United States. The rapid delivery system was designed to enable the retailers to improve service while holding less inventory. Six years later, the company had not seen the inventory reductions and reduced the service promise to 48 to 72 hours. The rapid delivery system never achieved its full potential because the marketing organization still provided the customers with incentives to buy in large volumes.[14] This example shows that failure to manage all the touches might diminish the impact of supply chain initiatives. Failure to include all functions has a cost. Those left out have the potential to maliciously or inadvertently undermine the initiatives. Using the GSCF framework increases the likelihood of success because all functions are involved in the planning and implementation of the initiative.

Failure to include all functions has a cost. Those left out have the potential to maliciously or inadvertently undermine the initiatives.

Process and Performance Benchmarking

In conversations with users of SCOR, a perceived strength is the set of benchmarking tools. The concept of benchmarking has received considerable

[14] Lambert, Douglas M. and Renan Burduroglu, "Measuring and Selling the Value of Logistics," *The International Journal of Logistics Management,* Vol. 11, No. 1 (2000), pp. 1-17.

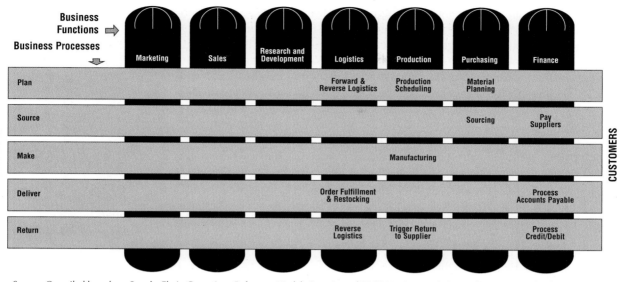

Figure 16-4
Functional Involvement in the SCOR Processes

Business Functions ➡
Business Processes ⬇

| | Marketing | Sales | Research and Development | Logistics | Production | Purchasing | Finance |

SUPPLIERS / **CUSTOMERS**

Plan — Forward & Reverse Logistics | Production Scheduling | Material Planning

Source — Sourcing | Pay Suppliers

Make — Manufacturing

Deliver — Order Fulfillment & Restocking | Process Accounts Payable

Return — Reverse Logistics | Trigger Return to Supplier | Process Credit/Debit

Source: Compiled based on: Supply-Chain Operations Reference Model. Overview of SCOR Version 8.0 © Copyright 2006, Supply-Chain Council; and, Bolstorff, Peter and Robert Rosenbaum, *Supply Chain Excellence: a Handbook for Dramatic Improvement Using the SCOR Model*, New York: AMACOM, 2003.

attention in both the management and research communities.[15] Most consider two types of benchmarking: performance and process benchmarking.[16] Performance benchmarking is about learning how competitors or firms in comparable industries are performing on key operational metrics such as inventory turns or fill rates, while process benchmarking, or what SCOR calls best-practice analysis, is concerned with learning about and duplicating best practices.

To offer assistance with performance benchmarking, the SCC, the organization that leads the development of SCOR, provides a source of data and information compiled from its members. Some managers have found the SCC data to be useful in their benchmarking efforts. However, there are issues related to the accuracy and use of these data.[17] Specifically, SCC collects these data by survey and while they provide very detailed instructions on how the numbers are to be developed, there should be concerns about the effort that managers expend on reworking their organization's data to fit the SCC's specifications.

Some managers have found the SCC data to be useful in their benchmarking efforts.

SCOR users also find value in the SCC's best-practice analysis. In line with the focus of SCOR, this list of best practices includes tools primarily aimed at improving transactional efficiency in the supply chain, such as activity-based

---

[15] Dattakumar, R. and R. Jagadeesh, "A Review of Literature on Benchmarking," *Benchmarking: An International Journal*, Vol. 10, No. 3 (2003), pp. 176-209.

[16] Bhutta, Khurrum S. and Faizul Huq, "Benchmarking - Best Practices: an Integrated Approach," *Benchmarking: an International Journal*, Vol. 6, No. 3 (1999), pp. 176-209.

[17] Hammer, Michael and James Champy, *Reengineering the Corporation: a Manifesto for Business Revolution*, New York, NY: Harper Business, 1993; David Longbottom, "Benchmarking in the UK: an Empirical Study of Practitioners and Academics," *Benchmarking: an International Journal*, Vol. 7, No. 2 (2000), pp. 98-117; Andrew Cox and Ian Thompson, "On the Appropriateness of Benchmarking," *Journal of General Management*, Vol. 23, No. 3 (1998), pp. 1-19; and, Andrew Campbell, "Tailored, Not Benchmarked," *Harvard Business Review*, Vol. 77, No. 2 (1999), pp. 41-47.

costing, advanced-shipping notification, Kanban and supplier certification programs. Information on how to implement these practices can be obtained through the SCC. In this way, the SCC might provide value to those implementing the GSCF framework, as the teams evaluate these best practices in the context of the eight supply chain management processes. For example, CPFR might be a practice implemented in the context of the demand management process. However, some managers find that process benchmarking might stifle creativity.

A drawback to benchmarking best practices is a lack of creativity and the possibility of missing an opportunity to completely change the process. The real strength of the GSCF framework is to start with the objectives and develop strategies and tactics to achieve them in a rapidly changing business environment. The GSCF framework has the potential to create greater value through leading change and/or being the first mover. (Ernie Elliot, Rear Admiral Retired, Supply Corps, USN; VP Supply Chain, xpedx, an International Paper Company).

"The GSCF framework has the potential to create greater value through leading change and/or being the first mover."

To perform process benchmarking using the GSCF framework, management can rely on the assessment tools for each of the eight supply chain management processes. The GSCF processes represent the combined knowledge of the executives that participated in the Forum's meetings over the past 15 years. In other words, the sub-processes and activities are the best practices to successfully manage a business and develop sustained competitive advantages.

Since the implementation of an improvement initiative is costly, management should not pursue one just because a competitor, known or unknown, is doing it. Management should identify to what extent each process needs to be formalized. Assessment tools for the supply chain management processes have been developed.[18] The assessment tools are designed to enable management to evaluate their firms' current business practices in terms of these processes and identify improvement opportunities. The methodology for conducting an assessment using the assessment tools is explained in Chapter 10.

Value Creation

Managers have four ways to create value: increase revenue, reduce operating cost, reduce working capital, and increase asset efficiency. The two frameworks use different approaches to measuring how the efforts of supply chain management can be used to create value.

In the GSCF framework, operational measures are tied to the firm's EVA and to profitability reports for customers and suppliers. Therefore, central to the successful implementation of the GSCF framework is the identification of the revenue implications associated with all activities performed within the firm and by the firm's supply chain members. This will enable the development of profitability reports which provide information about the value that each key supplier provides to the customer as well as the value that the customer provides to each of the key suppliers. The GSCF framework is intended not only to measure cost reduction and increased asset utilization but also to identify the revenue implications from closely managing relationships with key suppliers and customers. For example, including customers in the product development and commercialization process should shorten time to market and yield products that

---

[18] For more information, see Appendices A through H of this chapter.

better meet customer requirements, generating more profit.

Because the objective of SCOR is operational efficiency, the drivers of value creation are focused on cost reductions and improvements in asset utilization. This makes measurement easier because it tends to be less subjective to determine how much will be saved by a particular program than to estimate how a segment of customers will respond to a service improvement, a new marketing effort, or a new product. Also, cost reductions will yield large savings when inefficiencies are present. However, when efficiency levels are high, incremental improvements tend to be smaller. Thus, managers of firms with lower levels of efficiency might find bigger and more immediate benefits from the implementation of SCOR, while those that have achieved high levels of internal efficiency will find more value focusing on managing relationships outside the firm, as prescribed in the GSCF framework. The GSCF framework has the advantage of considering revenue generation as well as cost reduction. For long-term financial success, it is necessary to focus on revenue enhancement.

Summary

While the GSCF and SCOR frameworks both focus on the implementation of cross-functional processes in the supply chain, the GSCF framework is more inclusive since all business functions are involved and a broader set of activities is included. In addition, the GSCF framework provides a mechanism for considering revenue generation, rather than focusing just on cost reductions.

In 2004, the SCC announced the formation of two new special interest groups: the Design-Chain Council and the Customer-Chain Council.[19] The Design-Chain Council developed DCOR, a new reference model with five processes: plan, research, design, integrate and amend.[20] The Customer-Chain Council has not yet released CCOR.[21] The addition of these councils and models appears to indicate that the SCC has reached the conclusion that the SCOR model is an incomplete supply chain management framework. While the creation of these new models has increased the breadth of activities considered by the SCC, they still fall short of presenting a fully integrated approach to managing the supply chain. DCOR focuses on organizing the operational steps of a product development project (similar to part of the operational product development and commercialization process in the GSCF framework). It does not seem to address cross-functional involvement and provides no explicit interfaces with the other reference models nor does it describe the role of the corporate functions in the processes. In addition, the metrics designed in DCOR are focused on cost, labor and asset utilization.[22] It is a major failing to not focus on the profit contribution of new products and product extensions, since they are widely recognized as the lifeblood of the business.[23]

The three reference models, SCOR, DCOR and CCOR, appear to be independent. Scott Stephens (former Chief Technology Officer of the SCC)

---

[19] Supply Chain Council news release, June 4, 2004, available at www.supply-chain.org.

[20] Supply Chain Council news release, May 2006, available at www.supply-chain.org.

[21] According to the Model Development FAQs page of www.supply-chain.org, in December 2007.

[22] Nyere, John, "The Design-Chain Operations Reference-Model", available at www.supply-chain.org.

[23] Crawford, C. Merle, and Anthony Di Benedetto, *New Products Management*, 8th Edition, New York: McGraw-Hill, 2006.

developed an integrated business reference framework and presented it at Supply Chain World 2006.[24] It shows the three models are connected to the business plan but the explicit connections between the three models have not been delineated. The risk is that dividing the supply chain management processes into these three models fractionalizes managers' attention and create larger silos, rather than encouraging cross-functional integration which ventilates the silos.

Guidelines for Implementing the GSCF Framework

All organizations exist in one or more supply chains, but few managers truly understand the underlying business relationships that take place with their key customers and suppliers.[25] Thus, most mangers have a fragmented approach to supply chain management. As managers develop the capabilities for implementing the GSCF framework, they must start with a clear understanding of the current state of their organization with respect to the supply chain management processes and decide how best to lead their organization with implementation of the framework. Managers will require skills and tools that support both assessment of the processes and change management.

Assessment of the Supply Chain Management Processes

Self-assessment has been popularized by various high profile quality awards such as the Deming Prize and Malcolm Baldridge National Quality Award.[26] Self-assessment is a comprehensive, systematic and regular review of an organization's activities and results compared to a model of business excellence.[27] When implementing the GSCF framework, self-assessment allows management to identify the firm's capabilities and areas for improvement.

Self-assessment will be an important tool for managers to use during implementation of the GSCF framework.

Why should managers assess their firm's supply chain management activities prior to implementing the GSCF framework? Self-assessments are valuable when managers sense a performance problem, but lack an understanding of its severity or its source.[28] The self-assessment of a firm's supply chain management processes should serve as an information system for managers as they begin the implementation of the GSCF framework. In addition, the self-assessment should provide the following benefits:[29]

- Measure and target improvements related to the GSCF framework implementation.

---

[24] As shown in: Nyere, John, "The Design-Chain Operations Reference-Model," available at www.supply-chain.org.

[25] Handfield, Robert B. and Ernest L. Nichols, Jr., *Supply Chain Redesign: Converting Your Supply Chain into an Integrated Value System*, Upper Saddle River, NJ: Financial Times Prentice Hall, 2002.

[26] Lascelle, D. and R. Peacock, *Self Assessment for Business Excellence*, London, UK: McGraw Hill, 1996.

[27] European Foundation for Quality Management, 1994.

[28] Ford, Matthew W. and James R. Evans, "Models for Organizational Self-Assessment," *Business Horizons*, Vol. 45, No. 6 (2002), pp. 25-33.

[29] Tennant, Charles and Paul Roberts, "The Creation and Application of a Self-Assessment Process for New Product Introduction," *International Journal of Project Management*, Vol. 21, No. 1 (2003), pp. 77-87; and, Francisco B. Benavent, "TQM Self-Assessment Evolves and Promotes Strategic Learning at Ericsson España S.A.," *Journal of Organizational Excellence*, Vol. 22, No. 2 (2003), pp. 65-75.

- Highlight best practices with respect to the management of successful relationships and implementation of the supply chain management processes.
- Provide strategic direction for implementing the GSCF framework.
- Make inter-divisional comparisons for each business process.
- Facilitate the integration of supply chain management principles into other business practices.
- Foster learning of the GSCF framework in the organization.

Figure 16-5 provides an overview of the activities involved with a self-assessment of a firm's supply chain management processes.[30] The cyclic nature of the self-assessment enables management to improve the organization's position on a continuous basis.[31] Thus, an initial assessment should be performed prior to beginning implementation of the GSCF framework. In addition, there should be periodic assessments during implementation to provide management with an update of the progress being made.

Necessary criteria for a successful self-assessment of the firm's status with respect to implementing the GSCF framework should include:[32]
- Gaining commitment and support from all levels of organization.
- Evaluating actions taken from previous self-assessments.

Figure 16-5
Self-Assessment Process for the GSCF Framework

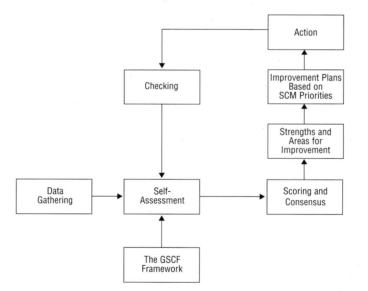

Source: Adapted from F. Balbastre and M. Moreno-Luzon, "Self-assessment Application and Learning in Organizations: A Special Reference to the Ontological Dimension," *Total Quality Management*, Vol. 14, No. 3 (2003), pp. 367-388.

[30] Adapted from F. Balbastre and M. Moreno-Luzon, "Self-assessment Application and Learning in Organizations: A Special Reference to the Ontological Dimension," *Total Quality Management*, Vol. 14, No. 3 (2003), pp. 367-388.

[31] Balbastre, F. and M. Moreno-Luzon, "Self-assessment Application and Learning in Organizations: A Special Reference to the Ontological Dimension," *Total Quality Management*, Vol. 14, No. 3 (2003), pp. 367-388.

[32] Ritchie, L. and B. G. Dale, "Self-assessment Using the Business Excellence Model: A Study of Practice and Process," *International Journal of Production Economics*, Vol. 66, No. 3 (2000), pp. 241-255.

- Increasing awareness of the use of the GSCF framework.
- Incorporating self-assessment into the implementation of the GSCF framework.
- Ensuring that self-assessment is not "added on" to employees existing workload.

Self-assessment will be an important tool for managers to use during implementation of the GSCF framework. Management could use the GSCF assessment tool or consider other options. Managers wishing to use other methods of self-assessment should consider the following questions:[33]

- Is the model from a conceptual domain similar to the area requiring assessment?
- Does the model relate to experience and real-life events?
- Does the model allow managers to understand process strengths and weaknesses, and guide them toward areas that need corrective action or improvement?
- Does the model's affiliation lend legitimacy to the model, which will enhance the self-assessment initiative?
- Does the model improve the probability of accurate conclusions and effective actions stemming from the self-assessment?

The methodology that was designed to conduct an assessment of one or more of the GSCF supply chain management processes is described in detail in Chapter 10.

Change Management

Implementing the GSCF framework will require managers to be skilled in the art of change management. While Chapter 13 provides specific steps for implementing and sustaining the supply chain management processes, it is also important for management to understand how to effectively create an environment for change within their firms. Several established change models are available to guide and instruct managers as they implement a change.[34] Probably the most well known is Kotter's strategic eight-step model for transforming organizations. This section provides a brief description of the model and provides guidance to managers as they lead organizational change focused on implementing the GSCF framework.

Implementing the GSCF framework will require managers to be skilled in the art of change management.

Kotter's model is based on a study of over 100 organizations varying in size and industry type. The model is focused strategically and is designed to help managers avoid mistakes when implementing change. The two key lessons from the model are that change goes through a series of phases, each lasting a considerable amount of time, and that critical mistakes in any of the phases can have a negative impact on the momentum of change. The eight steps of Kotter's model for transforming an organization are as follows:[35]

---

[33] Adapted from Ford, Matthew W. and James R. Evans, "Models for Organizational Self-Assessment," *Business Horizons*, Vol. 45, No. 6 (2002), pp. 25-33.

[34] See for example: Jick, T., *Implementing Change*, Note 9-191-114, Boston, MA:Harvard Business School Press, 1991; and, John P. Kotter, "Leading Change: Why Transformation Efforts Fail," *Harvard Business Review*, Vol. 74, No. 2 (1995), pp. 59-65.

[35] Mento, Anthony J., Raymond M. Jones, and Walter Dirndorfer, "A Change Management Process: Grounded in both Theory and Practice," *Journal of Change Management*, Vol. 3, No. 1 (2002), pp. 45-59.

- Establishing a sense of urgency.
- Forming a powerful guiding coalition.
- Creating a vision.
- Communicating the vision.
- Empowering others to act on the vision.
- Planning for and creating short-term wins.
- Consolidating improvements and producing still more change.
- Institutionalizing new approaches.

Establishing a sense of urgency. The establishment of a sense of urgency is essential because getting a change program started requires the enthusiastic cooperation of many individuals within the firm.[36] This is especially true when implementing the GSCF framework. Each of the eight supply chain management processes requires the support of all functions within a firm, as well as customers and suppliers. According to Kotter, the urgency rate within the organization is right when about 75% of a company's management is honestly convinced that business-as-usual is totally unacceptable.[37] Thus, when implementing one of the GSCF processes, management must build a compelling case for why change is needed. In addition, management must build this compelling case for the key supply chain members beyond the walls of the firm. This is best achieved by demonstrating how financial performance or competitive positioning is being affected negatively by the current system. The previous chapters provide examples of how each process can be tied back to financial performance measures such as EVA. In order to build a case, management must identify the financial consequences of not changing. HP Latin America has used the assessment process described in Chapter 10 as a starting point for building a sense of urgency to improve the demand management process and the order fulfillment process.

In order to build a case, management must identify the financial consequences of not changing.

Forming a powerful guiding coalition. Forming a powerful guiding coalition requires active support from the CEO level and a cross-functional leadership team. While a small group or team can begin the implementation of the GSCF framework, they will need the active involvement of upper management from all of the functions. Senior management needs to establish a guiding coalition, help the process team(s) develop a shared assessment of their organization's problems and opportunities, and create a minimum level of trust and communication. Moen Inc. began implementation of the GSCF order fulfillment process with their team launch program. This structured program provided an opportunity for a diverse group of cross-functional representatives to build momentum for the task of changing the firm's order fulfillment process to one that is in line with the GSCF framework. The off-site meeting launching the program allowed these managers who typically worked within their own functions to develop a level of trust and commitment with people from other functions. The steps for implementing the processes, highlighted in Chapter 13, specifically address this critical aspect of change management.

---

[36] Kotter, John P., "Leading Change: Why Transformation Efforts Fail," *Harvard Business Review*, Vol. 74, No. 2 (1995), pp. 59-65.

[37] Kotter, John P., "Leading Change: Why Transformation Efforts Fail," *Harvard Business Review*, Vol. 74, No. 2 (1995), pp. 59-65.

Creating a vision. The creation of a vision clarifies the direction in which an organization needs to move.[38] The chapters in this book can serve as an effective starting point for creating a vision within your organization. For example, management at Moen Inc. handed out copies of the order fulfillment process chapter to each member of the cross-functional team charged with developing the new process. The team members used significant time within the launch meeting to discuss the chapter and clarify the team's vision of where they wanted to move the order fulfillment process. Kotter suggests that a useful rule of thumb is to reach a point where you can communicate the vision to someone in five minutes or less and get a reaction that signifies both understanding and interest.[39] At Moen, having the key team members review the chapter and discuss the process enabled them to develop an increased ability to communicate the vision to others.

Communicating the vision. Communicating the vision requires that management goes beyond the typical mass e-mail announcing that a cross-functional team is developing a new approach to supply chain management. The successful change efforts leverage all existing communication channels to broadcast the vision. This could include newsletters, meetings, and training activities. Coca-Cola has developed a newsletter that specifically focuses on supplier relationship management and the successes that have been achieved implementing this process. One potential approach for communicating the vision throughout the organization is to provide training in the GSCF framework for employees in every business function. Several organizations have made investments in training programs designed specifically to communicate the GSCF process-based vision of supply chain management to employees. In addition, upper management must focus on "walking the talk." Managers who promote the values of the process-based, cross-functional approach of the GSCF framework must not revert to the functional perspective in their daily activities such as rewarding functional performance independently. Nothing undermines change more than behavior by high level individuals that is inconsistent with their words.[40]

Empowering others to act on the vision. Empowering others to act on the vision requires that employees are emboldened to try new approaches, to develop creative ideas, and to provide leadership. The only constraint is that the actions must fit within the vision established by the GSCF framework. Ultimately, the more people involved, the better the chances of succeeding with the implementation. Sharing the supply chain management vision requires not only communication, but the removal of potential obstacles to that vision. These obstacles can take the form of individuals, organizational structures, performance-appraisal systems, or job categories to name a few. As an example, management at Colgate-Palmolive wanted to have more involvement of a key supplier in the product development and commercialization process, but the existing organizational structure at the supplier was an obstacle. The supplier's account representative had one of Colgate's major competitors as a customer making it difficult to involve her on a

Nothing undermines change more than behavior by high level individuals that is inconsistent with their words.

---

[38] Kotter, John P., "Leading Change: Why Transformation Efforts Fail," *Harvard Business Review*, Vol. 74, No. 2 (1995), pp. 59-65.

[39] Kotter, John P., "Leading Change: Why Transformation Efforts Fail," *Harvard Business Review*, Vol. 74, No. 2 (1995), pp. 59-65.

[40] Kotter, John P., "Leading Change: Why Transformation Efforts Fail," *Harvard Business Review*, Vol. 74, No. 2 (1995), pp. 59-65.

product development and commercialization team. At Colgate's request the supplier assigned a dedicated account representative which provided the level of trust and safeguards required to include the supplier on the team. In addition, the supplier agreed that the R&D people who worked on Colgate's new product development would not work on projects with Colgate's direct competitors.

Planning for and creating short-term wins. Planning for and creating short-term wins involves managers charged with implementing the GSCF processes to quickly identify areas where the implementation can provide examples of improvement. Implementing the GSCF framework or an individual process within the framework will take time. Thus, implementation efforts might lose momentum if there are no short-term goals to meet and celebrate. Without short-term wins, people might give up or join the ranks of those who have been resisting change. As part of the management team's efforts to implement the order fulfillment process at Moen Inc., the team focused initially on documenting improvements in the existing process that were achieved as part of the implementation. These improvements demonstrated that the team was making measurable progress and enabled them to reinforce the value of the implementation. The team leadership also drove the team to increase the expectations for improvements over time in order to expand the management's perspective beyond process improvement to the implementation of the complete process. Coca-Cola has used some of the mapping techniques described in Chapter 11 to realize short-term improvements that help support their process implementation efforts.

Consolidating improvements and producing still more change. Managers must consolidate improvements and produce more change. Instead of declaring victory, leaders of successful change efforts use the credibility afforded by the short-term wins to tackle even bigger problems.[41] Two key aspects of this step for those implementing the GSCF framework are to realize that the changes will not take place overnight and that the hiring, promoting and development of employees must be supportive of the new vision. The natural tendency of change teams is to want to see quick implementation of the new framework. This can lead to failure of the effort because team members become frustrated with the pace of change. Leadership should look continuously to reinvigorate the process with new projects, themes and change agents that are consistent with the overall goal of implementing the GSCF framework.

Institutionalizing new approaches. Focusing on institutionalizing new approaches involves articulating connections between the new supply chain management approach and overall corporate success. In addition, there needs to be a means for ensuring leadership development and succession so that the GSCF framework reaches its full potential. It is important that the GSCF framework is seen throughout the organization as the way things are done. Thus, as progress is made implementing the framework, it is critical that the connection with improved corporate performance is communicated up and down the organization. As part of this, employee reward systems should include some compensation based on the financial impact of employees' process activities and not just their functional activities.

...employee reward systems should include some compensation based on the financial impact of employees' process activities and not just their functional activities.

---

[41] Kotter, John P., "Leading Change: Why Transformation Efforts Fail," *Harvard Business Review*, Vol. 74, No. 2 (1995), pp. 59-65.

Conclusions

In this chapter, we compared the GSCF framework with the SCOR framework developed by the Supply-Chain Council. Both frameworks acknowledge that the supply chain is a network of companies, or independent business units, from end-users to original suppliers and suggest the implementation of cross-functional business processes. However, the approach to business process implementation prescribed by SCOR and GSCF differ and they represent distinct ways of managing the business; SCOR is focused on achieving transactional efficiency within the realm of purchasing, manufacturing, and distribution; while GSCF focuses on relationship management and integrating all activities within the firm and with key members of the supply chain.

Guidelines for implementing the GSCF supply chain management framework were presented. Since change management is particularly important as companies implement supply chain management, the chapter ended with a section on this topic.

At the Spring 2004 meeting of The Global Supply Chain Forum, a series of break-out sessions were devoted to the topic "the supply chain of the future". At the end of the day, the conclusion of the group was that when an organization's management had successfully implemented all eight of the SCM processes, they would have achieved the supply chain of the future and would be able to respond to whatever challenges the business might face. Where is your company in terms of successful implementation of cross-functional business processes? In order to create the most value for the company's shareholders and the whole supply chain including consumers/end-users, management must take action to integrate the supply chain. The time for action is now.

In order to create the most value for the company's shareholders and the whole supply chain including consumers/end-users, management must take action to integrate the supply chain. The time for action is now.

Assessment Tool for the Customer Relationship Management Process

General Information

This assessment tool is designed to identify opportunities in your organization's customer relationship management process. It highlights important aspects of the strategic and operational sub-processes within customer relationship management. Management can use this tool to identify process strengths and weaknesses, and then focus their efforts on those areas where improvement efforts will drive the most benefits.

Directions

A cross-functional management team should complete each item in the assessment, the score, the importance, and the justification.

Score: The score for the item is assessed on a 5-point scale.

1 = you agree with the statement written in column 1.

2 = you believe the organization is somewhere between the statements in columns 1 and 3.

3 = you agree with the statement written in column 3.

4 = you believe the organization is somewhere between the statements in columns 3 and 5.

5 = you agree with the statement written in column 5.

The scale includes descriptions for 1, 3, and 5. Intermediate columns are included to accommodate ratings that fall between the scale points. Check the box corresponding to the score of the item. If the respondent is not sure how to score the item, check the "Don't Know" box.

Importance: The importance of the item is assessed on a 3-point scale.

3 = Critical: Item is essential for the success of the customer relationship management process within your organization.

2 = Important: Item is important but not essential for the success of the customer relationship management process within your organization.

1 = Minor Importance: Item is of minor importance for the success of the customer relationship management process within your organization.

Justification: Provide justification for your score and importance rating for each item in the space provided, i.e., why did you score the items the way you did?

Strategic Sub-Processes

S–1. Review Corporate and Marketing Strategy

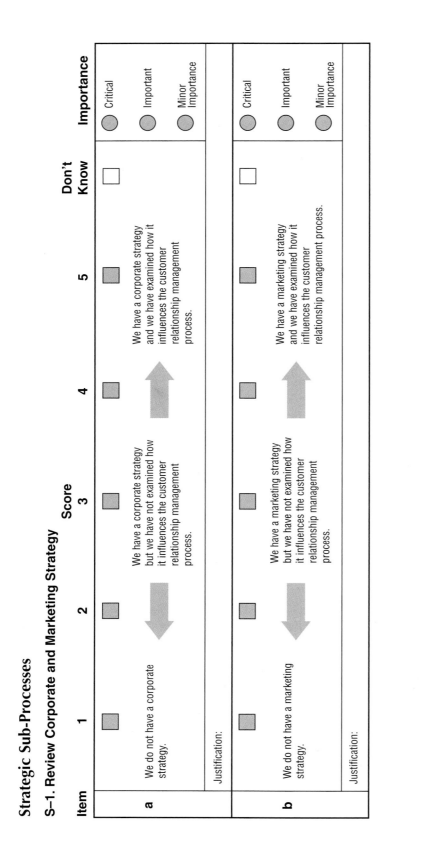

Item	1	2	Score 3	4	5	Don't Know	Importance
a	☐ We do not have a corporate strategy.	☐	☐ We have a corporate strategy but we have not examined how it influences the customer relationship management process.	☐	☐ We have a corporate strategy and we have examined how it influences the customer relationship management process.	☐	● Critical ● Important ● Minor Importance
Justification:							
b	☐ We do not have a marketing strategy.	☐	☐ We have a marketing strategy but we have not examined how it influences the customer relationship management process.	☐	☐ We have a marketing strategy and we have examined how it influences the customer relationship management process.	☐	● Critical ● Important ● Minor Importance
Justification:							

S-2. Identify Criteria for Segmenting Customers

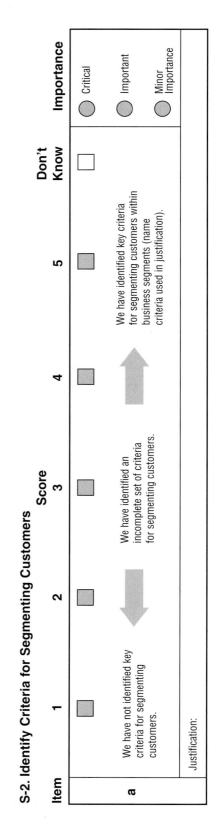

Item	1	2	Score 3	4	5	Don't Know	Importance
a	☐ We have not identified key criteria for segmenting customers.	☐	☐ We have identified an incomplete set of criteria for segmenting customers.	☐	☐ We have identified key criteria for segmenting customers within business segments (name criteria used in justification).	☐	● Critical ● Important ● Minor Importance
Justification:							

S-3. Provide Guidelines for the Degree of Customization in the Product and Service Agreement (PSA)

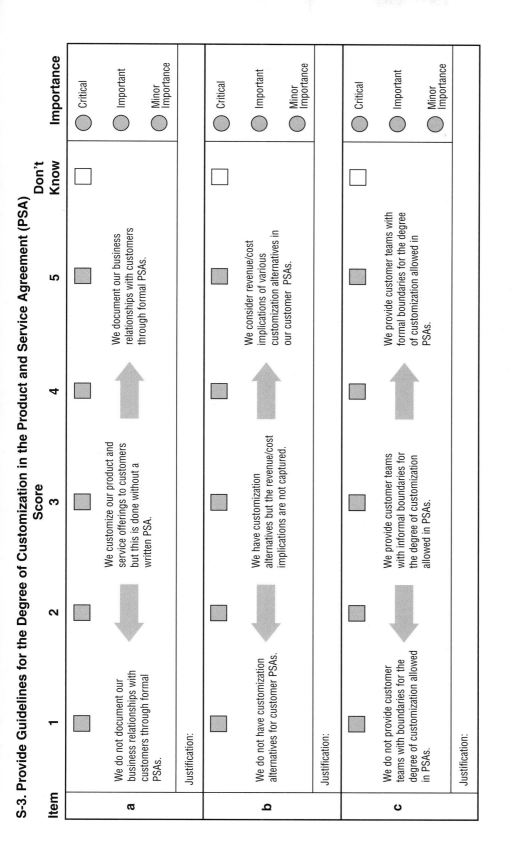

Item	1	2	3	4	5	Don't Know	Importance
a	We do not document our business relationships with customers through formal PSAs.		We customize our product and service offerings to customers but this is done without a written PSA.		We document our business relationships with customers through formal PSAs.		Critical / Important / Minor Importance
Justification:							
b	We do not have customization alternatives for customer PSAs.		We have customization alternatives but the revenue/cost implications are not captured.		We consider revenue/cost implications of various customization alternatives in our customer PSAs.		Critical / Important / Minor Importance
Justification:							
c	We do not provide customer teams with boundaries for the degree of customization allowed in PSAs.		We provide customer teams with informal boundaries for the degree of customization allowed in PSAs.		We provide customer teams with formal boundaries for the degree of customization allowed in PSAs.		Critical / Important / Minor Importance
Justification:							

S-4. Develop Framework of Metrics

Item	Score 1	2	3	4	5	Don't Know	Importance
a	☐ We do not have formal customer relationship management metrics.	☐	☐ We do not relate our customer relationship management metrics to financial performance.	☐	☐ We have formal metrics focused on customer relationship management and we understand how they impact our firm's EVA.	☐	◯ Critical ◯ Important ◯ Minor Importance
Justification:							
b	☐ We do not have formal performance goals for customer relationship management.	☐	☐ We have formal performance goals relating to customer relationship management that are communicated internally.	☐	☐ We have formal performance goals relating to customer relationship management that are communicated throughout the firm and to customers.	☐	◯ Critical ◯ Important ◯ Minor Importance
Justification:							
c	☐ We do not have profitability reports by customer.	☐	☐ We have customer profitability reports but they contain many cost allocations.	☐	☐ We have the capability to measure customer profitability on a revenue minus avoidable cost basis.	☐	◯ Critical ◯ Important ◯ Minor Importance
Justification:							
d	☐ We do not know what impact we have on a customer's profitability.	☐	☐ We have a limited capability to measure the impact our business has on a customer's profitability.	☐	☐ We have the capability to measure the impact our business has on a customer's profitability.	☐	◯ Critical ◯ Important ◯ Minor Importance
Justification:							

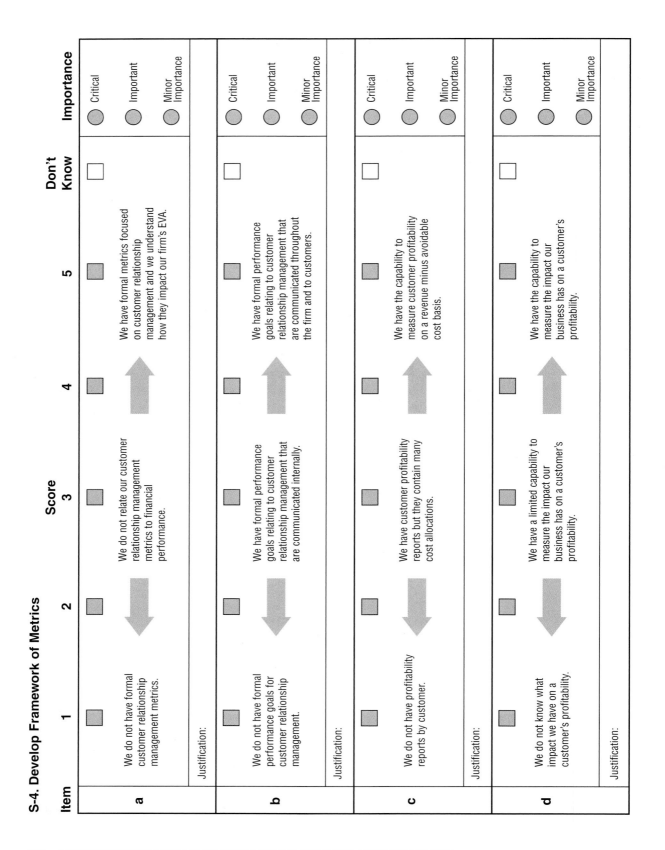

S-4. Develop Framework of Metrics (continued)

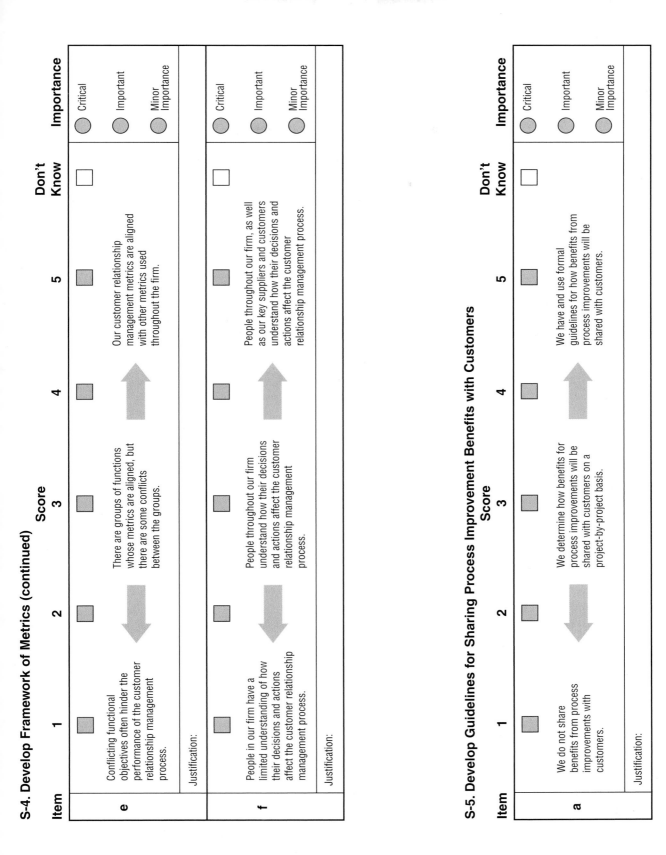

Item	1	2	Score 3	4	5	Don't Know	Importance
e	Conflicting functional objectives often hinder the performance of the customer relationship management process.		There are groups of functions whose metrics are aligned, but there are some conflicts between the groups.		Our customer relationship management metrics are aligned with other metrics used throughout the firm.	☐	● Critical ● Important ● Minor Importance
Justification:							
f	People in our firm have a limited understanding of how their decisions and actions affect the customer relationship management process.		People throughout our firm understand how their decisions and actions affect the customer relationship management process.		People throughout our firm, as well as our key suppliers and customers understand how their decisions and actions affect the customer relationship management process.	☐	● Critical ● Important ● Minor Importance
Justification:							

S-5. Develop Guidelines for Sharing Process Improvement Benefits with Customers

Item	1	2	Score 3	4	5	Don't Know	Importance
a	We do not share benefits from process improvements with customers.		We determine how benefits for process improvements will be shared with customers on a project-by-project basis.		We have and use formal guidelines for how benefits from process improvements will be shared with customers.	☐	● Critical ● Important ● Minor Importance
Justification:							

Operational Sub-Processes

O-1. Segment Customers

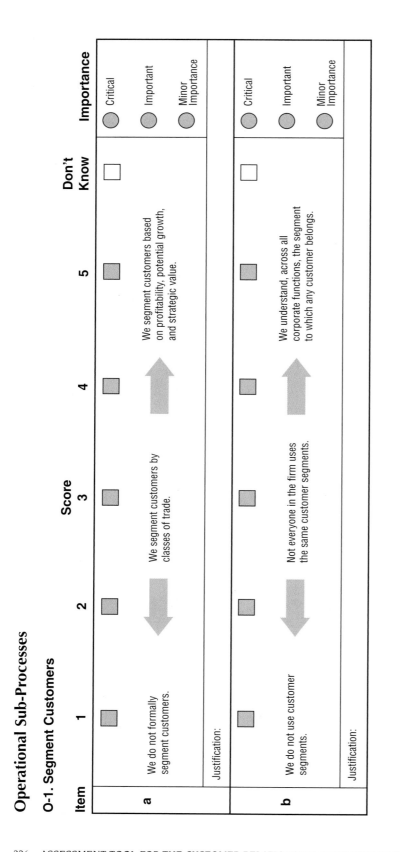

Item	Score					Don't Know	Importance
	1	2	3	4	5		

a
- (Score 1) We do not formally segment customers.
- (Score 3) We segment customers by classes of trade.
- (Score 5) We segment customers based on profitability, potential growth, and strategic value.

Importance: ○ Critical ○ Important ○ Minor Importance

Justification:

b
- (Score 1) We do not use customer segments.
- (Score 3) Not everyone in the firm uses the same customer segments.
- (Score 5) We understand, across all corporate functions, the segment to which any customer belongs.

Importance: ○ Critical ○ Important ○ Minor Importance

Justification:

O-2. Prepare the Account/Segment Management Team

Item	Score					Don't Know	Importance

Item	1	2	3	4	5	Don't Know	Importance
a	All customers have an assigned sales representative who manages the account independently with infrequent interaction from other functions.	➡	When the sales representative identifies problems or opportunities that require functional expertise, they seek out the appropriate person for an answer.		We have an account manager and a cross-functional team assigned to key customers and segments of other customers.	☐	◕ Critical ◕ Important ◕ Minor Importance
	Comment:						
b	We do not have cross-functional customer teams.	➡	We have an informal process for determining cross-functional membership for customer teams.		We have a formal process for determining cross-functional membership for customer teams.	☐	◕ Critical ◕ Important ◕ Minor Importance
	Justification:						

O-3. Internally Review the Accounts

Item	Score					Don't Know	Importance

Item	1	2	3	4	5	Don't Know	Importance
a	We do not have a process for internally reviewing customers to look for opportunities.	➡	We have a process for internally reviewing customers to look for opportunities, but it is not cross-functional.		We have a cross-functional process for internally reviewing customers to look for opportunities.	☐	◕ Critical ◕ Important ◕ Minor Importance
	Justification:						

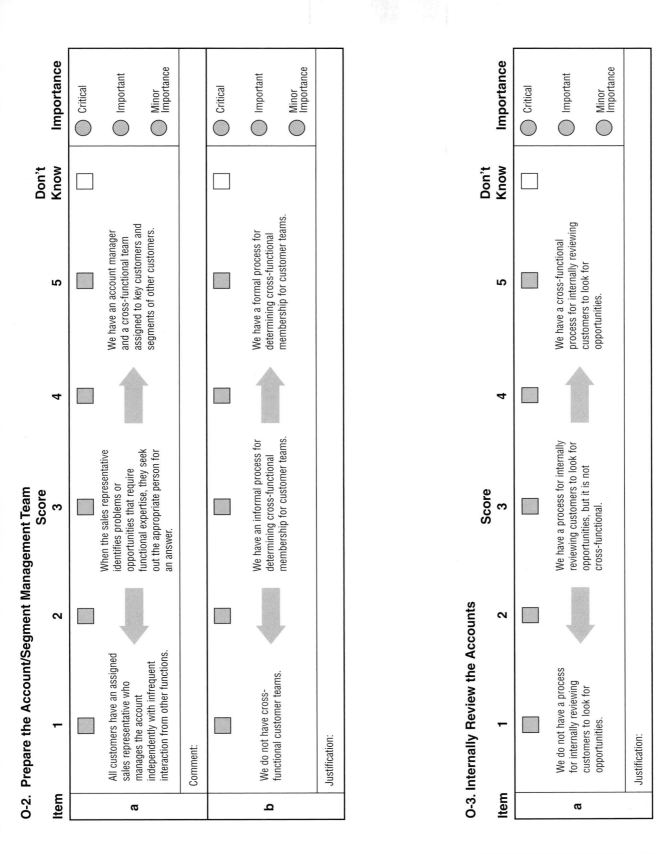

O-4. Identify Opportunities with the Accounts

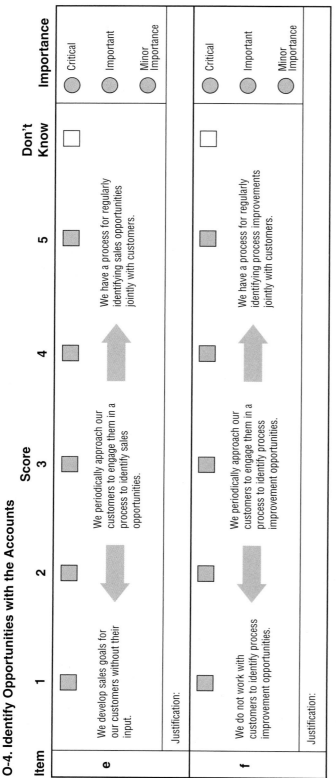

Item		Score					Don't Know	Importance
	1	2	3	4	5			
e	☐	☐	☐	☐	☐		☐	○ Critical ○ Important ○ Minor Importance

We develop sales goals for our customers without their input.

We periodically approach our customers to engage them in a process to identify sales opportunities.

We have a process for regularly identifying sales opportunities jointly with customers.

Justification:

| f | ☐ | ☐ | ☐ | ☐ | ☐ | | ☐ | ○ Critical ○ Important ○ Minor Importance |

We do not work with customers to identify process improvement opportunities.

We periodically approach our customers to engage them in a process to identify process improvement opportunities.

We have a process for regularly identifying process improvements jointly with customers.

Justification:

O-5. Develop the Product and Service Agreement

Item		Score					Don't Know	Importance

a

1	2	3	4	5

We do not develop formal PSAs for our customers.

⬇

We have standard PSAs that are given to all customers.

⬆

We customize PSAs for each key customer or customer segment based on their needs and our profit goals.

Importance:
- ⬤ Critical
- ⬤ Important
- ⬤ Minor Importance

Justification:

b

We do not have PSAs with our customers.

⬇

PSAs are communicated across corporate functions but employees do not execute their tasks differently based on them.

⬆

PSAs are communicated across corporate functions and employees execute their tasks differently based on the features of the PSAs.

Importance:
- ⬤ Critical
- ⬤ Important
- ⬤ Minor Importance

Justification:

O-6. Implement the Product and Service Agreement

Item		Score					Don't Know	Importance

a

1	2	3	4	5

Management efforts are focused on the fulfillment of each business transaction and handling emergency situations.

⬇

Based on the PSA, improvement projects are identified and implemented on an ad-hoc basis.

⬆

Based on the PSA, action items are developed and implementation is monitored jointly at regular meetings with customers.

Importance:
- ⬤ Critical
- ⬤ Important
- ⬤ Minor Importance

Justification:

O-7. Measure Performance and Generate Profitability Reports

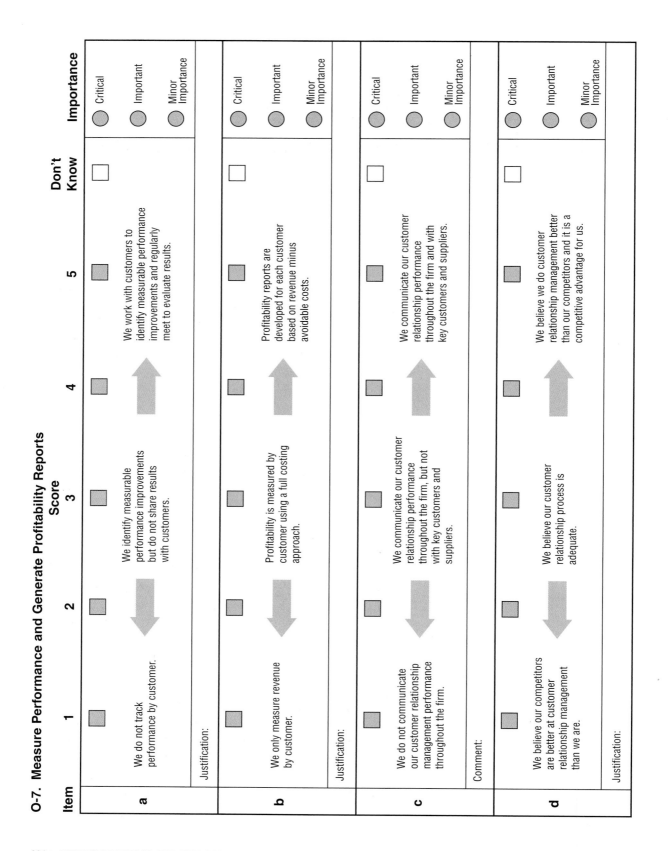

Item		Score					Don't Know	Importance
		1	2	3	4	5		

a — We do not track performance by customer. → We identify measurable performance improvements but do not share results with customers. → We work with customers to identify measurable performance improvements and regularly meet to evaluate results.
Importance: ● Critical ● Important ● Minor Importance

Justification:

b — We only measure revenue by customer. → Profitability is measured by customer using a full costing approach. → Profitability reports are developed for each customer based on revenue minus avoidable costs.
Importance: ● Critical ● Important ● Minor Importance

Justification:

c — We do not communicate our customer relationship management performance throughout the firm. → We communicate our customer relationship performance throughout the firm, but not with key customers and suppliers. → We communicate our customer relationship performance throughout the firm and with key customers and suppliers.
Importance: ● Critical ● Important ● Minor Importance

Comment:

d — We believe our competitors are better at customer relationship management than we are. → We believe our customer relationship process is adequate. → We believe we do customer relationship management better than our competitors and it is a competitive advantage for us.
Importance: ● Critical ● Important ● Minor Importance

Justification:

APPENDIX B: Assessment Tool for the Supplier Relationship Management Process

General Information

This assessment tool is designed to identify opportunities in your organization's supplier relationship management process. It highlights important aspects of the strategic and operational sub-processes within supplier relationship management. Management can use this tool to identify process strengths and weaknesses, and then focus their efforts on those areas where improvement efforts will drive the most benefits.

Directions

A cross-functional management team should complete each item in the assessment, the score, the importance, and the justification.

Score: The score for the item is assessed on a 5-point scale.

1 = you agree with the statement written in column 1.

2 = you believe the organization is somewhere between the statements in columns 1 and 3.

3 = you agree with the statement written in column 3.

4 = you believe the organization is somewhere between the statements in columns 3 and 5.

5 = you agree with the statement written in column 5.

The scale includes descriptions for 1, 3, and 5. Intermediate columns are included to accommodate ratings that fall between the scale points. Check the box corresponding to the score of the item. If the respondent is not sure how to score the item, check the "Don't Know" box.

Importance: The importance of the item is assessed on a 3-point scale.

3 = Critical: Item is essential for the success of the supplier relationship management process within your organization.

2 = Important: Item is important but not essential for the success of the supplier relationship management process within your organization.

1 = Minor Importance: Item is of minor importance for the success of the supplier relationship management process within your organization.

Justification: Provide justification for your score and importance rating for each item in the space provided, i.e., why did you score the items the way you did?

Strategic Sub-Processes

S–1. Review Corporate, Marketing, Manufacturing and Sourcing Strategies

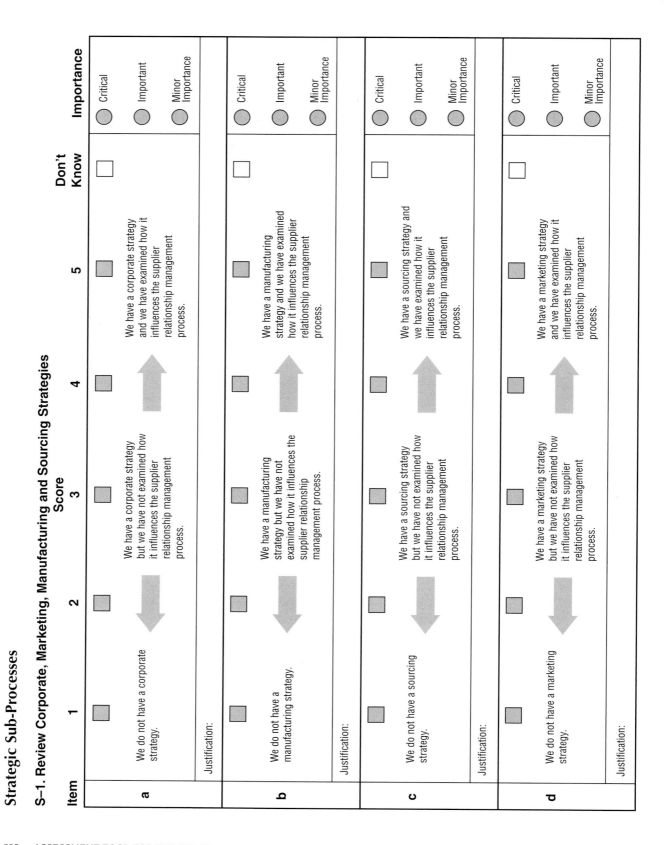

Item	1	2	3	4	5	Don't Know	Importance
a	We do not have a corporate strategy.		We have a corporate strategy but we have not examined how it influences the supplier relationship management process.		We have a corporate strategy and we have examined how it influences the supplier relationship management process.		◐ Critical / ◐ Important / ◐ Minor Importance
	Justification:						
b	We do not have a manufacturing strategy.		We have a manufacturing strategy but we have not examined how it influences the supplier relationship management process.		We have a manufacturing strategy and we have examined how it influences the supplier relationship management process.		◐ Critical / ◐ Important / ◐ Minor Importance
	Justification:						
c	We do not have a sourcing strategy.		We have a sourcing strategy but we have not examined how it influences the supplier relationship management process.		We have a sourcing strategy and we have examined how it influences the supplier relationship management process.		◐ Critical / ◐ Important / ◐ Minor Importance
	Justification:						
d	We do not have a marketing strategy.		We have a marketing strategy but we have not examined how it influences the supplier relationship management process.		We have a marketing strategy and we have examined how it influences the supplier relationship management process.		◐ Critical / ◐ Important / ◐ Minor Importance
	Justification:						

S-2. Identify Criteria for Segmenting Suppliers

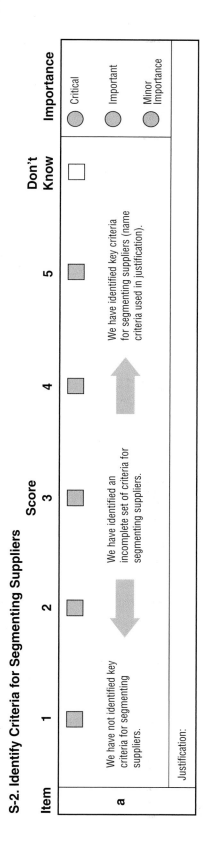

Item	1	2	3	4	5	Don't Know	Importance

Score

	1	2	3	4	5	Don't Know	Importance

a

We have not identified key criteria for segmenting suppliers.

We have identified an incomplete set of criteria for segmenting suppliers.

We have identified key criteria for segmenting suppliers (name criteria used in justification).

Critical
Important
Minor Importance

Justification:

S-3. Provide Guidelines for the Degree of Customization in the Product and Service Agreement

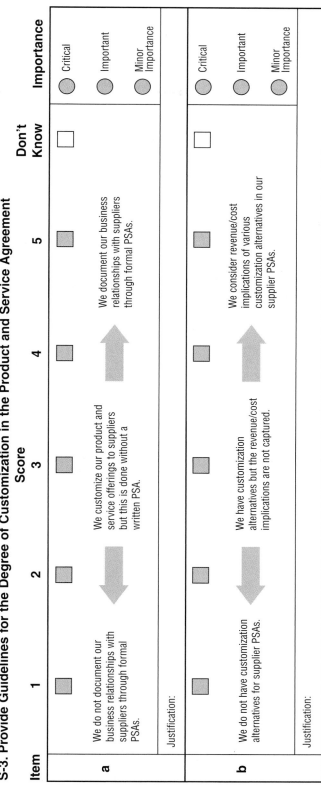

Score

Item	1	2	3	4	5	Don't Know	Importance

a

We do not document our business relationships with suppliers through formal PSAs.

We customize our product and service offerings to suppliers but this is done without a written PSA.

We document our business relationships with suppliers through formal PSAs.

Critical
Important
Minor Importance

Justification:

b

We do not have customization alternatives for supplier PSAs.

We have customization alternatives but the revenue/cost implications are not captured.

We consider revenue/cost implications of various customization alternatives in our supplier PSAs.

Critical
Important
Minor Importance

Justification:

S-3. Provide Guidelines for the Degree of Customization in the Product and Service Agreement (continued)

Item	1	2	Score 3	4	5	Don't Know	Importance
c	We do not provide supplier teams with boundaries for the degree of customization desired in PSAs.		We provide supplier teams with informal boundaries for the degree of customization desired in PSAs.		We provide supplier teams with formal boundaries for the degree of customization desired in PSAs.	☐	◯ Critical ◯ Important ◯ Minor Importance
Justification:							

S-4. Develop Framework of Metrics

Item	1	2	Score 3	4	5	Don't Know	Importance
a	We do not have formal supplier relationship management metrics.		We do not relate our supplier relationship management metrics to financial performance.		We have formal metrics focused on supplier relationship management and we understand how they impact our firm's EVA.	☐	◯ Critical ◯ Important ◯ Minor Importance
Justification:							
b	We do not have formal performance goals for supplier relationship management.		We have formal performance goals relating to supplier relationship management that are communicated internally.		We have formal performance goals relating to supplier relationship management that are communicated throughout the firm and to suppliers.	☐	◯ Critical ◯ Important ◯ Minor Importance
Justification:							

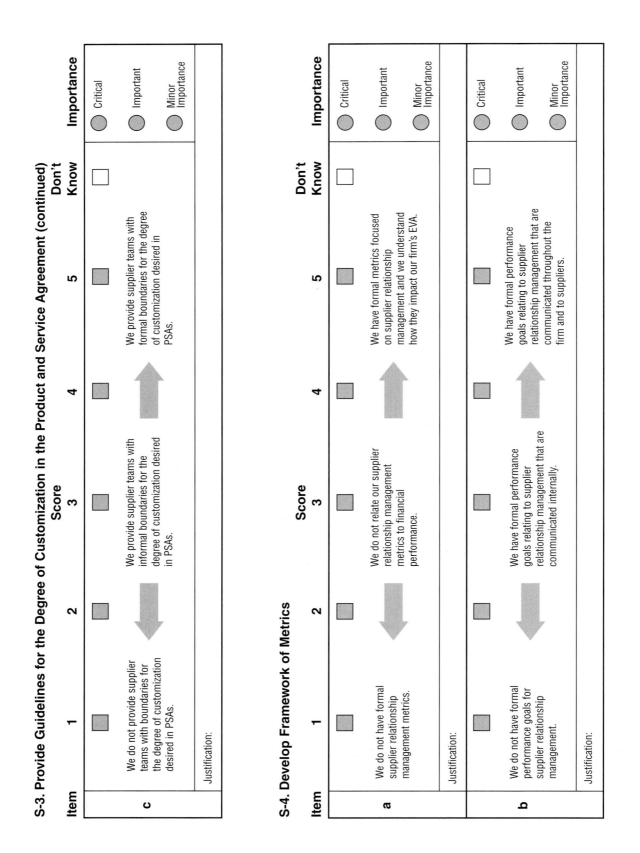

S-4. Develop Framework of Metrics (continued)

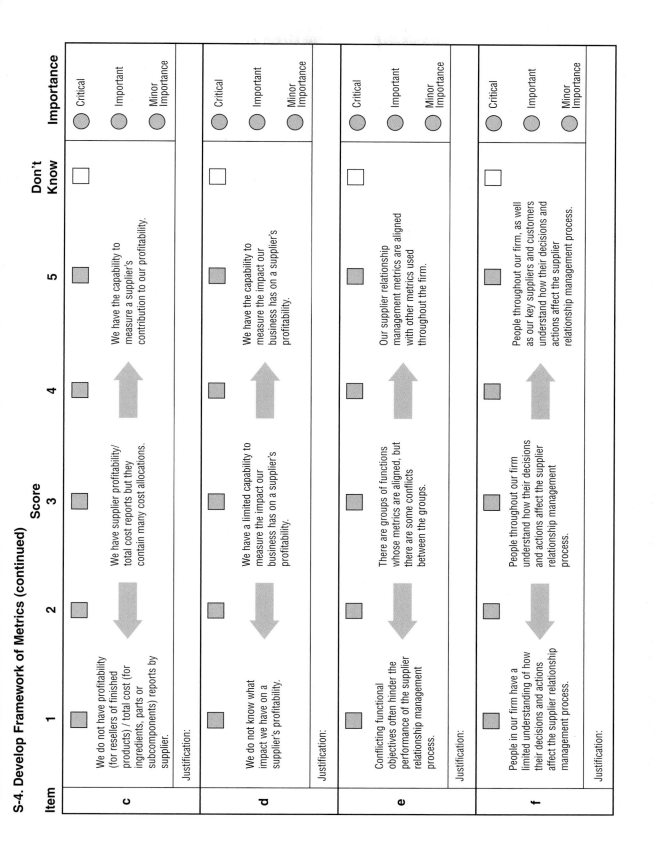

Item	Score 1	2	3	4	5	Don't Know	Importance

c

Score 1: We do not have profitability (for resellers of finished products) / total cost (for ingredients, parts or subcomponents) reports by supplier.

Score 3: We have supplier profitability/total cost reports but they contain many cost allocations.

Score 5: We have the capability to measure a supplier's contribution to our profitability.

Importance: ○ Critical ○ Important ○ Minor Importance

Justification:

d

Score 1: We do not know what impact we have on a supplier's profitability.

Score 3: We have a limited capability to measure the impact our business has on a supplier's profitability.

Score 5: We have the capability to measure the impact our business has on a supplier's profitability.

Importance: ○ Critical ○ Important ○ Minor Importance

Justification:

e

Score 1: Conflicting functional objectives often hinder the performance of the supplier relationship management process.

Score 3: There are groups of functions whose metrics are aligned, but there are some conflicts between the groups.

Score 5: Our supplier relationship management metrics are aligned with other metrics used throughout the firm.

Importance: ○ Critical ○ Important ○ Minor Importance

Justification:

f

Score 1: People in our firm have a limited understanding of how their decisions and actions affect the supplier relationship management process.

Score 3: People throughout our firm understand how their decisions and actions affect the supplier relationship management process.

Score 5: People throughout our firm, as well as our key suppliers and customers understand how their decisions and actions affect the supplier relationship management process.

Importance: ○ Critical ○ Important ○ Minor Importance

Justification:

S-5. Develop Guidelines for Sharing Process Improvement Benefits with Suppliers

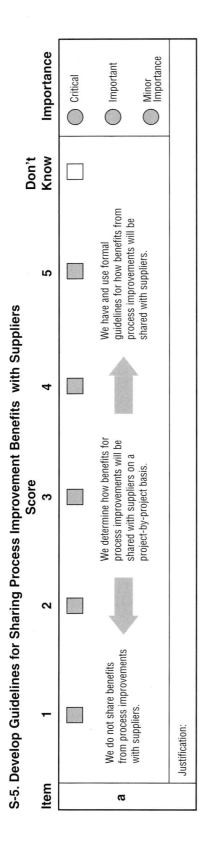

Item	Score 1	2	3	4	5	Don't Know	Importance
a	We do not share benefits from process improvements with suppliers.		We determine how benefits for process improvements will be shared with suppliers on a project-by-project basis.		We have and use formal guidelines for how benefits from process improvements will be shared with suppliers.	☐	● Critical ● Important ● Minor Importance
Justification:							

Operational Sub-Processes

O-1. Segment Suppliers

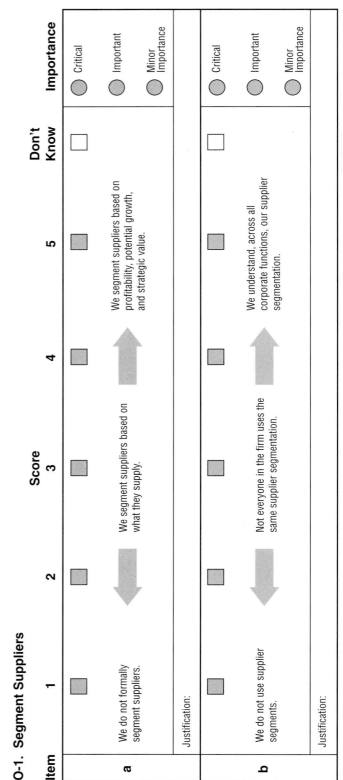

Item	Score 1	2	3	4	5	Don't Know	Importance
a	We do not formally segment suppliers.		We segment suppliers based on what they supply.		We segment suppliers based on profitability, potential growth, and strategic value.	☐	● Critical ● Important ● Minor Importance
Justification:							
b	We do not use supplier segments.		Not everyone in the firm uses the same supplier segmentation.		We understand, across all corporate functions, our supplier segmentation.	☐	● Critical ● Important ● Minor Importance
Justification:							

O-2. Prepare the Supplier/Segment Management Team

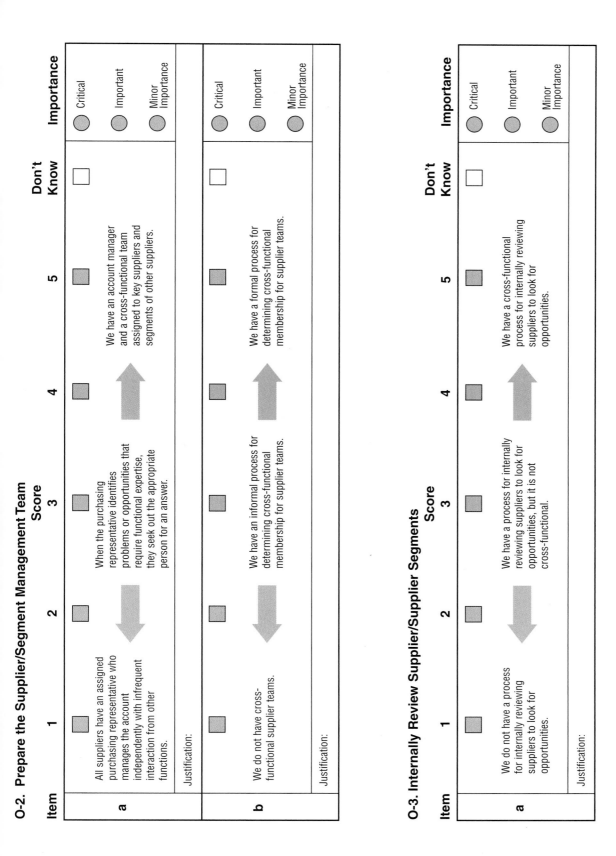

Item	Score 1	2	3	4	5	Don't Know	Importance
a	All suppliers have an assigned purchasing representative who manages the account independently with infrequent interaction from other functions.		When the purchasing representative identifies problems or opportunities that require functional expertise, they seek out the appropriate person for an answer.		We have an account manager and a cross-functional team assigned to key suppliers and segments of other suppliers.		Critical / Important / Minor Importance

Justification:

Item	Score 1	2	3	4	5	Don't Know	Importance
b	We do not have cross-functional supplier teams.		We have an informal process for determining cross-functional membership for supplier teams.		We have a formal process for determining cross-functional membership for supplier teams.		Critical / Important / Minor Importance

Justification:

O-3. Internally Review Supplier/Supplier Segments

Item	Score 1	2	3	4	5	Don't Know	Importance
a	We do not have a process for internally reviewing suppliers to look for opportunities.		We have a process for internally reviewing suppliers to look for opportunities, but it is not cross-functional.		We have a cross-functional process for internally reviewing suppliers to look for opportunities.		Critical / Important / Minor Importance

Justification:

O-4. Identify Opportunities with Suppliers

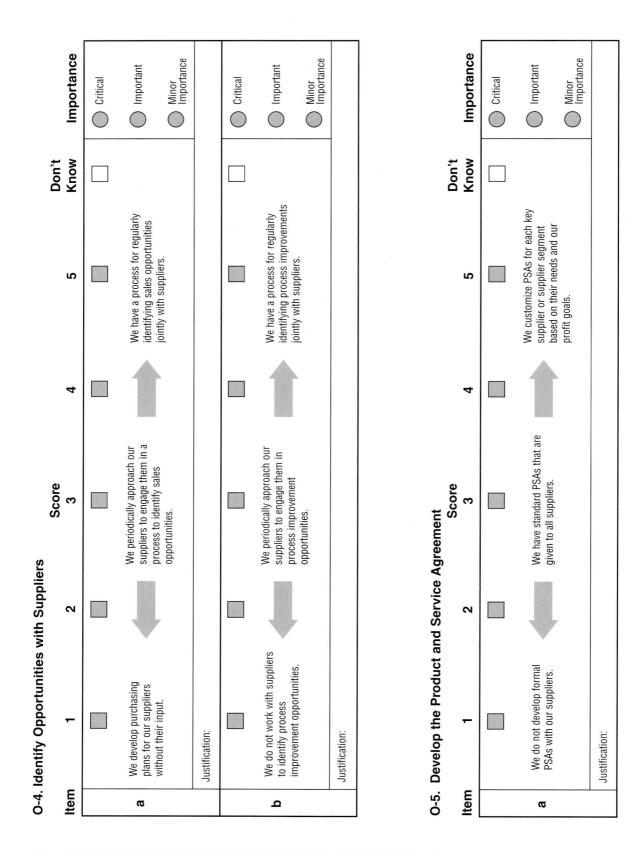

Item		Score				Don't Know	Importance
	1	2	3	4	5		☐ Critical / ☐ Important / ☐ Minor Importance
a	We develop purchasing plans for our suppliers without their input.		We periodically approach our suppliers to engage them in a process to identify sales opportunities.		We have a process for regularly identifying sales opportunities jointly with suppliers.		
	Justification:						
b	We do not work with suppliers to identify process improvement opportunities.		We periodically approach our suppliers to engage them in process improvement opportunities.		We have a process for regularly identifying process improvements jointly with suppliers.		
	Justification:						

O-5. Develop the Product and Service Agreement

Item		Score				Don't Know	Importance
	1	2	3	4	5		☐ Critical / ☐ Important / ☐ Minor Importance
a	We do not develop formal PSAs with our suppliers.		We have standard PSAs that are given to all suppliers.		We customize PSAs for each key supplier or supplier segment based on their needs and our profit goals.		
	Justification:						

O-5. Develop the Product and Service Agreement (continued)

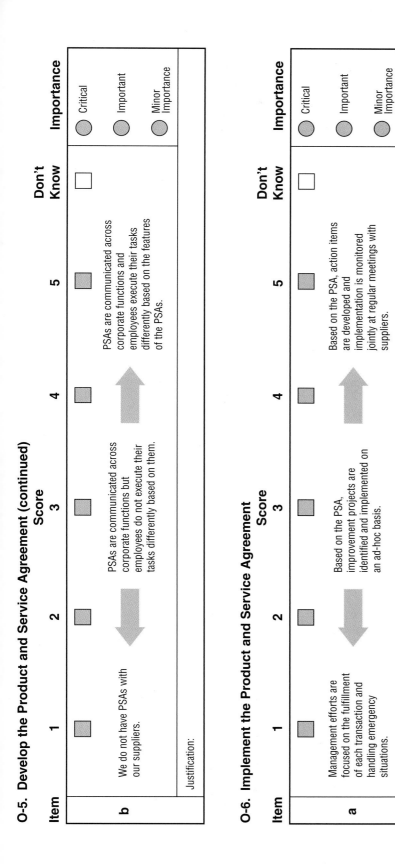

Item	Score					Don't Know	Importance
	1	2	3	4	5		
b	We do not have PSAs with our suppliers.		PSAs are communicated across corporate functions but employees do not execute their tasks differently based on them.		PSAs are communicated across corporate functions and employees execute their tasks differently based on the features of the PSAs.		● Critical ● Important ● Minor Importance

Justification:

O-6. Implement the Product and Service Agreement

Item	Score					Don't Know	Importance
	1	2	3	4	5		
a	Management efforts are focused on the fulfillment of each transaction and handling emergency situations.		Based on the PSA, improvement projects are identified and implemented on an ad-hoc basis.		Based on the PSA, action items are developed and implementation is monitored jointly at regular meetings with suppliers.		● Critical ● Important ● Minor Importance

Justification:

O-7. Measure Performance and Generate Supplier Cost/Profitability Reports

Item	1	2	3	4	5	Don't Know	Importance
a	☐	☐	☐	☐	☐	☐	○ Critical ○ Important ○ Minor Importance
	We do not track performance by supplier.		We identify measurable performance improvements but do not share results with suppliers.		We work with suppliers to identify measurable performance improvements and regularly meet to evaluate results.		
	Justification:						
b	☐	☐	☐	☐	☐	☐	○ Critical ○ Important ○ Minor Importance
	We only measure suppliers based on the price of items purchased.		Suppliers are measured using service performance and some cost data.		Suppliers are evaluated based on total delivered cost and when appropriate using profitability reports based on revenue minus avoidable costs.		
	Justification:						
c	☐	☐	☐	☐	☐	☐	○ Critical ○ Important ○ Minor Importance
	We do not communicate our supplier relationship management performance throughout the firm.		We communicate our supplier relationship management performance throughout the firm, but not with key customers and suppliers.		We communicate our supplier relationship management performance throughout the firm and with key customers and suppliers.		
	Justification:						
d	☐	☐	☐	☐	☐	☐	○ Critical ○ Important ○ Minor Importance
	We believe our competitors are better at supplier relationship management than we are.		We believe our supplier relationship management process is adequate.		We believe that our supplier relationship management process is better than our competitors and it is a competitive advantage for us.		
	Justification:						

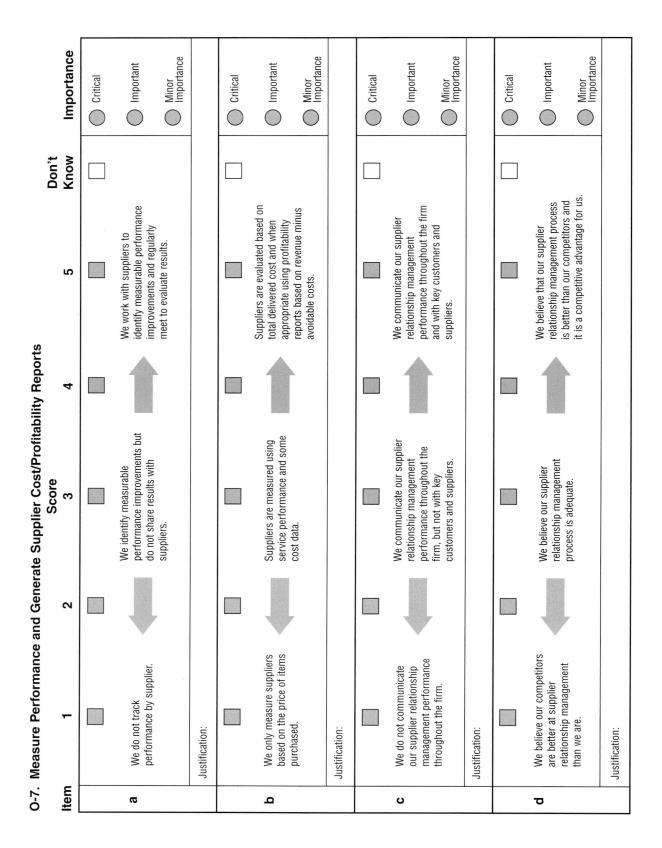

APPENDIX C: Assessment Tool for the Customer Service Management Process

General Information

This assessment tool is designed to identify opportunities in your organization's customer service management process. It highlights important aspects of the strategic and operational sub-processes within customer service management. Management can use this tool to identify process strengths and weaknesses, and then focus their efforts on those areas where improvement efforts will drive the most benefits.

Directions

A cross-functional management team should complete each item in the assessment, the score, the importance, and the justification.

Score: The score for the item is assessed on a 5-point scale.

1 = **you agree with the statement written in column 1.**
2 = **you believe the organization is somewhere between the statements in columns 1 and 3.**
3 = **you agree with the statement written in column 3.**
4 = **you believe the organization is somewhere between the statements in columns 3 and 5.**
5 = **you agree with the statement written in column 5.**

The scale includes descriptions for 1, 3, and 5. Intermediate columns are included to accommodate ratings that fall between the scale points. Check the box corresponding to the score of the item. If the respondent is not sure how to score the item, check the "Don't Know" box.

Importance: The importance of the item is assessed on a 3-point scale.

3 = **Critical:** Item is essential for the success of the customer service management process within your organization.
2 = **Important:** Item is important but not essential for the success of the customer service management process within your organization.
1 = **Minor Importance:** Item is of minor importance for the success of the customer service management process within your organization.

Justification: Provide justification for your score and importance rating for each item in the space provided, i.e., why did you score the items the way you did?

Strategic Sub-Processes
S–1. Develop Customer Service Strategy

Item	Score					Don't Know	Importance

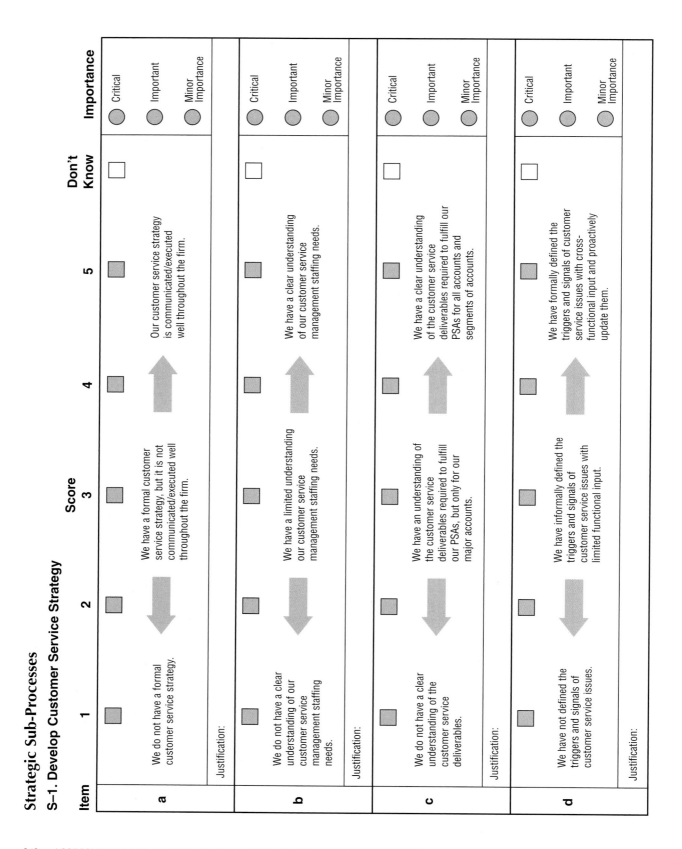

a

1 ☐

2 ☐ We do not have a formal customer service strategy.

3 ☐ We have a formal customer service strategy, but it is not communicated/executed well throughout the firm.

4 ☐

5 ☐ Our customer service strategy is communicated/executed well throughout the firm.

Don't Know ☐

Importance: ○ Critical ○ Important ○ Minor Importance

Justification:

b

1 ☐ We do not have a clear understanding of our customer service management staffing needs.

2 ☐

3 ☐ We have a limited understanding of our customer service management staffing needs.

4 ☐

5 ☐ We have a clear understanding of our customer service management staffing needs.

Don't Know ☐

Importance: ○ Critical ○ Important ○ Minor Importance

Justification:

c

1 ☐ We do not have a clear understanding of the customer service deliverables.

2 ☐

3 ☐ We have an understanding of the customer service deliverables required to fulfill our PSAs, but only for our major accounts.

4 ☐

5 ☐ We have a clear understanding of the customer service deliverables required to fulfill our PSAs for all accounts and segments of accounts.

Don't Know ☐

Importance: ○ Critical ○ Important ○ Minor Importance

Justification:

d

1 ☐ We have not defined the triggers and signals of customer service issues.

2 ☐

3 ☐ We have informally defined the triggers and signals of customer service issues with limited functional input.

4 ☐

5 ☐ We have formally defined the triggers and signals of customer service issues with cross-functional input and proactively update them.

Don't Know ☐

Importance: ○ Critical ○ Important ○ Minor Importance

Justification:

S-2. Develop Response Procedures

Item		Score					Don't Know	Importance
	1	2	3	4	5			

a — Score 1: Each customer service representative determines the appropriate response to a customer service inquiry and there is no oversight of their actions.
Score 3: We have developed consistent response procedures for primary customer service inquiries, but they are not systematically followed.
Score 5: We have developed consistent response procedures for our customer service inquires and all customer service representatives are trained to systematically follow them.
Don't Know ☐
Importance: ○ Critical ○ Important ○ Minor Importance
Justification:

b — Score 1: We do not analyze customer service inquires in order to identify events that require a consistent response.
Score 3: We informally analyze customer service inquires in order to identify events that require a consistent response.
Score 5: We formally analyze customer service inquires in order to identify events that require a consistent response.
Don't Know ☐
Importance: ○ Critical ○ Important ○ Minor Importance
Justification:

c — Score 1: We have a limited understanding of the internal coordination required to respond to various customer service events.
Score 3: We have a fairly good understanding of the internal coordination required to respond to various customer service events.
Score 5: We have a clear understanding of the coordination in the supply chain that is required to respond to various customer service events.
Don't Know ☐
Importance: ○ Critical ○ Important ○ Minor Importance
Justification:

d — Score 1: We have a limited understanding of the external coordination required to respond to various customer service events.
Score 3: We have a fairly good understanding of the external coordination required to respond to various customer service events.
Score 5: We have a clear understanding of the external coordination required to respond to various customer service events.
Don't Know ☐
Importance: ○ Critical ○ Important ○ Minor Importance
Justification:

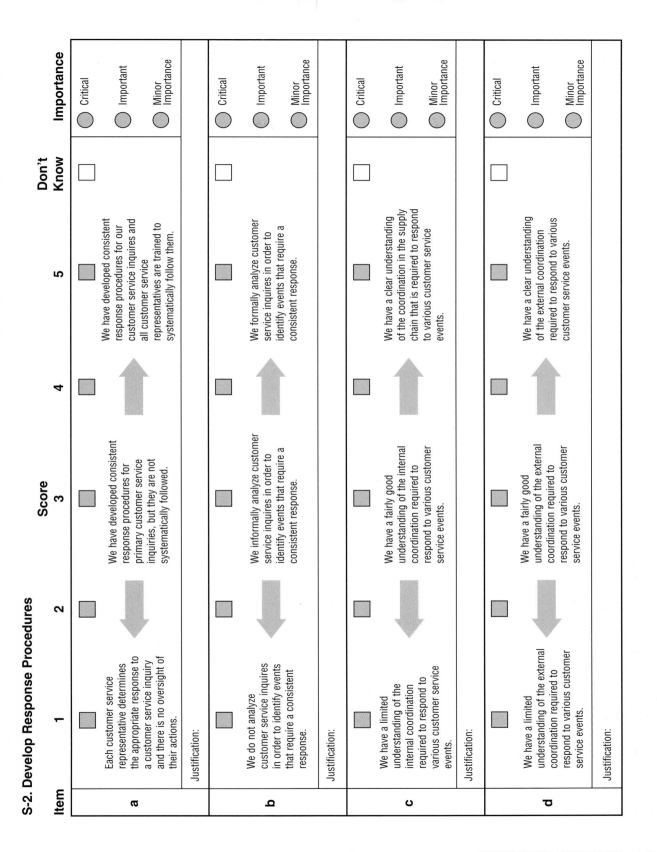

S–2. Develop Response Procedures (continued)

Item		Score				Don't Know	Importance
	1	2	3	4	5		

Item				
e	☐ **1** We determine appropriate response procedures for customer service events after they have occurred.	☐ **2** / ☐ **3** We proactively determine appropriate response procedures for major customer service events.	☐ **4** / ☐ **5** We proactively determine appropriate response procedures for a comprehensive set of customer service events.	Don't Know ☐

Importance:
- ◯ Critical
- ◯ Important
- ◯ Minor Importance

Justification:

S–3. Develop Infrastructure for Implementing Response Procedures

Item		Score				Don't Know	Importance
	1	2	3	4	5		

| **a** | ☐ **1** We are neither effective nor efficient in collecting relevant data regarding customer service events. | ☐ **2** / ☐ **3** We collect customer service event data internally but don't proactively obtain data from our suppliers or customers. | ☐ **4** / ☐ **5** We collect customer service event data effectively and efficiently, both internally and from suppliers and/or customers. | Don't Know ☐ |

Importance:
- ◯ Critical
- ◯ Important
- ◯ Minor Importance

Justification:

| **b** | ☐ **1** We are unable to proactively respond to customer service issues. | ☐ **2** / ☐ **3** On an ad-hoc basis, we are able to identify and respond to some customer service issues prior to the customer being impacted. | ☐ **4** / ☐ **5** We have mechanisms in place for identifying and responding to some customer service issues prior to the customer being impacted. | Don't Know ☐ |

Importance:
- ◯ Critical
- ◯ Important
- ◯ Minor Importance

Justification:

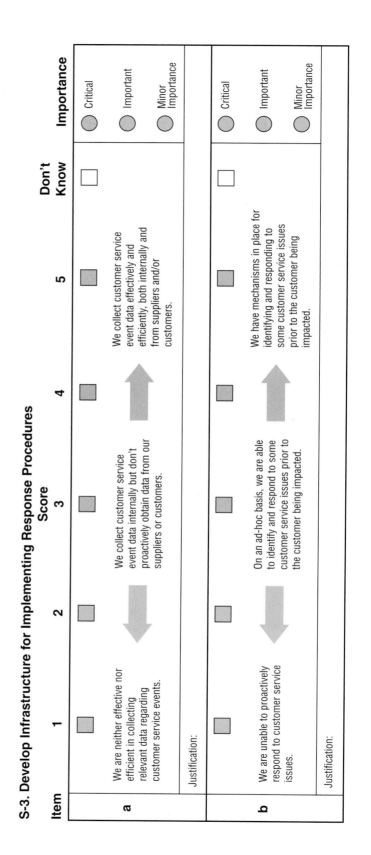

S-3. Develop Infrastructure for Implementing Response Procedures (continued)

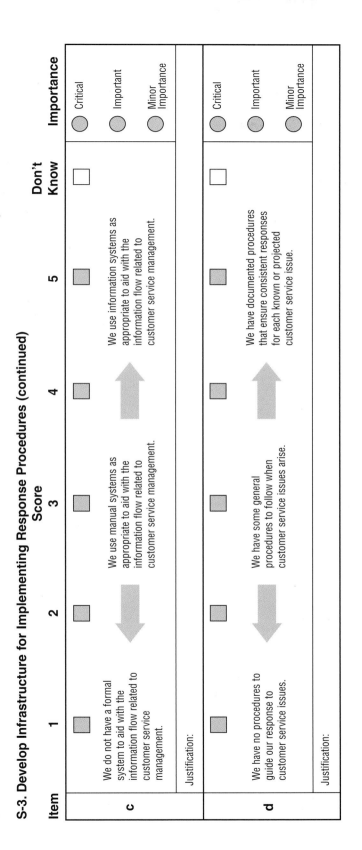

Item		Score					Don't Know	Importance
	1	2	3	4	5			

c — We do not have a formal system to aid with the information flow related to customer service management. → We use manual systems as appropriate to aid with the information flow related to customer service management. → We use information systems as appropriate to aid with the information flow related to customer service management.

Critical / Important / Minor Importance

Justification:

d — We have no procedures to guide our response to customer service issues. → We have some general procedures to follow when customer service issues arise. → We have documented procedures that ensure consistent responses for each known or projected customer service issue.

Critical / Important / Minor Importance

Justification:

S-4. Develop Framework of Metrics

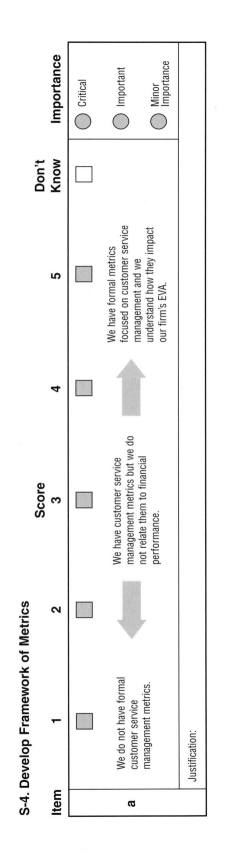

Item		Score					Don't Know	Importance
	1	2	3	4	5			

a — We do not have formal customer service management metrics. → We have customer service management metrics but we do not relate them to financial performance. → We have formal metrics focused on customer service management and we understand how they impact our firm's EVA.

Critical / Important / Minor Importance

Justification:

S-4. Develop Framework of Metrics (continued)

Item	1	2	Score 3	4	5	Don't Know	Importance
b	☒ We do not have formal performance goals for customer service management.	☒	☒ We have formal performance goals relating to customer service management that are communicated internally.	☒	☒ We have formal performance goals relating to customer service management that are communicated throughout the firm and to suppliers and customers.	☐	○ Critical ○ Important ○ Minor Importance
Justification:							
c	☒ Conflicting functional objectives often hinder the performance of the customer service management process.	☒	☒ There are groups of functions whose metrics are aligned, but there are some conflicts between the groups.	☒	☒ Our customer service management metrics are aligned with other metrics used throughout the firm.	☐	○ Critical ○ Important ○ Minor Importance
Justification:							
d	☒ People in our firm have a limited understanding of how their decisions and actions affect the customer service management process.	☒	☒ People throughout our firm understand how their decisions and actions affect the customer service management process.	☒	☒ People throughout our firm, as well as our key suppliers and customers understand how their decisions and actions affect the customer service management process.	☐	○ Critical ○ Important ○ Minor Importance
Justification:							

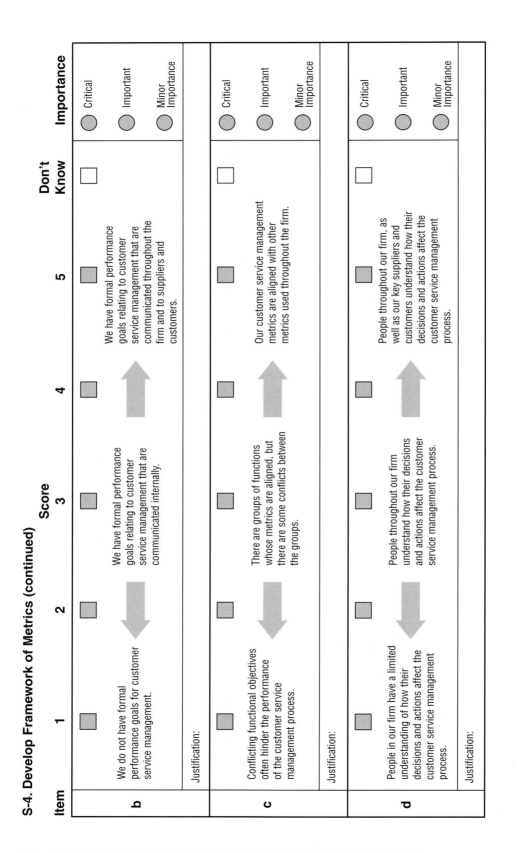

Operational Sub-Processes

O-1. Recognize Event

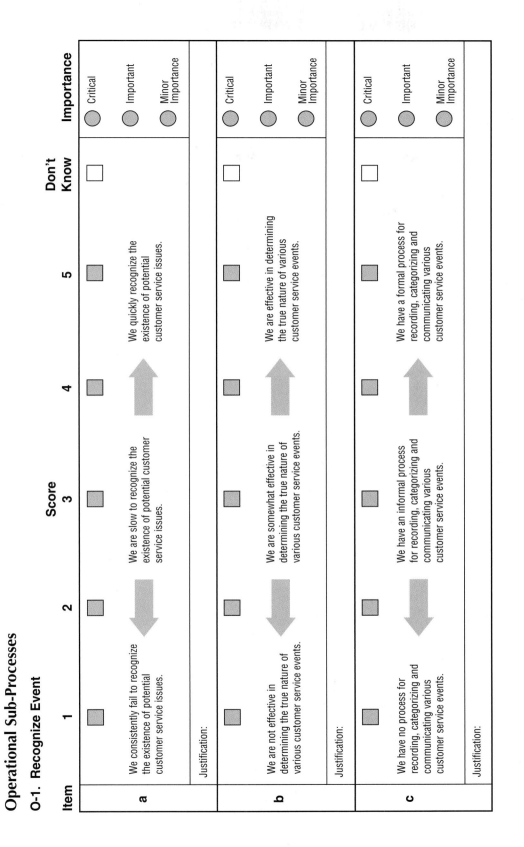

Item		Score						Don't Know	Importance
		1	2	3	4	5			

a — We consistently fail to recognize the existence of potential customer service issues.
We are slow to recognize the existence of potential customer service issues.
We quickly recognize the existence of potential customer service issues.

Justification:

b — We are not effective in determining the true nature of various customer service events.
We are somewhat effective in determining the true nature of various customer service events.
We are effective in determining the true nature of various customer service events.

Justification:

c — We have no process for recording, categorizing and communicating various customer service events.
We have an informal process for recording, categorizing and communicating various customer service events.
We have a formal process for recording, categorizing and communicating various customer service events.

Justification:

Importance: Critical / Important / Minor Importance

O-2. Evaluate Situation and Alternatives

Item	Score 1	2	3	4	5	Don't Know	Importance
a	□ We do not effectively coordinate across functions to determine alternative actions to customer service events.	□	□ We are somewhat effective in coordinating across functions to determine alternative actions to customer service events.	□	□ We effectively coordinate across functions to determine alternative actions to customer service events.	☐	○ Critical ○ Important ○ Minor Importance
	Justification:						
b	□ We are not efficient in deciding how to respond to various customer service events.	□	□ We are somewhat efficient in deciding how to respond to various customer service events.	□	□ We efficiently decide how to respond to various customer service events.	☐	○ Critical ○ Important ○ Minor Importance
	Justification:						
c	□ We are not effective in evaluating alternatives for managing a customer service event in a way that is least disruptive to the customer and internal operations.	□	□ We are somewhat effective in evaluating alternatives for managing a customer service event in a way that is least disruptive to the customer and internal operations.	□	□ We are effective in evaluating alternatives for managing a customer service event in a way that is least disruptive to the customer and internal operations.	☐	○ Critical ○ Important ○ Minor Importance
	Justification:						
d	□ We are frequently reevaluating situations and alternatives for events that have already occurred several times in the past.	□	□ We sometimes reevaluate situations and alternatives for events that have already occurred several times in the past.	□	□ We rarely reevaluate situations and alternatives for events that have already occurred several times in the past.	☐	○ Critical ○ Important ○ Minor Importance
	Justification:						

O-3. Implement Solution

Item		Score					Don't Know	Importance

a

Score:
- 1: We do not effectively determine the implementation steps required to solve a customer service issue.
- 2: ☐
- 3: We are somewhat effective in determining the implementation steps required to solve a customer service issue.
- 4: ☐
- 5: We effectively determine the implementation steps required to solve a customer service issue.
- Don't Know: ☐

Importance:
- ● Critical
- ● Important
- ● Minor Importance

Justification:

b

Score:
- 1: We do a poor job of coordinating with business process owners or function managers when responding to a customer service event.
- 2: ☐
- 3: We do a fair job of coordinating with business process owners or function managers when responding to a customer service event.
- 4: ☐
- 5: We do an excellent job of coordinating with business process owners or function managers when responding to a customer service event.
- Don't Know: ☐

Importance:
- ● Critical
- ● Important
- ● Minor Importance

Justification:

O-4. Monitor and Report

Item		Score					Don't Know	Importance

a

Score:
- 1: We do not monitor the evolution of various customer service events.
- 2: ☐
- 3: We monitor the evolution of major customer service events.
- 4: ☐
- 5: We monitor the evolution of all customer service events.
- Don't Know: ☐

Importance:
- ● Critical
- ● Important
- ● Minor Importance

Justification:

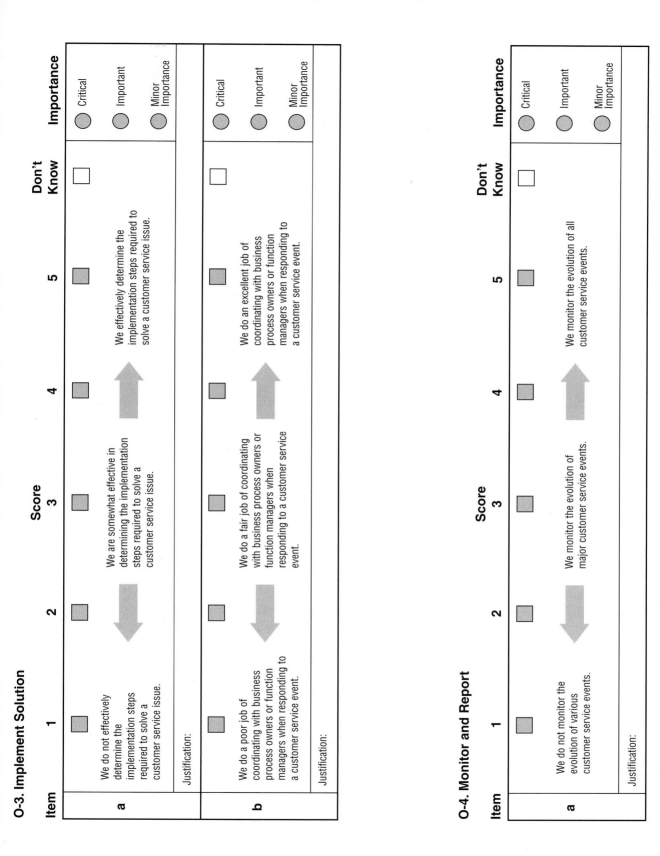

O-4. Monitor and Report (continued)

Item	1	2	Score 3	4	5	Don't Know	Importance
b	We do not record customer service events.		We manually track customer service events.		We electronically track customer service events.	☐	◯ Critical ◯ Important ◯ Minor Importance
	Justification:						
c	We are very inflexible when it comes to responding to customer service events.		We believe there are opportunities to improve our internal ability to respond to customer service events.		We have developed an appropriate level of flexibility within our firm to respond to customer service events.	☐	◯ Critical ◯ Important ◯ Minor Importance
	Justification:						
d	We do not work with suppliers and customers to improve flexibility so that we can better respond to customer service events.		We have identified opportunities to work with suppliers and customers more closely to improve flexibility so that we can better respond to customer service events.		We have worked with suppliers and customers to develop an appropriate level of flexibility throughout the supply chain so that we can better respond to customer service events.	☐	◯ Critical ◯ Important ◯ Minor Importance
	Justification:						
e	We do not keep our customers informed of our response to customer service events.		We keep our customers informed of our response to customer service events if they ask.		We proactively keep our customers informed of our response to customer service events.	☐	◯ Critical ◯ Important ◯ Minor Importance
	Justification:						

O-4. Monitor and Report (continued)

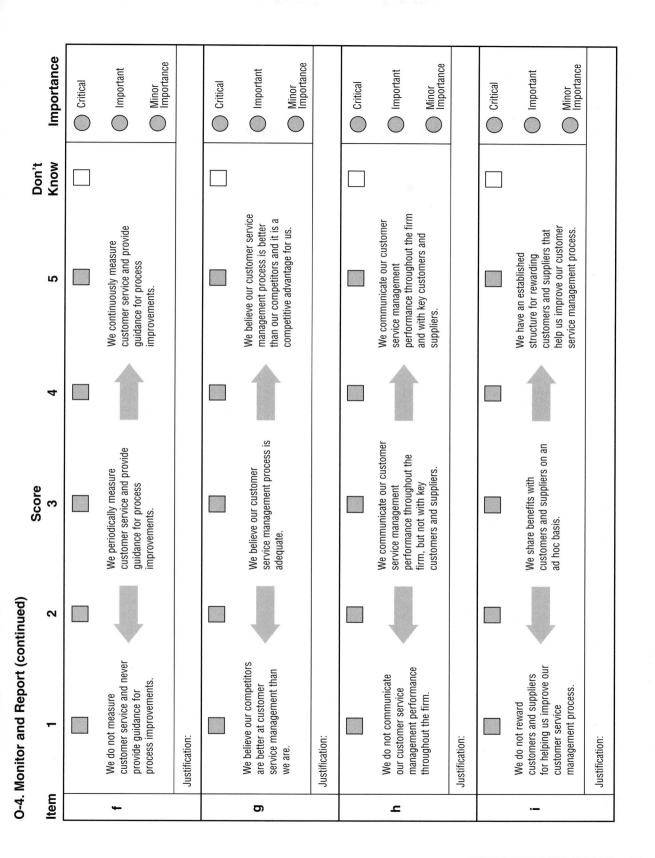

Item	1	2	Score 3	4	5	Don't Know	Importance
f	We do not measure customer service and never provide guidance for process improvements.		We periodically measure customer service and provide guidance for process improvements.		We continuously measure customer service and provide guidance for process improvements.	☐	◯ Critical ◯ Important ◯ Minor Importance
	Justification:						
g	We believe our competitors are better at customer service management than we are.		We believe our customer service management process is adequate.		We believe our customer service management process is better than our competitors and it is a competitive advantage for us.	☐	◯ Critical ◯ Important ◯ Minor Importance
	Justification:						
h	We do not communicate our customer service management performance throughout the firm.		We communicate our customer service management performance throughout the firm, but not with key customers and suppliers.		We communicate our customer service management performance throughout the firm and with key customers and suppliers.	☐	◯ Critical ◯ Important ◯ Minor Importance
	Justification:						
i	We do not reward customers and suppliers for helping us improve our customer service management process.		We share benefits with customers and suppliers on an ad hoc basis.		We have an established structure for rewarding customers and suppliers that help us improve our customer service management process.	☐	◯ Critical ◯ Important ◯ Minor Importance
	Justification:						

APPENDIX D: Assessment Tool for the Demand Management Process

General Information

This assessment tool is designed to identify opportunities in your organization's demand management process. It highlights important aspects of the strategic and operational sub-processes within demand management. Management can use this tool to identify process strengths and weaknesses, and then focus their efforts on those areas where improvement efforts will drive most benefits.

Directions

A cross-functional management team should complete each item in the assessment, the score, the importance, and the justification.

Score: The score for the item is assessed on a 5-point scale.

1 = **you agree with the statement written in column 1.**

2 = **you believe the organization is somewhere between the statements in columns 1 and 3.**

3 = **you agree with the statement written in column 3.**

4 = **you believe the organization is somewhere between the statements in columns 3 and 5.**

5 = **you agree with the statement written in column 5.**

The scale includes descriptions for 1, 3, and 5. Intermediate columns are included to accommodate ratings that fall between the scale points. Check the box corresponding to the score of the item. If the respondent is not sure how to score the item, check the "Don't Know" box.

Importance: The importance of the item is assessed on a 3-point scale.

3 = **Critical:** Item is essential for the success of the demand management process within your organization.

2 = **Important:** Item is important but not essential for the success of the demand management process within your organization.

1 = **Minor Importance:** Item is of minor importance for the success of the demand management process within your organization.

Justification: Provide justification for your score and importance rating for each item in the space provided, i.e., why did you score the items the way you did?

Strategic Sub-Processes

S–1. Determine Demand Management Goals and Strategy

Item		Score					Don't Know	Importance
		1	2	3	4	5		

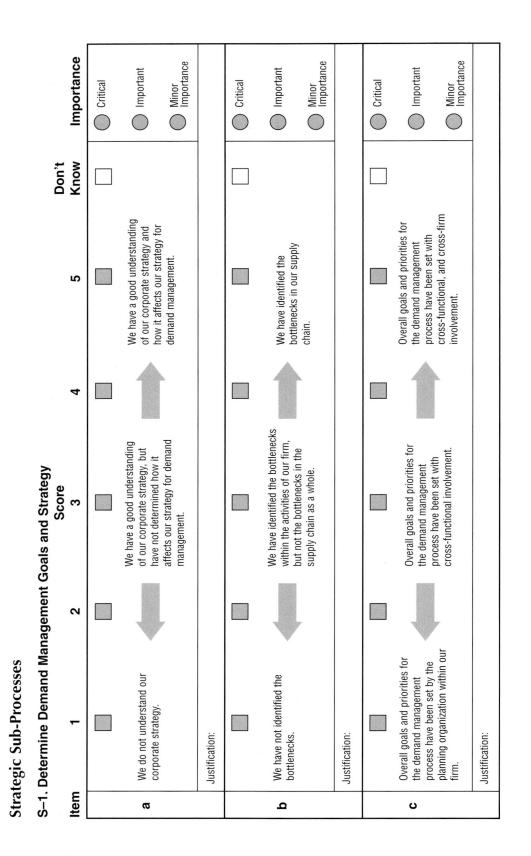

a — We do not understand our corporate strategy.

We have a good understanding of our corporate strategy, but have not determined how it affects our strategy for demand management.

We have a good understanding of our corporate strategy and how it affects our strategy for demand management.

Justification:

b — We have not identified the bottlenecks.

We have identified the bottlenecks within the activities of our firm, but not the bottlenecks in the supply chain as a whole.

We have identified the bottlenecks in our supply chain.

Justification:

c — Overall goals and priorities for the demand management process have been set by the planning organization within our firm.

Overall goals and priorities for the demand management process have been set with cross-functional involvement.

Overall goals and priorities for the demand management process have been set with cross-functional, and cross-firm involvement.

Justification:

Importance:
- Critical
- Important
- Minor Importance

S-2. Determine Forecasting Procedures

Item	Score 1	2	3	4	5	Don't Know	Importance
a	☐ We do not develop formal forecasts for planning purposes.	☐	☐ We use forecasts for planning, but different functional areas in our firm use their own forecasts and there is no coordination.	☐	☐ Our forecasts are coordinated within the firm such that different functional areas are planning based on the same numbers.	☐	◯ Critical ◯ Important ◯ Minor Importance
Justification:							
b	☐ We have not evaluated what additional data sources could improve our forecasting process.	☐	☐ We collect data from several sources and use it to develop forecasts, but we have not evaluated the value of each source.	☐	☐ We know what sources of data are available, have evaluated the value of each source.	☐	◯ Critical ◯ Important ◯ Minor Importance
Justification:							
c	☐ We have not analyzed the appropriateness of VMI and CPFR.	☐	☐ We have analyzed the appropriateness of VMI and CPFR but we have not yet implemented them to their fullest potential.	☐	☐ We have analyzed the appropriateness of VMI and CPFR and implemented them to their fullest potential.	☐	◯ Critical ◯ Important ◯ Minor Importance
Justification:							
d	☐ We use the same forecasting methods for all our products.	☐	☐ We choose forecasting methods based on product family.	☐	☐ We choose forecasting methods based on product segmentation (e.g. demand pattern, channel, uncertainty)	☐	◯ Critical ◯ Important ◯ Minor Importance
Justification:							

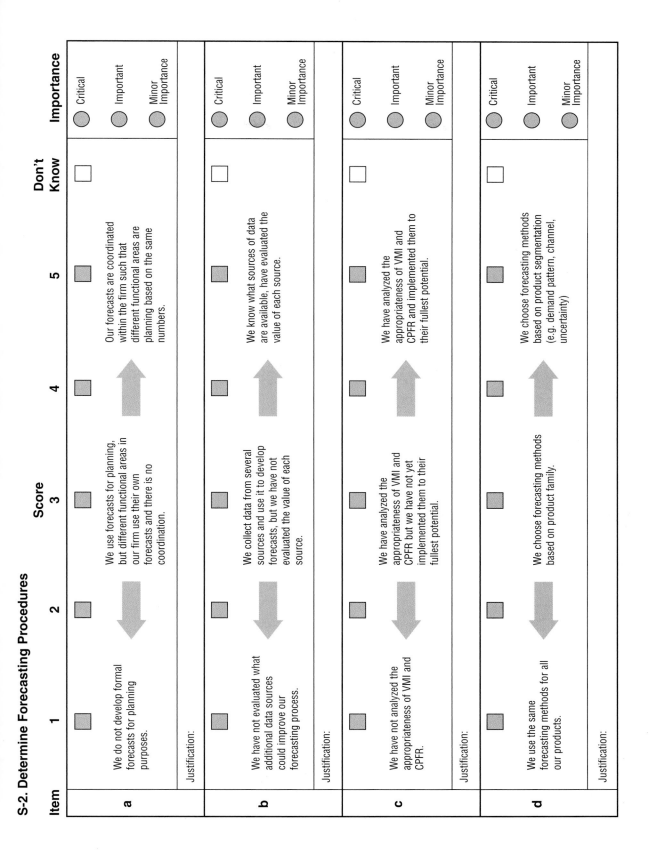

S-2. Determine Forecasting Procedures (continued)

Item		Score					Don't Know	Importance
	1	2	3	4	5			

Item					
e	☐ (1)	☐ (2)	☐ (3)	☐ (4)	☐ (5)	☐ Don't Know
	We do not re-evaluate our choice of forecasting methods.	⬇	We re-evaluate our choice of forecasting methods once problems arise.	⬆	We re-evaluate our choice of forecasting methods regularly.	

Importance:
- 🔘 Critical
- 🔘 Important
- 🔘 Minor Importance

Justification:

S-3. Plan Information Flow

Item		Score					Don't Know	Importance
	1	2	3	4	5			

a	☐ (1)	☐ (2)	☐ (3)	☐ (4)	☐ (5)	☐ Don't Know
	We have not designed an effective system for collecting input data for the forecast.	⬇	We have designed a system for collecting input data from internal sources for the forecast.	⬆	We have designed a system for collecting input data from internal and external sources for the forecast.	

Importance:
- 🔘 Critical
- 🔘 Important
- 🔘 Minor Importance

Justification:

b	☐ (1)	☐ (2)	☐ (3)	☐ (4)	☐ (5)	☐ Don't Know
	We have not designed an effective system for sharing forecast data with everyone who needs it.	⬇	We have evaluated who in the firm needs forecast information, and we have designed a system to share it effectively.	⬆	We have evaluated, both internally and externally, who needs forecast information, and we have designed a system to share it effectively.	

Importance:
- 🔘 Critical
- 🔘 Important
- 🔘 Minor Importance

Justification:

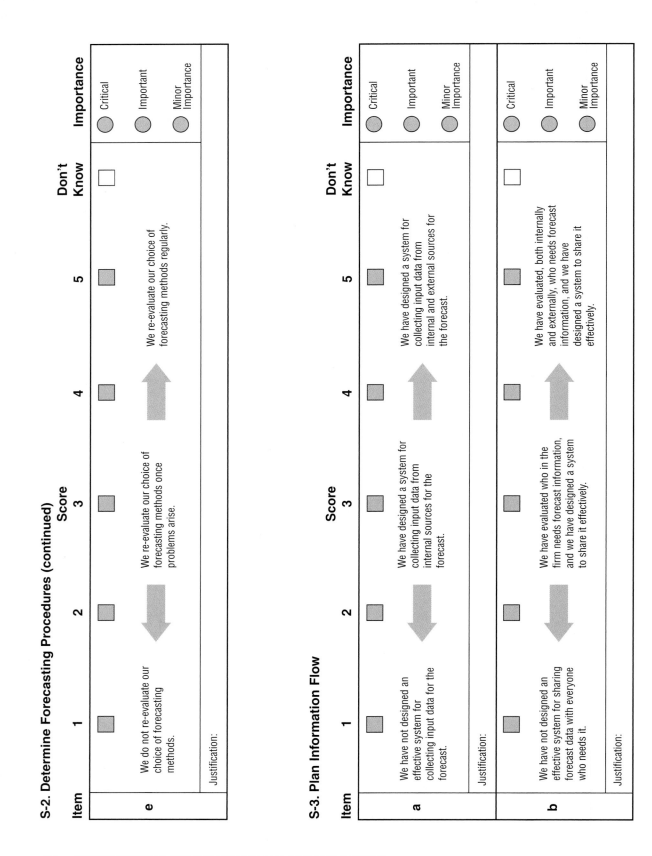

S-3. Plan Information Flow (continued)

Item		Score					Don't Know	Importance
	1	2	3	4	5			
c	We do not consider how forecast information can influence our business strategy.		Forecast information is used strategically within the function where the forecast is developed.		We understand how forecast information can influence our business strategy and share relevant information with key decision makers in the firm.		☐	◐ Critical
								◐ Important
								◐ Minor Importance
Justification:								

S-4. Determine Synchronization Procedures

Item		Score					Don't Know	Importance
	1	2	3	4	5			
a	We do not have formal synchronization procedures in place to match supply with demand.		We have consistent synchronization procedures that involve cross-functional input and execution.		We have consistent synchronization procedures that are cross-functional and also include input from appropriate suppliers and/or customers.		☐	◐ Critical
								◐ Important
								◐ Minor Importance
Justification:								
b	We make allocation and stockpiling decisions without cross-functional input.		We make allocation and stockpiling decisions with cross-functional input but we don't have firm policies in place.		We have allocation policies based on customer segmentation and stockpiling policies based on profitability, and we adhere to these policies.		☐	◐ Critical
								◐ Important
								◐ Minor Importance
Justification:								

S-4. Determine Synchronization Procedures (continued)

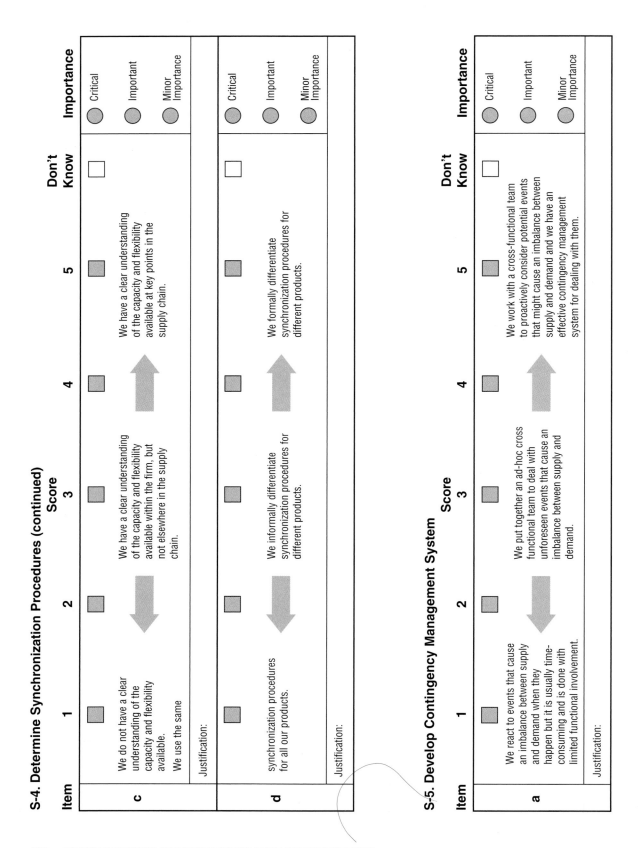

Item	Score 1	Score 2	Score 3	Score 4	Score 5	Don't Know	Importance
c	We do not have a clear understanding of the capacity and flexibility available. We use the same		We have a clear understanding of the capacity and flexibility available within the firm, but not elsewhere in the supply chain.		We have a clear understanding of the capacity and flexibility available at key points in the supply chain.	☐	○ Critical ○ Important ○ Minor Importance

Justification:

Item	Score 1	Score 2	Score 3	Score 4	Score 5	Don't Know	Importance
d	synchronization procedures for all our products.		We informally differentiate synchronization procedures for different products.		We formally differentiate synchronization procedures for different products.	☐	○ Critical ○ Important ○ Minor Importance

Justification:

S-5. Develop Contingency Management System

Item	Score 1	Score 2	Score 3	Score 4	Score 5	Don't Know	Importance
a	We react to events that cause an imbalance between supply and demand when they happen but it is usually time-consuming and is done with limited functional involvement.		We put together an ad-hoc cross functional team to deal with unforeseen events that cause an imbalance between supply and demand.		We work with a cross-functional team to proactively consider potential events that might cause an imbalance between supply and demand and we have an effective contingency management system for dealing with them.	☐	○ Critical ○ Important ○ Minor Importance

Justification:

S-6. Develop Framework of Metrics

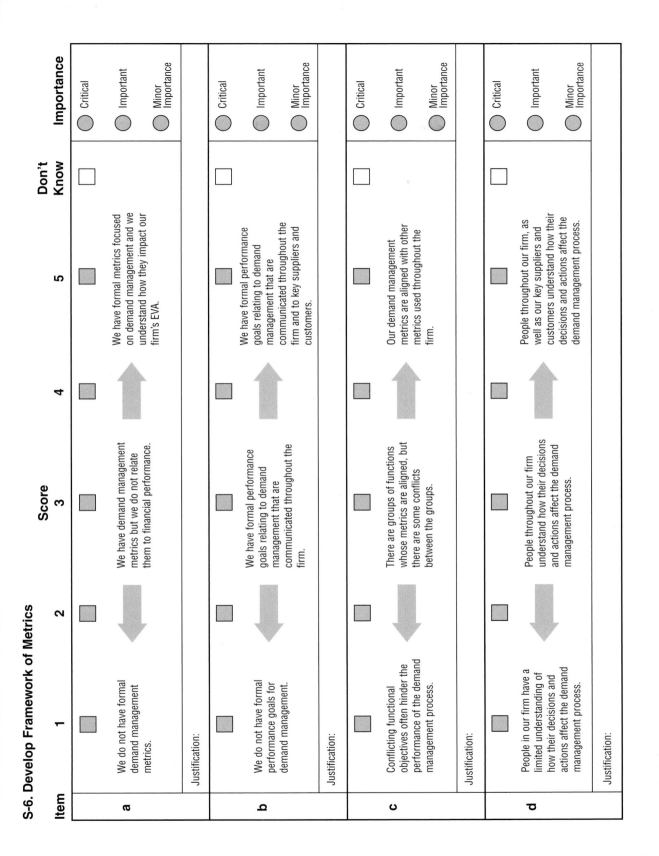

Item	Score 1	2	3	4	5	Don't Know	Importance
a	We do not have formal demand management metrics.		We have demand management metrics but we do not relate them to financial performance.		We have formal metrics focused on demand management and we understand how they impact our firm's EVA.		Critical / Important / Minor Importance
Justification:							
b	We do not have formal performance goals for demand management.		We have formal performance goals relating to demand management that are communicated throughout the firm.		We have formal performance goals relating to demand management that are communicated throughout the firm and to key suppliers and customers.		Critical / Important / Minor Importance
Justification:							
c	Conflicting functional objectives often hinder the performance of the demand management process.		There are groups of functions whose metrics are aligned, but there are some conflicts between the groups.		Our demand management metrics are aligned with other metrics used throughout the firm.		Critical / Important / Minor Importance
Justification:							
d	People in our firm have a limited understanding of how their decisions and actions affect the demand management process.		People throughout our firm understand how their decisions and actions affect the demand management process.		People throughout our firm, as well as our key suppliers and customers understand how their decisions and actions affect the demand management process.		Critical / Important / Minor Importance
Justification:							

Operational Sub-Processes

O-1. Collect Data / Information

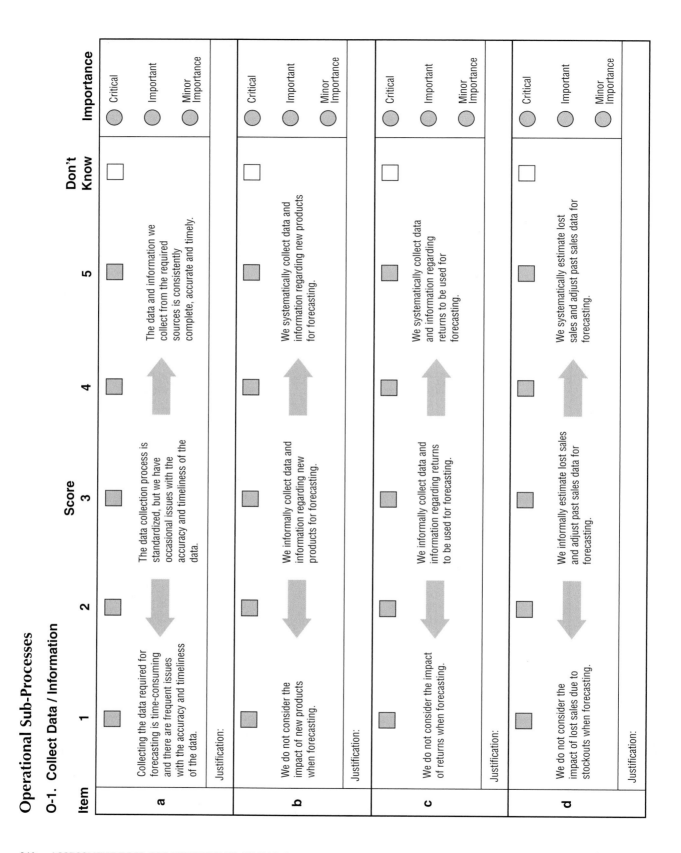

Item	1	2	3	4	5	Don't Know	Importance
a	Collecting the data required for forecasting is time-consuming and there are frequent issues with the accuracy and timeliness of the data.		The data collection process is standardized, but we have occasional issues with the accuracy and timeliness of the data.		The data and information we collect from the required sources is consistently complete, accurate and timely.	☐	◯ Critical ◯ Important ◯ Minor Importance
	Justification:						
b	We do not consider the impact of new products when forecasting.		We informally collect data and information regarding new products for forecasting.		We systematically collect data and information regarding new products for forecasting.	☐	◯ Critical ◯ Important ◯ Minor Importance
	Justification:						
c	We do not consider the impact of returns when forecasting.		We informally collect data and information regarding returns to be used for forecasting.		We systematically collect data and information regarding returns to be used for forecasting.	☐	◯ Critical ◯ Important ◯ Minor Importance
	Justification:						
d	We do not consider the impact of lost sales due to stockouts when forecasting.		We informally estimate lost sales and adjust past sales data for forecasting.		We systematically estimate lost sales and adjust past sales data for forecasting.	☐	◯ Critical ◯ Important ◯ Minor Importance
	Justification:						

Score

O-2. Forecast

Item	Score					Don't Know	Importance
	1	2	3	4	5		
a	There is a lot of variability in our forecast accuracy from period to period.		There is some variability in our forecast accuracy from period to period.		Our forecast accuracy is very consistent from period to period.	☐	○ Critical ○ Important ○ Minor Importance
Justification:							
b	Our forecast accuracy is worsening over time.		Our forecast accuracy has remained stable over time.		Our forecast accuracy has been improving over time.	☐	○ Critical ○ Important ○ Minor Importance
Justification:							
c	We do not track forecast errors.		We track forecast errors but we do not analyze them to help improve our forecast accuracy.		We track and analyze forecast errors and use that information to improve our forecast accuracy.	☐	○ Critical ○ Important ○ Minor Importance
Justification:							
d	We have significant opportunities to improve our forecasting process.		We have limited opportunities to improve our forecasting process.		It would not be cost effective to try to improve our forecasting process any more.	☐	○ Critical ○ Important ○ Minor Importance
Justification:							

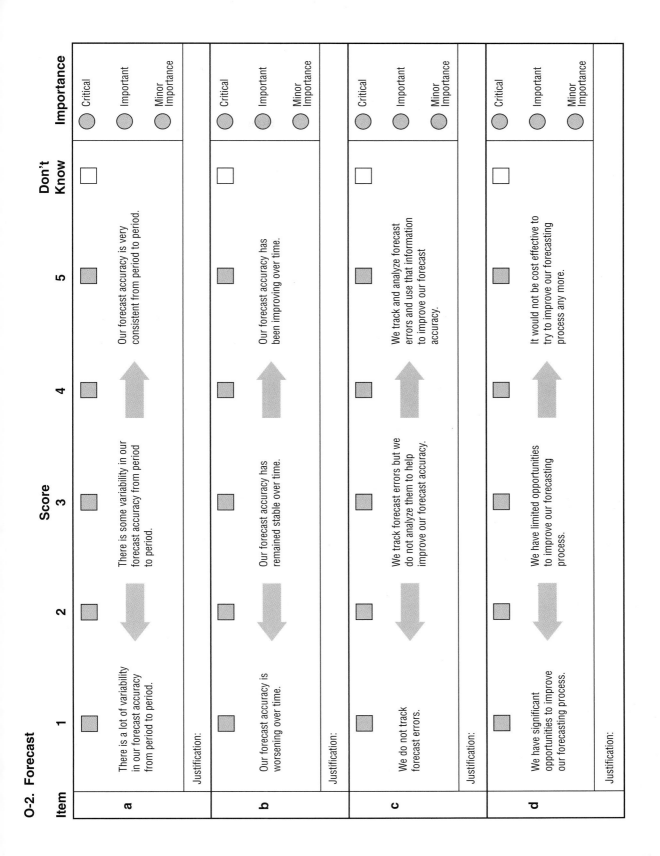

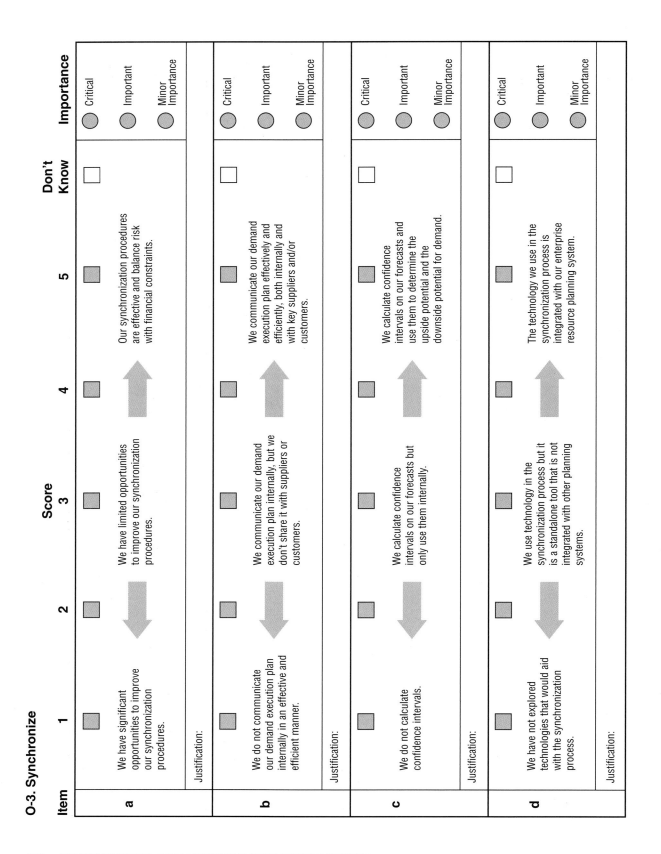

O-3. Synchronize

Item	Score 1	2	3	4	5	Don't Know	Importance
a	We have significant opportunities to improve our synchronization procedures.		We have limited opportunities to improve our synchronization procedures.		Our synchronization procedures are effective and balance risk with financial constraints.	☐	○ Critical ○ Important ○ Minor Importance
Justification:							
b	We do not communicate our demand execution plan internally in an effective and efficient manner.		We communicate our demand execution plan internally, but we don't share it with suppliers or customers.		We communicate our demand execution plan effectively and efficiently, both internally and with key suppliers and/or customers.	☐	○ Critical ○ Important ○ Minor Importance
Justification:							
c	We do not calculate confidence intervals.		We calculate confidence intervals on our forecasts but only use them internally.		We calculate confidence intervals on our forecasts and use them to determine the upside potential and the downside potential for demand.	☐	○ Critical ○ Important ○ Minor Importance
Justification:							
d	We have not explored technologies that would aid with the synchronization process.		We use technology in the synchronization process but it is a standalone tool that is not integrated with other planning systems.		The technology we use in the synchronization process is integrated with our enterprise resource planning system.	☐	○ Critical ○ Important ○ Minor Importance
Justification:							

O-4. Reduce Variability and Increase Flexibility

Item	Score 1	2	3	4	5	Don't Know	Importance
a	We have not evaluated how our policies and sales practices add variability to demand.	We have made efforts to reduce controllable demand variability but more opportunities exist.			We have minimized the demand variability that we control internally.	☐	◯ Critical ◯ Important ◯ Minor Importance
	Justification:						
b	We assume customer demand is an input that cannot be affected.	We believe there are opportunities to work with customers more closely to manage demand variability.			We work closely with our key customers to manage demand variability.	☐	◯ Critical ◯ Important ◯ Minor Importance
	Justification:						
c	We experience considerable strain when we need to respond to unexpected changes to demand.	We believe there are opportunities to improve our internal ability to respond to demand.			We have developed an appropriate level of flexibility within our firm.	☐	◯ Critical ◯ Important ◯ Minor Importance
	Justification:						
d	We have not worked with suppliers and customers to improve our flexibility to respond to unexpected changes in demand.	We have worked with key customers and suppliers to improve our flexibility but there are more opportunities to do so.			We have worked with suppliers and customers to develop an appropriate level of flexibility throughout the supply chain so that we can best meet demand.	☐	◯ Critical ◯ Important ◯ Minor Importance
	Justification:						

O-5. Measure Performance

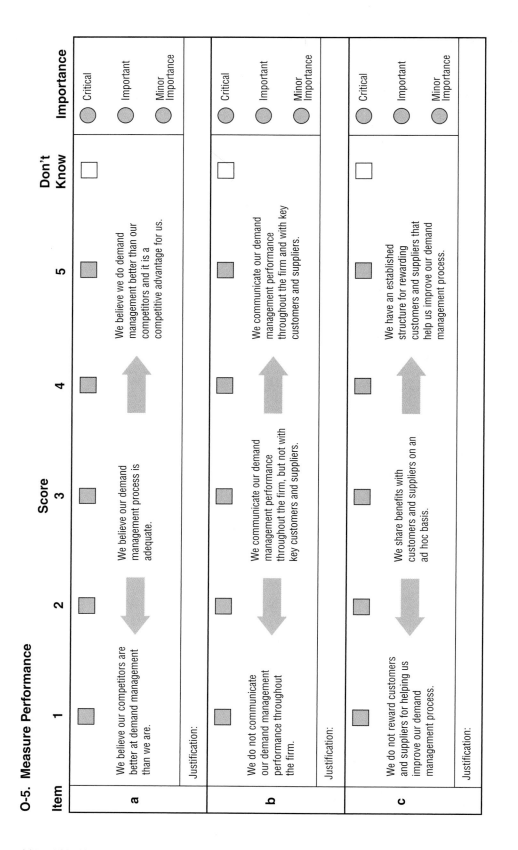

Item	Score 1	2	3	4	5	Don't Know	Importance
a	☐ We believe our competitors are better at demand management than we are.	☐	☐ We believe our demand management process is adequate.	☐	☐ We believe we do demand management better than our competitors and it is a competitive advantage for us.	☐	○ Critical ○ Important ○ Minor Importance
	Justification:						
b	☐ We do not communicate our demand management performance throughout the firm.	☐	☐ We communicate our demand management performance throughout the firm, but not with key customers and suppliers.	☐	☐ We communicate our demand management performance throughout the firm and with key customers and suppliers.	☐	○ Critical ○ Important ○ Minor Importance
	Justification:						
c	☐ We do not reward customers and suppliers for helping us improve our demand management process.	☐	☐ We share benefits with customers and suppliers on an ad hoc basis.	☐	☐ We have an established structure for rewarding customers and suppliers that help us improve our demand management process.	☐	○ Critical ○ Important ○ Minor Importance
	Justification:						

APPENDIX E: Assessment Tool for the Order Fulfillment Process

General Information

This assessment tool is designed to identify opportunities in your organization's order fulfillment process. It highlights important aspects of the strategic and operational sub-processes within order fulfillment. Management can use this tool to identify process strengths and weaknesses, and then focus their efforts on those areas where improvement efforts will drive the most benefits.

Directions

A cross-functional management team should complete each item in the assessment, the score, the importance, and the justification.

Score: The score for the item is assessed on a 5-point scale.

1 = **you agree with the statement written in column 1.**

2 = **you believe the organization is somewhere between the statements in columns 1 and 3.**

3 = **you agree with the statement written in column 3.**

4 = **you believe the organization is somewhere between the statements in columns 3 and 5.**

5 = **you agree with the statement written in column 5.**

The scale includes descriptions for 1, 3, and 5. Intermediate columns are included to accommodate ratings that fall between the scale points. Check the box corresponding to the score of the item. If the respondent is not sure how to score the item, check the "Don't Know" box.

Importance: The importance of the item is assessed on a 3-point scale.

3 = **Critical:** Item is essential for the success of the order fulfillment process within your organization.

2 = **Important:** Item is important but not essential for the success of the order fulfillment process within your organization.

1 = **Minor Importance:** Item is of minor importance for the success of the order fulfillment process within your organization.

Justification: Provide justification for your score and importance rating for each item in the space provided, i.e., why did you score the items the way you did?

Strategic Sub-Processes

S–1. Review Corporate and Marketing Strategy

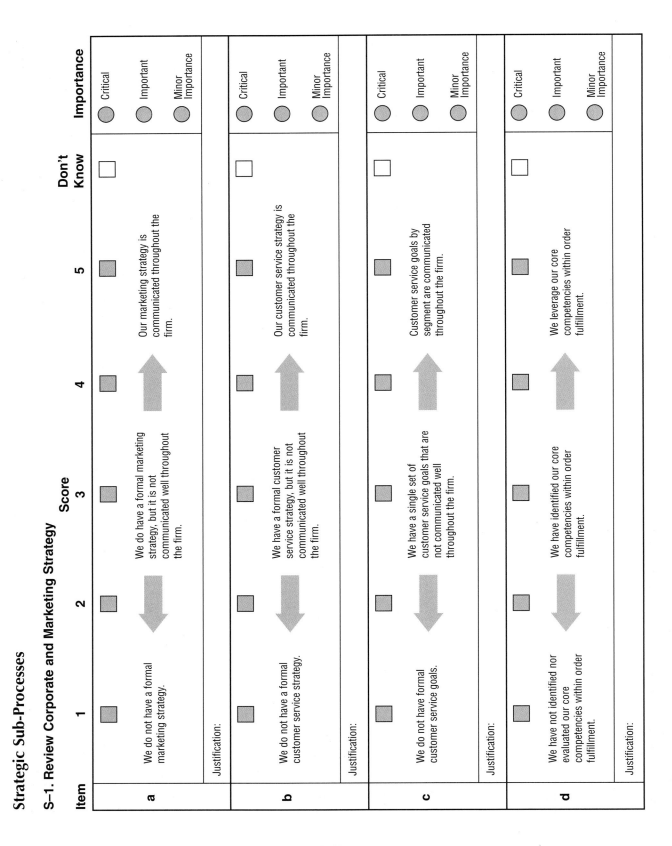

Item		1	2	Score 3	4	5	Don't Know	Importance
a		We do not have a formal marketing strategy.		We do have a formal marketing strategy, but it is not communicated well throughout the firm.		Our marketing strategy is communicated throughout the firm.	☐	◉ Critical ◉ Important ◉ Minor Importance
	Justification:							
b		We do not have a formal customer service strategy.		We have a formal customer service strategy, but it is not communicated well throughout the firm.		Our customer service strategy is communicated throughout the firm.	☐	◉ Critical ◉ Important ◉ Minor Importance
	Justification:							
c		We do not have formal customer service goals.		We have a single set of customer service goals that are not communicated well throughout the firm.		Customer service goals by segment are communicated throughout the firm.	☐	◉ Critical ◉ Important ◉ Minor Importance
	Justification:							
d		We have not identified nor evaluated our core competencies within order fulfillment.		We have identified our core competencies within order fulfillment.		We leverage our core competencies within order fulfillment.	☐	◉ Critical ◉ Important ◉ Minor Importance
	Justification:							

S–1. Review Corporate and Marketing Strategy (continued)

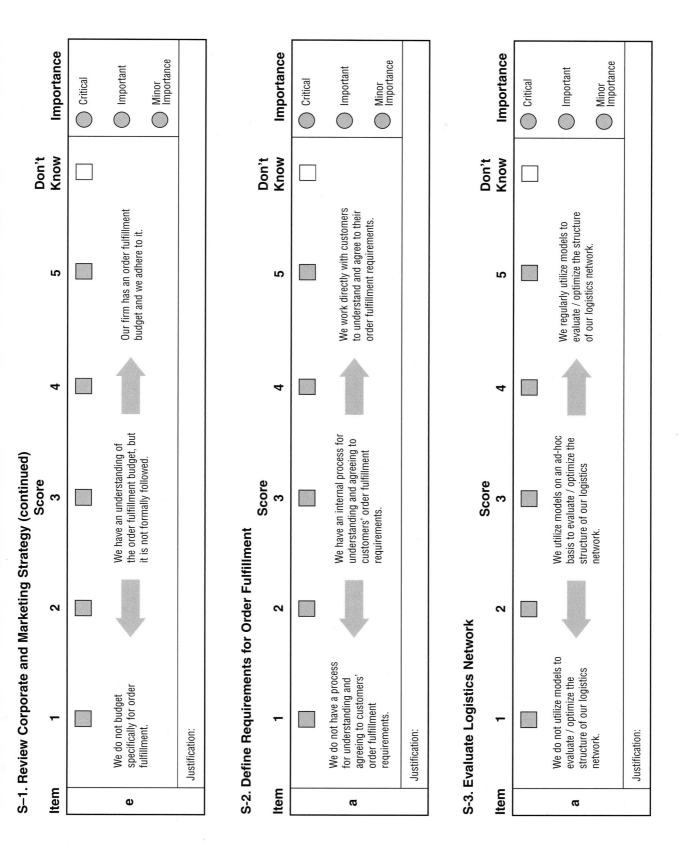

Item	Score					Don't Know	Importance
	1	2	3	4	5		
e	We do not budget specifically for order fulfillment.		We have an understanding of the order fulfillment budget, but it is not formally followed.		Our firm has an order fulfillment budget and we adhere to it.	☐	⬤ Critical ⬤ Important ⬤ Minor Importance

Justification:

S–2. Define Requirements for Order Fulfillment

Item	Score					Don't Know	Importance
	1	2	3	4	5		
a	We do not have a process for understanding and agreeing to customers' order fulfillment requirements.		We have an internal process for understanding and agreeing to customers' order fulfillment requirements.		We work directly with customers to understand and agree to their order fulfillment requirements.	☐	⬤ Critical ⬤ Important ⬤ Minor Importance

Justification:

S–3. Evaluate Logistics Network

Item	Score					Don't Know	Importance
	1	2	3	4	5		
a	We do not utilize models to evaluate / optimize the structure of our logistics network.		We utilize models on an ad-hoc basis to evaluate / optimize the structure of our logistics network.		We regularly utilize models to evaluate / optimize the structure of our logistics network.	☐	⬤ Critical ⬤ Important ⬤ Minor Importance

Justification:

S-4. Define Plan for Order Fulfillment

Item	Score 1	2	3	4	5	Don't Know	Importance
a	☐ All customers are treated equally in terms of our order fulfillment terms and policies.	☐	☐ We differentiate order fulfillment terms and policies for each customer segment based on class of trade.	☐	☐ We differentiate order fulfillment terms and policies for each customer segment based on profitability or future contribution to the firm.	☐	○ Critical ○ Important ○ Minor Importance
	Justification:						
b	☐ We do not have rules for allocating products, and as a result, we tend to allocate based on subjective factors.	☐	☐ We do not have established rules for allocating products, but we analyze situations with cross-functional input as they occur and make appropriate decisions as necessary.	☐	☐ We establish rules for how product is allocated between customers / customer segments, which are reviewed periodically by a cross-functional team.	☐	○ Critical ○ Important ○ Minor Importance
	Justification:						
c	☐ We have not evaluated the role of technology within order fulfillment.	☐	☐ We have assessed but we have not yet implemented appropriate technology to support our order fulfillment activities.	☐	☐ We have assessed and are utilizing technology appropriately to support our order fulfillment activities.	☐	○ Critical ○ Important ○ Minor Importance
	Justification:						
d	☐ We experience considerable demand variability as a result of our ordering rules.	☐	☐ We experience some demand variability as a result of our ordering rules.	☐	☐ We have established ordering rules that minimize demand variability (e.g. payment terms, minimum order sizes, etc.).	☐	○ Critical ○ Important ○ Minor Importance
	Justification:						

S-5. Develop Framework of Metrics

Item	1	2	3	Score 4	5	Don't Know	Importance

a

1	We do not have formal order fulfillment metrics.
3	We have our order fulfillment metrics but we do not relate them to financial performance.
5	We have formal metrics focused on order fulfillment and we understand how they impact our firm's EVA.

Justification:

Importance: Critical / Important / Minor Importance

b

1	We do not have formal performance goals for order fulfillment.
3	We have formal performance goals relating to order fulfillment that are communicated internally.
5	We have formal performance goals relating to order fulfillment that are communicated throughout the firm and to customers.

Justification:

Importance: Critical / Important / Minor Importance

c

1	Conflicting functional objectives often hinder the performance of the order fulfillment process.
3	There are groups of functions whose metrics are aligned, but there are some conflicts between the groups.
5	Our order fulfillment metrics are aligned with other metrics used throughout the firm.

Justification:

Importance: Critical / Important / Minor Importance

d

1	People in our firm have a limited understanding of how their decisions and actions affect the order fulfillment process.
3	People throughout our firm understand how their decisions and actions affect the order fulfillment process.
5	People throughout our firm, as well as our key suppliers and customers understand how their decisions and actions affect the order fulfillment process.

Justification:

Importance: Critical / Important / Minor Importance

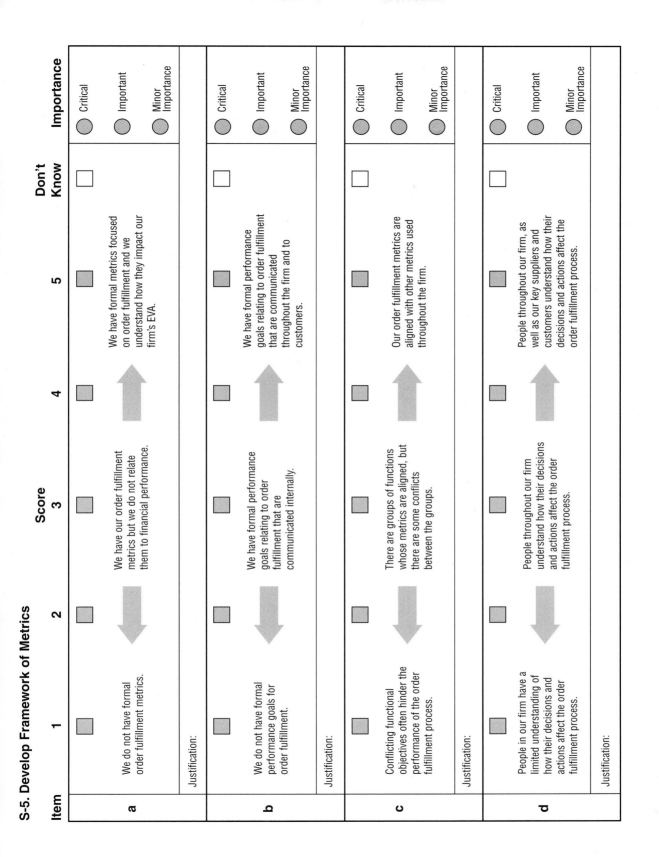

Operational Sub-Processes

O-1. Generate and Communicate Order

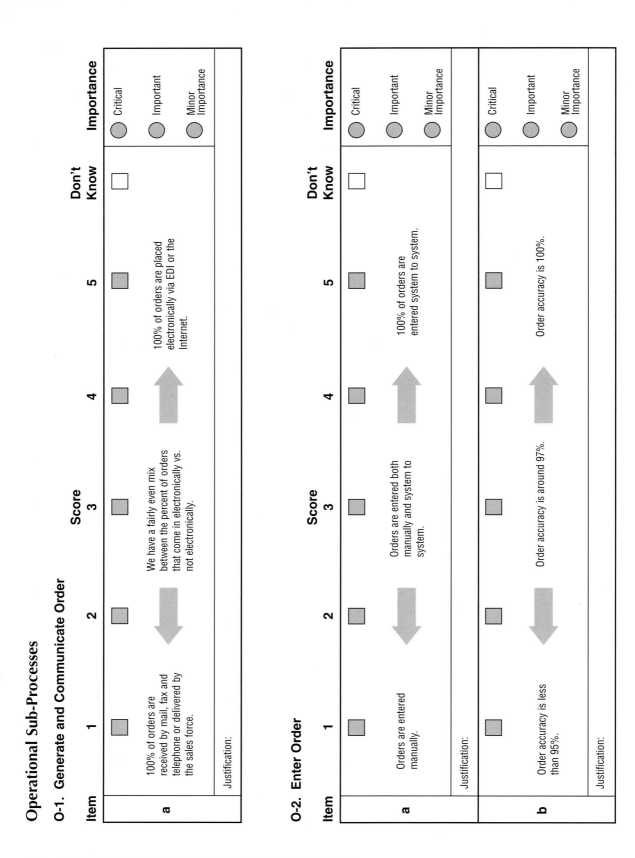

Item	1	2	Score 3	4	5	Don't Know	Importance
a	100% of orders are received by mail, fax and telephone or delivered by the sales force.		We have a fairly even mix between the percent of orders that come in electronically vs. not electronically.		100% of orders are placed electronically via EDI or the Internet.		● Critical ● Important ● Minor Importance
Justification:							

O-2. Enter Order

Item	1	2	Score 3	4	5	Don't Know	Importance
a	Orders are entered manually.		Orders are entered both manually and system to system.		100% of orders are entered system to system.		● Critical ● Important ● Minor Importance
Justification:							
b	Order accuracy is less than 95%.		Order accuracy is around 97%.		Order accuracy is 100%.		● Critical ● Important ● Minor Importance
Justification:							

O-2. Enter Order (continued)

Item		Score					Don't Know	Importance
	1	**2**	**3**	**4**	**5**			
c	☐	☐	☐	☐	☐	☐	◯ Critical
	Order entry delays of more than 24 hours are common.		Order entry delays of between 12 and 24 hours are common.		All orders are entered upon receipt.			◯ Important
								◯ Minor Importance
Justification:								

O-3. Process Order

Item		Score					Don't Know	Importance
	1	**2**	**3**	**4**	**5**			
a	☐	☐	☐	☐	☐	☐	◯ Critical
	Customer orders are often delayed for credit checks, inventory checks, and order flow and transportation planning.		Our credit and inventory checks are not automated but they are done efficiently and effectively.		Our order processing system automatically checks credit and inventory availability, and plans order flow and transportation.			◯ Important
								◯ Minor Importance
Justification:								

O-4. Handle Documents

Item		Score					Don't Know	Importance
	1	**2**	**3**	**4**	**5**			
a	☐	☐	☐	☐	☐	☐	◯ Critical
	Customer orders are not formally acknowledged		Customer orders are formally acknowledged, but there is a short delay.		Customer orders are automatically acknowledged upon receipt.			◯ Important
								◯ Minor Importance
Justification:								

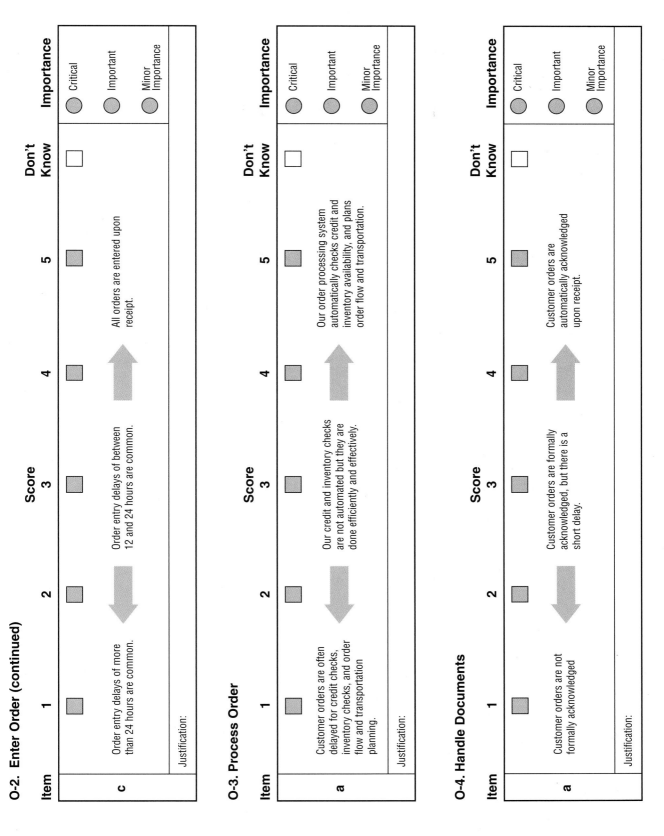

O-5. Fill Order

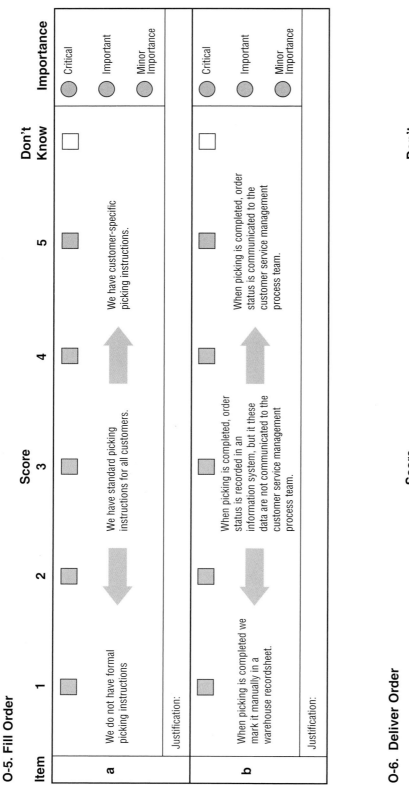

Item	1	2	Score 3	4	5	Don't Know	Importance
a	We do not have formal picking instructions		We have standard picking instructions for all customers.		We have customer-specific picking instructions.	☐	◉ Critical ◉ Important ◉ Minor Importance
	Justification:						
b	When picking is completed we mark it manually in a warehouse recordsheet.		When picking is completed, order status is recorded in an information system, but it these data are not communicated to the customer service management process team.		When picking is completed, order status is communicated to the customer service management process team.	☐	◉ Critical ◉ Important ◉ Minor Importance
	Justification:						

O-6. Deliver Order

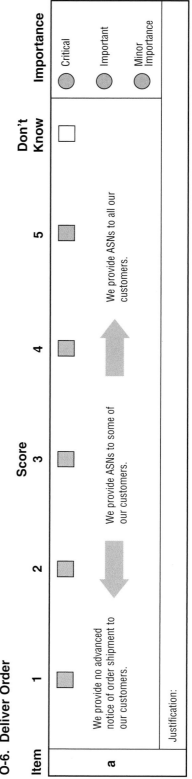

Item	1	2	Score 3	4	5	Don't Know	Importance
a	We provide no advanced notice of order shipment to our customers.		We provide ASNs to some of our customers.		We provide ASNs to all our customers.	☐	◉ Critical ◉ Important ◉ Minor Importance
	Justification:						

O-6. Deliver Order (continued)

Item	Score					Don't Know	Importance
	1	2	3	4	5		

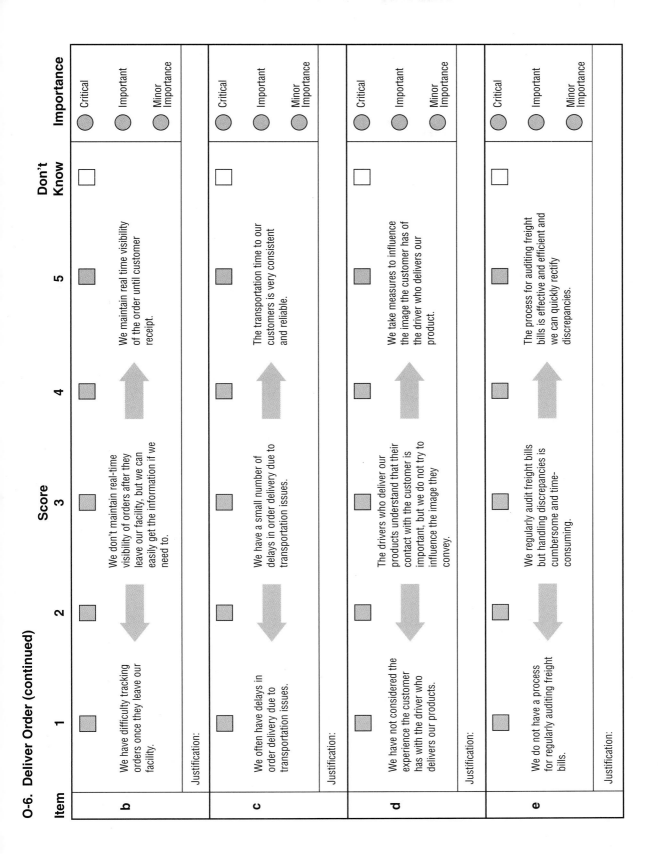

b — ◻ (1) We have difficulty tracking orders once they leave our facility. → ◻ (3) We don't maintain real-time visibility of orders after they leave our facility, but we can easily get the information if we need to. → ◻ (5) We maintain real time visibility of the order until customer receipt. ☐ Don't Know ○ Critical ○ Important ○ Minor Importance

Justification:

c — ◻ (1) We often have delays in order delivery due to transportation issues. → ◻ (3) We have a small number of delays in order delivery due to transportation issues. → ◻ (5) The transportation time to our customers is very consistent and reliable. ☐ Don't Know ○ Critical ○ Important ○ Minor Importance

Justification:

d — ◻ (1) We have not considered the experience the customer has with the driver who delivers our products. → ◻ (3) The drivers who deliver our products understand that their contact with the customer is important, but we do not try to influence the image they convey. → ◻ (5) We take measures to influence the image the customer has of the driver who delivers our product. ☐ Don't Know ○ Critical ○ Important ○ Minor Importance

Justification:

e — ◻ (1) We do not have a process for regularly auditing freight bills. → ◻ (3) We regularly audit freight bills but handling discrepancies is cumbersome and time-consuming. → ◻ (5) The process for auditing freight bills is effective and efficient and we can quickly rectify discrepancies. ☐ Don't Know ○ Critical ○ Important ○ Minor Importance

Justification:

O-6. Deliver Order (continued)

Item	Score					Don't Know	Importance
	1	2	3	4	5		
f	Our transportation providers often complain that we do not pay our freight bills on-time.		We usually pay our freight bills on time but the process is very manual.		The paying of freight bills is automatic and managed by exception.	☐	⦿ Critical ⦿ Important ⦿ Minor Importance
Justification:							

O-7. Perform Post Delivery Activities and Measure Performance

Item	Score					Don't Know	Importance
	1	2	3	4	5		
a	We lack a comprehensive understanding of the distinct steps of our order fulfillment process.		We have identified and documented the current standard set of steps for fulfilling an order.		We have analyzed standard steps for fulfilling an order to ensure process efficiency.	☐	⦿ Critical ⦿ Important ⦿ Minor Importance
Justification:							
b	We do not know the average time and variability of the distinct steps involved with the fulfillment of customer orders.		We have measured the average time and variability of the distinct steps involved with the fulfillment of customer orders.		We have measured and analyzed the average time and variability of the distinct steps involved with the fulfillment of customer orders to ensure process efficiency.	☐	⦿ Critical ⦿ Important ⦿ Minor Importance
Justification:							

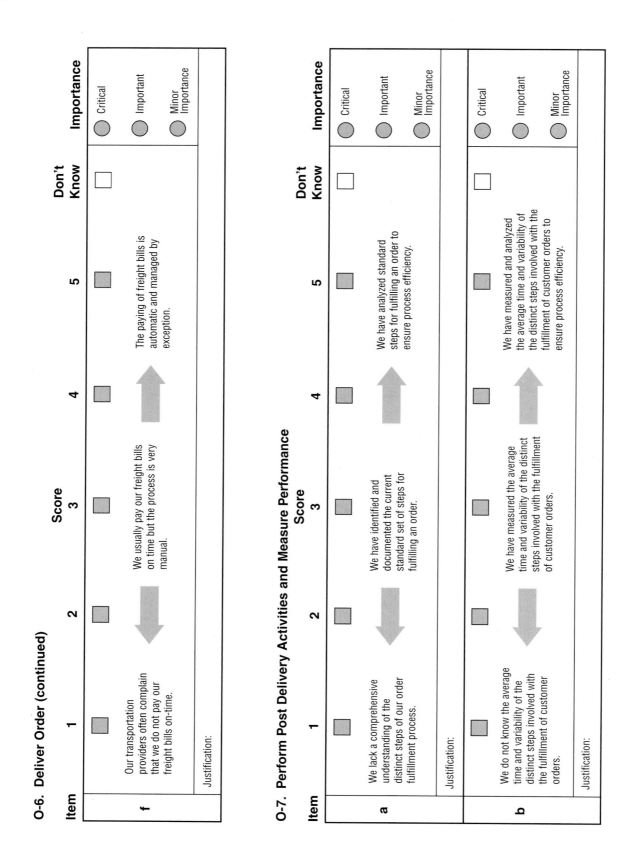

O-7. Perform Post Delivery Activities and Measure Performance (continued)

Item	Score 1	2	3	4	5	Don't Know	Importance

c

Score 1–2: Our customers often complain about the high variability in the overall time it takes us to fill an order.

Score 3: Our customers experience some variability in the overall time it takes to fill an order but it is not a source of complaints.

Score 4–5: Our customers experience very low variability in the overall time it takes us to fill an order.

Importance: ○ Critical ○ Important ○ Minor Importance

Justification:

d

Score 1–2: We are unable to quickly respond to customer requests regarding order status.

Score 3: Our customers have to contact us to get information regarding order status, but we can quickly respond to their requests.

Score 4–5: We are able to provide order tracking information to our customers. Our customers are able to access tracking information electronically.

Importance: ○ Critical ○ Important ○ Minor Importance

Justification:

e

Score 1–2: Our customers view our order fulfillment process as being inferior to that of our competitors.

Score 3: Our customers are satisfied with our order fulfillment process.

Score 4–5: Our customers view our order fulfillment process as being superior to that of our competitors and we believe it is a competitive advantage.

Importance: ○ Critical ○ Important ○ Minor Importance

Justification:

f

Score 1–2: We do not communicate our order fulfillment performance throughout the firm.

Score 3: We communicate our order fulfillment performance throughout the firm, but not with key customers and suppliers.

Score 4–5: We communicate our order fulfillment performance throughout the firm and with key customers and suppliers.

Importance: ○ Critical ○ Important ○ Minor Importance

Justification:

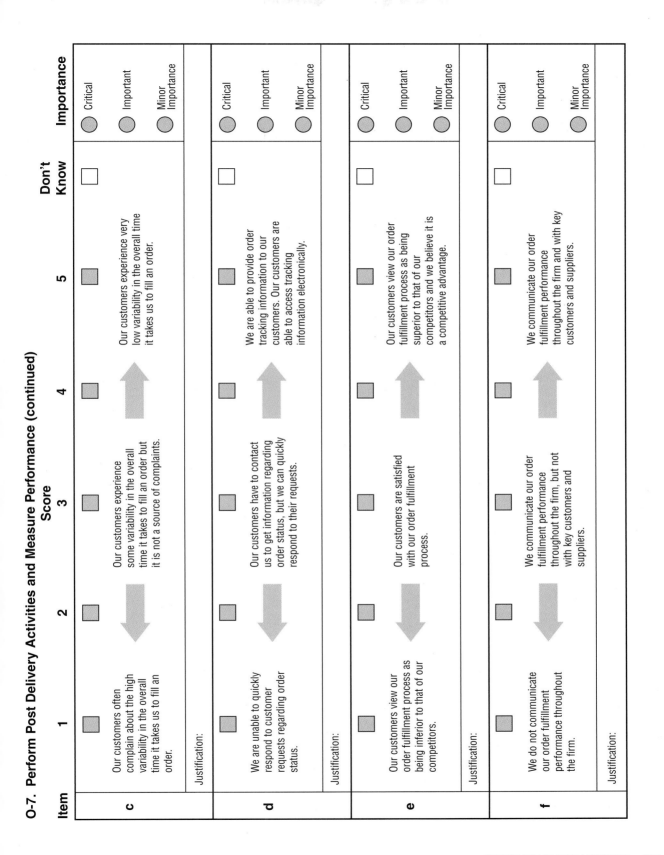

O-7. Perform Post Delivery Activities and Measure Performance (continued)

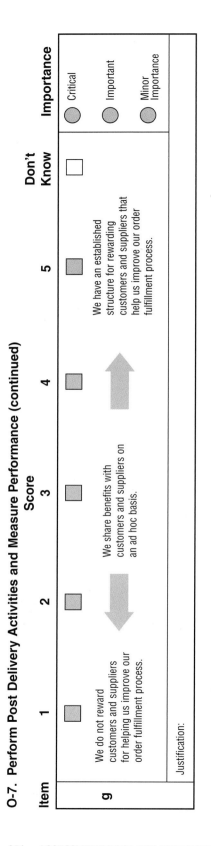

Item	Score					Don't Know	Importance
	1	2	3	4	5		

g

We do not reward customers and suppliers for helping us improve our order fulfillment process.

We share benefits with customers and suppliers on an ad hoc basis.

We have an established structure for rewarding customers and suppliers that help us improve our order fulfillment process.

Importance: ⬤ Critical ⬤ Important ⬤ Minor Importance

Justification:

APPENDIX F: Assessment Tool for the Manufacturing Flow Management Process

General Information

This assessment tool is designed to identify opportunities in your organization's manufacturing flow management process. It highlights important aspects of the strategic and operational sub-processes within manufacturing flow management. Management can use this tool to identify process strengths and weaknesses, and then focus their efforts on those areas where improvement efforts will drive the most benefits.

Directions

A cross-functional management team should complete each item in the assessment, the score, the importance, and the justification.

Score: The score for the item is assessed on a 5-point scale.

1 = you agree with the statement written in column 1.

2 = you believe the organization is somewhere between the statements in columns 1 and 3.

3 = you agree with the statement written in column 3.

4 = you believe the organization is somewhere between the statements in columns 3 and 5.

5 = you agree with the statement written in column 5.

The scale includes descriptions for 1, 3, and 5. Intermediate columns are included to accommodate ratings that fall between the scale points. Check the box corresponding to the score of the item. If the respondent is not sure how to score the item, check the "Don't Know" box.

Importance: The importance of the item is assessed on a 3-point scale.

3 = Critical: Item is essential for the success of the manufacturing flow management process within your organization.

2 = Important: Item is important but not essential for the success of the manufacturing flow management process within your organization.

1 = Minor Importance: Item is of minor importance for the success of the manufacturing flow management process within your organization.

Justification: Provide justification for your score and importance rating for each item in the space provided, i.e., why did you score the items the way you did?

Strategic Sub-Processes

S–1. Review Manufacturing, Sourcing, Marketing, and Logistics Strategies

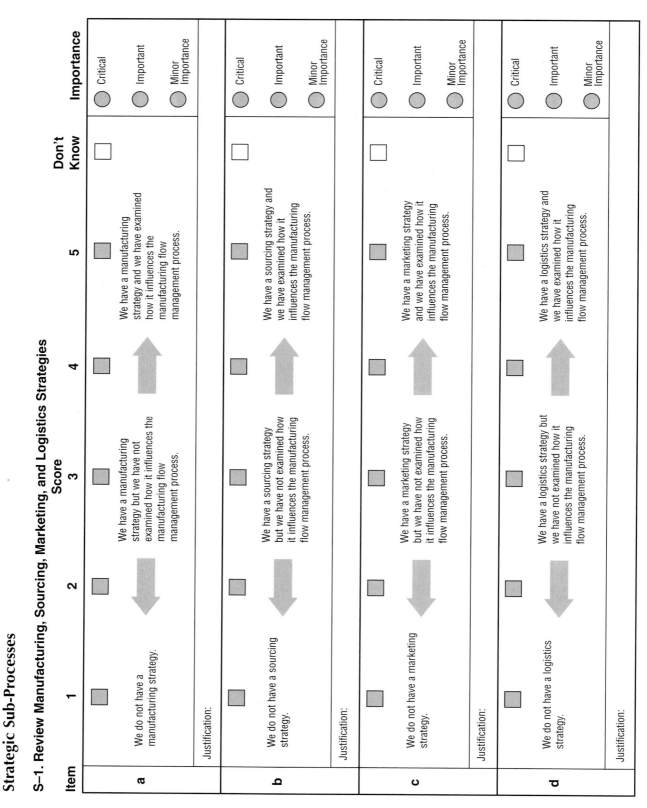

Item	1	2	3	4	5	Don't Know	Importance

a — We do not have a manufacturing strategy. / We have a manufacturing strategy but we have not examined how it influences the manufacturing flow management process. / We have a manufacturing strategy and we have examined how it influences the manufacturing flow management process.

Critical, Important, Minor Importance

Justification:

b — We do not have a sourcing strategy. / We have a sourcing strategy but we have not examined how it influences the manufacturing flow management process. / We have a sourcing strategy and we have examined how it influences the manufacturing flow management process.

Critical, Important, Minor Importance

Justification:

c — We do not have a marketing strategy. / We have a marketing strategy but we have not examined how it influences the manufacturing flow management process. / We have a marketing strategy and we have examined how it influences the manufacturing flow management process.

Critical, Important, Minor Importance

Justification:

d — We do not have a logistics strategy. / We have a logistics strategy but we have not examined how it influences the manufacturing flow management process. / We have a logistics strategy and we have examined how it influences the manufacturing flow management process.

Critical, Important, Minor Importance

Justification:

S-1. Review Manufacturing, Sourcing, Marketing, and Logistics Strategies (continued)

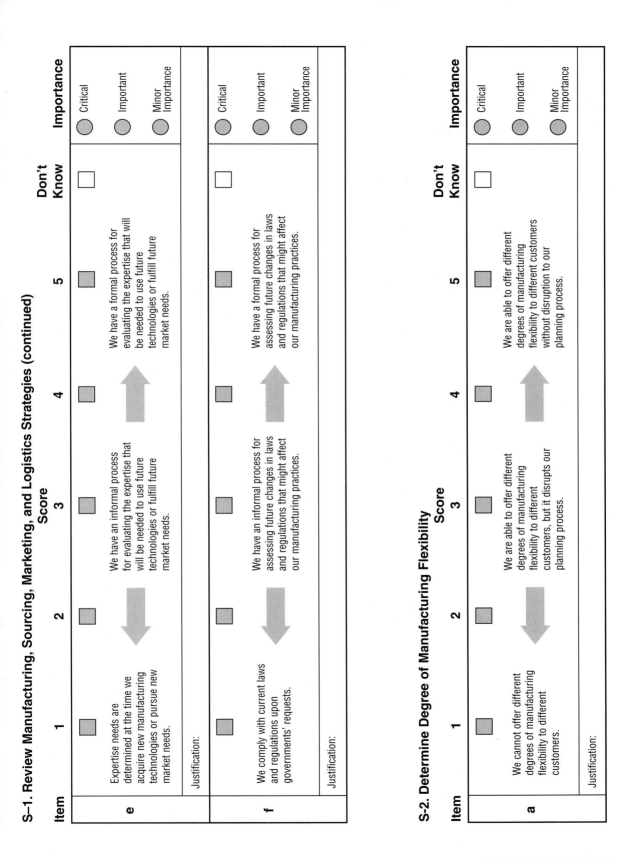

Item	Score					Don't Know	Importance

e — Score 1: Expertise needs are determined at the time we acquire new manufacturing technologies or pursue new market needs. Score 3: We have an informal process for evaluating the expertise that will be needed to use future technologies or fulfill future market needs. Score 5: We have a formal process for evaluating the expertise that will be needed to use future technologies or fulfill future market needs.

Importance: Critical / Important / Minor Importance

Justification:

f — Score 1: We comply with current laws and regulations upon governments' requests. Score 3: We have an informal process for assessing future changes in laws and regulations that might affect our manufacturing practices. Score 5: We have a formal process for assessing future changes in laws and regulations that might affect our manufacturing practices.

Importance: Critical / Important / Minor Importance

Justification:

S-2. Determine Degree of Manufacturing Flexibility

Item	Score					Don't Know	Importance

a — Score 1: We cannot offer different degrees of manufacturing flexibility to different customers. Score 3: We are able to offer different degrees of manufacturing flexibility to different customers, but it disrupts our planning process. Score 5: We are able to offer different degrees of manufacturing flexibility to different customers without disruption to our planning process.

Importance: Critical / Important / Minor Importance

Justification:

S-2. Determine Degree of Manufacturing Flexibility (continued)

Item	1	2	3	4	5	Don't Know	Importance
b	We do not evaluate manufacturing flexibility requirements.		Manufacturing flexibility requirements are set by the manufacturing function.		Manufacturing flexibility requirements are determined by a cross-functional team.	☐	○ Critical ○ Important ○ Minor Importance
	Justification:						
c	Quality policies and controls are not standardized.		We have standard quality policies and controls which are offered to all customers.		Quality policies and controls are standardized for segments of customers, and jointly established with key customers.	☐	○ Critical ○ Important ○ Minor Importance
	Justification:						
d	We do not plan for capacity growth for the future.		We informally plan for capacity growth in order to support the manufacturing flexibility requirements in the future.		We formally plan for capacity growth in order to support the manufacturing flexibility requirements in the future.	☐	○ Critical ○ Important ○ Minor Importance
	Justification:						
e	Make/buy decisions are based only on price with a short-term focus.		Make/buy decisions are based on multiple criteria, but with a short-term focus.		Make/buy decisions are based on multiple criteria, with a long-term focus.	☐	○ Critical ○ Important ○ Minor Importance
	Justification:						

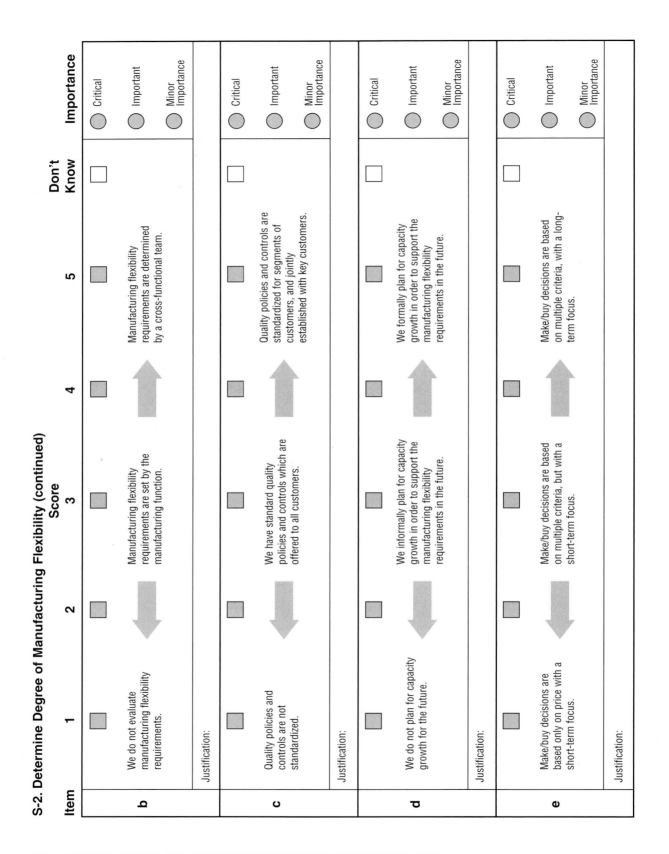

S-3. Determine Push / Pull Boundaries

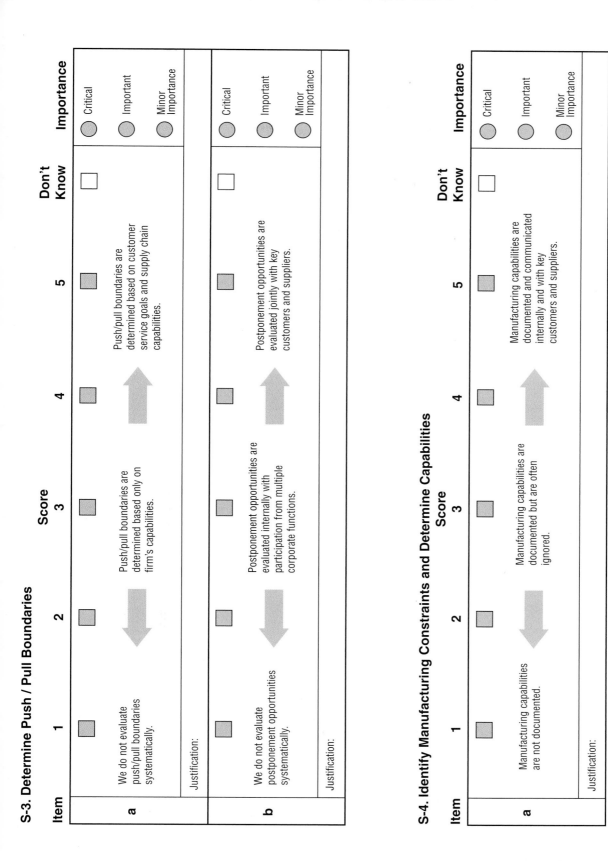

Item	Score 1	2	3	4	5	Don't Know	Importance
a	We do not evaluate push/pull boundaries systematically.		Push/pull boundaries are determined based only on firm's capabilities.		Push/pull boundaries are determined based on customer service goals and supply chain capabilities.	☐	◯ Critical ◯ Important ◯ Minor Importance
Justification:							
b	We do not evaluate postponement opportunities systematically.		Postponement opportunities are evaluated internally with participation from multiple corporate functions.		Postponement opportunities are evaluated jointly with key customers and suppliers.	☐	◯ Critical ◯ Important ◯ Minor Importance
Justification:							

S-4. Identify Manufacturing Constraints and Determine Capabilities

Item	Score 1	2	3	4	5	Don't Know	Importance
a	Manufacturing capabilities are not documented.		Manufacturing capabilities are documented but are often ignored.		Manufacturing capabilities are documented and communicated internally and with key customers and suppliers.	☐	◯ Critical ◯ Important ◯ Minor Importance
Justification:							

S-4. Identify Manufacturing Constraints and Determine Capabilities (continued)

Item	Score 1	2	3	4	5	Don't Know	Importance
b	☐ Decisions regarding stock levels are based only on local information.	☐	☐ Decision-making regarding stock levels is centralized.	☐	☐ Decision-making regarding stock levels is centralized, but adjustments can be made based on local information.	☐	◯ Critical ◯ Important ◯ Minor Importance
Justification:							
c	☐ We do not have disposal/disposition guidelines.	☐	☐ Each manager is responsible for determining disposal/disposition guidelines.	☐	☐ We have formal disposal/disposition guidelines.	☐	◯ Critical ◯ Important ◯ Minor Importance
Justification:							
d	☐ Customer service representatives make decisions regarding customer requests without any input from manufacturing.	☐	☐ Customer service representatives usually have to contact someone in manufacturing to help them assess whether customer requests can be fulfilled.	☐	☐ We have established and communicated guidelines so that customer service representatives know which customer requests can be fulfilled without further evaluation.	☐	◯ Critical ◯ Important ◯ Minor Importance
Justification:							
e	☐ Manufacturing constraints and capabilities are not formally documented.	☐	☐ We have developed mechanisms to communicate our manufacturing capabilities on an as-needed basis.	☐	☐ We have developed mechanisms that communicate real-time information about our manufacturing capabilities.	☐	◯ Critical ◯ Important ◯ Minor Importance
Justification:							

S-5. Develop Framework of Metrics

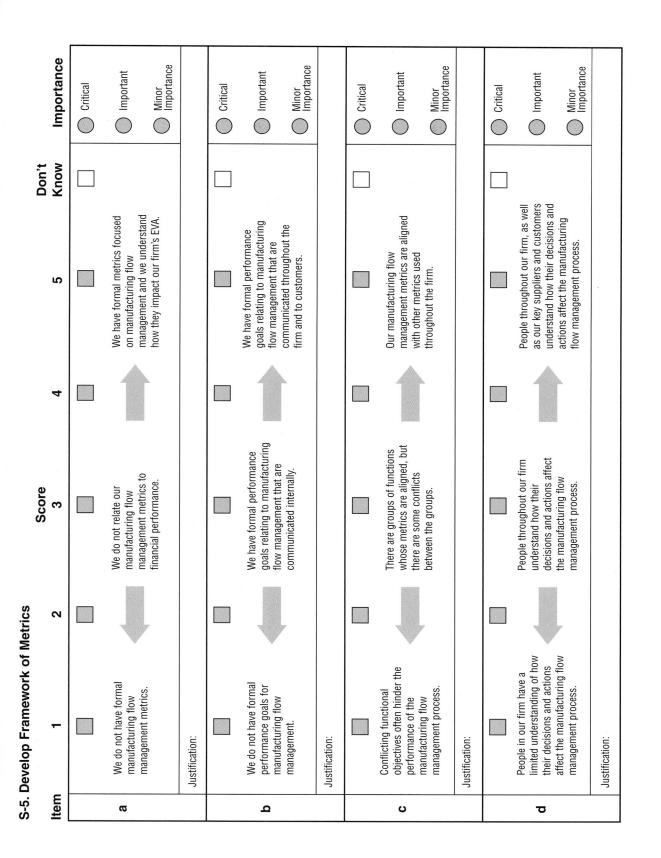

Item	Score 1		2	3		4	5	Don't Know	Importance
a	☐ We do not have formal manufacturing flow management metrics.		☐	☐ We do not relate our manufacturing flow management metrics to financial performance.		☐	☐ We have formal metrics focused on manufacturing flow management and we understand how they impact our firm's EVA.	☐	◉ Critical ◉ Important ◉ Minor Importance
	Justification:								
b	☐ We do not have formal performance goals for manufacturing flow management.		☐	☐ We have formal performance goals relating to manufacturing flow management that are communicated internally.		☐	☐ We have formal performance goals relating to manufacturing flow management that are communicated throughout the firm and to customers.	☐	◉ Critical ◉ Important ◉ Minor Importance
	Justification:								
c	☐ Conflicting functional objectives often hinder the performance of the manufacturing flow management process.		☐	☐ There are groups of functions whose metrics are aligned, but there are some conflicts between the groups.		☐	☐ Our manufacturing flow management metrics are aligned with other metrics used throughout the firm.	☐	◉ Critical ◉ Important ◉ Minor Importance
	Justification:								
d	☐ People in our firm have a limited understanding of how their decisions and actions affect the manufacturing flow management process.		☐	☐ People throughout our firm understand how their decisions and actions affect the manufacturing flow management process.		☐	☐ People throughout our firm, as well as our key suppliers and customers understand how their decisions and actions affect the manufacturing flow management process.	☐	◉ Critical ◉ Important ◉ Minor Importance
	Justification:								

Operational Sub-Processes

O-1. Determine Routing and Velocity through Manufacturing

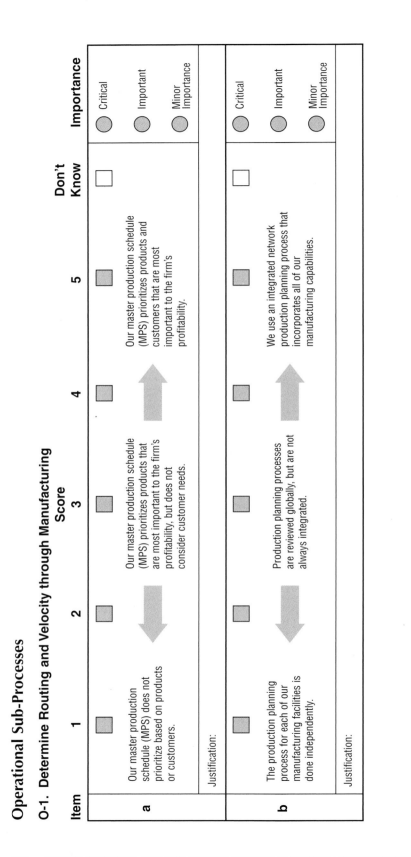

Item		Score					Don't Know		Importance
	1	2	3	4	5			
a	Our master production schedule (MPS) does not prioritize based on products or customers.		Our master production schedule (MPS) prioritizes products that are most important to the firm's profitability, but does not consider customer needs.		Our master production schedule (MPS) prioritizes products and customers that are most important to the firm's profitability.			○ Critical ○ Important ○ Minor Importance
	Justification:							
b	The production planning process for each of our manufacturing facilities is done independently.		Production planning processes are reviewed globally, but are not always integrated.		We use an integrated network production planning process that incorporates all of our manufacturing capabilities.			○ Critical ○ Important ○ Minor Importance
	Justification:							

O-2. Plan Manufacturing and Material Flow

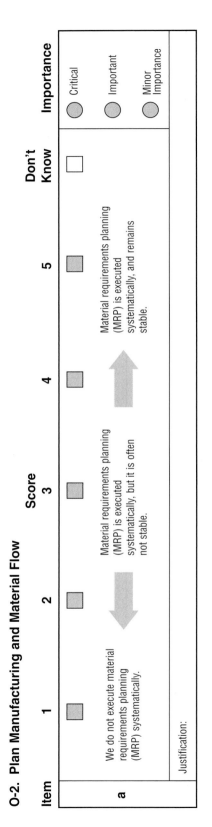

Item		Score					Don't Know		Importance
	1	2	3	4	5			
a	We do not execute material requirements planning (MRP) systematically.		Material requirements planning (MRP) is executed systematically, but it is often not stable.		Material requirements planning (MRP) is executed systematically, and remains stable.			○ Critical ○ Important ○ Minor Importance
	Justification:							

O-2. Plan Manufacturing and Material Flow (continued)

Item		Score					Don't Know	Importance
		1	2	3	4	5		

b

We do not develop detailed capacity plans for each manufacturing facility.

We develop detailed capacity plans, but conflicts are resolved without considering cross-functional input.

We develop detailed capacity plans, and conflicts are resolved with cross-functional input.

Importance: ● Critical   ● Important   ● Minor Importance

Justification:

O-3. Execute Capacity and Demand Plans

Item		Score					Don't Know	Importance
		1	2	3	4	5		

a

Our inventory records are not accurate and we frequently face disruptions in manufacturing due to these inaccuracies.

Our inventory records are fairly accurate and we occasionally face disruptions in manufacturing due to these inaccuracies.

Our inventory records are sufficiently accurate and we rarely face disruptions in manufacturing due to data inaccuracies.

Importance: ● Critical   ● Important   ● Minor Importance

Justification:

b

We frequently face disruptions in manufacturing due to inventory management issues.

We occasionally face disruptions in manufacturing due to inventory management issues.

We rarely face disruptions in manufacturing due to inventory management issues.

Importance: ● Critical   ● Important   ● Minor Importance

Justification:

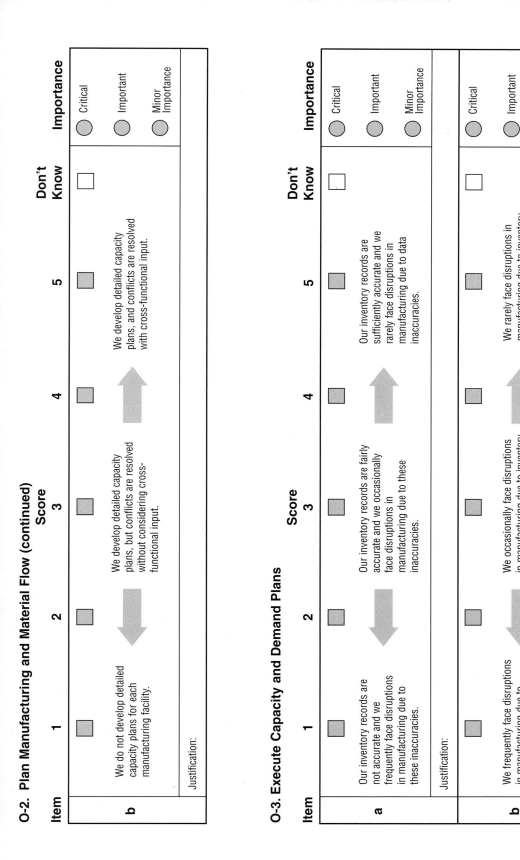

O-4. Measure Performance

Item		Score					Don't Know	Importance
	1	2	3	4	5			

a

1: We believe our competitors are better at manufacturing flow management than we are.

3: We believe our manufacturing flow management process is adequate.

5: We believe we do manufacturing flow management better than our competitors and it is a competitive advantage for us.

Don't Know ☐

Importance: ● Critical ● Important ● Minor Importance

Justification:

b

1: We do not communicate our manufacturing flow management performance throughout the firm.

3: We communicate our manufacturing flow management performance throughout the firm, but not with key customers and suppliers.

5: We communicate our manufacturing flow management performance throughout the firm and with key customers and suppliers.

Don't Know ☐

Importance: ● Critical ● Important ● Minor Importance

Justification:

c

1: We do not reward customers and suppliers for helping us improve our manufacturing flow management process.

3: We share benefits with customers and suppliers on an ad hoc basis.

5: We have an established structure for rewarding customers and suppliers that help us improve our manufacturing flow management process.

Don't Know ☐

Importance: ● Critical ● Important ● Minor Importance

Justification:

d

1: We do not evaluate past exceptions and emergency situations.

3: We regularly evaluate past exceptions and emergency situations, but do not measure their cost/revenue implications.

5: We regularly evaluate past exceptions and emergency situations, assess the cost/revenue implications, and make changes to avoid them in the future.

Don't Know ☐

Importance: ● Critical ● Important ● Minor Importance

Justification:

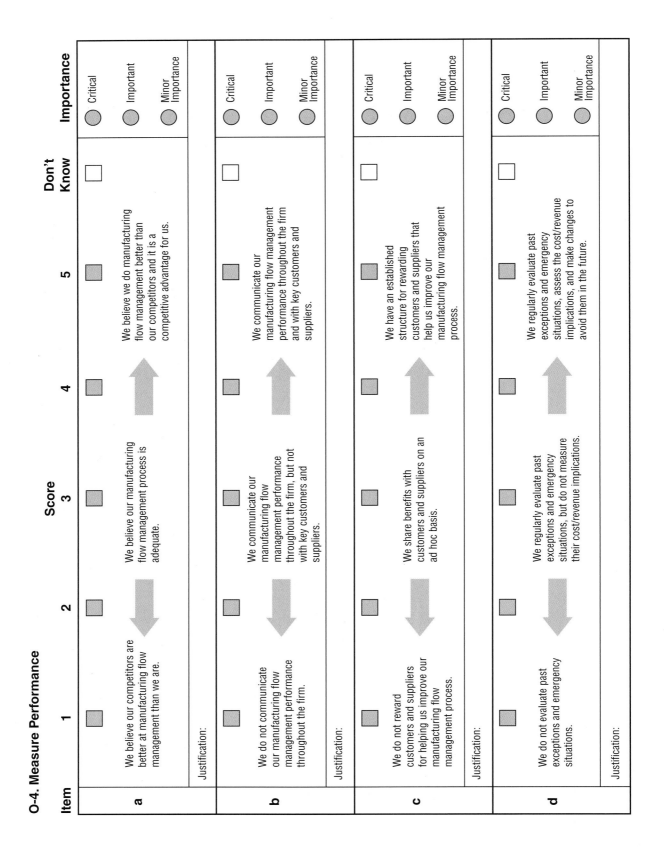

APPENDIX G: Assessment Tool for the Product Development and Commercialization Process

General Information

This assessment tool is designed to identify opportunities in your organization's product development and commercialization process. It highlights important aspects of the strategic and operational sub-processes within product development and commercialization. Management can use this tool to identify process strengths and weaknesses, and then focus their efforts on those areas where improvement efforts will drive the most benefits.

Directions

A cross-functional management team should complete each item in the assessment, the score, the importance, and the justification.

Score: The score for the item is assessed on a 5-point scale.

1 = **you agree with the statement written in column 1.**

2 = **you believe the organization is somewhere between the statements in columns 1 and 3.**

3 = **you agree with the statement written in column 3.**

4 = **you believe the organization is somewhere between the statements in columns 3 and 5.**

5 = **you agree with the statement written in column 5.**

The scale includes descriptions for 1, 3, and 5. Intermediate columns are included to accommodate ratings that fall between the scale points. Check the box corresponding to the score of the item. If the respondent is not sure how to score the item, check the "Don't Know" box.

Importance: The importance of the item is assessed on a 3-point scale.

3 = **Critical:** Item is essential for the success of the product development and commercialization process within your organization.

2 = **Important:** Item is important but not essential for the success of the product development and commercialization process within your organization.

1 = **Minor Importance:** Item is of minor importance for the success of the product development and commercialization process within your organization.

Justification: Provide justification for your score and importance rating for each item in the space provided, i.e., why did you score the items the way you did?

Strategic Sub-Processes

S-1. Review Corporate, Marketing, Manufacturing and Sourcing Strategies

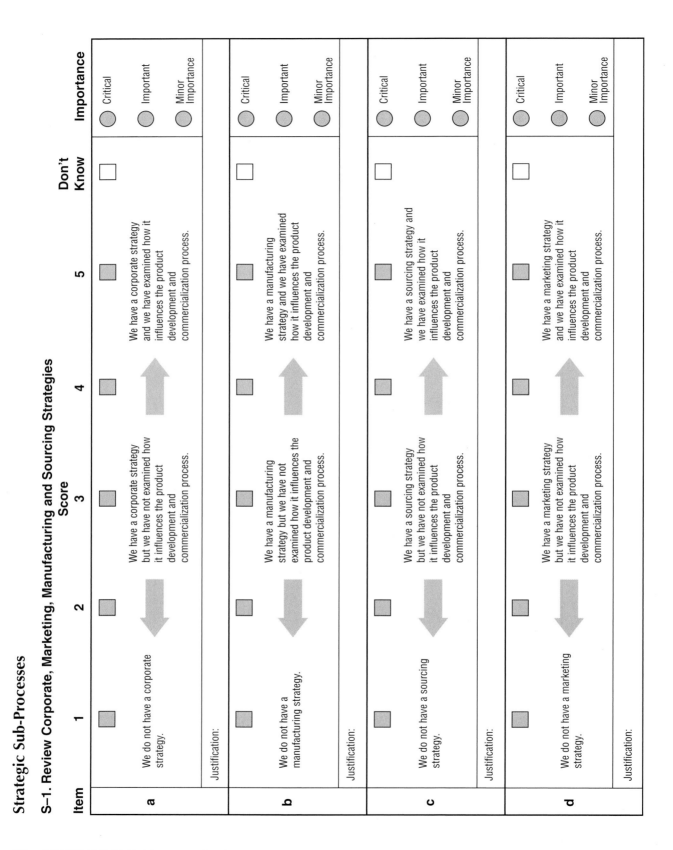

Item	Score					Don't Know	Importance
	1	2	3	4	5		
a	We do not have a corporate strategy.		We have a corporate strategy but we have not examined how it influences the product development and commercialization process.		We have a corporate strategy and we have examined how it influences the product development and commercialization process.	☐	○ Critical ○ Important ○ Minor Importance
Justification:							
b	We do not have a manufacturing strategy.		We have a manufacturing strategy but we have not examined how it influences the product development and commercialization process.		We have a manufacturing strategy and we have examined how it influences the product development and commercialization process.	☐	○ Critical ○ Important ○ Minor Importance
Justification:							
c	We do not have a sourcing strategy.		We have a sourcing strategy but we have not examined how it influences the product development and commercialization process.		We have a sourcing strategy and we have examined how it influences the product development and commercialization process.	☐	○ Critical ○ Important ○ Minor Importance
Justification:							
d	We do not have a marketing strategy.		We have a marketing strategy but we have not examined how it influences the product development and commercialization process.		We have a marketing strategy and we have examined how it influences the product development and commercialization process.	☐	○ Critical ○ Important ○ Minor Importance
Justification:							

S–1. Review Corporate, Marketing, Manufacturing and Sourcing Strategies (continued)

Item	Score 1	2	3	4	5	Don't Know	Importance
e	☐ We do not review the product needs of our key customer segments.	☐	☐ We periodically perform an internal review of the product needs of our key customer segments.	☐	☐ We regularly meet with key customer segments to review their product needs.	☐	◉ Critical ◉ Important ◉ Minor Importance
	Justification:						
f	☐ We have no understanding of the supply chain constraints and capabilities as they relate to product development activities.	☐	☐ We have a limited understanding of the supply chain constraints and capabilities as they relate to product development activities.	☐	☐ We have an extensive (cross-functional) understanding of the supply chain constraints and capabilities as they relate to product development activities.	☐	◉ Critical ◉ Important ◉ Minor Importance
	Justification:						

S–2. Develop Idea Generation and Screening Processes

Item	Score 1	2	3	4	5	Don't Know	Importance
a	☐ We do not consider customer feedback with respect to product development activities.	☐	☐ We informally consider customer feedback in our product development activities.	☐	☐ We have a formal customer feedback program that serves as input into our product development and commercialization process.	☐	◉ Critical ◉ Important ◉ Minor Importance
	Justification:						

S–2. Develop Idea Generation and Screening Processes (continued)

Item	1	2	3	4	5	Don't Know	Importance
b	☐ We do not offer incentives for new product ideas.	☐	☐ We provide incentives for new product ideas that come from our employees.	☐	☐ We provide incentives for new product ideas that come from employees, suppliers and customers.	☐	○ Critical ○ Important ○ Minor Importance
	Justification:						
c	☐ We rely on a very limited number of sources for developing new product ideas.	☐	☐ We use several sources for developing new product ideas, but there is room for improvement.	☐	☐ We have evaluated the value of all potential sources of new product ideas and use them appropriately.	☐	○ Critical ○ Important ○ Minor Importance
	Justification:						
d	☐ We do not have an explicit methodology for developing new product ideas.	☐	☐ We have informal procedures for developing new product ideas.	☐	☐ We have an explicit methodology for developing new product ideas.	☐	○ Critical ○ Important ○ Minor Importance
	Justification:						
e	☐ We do not re-evaluate our choice of sources for new product ideas.	☐	☐ We re-evaluate our choice of sources for new product ideas once problems arise.	☐	☐ We re-evaluate our choice of sources for new product ideas regularly.	☐	○ Critical ○ Important ○ Minor Importance
	Justification:						

S–3. Establish Guidelines for Cross-Functional Product Development Team Membership

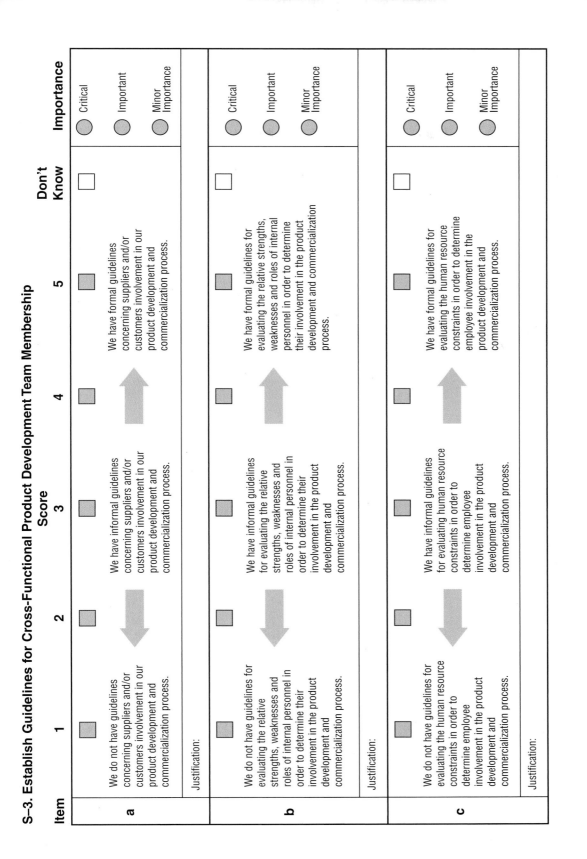

Item	Score					Don't Know	Importance

a

1 — We do not have guidelines concerning suppliers and/or customers involvement in our product development and commercialization process.

3 — We have informal guidelines concerning suppliers and/or customers involvement in our product development and commercialization process.

5 — We have formal guidelines concerning suppliers and/or customers involvement in our product development and commercialization process.

Importance: ○ Critical ○ Important ○ Minor Importance

Justification:

b

1 — We do not have guidelines for evaluating the relative strengths, weaknesses and roles of internal personnel in order to determine their involvement in the product development and commercialization process.

3 — We have informal guidelines for evaluating the relative strengths, weaknesses and roles of internal personnel in order to determine their involvement in the product development and commercialization process.

5 — We have formal guidelines for evaluating the relative strengths, weaknesses and roles of internal personnel in order to determine their involvement in the product development and commercialization process.

Importance: ○ Critical ○ Important ○ Minor Importance

Justification:

c

1 — We do not have guidelines for evaluating the human resource constraints in order to determine employee involvement in the product development and commercialization process.

3 — We have informal guidelines for evaluating human resource constraints in order to determine employee involvement in the product development and commercialization process.

5 — We have formal guidelines for evaluating the human resource constraints in order to determine employee involvement in the product development and commercialization process.

Importance: ○ Critical ○ Important ○ Minor Importance

Justification:

S–4. Identify Product Rollout Issues and Constraints

Item	Score 1	2	3	4	5	Don't Know	Importance
a	We do not have formal procedures in place to identify product rollout issues and constraints.		We have consistent procedures that involve cross-functional input to identify product rollout issues and constraints.		We have consistent procedures that are cross-functional and also include input from appropriate suppliers and/or customers to identify product rollout issues and constraints.	☐	○ Critical ○ Important ○ Minor Importance
	Justification:						
b	We do not consider potential problems associated with market and promotion planning for product rollouts.		We informally consider potential problems associated with market and promotion planning for product rollouts.		We formally consider potential problems associated with market and promotion planning for product rollouts.	☐	○ Critical ○ Important ○ Minor Importance
	Justification:						
c	We do not consider potential problems associated with sales force training for product rollouts.		We informally consider potential problems associated with sales force training for product rollouts.		We formally consider potential problems associated with sales force training for product rollouts.	☐	○ Critical ○ Important ○ Minor Importance
	Justification:						
d	We do not consider potential problems associated with transportation planning for product rollouts.		We informally consider potential problems associated with transportation planning for product rollouts.		We formally consider potential problems associated with transportation planning for product rollouts.	☐	○ Critical ○ Important ○ Minor Importance
	Justification:						

S–4. Identify Product Rollout Issues and Constraints (continued)

Item	Score 1	2	3	4	5	Don't Know	Importance

e

Score 1: We do not consider potential problems associated with inventory deployment for product rollouts.

Score 3: We informally consider potential problems associated with inventory deployment for product rollouts.

Score 5: We formally consider potential problems associated with inventory deployment for product rollouts.

Don't Know: ☐

Importance: ● Critical ● Important ● Minor Importance

Justification:

S–5. Establish New Product Project Guidelines

Item	Score 1	2	3	4	5	Don't Know	Importance

a

Score 1: We do not have guidelines for establishing product time-to-market expectations for our product development and commercialization process.

Score 3: We have informal guidelines for establishing time-to-market expectations for our product development and commercialization process.

Score 5: We have formal guidelines for establishing time-to-market expectations for our product development and commercialization process.

Don't Know: ☐

Importance: ● Critical ● Important ● Minor Importance

Justification:

b

Score 1: We do not have guidelines for establishing product profitability targets for our product development and commercialization process.

Score 3: We have informal guidelines for establishing product profitability targets for our product development and commercialization process.

Score 5: We have formal guidelines for establishing product profitability targets for our product development and commercialization process.

Importance: ● Critical ● Important ● Minor Importance

Justification:

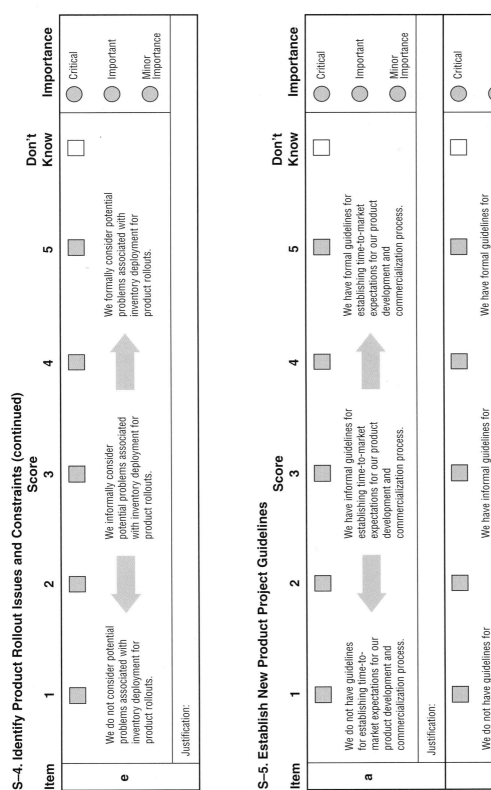

S–5. Establish New Product Project Guidelines (continued)

Item	Score 1	2	3	4	5	Don't Know	Importance
c	We do not have procedures to consider the drain on human resources of our product development and commercialization process.		We have informal procedures to consider the drain on human resources of our product development and commercialization process.		We have formal procedures to consider the drain on human resources of our product development and commercialization process.		○ Critical ○ Important ○ Minor Importance
	Justification:						
d	We do not have procedures for assessing the strategic fit of new products.		We have informal procedures for assessing the strategic fit of new products.		We have formal procedures for assessing the strategic fit of new products.		○ Critical ○ Important ○ Minor Importance
	Justification:						

S–6. Develop Framework of Metrics

Item	Score 1	2	3	4	5	Don't Know	Importance
a	We do not have formal product development and commercialization metrics.		We have product development and commercialization metrics but we do not relate them to financial performance.		We have formal metrics focused on product development and commercialization and we understand how they impact our firm's EVA.		○ Critical ○ Important ○ Minor Importance
	Justification:						

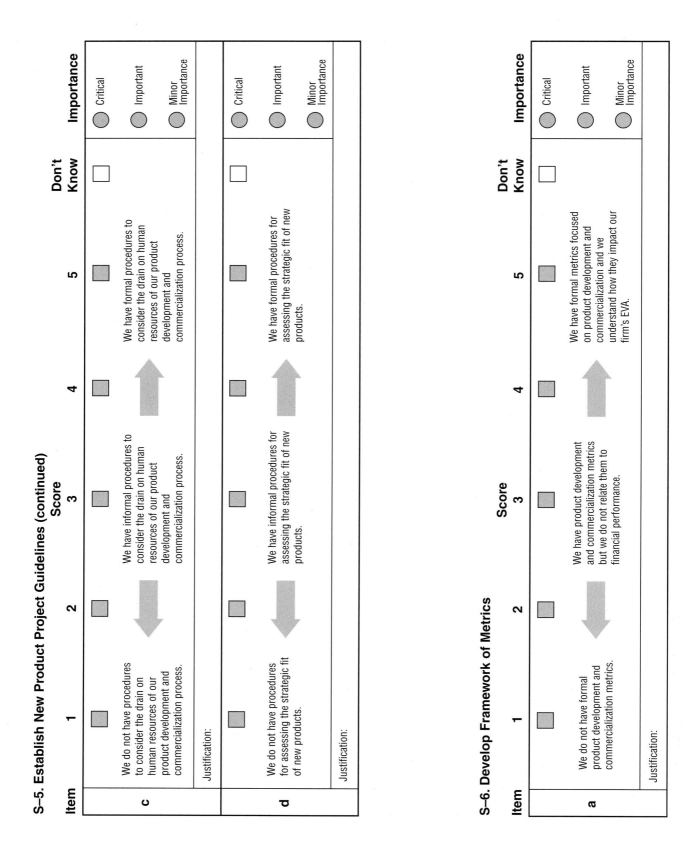

S–6. Develop Framework of Metrics (continued)

Item	Score 1	2	3	4	5	Don't Know	Importance
b	☐	☐ We do not have formal performance goals for product development and commercialization.	☐ We have formal performance goals relating to product development and commercialization that are communicated internally.	☐	☐ We have formal performance goals relating to product development and commercialization that are communicated throughout the firm and to suppliers and customers.	☐	◑ Critical ◑ Important ◑ Minor Importance
	Justification:						
c	☐ Conflicting functional objectives often hinder the performance of the product development and commercialization process.	☐	☐ There are groups of functions whose metrics are aligned, but there are some conflicts between the groups.	☐	☐ Our product development and commercialization metrics are aligned with other metrics used throughout the firm.	☐	◑ Critical ◑ Important ◑ Minor Importance
	Justification:						
d	☐ People in our firm have a limited understanding of how their decisions and actions affect the product development and commercialization process.	☐	☐ People throughout our firm understand how their decisions and actions affect the product development and commercialization process.	☐	☐ People throughout our firm, as well as our key suppliers and customers understand how their decisions and actions affect the product development and commercialization process.	☐	◑ Critical ◑ Important ◑ Minor Importance
	Justification:						

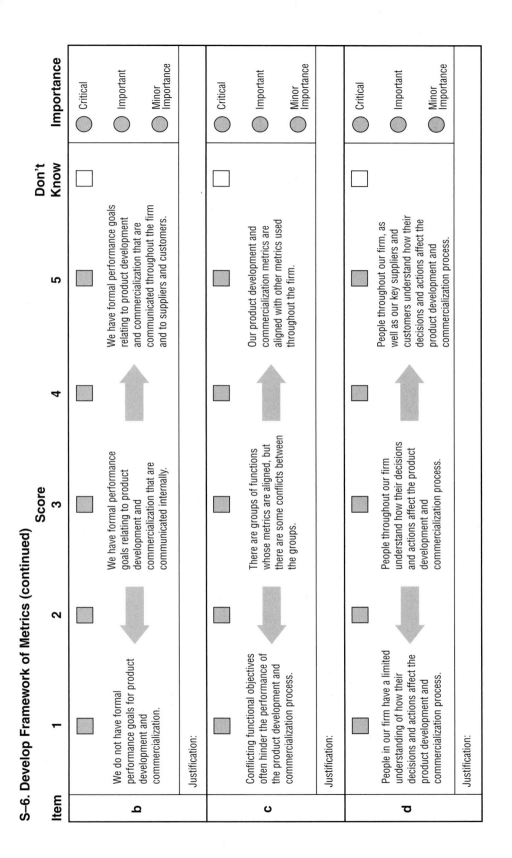

Operational Sub-Processes

O–1. Define New Products and Assess Fit

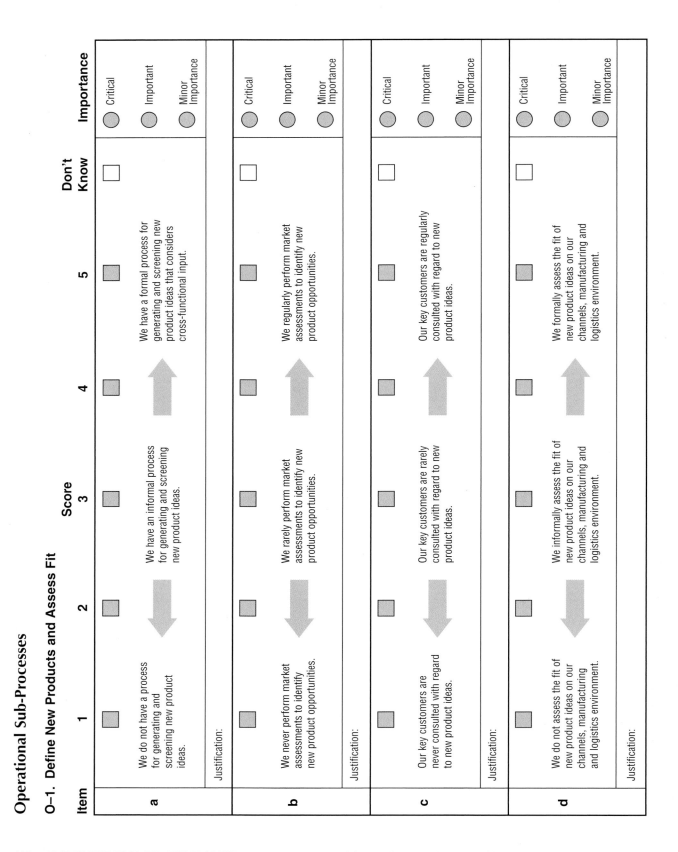

Item	Score 1	Score 2	Score 3	Score 4	Score 5	Don't Know	Importance
a	☐ We do not have a process for generating and screening new product ideas.	☐	☐ We have an informal process for generating and screening new product ideas.	☐	☐ We have a formal process for generating and screening new product ideas that considers cross-functional input.	☐	◯ Critical ◯ Important ◯ Minor Importance
Justification:							
b	☐ We never perform market assessments to identify new product opportunities.	☐	☐ We rarely perform market assessments to identify new product opportunities.	☐	☐ We regularly perform market assessments to identify new product opportunities.	☐	◯ Critical ◯ Important ◯ Minor Importance
Justification:							
c	☐ Our key customers are never consulted with regard to new product ideas.	☐	☐ Our key customers are rarely consulted with regard to new product ideas.	☐	☐ Our key customers are regularly consulted with regard to new product ideas.	☐	◯ Critical ◯ Important ◯ Minor Importance
Justification:							
d	☐ We do not assess the fit of new product ideas on our channels, manufacturing and logistics environment.	☐	☐ We informally assess the fit of new product ideas on our channels, manufacturing and logistics environment.	☐	☐ We formally assess the fit of new product ideas on our channels, manufacturing and logistics environment.	☐	◯ Critical ◯ Important ◯ Minor Importance
Justification:							

O-2. Establish Cross-Functional Product Development Team

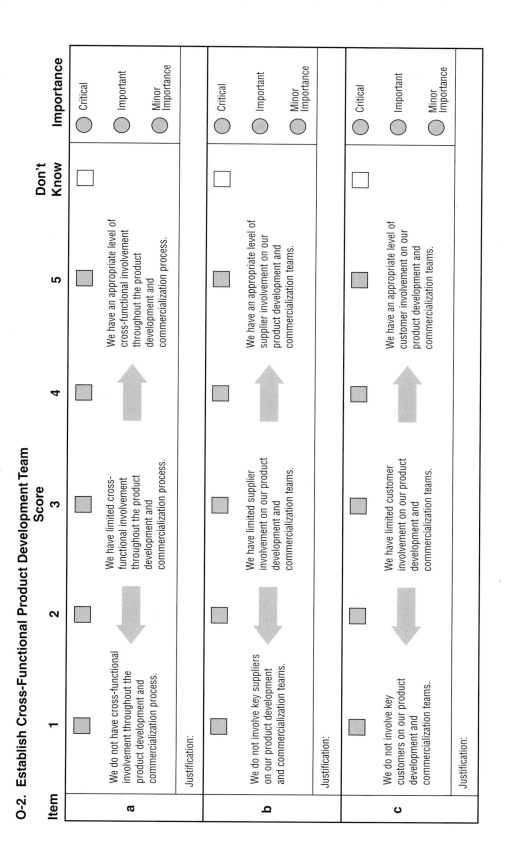

Item	Score					Don't Know	Importance

a — Score 1–2: We do not have cross-functional involvement throughout the product development and commercialization process. Score 3: We have limited cross-functional involvement throughout the product development and commercialization process. Score 4–5: We have an appropriate level of cross-functional involvement throughout the product development and commercialization process.

Justification:

b — Score 1–2: We do not involve key suppliers on our product development and commercialization teams. Score 3: We have limited supplier involvement on our product development and commercialization teams. Score 4–5: We have an appropriate level of supplier involvement on our product development and commercialization teams.

Justification:

c — Score 1–2: We do not involve key customers on our product development and commercialization teams. Score 3: We have limited customer involvement on our product development and commercialization teams. Score 4–5: We have an appropriate level of customer involvement on our product development and commercialization teams.

Justification:

Importance options for each item: Critical, Important, Minor Importance

O-3. Formalize New Product Development Project

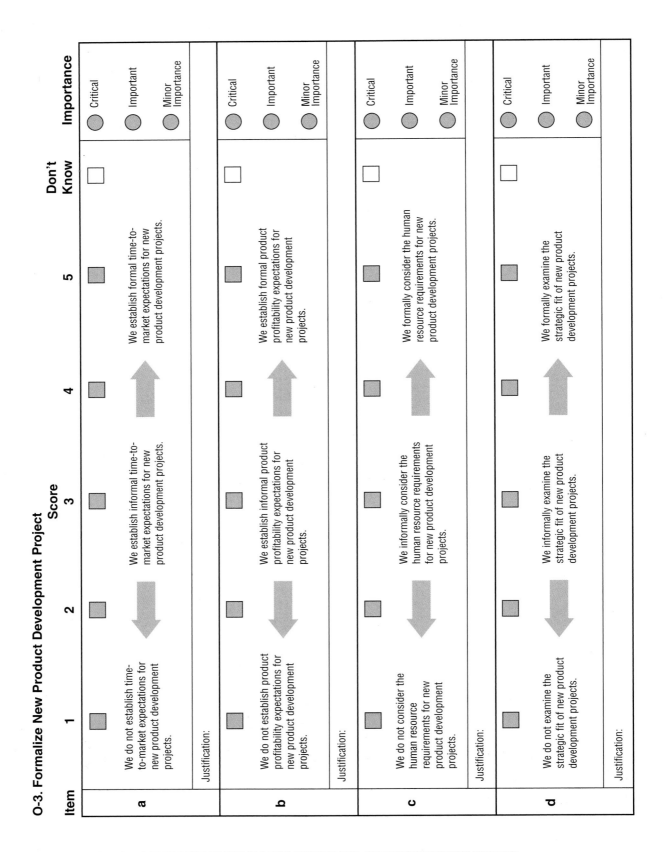

Item		Score 1	2	3	4	5	Don't Know	Importance
a		We do not establish time-to-market expectations for new product development projects.		We establish informal time-to-market expectations for new product development projects.		We establish formal time-to-market expectations for new product development projects.	☐	◯ Critical ◯ Important ◯ Minor Importance
	Justification:							
b		We do not establish product profitability expectations for new product development projects.		We establish informal product profitability expectations for new product development projects.		We establish formal product profitability expectations for new product development projects.	☐	◯ Critical ◯ Important ◯ Minor Importance
	Justification:							
c		We do not consider the human resource requirements for new product development projects.		We informally consider the human resource requirements for new product development projects.		We formally consider the human resource requirements for new product development projects.	☐	◯ Critical ◯ Important ◯ Minor Importance
	Justification:							
d		We do not examine the strategic fit of new product development projects.		We informally examine the strategic fit of new product development projects.		We formally examine the strategic fit of new product development projects.	☐	◯ Critical ◯ Important ◯ Minor Importance
	Justification:							

O-4. Design, Build and Test Prototypes

Item		Score 1	2	3	4	5	Don't Know	Importance
a		⬜	⬜	⬜ We sometimes design and build prototypes as part of our product development process.	⬜	⬜ We systematically design and build prototypes as part of our product development process.	⬜	⚫ Critical ⚫ Important ⚫ Minor Importance
		We do not design and build prototypes.						
	Justification:							
b		⬜	⬜	⬜ We have limited involvement with suppliers on the design and building of prototypes.	⬜	⬜ We have an appropriate level of involvement with suppliers on the design and building of prototypes.	⬜	⚫ Critical ⚫ Important ⚫ Minor Importance
		We do not work with suppliers on the design and building of prototypes.						
	Justification:							
c		⬜	⬜	⬜ We rarely work with suppliers to perform a value analysis to determine what portions of the product design and rollout process truly add value.	⬜	⬜ We have an appropriate level of involvement by suppliers in order to perform a value analysis to determine what portions of the product design and rollout process truly add value.	⬜	⚫ Critical ⚫ Important ⚫ Minor Importance
		We never work with suppliers to perform a value analysis to determine what portions of the product design and rollout process truly add value.						
	Justification:							
d		⬜	⬜	⬜ We have informal procedures for sourcing prototype materials.	⬜	⬜ We have formal procedures for sourcing prototype materials.	⬜	⚫ Critical ⚫ Important ⚫ Minor Importance
		We have no procedures for sourcing prototype materials.						
	Justification:							

O-4. Design, Build and Test Prototypes (continued)

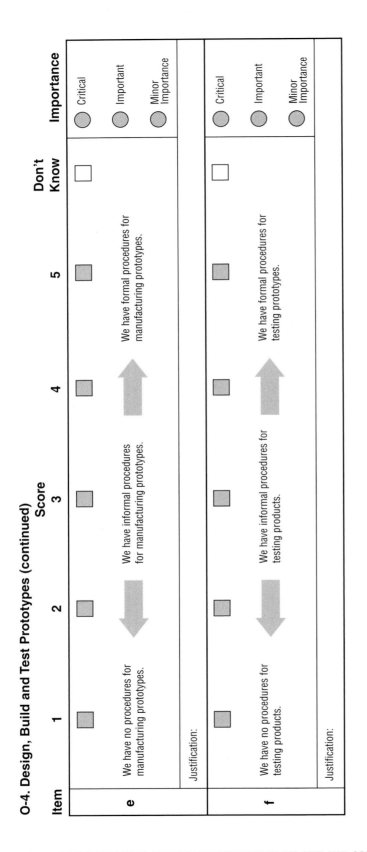

Item	Score					Don't Know	Importance
	1	2	3	4	5		

e — We have no procedures for manufacturing prototypes. → We have informal procedures for manufacturing prototypes. → We have formal procedures for manufacturing prototypes.

Importance: ○ Critical ○ Important ○ Minor Importance

Justification:

f — We have no procedures for testing products. → We have informal procedures for testing products. → We have formal procedures for testing prototypes.

Importance: ○ Critical ○ Important ○ Minor Importance

Justification:

O-5. Evaluate Make/Buy Decision

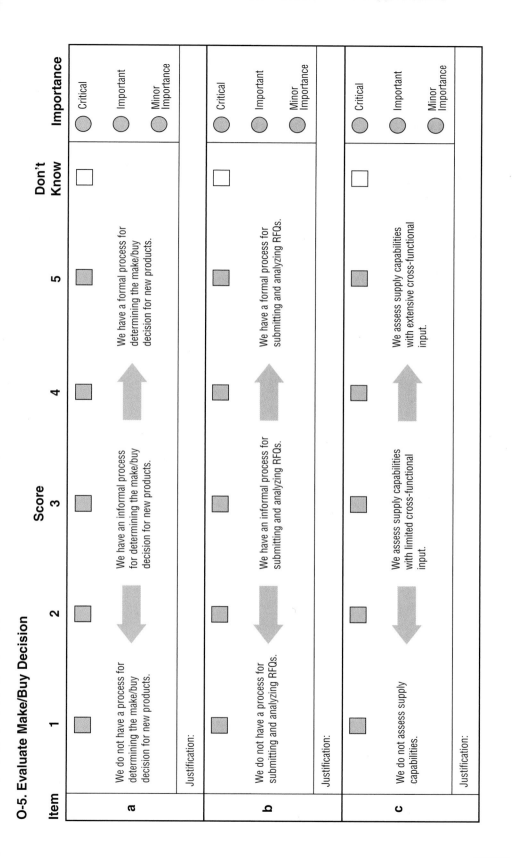

Item		Score					Don't Know	Importance
	1	2	3	4	5			

a — 1: We do not have a process for determining the make/buy decision for new products. — 3: We have an informal process for determining the make/buy decision for new products. — 5: We have a formal process for determining the make/buy decision for new products.

Justification:

Importance: Critical / Important / Minor Importance

b — 1: We do not have a process for submitting and analyzing RFQs. — 3: We have an informal process for submitting and analyzing RFQs. — 5: We have a formal process for submitting and analyzing RFQs.

Justification:

Importance: Critical / Important / Minor Importance

c — 1: We do not assess supply capabilities. — 3: We assess supply capabilities with limited cross-functional input. — 5: We assess supply capabilities with extensive cross-functional input.

Justification:

Importance: Critical / Important / Minor Importance

O-6. Determine Channels

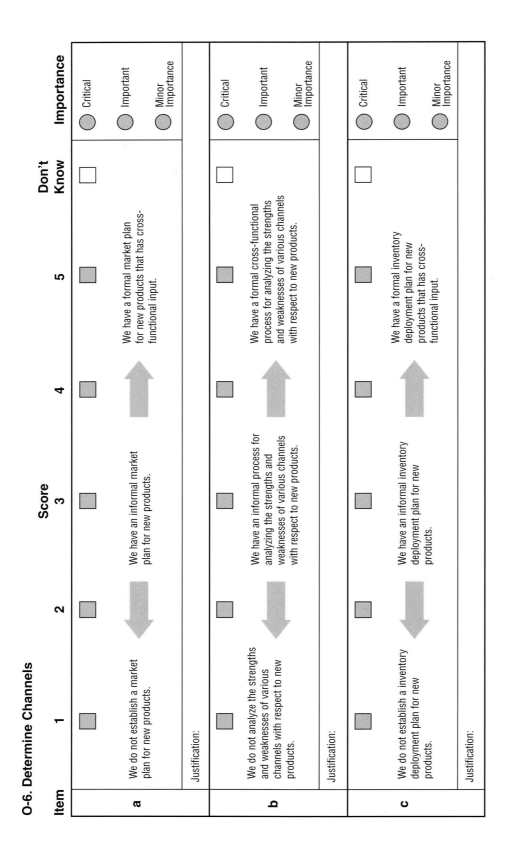

Item		Score					Don't Know	Importance
	1	2	3	4	5			
a	☐	☐	☐	☐	☐		☐	◯ Critical ◯ Important ◯ Minor Importance
	We do not establish a market plan for new products.		We have an informal market plan for new products.		We have a formal market plan for new products that has cross-functional input.			
Justification:								
b	☐	☐	☐	☐	☐		☐	◯ Critical ◯ Important ◯ Minor Importance
	We do not analyze the strengths and weaknesses of various channels with respect to new products.		We have an informal process for analyzing the strengths and weaknesses of various channels with respect to new products.		We have a formal cross-functional process for analyzing the strengths and weaknesses of various channels with respect to new products.			
Justification:								
c	☐	☐	☐	☐	☐		☐	◯ Critical ◯ Important ◯ Minor Importance
	We do not establish a inventory deployment plan for new products.		We have an informal inventory deployment plan for new products.		We have a formal inventory deployment plan for new products that has cross-functional input.			
Justification:								

O-7. Rollout Product

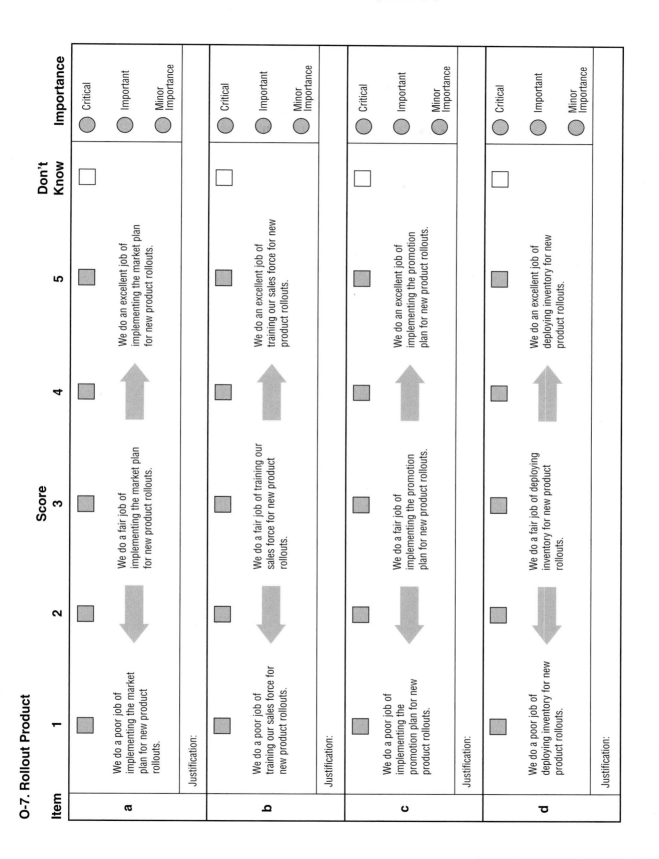

Item		Score					Don't Know	Importance
		1	2	3	4	5		

a — We do a poor job of implementing the market plan for new product rollouts. / We do a fair job of implementing the market plan for new product rollouts. / We do an excellent job of implementing the market plan for new product rollouts.

Justification:

Importance: Critical / Important / Minor Importance

b — We do a poor job of training our sales force for new product rollouts. / We do a fair job of training our sales force for new product rollouts. / We do an excellent job of training our sales force for new product rollouts.

Justification:

Importance: Critical / Important / Minor Importance

c — We do a poor job of implementing the promotion plan for new product rollouts. / We do a fair job of implementing the promotion plan for new product rollouts. / We do an excellent job of implementing the promotion plan for new product rollouts.

Justification:

Importance: Critical / Important / Minor Importance

d — We do a poor job of deploying inventory for new product rollouts. / We do a fair job of deploying inventory for new product rollouts. / We do an excellent job of deploying inventory for new product rollouts.

Justification:

Importance: Critical / Important / Minor Importance

O-7. Rollout Product (continued)

Item	Score					Don't Know	Importance

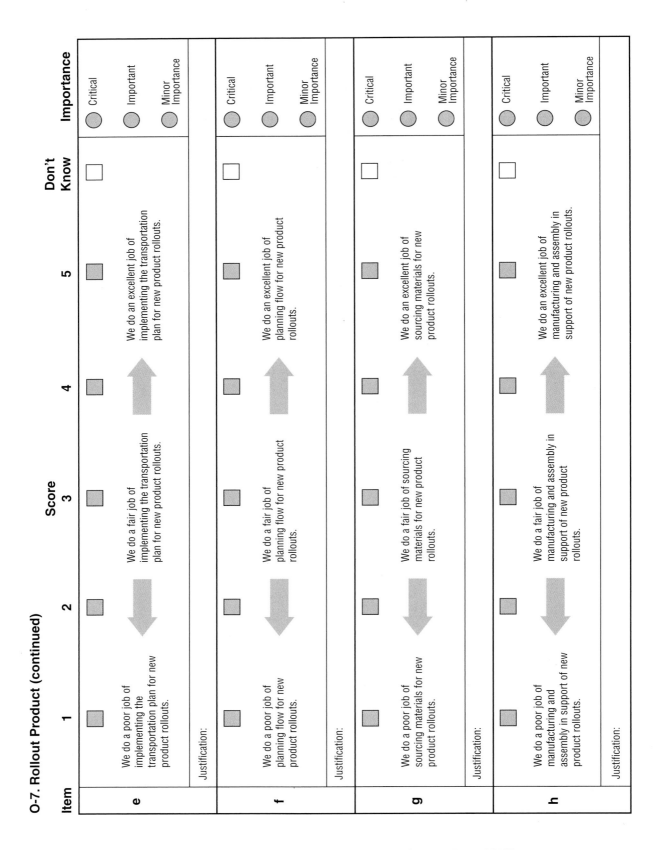

e — We do a poor job of implementing the transportation plan for new product rollouts.

We do a fair job of implementing the transportation plan for new product rollouts.

We do an excellent job of implementing the transportation plan for new product rollouts.

○ Critical
○ Important
○ Minor Importance

Justification:

f — We do a poor job of planning flow for new product rollouts.

We do a fair job of planning flow for new product rollouts.

We do an excellent job of planning flow for new product rollouts.

○ Critical
○ Important
○ Minor Importance

Justification:

g — We do a poor job of sourcing materials for new product rollouts.

We do a fair job of sourcing materials for new product rollouts.

We do an excellent job of sourcing materials for new product rollouts.

○ Critical
○ Important
○ Minor Importance

Justification:

h — We do a poor job of manufacturing and assembly in support of new product rollouts.

We do a fair job of manufacturing and assembly in support of new product rollouts.

We do an excellent job of manufacturing and assembly in support of new product rollouts.

○ Critical
○ Important
○ Minor Importance

Justification:

O-8. Measure Performance

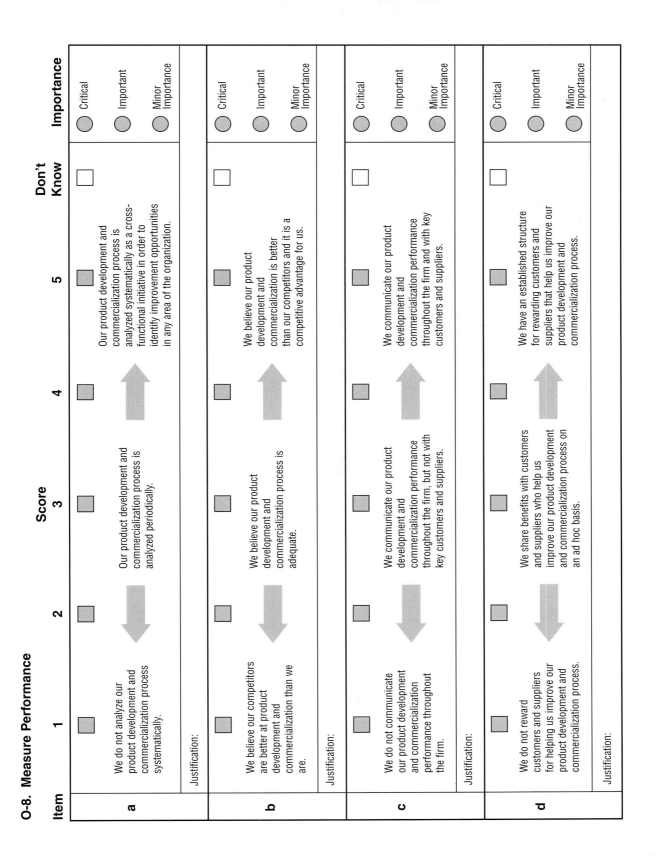

Item	Score					Don't Know	Importance

a

1 — We do not analyze our product development and commercialization process systematically.

3 — Our product development and commercialization process is analyzed periodically.

5 — Our product development and commercialization process is analyzed systematically as a cross-functional initiative in order to identify improvement opportunities in any area of the organization.

Importance: ○ Critical ○ Important ○ Minor Importance

Justification:

b

1 — We believe our competitors are better at product development and commercialization than we are.

3 — We believe our product development and commercialization process is adequate.

5 — We believe our product development and commercialization is better than our competitors and it is a competitive advantage for us.

Importance: ○ Critical ○ Important ○ Minor Importance

Justification:

c

1 — We do not communicate our product development and commercialization performance throughout the firm.

3 — We communicate our product development and commercialization performance throughout the firm, but not with key customers and suppliers.

5 — We communicate our product development and commercialization performance throughout the firm and with key customers and suppliers.

Importance: ○ Critical ○ Important ○ Minor Importance

Justification:

d

1 — We do not reward customers and suppliers for helping us improve our product development and commercialization process.

3 — We share benefits with customers and suppliers who help us improve our product development and commercialization process on an ad hoc basis.

5 — We have an established structure for rewarding customers and suppliers that help us improve our product development and commercialization process.

Importance: ○ Critical ○ Important ○ Minor Importance

Justification:

APPENDIX H: Assessment Tool for the Returns Management Process

General Information

This assessment tool is designed to identify opportunities in your organization's returns management process. It highlights important aspects of the strategic and operational sub-processes within returns management. Management can use this tool to identify process strengths and weaknesses, and then focus their efforts on those areas where improvement efforts will drive the most benefits.

Directions

A cross-functional management team should complete each item in the assessment, the score, the importance, and the justification.

Score: The score for the item is assessed on a 5-point scale.

1 = you agree with the statement written in column 1.

2 = you believe the organization is somewhere between the statements in columns 1 and 3.

3 = you agree with the statement written in column 3.

4 = you believe the organization is somewhere between the statements in columns 3 and 5.

5 = you agree with the statement written in column 5.

The scale includes descriptions for 1, 3, and 5. Intermediate columns are included to accommodate ratings that fall between the scale points. Check the box corresponding to the score of the item. If the respondent is not sure how to score the item, check the "Don't Know" box.

Importance: The importance of the item is assessed on a 3-point scale.

3 = **Critical:** Item is essential for the success of the returns management process within your organization.

2 = **Important:** Item is important but not essential for the success of the returns management process within your organization.

1 = **Minor Importance:** Item is of minor importance for the success of the returns management process within your organization.

Justification: Provide justification for your score and importance rating for each item in the space provided, i.e., why did you score the items the way you did?

Strategic Sub-Processes

S–1. Determine Returns Management Goals and Strategy

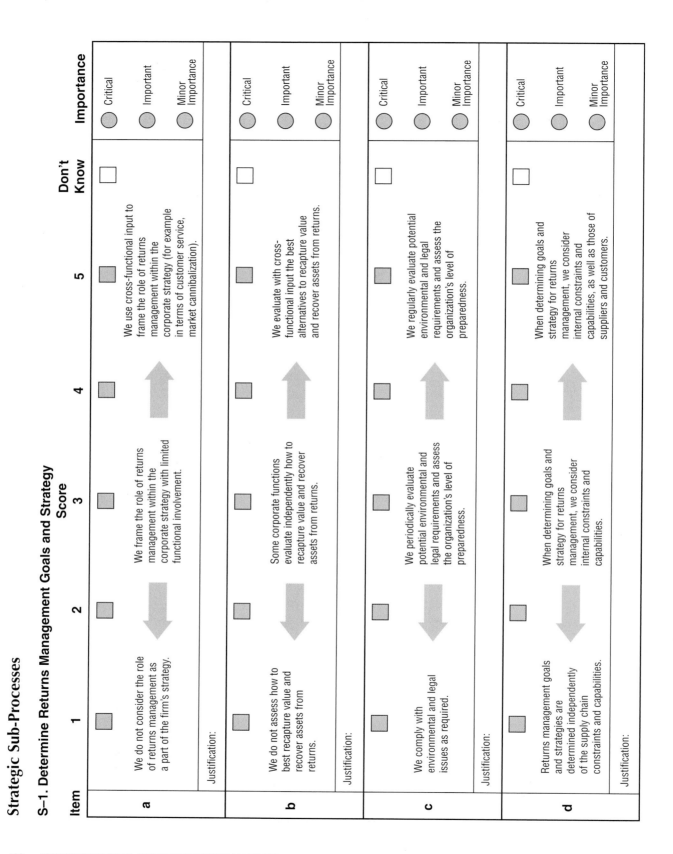

Item	Score					Don't Know	Importance
	1	2	3	4	5		

a
- 1: We do not consider the role of returns management as a part of the firm's strategy.
- 3: We frame the role of returns management within the corporate strategy with limited functional involvement.
- 5: We use cross-functional input to frame the role of returns management within the corporate strategy (for example in terms of customer service, market cannibalization).
- Importance: Critical / Important / Minor Importance

Justification:

b
- 1: We do not assess how to best recapture value and recover assets from returns.
- 3: Some corporate functions evaluate independently how to recapture value and recover assets from returns.
- 5: We evaluate with cross-functional input the best alternatives to recapture value and recover assets from returns.
- Importance: Critical / Important / Minor Importance

Justification:

c
- 1: We comply with environmental and legal issues as required.
- 3: We periodically evaluate potential environmental and legal requirements and assess the organization's level of preparedness.
- 5: We regularly evaluate potential environmental and legal requirements and assess the organization's level of preparedness.
- Importance: Critical / Important / Minor Importance

Justification:

d
- 1: Returns management goals and strategies are determined independently of the supply chain constraints and capabilities.
- 3: When determining goals and strategy for returns management, we consider internal constraints and capabilities.
- 5: When determining goals and strategy for returns management, we consider internal constraints and capabilities, as well as those of suppliers and customers.
- Importance: Critical / Important / Minor Importance

Justification:

S-2. Develop Avoidance, Gatekeeping and Disposition Guidelines

Item	Score 1	2	3	4	5	Don't Know	Importance
a	☐ We have not identified types of returns.	☐	☐ We handle product returns as one type and reusable containers as the other type of return.	☐	☐ We have identified types of returns with the input of a cross-functional management team.	☐	◯ Critical ◯ Important ◯ Minor Importance
	Justification:						
b	☐ We do not look for avoidance opportunities.	☐	☐ We informally identify and review avoidance opportunities with limited cross-functional input.	☐	☐ We have formal procedures for identifying and reviewing avoidance opportunities with cross-functional input.	☐	◯ Critical ◯ Important ◯ Minor Importance
	Justification:						
c	☐ We do not have formal (published) returns policies.	☐	☐ Our returns policies focus on financial aspects such as refunds and account credits.	☐	☐ We have developed refund policies as well as gatekeeping policies.	☐	◯ Critical ◯ Important ◯ Minor Importance
	Justification:						
d	☐ We do not have formal disposition guidelines.	☐	☐ Disposition guidelines are developed within a functional department, and not coordinated with customers and suppliers.	☐	☐ Disposition guidelines are developed with the input of a cross-functional team and involve key customers and suppliers.	☐	◯ Critical ◯ Important ◯ Minor Importance
	Justification:						

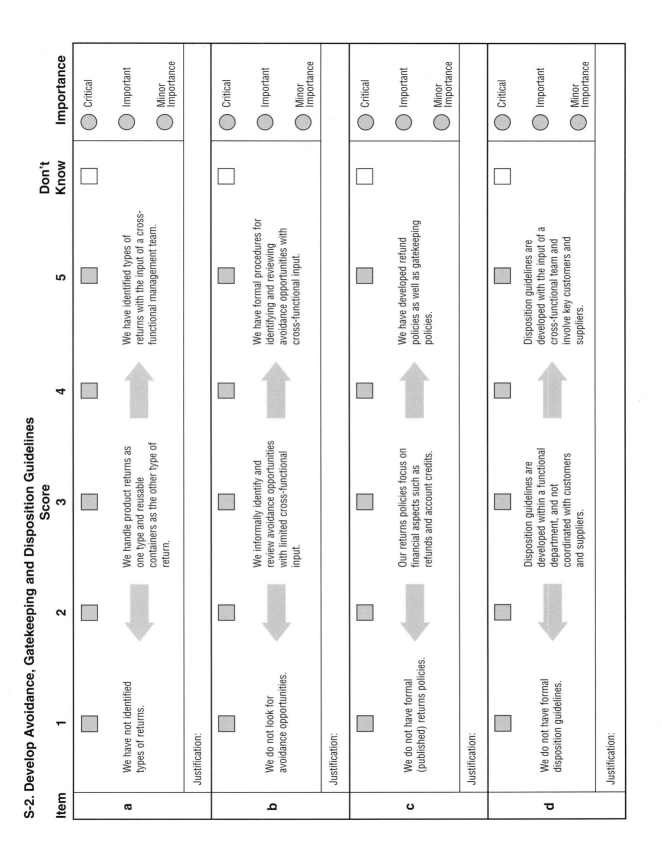

S-3. Develop Returns Network and Flow Options

Item	1	2	3	Score 4	5	Don't Know	Importance

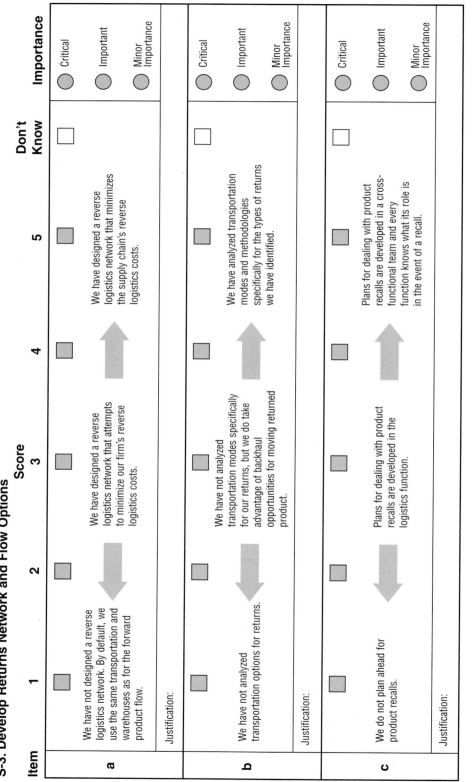

a

We have not designed a reverse logistics network. By default, we use the same transportation and warehouses as for the forward product flow. (1)

We have designed a reverse logistics network that attempts to minimize our firm's reverse logistics costs. (3)

We have designed a reverse logistics network that minimizes the supply chain's reverse logistics costs. (5)

Justification:

Importance: ○ Critical ○ Important ○ Minor Importance

b

We have not analyzed transportation options for returns. (1)

We have not analyzed transportation modes specifically for our returns, but we do take advantage of backhaul opportunities for moving returned product. (3)

We have analyzed transportation modes and methodologies specifically for the types of returns we have identified. (5)

Justification:

Importance: ○ Critical ○ Important ○ Minor Importance

c

We do not plan ahead for product recalls. (1)

Plans for dealing with product recalls are developed in the logistics function. (3)

Plans for dealing with product recalls are developed in a cross-functional team and every function knows what its role is in the event of a recall. (5)

Justification:

Importance: ○ Critical ○ Important ○ Minor Importance

S-4. Develop Credit Rules

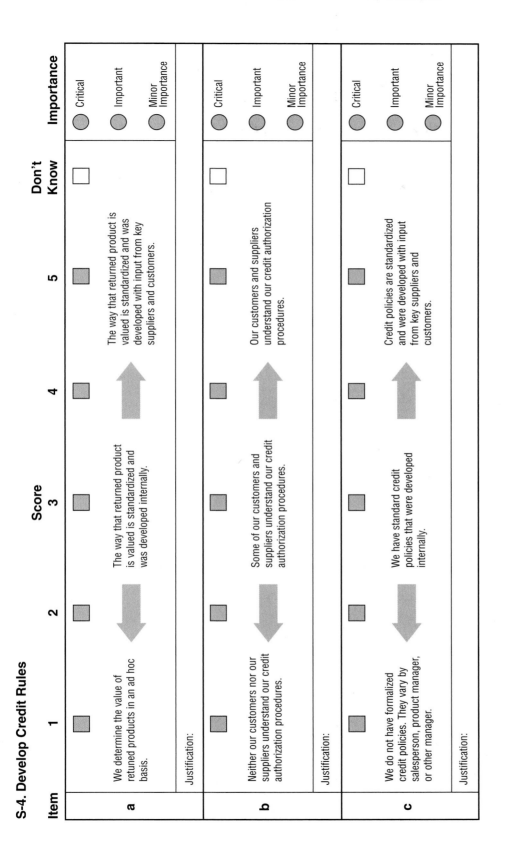

Item	Score					Don't Know	Importance

a — We determine the value of returned products in an ad hoc basis.

The way that returned product is valued is standardized and was developed internally.

The way that returned product is valued is standardized and was developed with input from key suppliers and customers.

Justification:

b — Neither our customers nor our suppliers understand our credit authorization procedures.

Some of our customers and suppliers understand our credit authorization procedures.

Our customers and suppliers understand our credit authorization procedures.

Justification:

c — We do not have formalized credit policies. They vary by salesperson, product manager, or other manager.

We have standard credit policies that were developed internally.

Credit policies are standardized and were developed with input from key suppliers and customers.

Justification:

Importance: Critical / Important / Minor Importance

S-5. Determine Secondary Markets

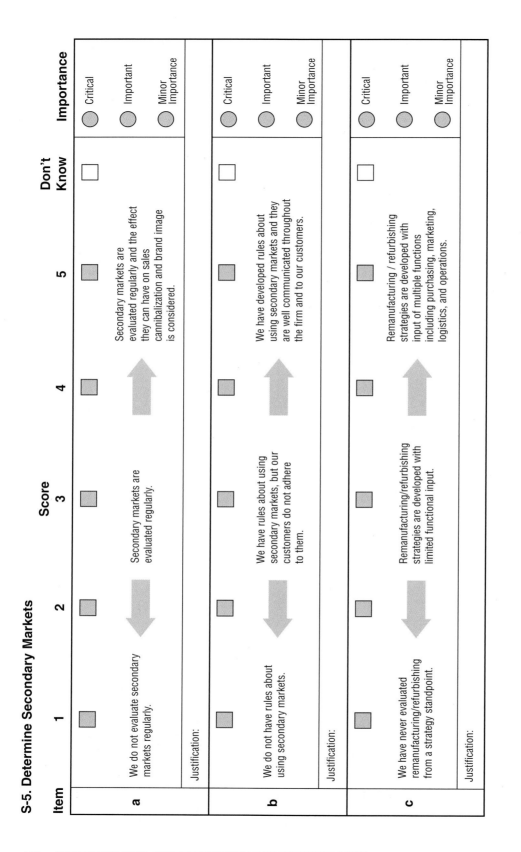

Item		Score					Don't Know	Importance
		1	2	3	4	5		
a		☐	☐	☐	☐	☐	☐	◉ Critical ◉ Important ◉ Minor Importance
	We do not evaluate secondary markets regularly.			Secondary markets are evaluated regularly.		Secondary markets are evaluated regularly and the effect they can have on sales cannibalization and brand image is considered.		
	Justification:							
b		☐	☐	☐	☐	☐	☐	◉ Critical ◉ Important ◉ Minor Importance
	We do not have rules about using secondary markets.			We have rules about using secondary markets, but our customers do not adhere to them.		We have developed rules about using secondary markets and they are well communicated throughout the firm and to our customers.		
	Justification:							
c		☐	☐	☐	☐	☐	☐	◉ Critical ◉ Important ◉ Minor Importance
	We have never evaluated remanufacturing/refurbishing from a strategy standpoint.			Remanufacturing/refurbishing strategies are developed with limited functional input.		Remanufacturing / refurbishing strategies are developed with input of multiple functions including purchasing, marketing, logistics, and operations.		
	Justification:							

S-6. Develop Framework of Metrics

Item	Score 1	2	3	4	5	Don't Know	Importance
a	We do not have formal returns management metrics.		We have returns management metrics but we do not relate them to financial performance.		We have formal metrics focused on returns management and we understand how they impact our firm's EVA.	☐	◯ Critical ◯ Important ◯ Minor Importance
Justification:							
b	We do not have formal performance goals for returns management.		We have formal performance goals relating to returns management that are communicated internally.		We have formal performance goals relating to returns management that are communicated throughout the firm and to key suppliers and customers.	☐	◯ Critical ◯ Important ◯ Minor Importance
Justification:							
c	Conflicting functional objectives often hinder the performance of the returns management process.		There are groups of functions whose metrics are aligned, but there are some conflicts between the groups.		Our returns management metrics are aligned with other metrics used throughout the firm.	☐	◯ Critical ◯ Important ◯ Minor Importance
Justification:							
d	People in our firm have a limited understanding of how their decisions and actions affect the returns management process.		People throughout our firm understand how their decisions and actions affect the returns management process.		People throughout our firm, as well as our key suppliers and customers understand how their decisions and actions affect the returns management process.	☐	◯ Critical ◯ Important ◯ Minor Importance
Justification:							

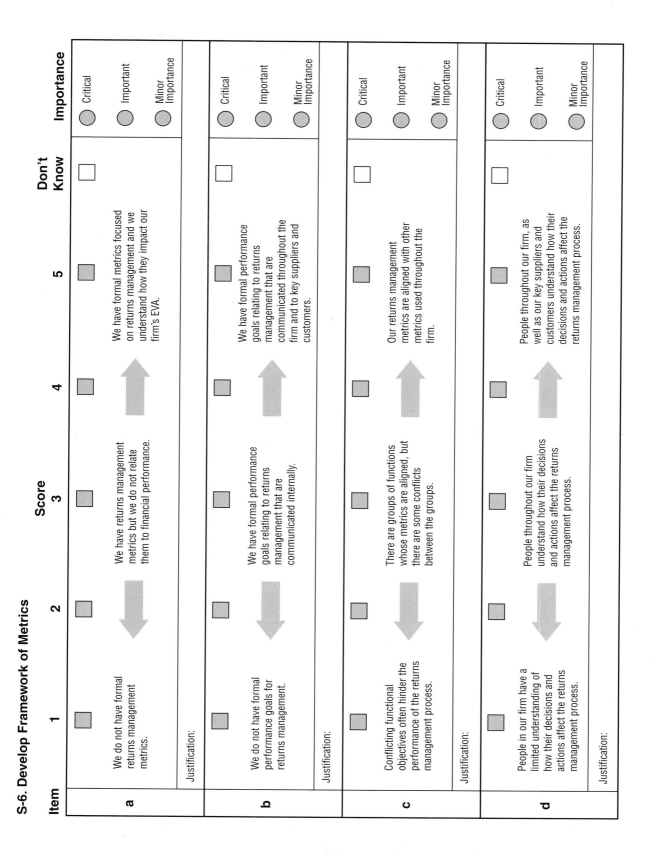

Operational Sub-Processes

O-1. Receive Return Request

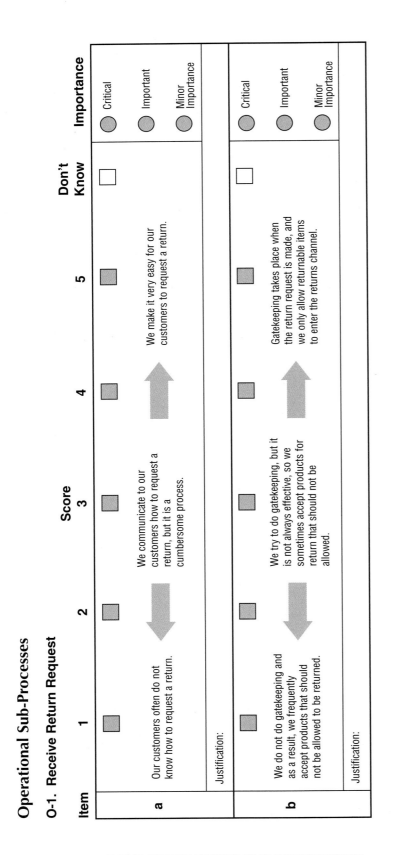

Item	Score					Don't Know	Importance

a — Our customers often do not know how to request a return.

We communicate to our customers how to request a return, but it is a cumbersome process.

We make it very easy for our customers to request a return.

Justification:

b — We do not do gatekeeping and as a result, we frequently accept products that should not be returned.

We try to do gatekeeping, but it is not always effective, so we sometimes accept products for return that should not be allowed.

Gatekeeping takes place when the return request is made, and we only allow returnable items to enter the returns channel.

Justification:

Importance: Critical / Important / Minor Importance

O-2. Determine Routing

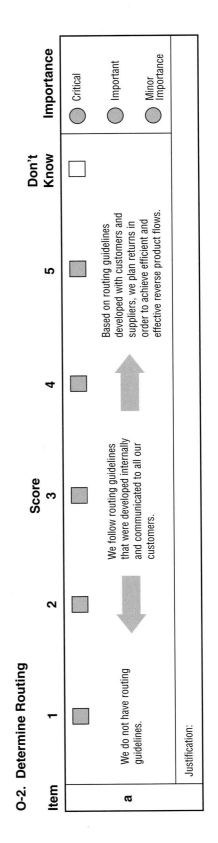

Item	Score					Don't Know	Importance

a — We do not have routing guidelines.

We follow routing guidelines that were developed internally and communicated to all our customers.

Based on routing guidelines developed with customers and suppliers, we plan returns in order to achieve efficient and effective reverse product flows.

Justification:

Importance: Critical / Important / Minor Importance

O-2. Determine Routing (continued)

Item		Score					Don't Know	Importance
	1	2	3	4	5			

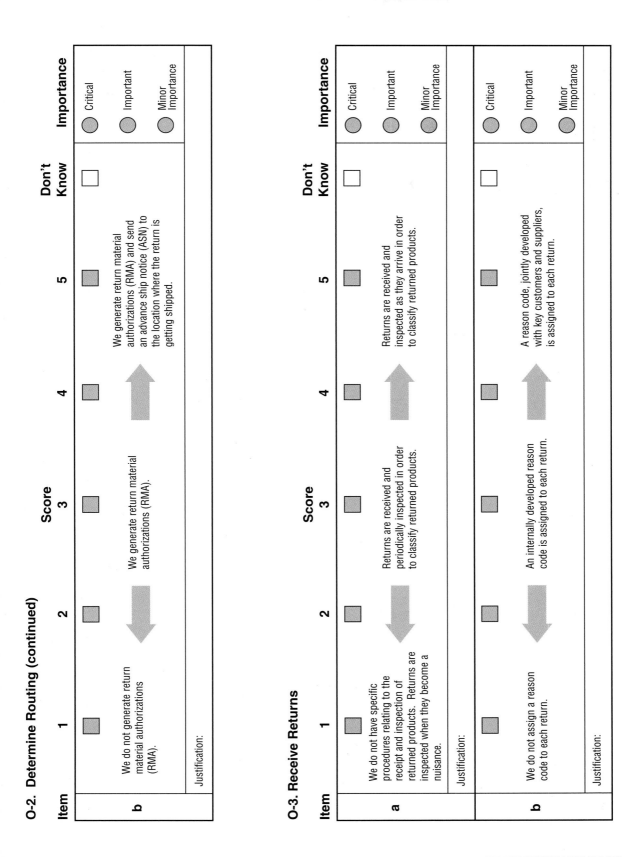

b

We do not generate return material authorizations (RMA).

We generate return material authorizations (RMA).

We generate return material authorizations (RMA) and send an advance ship notice (ASN) to the location where the return is getting shipped.

⬤ Critical
⬤ Important
⬤ Minor Importance

Justification:

O-3. Receive Returns

Item		Score					Don't Know	Importance
	1	2	3	4	5			

a

We do not have specific procedures relating to the receipt and inspection of returned products. Returns are inspected when they become a nuisance.

Returns are received and periodically inspected in order to classify returned products.

Returns are received and inspected as they arrive in order to classify returned products.

⬤ Critical
⬤ Important
⬤ Minor Importance

Justification:

b

We do not assign a reason code to each return.

An internally developed reason code is assigned to each return.

A reason code, jointly developed with key customers and suppliers, is assigned to each return.

⬤ Critical
⬤ Important
⬤ Minor Importance

Justification:

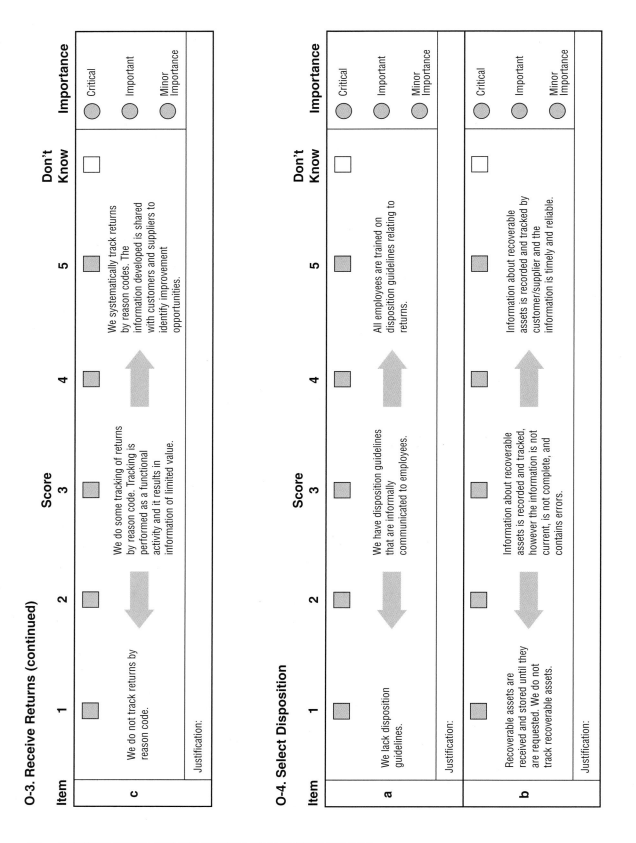

O-3. Receive Returns (continued)

Item	Score					Don't Know	Importance
	1	2	3	4	5		
c	We do not track returns by reason code.		We do some tracking of returns by reason code. Tracking is performed as a functional activity and it results in information of limited value.		We systematically track returns by reason codes. The information developed is shared with customers and suppliers to identify improvement opportunities.	☐	● Critical ● Important ● Minor Importance
Justification:							

O-4. Select Disposition

Item	Score					Don't Know	Importance
	1	2	3	4	5		
a	We lack disposition guidelines.		We have disposition guidelines that are informally communicated to employees.		All employees are trained on disposition guidelines relating to returns.	☐	● Critical ● Important ● Minor Importance
Justification:							
b	Recoverable assets are received and stored until they are requested. We do not track recoverable assets.		Information about recoverable assets is recorded and tracked, however the information is not current, is not complete, and contains errors.		Information about recoverable assets is recorded and tracked by customer/supplier and the information is timely and reliable.	☐	● Critical ● Important ● Minor Importance
Justification:							

O-5. Credit Customer / Supplier

Item	Score					Don't Know	Importance

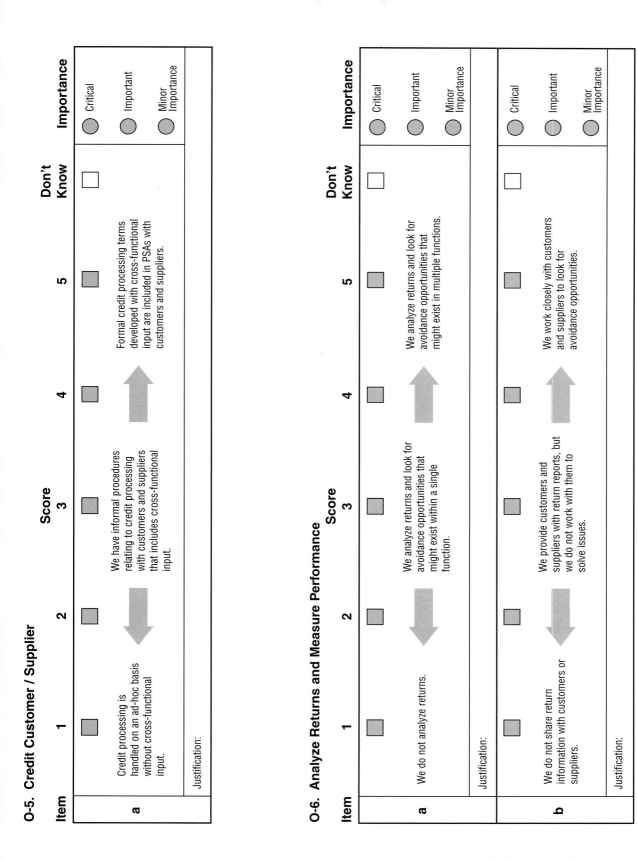

a

Credit processing is handled on an ad-hoc basis without cross-functional input.

We have informal procedures relating to credit processing with customers and suppliers that includes cross-functional input.

Formal credit processing terms developed with cross-functional input are included in PSAs with customers and suppliers.

Justification:

O-6. Analyze Returns and Measure Performance

a

We do not analyze returns.

We analyze returns and look for avoidance opportunities that might exist within a single function.

We analyze returns and look for avoidance opportunities that might exist in multiple functions.

Justification:

b

We do not share return information with customers or suppliers.

We provide customers and suppliers with return reports, but we do not work with them to solve issues.

We work closely with customers and suppliers to look for avoidance opportunities.

Justification:

Score: 1, 2, 3, 4, 5

Importance: Critical, Important, Minor Importance

Don't Know

O-6. Analyze Returns and Measure Performance (continued)

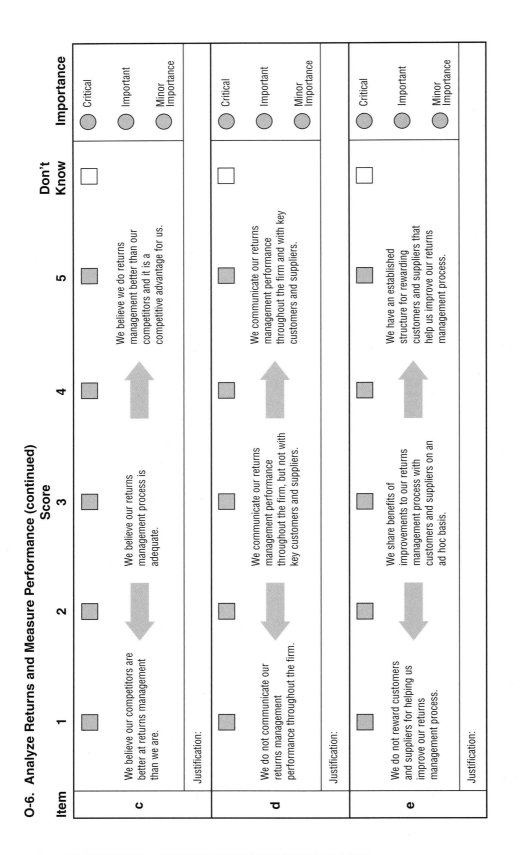

Item	Score 1	2	3	4	5	Don't Know	Importance
c	☐ We believe our competitors are better at returns management than we are.	☐	☐ We believe our returns management process is adequate.	☐	☐ We believe we do returns management better than our competitors and it is a competitive advantage for us.	☐	○ Critical ○ Important ○ Minor Importance
	Justification:						
d	☐ We do not communicate our returns management performance throughout the firm.	☐	☐ We communicate our returns management performance throughout the firm, but not with key customers and suppliers.	☐	☐ We communicate our returns management performance throughout the firm and with key customers and suppliers.	☐	○ Critical ○ Important ○ Minor Importance
	Justification:						
e	☐ We do not reward customers and suppliers for helping us improve our returns management process.	☐	☐ We share benefits of improvements to our returns management process with customers and suppliers on an ad hoc basis.	☐	☐ We have an established structure for rewarding customers and suppliers that help us improve our returns management process.	☐	○ Critical ○ Important ○ Minor Importance
	Justification:						

Author Index

Company Index

Subject Index